Accounting
for
Management Control:
An Introduction

Charles T. Horngren, Ph.D., C.P.A.

Professor of Accounting
University of Chicago

PRENTICE-HALL, INC.
Englewood Cliffs, New Jersey

To my wife

Preface

THIS BOOK IS AN INTRODUCTION TO INTERNAL ACCOUNTING—
most often called management accounting. The important
topics with which it deals are those that all students of
business should study. The book is written primarily for
undergraduates who have had one or two terms of basic
accounting. It is appropriate for a one-semester course in
managerial accounting at either the undergraduate or grad-
uate level. My twin goals have been to choose relevant subject matter and to present it clearly.

A student of business will be educationally short-changed
unless he acquires a knowledge and appreciation of the ways
in which accounting can help managers to operate effectively. Because accounting is so pervasive, an understanding
of its usefulness—and its limitations, also—is desirable
whether the student eventually becomes a company president, a production manager, a public accountant, a sales
manager, a controller, or a politician. The study of accounting for planning and control can be especially fruitful because it is viewed through the eyes of the managers who are
subject to accounting measures of performance and who are
often heavily dependent on accounting information for
guidance in decision making. There is no escaping the
linkage of accounting and management. That is why the
study of internal accounting is important. That is why such

iii

courses are increasingly required of all undergraduate students of business.

Modern accounting provides incisive help for the entire process of management—planning, controlling, and special decision making. The accumulation of figures (*score keeping*) is only one aspect of accounting. The emphasis of this book is on the accountant's positive responsibility for objective analysis and interpretation (*attention directing* and *problem solving*). This book informs managers and future managers of what to expect and demand of the accounting function. It informs accountants and future accountants of their major professional obligations to managers.

What subject matter deserves emphasis in a book such as this? We should be concerned with subjects of prime managerial significance, subjects that from the outset intrigue the student and ignite his curiosity: the interdependence and the mutual interests of accountants and managers; the over-all financial measures of performance; the basic patterns of cost behavior; cost-volume-profit relationships; flexible budgets; standards; responsibility accounting; the effects of cost systems on personal motivation; techniques for evaluating individual performance; and techniques for aiding long-range planning and the making of special decisions.

Perspective is gained by emphasizing the accountant's role in an organization. The student sees that the accountant must perform three jobs simultaneously: score keeping, attention directing, and problem solving. And he will begin to understand why accounting's major contributions to management arise from attention directing and problem solving.

This book attempts a balanced, flexible approach. For example, it deals as much with retail, wholesale, selling, and administrative situations as it does with manufacturing. The fundamental accounting concepts and techniques for planning and control are applicable to all types and functions of organizations, not just to manufacturing. This more general approach enables the student to relate more easily the book's examples and problems to his particular interests. Moreover, many valuable concepts (for example, master budgets) are more easily grasped if they are not complicated by intricate manufacturing situations.

Stress is on planning and control, not on product costing for purposes of inventory valuation and income determination. This approach, which excludes the troublesome but unimportant complications introduced by changes in inventory levels, simplifies the presentation of planning and control techniques in the classroom. Instead of the simultaneous discussion of costs for control and for product costing found in most texts, this text presents control thoroughly without dwelling on product costing at all until Chapter 15. At that point, the implications of overhead application for product costing, as well as a comparison of actual-normal, direct, and standard costing, may be made in perspective and in relation to management policy decisions regarding the "best" inventory valuation method.

This book has three parts. In Part One (Chapters 2-5), we review, interpret, and appraise basic accounting, dealing mainly with the stewardship responsibilities of management. Chapter 4 features an easy, almost foolproof, technique for the preparation of the funds statement. It also highlights the analytical uses of the statement.

Part Two is the nucleus of the book. It emphasizes the attention-directing and problem-solving functions of accounting in relation to current planning and control, evaluation of performance, special decisions, and long-range planning. Stress is on cost analysis rather than on cost record keeping.

Part Three contains chapters on income tax planning and on quantitative techniques. Both topics are important, but the decision to study them will depend on the teacher's preferences and on the student's background.

Two special features contribute to the clarity of the presentation. First, every chapter has a "Summary Problem for Your Review," followed by a complete solution in which the chapter's important concepts and techniques are stressed. The student is to: (1) study the chapter; (2) attempt to solve the review problem; (3) consult the solution after making an honest attempt to achieve his own solution; and (4) solve the homework problems. This plan provides a built-in check of the student's comprehension, helps his preparation for class, and minimizes the classroom discussion of issues which can bog down the session. More material can be covered in a single session, and a more thorough course is possible.

Second, the homework problems have been carefully prepared and fully tested in the classroom. The choice and development of appropriate, stimulating problems has been regarded as a key phase of this book's preparation. First-rate homework material is crucial to the success of any accounting course.

The assignment material has been organized quite differently than in typical textbooks. Each chapter's assignment material is divided into two groups: *essential* and *additional*.* The first group of problems is designed to convey the fundamental concepts and techniques of the chapter. This material should be covered in its entirety. In some chapters, the essential group contains only two problems; in other chapters, it contains as many as eight. This essential assignment material will suffice as a solid introduction to the primary concepts of accounting for manage-

* A fuller explanation of the organization of the assignment material accompanies the assignment following Chapter 1.

ment control. All assignment material has been tested in the classroom and checked and rechecked for appropriateness, difficulty, and technical errors. The additional assignment material in each chapter is accompanied by a descriptive note that points out the particular characteristics of specific problems.

Among other features intended to enhance clarity and flexibility are the opening statements in each chapter which serve as introductions, the summaries at the end of each chapter, and the Glossary of fundamental terms at the end of the book.

Alternative Ways of Using This Book

How much time should be spent on each of the various chapters? The answer to such a question must always be tentative, because the background of students varies and because teachers never completely agree on the relative importance of various topics or on the proper sequence of presentation. This book is flexible enough to permit the instructor to use a variety of chapter sequences and to place emphasis on varying assignments. Alternative schedules for assignment material are shown on page vii. Various combinations of these alternatives are also possible.

Some instructors may be able to cover all the chapters in one term. In my view, Alternative 1, Sequence A: (Chapter 1 plus Part Two) will provide the basis for a course that is aimed wholly at the management uses of accounting.

The instructor can, if he wishes, employ any of the following variations: (1) assign Chapter 15 (Product Costing) at any point after Chapter 8 (Cost Behavior: A Closer Look); (2) assign appropriate sections on income tax planning from Chapter 16 simultaneously with the sections on capital budgeting in Chapter 14; (3) skip or dwell on various parts of Chapters 2-5 depending on the students' backgrounds; and (4) omit Chapter 15 (Multipurpose Accounting Systems, Product Costing, and Overhead Application) in classes where the techniques of inventory valuation are not as important as other topics.

The list of students and professors at the University of Chicago and elsewhere who deserve acknowledgment for ideas, assistance, and assorted assignment material is too long to enumerate here without slighting somebody. Nevertheless, I shall mention the names of those who gave considerable help.

My special appreciation goes to the students who studied the manuscript, who worked so many, many problems, and who provided ideas for clarifying material as well as for assignment material.

Among the students who rendered conscientious critical and clerical assistance were James Alic, James Bergeron, John Gannon, Robert Grose, Thomas Johnson, Bernard Katz, James Livingston, Bernard McFall, Stephen Nelick, William Ross, and especially Alfred Collins.

ALTERNATE SUGGESTED ASSIGNMENT SCHEDULES

Alternative 1 *				Alternative 2 †			
Sequence A		Sequence B		Sequence A		Sequence B	
Chapter	Sessions	Chapter	Sessions	Chapter	Sessions	Chapter	Sessions
1	1.0	1	1.0	1	1.0	1	1.0
2–5	skip	2–5	skip	2	1.0	2	1.0
6	1.5	6	1.5	3	2.0	3	2.0
7	1.0	7	1.0	4	2.0	6	2.0
8	3.5	8	3.5	5	1.0	7	1.0
9	3.0	15 ‡ ||	3.0	6	2.0	8	3.5
10	4.0	9	3.0	7	1.0	9	3.0
11	1.5	15 § ||	2.0	8	3.5	10	4.0
12	2.0	10	4.0	9	3.0	11	1.5
13	3.5	11	1.5	10	3.0	12	2.0
14	4.0	12	2.0	11	1.5	13	2.5
15 ||	5.0	13	3.5	12	1.0	14	3.5
		14	4.0	13	2.5	4	2.0
16,17	Optional	16,17	Optional	14	3.5	5	1.0
Total	30.0 ¶		30.0		30.0		30.0

* For students with a relatively strong background in elementary accounting, perhaps two terms taken immediately prior to his course.

† For students with a relatively weak background in elementary accounting, perhaps only one term, or when there has been a substantial lapse of time between elementary accounting and this course.

‡ To the Section of Chapter 15 on *Standard Costs for Product Costing*.

§ From *Standard Costs for Product Costing* on.

\|\| Can be omitted.

¶ Thirty sessions used for illustrative purposes; for fewer or more sessions, the relative time devoted to each topic would be unchanged.

The comments of the following reviewers have been extremely helpful: James B. Bower, The University of Wisconsin; Jay Cook, Washington and Lee University; Dennis Gordon, The University of Akron; and Leonard Morrissey, Dartmouth College.

The superb secretarial work of Raymonde Rousselot is much appreciated.

My debts to specific professors and authors are acknowledged in appropriate passages in the book. My thanks to the American Institute of Certified Public Accountants, the National Association of Accountants, and the Society of Industrial and Cost Accountants of Canada for their generous permission to use some of their problems and to quote from their publications.

CHARLES T. HORNGREN

Contents

ix

ments: *Balance sheet classification; Carrying value; Lower of cost or market; Exchanges and conversions; Sales.* LONG-LIVED ASSETS: General characteristics; Tangible, or fixed, assets; Intangible assets. LIABILITIES. STOCKHOLDERS' EQUITY: General characteristics; Reserves; Net income and retained earnings. SUMMARY. SUMMARY PROBLEMS FOR YOUR REVIEW. ASSIGNMENT MATERIAL.

Part 2. The Core of Accounting for Planning and Control

Part 3. Selected Topics for Further Study

PART ONE

Score Keeping
Stewardship
and Evaluation

CHAPTER 1

Perspective: Score Keeping
Attention Directing
and Problem Solving

AS THE PREFACE INDICATES, THE OBJECTIVE OF THIS BOOK IS to develop your knowledge and appreciation of how accounting helps managers to operate effectively. Accounting and management are inextricably linked. That is why the study of internal accounting is important, regardless of whether you ultimately become an accountant or a manager.

The objective of this chapter is to view the accountant's role in an organization in perspective. We shall see that the accountant must fulfill three jobs simultaneously: score keeping, attention directing, and problem solving. We also will begin to understand why attention directing and problem solving provide the major benefits which management derives from accounting.

DISTINCTIVE PURPOSES OF ACCOUNTING FOR PLANNING AND CONTROL

Three Broad Purposes of an Accounting System

The accounting system is the major quantitative information system in almost every organization. An effective accounting system provides information for three broad purposes: (1) internal reporting to managers, for use in planning and controlling current operations; (2) internal report-

3

ing to managers, for use in making special decisions and in formulating long-range plans; and (3) external reporting to stockholders, government and other outside parties.

Both management (internal parties) and the external parties share an interest in all three important purposes, but the emphases of financial accounting and of management (internal) accounting differ. Financial accounting has been mainly concerned with the third purpose and has traditionally been oriented toward the historical, stewardship aspects of external reporting. The distinguishing feature of management accounting—of accounting for planning and control—is its emphasis on the first and second purposes.

An accounting system should help executives to select short-run and long-run goals, formulate plans for attaining those goals, investigate reasons for deviations from those goals, and reselect goals. Internal accounting is concerned with the accumulation, classification, and interpretation of information which assists individual executives to fulfill organizational objectives as revealed explicitly or implicitly by top management.

Types of Information Supplied by Accounting

What information should the management accountant supply? The types of information needed have been neatly described in a study of seven large companies with geographically dispersed operations, made by H. A. Simon and his associates. Their approach would probably prove fruitful to any company:

> By observation of the actual decision-making process, specific types of data needs were identified at particular organizational levels—the vice presidential level, the level of the factory manager, and the level of the factory head [foreman], for example—each involving quite distinct problems of communication for the accounting department.[1]

The Simon research team found that three types of information, each serving a different purpose, often at various management levels, raise and help to answer three basic questions:

1. Scorecard questions: Am I doing well or badly?
2. Attention-directing questions: What problems should I look into?
3. Problem-solving questions: Of the several ways of doing the job, which is the best?

The scorecard and attention directing uses of data are closely related. The same data may serve a scorecard function for a foreman and an

---

[1] H. A. Simon, *Administrative Behavior*, 2nd ed. (New York: The Macmillan Company, 1957), p. 20. For the complete study see H. A. Simon, H. Guetzkow, G. Kozmetsky, and G. Tyndall, *Centralization vs. Decentralization in Organizing The Controller's Department* (New York: Controllership Foundation, Inc., 1954). This perceptive study is much broader than its title implies.

attention-directing function for his superior. For example, many accounting systems provide performance reports in which actual results are compared with previously determined budgets or standards. Such a performance report often helps to answer scorecard questions and attention directing questions simultaneously. Furthermore, the actual results collected serve not only control purposes but also the traditional needs of financial accounting, which is chiefly concerned with the answering of scorecard questions. This collection, classification, and reporting of data is the task that dominates day-to-day accounting.

Problem solving data may be used in long-range planning and in making special, nonrecurring decisions, such as whether to make or buy parts, replace equipment, add or drop a product, etc. These decisions often require expert advice from specialists such as industrial engineers, budgetary accountants, statisticians, and others.

In sum, the accountant's task of supplying information has three facets:
1. *Score keeping.* The accumulation of data. This aspect of accounting enables both internal and external parties to evaluate organizational performance and position.
2. *Attention directing.* The reporting and interpreting of information which helps managers to focus on operating problems, imperfections, inefficiencies, and opportunities. This aspect of accounting helps managers to concern themselves with important aspects of operations promptly enough for effective action either through perceptive planning or through astute day-to-day supervision. Attention directing is commonly associated with current planning and control and with the analysis and investigation of recurring, routine internal accounting reports.
3. *Problem solving.* This aspect of accounting involves the concise quantification of the relative merits of possible courses of action, often with recommendations as to the best procedure. Problem solving is commonly associated with nonrecurring decisions, situations that require special accounting analyses or reports.

The above distinctions sometimes overlap or merge. Consequently, it is often difficult to pinpoint a particular accounting task as being score keeping, attention directing, or problem solving. Nevertheless, attempts to make these distinctions provide insight into the objectives and tasks of both accountants and managers.

Management Accounting and the Over-all Information System

These three uses of data may be related to the broad purposes of the accounting system. The business information system of the future is likely to be a single, multiple-purpose system with a highly selective reporting scheme. It will be tightly integrated and will serve three main purposes: (1) routine reporting to management, primarily for planning and controlling current operations (score keeping and attention directing); (2) special reporting to management, primarily for long-range planning and nonrecurring decisions (problem solving); and (3) routine reporting on financial results, primarily for external parties (score keeping). Although such a system can probably be designed in a self-contained, integrated manner to serve routine purposes simultaneously, its function of providing information about special problems will always entail preparing much data that will not lie within the system.

THE MANAGEMENT PROCESS

Management by Exception

The manager needs to have an over-all perspective, a perception of the goals of the organization as a whole and of the goals of his own department within that organization. He needs a plan for attaining these objectives. He needs to execute the plan and to follow it up with an appraisal of how well actual performance conformed to his plan. Then he can formulate new plans based on his experience and on contemplated new conditions.

The left-hand side of Exhibit 1-1 clearly demonstrates the planning

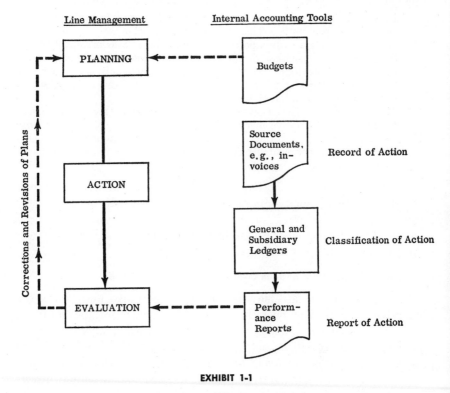

EXHIBIT 1-1

Accounting Framework for Planning and Control

and control cycle. *Planning* (the top box) means the selecting of objectives and the means for their attainment. It provides the answers to two questions: What is desired? When and how is it to be accomplished? *Controlling* (the two boxes immediately below) means adherence to plans through action and evaluation. The notion of control advocated here implies that plans already exist and that a continuous cycle interlocks planning and control so that evaluation of results sparks correction and revision of plans. Planning is more vital than control because superior control is fruitless if faulty plans are being implemented. The two are so intertwined that it seems artificial to draw rigid lines of separation between them, yet at times we will find it useful to concentrate on one or the other phase of the planning-control cycle.

The right-hand side of Exhibit 1-1 shows that accounting formalizes plans by expressing them in the language of figures as *budgets*. Accounting formalizes control as *performance reports* (the last box), which compare results with plans and which spotlight exceptions (i.e., deviations or variances from plans). Exhibit 1-2 shows the form of a simple performance report.

EXHIBIT 1-2

Performance Report

	Budgeted Amounts	Actual Amounts	Deviations or Variances	Explanation
Sales	xxx	xxx	xx	—
Various expenses	xxx	xxx	xx	—
Net income	xxx	xxx	xx	—

Such reports spur investigation of exceptions. Operations are then brought into conformity with the plans, or the plans are revised. This is an example of management by exception.

Management by exception means that the executive's attention and effort are concentrated on the significant deviations from expected results and that the information system highlights the areas most in need of investigation. Management should not ordinarily be concerned with results that conform closely to plans.

Illustration of the Budget and the Performance Report

An assembly department constructs electric fans. The assembly of the parts and the installation of the electric motor are basically hand operations. Each fan is inspected before being transferred to the painting department. In light of the present sales forecast, a production schedule of 4,000 window fans and 6,000 table fans is planned for the coming month. Cost classifications are shown in Exhibit 1-3, the Assembly Department Budget.

EXHIBIT 1-3

Assembly Department Budget
For the Month Ending Mar. 31, 19x1

Material (detailed by type: metal stampings, motors, etc.)	$ 38,000
Assembly labor (detailed by job classification, number of workers, etc.)	73,000
Other labor (foremen, inspectors)	12,000
Utilities, maintenance, etc.	7,500
Supplies (small tools, lubricants, etc.)	2,500
Total	$133,000

The operating plan (the department budget) for the coming month is prepared in conferences attended by the foreman, his supervisor, and an accountant. Each of the costs subject to the foreman's control is scrutinized. Its average amount for the past few months is often used as a guide, especially if past performance has been reasonably efficient. However, the budget is a *forecast* of costs. Each cost is projected in the light of trends, price changes, alterations in product mix, specifications, labor methods, and changes in production volume from month to month. The budget is then formulated, and it becomes the foreman's target for the month.

As actual factory costs are incurred during the month, the accounting department collects them and classifies them by departments. At the end of the month (or perhaps weekly, or even daily, for such key items as materials or assembly labor), the accounting department prepares an Assembly Department Performance Report (Exhibit 1-4). In practice, this report may be very detailed and would contain explanations of any variances from the budget.

EXHIBIT 1-4

Assembly Department Performance Report
For the Month Ending Mar. 31, 19x1

	Budget	*Actual*	*Variance*	
Material (detailed by type: metal stampings, motors, etc.)	$ 38,000	$ 39,000	$1,000	*U*
Assembly labor (detailed by job classification, number of workers, etc.)	73,000	74,300	1,300	*U*
Other labor (foremen, inspectors)	12,000	11,200	800	*F*
Utilities, maintenance, etc.	7,500	7,400	100	*F*
Supplies (small tools, lubricants, etc.)	2,500	2,600	100	*U*
Total	$133,000	$134,500	$1,500	*U*

U = Unfavorable
F = Favorable

The foreman and his superiors use this report to help appraise performance. The spotlight is cast on the variances—the deviations from the budget. It is through management's investigation of these variances that better ways of doing things are discovered. The budget is an aid to planning; the performance report is the tool that aids controlling. The accounting system thus helps to direct managerial attention to the exceptions. Exhibit 1-1 shows that accounting does *not* do the controlling. Controlling consists of action performed by the managers and their workmen and of the evaluation which follows action. Accounting assists the managerial control function by providing a prompt record of the action and by systematically pinpointing trouble spots. This management-by-exception approach frees managers from needless concern with those phases of operations that are functioning effectively.

ROLE OF THE ACCOUNTANT IN THE ORGANIZATION

Line and Staff Authority

Except for exerting line authority over his own department, the chief accounting executive generally fills a staff role in his company, as contrasted with the line roles of sales and production executives. Most companies have the production and sale of goods as their basic objectives. *Line managers are directly responsible* for attaining these objectives as efficiently as possible.

Staff elements of organizations arise when the scope of the line manager's responsibility and duties enlarges to such a degree that he needs specialized help to operate effectively. When a department's primary task is advice and service to other departments, it is a staff department. *Staff authority is indirectly related* to the major objectives of the organization.

The accounting function is usually a staff function. The accounting department has responsibility for providing line managers, and also other staff managers, with specialized service, including advice and help in budgeting, controlling, pricing, and the making of special decisions. The accounting department does not exercise direct authority over line departments: its authority to prescribe uniform accounting and reporting methods is delegated to the controller by top line management. The uniform accounting procedure is authorized by the company president and is installed for him by the controller. When the controller prescribes the line department's role in supplying accounting information, he is not speaking as the controller, a staff man; he is speaking for top line management.

Theoretically, the controller's decisions regarding the best accounting procedures to be followed by line people are transmitted to the president. In turn, the president communicates these procedures through a manual of instructions which comes down through the line chain of command to all people affected by the procedures. In practice, the daily work of the controller, and his face-to-face relationships with the production manager or foreman, may require him to direct how production records should be

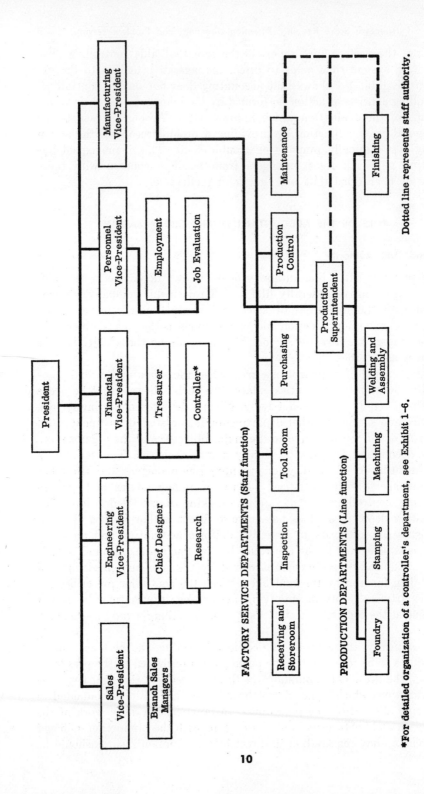

FACTORY SERVICE DEPARTMENTS (Staff function)

PRODUCTION DEPARTMENTS (Line function)

Dotted line represents staff authority.

*For detailed organization of a controller's department, see Exhibit 1-6.

EXHIBIT 1-5

Organization Chart of a Manufacturing Company

10

kept or how work tickets should be completed. The controller usually holds delegated authority from top line management over such matters.

Exhibit 1-5 shows the general organizational relationship described above. Exhibit 1-6 shows how a controller's own department may be organized.

The Controller

The title of controller is applied to various accounting positions, the stature and duties of which vary from company to company. In some firms, the controller is little more than a glorified bookkeeper who compiles data, primarily for conventional balance sheets and income statements. In other firms (General Electric) he is a key executive who aids managerial planning and control in 104 company subdivisions. In most firms, he has a status somewhere between these two extremes. For example, his opinion on the tax implications of certain management decisions may be carefully weighed, yet his opinion on other aspects of these decisions may not be sought. In this book, "controller" means the chief accounting executive. We have already seen that the modern controller does not do any controlling in terms of line authority, except over his own department. Yet the modern concept of controllership maintains that, in a special sense, the controller *does* control: by reporting and interpreting relevant data, the controller exerts a force or influence or projects an attitude that impels management toward logical decisions which are consistent with its objectives.

The controller has been compared to the ship's navigator. The navigator is especially trained to assist the captain. Without the navigator, the ship may go aground on reefs or miss its destination entirely. He guides the captain and informs him as to how well the ship is being steered, but the captain exerts his right to command.

Difficulties of Human Relations

Line and staff relationships often result in friction because of a lack of understanding of such relationships on the part of both line and staff executives. Line executives complain that staff men are too distant to understand their problems or that they want to seize line authority, that they lack perspective, and that they always take credit but never bear the blame. Staff executives complain that line managers are too resistant to change, do not take advantage of staff help, and do not give staff enough authority.

As a staff man, the successful internal accountant is alert to the sources of friction between line and staff. He avoids assuming line authority and thus losing the objectivity that should be one of his most appealing characteristics. He foresees the ultimate impact of any change in accounting procedures on the line manager's attitudes and willingness to cooperate.

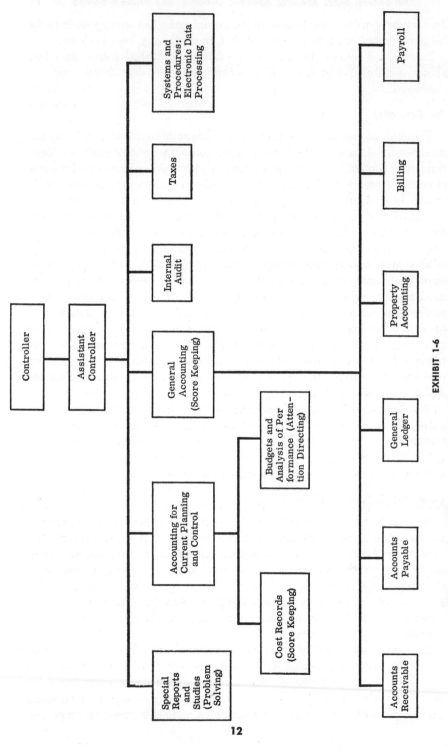

EXHIBIT 1-6

Organization Chart of a Controller's Department

The crucial problem of human relations is examined more carefully in Chapter 12.

Importance of Accurate Source Documents

Managerial accounting records are only as accurate as their source documents (e.g., requisitions and time cards). Most source documents are initiated by line managers or their subordinates. Unless the line manager appreciates the necessity for the source documents that he originates, and the benefits they make possible, any accounting system, no matter how elaborate, will be rendered nearly useless. The importance of accurate source documents cannot be overemphasized.

SUMMARY

An understanding of the over-all purposes of the accounting system provides perspective for the study of the usefulness of accounting to management. The accounting system of the future is likely to be a multiple-purpose system with a highly selective reporting scheme. It will be highly integrated and will serve three main purposes: (1) routine reporting to management, primarily for planning and controlling current operations (score keeping and attention directing); (2) special reporting to management, primarily for long-range planning and nonrecurring decisions (problem solving); and (3) routine reporting on financial results, oriented primarily for external parties (score keeping). The first two purposes are the distinguishing characteristics of internal accounting for planning and control.

Internal accounting is interwoven with management itself. Accounting is a service function. Internal accounting is not management as ordinarily conceived, but it helps management do a better job.

The chief of internal accounting is usually called the *controller*. His responsibilities usually encompass all phases of accounting, including income taxes and routine reporting to outside parties. But accounting techniques for planning and control are his main tools for helping managers to get things done. Besides being a combination score keeper, attention director, and problem solver, he must constantly exert an objective influence without seizing or accepting line authority. The human or organizational facets of his work often provide his most challenging and delicate tasks.

It is apparent that both accountants and managers must try to become as familiar as possible with all phases of their organizations and with the viewpoints of all levels of management. In this way, they are more likely to maximize their individual, mutual, and over-all organizational effectiveness. Operating managers should try to see the usefulness and potentialities of internal accounting techniques and reports. Accountants should try to supply relevant information—information which will help managers to distinguish over-all organizational objectives and assist them in making wise decisions. The attention-directing and problem-solving functions are the distinguishing features of management (internal) accounting.

SUMMARY PROBLEMS FOR YOUR REVIEW

PROBLEMS

(Try to solve these problems before examining the solutions that follow.)

1. The score-keeping, attention-directing, and problem-solving duties of the accountant have been described in this chapter and elsewhere in the literature. The accountant's usefulness to management is said to be directly influenced by how good an attention director and problem solver he is.

   Evaluate this contention by specifically relating the accountant's duties to the duties of operating management.

2. Using the organization charts in this chapter (Exhibits 1-5 and 1-6) answer the following questions:

   a. Do the following have line or staff authority over the machining foreman: maintenance foreman, manufacturing vice-president, production superintendent, purchasing agent, storekeeper, personnel vice-president, president, chief budgetary accountant, chief internal auditor?

   b. What is the general role of service departments in an organization? How are they distinguished from operating or producing departments?

   c. Does the controller have line or staff authority over the cost accountants? The accounts receivable clerks?

   d. What is probably the *major duty* (score keeping, attention directing, or problem solving) of the following:

Payroll clerk	Budgetary accountant
Accounts receivable clerk	Cost analyst
Cost record clerk	Head of special reports and studies
Head of general accounting	Head of accounting for planning
Head of taxes	and control
Head of internal auditing	Controller

SOLUTIONS

1. Operating managers may have to be good score keepers, but their major duties are to concentrate on the day-to-day problems that most need attention, to make longer-range plans, and to arrive at special decisions. Accordingly, because the manager is concerned mainly with attention directing and problem solving, he will obtain the most benefit from the alert internal accountant who is a useful attention director and problem solver.

2. *a.* The only executives having line authority over the machining foreman are the president, the manufacturing vice-president, and the production superintendent.

b. A typical company's major purpose is to produce and sell goods or services. Unless a department is directly concerned with producing or selling, it is called a service or staff department. Service departments exist only to help the production and sales departments with their major tasks: the efficient production and sale of goods or services.

c. The controller has line authority over all members of his own department, all those shown in the controller's organization chart (Exhibit 1-6).

d. The major duty of the first five—through the head of taxes—is typically score keeping. Attention directing is probably the major duty of the next three. Problem solving is probably the primary duty of the head of special reports and studies. The head of accounting for planning and control and the controller should be concerned with all three duties: score keeping, attention directing, and problem solving. However, there is a perpetual danger that day-to-day pressures will emphasize score keeping. Therefore, accountants and managers should constantly see that attention directing and problem solving are also stressed. Otherwise, the major management benefits of an accounting system may be lost.

ASSIGNMENT MATERIAL

The assignment material for each chapter is divided into two groups: *essential* and *additional*. The first group consists of carefully designed, relatively straightforward material aimed at conveying the fundamental concepts and techniques of the particular chapter. These assignments provide a solid introduction to the major concepts of accounting for management control; consequently, the essential group should be covered in its entirety.

The first question in each chapter usually concerns terminology, an extremely important and often troublesome phase of the learning process. A fuzzy understanding of terms hampers the learning of concepts. Many instructors will not require written answers to the question on terminology; in this case, the reader should check his comprehension of new terms by consulting the Glossary at the end of the book.

The second group of assignment material in each chapter should not be regarded as inferior to the essential group. Many of these problems can be substituted for ones in the essential group. Some, such as Problem 1-20, probe the chapter's contents more deeply than those in the essential group. Others, such as Problems 16-20 and 16-21, dwell on particular aspects of a concept. Comments on the merits of individual problems or cases in the second group will be found at the beginning of the Additional Assignment Material in each chapter.

ESSENTIAL ASSIGNMENT MATERIAL

1-1. *Terminology.* Define the following terms: score keeping; attention directing; problem solving; management by exception; planning; controlling; performance report; budget; variance; line authority; staff authority; controller; comptroller; source document.

1-2. *Role of the accountant in the organization: line and staff functions.*
    1. Of the following, who have line authority over a cost record clerk: budgetary accountant; head of accounting for current planning and control; head of general accounting; controller; storekeeper; production

        superintendent; manufacturing vice-president; president; production control chief?

    2. Of the following, who have line authority over an assembler: stamping foreman; assembly foreman; production superintendent; production control chief; storekeeper; manufacturing vice-president; engineering vice-president; president; controller; budgetary accountant; cost record clerk?

1-3. *Score keeping, attention directing, and problem solving.* For each of the following, identify the function the accountant is performing: i.e., score keeping, attention directing, or problem solving. *Also state* whether the departments mentioned are service or production departments.

    1. Processing the weekly payroll for the maintenance department.
    2. Explaining the welding foreman's performance report.
    3. Analyzing the costs of several different ways to blend raw materials in the foundry.
    4. Tallying sales, by branches, for the sales vice-president.
    5. Analyzing, for the president, the impact on net income of a contemplated new product.
    6. Interpreting why a branch did not meet its sales quota.
    7. Interpreting variances on a machining foreman's performance report.
    8. Preparing the budget for research and development.
    9. Adjusting journal entries for depreciation on the personnel manager's office equipment.
    10. Preparing a customer's monthly statement.

ADDITIONAL ASSIGNMENT MATERIAL

    Note: Problems 1-19 and 1-20 press somewhat beyond the boundaries of this chapter but provide a bird's-eye view of what is forthcoming.

1-4. "The accounting system is intertwined with operating management. Business operations would be a hopeless tangle without the paperwork that is so often regarded with disdain." Do you agree? Explain, giving examples.
1-5. What are the three broad purposes of an accounting system?
1-6. "The emphases of financial accounting and management accounting differ." Explain.
1-7. Distinguish among score keeping, attention directing, and problem solving.
1-8. Give examples of special nonrecurring decisions and of long-range planning.
1-9. Briefly describe the probable business information system of the future.
1-10. "Planning is much more vital than control." Do you agree? Explain.
1-11. Distinguish among a source document, a subsidiary ledger, and a general ledger.
1-12. Distinguish among a budget, a performance report, and a variance.
1-13. "Management by exception means abdicating management responsibility for planning and control." Do you agree? Explain.
1-14. "Good accounting provides automatic control of operations." Do you agree? Explain.
1-15. Distinguish between line and staff authority.
1-16. "The controller does control in a special sense." Explain.
1-17. "The importance of accurate source documents cannot be overemphasized." Explain.
1-18. *Organization chart.* Draw an organization chart for a single-factory com-

pany with the following personnel. Which represent factory service departments? Producing departments?

Punch press foreman	Personnel vice-president
Vice-president and controller	Maintenance foreman
Storekeeper	Sales vice-president
Drill press foreman	Production control chief
Production superintendent	Production planning chief
Chairman of the board	Assembly foreman
Engineering vice-president	Purchasing agent
Manufacturing vice-president	Secretary and treasurer
President	

1-19. *Score keeping, attention directing, and problem solving.* Internal (management) accounting tends to emphasize the attention-directing and problem-solving functions of accounting. However, there are many companies that have accounting systems that are oriented almost exclusively to score keeping. For example, one critic has stated:

> Very few people in business have had the opportunity to reflect on the way in which the accounting model developed, particularly on how an instrument well adapted to detect fraud and measure tax liability has gradually been used as a general information source. Having become accustomed to information presented in this form, business people have adapted their concepts and patterns of thought and communication to it rather than adapting the information to the job or person. When one suggests the reverse process, as now seems not only logical but well within economic limits, he must expect a real reluctance to abandon a pattern of behavior that has a long history of working apparently quite well.[2]

Considering the introductory material in this chapter, comment on this quotation, particularly on the meaning and implications of the last quoted sentence for today's and tomorrow's controllers.

1-20. *Selection of performance report and possible reasons for variances.* Charles Nardley is the general manager of a sizable product division of a mammoth corporation. Formerly, he was sales manager of the division. He is a sales-oriented executive and has little patience with heavily detailed accounting reports. Yet he wants to know what phases of production are most in need of top management attention.

All of the following three performance reports have an attached explanation of variances, not shown here. As the controller of this division, which performance report would you be inclined to submit to Nardley? Why? Why do some of the totals differ from others? Do any of the relationships shown suggest possible reasons for certain variances?

---

[2] William R. Fair, "The Next Step in Management Controls," in Donald G. Malcom and Alan J. Rowe, eds., *Management Control Systems* (New York: John Wiley & Sons, Inc., 1960), pp. 229-30.

LARGE CORPORATION
Sizable Division
Performance Report
For the Week Ended Jan. 24, 19x1

Production scheduled: 104,000 RF transformers
Production achieved: 100,000 RF transformers

F = Favorable Variance
U = Unfavorable Variance

Performance Report A:	Budget*	Actual	Variance	
Materials	$ 93,000	$ 93,500	$ 500	U
Labor	42,300	43,980	1,680	U
Other factory costs	14,700	16,520	1,820	U
	$150,000	$154,000	$4,000	U

* Based on 100,000 units.

Performance Report B:				
Two-gang variable condensers	$ 50,000	$ 50,200	$ 200	U
Other materials	43,000	43,300	300	U
Machine operators and coil winders	800	830	30	U
Assemblers	28,800	29,950	1,150	U
Testers	12,700	13,200	500	U
Rework	3,500	5,100	1,600	U
Power	7,000	7,100	100	U
Supplies	2,500	2,550	50	U
Indirect labor	1,700	1,770	70	U
	$150,000	$154,000	$4,000	U

Performance Report C:				
Aluminum chassis	$ 8,000	$ 8,000	$ —	
Two-gang variable condenser	50,000	50,200	200	U
Coil forms	8,000	8,000	—	
Copper wire, size 20	3,000	3,250	250	U
Paddler capacitor	8,000	8,000	—	
Tube socket	10,000	10,000	—	
Fixed capacitor	5,000	5,050	50	U
Three-strip terminal board	1,000	1,000	—	
Machine operators	500	520	20	U
Coil winders	300	310	10	U
Assemblers, stage 1	9,600	9,960	360	U
Assemblers, stage 2	19,200	19,990	790	U
Testers	12,700	13,200	500	U
Rework	3,500	5,100	1,600	U
Power	7,000	7,100	100	U
Supplies	2,500	2,550	50	U
Indirect labor	1,700	1,770	70	U
Depreciation	10,000	10,000	—	
Factory insurance	400	400	—	
Municipal property taxes	4,000	4,000	—	
Indirect labor	8,500	8,500	—	
	$172,900	$176,900	$4,000	U

CHAPTER 2

Basic
Accounting
Concepts

MANY OF YOU HAVE RECENTLY COMPLETED A COURSE IN BASIC accounting; others may have studied it some time ago. In either event, a short review is in order. This chapter is designed to give an over-all view of some fundamental concepts of accounting, with special emphasis on external corporate reporting—that is, on the manager's custodial or stewardship responsibilities for the assets entrusted to him. This type of reporting is basically a score-keeping task.

UNDERLYING CONCEPTS

The first few sessions of your course in elementary accounting probably dealt with transactions (those events that accountants deem worthy of formal recording), the balance sheet equation, the components of an income statement, and a variety of technical terms—asset, equity, liability, revenue, expense, net income, retained income, adjustments, and so forth. A conceptual framework, developed through the years by individuals and professional societies, underlies the terminology and procedures that you learned. Although these concepts are constantly being reevaluated by many accounting practitioners and academicians, they enjoy widespread acceptance by professional accountants.

The Entity

The accounting process focuses upon events as they affect a specific area of attention and effort—an organization. This entity may be a consolidated group of many interrelated corporations, a single corporation, a tax district, a department, or a paper-making machine. The concept of an entity helps the accountant relate events to a sharply defined unit of activity. For example, one of the first things you learned was to separate business transactions from personal transactions. A sale of groceries is an accounting transaction for a grocery store (the entity), but the owner's alimony payment by personal check of the owner is not.

Going Concern

To view an entity as a going concern is to assume that it will continue indefinitely or at least that it will not be liquidated in the near future. This notion implies that existing *resources,* such as fixed assets, *will be used* to fulfill the general purposes of a continuing concern, *rather than sold* in tomorrow's real estate or equipment markets. It also implies that existing liabilities will be paid at maturity in an orderly manner.

Monetary Measures

The monetary unit (the dollar, in the United States and Canada) is the principal means for measuring assets and equities. It is the common denominator for quantifying the effects of a wide variety of transactions. Accountants record, classify, summarize, and report in terms of the dollar.

Such measurement assumes that the principal counter—the dollar—is an unchanging yardstick. Yet we all know that a 1960 dollar does not have the same purchasing power as a 1950 or 1940 dollar. Therefore, accounting statements that include different dollars must be interpreted and compared with full consciousness of the limitations of the basic measurement unit. (For an expanded discussion, see Chapter 5.)

Accountants have been extensively criticized for not making explicit and formal adjustments to remedy the defects of their measuring unit. In the face of this, they maintain that price level adjustments would lessen objectivity and would add to general confusion. They claim that the price level problem has been exaggerated, and that the adjustments would not significantly affect the vast bulk of corporate statements because most accounts are in current or nearly current dollars.

Consistency

In reporting information, accountants are often free to select any one of a variety of procedures, all of which conform to "generally accepted accounting principles." There are, for example, various inventory cost-flow assumptions and various methods of allocating depreciation. Unless they are informed otherwise, users of financial statements assume that the particular procedures adopted by a given organization are consistent from year to year. If consistency could not be assumed, chaos would result. An organization could, for example, switch at whim from a first-in, first-out accounting of inventory to a last-in, first-out accounting, and back again.

Although consistency is desirable, it does not in itself constitute virtue. An accounting procedure can be consistently wrong. A company could, for example, consistently write off all acquisitions of fixed assets as expenses in the year of purchase. What is desired is described as "generally accepted accounting principles applied on a basis consistent with that of the preceding year." Where such consistency is not maintained, adequate disclosure and explanation should be mandatory.

Realization

The realization concept usually pertains to the recording of revenue from sales of products and services to customers. When is revenue realized—when the inventory is acquired, when the order is received, when the order is put into process, when it is finished, when it is delivered, or when the revenue is collected? Generally, the accountant has maintained that revenue is recognized when the goods or services are delivered, despite the fact that delivery is only one of a series of events related to the sale. He defends this entrenched practice by pointing out that, for most businesses, delivery is the occasion which validates a legal claim against the customer for goods or services rendered. He maintains that although the importance of purchasing, production, and distribution may differ from business to business, revenue is generally regarded as an indivisible totality. In this sense, revenue cannot be allocated in bits and pieces to individual business functions.

There are two major exceptions to the notion that an exchange (delivery, in most cases) is needed to justify the realization of revenue. First, long-run construction contracts often necessitate a percentage-of-completion method. For example, the builder of an ocean liner or a huge office building may portray his performance better by spreading prospective revenues, related costs, and resulting net income over the life of the contract in proportion to the work accomplished. Otherwise, all of the net income would appear in one chunk upon completion of the project, as if it were earned on a single day. Second, depending on the uncertainties involved, revenue is regarded as being realized under long-run installment contracts in proportion to the cash collections. In the first instance, revenue is realized earlier than under the general realization test; in the second instance, revenue is realized later.

Objectivity

Accountants seek and prize objectivity as one of their principal strengths and regard it as an essential characteristic of measurement. Objectivity is freedom from bias—it results in accuracy that is supported by convincing evidence which can be verified by independent accountants. It is a relative rather than an absolute concept. Some measurements can be extremely objective (such as cash in a cash register) in the sense that their accuracy can be checked exactly by a dozen CPA's. But there are gradations of objectivity. A dozen CPA's are less likely to arrive at the same balances for receivables, inventories, plant and equipment, and intangible assets, respectively. Yet they strive for measurement rules that will produce reasonable results, as objectively determined as possible. That is why accountants are generally satisfied with existing tests of realization.

Many critics of existing accounting practices want to trade objectivity (accuracy) for what they conceive as more relevant or valid information. For example, the accounting literature is peppered with suggestions that accounting should attempt to measure "economic income," even though objectivity may be lessened. This particular suggestion often involves introducing asset valuations at replacement costs, when these are higher than historical costs. The accounting profession has generally rejected these suggestions, even when reliable replacement market price quotations are available, because no evidence short of a bona fide sale is regarded as sufficient to justify income recognition.

Conservatism

In a technical sense, conservatism means selecting that method of measurement which yields the gloomiest immediate results. This attitude is reflected in such working rules as: "Anticipate no gains, but provide for all possible losses," and "If in doubt, write it off."

Accountants regard the historical costs of acquiring an asset as the ceiling for its valuation. Assets may be written up only upon an exchange, but they may be written down without an exchange. For example, consider the lower-of-cost-or-market procedures. Inventories are written down when replacement costs decline, but they are never written up when replacement costs increase.

Conservatism has been criticized as being inherently inconsistent. If replacement market prices are sufficiently objective and verifiable to justify write-downs, why aren't they just as valid for write-ups? Furthermore, the critics maintain, conservatism is not a fundamental concept. Accounting reports should try to present the most accurate picture possible—neither too high nor too low. Accountants defend their attitude by saying that erring in the direction of conservatism has less severe economic and social consequences than erring in the direction of overstating net income.

Matching

Many accountants claim that the principal concern of accounting is the periodic matching of accomplishments (as measured by the selling prices of goods and services rendered) with efforts (as measured by the costs of the goods and services rendered). Much of the accountant's work deals with the difficult measurement problems that must be overcome in the evaluation of an organization's performance—the relationship between efforts and accomplishments—during a given span of time.

Disclosure

Accountants are obliged to transmit all significant financial data, preferably in the body of the financial reports but also in explanatory footnotes. Especially since they may disagree about which particular inventory or depreciation method is best, accountants should disclose all the major facts so that the user can make his own adjustments and comparisons. The need for ample disclosure is paramount. There is no rule against providing supplementary information on price level adjustments, depreciation methods, or market values. A working rule should be: "When in doubt, disclose." Disclosure is perhaps one of the most important of the underlying concepts.

TERMINOLOGY

Accountants have very special meanings for their technical terms, and a large part of the course in basic accounting is devoted to the accountant's language. Some of the fundamental terms will now be reviewed.

Assets

Assets are economic resources that are expected to benefit the future activities of the entity. Assets may be viewed as bundles of services awaiting future use or expiration. It is helpful to think of assets, other than cash and receivables, as prepaid or stored costs (for example, inventories or fixed assets) which are carried forward to future periods rather than immediately charged against revenue.

Expired Costs

Expired costs, according to the Committee on Concepts and Standards of the American Accounting Association, are

> . . . those having no discernible benefit to future operations. They may be classified as "expense" or "loss." Expense is the expired cost, directly or in-

directly related to a given fiscal period, of the flow of goods or services into the market and of related operations. Loss is expired cost not beneficial to the revenue-producing activities of the enterprise.[1]

Most expired costs belong in the expense category rather than in the loss category. Examples of expenses are the cost of goods sold and the expired insurance on salesmen's cars. Examples of losses are losses from flood and theft not covered by insurance. Losses, unlike expenses, are not of direct benefit in the obtaining of revenue in a given period and they are generally nonrecurring.

To summarize, expenses and losses are used-up assets. Most assets may be conveniently viewed as costs which are held back from the expense stream and carried on the balance sheet to await release as expense in some future period. As inventories are used, for example, their cost becomes an expense which is charged as cost of goods sold. As delivery trucks are used, their original cost becomes an expense which is charged as depreciation.

Revenue

Revenue, according to the Committee on Concepts and Standards, is,

. . . the monetary expression of the aggregate of products or services transferred by an enterprise to its customers during a period of time.[2]

The major source of revenue is the sale of products or services.

Net Income

Net income is the change in net assets which reflects the excess of revenue and other income over related expenses and losses. Essentially it is the result of a process by which revenue, as it is realized, is matched with related expired costs. Costs expire. They become expenses or losses as they benefit a given period or as they may no longer be justifiably carried forward as assets. Net income, then, is the residual amount— the result of the matching of efforts (i.e., expenses) and accomplishments (i.e., revenue).

Accrual Basis and Cash Basis

The conceptually proper method of income determination is the *accrual basis*. Revenue is recognized as it is realized; expenses are recognized in the period during which the costs expire.

In accounting on the *cash basis*, revenue is recognized as cash is collected and most expenses are recognized in the period during which the

---

[1] "Accounting and Reporting Standards for Corporate Financial Statements, 1957 Revision," *Accounting Review*, October, 1957, p. 541.

[2] *Ibid.*, p. 540.

cash is disbursed. Depreciation is an exception. It is usually recognized as an expense under either the accrual or the cash method.

Adjusting Entries

Accounting on the accrual basis is usually achieved with the significant help of adjusting entries. (As you may recall, these entries usually prove troublesome to the beginning student.) The principal adjusting entries are for prepayments, accruals, deferrals, bad debt allowances, and depreciation. All of them have an important common characteristic. They reflect implicit transactions, in contrast to the explicit transactions that trigger nearly all the day-to-day routine entries.

To illustrate: Entries for sales, purchases, cash receipts, and cash disbursements are supported by explicit evidence. This evidence is usually in the form of source documents (for example, sales slips, purchase invoices, employee time records, customer's payments, or outgoing payments). On the other hand, adjusting entries for accrued interest, accrued wages, prepaid insurance, subscriptions collected in advance, depreciation, and the like are prepared from special schedules or memoranda that recognize events (like the passage of time) that are overlooked in day-to-day recording.

Adjusting entries refine the accountant's accuracy and provide a more meaningful measure of efforts, accomplishments, and financial position. They are an essential part of accrual accounting.

Value

Caution should be employed in the use of the word "value," because it is a word of many meanings and because it can usually be replaced by a more precise word. Whenever you are tempted to use "value," try to find a different term. You will be less vague, for example, if you refer to the costs of fixed assets and inventories rather than to their values. However, you may say "value" when it is accepted current usage, provided you modify the word by another descriptive word (market value, net realizable value).

SUMMARY

There is an underlying structure that provides a conceptual basis for accounting practice. The major ideas that guide accountants in their recording, classifying, and reporting are the entity, going concern, monetary measures, consistency, realization, objectivity, conservatism, matching, and disclosure.

Accountants have precise meanings for the terms they use. Among the more important terms are assets, expired costs, expense, loss, revenue, net income, accrual basis, and adjusting entries. The word "value," used alone, is vague. It should not be used loosely.

SUMMARY PROBLEM FOR YOUR REVIEW

PROBLEM

The aim of this problem is to review over-all fundamental accounting relationships, with special emphasis on the relation of cash inflow and outflow to the accrual concept of net income. The solution techniques were not discussed in the body of this chapter; they are demonstrated in this chapter's Appendix II.

(*Try to solve the problem before examining the solution that follows.*)

The Cavaretta Cashew Co. presents the following data:

*Partial Trial Balance
after All Adjustments and Closing**
19x4

	Jan. 1	Dec. 31
Cash	$ 22,000	$ 13,000
Accounts receivable	34,000	60,000
Inventory	80,000	68,000
Accounts payable	40,000	56,000
Fixed assets	71,000	78,000
Accumulated depreciation	11,000	17,000
Prepaid operating expenses	4,000	2,000
Note payable to bank	—	10,000
Cavaretta, capital	160,000	138,000

* The bookkeeper entered all adjustments, as of Dec. 31, except the one for interest.

Analysis of the cash transactions reveals:

Cash received from:	
Customers	$374,000
Cavaretta, additional investment	50,000
Bank loan on Dec. 1, 19x4 (due Apr. 1, 19x5;	
6% interest payable at maturity)	10,000
Cash paid out for:	
Merchandise	$224,000
Operating expenses	108,000
Fixed assets	7,000
Cavaretta, capital withdrawal	104,000

Required:

Prepare, in good form, as detailed an income statement for the year 19x4 as the data permit. If you have trouble, study Appendix II.

SOLUTION

CAVARETTA CASHEW CO.

Income Statement
For the Year Ending Dec. 31, 19x4

Sales (A)*		$400,000
Less cost of goods sold:		
Inventory, Jan. 1, 19x4	$ 80,000	
Purchases (B)*	240,000	
Available for sale	$320,000	
Inventory, Dec. 31, 19x4	68,000	252,000
Gross margin		$148,000
Less operating expenses:		
Depreciation	$ 6,000	
Miscellaneous (C)*	110,000	116,000
Net operating income		$ 32,000
Less interest expense (D)*		50
Net income		$ 31,950

* Letters are keyed to Supporting T-Account Analysis which follows.

Supporting T-Account Analysis

(A)   Accounts Receivable

Net change 26,000	
Sales X	Collections 374,000

$X = \$400,000$

(B)   Accounts Payable

	Net change 16,000
Payments 224,000	Purchases X

$X = \$240,000$

(C)   Prepaid Operating Expenses

	Net change 2,000
Payments 108,000	Write-offs X

$X = \$110,000$

(D) $.06 \times \$10,000 \times \frac{1}{12} = \$50$

The above analysis should suffice for obtaining the key income statement items. A more thorough T-account analysis follows:

Complete Analysis of T Accounts

Cash

			9,000
(1)	374,000	(4)	224,000
(2)	50,000	(5)	108,000
(3)	10,000	(6)	7,000
		(7)	104,000

Accounts Receivable

	26,000		
(8)	400,000	(1)	374,000

Inventory

			12,000
(9B)	68,000	(9A)	80,000

Fixed Assets

	7,000		
(6)	7,000		

Accumulated Depreciation

			6,000
		(12)	6,000

Prepaid Operating Expenses

			2,000
(5)	108,000	(11)	110,000

Accounts Payable

			16,000
(4)	224,000	(10)	240,000

Note Payable

			10,000
		(3)	10,000

Cavaretta, Capital

	22,000		
(7)	104,000	(2)	50,000
		(13)	32,000*

Net Income Summary

(9A)	80,000	(8)	400,000
(10)	240,000	(9B)	68,000
(11)	110,000		
(12)	6,000		
(13)	32,000*		

* Note that all adjustments, except the $50 interest accrual, were entered. If this had been entered, the ending capital account balance would have been $137,950 instead of $138,000 and Entry (13) would be $31,950 instead of $32,000.

APPENDICES

I. Fundamental Accounting Relationships: Points to Remember

The following reminders are for those of you who feel rusty about basic accounting relationships. Nearly all these points were probably covered during the initial weeks of your first course.

Terminology

The terms grouped below have similar meanings and are often used interchangeably:

1. Balance sheet; position statement; statement of financial position; statement of financial condition.
2. Income statement; report of earnings; statement of operations; statement of profit and loss; statement of income.

3. Reconciliation of retained earnings; statement of surplus; statement of retained earnings; reconciliation of proprietor's capital.
4. Assets; properties; resources.
5. Equities; claims; interests; liabilities and net worth; sources; liabilities and stockholders' equity.
6. Liabilities; outside claims; outsider interests.
7. Stockholders' equity; net worth; proprietorship; ownership claims; ownership equity; ownership interests; capital stock and surplus; capital.
8. Retained earnings; retained income; earned surplus; reinvested earnings.
9. Revenue; sales.
10. Cost of goods sold; cost of sales; merchandise cost of goods sold.

Some Fundamentals

1.
$$\text{Assets } (A) = \text{Liabilities } (L) + \text{Stockholders' equity } (SE) \tag{1}$$

But SE equals original ownership claim plus the increase in ownership claim due to profitable operations. That is, SE equals the claim arising from *contributed capital* plus the claim arising from *accumulated capital*, the forced reinvestment of earnings.

Therefore
$$A = L + \text{Capital stock} + \text{Retained earnings} \tag{2}$$

But, ignoring dividends for the moment, Retained earnings equals Revenue minus Expenses.

Therefore
$$A = L + \text{Capital stock} + \text{Revenue} - \text{Expenses} \tag{3}$$

Transposing
$$A + \text{Expenses} = L + \text{Capital stock} + \text{Revenue} \tag{4}$$

Finally
$$\text{Left} = \text{Right} \tag{5}$$
$$\text{Debit} = \text{Credit}$$

2. *Debit* means one thing, and one thing only—"left" (not "bad," "something coming," etc.). *Credit* means one thing and one thing only—"right" (not "good," "something owed," etc.).
3. *Revenue* and *expense accounts* are nothing more than subdivisions of stockholders' equity—temporary stockholders' equity accounts, as it were. Their purpose is to summarize the volume of sales and the various expenses, so that management is kept informed of the reasons for the constant increases and decreases in stockholders' equity in the course of ordinary operations. In this way comparisons can be made, standards or goals can be set, and control can be better exercised.
4. Assets are traditionally carried as left-hand balances. Why do assets and expenses both carry debit balances? They carry left-hand balances for different reasons. *Expenses* are temporary stockholders' equity accounts. Decreases in stockholders' equity are entered on the left side of the accounts because they offset the normal (i.e., right-hand) stockholders' equity balances. Because expenses decrease stockholders' equity, they are carried as left-hand balances.
5. *Retained earnings* (earned surplus) are not a pot of cash that is awaiting distribution to stockholders. Following is an example of the meaning of balance sheet relationships:

Step 1. Assume an opening balance sheet of:

Cash	$100	Capital stock	$100

Step 2. Purchase inventory for $50 cash. The balance now reads:

Cash	$ 50	Capital stock	$100
Inventory	50		
	$100		

Step 3. Now sell the inventory for $80:

Cash	$130	Capital stock	$100
		Retained earnings	30
			$130

At this stage the retained earnings might be reflected by a $30 increase in cash. But the $30 in retained earnings connotes only a general claim against total assets. This may be clarified by the transaction which follows.

Step 4. Purchase equipment and inventory, in the amounts of $40 and $50, respectively. Now:

Cash	$ 40	Capital stock	$100
Inventory	50	Retained earnings	30
Equipment	40		$130
	$130		

Where is the $30 in retained earnings reflected? Is it reflected in cash, in inventory, or in equipment? The answer is indeterminate. This example helps to explain the nature of the retained earnings account. It is a *claim*, not a pot of gold. Retained earnings are increased by profitable operations, but the cash inflow from sales is an increment in assets (see *Step 3*). When the cash inflow takes place, management will use the cash, most often to buy more inventory or equipment (*Step 4*). Retained earnings are a *general* claim against *total* assets, *not* a preferred claim against cash or against any other asset.

6. *Withdrawals, or dividends,* are distributions of assets which reduce ownership claims. The cash assets that are distributed typically arose from profitable operations. Thus, dividends or withdrawals are often spoken of as "distributions of profits" or "distributions of retained income." Dividends are often erroneously described as being "paid *out of* retained income." In reality, ordinary dividends are distributions of assets, and liquidate a portion of the ownership claim. The distribution is made possible by profitable operations.

7. *A useful point of view:* Assets are measured as prepaid costs or stored-up costs. Expenses are used-up assets. Thus, assets are costs held back from the expense stream and carried on the balance sheet to await release as expenses in some future period. That is, assets represent services that will benefit future fiscal periods.

8. *Closing the books* is the mechanical bookkeeping act of clearing out all the balances in the *nominal* revenue and expense accounts by transferring their ending balances to the retained earnings account. Thus, it is a process of summarizing and transferring temporary stockholders' equity accounts.

After the books are closed, there are balances only in the *real* accounts (i.e., the accounts that appear in the balance sheet).

Closing the books is a practical necessity in that it excludes from revenue and expense accounts those data which do not pertain to the current fiscal period. After closing, all revenue and expense accounts have zero balances because the amounts have been transferred and summarized as one figure (i.e., net income for the year) which rests in the retained earnings account. Thus, the revenue and expense accounts are ready for the coming fiscal period.

An illustration of the closing process follows:

Step 1. Assume it is the end of the fiscal year, and the following balances are found in the general ledger revenue and expense accounts:

Sales	$100,000
Cost of goods sold	60,000
Rent	20,000
Wages	15,000

Assume also that there is a retained earnings balance (carried from previous fiscal periods) of $200,000.

Step 2. Now make the entry to close the books, as follows:

Debit: Sales	$100,000	
Credit: Cost of goods sold		$60,000
Rent		20,000
Wages		15,000
Retained earnings		5,000

Visualize the postings of this entry: *All* revenue and expense accounts will now have zero balances, and retained earnings will be increased by $5,000, the net income for the year.

Did stockholders' equity change in total? No. What happened? All that occurred was the mechanical act of *transferring* and *summarizing* the amounts in the temporary stockholders' equity accounts to the permanent stockholders' equity account (i.e., retained earnings). Rather than clutter the retained earnings account with the burdensome details of all specific revenues and expenses, these data are summarized and carried as one figure (i.e., net income) in the retained earnings account.

Step 3. When the new fiscal period begins, brand new revenue and expense accounts are created. These are used until the end of the fiscal period. Then they are closed and transferred to retained earnings. The same procedure is followed year after year.

II. Problem Solving Techniques

Cash versus Accrual Basis

In the body of Chapter 2, we briefly discussed the accrual and the cash bases for matching revenues and expenses. In practice, accountants often face the problem of using accounting records kept on a cash basis as a starting point for preparing financial statements on an accrual basis. Accountants must be able to change from one to the other, often from the cash to the accrual basis. The correction of errors or the adjusting of incomplete records, also, often involves the relationship of cash flow to revenue or expense recognition.

Our interest in these techniques is not primarily to develop your bookkeeping ability. Rather, it is to help you realize that the use of accrual accounting, rather than cash accounting, makes possible a more refined evaluation of performance.

Below are two short problems. The solutions, and some comments about technique, follow. Before glancing at the solutions and comments, attempt to get the answers on scratch paper.

Question 1. From the following information, calculate the gross sales for May:

Accounts receivable, May 1	$15,000	Cash discounts allowed on credit	
Accounts receivable, May 31	14,600	sales	$100
Collections on account	8,050	Write-offs of accounts receivable	300
Cash sales	3,000	Allowances on sales	200

Question 2. From the following information calculate the cost of goods sold for the year. Assume that cash discounts are treated as offsets against purchases rather than as other income:

Accounts payable		Inventory, Dec. 31	$13,000
(for merchandise), Jan. 1	$20,000	Cash discounts taken on credit	
Accounts payable, Dec. 31	22,000	purchases	500
Cash payments on account	50,000	Purchase returns	2,000
Inventory, Jan. 1	11,000	Cash purchases	5,000

Similar questions used in class tests have resulted in a very high percentage of error. Likelihood of error may be minimized through the use of key T accounts as work sheets for cash versus accrual and incomplete record problems. The use of key T accounts offers the following advantages:

1. You work with a familiar device.

2. T accounts are constructed with built-in checks on accuracy.

Solution to Question 1

Step 1. Enter all knowns in the key T account. A knowledge of the usual components of such an account is essential.

Accounts Receivable

Balance, May 1	15,000	Write-offs	300
Gross credit sales	X	Allowance on sales	200
		Discounts allowed	100*
		Collections	8,050
Total debits	(15,000 + X)	*Total credits*	8,650
Balance, May 31	14,600		

* This bracket is used to highlight the analytical usefulness of subdividing the credit to Accounts Receivable arising from collections subject to cash discounts. For example, if a $1,000 debt subject to a 2 per cent cash discount were collected, the journal entry would be:

Cash	980	
Cash discounts allowed	20	
Accounts receivable		1,000

For analytical purposes, the $1,000 credit is subdivided into $980 and $20, even though the real-life posting would be a lump sum of $1,000.

Step 2. Find the unknown by solving for X. Simple arithmetic will yield the answer, but the following solution illustrates the algebraic nature of relationships in a debit balance account:

$$Total\ debits - Total\ credits = Balance$$
$$(\$15,000 + X) - \$8,650 = \$14,600$$
$$\$15,000 + X = \$23,250$$
$$X = \$\ 8,250$$

Credit Sales plus Cash Sales equals Gross Sales: $8,250 plus $3,000 equals *$11,250.*

Alternate Solution to Question 1

Working with the net *change* in the beginning and ending balance of a particular account is a less awkward procedure to problems of this type. To show how this is done, let us rework the solution to Question 1.

The algebraic nature of the relationships in the Accounts Receivable can be used to show the following:

Beginning balances + Current debits − Current credits = Ending balance   (1)
or   Current debits − Current credits = Ending balance
                                                                        − Beginning balance   (2)

Equation (2) can be used as a basic approach to cash versus accrual problems. The steps to be taken, therefore, are:

Step 1. Insert the *net change* in the balances at the *top* of the account, drawing a single line below the net change as indicated.

Accounts Receivable

Increase	*Decrease*
	400

Step 2. Enter all other known items in the T account.

Accounts Receivable

		Net change	400
Gross credit sales	X	Write-offs	300
		Allowance on sales	200
		Discounts allowed	$\{$ 100
		Collections	$\{$ 8,050
Total current debits	X	*Total current credits*	8,650

If a correct analysis is made, the difference between the Total Current Debits and Total Current Credits should equal the Net Change at the top of the account.

Step 3. Find the unknown.

$$\textit{Current debits} - \textit{Current credits} = \textit{Ending balance} - \textit{Beginning balance}$$
$$X - \$8,650 \qquad = -\$400^*$$
$$X = -\$400 + \$8,650$$
$$X = \$8,250$$

* \$14,600 − \$15,000 = −\$400

Solution to Question 2

Steps 1 and 2. Enter the net change at the proper side of the top of the T account, and then enter all other known items:

Accounts Payable

Decrease		*Increase*	
			2,000
Purchase returns	2,000	Credit purchases	X
Discounts taken	⎰ 500		
Cash payments	⎱ 50,000		
	52,500		X

Step 3. Obtain the unknown:

$$\textit{Current credits} - \textit{Current debits} = \textit{Net change in balance}$$
$$X - \$52,500 \qquad = \$\ 2,000$$
$$X = \$54,500$$

Total Credit Purchases plus Cash Purchases equals \$54,500 plus \$5,000, or \$59,500.

Step 4. Many students overlook the necessity for getting the cost of goods sold. They stop after the third step. Never forget the requirements of the problem.

Inventory, Jan. 1			\$11,000
Purchases		\$59,500	
Returns	\$2,000		
Discounts	500	2,500	57,000
			\$68,000
Inventory, Dec. 31			13,000
Cost of goods sold			\$55,000

This key T-account technique may be used to advantage in many problem situations.

Statement of Cash Receipts and Disbursements

It is helpful to remember that a statement of cash receipts and disbursements is merely a formal reproduction and analysis of the content of a cash account. The use of a cash T account together with other key T accounts as a work sheet is often the most efficient means of solving problems requiring such a statement.

Correction of Errors

Problems involving the correction of errors test practical comprehension of the accrual basis of accounting. Problems of this sort are helpful because they:

(1) present unfamiliar situations; (2) require more pervasive thought than problems of a more stereotyped nature; and (3) require not only knowledge of correct methods, but also the ability to work from the incorrect to the correct method (usually through adjusting or correcting entries).

The most troublesome errors are frequently those that affect two or more fiscal periods. These errors may be divided into two major types:

1. *Counterbalancing errors.* These are omissions or misstatements in one fiscal period which are counterbalanced by offsetting errors in the ordinary bookkeeping process in the next period. Examples are errors affecting accruals, prepayments, deferrals, and inventories. Such errors affect income by identical and offsetting amounts in successive periods; they also affect the balance sheet of the first period, but not the second.

   For example, the omission of $1,000 of accrued salaries would: (1) overstate income and understate year-end liabilities by $1,000 in the first year; and (2) understate income by $1,000 and have no effect on year-end liabilities in the second year. Note that the retained earnings balance at the end of the second year would be correct (ignoring income tax considerations). The total of the two incorrect net incomes will be identical with the total of the two correct net incomes.

2. Some errors are not counterbalanced in the ordinary bookkeeping process. Thus, until specific correcting entries are made, all subsequent balance sheets will be in error. Examples of such errors are erroneous depreciation estimates, charging original bond discounts directly to retained earnings, capitalizing repairs, and charging capital outlays to expense.

   For example, an excessive depreciation expense of $2,000 in one year would: (1) understate income, assets, and retained earnings by $2,000 in that year; and (2) would continue as an understatement of assets and retained earnings on successive balance sheets for the life of the fixed asset. Observe that income for subsequent years would not be affected unless the same error is committed again.

Inventory Shortages, Fire Losses, Incomplete Records

Most problems involving inventory losses present a great amount of factual information. You must pick and choose the relevant from the irrelevant in working toward the unknown inventory figure. Essentially, most of these problems require a recasting of the conventional cost-of-goods-sold section and working from given amounts to the unknown inventory amount.

One effective way to solve these problems involves preparing a schedule of the conventional sales and cost-of-goods-sold section of the income statement.

Sales		$1,000 (100%)
Less cost of sales:		
Beginning inventory	$ 400	
Purchases	1,500	
Available for sale	$1,900	
Ending inventory	X	
Cost of sales		Y
Gross profit		Z (40%)

The facts in a problem will supply sufficient figures so that you may fill in the conventional schedule with known figures and then obtain the unknown, either by working from the bottom (i.e., Gross Profit) up or from the top (i.e., Sales) down.

The use of the gross profit relationship is usually an integral part of the solution to such problems. Unless otherwise stated, any gross profit percentage given is based upon *net sales*, not cost. In the above schedule, Gross Profit is 40 per cent. Cost of Sales must be 60 per cent of sales, or $600. Therefore, the Ending Inventory must be $1,300.

The gross profit relationship may also be stated algebraically. If you have facility with algebra, you may prefer to use equations such as the following:

$$\text{Cost of sales} = \text{Net sales} - \text{Gross profit}$$

and

$$\text{Cost of sales} = \text{Beginning inventory} + \text{Net purchases} - \text{Ending inventory}$$

ASSIGNMENT MATERIAL

ESSENTIAL ASSIGNMENT MATERIAL

2-1. *Adjusting and Correcting Entries.* The following is an Unadjusted Trial Balance as of Dec. 31, 19x2:

MANTLE CLOAK COMPANY

Unadjusted Trial Balance
Dec. 31, 19x2

Account Number			
1.	Cash	$ 5,000	
2.	Note receivable	1,000	
3.	Accounts receivable	10,300	
4.	Allowance for bad debts		$ 300
5.	Inventory balance, as of Jan. 1, 19x2	20,000	
6.	Unexpired insurance	600	
7.	Office supplies on hand		
8.	Unexpired rent		
9.	Equipment	4,000	
10.	Accumulated depreciation on equipment		500
11.	Accounts payable		10,000
12.	Long-term 5 per cent mortgage payable		3,000
13.	Accrued interest payable		
14.	Accrued wages payable		
15.	Mantle capital		18,500
16.	Sales		120,000
17.	Sales returns	1,000	
18.	Sales discounts	1,000	
19.	Purchases	71,000	
20.	Purchase returns		1,000
21.	Wages	22,000	
22.	Rent and heat	10,000	
23.	Bad debts expense		
24.	Other operating expenses	7,000	
25.	Supplies expense	400	
26.	Insurance expense		
27.	Depreciation		
28.	Interest expense		
		$153,300	$153,300

Required:

For each of the following items (1) through (12) prepare the necessary entries. Select only from the accounts listed in the Trial Balance. The same account may be used in several answers. Answer by using account *numbers*. For example, Item (1) would call for a debit to Cash (1) for $100, a debit to Equipment (9) for $300, and a credit to Mantle Capital (15) for $400. (*Note:* The accounts that carry no balances are listed in the table for your convenience in making adjustments. All accounts needed to answer the questions are included.)

(1) On Dec. 30, the owner invested $100 in cash plus equipment valued at $300. The bookkeeper has not recorded the transaction.

(2) Unexpired insurance was $450 on Dec. 31, 19x2.

(3) The interest on the mortgage is payable yearly on Jan. 2. (Adjust for a *full year's* interest. Don't refine the arithmetic for one or two days' interest.)

(4) Wages of sales clerks earned, but not paid, amount to $100.

(5) A physical count of the office supplies revealed that there is a balance of $300 on hand as of Dec. 31, 19x2.

(6) It is estimated that the Allowance for Bad Debts should be *increased* by an amount equal to one-half of 1 per cent of 19x2 gross sales.

(7) The equipment cost is being allocated to operations on the basis of an estimated useful life of 20 years and no residual value.

(8) Mantle withdrew $500 in cash on Dec. 31. The bookkeeper has not recorded the transaction.

(9) A $500 rental charge for January, 19x3, was paid in cash to the DiMaggio Realty Company on Dec. 31. The Mantle Company bookkeeper did not record the transaction.

(10) A correct entry was made, early in December, for $1,000 worth of goods sold to a customer on open account. The customer returned these goods on Dec. 29. The bookkeeper has made no entry for the latter transaction, although a credit memo was issued, Dec. 31.

(11) On Dec. 20, a customer paid the Mantle Company $980 for a $1,000 invoice, deducting a 2 per cent discount. The bookkeeper made the appropriate entries. On Dec. 30, Mr. Mantle discovered that the customer should have paid the full $1,000 because the discount period had expired on Dec. 17. He sent the customer another invoice for the extra $20. The bookkeeper has not recorded the latter transaction.

(12) There was a $1,000 payroll robbery on Dec. 15. Wages had been debited for $1,000 and Cash credited for $1,000 for the original payroll. A substitute payroll was made up on Dec. 16, Wages again debited for $1,000, and Cash again credited for $1,000. However, the loss was covered by insurance. On Dec. 20, the insurance company remitted $1,000 and the Mantle bookkeeper debited Cash and credited Sales.

2-2. *Converting from accrual to cash basis.* The Vatter Athletic Club presents the following statements at the end of the calendar year 19x2:

Comparative Balance Sheets

Dec. 31	19x1	19x2
Cash	$ 1,100	$ 9,170
Dues receivable	2,500	3,000
Investments	8,000	3,000
Furniture and fixtures	500	900
Accumulated depreciation on furniture and fixtures	—	(100)
Accrued interest receivable	100	200
Supplies	100	250
Totals	$12,300	$16,420
Accounts payable (supplies only)	$ 1,500	$ 1,300
Notes payable	300	50
Accrued general expenses	400	450
Dues received in advance	100	—
Members' equity	10,000	14,620
Totals	$12,300	$16,420

Statement of Income

Revenue:		
Dues	$8,000	
Interest	700	
Donations	520	
		$9,220
Expenses:		
General expenses	$2,000	
Supplies consumed	1,500	
Depreciation	100	
Loss on sale of investments	1,000	4,600
		$4,620

Required:

Assuming that only supplies were purchased on account during the year, answer the following questions:

1. How much cash was received as payments for dues during the year?
2. How much cash was received as payments for interest during the year?
3. How much cash was received upon sale of the investments?
4. How much cash was disbursed for general expenses for the year?
5. How much cash was disbursed for supplies during the year?

ADDITIONAL ASSIGNMENT MATERIAL

Note: All of these problems are relatively simple, in the sense that they constitute a review of the fundamentals of accrual accounting in relation to cash flow and in relation to the effects of errors. Problems 2-25 and 2-26 are probably the most elementary. Problem 2-38 is the most comprehensive. Problem 2-39 is a recapitulation of the provocative issues raised by the financial statements of the

Lyndon Johnson family; it fuses in one situation all the basic concepts covered in this chapter.

2-3. Give five examples of accounting entities.

2-4. Define the going concern.

2-5. What is the major criticism of the dollar as the principal accounting measure?

2-6. Define consistency.

2-7. What are the two major exceptions to the idea that an exchange is needed to justify the realization of revenue?

2-8. What does the accountant mean by objectivity?

2-9. Define conservatism.

2-10. How important is disclosure in relation to other fundamental accounting concepts?

2-11. Criticize: "Assets are things of value owned by the entity."

2-12. Distinguish between an expense and a loss.

2-13. Criticize: "Net income is the difference in the ownership capital amount balances at two points in time."

2-14. Distinguish between the accrual basis and the cash basis.

2-15. How do adjusting entries differ from routine entries?

2-16. Why is it better to refer to the *costs,* rather than *values,* of assets like plant or inventories?

2-17. Give at least two synonymous terms for each of the following: balance sheet; income statement; assets.

2-18. Give at least three other terms for retained earnings.

2-19. Criticize: "As a stockholder, I have a right to more dividends. You have millions stashed away in Retained Earnings. It's about time that you let the true owners get their hands on that pot of gold."

2-20. Criticize: "Dividends are distributions of profits."

2-21. Describe closing the books in two sentences.

2-22. What are the two major types of errors that affect two or more fiscal periods?

2-23. If gross profit is 60 per cent, express the relationship of cost of goods sold to gross profit in percentage terms.

2-24. *Conservatism and consistency.* (CPA, Adapted.) The new president and the controller of a chain of independent gasoline stations are having a dispute regarding the first-year operating losses of new gasoline stations. The president favors amortization of such losses over a three-year period, but the controller does not favor regarding such losses as an asset. The president maintains that amortization is industry practice and that such accounting would be conservative and consistent with industry practice.

Evaluate the president's use of the words "conservative" and "consistent" from the standpoint of accounting terminology. What accounting treatment do you recommend? Why?

2-25. *Balance sheet equation: solving for unknowns.* (Prepared by James March.) Compute the unknowns (X, Y, and Z) in the following (*a* through *g*).

Given	a	b	c	d	e	f	g
Assets at beginning of period		$10,000				Z	$ 8,200
Assets at end of period		11,000					9,600
Liabilities at beginning of period		6,000				$ 2,000	4,000
Liabilities at end of period		Y					6,000
Proprietorship at beginning of period	$5,000						X
Proprietorship at end of period	X	5,000				10,000	
Sales			$15,000		X	14,000	20,000
Inventory at beginning of period			6,000	$ 8,000		Y	
Inventory at end of period			7,000	6,000		7,000	
Purchases			10,000	10,000		6,000	
Gross profit			Y		2,000	6,000	
Cost of goods sold			X	X	4,500	X	Z
Other expenses			4,000			4,000	5,000
Net profit	3,000	X	Z				Y
Withdrawals	1,000					1,500	400
Additional investments						5,000	

2-26. *Matching transactions and accounts.* Listed below are a series of accounts which are numbered for identification. At the right are columns in which you are to write the identification numbers of the accounts affected by the transactions described. The same account may be used in several answers. Answer all; omit none.

1. Cash
2. Accounts receivable
3. Inventory
4. Equipment
5. Allowance for depreciation of equipment
6. Prepaid insurance
7. Accounts payable

8. Notes payable
9. Wages payable
10. Accrued interest payable
11. Common stock
12. Retained earnings
13. Operating expenses
14. Cost of goods sold
15. Sales

	Debit	Credit
a. Purchased new equipment for cash plus a short-term note.	4	1, 8
b. Paid cash for salaries and wages. Part of this payment was for work done during the last fiscal period.		
c. Made sales on credit. Inventory is accounted for by a perpetual system.		
d. Collected cash from customers on account.		
e. Paid some old trade bills with cash.		
f. Purchased three-year insurance policy on credit.		
g. Sold for cash some old equipment at book value. (*Note:* Book value is the difference between original cost and accumulated depreciation.)		
h. Paid off note owed to bank, together with interest accrued during last fiscal period and interest incurred during this fiscal period.		

i. Paid freight-in charges in cash for inventory that arrived today.   _____ _____
j. Bought regular merchandise on credit.   _____ _____
k. In order to secure additional funds, 400 new shares of common stock were sold for cash.   _____ _____
l. Some insurance premiums have expired and an adjusting entry is required.   _____ _____
m. Paid cash for ad in today's *Chicago Tribune*.   _____ _____
n. Recorded the entry for depreciation on equipment for the current fiscal period.   _____ _____

2-27. *Effects of error.* The bookkeeper of a certain firm, the Dark Co., included the cost of a new motor truck, purchased on Dec. 30 for $5,000 to be paid in January, as an operating expense instead of as an addition to the proper asset account. What was the effect of this error ("no effect," "overstated," or "understated"—use symbols n, o, or u, respectively) on:

1. Operating expenses for the year ended Dec. 31.   _____
2. Net profit from operations for the year.   _____
3. Retained earnings as of Dec. 31 after the books are closed.   _____
4. Total liabilities as of Dec. 31.   _____
5. Total assets as of Dec. 31.   _____

2-28. *Find unknowns in Cost of Goods Sold section.* For each of the following Cases (1 through 4), find the unknowns, designated by letters A through G.

	Case 1	Case 2	Case 3	Case 4
Inventory, Jan. 1	B	$ 50,000	$20,000	$15,000
Freight in		3,000	1,000	2,000
Gross purchases	$ 70,000	90,000	E	67,000
Gross sales	100,000	130,000		G
Returned purchases		2,000	2,000	3,000
Sales discounts			1,000	2,000
Purchase discounts		2,000	1,000	1,000
Freight out		4,000	2,000	1,400
Gross profit	20,000	C		25,000
Sales returns			5,000	4,000
Inventory, Dec. 31	30,000	D	30,000	F
Cost of goods sold	A	110,000	50,000	80,000
Accounts receivable, Jan. 1	8,000	15,200	3,000	7,500
Accounts receivable, Dec. 31	10,300	17,000	3,100	6,600
Accounts payable, Jan. 1	3,650	12,150	4,050	3,900
Accounts payable, Dec. 31	7,000	9,840	4,200	1,200

2-29. *Converting from cash to accrual basis.* From the following data, calculate the rent revenue earned balance on the accrual basis to be reported in the income statement for the month of December. Rent collections during December were $3,000. The data pertain to a real estate company's operations.

	Dec. 1	Dec. 31
Deferred rental revenue	$200	$2,000
Accrued rent receivable	300	600

2-30. *Compute rent revenue.* From the following data, calculate the rent revenue earned balance on the accrual basis to be reported in the income statement for the month of December. Rent collections during December were $5,000. The data pertain to a real estate company's operations:

	Dec. 1	Dec. 31
Deferred rental revenue	$200	$2,000
Accrued rent receivable	500	800

2-31. *Converting from accrual to cash basis.* The following account balances were taken from the ledger of the Brown Distributing Co. on the dates indicated:

	Jan. 1, 19x1	Dec. 31, 19x1
Accounts payable	$16,500	$ 14,000
Notes receivable	2,000	1,000
Purchases		166,000
Accounts receivable	26,200	20,400
Sales		205,000
Returned purchases and allowances		2,500

Additional information:

Purchases and sales are all on account with no discounts.

Accounts payable reflect transactions with merchandise creditors only.

Notes receivable totaling $4,000 were accepted in settlement of open accounts.

No accounts receivable were written off as uncollectible during 19x1.

Required:

1. Compute the amount of cash collected on:
   a. Accounts Receivable.
   b. Notes Receivable (ignore interest).
2. Compute the amount paid to merchandise creditors.

2-32. *Conversion from accrual to cash basis.* From the following data, calculate the cash collected for subscriptions for the month of December. The Subscription Revenue Earned balance that was reported in the income statement for the month of December was $200,000. These data pertain to a magazine company's operations:

	Dec. 1	Dec. 31
Deferred subscription revenue	$100,000	$170,000
Accrued subscriptions receivable	9,000	7,000

2-33. *Cost of inventory destroyed by fire.* R. Kelly requires an estimate of the cost of merchandise lost by fire on Mar. 7. Merchandise inventory on Jan. 1 was $40,000. Purchases since Jan. 1 were $35,000; freight in, $3,000; purchase returns and allowances, $2,000. Sales are made at a gross profit of 25 per cent of *sales* and totaled $42,000 up to Mar. 7. What was the cost of the merchandise destroyed?

2-34. *Gross profit computations and inventory costs.* On Jan. 15, 19x4, P. Warner valued his inventory at cost, $18,000. His statements are based on the calendar year, so you find it necessary to establish an inventory figure as of Jan. 1, 19x4. You find that from Jan. 2 to Jan. 15, sales were $60,000; sales returns, $1,500; goods purchased and placed in stock, $54,000; goods removed from stock and returned to vendors, $2,000; freight in, $500. Calculate the inventory cost as of Jan. 1, assuming that goods are marked to sell at 30 per cent above cost.

2-35. *Effects of errors.* What will be the effect—overstated (*o*), understated (*u*), no effect (*n*)—upon the income statements of the present and future periods if:

	Present	Future
1. Deferred charges are ignored?	_____	_____
2. Accrued expenses are ignored?	_____	_____
3. Deferred credits are ignored?	_____	_____
4. Accrued income is ignored?	_____	_____

2-36. *Effects of errors.* Assume a going concern and analyze the effect of the following errors on the net profit figures for 19x1 and 19x2. Choose one of three answers: understated (*u*), overstated (*o*), or no effect (*n*). Problem *a* has been answered as an illustration.

a. EXAMPLE: Failure to adjust at end of 19x1 for sales salaries accrued. 19x1: *o*; 19x2: *u*. (*Explanation:* In 19x1, expenses would be understated and profits overstated. This error would carry forward so that expenses in 19x2 would be overstated and profits understated.)

b. Failure to adjust at end of 19x1 for interest earned but not received on notes receivable.

c. Omission of Depreciation on Office Machines in 19x1 only. Ordinary depreciation was taken in 19x2.

d. Machinery, cost price $500, bought in 19x1, was not entered in the books until paid for in 19x2. Ignore depreciation; answer in terms of the specific error described.

e. Failure to adjust for the following at end of 19x2: Physical count of office supplies, $100. Office Supplies, an asset account, was charged for purchases of supplies and had an unadjusted balance of $300.

f. Three months' rent, collected in advance in December, 19x1, for the first quarter of 19x2 was credited directly to Rent Earned in 19x1. No adjustment was made for the unearned rent at the end of 19x1.

2-37. *Product development costs and income measurement.* Comment on the following: (from *Chicago Tribune*, May 14, 1963):

Sales of Motorola, Inc. in the first quarter of the year set a new record for the period, but extraordinary design and pre-production costs on a color television tube . . . pared profits.

Motorola's first quarter sales were $80,590,096, up 4 per cent from the old first quarter high. . . . Net profit in the period was $1,356,667 . . . compared with $2,455,944 in the first 1962 quarter.

He said that total investment ¦ . . . in the project will exceed 4 million dollars. Much of this amount was to be spent in the first 1963 quarter.

2-38. *Effects of adjustments and corrections.* Listed below are a series of accounts which are numbered for identification. All accounts needed to answer the parts of this question are included. Prepare an answer sheet with columns in which you are to write the identification numbers of the accounts affected by your answers. The same account may be used in several answers.

1. Cash	18. Accrued interest payable
2. Accounts receivable	19. Deferred subscription revenue
3. Notes receivable	20. Capital
4. Inventory	21. Sales
5. Accrued interest receivable	22. Sales discounts
6. Accrued rent receivable	23. Sales returns and allowances
7. Fuel on hand	24. Purchases
8. Unexpired rent	25. Purchase discounts
9. Unexpired insurance	26. Purchase returns and allowances
10. Unexpired repairs and maintenance	27. Fuel expense
nance	28. Salaries and wages
11. Land	29. Insurance expense
12. Buildings	30. Repairs and maintenance expense
13. Machinery and equipment	31. Rent expense
14. Accounts payable	32. Social security tax expense
15. Notes payable	33. Rent revenue
16. Accrued wages and salaries payable	34. Subscription revenue
	35. Interest revenue
17. Accrued social security taxes payable	36. Interest expense

Required: Prepare any necessary adjusting or correcting entries called for by the following situations, *which were discovered at the end of the calendar year.* With respect to each situation, assume that no entries have been made regarding the situation other than those specifically described (i.e., no monthly adjustments have been made during the year). *Consider each situation separately.* These transactions were not necessarily conducted by one business firm.

Illustration: Purchased new equipment for $100 cash, plus a $300 short-term note. The bookkeeper failed to record the transaction. The answer would appear as follows:

	Account		*Amount*	
	Debit	*Credit*	*Debit*	*Credit*
Illustration	13	1,15	400	100,300
a.	——	——	——	——
b.	——	——	——	——
c.	——	——	——	——
etc.	——	——	——	——

a. A business made several purchases of fuel oil. Some purchases ($800) were debited to Fuel Expense, while others ($1,100) were charged to an asset account. An oil gauge revealed $400 of fuel on hand at the end of the year. There was no fuel on hand at the beginning of the year.

b. On Apr. 1, a business took out a fire insurance policy. The policy was for two years and the premium paid was $400. It was debited to Insurance Expense on Apr. 1.

c. On Dec. 1, $400 was paid in advance to the landlord for four months' rent. The tenant debited Unexpired Rent for $400 on Dec. 1. What adjustment is necessary on Dec. 31 on the tenant's books?

d. Machinery is repaired and maintained by an outside maintenance company on an annual fee basis, payable in advance. The $240 fee was paid in advance on Sept. 1 and charged to Repairs and Maintenance Expense. What adjustment is necessary on Dec. 31?

e. Office wages earned but not paid on Dec. 31 amount to $300. The bookkeeper recognized the accrual by debiting Salaries and Wages and crediting Sales Discounts. Prepare a *correcting* entry.

f. On Nov. 14, $800 of machinery was purchased. $200 cash was paid down and a 90-day, 5 per cent note payable was signed for the balance. The Nov. 14 transaction was properly recorded. Prepare the adjustment for the interest.

g. The employer's liability for his $325 share of social security taxes has not been recognized.

h. A publisher sells subscriptions to magazines. Customers pay in advance. Receipts are originally credited to Deferred Subscription Revenue. On Aug. 1, many one-year subscriptions were collected and recorded, amounting to $12,000.

i. On Dec. 30, certain merchandise was purchased for $1,000 on open account. The bookkeeper debited Machinery and Equipment and credited Accounts Payable for $1,000.

j. A 120-day, 7 per cent, $7,500 cash loan was made to a customer on Oct. 28. The Oct. 28 transaction was recorded correctly.

k. A correct entry was made early in December for $3,000 of goods purchased on open account. However, all the goods were returned to the supplier and a credit memo was received on Dec. 29. But our bookkeeper has made no entry for the latter transaction.

l. A $300 purchase of equipment on Dec. 5 was erroneously debited to Purchases. The credit was correctly made to Cash.

m. On Dec. 3, $11,000 worth of merchandise was purchased on open account and an appropriate entry was made. The bill was paid on Dec. 11, but the bookkeeper made an entry on that date debiting Purchases and crediting Cash.

n. On Dec. 12, a $3,500 sale, subject to a 2 per cent discount if paid within 10 days, was made and recorded. A check was received for $3,430 on Dec. 29. However, the bookkeeper has overlooked it and the cash receipt has not been journalized. Make the appropriate entry.

2-39. *The Case of the President's Wealth.* From the *Chicago Tribune*, Aug. 20, 1964:

Accountants acting on President Johnson's orders today reported his family wealth totaled $3,484,098.

The statement of capital, arrived at through conservative procedures of evaluation, contrasted with a recent estimate published by *Life* magazine, which put the total at 14 million dollars.

The family fortune, which is held in trust while the Johnsons are in the White House, was set forth in terms of book values. The figures represent original cost rather than current market values on what the holdings would be worth if sold now.

Announced by the White House press office, but turned over to reporters by a national accounting firm at their Washington branch office, the financial statement apparently was intended to still a flow of quasi-official and unofficial estimates of the Johnson fortune. . . .

Assets

Cash	$ 132,547
Bonds	398,540
Interest in Texas Broadcasting Corp.	2,543,838
Ranch properties and other real estate	525,791
Other assets, including insurance policies	82,054
Total assets	$3,682,770

Liabilities

Note payable on real estate holding, 5 per cent due 1971	$ 150,000
Accounts payable, accrued interest, and income taxes	48,672
Total liabilities	$ 198,672
Capital	$3,484,098

The report apportions the capital among the family, with $378,081 credited to the President; $2,126,298 to his wife Claudia T., who uses the name Lady Bird; $490,141 to their daughter Lynda Bird; and $489,578 to their daughter Luci Baines.

The statement said the family holdings—under the names of the President, his wife, and his two daughters, Lynda Bird and Luci Baines—had increased from $737,730 on January 1, 1954, a year after Johnson became Democratic leader of the Senate, to $3,484,098 on July 31 this year, a gain of $2,746,368. . . .

A covering letter addressed to Johnson said the statement was made "in conformity with generally accepted accounting principles applied on a consistent basis."

By far the largest part of the fortune was listed as the Johnsons' interest in the Texas Broadcasting Corporation, carried on the books as worth $2,543,838.

The accountants stated that this valuation was arrived at on the basis of the cost of the stock when the Johnsons bought control of the debt-ridden radio station between 1943 and 1947, plus accumulated earnings ploughed back as equity, less 25 per cent capital gains tax.

Editorial, *Chicago Tribune*, Saturday, August 22, 1964:

An accounting firm acting on Mr. Johnson's instructions and employing what it termed "generally accepted auditing standards" has released a statement putting the current worth of the Lyndon Johnson family at a little less than 3½ million dollars. . . .

Dean Burch, chairman of the Republican National Committee, has remarked that the method used to list the Johnson assets was comparable to placing the value of Manhattan Island at $24, the price at which it was purchased from the Indians. The Johnson accounting firm conceded that its report was "not intended to indicate the values that might be realized if the investment were sold."

In fact, it would be interesting to observe the response of the Johnson family if a syndicate of investors were to offer to take Texas Broadcasting off the family's hands at double the publicly reported worth of the operation. . . .

Evaluate the criticisms, making special reference to fundamental accounting concepts or "principles."

CHAPTER 3

Components
of Financial
Statements

FINANCIAL STATEMENTS ASSIST ONE TO EVALUATE A COMPANY'S
performance and financial position, thereby aiding in the
major analytical tasks of comparison and prediction. Most
persons investigating a company are concerned with more
than the value of its individual assets. They want to know
the outlook for income, growth, and financial strength.

A going concern is usually something more than the mere
sum of its parts. That is why investors generally consider
the over-all net income performance a better approach to
company evaluation than individual asset appraisal. Still,
the accountant has no choice but to measure individual
parts. He hopes that, in the process, his techniques of measuring individual items will produce measurements which will
assist the user to evaluate the company as a whole.

Financial statements are the results of the application of
many accounting measurement techniques to a stream of
transactions. Each transaction is analyzed separately; its
effects on two or more accounts are recorded, classified,
summarized, and periodically reported in the major financial statements. The characteristics of the various major
components of these statements will now be considered.

As we study the various balance sheet items, keep in
mind that the balance sheet (the position statement) is
intertwined with the income statement. A change in inven-

tory methods, for example, will simultaneously affect both the balance sheet and the income statement.

CURRENT ASSETS

General Characteristics

Current assets are those which are reasonably expected to be transformed into cash or to be sold or consumed during the normal operating cycle of the business. By this definition, the following items are current assets: cash; receivables; inventories; prepaid current expenses; temporary investments; ordinary installment and deferred receivables; and receivables from officers, employees and affiliates. The following items are not current assets: cash not available for current operations; long-term investments; long-term deferred charges; and the cash surrender value of life insurance. The emphasis is upon the working capital cycle, the unending movement from cash to inventory to receivables and back to cash. Those assets that are not directly interlocked with the working capital cycle are not classified as current assets.

Cash is ordinarily the easiest current asset to measure: it is the amount on hand, or on deposit, that is available for normal business use. Receivables are stated as the net amount expected to be collected after providing for estimated uncollectibles, discounts, returns, and price allowances. Inventories, which are generally the largest current asset, are measured at cost. Because of the complexity of measuring at cost, the bulk of our discussion of current assets will be concentrated on inventories.

Inventory Methods

DIFFICULTIES OF MEASURING COST. The choice of a specific method of inventory valuation has an important impact upon the measurement of income. Cost, determined in one of numerous ways, is the general basis for valuation of inventories. But the estimation of cost of the inventory, as it is purchased or used in manufacture, is entwined in a web of difficulties.

The determination of the cost of incoming materials or merchandise is an example. Is cost part or all of the following: invoice price, freight charges, handling, insurance, storage, purchasing department costs, other indirect or direct charges? Usually, the invoice price and the freight charges are regarded as inventory costs, but the other costs are not.

Once the cost is defined, there is the question of how to allocate these product costs in a given year—how to divide them between the goods sold and the goods still on hand. There are many variations and combinations of cost-flow assumptions: first in, first out; last in, first out; a variety of average cost methods; base stock; specific identification;

standard costs; retail method; and ultimate sales price less cost of disposition.

PERPETUAL AND PERIODIC INVENTORIES. There are two fundamental ways of accounting for inventories: perpetual and periodic. The *perpetual inventory method* keeps a running, continuous record which tracks inventories and the cost of goods sold on a day-to-day basis. Such a record facilitates managerial control and the preparation of interim financial statements. Physical inventory counts are taken at least once a year in order to check on the accuracy of the clerical records.

The *periodic inventory method* does not involve a day-to-day record of inventories. Instead, costs are broken down into logical categories, such as purchases, freight in, and purchase discounts. The cost of goods sold cannot be computed accurately until the ending inventories are determined by physical count and subtracted from the sum of the opening inventory and purchases. Exhibit 3-1 is a comparison of perpetual and periodic inventory methods.

EXHIBIT 3-1

Periodic Method		*Perpetual Method*	
Beginning inventories (by physical count)	xxx	Cost of goods sold (kept on a day-to-day basis rather than being determined periodically)*	xxx
Add: Purchases	xxx		
Cost of goods available for sale	xxx	* Such a condensed figure does not	
Less: Ending inventories (by physical count)	xxx	preclude the presentation of a supplementary schedule similar	
Cost of goods sold	xxx	to that on the left.	

VARIOUS COST-FLOW ASSUMPTIONS. With few exceptions, the differences between inventory methods deal with the timing of cost releases in relation to income determination. Where it is impractical to identify inventories in terms of specific usage or sales, some assumption is made for transferring certain costs out of inventory. The most commonly used assumption is one of the following three:

1. *First in, first out* (Fifo). The stock acquired earliest is assumed to be used first; the stock acquired latest is assumed to be still on hand.

2. *Last in, first out* (Lifo). The stock acquired earliest is assumed to be still on hand; the stock acquired latest is assumed to have been used immediately. In the Lifo method the most recent, or last, inventory costs is considered to be the cost of goods used or sold. The attempt is to match the current cost of materials against current sales. As compared to Fifo, the Lifo technique of valuing inventory results in the reporting of less income when prices are rising and more income when prices are falling.

3. *Average inventory.* One version of this general method is the *moving average* method. Each purchase is lumped with the former inventory balance, so that a new average unit price is arrived at and is used as the

cost of subsequent issues of inventory. This method may be used with a perpetual inventory system. A *weighted average* method is often used with a periodic inventory system. This average is computed by dividing the total cost of the beginning inventory plus purchases, by the total number of units in those two classes.

These methods are best understood through illustration. The problem chosen is adapted from a CPA examination.

PROBLEM

The Saunders Corp. uses raw material *A* in a manufacturing process. Information as to balances on hand, purchases, and requisitions of material *A* are given in the following table:

Raw Material A

Date	Received	Issued	Balance	Unit Price	Received	Issued	Balance
	Quantities				*Dollars*		
Jan. 1			100	$1.50			$150
Jan. 24	300		400	1.56	$468		
Feb. 8		80	320				
Mar. 16		140	180				
June 11	150		330	1.60	240		
Aug. 18		130	200				
Sept. 6		110	90				
Oct. 15	150		240	1.70	255		
Dec. 29		140	100				

Required:

1. If a perpetual inventory record of material *A* is operated on a Fifo basis, it will show a closing inventory of: (*a*) $150; (*b*) $152; (*c*) $159; (*d*) $162; (*e*) $170; (*f*) answer not given.

2. Assume that no perpetual inventory is maintained for material *A*, and that quantities are obtained by an annual physical count. The accounting records show purchases but not issues. On this assumption, the closing inventory on a Fifo basis will be: (*a*) $150; (*b*) $156; (*c*) $159; (*d*) $160; (*e*) $170; (*f*) answer not given.

3. Assume that no perpetual inventory is maintained for material *A*, and that quantities are obtained by an annual physical count. The accounting records show purchases but not issues. On this assumption, the closing inventory on a Lifo basis will be: (*a*) $150; (*b*) $152; (*c*) $156; (*d*) $160; (*e*) $170; (*f*) answer not given.

4. If a perpetual inventory record of material *A* is operated on a moving average basis, it will show a closing inventory which is: (*a*) Lower than on the Lifo basis; (*b*) lower than on the Fifo basis; (*c*) higher than on the Fifo basis; (*d*) answer not given.

5. The exact closing inventory in Question 4 is $_____.

6. Assume that no perpetual inventory is maintained and that quantities are obtained by an annual physical count. The accounting records show purchases but not issues. On this assumption, the closing inventory, on a weighted average basis, will be $_____.

Solution

1. **(e): $170.** Under Fifo, the ending inventory valuation may be most easily obtained by working back from the closing date until the number of units purchased equals the number of units in ending inventory. Then apply the appropriate unit purchase costs to obtain the total dollar amount. In this example, 100 units @ $1.70 = $170.

2. **(e): $170.** The answer is identical under the perpetual and periodic systems. Under a periodic inventory method, the files must be combed for recent invoices until 100 units are tallied. In this case, the most recent invoice would suffice. In other cases, more than one invoice may be needed to cover the 100 units in the ending inventory.

3. **(a):** 100 units @ $1.50 = $150. Under a periodic Lifo method, a *temporary* reduction below the number of units in the beginning inventory will have no effect upon the valuation of the ending inventory so long as the number of units counted at the end of the year is at least equal to the beginning inventory.

4. **(b):** Under Fifo, the earliest costs of material are assigned to the cost of sales and the latest costs of material are assigned to inventory. Unit prices have been rising during the period. Therefore, more of the earlier, lower-cost, units will be contained in the ending inventory under the moving average method than under Fifo.

5. **$165.125:** The moving average technique requires the computation of a new average unit cost after each acquisition. This unit cost is used for all issues until the next purchase is made:

Moving Average

Perpetual Method

Date	Received Units	Price	Amount	Issued Units	Price	Amount	Balance Units	Price	Amount
Jan. 1							100	$1.50000	$150.000
Jan. 24	300	$1.56	$468				400	1.54500	618.000
Feb. 8				80	$1.54500	$123.600	320	1.54500	494.400
Mar. 16				140	1.54500	216.300	180	1.54500	278.100
June 11	150	1.60	240				330	1.57000	518.100
Aug. 18				130	1.57000	204.100	200	1.57000	314.000
Sept. 6				110	1.57000	172.700	90	1.57000	141.300
Oct. 15	150	1.70	255				240	1.65125	396.300
Dec. 29				140	1.65125	231.175	100	1.65125	165.125

Recapitulation

Costs to account for: $150 + $468 + $240 + $255 = $1,113.000
Deduct: Issues   947.875
Ending balance $ 165.125

6. $159: (100 units × $1.59.)

Weighted Average*

Periodic Method

Date	Units	Unit Price	Dollars
Jan. 1	100	$1.50	$ 150
Jan. 24	300	1.56	468
June 11	150	1.60	240
Oct. 15	150	1.70	255
To account for	700		$1,113

Weighted unit cost = $1,113 ÷ 700   = $1.59
Costs released   600 @ $1.59 $ 954
Costs in ending inventory   100 @ $1.59   159
Costs accounted for $1,113

* The assumption of a weighted average is subject to criticism because the Oct. 15 purchase influences the costing of issues throughout the year, even though, strictly speaking, the cost of earlier issues would not have been affected by purchases made later in the year.

LIFO VERSUS FIFO. If unit prices did not fluctuate, all inventory methods would show identical results. But prices change, and these changes appear in the financial records in different ways, depending on the specific inventory methods used. Under Lifo, current purchase prices are reflected in current operating results; under Fifo, recognition of price effects is delayed. If prices are volatile, year-to-year incomes may differ dramatically under the two approaches to inventory valuation.

Balance sheet presentations are also affected by the choice of Lifo or Fifo. Under the Lifo method, older and older, and hence meaningless, inventory prices are shown, especially if stocks grow through the years. Under the Fifo method, the balance sheet tends to reflect current prices.

When prices are rising, Lifo shows less income than Fifo, thus minimizing income taxes. Also, Lifo permits the immediate influencing of net income by the timing of purchases, a feature that has not received the attention it deserves. For example, if prices are rising and a company desires, for income tax or other reasons, to show less income in a given year, all it need do is to buy a large amount of inventory near the end of the year—thus releasing, as expenses, higher costs than would ordinarily be released.

It should also be recognized that neither the Fifo nor the Lifo approach isolates and measures the effects of price fluctuations as special managerial problems. As Exhibit 3-2 shows, Fifo buries rises in price in the regular income figure and Lifo excludes the effects of price changes from the income statement. The $50 increase in the cost of materials is buried in the $300 Fifo gross margin figure and ignored in the $250 Lifo gross margin figure.

EXHIBIT 3-2

		Lifo		*Fifo*
Sales, 5,000 @ $.20		$1,000		$1,000
Inventory, beginning	1,000 @ $.10 = $100		$100	
Purchases	5,000 @ $.15 = 750		750	
	$850		$850	
Inventory, ending	1,000 @ $.10 = 100	750	1,000 @ $.15 = 150	700
Gross margin		$ 250		$ 300

LOWER OF COST OR MARKET. When the concept of the market price is superimposed upon a cost method, the combined method is often called the lower-of-cost-or-market method. That is, the current market price is compared to cost (derived by Fifo, weighted average, or other method), and the lower of the two is selected as the basis for the valuation of goods at a specific inventory date. *Market* generally means the replacement cost or its equivalent. It does not mean the ultimate selling price to customers.

Assume that an ending inventory is valued at $10,000 at cost and $7,000 at market. If the lower market price is indicative of lower ultimate sales prices, an inventory write-down of $3,000 is in order. $3,000 of the cost is considered to have expired during the current period because it cannot be justifiably carried forward to the future. Furthermore, the decision to purchase was probably made during the current period, but unfortunate fluctuations occurred in the replacement market during the same period. These downward price fluctuations caused the inventory to lose some utility, some revenue-producing power. (On the other hand, if *selling prices* are not also likely to fall, the revenue-producing power of the inventory will be maintained and no write-down would be justified.)

The new $7,000 valuation is what is left of the original cost of the inventory. In other words, the new market price becomes, for accounting purposes, the new cost of the inventory.

Compared to a strict cost method (see Exhibit 3-3), the lower-of-cost-or-market method results in less net income in the current period and more net income in the future period. Assuming that there are no sales in the second period shown in Exhibit 3-3, except for the disposal of the inventory in question, total income for both periods will be the same (ignoring income tax). Note that the total Margin for the two periods is $31,000, under both methods. The lower-of-cost-or-market method has been termed a conservative valuation method. However, it results in a favorable impact upon the net income of the next period.

EXHIBIT 3-3

	Cost		Lower of Cost or Market	
	Period 1	*Period 2*	*Period 1*	*Period 2*
Net sales	$100,000	$11,000	$100,000	$11,000
Cost of goods available	$ 80,000	$10,000	$ 80,000	$ 7,000
Ending inventory after write-down	10,000	—	7,000	—
Cost of sales*	$ 70,000	$10,000	$ 73,000	$ 7,000
Margin	$ 30,000	$ 1,000	$ 27,000	$ 4,000

* Cost of sales is increased by the $3,000 inventory write-down in this example. Many accountants favor isolating the write-down and deducting it separately after the ordinary gross margin.

Investments

BALANCE SHEET CLASSIFICATION. Investments are classified according to *purpose*. An investment is carried as a current asset if it is a temporary holding of otherwise idle cash; it is a part of a separate classification, Investments, if it is long-term in nature. Investments, as a classification, usually appear on the balance sheet between Current Assets and Fixed Assets.

CARRYING VALUE. Stocks held as long-term investments are generally carried at acquisition cost.

Bonds held as long-term investments are carried at acquisition cost, adjusted for amortization of premiums or discounts. (The process of amortization of discounts on investments is sometimes more accurately referred to as "accumulation" of discounts.) Premiums or discounts on bonds are rarely accounted for in separate ledger accounts. Instead, amortization is directly entered in the Investment in Bonds account.

LOWER OF COST OR MARKET. Accountants generally favor applying the lower-of-cost-or-market rule to the total portfolio of temporary investments.

Long-term investments in stocks should generally be shown at cost; bonds should be shown at cost, adjusted for amortization of discounts or premiums. Departure from these bases is necessary only when there has been a substantial and relatively permanent decline below the carrying value. A valuation account used when write-downs are made preserves the record of cost or cost adjusted for amortization.

The most informative presentation of either temporary or long-term investments would reveal both cost and cost adjusted for amortization and market values. The latter may appear parenthetically or in footnote form.

EXCHANGES AND CONVERSIONS. Stocks and bonds may be acquired by means other than cash. Examples are purchases made with fixed assets or with different types of securities (with other investments or by issuance of the acquiring company's own stocks or bonds). Such exchanges raise the question of: (1) the proper amount to be debited for the newly acquired securities; and (2) the recognition of gain or loss on the exchange.

In exchanges, the proper amount to be debited for the acquisition is the fair market value of either the outgoing or the incoming item, whichever is more objectively determinable. If fair market values are unavailable or indeterminate, the cost or book value of the item parted with may be regarded as the cost of the acquisition.

This procedure results in recognition of a gain or loss amounting to the difference between the cost of the new securities and the carrying value of the item exchanged for them. When a company issues its own additional stock in exchange for new securities, the gain or loss would affect paid-in capital rather than income.

No gain or loss is recognized, for tax purposes, when securities are exchanged pursuant to a conversion privilege. The majority opinion is that gain or loss should be recognized for financial accounting purposes, however. Market quotations, when available, are an objective basis for computing gain or loss on the conversion.

SALES. When holdings of the same security consist of purchases made at different unit prices, what cost should be released if a portion of the holdings are sold? Conventional ways of determining the cost to be assigned to securities sold include: (1) specific identification; (2) first in, first out; and (3) average cost. Average costs are not recognized for income tax purposes.

LONG-LIVED ASSETS

General Characteristics

Long-lived assets are not held primarily for resale. They represent future services to be used over a prolonged span of time. They are often divided into two groups: tangible and intangible. In general, the measure of usefulness at the time of acquisition is cost. The major difficulties of measurement center about the allocation of the cost of acquisition to the appropriate accounting periods.

Tangible, or Fixed, Assets

Those long-lived assets which are tangible, which can be physically seen and touched, are often called fixed assets. Their acquisition cost is the invoice amount, plus freight and installation, less discounts.

Depreciation is the estimated allocation of the cost of fixed assets to the particular periods or products that benefit from the utilization of the fixed asset. Accountants often stress that depreciation is a process of allocation of the original cost of acquisition; it is not a process of valuation in the layman's sense of the term. The ordinary balance sheet presentation (Exhibit 3-4) does not show replacement cost, resale value, or the price changes since acquisition.

EXHIBIT 3-4

Plant and equipment (at original acquisition cost)	xxx
Less: Accumulated depreciation (that portion of original cost which has already been charged to operations)	xxx
Net book value (that portion of original cost that will be charged to future operations)	xxx

The amount of original cost to be allocated as depreciation is the difference between the total acquisition cost and the estimated terminal value. The depreciation allocation may be made on the basis of time or service. The estimate of useful life, which is an important factor in determining the yearly allocation of depreciation, is influenced by estimates of physical wear and tear, technological change, and economic obsolescence.

The pattern of depreciation has a direct effect on the reported financial showing. Exhibit 3-5 is a comparison of the annual depreciation produced by four techniques. The asset has a cost (C) of $1,050, an estimated scrap value (s) of $50, and an estimated life (n) of five years. Results are rounded to the nearest dollar.

EXHIBIT 3-5

Annual Depreciation: Four Techniques

Year	Straight Line*	Declining Balance at Twice the Straight-line Rate†	Sum-of-years Digits‡	Formula: Fixed Percentage§
1	$ 200	$420	$ 333	$ 479
2	200	252	267	260
3	200	151	200	142
4	200	91	133	77
5	200	54	67	42
Total	$1,000	$968	$1,000	$1,000

* Rate, unadjusted for salvage: 20% ($1,050 − $50).
† 40% × $1,050; 40% ($1,050 − $420); etc.
‡ 5/15 ($1,050 − $50); 4/15 ($1,050 − $50); etc.
§ Rate $= 1 - \sqrt[n]{s/C} = 1 - \sqrt[5]{\$50/\$1,050} = 45.6\%$.
  45.6% × $1,050; 45.6% ($1,050 − $479); etc.

The totals reveal that three methods have allocated the same total amount of depreciation to the five-year period (an amount equal to cost minus scrap). However, the declining-balance method, which uses twice the straight-line rate unadjusted for scrap, will never fully depreciate the base.

Although straight line depreciation is the easiest method to understand,

there are theoretical and practical reasons for choosing one of the accelerated depreciation methods. Theoretically, the economic benefits from
most newly acquired fixed assets are bunched in the early years of their
useful life. And, as is explained more thoroughly in Chapter 16, earlier
write-offs of fixed asset costs have the practical advantage of producing
greater income tax deductions.

Intangible Assets

The acquisition costs of intangible assets (such as purchased good will,
trade names, secret processes, and patents) should be amortized over
their useful lives. Where the useful lives are estimated to be extremely
long, the acquisition costs are not amortized. However, accountants tend
to be extremely conservative about intangible assets, and most intangibles
are rapidly amortized.

The contrast between the accounting for tangible and intangible long-
lived assets raises some provocative and knotty theoretical issues. Accountants are sometimes overly concerned with physical objects or
contractual rights, tending to overlook the underlying reality of future
economic benefits.

This preoccupation with physical evidence often results in the expensing of outlays that should be treated as assets. Thus, expenditures for
research, advertising, employee training and the like are usually expensed,
although it seems clear that in an economic sense such expenditures represent future benefit. The difficulty of measuring future benefits is the
reason usually advanced for expensing these items.

LIABILITIES

Liabilities are obligations or responsibilities to pay assets or to perform
services. They are the claims or interests of outsiders. The reporting of
most liabilities is fairly straightforward and uniform: an attempt is made
to measure the amount currently needed to liquidate the claim.

Certain liabilities—such as long-term leases, deferred income taxes, and
pensions—entail thorny measurement problems that are beyond the scope
of this book. There is little economic difference, for example, between a
company which buys a building subject to an extremely heavy thirty-
year mortgage and another company which leases a similar building for
thirty years. The first company shows the building as an asset and the
mortgage as a liability. Under current accounting practice, the second
company does not enter either the fixed asset or the lease liability in its
formal books of account. The details of such leases are supposed to be
disclosed in footnotes. (See Chapter 5 for additional discussion of this
point.)

STOCKHOLDERS' EQUITY

General Characteristics

The interests or equities of owners represent residual claims to assets. Stockholders' equity arises from two main sources: (1) contributed capital; and (2) retained earnings. Balance sheet presentation often distinguishes these two sources. Note, in Exhibit 3-6, that total Contributed Capital is subdivided into legal capital and capital in excess of legal capital.

EXHIBIT 3-6

Stockholders' equity:

Common stock, $5 par value, authorized, 1,000,000 shares; issued and outstanding, 500,000 shares; stated or legal capital	$2,500,000
Additional contributions in excess of legal requirements (Paid-in surplus)	1,000,000
Total contributed capital	$3,500,000
Retained earnings	6,000,000
Total stockholders' equity	$9,500,000

The task of clear presentation is often complicated by state corporation laws. For example, an ordinary stock dividend (i.e., additional common stock issued as a dividend on existing common stock) frequently results in the transfer of an amount from Retained Earnings to Total Contributed Capital, and the distinction between contributed capital and retained earnings is blurred in the process.

Another example involves treasury stock. In essence, the purchase of treasury stock is a contraction of stockholders' equity; there is no basic difference between unissued stock and treasury stock. But legal requirements again affect the accounting. There has been a tendency in accounting practice to deduct treasury stock from the gross stockholders' equity to arrive at a net equity figure. Although such treatment is generally accepted, it fails to preserve the line of demarcation between contributed capital and retained earnings.

Exhibit 3-7 is a presentation of a complicated stockholders' equity section. Older terminology is in parentheses.

Reserves

You should be thoroughly familiar with the three broad types of reserves used in accounting:

1. *Asset valuation.* An offset to an asset. Examples: reserves for depreciation, depletion, bad debts, reduction of inventory or investments to market, deferred maintenance. "Allowance for . . ." is better terminology.
2. *Liability.* An estimate of a liability of indefinite or uncertain amount. Examples: reserves for income taxes, warranties, vacation pay. "Estimated liability for . . ." is better terminology.

EXHIBIT 3-7

Stockholders' Equity (Net Worth)
Dec. 31, 19x1

5 per cent preferred stock, $100 par value; authorized, 10,000 shares; issued and outstanding, 6,000 shares	$ 600,000	
Excess received over par value of preferred shares issued (Premium on preferred stock)	50,000	$ 650,000
Common stock, no par value, stated value $10 per share; authorized, 100,000 shares; issued, 80,000 shares, of which 5,000 shares are held in the treasury	$ 800,000	
Excess received over stated value of common shares issued (Paid-in surplus)	1,000,000	
Excess received over cost of common treasury stock (Paid-in surplus on treasury stock)	10,000	1,810,000
Total legal capital*		$2,460,000
Donated capital: plant site received from City of Champion (Donated surplus)		200,000
Total		$2,660,000
Retained earnings (Earned surplus):		
Reserve† for possible future price declines in inventory	$ 100,000	
Reserve for treasury stock	20,000	
Reserve for sinking fund	200,000	
Reserve for expansion	200,000	
Reserve for replacement of fixed assets	300,000	
Reserve for retirement of preferred stock	400,000	
Reserve for general contingencies	50,000	
Reserve for investment in working capital	200,000	
Unappropriated	790,000	
Total retained earnings		2,260,000
Excess of appraised value of fixed assets over cost (Appraisal surplus)		500,000
Subtotal		$5,420,000
Less: Cost of 5,000 shares of common stock reacquired and held in treasury (Treasury stock)		220,000
Stockholders' equity		$5,200,000

* Definitions of legal capital vary among states. Many states define legal capital as only the par or stated value of issued stock (see Exhibit 3-6 for the format under these conditions). Exhibit 3-7 would be changed to show preferred stock at par plus common stock at stated value. All Paid-in Surplus accounts would then follow.
† The term "appropriated" or "restricted" may be used in place of "reserve."

3. *Retained earnings reserve.* A restriction of dividend-paying power denoted by a specific subdivision of retained earnings. Examples: reserves for contingencies, possible price declines or increases, sinking fund, expansion, treasury stock, retirement of preferred stock. The American Institute of Certified Public Accountants (AICPA) maintains that the term "reserve" should be confined *solely* to this category.[1]
You should be aware that retained earnings reserves: (1) should be created by charging retained earnings, not income; (2) should never be used to relieve income of charges for expenses or losses; (3) should

[1] *Terminology Bulletin No. 1,* pp. 26-28, in *Accounting Research and Terminology Bulletins—Final Edition* (New York: American Institute of Certified Public Accountants, 1961).

never influence the determination of net income for any year; and (4) should be restored to retained earnings when no longer needed.

To summarize:

Type of Reserve	Creation		Disposition	
Asset valuation	Bad debts expense	xxx	Allowance for bad debts	xxx
	Allowance for bad debts	xxx	Accounts receivable	xxx
Liability	Income tax expense	xxx	Estimated income taxes	
	Estimated income taxes		payable	xxx
	payable	xxx	Cash	xxx
Retained earnings	Retained earnings	xxx	Reserve for contingencies	xxx
	Reserve for contingencies	xxx	Retained earnings	xxx

Net Income and Retained Earnings

Accountants disagree about the proper definition of net income. Some important points relating to the all-inclusive type of income statement versus the current operating performance type of statement have been discussed by the AICPA. As a general rule, the Institute maintains that all nonrecurring items of revenue and expense which are not material in amount should be credited or charged to income and thus appear on the income statement. Such an item would be material in amount if its inclusion in the determination of net income would impair the latter's significance "so that misleading inferences might be drawn therefrom." [2]

The Institute points out that the following items should be excluded from the determination of net income under all circumstances:

(a) Adjustments resulting from transactions in the company's own capital stock;
(b) Amounts transferred to and from accounts properly designated as surplus appropriations, such as charges and credits with respect to general purpose contingency reserves;
(c) Amounts deemed to represent excessive costs of fixed assets, and annual appropriations in contemplation of replacement of productive facilities at higher price levels; and
(d) Adjustments made pursuant to a quasi-reorganization.[3]

SUMMARY

Although most investors are interested in over-all income performance and financial status and are not interested in itemized measurements, the accountant has no choice but to measure individual parts. He hopes that

---

[2] *Research Bulletin No. 43, Restatement and Revision of Accounting Research Bulletins,* pp. 59-65, in *Accounting Research and Terminology Bulletins—Final Edition.*
[3] *Ibid.,* p. 64.

his measurement of individual items will produce measurements useful for evaluating the company as a whole.

Cash and receivables are measured as the net amount available or to be collected. In general, all other assets are valued at the cost of acquisition or less. The acquisition cost provides: (1) a record of all transactions entered into, at prices valid at the time of the events; (2) a reasonable measurement of financial commitment; and (3) a useful point of departure for allocation, adjustment, and interpretation. Acquisition cost is an objective measurement and is almost universally acceptable to business, legal, taxing, and regulatory authorities.

Accountants have long recognized that certain events during the asset-holding period may indicate the partial expiration of acquisition costs. Write-downs may be prompted by damage, obsolescence, deterioration, style changes, and specific price changes. No exchange is necessary to justify write-downs under the lower-of-cost-or-market rule, which is applied to marketable securities and inventories. Of course, the most frequent events which cause the expiration of acquisition costs are use, conversion, or sales.

Liabilities are usually measured as the amount currently needed to liquidate the claims. Stockholders' equity, the residual claim to assets, arises from two main sources: contributed capital and accumulated capital. The measurement of stockholders' equity represents a mixture of dollars of different purchasing power.

SUMMARY PROBLEMS FOR YOUR REVIEW

PROBLEMS

Since this chapter contains a variety of topics, the following questions stress the more important ideas, rather than specific techniques.

1. Cost prices have been rising, and the net income for a given company is $5,000 under one inventory method and $8,000 under another inventory method. Which of the two methods is last in, first out? Why?

2. A company bought some merchandise for $50,000 on Nov. 12. On Dec. 31, under a lower-of-cost-or-market procedure, this inventory was written down to $46,000, the replacement cost on that date. On Apr. 30, the inventory was still unsold, but the replacement cost was $53,000. What is the generally accepted inventory valuation on Apr. 30? Why?

3. Professor William A. Paton described the reserve for depreciation as being the "hole in a doughnut, which enlarges each year." Explain.

4. "There is little merit in subdividing retained earnings into reserve accounts. As a practical matter, the vast bulk of the retained earnings of a going concern will never be liquidated by cash dividends anyway." Do you agree? Explain.

5. What is the all-inclusive concept of income?

SOLUTIONS

1. The method showing a net income of $5,000 is last in, first out. If prices are rising, Lifo results in less net income because the more recent, higher, costs are released as expense first. The selection of an inventory valuation method is important to both investors and management, because it may have an important effect on the net income of any given year.

2. The inventory would be valued at $46,000. The lower-of-cost-or-market method is an approach to the timing of the release of the $50,000 historical cost to expense. The initial write-down from $50,000 to $46,000 is based on the notion that $4,000 of the original $50,000 could not be justifiably carried forward to the future as of Dec. 31. $46,000 becomes the new cost for any subsequent lower-of-cost-or-market comparisons. But the Apr. 30 market price of $53,000 is not below the $46,000 cost, so the latter remains untouched on Apr. 30. Historical costs are generally the *upper limit* of accounting valuations. Market prices are used solely to justify measurement of cost expirations. Once written down, the costs are not written up again, not even to restore an item to its initial historical cost.

3. Reserves for depreciation are commonly misunderstood, thought of as funds of cash being accumulated for replacement of fixed assets. A reserve for depreciation is really that portion of original cost which has already been charged to operations. Consequently, it can be likened to the hole in a doughnut. The original cost of the asset is the entire jelly-filled doughnut. An eager child may eat the jelly center first, thus creating a hole in the doughnut. The reserve (i.e., allowance) for depreciation is the hole. As time passes, the hole becomes larger.

4. Retained earnings reserves or appropriations restrict the dividend-paying powers of the corporation. They may also help explain retention of income. Sometimes such restrictions arise from legal contracts with bondholders or holders of preferred stock. Sometimes such restrictions are voluntarily imposed by the board of directors. An unfortunate connotation of this procedure is that any unappropriated retained earnings are soon likely to be liquidated in the form of cash dividends.

   The *entire* retained earnings account, including appropriations, reflects the continued use of assets generated by profitable operations. Retention is for the maintenance and enhancement of the competitive position of the enterprise. Any manager or investor who knows the rudiments of accounting and business administration knows that a large chunk of the resources acquired through profitable operations is permanently committed for legitimate corporate purposes and will never be distributed to the owners. The appropriating or restricting of retained earnings has no power to alter a fact. The fact is, for the going concern, that a large part of the retained earnings will never be liquidated.

5. The *all-inclusive* concept of income includes all items of revenue and expense in the determination of net income. In contrast, the *current operating performance* concept excludes from net income any nonrecurring items of revenue and expense which are material in amount.

ESSENTIAL ASSIGNMENT MATERIAL

3-1. *Lifo and Fifo.* The Kiner Coal Co. does not maintain a perpetual inventory system. The inventory of coal on June 30 shows 1,000 tons at $6 per ton. A physical inventory on July 31 shows a total of 1,200 tons on hand. Revenue from sales of coal for July totals $30,000. The following purchases were made during July:

July 5	2,000 Tons @ $7 per ton
July 15	500 Tons @ $8 per ton
July 25	600 Tons @ $9 per ton

Required: Compute the inventory value, as of July 31, using:

a. Lifo: last in, first out
b. Fifo: first in, first out

3-2. *Lower of cost or market.* The company uses cost or market, whichever is lower. There were no sales or purchases during the periods indicated, and there has been no change in the salability of the merchandise. At what amount would you value merchandise on the dates listed below:

	Invoice Cost	Replacement Cost
Dec. 31, 19x1	$100,000	$ 80,000
Apr. 30, 19x2	100,000	90,000
Aug. 31, 19x2	100,000	105,000
Dec. 31, 19x2	100,000	65,000

3-3. *Multiple choice: comparison of inventory methods.* (CPA Adapted.) The Berg Corp. *began business on Jan. 1, 19x4.* Information about its inventories under different valuation methods is shown below. Using this information, you are to choose the phrase which best answers each of the following questions. For each question, insert on an answer sheet *the number which identifies the answer* you select.

		Inventory		
	Lifo Cost	*Fifo Cost*	*Market*	*Lower of Specifically Identified Cost or Market*
Dec. 31, 19x4	$10,200	$10,000	$ 9,600	$ 8,900
Dec. 31, 19x5	9,100	9,000	8,800	8,500
Dec. 31, 19x6	10,300	11,000	12,000	10,900

1. The inventory basis which would show the *highest net income for 19x4* is: (a) Lifo cost; (b) Fifo cost; (c) Market; (d) Lower of cost or market.

2. The inventory basis which would show the *highest net income for 19x5*

is: (a) Lifo cost; (b) Fifo cost; (c) Market; (d) Lower of cost or market.

3. The inventory basis which would show the *lowest net income for the three years combined* is: (a) Lifo cost; (b) Fifo cost; (c) Market; (d) Lower of cost or market.

4. For the year 19x5, how much higher or lower would profits be on the *Fifo cost basis* than on the *lower-of-cost-or-market basis?* (a) $400 higher; (b) $400 lower; (c) $600 higher; (d) $600 lower; (e) $1,000 higher; (f) $1,000 lower; (g) $1,400 higher; (h) $1,400 lower.

5. On the basis of the information given, it appears that *the movement of prices* for the items in the inventory was: (a) Up in 19x4 and down in 19x6; (b) Up in both 19x4 and 19x6; (c) Down in 19x4 and up in 19x6; (d) Down in both 19x4 and 19x6.

3-4. *Correction of investment account.* Prepare journal entries correcting the following account. Cash dividends and stock dividends were credited to Dividend Income.

Temporary Investment in Basil Company Common Stock ($10 par value)

Jan. 15, 19x2 Acquired 200 shares $15,400	Oct. 3, 19x2 Sold the 20 shares of	
Feb. 20, 19x2 Received 20 shares as a stock dividend 200	dividend stock	$1,900

3-5. *Effects on stockholders' equity.* Indicate the effect (+, −, or O) on *total* stockholders' equity of General Motors Corp. of each of the following:

1. Declaration of a cash dividend.
2. Payment of (1).
3. Declaration of a stock dividend (common on common).
4. Issuance of a stock dividend (common on common).
5. Passing of a dividend on cumulative preferred stock.
6. Sale of 100 shares of General Motors by David Rockefeller to Tom Jones.
7. Operating loss for the period.
8. Purchase of 10 shares of treasury stock for $1,000 cash.
9. Sale of treasury stock, purchased in (8), for $1,200.
10. Sale of treasury stock, purchased in (8), for $900.
11. Creation of a reserve for contingencies.
12. Creation of a reserve for treasury stock.
13. Creation of a construction fund.
14. Creation of a reserve for current income taxes.
15. Creation of a reserve for depreciation.

ADDITIONAL ASSIGNMENT MATERIAL

Note: Problems 3-30 through 3-33 call for objective answers regarding a wide variety of situations. Problem 3-33 is a review of Chapters 2 and 3 and is the most complicated assignment problem for the two chapters.

3-6. Enumerate the items most commonly classified as current assets. Are the following included in the current asset category: cash surrender value of life insurance; deferred organization costs; unamortized discount on bonds payable?

3-7. List five inventory cost-flow assumptions.

3-8. Distinguish between the perpetual and periodic ways of accounting for inventories.

3-9. Briefly distinguish Fifo from Lifo.

3-10. What is the moving-average method of accounting for inventories?

3-11. Do Fifo or Lifo isolate and measure the effects of price fluctuations as special managerial problems?

3-12. What is meant by the term "market" in inventory accounting?

3-13. What are the relative effects on net income of a strict cost method and the lower-of-cost-or-market method?

3-14. "Sometimes 100 shares of stock should be classified as current assets and sometimes not." Explain.

3-15. What is the proper measure for an asset newly acquired through an exchange (e.g., an exchange of land for securities)? Explain.

3-16. What cost-flow assumptions are usually used in accounting for various sales of the same security?

3-17. Criticize: "Depreciation is the loss in value of a fixed asset over a given span of time."

3-18. What factors influence the estimate of useful life in depreciation accounting?

3-19. "Accountants sometimes are too concerned with physical objects or contractual rights." Explain.

3-20. What is the main objective in measuring liabilities?

3-21. What liabilities present the greatest measurement difficulties?

3-22. How may the distinction between contributed and accumulated capital be blurred by traditional accounting?

3-23. What are the three broad types of reserves?

3-24. What four rules should govern the accounting for retained earnings reserves?

3-25. Distinguish between the all-inclusive and the current operating performance concepts of income.

3-26. *Current assets, realization principles.* (CPA Adapted.) A proper determination of income requires a matching of expenses and revenues. The assignment of revenues to periods, however, is determined by the choice of the appropriate realization or recognition principles. While the point of sale or the time of providing a service is often considered the appropriate time of recognition, accountants have accepted other realization points. These others include the point of partial or full completion of production and the point of partial or full conversion into cash. Once the realization principle has been chosen, the matching principle requires an appropriate valuation of inventories and other assets and liabilities. For example, the valuation of accounts receivable at net selling price (the valuation of the asset received in exchange for the merchandise sold) implies that revenue has been realized at the point of sale or earlier.

For each of the following valuation bases or methods:

a. State the point at which revenue was realized.

b. Give an example or illustration of the correct usage of each.

c. State the accounting principle or reason involved in determining the realization point or valuation basis.

(1) Inventory recorded at cost.

(2) Accounts receivable recorded at selling price with an account called Deferred Gross Profit having a credit balance.

(3) Inventory recorded at selling price less a normal markup.

(4) Inventory recorded at the net figure of selling price less costs to complete.

(5) Inventory recorded at realization value (selling price).

3-27. *Used car inventory.* (CPA Adapted.) Your client, the Big Essex Agency, sells new and used cars and has a service department. At audit date, Apr. 30, 19x6, the used car inventory consisted of four cars.

	Used Car Number			
	1	*2*	*3*	*4*
Allowed on trade-in	$1,700	$2,400	$1,000	$1,400
Over-allowance*	300	300	200	200
Service department charges for work on car†	60	—	40	160
National Auto Dealers Association estimate of market value (at retail)				
At time of trade-in	1,600	2,200	875	1,200
At audit date	1,550	2,200	850	1,150
Probable sale price if sold during May, 19x6‡	1,600	2,150	825	1,300

* During the year, new cars were being sold at less than list where no trade-in was involved. The amounts in this line represent the discount that would have been allowed on the new car sold had that new car been sold for cash with no trade-in.

† The service department makes necessary repairs on used cars taken in trades and bills the used car department at cost plus a 33⅓ per cent markup. The amounts in this line are the bills from the service department.

‡ With the exception of cars 2 and 4, which are still on hand, the used cars were sold for cash during the first week of May, 19x6 at the amounts shown on this line.

Discuss the various factors which should be considered in assigning a value to the inventory of used cars. Indicate the computations needed to arrive at an acceptable inventory value for each car as of Apr. 30, 19x6.

3-28. *Creation and disposition of reserves.* Show how the items listed below are created and disposed of, using the following letters:

For Creation	*For Disposition*
A. By debit to an asset	*A.* Usually written off against the related asset
E. By debit to an expense	*I.* Carried indefinitely
R. By debit to retained earnings	*L.* Written off when the liability is liquidated
	R. Restored to retained earnings when its purpose is fulfilled
	O. Credited as other income to current net income

Each item below will have two answers, one for creation and one for disposition.

(1) Reserve for holiday pay.

(2) Reserve for contingencies.

(3) Reserve for possible future price declines in inventory.

(4) Reserve for redemption of S & H green merchandise savings stamps.

(5) Reserve for bad debts.

(6) Reserve for plant expansion.

(7) Reserve for bond sinking fund.

(8) Reserve for depletion.

(9) Reserve for income taxes.

(10) Reserve to reduce inventories from acquisition cost to current market price.

3-29. *Different concepts of income.* (CPA Adapted.) Information concerning the operations of a corporation may be presented in an income statement or in a combined statement of income and retained earnings. Income statements may be prepared on a current operating performance basis (earning power concept) or an all-inclusive basis (historical concept). Proponents of the two types of income statements do not agree upon the proper treatment of material extraordinary charges and credits.

Required:

a. Define "current operating performance" and "all-inclusive," as used above.

b. Explain the differences in content and organization of a current operating performance income statement and an all-inclusive income statement. Include a discussion of the proper treatment of material extraordinary charges and credits.

c. Give the principal arguments for the use of each of the three statements: all-inclusive income statement; current operating performance income statement; and combined statement of income and retained earnings.

3-30. *Balance sheet classification.* (CPA Adapted.) You have been asked to assist the chief accountant of the Chenault Corp. in the preparation of a balance sheet. The outline presented below represents the various classifications suggested by the chief accountant for the balance sheet; classification *o* has been added for items to be excluded from the balance sheet.

Assets		*Liabilities and Capital*	
a.	Current	g.	Current
b.	Investments	h.	Long-term
c.	Plant and equipment	i.	Other liabilities
d.	Intangibles	j.	Preferred stock
e.	Deferred charges	k.	Common stock
f.	Other assets	l.	Contributions in excess of par or stated value
		m.	Retained earnings
		n.	Other capital
		o.	Items excluded from the balance sheet.

Required:

Number an answer sheet, down the left margin, from (1) to (25).

Using the *letters* above, classify the following accounts according to the *preferred* balance sheet presentation. If the account is an offsetting or valuation account, mark an x before the letter. For example, Allowance for Doubtful Accounts would be x-a.

(1) Dividend payable (on Chenault's preferred stock).

(2) Plant construction in progress.

(3) Factory building (retired from use and held for sale).

(4) Reserve for higher plant replacement costs.

(5) Land (held for possible future building site).

(6) Merchandise inventory (held by Chenault Corp. on consignment).

(7) Stock dividend payable (in common stock to common stockholders and to be issued at par).

(8) Office supplies inventory.

(9) Sinking fund cash (First National Bank, trustee).

(10) Reserve for retirement of preferred stock.

(11) Installment sales accounts receivable (average collection period, 18 months).

(12) Reserve for possible decline in inventory value.

(13) Advances to officers (indefinite repayment date).

(14) Unredeemed merchandise coupons.

(15) Reserve for self-insurance.

(16) Inventory of small tools.

(17) Unissued common stock.

(18) Liability for loss on merchandise purchase commitments.

(19) Reserve to reduce inventory to market.

(20) Matured capital stock subscriptions (called by the board of directors and considered collectible).

(21) Common stock subscribed (Chenault Corp. stock).

(22) Reserve for sinking fund.

(23) Securities held as collateral.

(24) Bank overdraft.

(25) Contracts payable, retained percentage.

3-31. *General review: multiple choice.* (CPA Adapted.) Consider each of the items below. You are to indicate the nature of the account or accounts to be debited when recording each transaction using the preferred accounting treatment by choosing one of the answers from the lettered lists below. Prepayments should be recorded in balance sheet accounts. Disregard income tax considerations unless instructed otherwise.

a. Asset(s) only.

b. Accumulated amortization, depletion or depreciation only.

c. Expense only.

d. Asset(s) and expense.

e. Some other account or combination of accounts.

(1) The Talbot Co. spent $8,600 during the year for experimental purposes in connection with the development of its product. This is approximately the same amount that the company has been spending for this purpose annually for many years.

(2) In April, the West Co. paid $2,800 in cash because a suit was lost in defense of a patent infringement case.

(3) The Miller Co., plaintiff, paid $5,000 in legal fees in December, in connection with a successful infringement suit on its patent. No damages were awarded.

(4) The Placey Co. recently purchased land and two buildings at a total cost of $35,000, and entered the purchase on the books. Razing costs of $1,200 were incurred in removing the smaller building, which had an appraised value at acquisition of $6,200, in order to make room for new construction.

(5) In March, the Bijou Theatre bought projection equipment on the installment basis. The contract price was $23,610, payable $5,610 down and $2,250 a month for the next eight months. The cash price for this equipment was $22,530.

(6) On June 1, the Geneva Hotel installed a sprinkler system throughout the building at a cost of $13,000. As a result, the insurance rate was decreased by 40 per cent.

(7) The Dibble Co. traded its old machine, which had a net book value of $3,000 plus cash of $7,000, for a new one which had a fair market value of $9,000.

(8) A motor in one of Company B's trucks was overhauled at a cost of $600. It is expected that this will extend the life of the truck for two years.

(9) In order to improve production, machinery which had originally cost $130,000, including installation, was rearranged at a cost of $450.

(10) An improvement, which extended the life but not the usefulness of the asset, cost $6,000.

(11) Joe Donald and Frank Rice, maintenance repair men, spent five days in unloading and setting up a new $6,000 precision machine in the plant. Their wages for the five days totaled $240.

(12) The Edison Electric Co. recorded the first year's interest on 6 per cent, $100,000, ten-year bonds, sold a year ago at 94. The bonds were sold in order to finance the construction of a hydroelectric plant. Six months after the sale of the bonds, the hydroelectric plant was completed and operations were begun.

(13) The attic of the Business Building was finished at a cost of $3,000, to provide an additional office.

(14) The ABC Co., the owner of a building, purchased an old lease from tenants for $500, in order to occupy the building before expiration of the original lease four years hence.

(15) The Hiway Supermarket Co. erected a building at a cost of $25,000 on land owned by the Madison Syndicate. The Hiway Supermarket has a 25-year lease. All building costs, and six lease payments to the Madison Syndicate after the building was completed, have been charged to Suspense. You are correcting these entries as of June 30, the end of Hiway's fiscal year.

(16) In July, the Hiway Supermarket Co. [the same company as in item (15)], in accordance with the terms of its lease, paid the real estate tax based on the assessed value of the building and land. The estimated tax had been accrued, as of June 30, at $250 less than the actual tax.

(17) In July, the Hiway Supermarket Co. [same company as in item (15)] paid a special assessment. The special assessment provided funds for the construction of public streets in the area in which the market was located.

(18) In April, Fraser Investment Co. paid $1,700 to the Rio Grande Drilling Co. as part payment of its share of lease, drilling, and development costs in a successful oil-drilling venture.

(19) In September, Schaner & Vandegrift Co. purchased Fraser's interest in certain producing wells and undeveloped leases for $25,000.

(20) In December, Schaner & Vandegrift Co. paid $372 for operating expenses and $1,200 for completion costs of a new well. It is estimated that pipe used will have salvage value of $300.

3-32. *Balance sheet classification of reserves and funds.* Designate whether each of the following is essentially an: asset account (*A*); asset valuation account (*AV*); liability account (*L*); or retained earnings account (*R*).

(1) Reserve for sinking fund.

(2) Reserve for vacation pay.

(3) Reserve for possible future losses in foreign operations.

(4) Sinking fund for retirement of bonds.

(5) Reserve for employees' bonuses.

(6) Reserve for purchases of other companies.

(7) Construction fund.

(8) Reserve for impending economic recession.

(9) Reserve for replacement of facilities at higher price levels.

(10) Reserve to reduce investments from cost to market.

3-33. *Review problem for Chapters 2 and 3: multiple choice.* (Prepared by Kullervo Louhi. Data are from a CPA problem.) Trial Balances and a summary of Cash Receipts and Disbursements of the Harlan Co. appear below. The trial balance, as of Dec. 31, 19x3, is shown on a gross basis: that is, the totals of the debits and of the credits in each of the ledger accounts *including any balance from the after-closing trial balance of Dec. 31, 19x2*, are shown, rather than the final net balances of the accounts.

HARLAN CO.
Cash Receipts and Disbursements
For the Year 19x3

Receipts		*Disbursements*	
Cash balance, Jan. 1, 19x3	$ 21,000	Cash dividends paid	$ 4,000
Collections of accounts receivable	60,000	In settlement of accounts payable	44,260
Cash sales as per cash register tapes	15,000	Jan. 2, 19x3; cash involved in purchase of new machinery (balance paid in capital stock)	1,650
Proceeds from sale of investment	4,000	Net wages paid to employees	11,120
Proceeds from sale of equipment (Sold Jan. 1, 19x3)	800	Social security taxes: employees' and employer's shares	360
Proceeds from bank loan (face amount, $10,000; discounted on Nov. 1, 19x3, on a 6 per cent basis)	9,800	Withheld employees' income tax	700
Interest collected	600	Property taxes paid	600
Total beginning balance and receipts	$111,200	Purchase of investments	5,300
		Total disbursements	$67,990

HARLAN COMPANY
Trial Balances

	Dec. 31, 19x3		Dec. 31, 19x2	
	Debit	Credit	Debit	Credit
Cash	$111,200	$ 67,990	$21,000	
Customers' accounts	65,300	60,500	2,000	
Allowance for uncollectibles	500	1,300		$ 400
Investments	23,800	2,500	18,500	
Accrued interest receivable	400			
Merchandise	58,140	48,900	16,000	
Fixed assets	16,650	1,000	10,000	
Allowance for depreciation	100	2,565		1,000
Accounts payable to merchandise creditors	44,400	44,540		2,400
Bank loan		10,000		
Accrued personal property taxes	600	1,100		500
Capital stock		55,000		40,000
Retained earnings	14,000	39,695		23,200
Totals	$335,090	$335,090	$67,500	$67,500

1. Gross sales on credit in 19x3 amounted to: (a) $67,300; (b) $65,300; (c) $63,300; (d) $62,800; (e) $69,500.

2. Net merchandise cost of all sales in 19x3 was: (a) $16,000; (b) $42,140; (c) $58,140; (d) $48,760; (e) not determinable from the data.

3. The depreciation charge in 19x3 was: (a) $100; (b) $2,565; (c) $1,000; (d) $1,565; (e) none of the above.

4. From the data, it appears that depreciation is computed: (a) on a straight-line time basis; (b) as a constant percentage of a diminishing value; (c) as a diminishing percentage of a constant value; (d) as a percentage of sales; (e) the method of calculation is not determinable from the data.

5. Interest earned in 19x3 amounted to: (a) $1000; (b) $600; (c) $400; (d) none of the preceding amounts; (e) the amount is not determinable from the data.

6. Personal property tax expense accrued during 19x3 amounted to: (a) $1,100; (b) $600; (c) $500; (d) $100; (e) none of the above.

7. In addition to the capital stock given in exchange for fixed assets acquired, it appears that other capital stock: (a) has been sold for cash; (b) has been bought for cash; (c) has been issued as a stock dividend; (d) has been exchanged for certain investments; (e) none of the above.

8. Assuming no sales returns or allowances, the accounts receivable written off as worthless amounted to: (a) $1,300; (b) $400; (c) $500; (d) $1,800; (e) not determinable from the data.

9. The loss on the sale of equipment amounted to: (a) $1,000; (b) $800; (c) $200; (d) $100; (e) none of the above.

10. The estimated loss on uncollectible accounts in 19x3 amounted to: (a) $400; (b) $500; (c) $900; (d) $1,300; (e) no provision was made during the year.

11. In the transactions involving the debits to the Accounts Payable to Merchandise Creditors account, it appears probable that: (a) certain discounts were not taken; (b) an invoice was incorrectly entered; (c)

an invoice was incorrectly paid; (d) a purchase return or allowance was granted to the Harlan Co.; (e) none of the above happened.

12. The sale of investments resulted in: (a) a loss of $1,500; (b) a gain of $1,500; (c) a gain of $4,000; (d) no profit or loss; (e) none of the above.

13. Assuming that no adjustments or corrections for prior years were made during 19x3, the net profit for 19x3, according to the books, was: (a) $23,200; (b) $14,000; (c) $39,695; (d) $16,495; (e) $2,495.

14. With respect to the bank loan, it appears that: (a) all of the interest (discount) has been charged as an expense during 19x3, in error; (b) all of the interest (discount) has been correctly charged as an expense during 19x3; (c) none of the interest (discount) has been charged as an expense during 19x3, in error; (d) none of the interest (discount) has been charged as an expense during 19x3, correctly; (e) no interest (discount) is involved.

CHAPTER 4

Statements
of Funds Flow
and Cash Flow

PUBLISHED FINANCIAL INFORMATION MUST BE JUDGED BY ITS usefulness in facilitating analysis and interpretation. Recently, investors and accountants have shown increased interest in the so-called statement of sources and applications of funds (also called the funds statement, or statement of funds flow). Formerly, the funds statement was regarded as a sort of black sheep that was somehow supposed to relate the net income figure to the major changes in the balance sheet items.

The time has arrived for recognition of the funds statement as an integral part of the financial reporting family. Such statements, drafted with full cognizance of their uses and limitations, might aid considerably in solving some vexing analytical problems. The Accounting Principles Board of the American Institute of Certified Public Accountants has recommended that a statement of sources and applications of funds be included in corporate annual reports.[1] This opinion was reinforced by the New York Stock Exchange and the Directors of the Financial Analysts Federation.

---

[1] Accounting Principles Board, American Institute of Certified Public Accountants, Opinion No. 3, "The Statement of Source and Application of Funds," October, 1963.

STATEMENT OF FUNDS FLOW

Objectives of the Statement

The statement of funds flow shows directly information that can otherwise be obtained only by analysis and interpretation of the income and retained earnings statements and balance sheet. The funds statement summarizes the over-all investment and financing activities of a company. It shows the principal sources and applications of funds. Its major items usually include:

> *Sources of funds:*
> Operations (revenue, less charges against revenue requiring funds)
> Sales of long-lived assets
> ·Sales of investments in stocks or bonds
> Issuance of long-term debt or capital stock
>
> *Applications of funds:*
> Payment of dividends
> Redemption of long-term debt
> Repurchase of outstanding capital stock
> Purchase of noncurrent assets (investments, fixed assets, intangibles)

Financial analysts have cited the following information as being revealed by a funds statement: the major sources from which funds have been obtained (that is, profitable operations, borrowing, stockholder investment) ; clues as to the financial management habits of the executives (that is, management attitudes toward spending and financing) ; the proportion of funds applied to plant, dividends, debt retirement, etc.; indications of the impact of fund flows upon future dividend-paying probabilities; and an indication of the company's trend toward general financial strength or weakness.

Conceptual Framework

In the 1940's at the University of Chicago, Prof. William J. Vatter developed the conceptual and practical approaches to the funds statement that will now be described.[2] Exhibit 4-1 is a balance sheet set up in accordance with his method.

The frame of reference for this method is the natural division of the balance sheet into the Working Capital Segment (Current Assets and Current Liabilities) and the Nonworking Capital Segment (all noncurrent items). The task is then to trace or reconstruct the transactions "between" the two major segments of the balance sheet accounts.

A funds statement is an attempt to show the *causes* for the change in net working capital for a period. As Vatter has pointed out, the funds

---

[2] William J. Vatter, "Direct Method for the Preparation of Fund Statements," *Journal of Accountancy,* June, 1946, pp. 479-491.

EXHIBIT 4-1

SAMPLE COMPANY
Comparative Balance Sheets
Dec. 31, 19x1 and 19x2

Working Capital Segment

	19x1	19x2		19x1	19x2
Current assets	$200,000	$300,000	Current liabilities	$100,000	$160,000
			Net working capital	100,000	140,000
				$200,000	$300,000

Nonworking Capital Segment

	19x1	19x2		19x1	19x2
Investments	$ 40,000	$ 20,000	Long-term debt	$ 80,000	$110,000
Plant and equipment, net	220,000	250,000	Capital stock	200,000	200,000
Investment in working capital segment	100,000	140,000	Retained income	80,000	100,000
	$360,000	$410,000		$360,000	$410,000

statement is a report of the additions and subtractions to the net working capital, as reflected in transfers of capital into or out of the working capital segment. By analyzing the transactions recorded in the noncurrent accounts, you may isolate the items having an impact upon working capital, and hence upon the funds statement.

Definition of Funds

Although there is some disagreement on how funds should be defined, "net working capital" is by far the most widely used definition. Where this definition is used, the statement is best called a statement of changes in net working capital.

Net working capital is the excess of current assets over current liabilities. Besides cash, receivables, and inventories, *current assets* include the following: prepaid current expenses; temporary investments; ordinary installment and deferred receivables; and current receivables from officers, employees, and affiliates. The following items should be excluded from current assets: cash not available for current operations; long-term investments; long-term deferred charges; and cash surrender value of life insurance.

Current liabilities include the usual payables, plus the following items (if payable within twelve months): income taxes; serial note maturities; collections in advance for goods or services to be delivered; estimated liabilities for product warranties or guarantees.

T-Account Approach

We shall illustrate the T-account approach to preparing a statement of sources and applications of net working capital (funds).

Problem

From the following trial balances prepare a statement of changes in sources and applications of net working capital (funds).

	Dec. 31	
Assets:	*19x1*	*19x2*
Cash	$ 80,000	$ 40,000
Receivables	100,000	140,000
Inventories	250,000	351,000
Prepaid expenses	20,000	10,000
Fixed assets, net	1,000,000	1,566,000
Goodwill	650,000	60,000
Total assets	$2,100,000	$2,167,000

	Dec. 31	
Liabilities:	*19x1*	*19x2*
Accounts payable	$ 120,000	$ 180,000
Wages payable	10,000	5,000
Miscellaneous current liabilities	70,000	65,000
Long-term bonds payable	100,000	250,000
Capital stock, at par value	800,000	1,000,000
Paid-in capital in excess of par value of stock	300,000	200,000
Retained income	700,000	467,000
Total equities	$2,100,000	$2,167,000

On Mar. 31, 19x2, $600,000 of goodwill was charged off—$300,000 to paid-in capital and $300,000 to retained income. (There is much theoretical disagreement as to the proper accounting for goodwill. In practice, the tendency is to write it off as a lump sum or to amortize it rapidly.)

In the first half of 19x2, the company bought the assets of another business—$100,000 worth of equipment and $50,000 worth of inventory and accounts receivable. The amount paid was $170,000, the excess of $20,000 being considered the cost of the goodwill acquired. Various other cash purchases of equipment totaled $550,000.

Old machinery was sold for $1,000; it originally cost $12,000 and $8,000 depreciation had been accumulated.

Early in 19x2, the company received $400,000 cash for a new issue of capital stock which had a par value of $200,000. Long-term bonds were also issued for $150,000 cash.

Net income was $317,000, after deductions of $80,000 for depreciation, $10,000 for amortization of goodwill, and a deduction for the loss on the sale of machinery.

Steps in Preparation

First, compute the change in net working capital:

EXHIBIT 4-2

Computation of Changes in Net Working Capital

	Dec. 31		Increase
	19x1	*19x2*	*(Decrease)*
Current assets:			
Cash	$ 80,000	$ 40,000	$ (40,000)
Receivables	100,000	140,000	40,000
Inventories	250,000	351,000	101,000
Prepaid expenses	20,000	10,000	(10,000)
Total	$450,000	$541,000	$ 91,000
Less: Current liabilities:			
Accounts payable	$120,000	$180,000	$ 60,000
Wages payable	10,000	5,000	(5,000)
Miscellaneous	70,000	65,000	(5,000)
Net working capital	$250,000	$291,000	$ 41,000

This technique for solving the problem centers on the relationship between the net working capital T account and all nonworking capital accounts. The *net change* in the individual balances is entered at the top of each account, a single line being drawn below each entry as indicated. (This step is keyed by the letter *B* in the T accounts [Exhibit 4-3] that follow.)

This approach explains the change in net working capital by analyzing the influence of the changes in the nonworking capital accounts. Attention is concentrated upon the reconstruction of entries in the noncurrent accounts as they affect net working capital.

Let us examine the entries in Exhibit 4-3 step by step. The postings are keyed numerically.

1. A good starting point is net income and its relationship to net working capital (i.e., funds) provided by operations. A summary of the net income effect is entered: debit Net Working Capital, credit Retained Income. But Net Income does not directly reflect the impact of operations on Net Working Capital. Net income is a residual figure, the difference between revenue and all expenses and losses—including some expenses and losses (e.g., depreciation, amortization, and losses on the disposal of long-term assets) which do not affect Net Working Capital.

Our purpose is to ascertain the net effect of operations on Net Working Capital. The most straightforward way to accomplish this is to begin with the total sales figure and then deduct all the operating expenses that drained working capital (e.g., cost of goods sold, selling and administrative expenses, etc.). This is a cumbersome way of arriving at funds provided by operations, so accountants use a shortcut. Instead of beginning with the Sales total on the income statement and working down ($A - B - C$ in Exhibit 4-4), accountants usually start with Net Income and work up ($E + D$ in Exhibit 4-4) toward the entry Net Funds Provided

EXHIBIT 4-3

T-Account Approach to Sample Problem

Net Working Capital

Increases B. 41,000			Decreases	
		Sources	Applications	
Operations:			5. Purchase of equipment	100,000
1. Net income	317,000		5. Purchase of goodwill	20,000
2. Depreciation	80,000		7. Various purchases of plant	
3. Amortization	10,000		and equipment	550,000
6. Loss on machinery	3,000	410,000	9. Cash dividends paid	250,000
Other Sources:				
6. Proceeds of machinery sale		1,000		
8. Issuance of capital stock		400,000		
8. Issuance of long-term bonds		150,000		

Fixed Assets (Net)		Goodwill	
B. 566,000			B. 590,000
5. Purchase 100,000	2. Depreciation 80,000	5. Purchase 20,000	3. Amortization 10,000
7. Purchases 550,000	6. Sales 4,000		4. Write-off 600,000

Long-term Bonds Payable		Capital Stock	
	B. 150,000		B. 200,000
	8. Issuance 150,000		8. Issuance 200,000

Paid-in Capital		Retained Income	
B. 100,000		B. 233,000	
4. Write-off of goodwill 300,000	8. Issuance of stock 200,000	4. Write-off of goodwill 300,000	1. Net income 317,000
		9. Cash dividends 250,000	

by Operations. That is, they add back all charges not requiring working capital.

This shortcut is used in the Net Working Capital T account (see Exhibit 4-3). Notice that Increases are divided into two major sections: Operations and Other Sources. Sufficient space should be allowed in the Operations section for shortcut adjustments to net income to obtain the

EXHIBIT 4-4

Analysis of Income Statement
to Show Effects of Operations on Working Capital

(A)	Sales		xxx,xxx
(B)	Less: Cost of goods sold (detailed)		xxx,xxx
	Gross profit		xxx,xxx
(C)	Less: Operating expenses requiring working capital (detailed)		xxx,xxx

$\left(\begin{array}{l}desired\\figure\end{array}\right)$ ⟶ Net funds provided by operations $410,000

(D)	Less: Operating charges not requiring working capital:		
	Depreciation	$80,000	
	Amortization of goodwill	10,000	
	Loss on disposal on noncurrent assets	3,000	93,000
(E)	Net income		$317,000

---

funds provided by operations. The subtotal ($410,000 in Exhibit 4-4) will then be the funds provided by operations.

2. Depreciation:

Net working capital (adjustment to net income) $ 80,000	
Fixed assets (net)	$ 80,000

3. Amortization:

Net working capital (adjustment to net income) $ 10,000	
Goodwill	$ 10,000

4. Write-off of goodwill (no effect on working capital):

Retained income	$300,000	
Paid-in capital	300,000	
Goodwill		$600,000

5. Purchase of assets:

Fixed assets	$100,000	
Goodwill	20,000	
Net working capital		$120,000*

> * Note that the purchase of inventory and receivables had no effect on net working capital. The purchase was merely an exchange of current assets for current assets.

6. Sale of old machinery:

Net working capital (cash received)	$ 1,000	
Net working capital (adjustment to net income)	3,000	
Fixed assets (net)		$ 4,000

7. Various purchases of fixed assets:

Fixed assets	$550,000	
Net working capital		$550,000

8. Issuance of equities:

Net working capital	$400,000	
Capital stock		$200,000
Paid-in capital		200,000
Net working capital	$150,000	
Long-term bonds payable		$150,000

9. Note that, at this point, all explicit information has been entered in the pertinent accounts. A preliminary addition of the debits and credits below the line in each account will show that all changes in all accounts have been explained, except in the Net Working Capital account and the Retained Income account. Therefore, a hidden, implicit transaction is derived after all explicit, explained transactions have been posted. That transaction must be the payment of cash dividends:

Retained income	$250,000	
Net working capital		$250,000

Now all changes have been accounted for. All the ingredients of a funds statement are in the Net Working Capital T account of Exhibit 4-3. The difference between the debits and credits below the line in Net Working Capital is now equal to the $41,000 change that appears at the top of the account. From Exhibit 4-2 and the Net Working Capital T account of Exhibit 4-3, a funds statement (Exhibit 4-5) may be prepared:

EXHIBIT 4-5

SAMPLE COMPANY
Statement of Sources and Applications of Net Working Capital (Funds)
For the Year Ending Dec. 31, 19x2

Sources of net working capital:			
From operations:			
Net income		$317,000	
Add charges not requiring working capital:			
Depreciation	$ 80,000		
Amortization of goodwill	10,000		
Loss on sale of machinery	3,000	93,000	
Total funds (net working capital) provided by operations		$410,000	
From sale of machinery		1,000	
From issuance of capital stock		400,000	
From issuance of long-term bonds payable		150,000	
Total sources of net working capital			$961,000
Applications of net working capital:			
To purchase of business:			
Equipment	$100,000		
Goodwill	20,000		
Net funds applied to purchase		$120,000	
Various purchases of plant and equipment		550,000	
Cash dividends paid		250,000	
Total applications of net working capital			$920,000
Net increase in net working capital (see Exhibit 4-2)			$ 41,000

Shortened T-Account Method

An examination of the previous example reveals that most of the transactions affecting both working capital and noncurrent acounts may be posted directly to the Net Working Capital T account without formally completing the entries in all noncurrent T accounts. By wise use of the additional information in the problem itself, plus a scanning of the changes in noncurrent items, you can produce most of the sources and applications directly. T accounts for Fixed Assets and Retained Income will still be helpful in most instances, however.

An example of the shortened approach, using the same illustrative problem, follows:

EXHIBIT 4-6

Shortened T-Account Method

Net Working Capital

Increases			Decreases	
		B. 41,000		
		Sources	Applications	
Operations:				
1. Net income	317,000		5. Purchase of equipment	100,000
2. Depreciation	80,000		5. Purchase of goodwill	20,000
3. Amortization	10,000		7. Various purchases of plant	
6. Loss on machinery	3,000	410,000	and equipment	550,000
Other Sources:			9. Cash dividends paid	250,000
6. Proceeds of machinery sale		1,000		
8. Issuance of capital stock		400,000		
8. Issuance of long-term bonds		150,000		

Fixed Assets (Net)			Retained Income	
B. 566,000			B. 233,000	
5. Purchase	2. Depreciation		4. Write-off of	1. Net income
100,000	80,000		goodwill 300,000	317,000
7. Purchases	6. Sale		9. Cash dividends	
550,000	4,000		250,000	

After net changes in T accounts for Net Working Capital, Fixed Assets, and Retained Income, have been entered, additional information is scanned. Fund flow effects are picked out, and all entries are labeled for later reference. Let us examine the entries which are, again, posted numerically.

> 1, 2, and 3. Enter the net income and the adjustments thereto, to get funds provided by operations.
> 4. The write-off of goodwill had no effect on net working capital.
> 5. Purchase of assets: equipment and goodwill.

6. Sale of old machinery.
7. Various purchases of fixed assets.
8. Issuances of stock and bonds.
9. The balance in Retained Income is now $17,000, but the net change is a decrease of $233,000. The payment of cash dividends in the amount of $250,000 is therefore an implied transaction—the only apparent explanation for the $41,000 net increase in Net Working Capital and the $233,000 net decrease in Retained Income.

This method saves time and helps to isolate hidden transactions. But it must be remembered that it is merely a shortcut version of the complete T-account method illustrated previously.

Summary of Approach

Funds statements may be derived from T accounts as well as from bulky working papers. The major advantages of the T-account approach are: (1) it saves time; and (2) working with T accounts helps to clarify one's thinking about the whole subject of funds statements.

The frame of reference for this method is the natural division of the balance sheet into the working capital segment and the nonworking capital segment (all noncurrent accounts). The task then is to trace or to reconstruct the transactions between the two segments of the balance sheet accounts.

A summary of the steps follows:

1. Determine the net increase or decrease in working capital.
2. Enter the increase or decrease at the top of a Net Working Capital T account.
3. Enter net increases or decreases in noncurrent accounts at the top of individual T accounts. It is not always necessary to use all noncurrent accounts. The relationship, or lack of one, between the changes in many noncurrent accounts and net working capital is often so obvious that the actual setting up of T accounts is unnecessary. All that needs to be done is to enter the source or application in the working capital T account. However, in most cases it is helpful to use T accounts for fixed assets and retained earnings.
4. Reconstruct the entries in noncurrent accounts that affect working capital. First, consult the additional information in the problem. Second, by scanning the noncurrent accounts for unexplained changes, reconstruct the hidden transactions.
5. Using the working capital T account, prepare the formal funds statement.

Pitfalls to Avoid

1. Be certain that there is an appropriate classification of current assets and current liabilities before you compute changes in net working capital.
2. In almost all situations where there is a net loss, there will still be funds provided by operations. Depreciation and other nonworking capital charges are deducted in the computation of a net loss. When these are added back to the final net loss figure, the result shows a positive amount

of funds provided by operations. The following hypothetical Net Working Capital T account illustrates this point:

Net Working Capital

		40,000		
Operations:				
Net loss	(10,000)		Dividends	25,000
Depreciation	25,000	15,000		
Other sources:				
Sale of bonds		50,000		

3. One of the major features of funds statement problems is the presence of transactions which are not explicitly stated and which must be derived from analysis of the changes in noncurrent accounts. First, all explicit additional information is traced. Then the implicit, hidden transactions are reconstructed by a step-by-step consideration of all the unexplained changes in noncurrent accounts.

4. The formal presentation of the funds statement should include a subtotal of funds provided by operations. The mere listing of net income, depreciation, amortization, etc. as sources of funds indicates a misunderstanding of the relationship between depreciation and the flow of funds. Depreciation is not a source of funds. If it were, a company could obtain all the funds it needs simply by arbitrarily increasing its depreciation charges. The biggest source of funds is usually operations.

Limitations of the Statement

A statement of the flow of funds supposedly portrays the financial management habits of a company. However, a strictly held definition of *funds* as "net working capital" often results in the exclusion of important financial transactions from a funds flow statement. For example, the conversion of bonds into stock, the issuance of stock dividends, the declaration of a split in stock, the exchange of noncurrent assets for other noncurrent assets, and the acquisition of property for cash plus a substantial mortgage can all be ignored or only partially reported in a funds statement in which funds are equated with net working capital.

The disadvantages of defining funds as working capital have led to a variety of substitute definitions. Among them are "cash," "net liquid assets, exclusive of inventories," and "all financial resources." All have various strengths and weaknesses.

"All financial resources" is a broader concept than net working capital and would incorporate nearly all the relevant financial transactions, but it presents some difficulties. For example, some accountants support the notion that a stock dividend (common on common) should be reported as a source of funds and as a use of funds, since it is equivalent to paying a cash dividend which is immediately reinvested in the corporation by the stockholder. Other accountants would exclude such a transaction from an "all financial resources" concept.

Fortunately, there is a workable, satisfactory compromise in these situations. It probably would be best to retain the net working capital notion that is so entrenched as a definition of funds. At the same time, pertinent financial transactions not directly influencing net working capital should be reported parenthetically or in footnotes. If a company buys a building for $100,000, subject to a $60,000 mortgage, for example, an informative report would read as follows:

Funds applied:		
To purchase of building	$100,000	
Less mortgage payable	60,000	
Net working capital currently applied		$40,000

STATEMENT OF CASH FLOW

The Cash Flow Statement (Exhibit 4-7) is similar to a Statement of Sources and Applications of Funds (Exhibit 4-5), but the two differ in scope. As we have just seen, the funds statement is a summary explanation of transactions that have a direct impact upon *net working capital*. The cash flow statement is a summary explanation of transactions that have a direct impact upon *cash*, a narrower concept.

Essentially, this means that Cash, rather than Net Working Capital, is the master T account. Furthermore, it requires analyzing changes in all balance sheet items other than cash, in order to determine the impact of such changes on cash. The preparation of a cash flow statement involves reconstructing the cash transactions in the same manner in which the funds transactions are reconstructed for a funds flow statement.

The most difficult part of preparing a cash flow statement is the step-by-step analysis of all the items in the income statement, so that the net income, which has been computed on an accrual basis, may be

EXHIBIT 4-7

Cash Flow Statement

Cash was provided by:		
Operations (see schedule)		xxx
Issuance of capital stock		xxx
Issuance of bonds		xxx
Sale of investments		xxx
Total		xxx
Cash was applied to:		
Acquisition of plant and equipment	xxx	
Decrease of short-term bank loans	xxx	
Payment of long-term notes	xxx	
Payment of dividends	xxx	xxx
Increase (or decrease) in cash balance		xxx

converted to a cash flow from operations. Probably the easiest way to begin is with cash inflow from sales. Then translate all expenses into cash outflow. This analysis may be conducted on the left side of the master Cash T account; it is similar to the analysis conducted on the left side of the master Net Working Capital account in order to compute funds provided by operations.

In converting income statement items to the cash basis, remember that declines in inventories, prepayments of payables, and increases in payables will result in a smaller outflow of cash for current operations. Increases in receivables means that current sales are not all being immediately transformed into cash inflows.

SUMMARY

Statements of funds flow and cash flow are increasing in importance because they yield direct insights into the financial management policies of a company.

Statements of funds flow are better called Statements Explaining the Change in Net Working Capital or Statements of Sources and Applications of Net Working Capital, because net working capital is the most widely used definition of funds. Pertinent financial transactions which do not directly influence net working capital should be disclosed parenthetically or in footnotes.

SUMMARY PROBLEM FOR YOUR REVIEW

PROBLEM

The Buretta Co. has prepared the following data:

Trial Balances
Dec. 31
(In millions)

Debits	19x1	19x2	Change
Cash	$20	$ 7	$(13)
Accounts receivable	5	20	15
Inventory	15	40	25
Prepaid general expenses	2	4	2
Fixed assets, net	50	91	41
	$92	$162	$ 70
Credits			
Accounts payable for merchandise	$14	$ 39	$ 25
Accrued property tax payable	1	3	2
Mortgage payable in 19x9	—	40	40
Capital stock	70	70	—
Retained earnings	7	10	3
	$92	$162	$ 70

BURETTA CO.
Income Statement and Reconciliation of Retained Earnings
For the Year Ending Dec. 31, 19x2
(In millions)

Sales		$100
Less cost of goods sold:		
Inventory, Dec. 31, 19x1	$ 15	
Purchases	98	
Cost of goods available for sale	$113	
Inventory, Dec. 31, 19x2	40	73
Gross profit		$ 27
Less other expenses:		
General expenses	$ 11	
Depreciation	8	
Property taxes	4	23
Net income		$ 4
Dividends		1
Net income of the period retained		$ 3
Retained earnings, Dec. 31, 19x1		7
Retained earnings, Dec. 31, 19x2		$ 10

On Dec. 28, 19x2, Buretta paid $9,000,000 in cash and signed a $40,000,000 mortgage on a new building acquired to accommodate an expansion of operations.

In view of the fact that the net income of $4,000,000 was the highest in the company's history, Mr. Buretta, the chairman of the board, was perplexed by the company's extremely low cash balance.

Required:

1. Submit a statement of sources and applications of funds (net working capital), together with your supporting work.
2. Submit a statement of cash flow (cash receipts and disbursements), together with your supporting work.
3. Prepare, for Mr. Buretta, a brief explanation of why cash has decreased even though net working capital has increased and net income was $4,000,000.

SOLUTION

1.

BURETTA CO.
Statement of Sources and Applications of Net Working Capital (Funds)
For the Year Ending Dec. 31, 19x2

Sources:			
Funds provided by operations:			
Net income		$4,000,000	
Add depreciation, which was deducted in the computation of net income, but which does not require net working capital		8,000,000	$12,000,000
Applications:			
Dividends		$1,000,000	
Purchase of fixed assets	$49,000,000		
Less mortgage	40,000,000		
Net working capital currently applied		9,000,000	10,000,000
Net increase in net working capital			$ 2,000,000

Net working capital:
Dec. 31, 19x2 (in millions): ($7 + $20 + $40 + $4) − ($39 + $3) = $29
Dec. 31, 19x1 (in millions): ($20 + $5 + $15 + $2) − ($14 + $1) = $27
Net change = $ 2

Net Working Capital (In millions)

Increase			*Decreases*	
		2		
Operations:				
1. Net income	4		3. Dividends	1
2. Depreciation	8	12	4. Purchase of fixed assets	9
Other sources:				
None directly, but note how mortgage financing appears on the formal statement				

	Fixed Assets (Net)				Mortgage Payable	
	41					40
4.	49	2.	8		4.	40

	Capital Stock			Retained Earnings	
		0			3
			3.	1	1.	4

2.

BURETTA CO.
Statement of Cash Flow (Cash Receipts and Disbursements)
For the Year Ending Dec. 31, 19x2

Cash balance, Dec. 31, 19x1			$20,000,000
Receipts:			
From operations:			
Collections from customers		$85,000,000	
Operating disbursements:			
Merchandise	$73,000,000		
General expenses	13,000,000		
Property taxes	2,000,000	88,000,000	(3,000,000)*
Cash available for use			$17,000,000
Disbursements:			
Dividends		$ 1,000,000	
Purchase of fixed assets	$49,000,000		
Less mortgage	40,000,000		
Net cash payment		9,000,000	10,000,000
Cash balance, Dec. 31, 19x2			$ 7,000,000

* This is normally positive, that is, operations usually provide cash rather than drain cash.

Supporting Work (In millions)

Cash

			13

Receipts		*Disbursements*	
Operations:		*Operations:*	
Sales per income statement 100		Purchases:	
Less rise in receivables (15)		Per income statement 98	
1. Net inflow	85	Rise in payables (25)	
		2. Net outflow	73
		General expenses:	
		Per income statement 11	
		Rise in prepayments 2	
		3. Net outflow	13
		Property taxes:	
		Per income statement 4	
		Rise in accrual (2)	
		4. Net outflow	2
		Other:	
		5. Dividends	1
		6. Purchase of fixed assets	9

Accounts Receivable

			15
Sales	100	1.	85

Accounts Payable

			25
2.	73	Purchases	98

Inventory

	25		
Purchases	98	Cost of goods sold	73

Accrued Property Tax Payable

			2
4. Payments	2	Accruals	4

Prepaid General Expenses

	2		
3. Payments	13	Write-offs to expenses	11

Mortgage Payable

			40
		6.	40

Fixed Assets (Net)

	41		
6.	49	Depreciation	8

Capital Stock

			0

Retained Earnings

			3
5.	1	Net income	4

3.

To Mr. Buretta:

Severe squeezes on cash commonly accompany quick corporate growth. There may be ample net income and funds provided by operations, but the heavy demand for cash to expand fixed assets, inventories, and receivables may diminish the cash on hand despite profitable operations. That is why so many so-called growth companies usually pay little or no dividends.

ASSIGNMENT MATERIAL

ESSENTIAL ASSIGNMENT MATERIAL

4-1. *Statement of sources and applications of funds.* The following comparative trial balances and additional information pertain to the Quick Manufacturing Co. Using the T-account approach, prepare a statement of sources and applications of net working capital (funds) for the year, 19x2. This includes preparation of the final statement in good form.

QUICK MANUFACTURING CO.
Comparative Trial Balances

	Dec. 31	
	19x1	*19x2*
Debits:		
Cash	$ 50,000	$ 43,000
Receivables	65,000	76,000
Inventories	98,000	118,000
Prepaid rent	7,000	5,000
Patents	48,000	50,000
Fixed assets	182,000	205,000
	$450,000	$497,000
Credits:		
Accounts payable	$ 63,000	$ 71,000
Taxes payable	18,000	20,000
Bank loan	16,000	25,000
4 per cent serial bonds (current)	20,000	20,000
Accumulated depreciation	76,000	82,000
4 per cent serial bonds (noncurrent)	20,000	—
Capital stock ($10 par value)	100,000	110,000
Paid-in capital	50,000	55,000
Retained earnings	87,000	114,000
	$450,000	$497,000

Additional information pertaining to 19x2:

1. Old machinery, having a book value of $22,000 and accumulated depreciation of $18,000, was sold for $5,000.
2. In late December, another patent was acquired, at a cost of $5,000.
3. Net income amounted to $27,000, after deductions amounting to $24,000

for depreciation and $3,000 for amortization of patents. No dividends were paid during 19x2.

4. During the year the company received $15,000 for a new issue of 1,000 shares of capital stock.

4-2. *Statement of sources and applications of funds.* From the balance sheet of the WJV Co. for the years ending Dec. 31, 19x4 and 19x5 and the additional information presented below, prepare a statement of sources and applications of net working capital (funds). Use the T-account approach and include the final statement in good form in your answer.

WJV CO.
Comparative Balance Sheets

		Dec. 31		
Assets		*19x4*		*19x5*
Cash		$ 62,000		$ 80,000
Marketable securities		28,000		—
Accounts receivable		95,000		91,500
Inventories		126,000		114,000
Prepaid insurance		4,000		6,000
Total current assets		$315,000		$291,500
Long term notes receivable		55,000		50,000
Plant, property, and equipment	$285,000		$365,000	
Less: Accumulated depreciation	112,000	173,000	126,000	239,000
		$543,000		$580,500
Liabilities				
Accounts and notes payable		$106,000		$110,000
Taxes payable		38,000		35,000
Dividends payable		—		32,000
Total current liabilities		$144,000		$177,000
4½ per cent debentures	$ 50,000		$ 50,000	
Less: Unamortized discount	5,000	45,000	4,500	45,500
Capital stock ($5 par value)		80,000		80,000
Paid-in surplus		112,000		112,000
Retained earnings		162,000		166,000
		$543,000		$580,500

Additional information:

1. Net income for the year 19x5 amounted to $36,000.

2. On June 30, 19x5, a boiler exploded and was completely demolished. The boiler, which was four years old on Dec. 31, 19x4, originally cost $20,000 and was being depreciated on a straight-line basis according to a ten-year life estimate. Proceeds from an insurance policy covering the boiler amounted to $10,000.

4-3. *Multiple choice.* Select the best possible answer from the following lettered choices in answering the numbered questions below:

The following type of information is usually found in a statement of sources and applications of funds:

Sources

a. Operations: added to Net Income to obtain Funds Provided by Operations.

b. Operations: deducted from Net Income to obtain Funds Provided by Operations.

c. Increases in long-term liabilities.

d. Sales of noncurrent assets.   CASH

Applications

e. Cash dividends or withdrawals by owners.

f. Reductions in long-term liabilities.

g. Retirement of capital stock.

h. Increases in noncurrent assets.

Neither

i. Does not ordinarily appear in a conventional statement of sources and applications of funds.

Indicate the presentation, if any, of each of the following in a statement of sources and applications of funds:

i (1) Increase in allowance for uncollectible accounts.

a (2) Increase in accumulated depreciation.

d(3) Gain on sale of machinery.

d(4) Issuance of bonds for cash.

? — e(5) Declaration of a cash dividend on common stock. The dividend has not been paid at the close of the fiscal year.

b (6) Gain on sale of investments.

i (7) Purchase discounts on merchandise.

a (8) Amortization of patent charged to royalty revenues.

i (9) Acquisition of a factory site by donation from a city.

i (10) Issuance of stock to founders for promotional services.

b (11) Uninsured loss of a warehouse, by fire.

i (12) Uninsured loss of merchandise stored in the warehouse, by fire.

a (13) Loss on sale of investments.

i (14) Issuance of common stock in conversion of bonds.

i (15) Collection of accounts receivable.

d (16) Proceeds from sale of equipment at less than book value.

ADDITIONAL ASSIGNMENT MATERIAL

Note: Problems 4-24, 4-27, and 4-28 are especially recommended. Problem 4-27 is unusual because it works backward, giving a funds statement as a framework for computing other items. Problem 4-28 requires a cash flow statement as well as a funds statement. Cash flow has not been emphasized in the Assignment Material for Chapter 4 because the subject is covered thoroughly in the problems on cash budgeting in Chapter 6.

4-4. What are the major sources of funds? Applications?

4-5. What type of insights are provided by a funds statement?

4-6. Define a funds statement.

4-7. What is net working capital?

4-8. What are some examples of expenses and losses not affecting working capital?

4-9. What are the two major ways of computing funds provided by operations?

4-10. "The ordinary purchase of inventory has no effect on working capital." Why?

4-11. "Net losses mean drains on working capital." Do you agree? Explain.

4-12. "Depreciation is usually a big source of funds." Do you agree? Explain.

4-13. What are some weaknesses of the idea that funds are net working capital?

4-14. Give other definitions of funds.

4-15. What is the major difference between a funds statement and a cash flow statement?

4-16. Criticize the following presentation of part of a funds statement:

> Sources:
> | | |
> |---|---:|
> | Sales | $100,000 |
> | Less expenses requiring working capital | 70,000 |
> | Funds provided by operations | $ 30,000 |

4-17. The gain on the sale of a fixed asset represents part of the funds received by the X company. How should this item be presented on a fund statement? Why?

4-18. What are the effects on fund flows of the following transaction: The purchase of fixed assets at a cost of $100,000, of inventories at a cost of $200,000, and of receivables at a cost of $50,000, paid for by the assumption of a $70,000 mortgage on the fixed assets and the giving of a 90-day promissory note for $280,000.

4-19. The net income of the Lear Co. was $1,500,000. Included on the income statement are the following:

Uninsured loss of inventory, by flood	$100,000
Gain on the sale of equipment	200,000
Bad debt expense	50,000
Dividend income	10,000
Interest income, including $5,000 not yet received	20,000
Amortization of patents	50,000
Depreciation	400,000

Compute the funds provided by operations, assuming that interest and dividend income are a part of operating income.

4-20. *Components of net working capital.* Use the letter *I* to indicate which of the following items would be included in the computation of net working capital of the Mammoth Co. on Dec. 31, 19x4. Use the letter *E* to indicate which accounts would be excluded.

1. Retained earnings
2. Income tax payable
3. Accounts receivable
4. Office supplies inventory

5. Bonds payable Oct. 31, 19x5
6. Merchandise inventory
7. Investment in stock of subsidiary
8. Unexpired insurance
9. Cash surrender value of life insurance
10. Note payable June 1, 19x8
11. Sinking fund for redemption of preferred stock
12. Accrued vacation pay
13. Rent collected in advance
14. Cash dividend payable
15. Stock dividend payable
16. Arrearages on cumulative preferred dividends
17. Bond interest payable
18. Serial notes payable, $100,000; payable in four annual installments, beginning June 30, 19x5

4-21. *Cash flow and reported income.* The owner of a small manufacturing company is mystified by his accounting statements. His accountant has informed him that the company's net income hovers around zero each year. Cash has increased steadily since the inception of the business six years ago, so the owner believes that the company must be profitable. Inventories, receivables, payables, long-term debt, and capital stock have not changed perceptibly. No dividends have been paid.

Explain briefly why cash has increased in the face of zero profits. Give illustrations of transactions that would clarify your explanation.

4-22. *Effect on funds flow of fixed asset transactions.* The Camfield Co. balance sheets contained the following:

	Dec. 31	
	19x4	*19x5*
Fixed assets, at original cost	$563,000	$785,000
Accumulated depreciation	434,000	536,000

A $10,000 gain on the sale of fixed assets and a depreciation expense of $140,000 were shown on the 19x5 income statement. Expenditures for new plant and equipment during 19x5 were $300,000.

Compute the original cost and accumulated depreciation of the fixed assets sold during 19x5. Also compute the proceeds of the sale and give the journal entry for the sale.

4-23. *Criticize working capital statement.* (CPA Adapted.) You are to criticize the accompanying statement, considering mainly its function and content. (There are differences of opinion concerning the general form of such a statement and the terminology used. You need not concern yourself with these matters in your criticism except if you believe them to be essential to the accomplishment of the statement's function.) Mention in your discussion the specific items which the data lead you to believe: (*a*) may have been omitted incorrectly from the statement; or (*b*) should have been excluded from the statement. For *each* item which you mention, give your reason for inclusion or deletion and state how you would treat the item.

You need not prepare a revised statement. (There are no arithmetical errors in the statement.)

ENAK MANUFACTURING CO., INC.
Statement Showing Causes of Net Change in Working Capital

Funds were obtained from:

Operations (net income transferred to retained earnings)		$179,001.12
Current assets used up in year's operations		
Cash on hand and in banks	$ 33,427.73	
Postal stamps	20.00	33,447.73
Increase in common stock outstanding	$ 10,000.00	
Increase in capital surplus	20,000.00	30,000.00
		$242,448.85

Funds were applied to:

Payments of cash dividends		$ 35,442.00
Declaration of stock dividends (not yet issued)		27,400.00
Investment in additions to		
Accounts receivable—Trade	$ 10,004.43	
Notes receivable—Trade	2,500.00	
Inventories	101,442.21	
Marketable securities	10,440.00	
Cash surrender value of life insurance	1,141.25	
Fixed assets (net increase)	15,142.50	
Patents	20,000.00	
Prepaid expense	2,453.03	
Total		163,122.42
Payments of serial-bond maturities		10,000.00
Reduction in current liabilities		6,484.43
		$242,448.85

4-24. *Statement of sources and applications of funds: implicit transactions.* From the following information, prepare a statement of sources and applications of funds.

LIPPERT CO.
Trial Balance
(In thousands of dollars)

	Dec. 31	
Debits	*19x2*	*19x1*
Current assets	$140	$120
Fixed assets	172	270
Total debits	$312	$390
Credits		
Accumulated depreciation	$ 12	$ 32
Current liabilities	90	165
Capital stock	195	180
Retained earnings	15	13
Total credits	$312	$390

Depreciation expense was $8,000. Cash dividends were $15,000. In addition, dividends in common shares of $5,000 were charged to retained earnings. New equipment was purchased for $30,000 in cash. A $3,000 loss on the sale of old equipment was charged against net income. The depreciation accumulated on the old equipment was $28,000.

4-25. *Comprehensive statement of sources and applications of funds.* (CPA Adapted.) The net changes in the balance sheet accounts of *X* Co. for the year 19x0 are shown below:

	Debit	Credit
Investments		$25,000
Land	$ 3,200	
Buildings	35,000	
Machinery	6,000	
Office equipment		1,500
Allowance for depreciation:		
Buildings		2,000
Machinery		900
Office equipment	600	
Discount on bonds	2,000	
Bonds payable		40,000
Capital stock—preferred	10,000	
Capital stock—common		12,400
Premium on common stock		5,600
Retained earnings		6,800
Working capital	37,400	
	$94,200	$94,200

Additional information:

1. Cash dividends of $18,000 were declared Dec. 15, 19x0, payable Jan. 15, 19x1. A 2 per cent stock dividend was issued Mar. 31, 19x0 when the market value was $12.50 per share.
2. The investments were sold for $27,500.
3. A building which cost $45,000 and had a depreciated basis of $40,500 was sold for $50,000.
4. The following entry was made to record an exchange of an old machine for a new one:

Machinery	$13,000	
Allowance for depreciation—Machinery	5,000	
Machinery		$ 7,000
Cash		11,000

5. A fully depreciated office machine which cost $1,500 was written off.
6. Preferred stock of $10,000 par value was redeemed for $10,200.
7. The company sold 1,000 shares of its common stock (par value, $10) on June 15, 19x0, for $15 a share. There were 13,240 shares outstanding on Dec. 31, 19x0.

Required:

Statement of sources and applications of funds (net working capital) for the year 19x0. Use the T-account approach.

4-26. *Case study: interpretation of funds statement.* (SICA Adapted.) The controller of Elsta Co. Ltd. has asked you to comment on the statement of source and application of funds you prepared recently for him. Here is the statement:

ELSTA CO. LTD., WHOLESALERS,
Statement of Source and Application of Funds
For the Year Ending Dec. 31, 19x2

Funds were derived from:
Operations

Net profit for the year		$350,000	
Add: Expenses not requiring current cash outlay			
Depreciation	$90,000		
Amortization of bond discount	7,000	97,000	$ 447,000
Sale of investments			202,000
Total funds derived			$ 649,000

Funds were applied to:

Buildings and equipment purchased	$702,000	
Preferred shares retired		
(1,000 shares @ $105)	105,000	
Bonds redeemed (3,500 @ $102)	357,000	
Dividends paid, preferred and common	280,000	1,444,000
Net decrease in working capital*		$ 795,000

* The net decrease in working capital was made up as follows:

	Dec. 31		Working Capital	
	19x1	*19x2*	*Increase*	*Decrease*
Cash on hand and in bank	$ 126,000	$ 86,000	$	$ 40,000
Accounts receivable	1,650,000	1,690,000	40,000	
Inventories	1,295,000	850,000		445,000
	$3,071,000	$2,626,000	$40,000	$485,000
Bank loan (secured)		$ 100,000		$100,000
Accounts payable	$1,900,000	2,150,000		250,000
	$1,900,000	$2,250,000		$350,000
Working capital	$1,171,000	$ 376,000	$40,000	$835,000
				40,000
Net decrease in working capital				$795,000

Before making your comments on the above statement you obtain the following information from the company's records:

	19x0	*19x1*	*19x2*
Sales	$17,100,000	$14,100,000	$15,600,000
Cost of sales	$13,000,000	$11,000,000	$12,000,000

Sales of the company are approximately uniform each month and are expected to be $16,600,000 in 19x3. It is expected that the ratio of cost of sales to sales will be the average of this ratio for the past three years.

Required:

The letter which you would prepare to bring to the controller's attention any conclusions as to the company's financial policy which may be drawn from the above analysis.

4-27. *Using a funds statement to reconstruct net income and a balance sheet.* The following funds statement and additional information pertain to the operations of the Turner Corp. during 19x1.

TURNER CORP.
Statement of Sources and Applications of Net Working Capital (Funds)
For the Year Ending Dec. 31, 19x1

Sources of net working capital:		
Funds provided by operations	$ 51,500	
From issue of 20-year bonds	100,000	
From issue of common stock (15,000 shares		
@ $10 par value)	240,000	
Total sources of net working capital		$391,500
Applications of net working capital:		
For acquisition of plant and equipment	$170,000	
For payment of dividends	15,000	
Total applications of net working capital		185,000
Net increase in working capital		$206,500

Additional information:

1. The Turner Corp. was incorporated on Jan. 2, 19x1.
2. All plant and equipment was purchased on Jan. 2. The estimated life of the assets is ten years. Turner uses straight line depreciation.
3. On June 30, a $10,000 machine was destroyed by fire.

Required:

(a) From the above information compute the Turner Corp. net income for 19x1.
(b) Prepare a balance sheet, as of Dec. 31, 19x1, *in as much detail as possible.* (Hint: Current assets and current liabilities cannot be separately determined. Therefore, treat the difference, net working capital, as a single item in the balance sheet.)

4-28. *Comprehensive problem on funds statements and cash flow statements.* The following data pertain to the Knickelbine Co.:

	Trial Balances Dec. 31	
Debits	*19x0*	*19x1*
Cash	$ 20,000	?
Accounts receivable	18,000	$23,000
Inventory	35,000	29,500
Accrued interest receivable	300	—
Prepaid miscellaneous expenses	2,000	3,200
Fixed assets, net	28,000	24,000
	$103,300	?

Credits

Accounts payable for merchandise	$ 33,000	$40,000
Accrued property tax payable	550	580
Mortgage payable*	35,000	30,000
Capital stock	10,000	20,000
Retained earnings	24,750	? 46300
	$103,300	?

* This company was given an interest-free mortgage to encourage it to begin operations in its present location. The principal is payable in a $5,000 installment in 19x1 and in $7,500 annual installments thereafter.

Other information:

Sales	$211,100	Property taxes	$ 700
Purchases	121,000	Interest income	400
Miscellaneous expenses	55,500	Dividends paid	1,250
Depreciation	6,000		

Additional capital stock of $15,000 was issued early in the year, but $5,000 of stock was retired in November, 19x1.

Required:

1. Income statement and reconciliation of retained earnings.
2. Statement of sources and applications of funds, together with supporting work. You may omit a formal schedule of the details of working capital.
3. Statement of cash flow (cash receipts and disbursements), together with supporting work.

CHAPTER 5

Analysis
and Interpretation
of Financial Statements

FINANCIAL STATEMENTS SHOULD FACILITATE COMPARISON AND prediction, the two major analytical tasks of both internal and external users. In this chapter, we consider some techniques and ratios commonly used in financial analysis and interpretation. Although internal and external users share an interest in these techniques, our present emphasis is on external uses, particularly because internal uses—evaluation of management performance—are discussed at length in subsequent chapters. The techniques discussed in this chapter will be helpful both to managers and to investors.

THE ANALYSTS' GENERAL APPROACH

Focus of Interest and Sources of Information

Published financial statements are properly oriented toward the long-term investor, who is mainly interested in long-term earning power. Short-term creditors, such as major suppliers or banks, are usually more interested in the short-run ability of the corporation to satisfy its obligations as they mature. The amount of time allotted by the analyst and the quantity of information he seeks depend directly on the size of the investment he is considering and on his general familiarity with the company. Financial analysts usually use a company's annual report as the springboard for their review.

Heavy commitments, either in investments in common stock or in the form of large bank loans to a new customer, are preceded by thorough investigations, utilizing many sources of information: personal interviews with management, prospectuses (i.e., detailed financial descriptions), statistical services, annual detailed (Form 10-K) reports to the Securities and Exchange Commission, and subscriptions to the services of investment research organizations that have the contacts necessary for obtaining the desired information. The trade creditor, on the other hand, cannot allot the time or resources for a thorough investigation of every customer. He relies mostly on personal experience with customers and reports from credit agencies.

Comparison and Prediction

The financial analyst is an investor or an adviser to investors. His primary reason for analyzing quantitative data is to secure clues to *future* performance. He is a predictor. Comparison is an essential step in the prediction process—comparison of changing over-all economic conditions, comparison of industries, comparison of firms within industries, comparison of divisions within firms, and comparison of specific company financial data through the months or years.

The following is a summary of the financial analysts' approach to financial data:

1. Analysts look for trends and changes in major items. They compare years, products, and similar firms. Their figures are condensed: Anything under $100,000 (and sometimes $1 million) is generally regarded as insignificant.
2. The income statement is regarded as the most important reflector of the operations of the firm. There is a definite tendency to think in terms of "normal earning power," but all components of the statement are examined carefully. The items of greatest interest include: sales and sales breakdowns; cost of goods sold, inventory valuations, and gross margin; operating expenses, such as research, long-term rentals, and depreciation; nonrecurring items; foreign operations; income taxes; and net income. The most important income statement ratio is considered to be the per cent of net operating profit before income taxes to sales. [See the right-hand side of Eq. (3), p. 104.]
3. The analysts' concern with the balance sheet centers about the current working capital position and the capitalization structure. Analysts look for an adequate current position. They scrutinize the capitalization structure and any trends therein. The ratios most often employed are the current ratio [see Eq. (17), p. 112] and percentage breakdowns of capitalization structures [by book values, Eq. (12), and market values]. Reserves are scanned, and reclassified where it is deemed necessary.
4. Analysts are very much interested in sources and applications of funds. If funds statements are not included in corporate annual reports, they either draft makeshift funds statements or analyze comparative balance sheets in such a way that their written words amount to a funds flow analysis. Almost every written analysis contains an estimate of sources

and applications of funds over the past five to seven years and an estimate of fund flow for at least one year into the future.

The analyst emphasizes the flow of funds because it offers the clearest quantitative insight into the financial policies of the firm and into the future outlook for dividends. Consequently it appears, from the *uses* of quantitative data by analysts, that the funds statement ranks along with the income statement and the balance sheet as an essential financial statement.

The funds-flow thinking of the analyst is reflected in his treatment of fixed assets. The balance sheet values of fixed assets are all but ignored. Attention is concentrated on capital expenditures over the past five to seven years and, even more important, on planned capital expenditures. The sources of the funds for capital requirements are also estimated. The probable impact of capital expenditures on financial position, sales, earnings, and dividends is invariably discussed by analysts in their written reports.

Overemphasis of a Single Figure

The income statement is the center of analytical attention. Security analysts want to know what future earnings and dividends per share are going to be and whether the company will be able to meet its financial obligations.

An intelligent analyst will not be satisfied merely with a figure for earnings per share [Eq. (7)]. He is interested in interpreting that figure, in extracting the full story behind the figure. There is a danger in overemphasizing any single figure; modern business operations are too complex to be portrayed by a lone measure. The analyst must interpret *any* net income figure in light of the future prospects of each of its determinants and with a view to company plans and obligations.

Character of Income

Specifically, what is it that the analyst wants to know and struggles to project? He wants to know the character of the reported income as it bears on the future: the nature of the various ingredients of the income statement.

In studying revenue, the analyst considers each product line in the light of the following factors: capital investment needs, pricing changes, stability, research productivity, competitive situation, and general business conditions. In studying expenses, he considers questions like the following: What are the cost behavior patterns? Are some expenses postponable? Which expenses vary with volume and which do not? Which types of expense may be eliminated if there is a drastic decrease in revenue? What is the ratio between expenses and sales in various product lines?

What about labor conditions and cost-control techniques? What about research outlays and attitudes toward research?

If the above factors can be estimated with some degree of confidence, the net income—a residual, the result of subtracting expenses from revenue—may be projected. (Such work is admittedly an imposing undertaking.) And then, what of the disposition of the probable income? The analyst will isolate depreciation when it is relatively important, and compare it with planned or needed capital expenditures and with the retirement of debt arising from past capital expenditures. He will wonder if depreciation is adequate for those outlays. He will also try to estimate the probable return on additional dollars committed to plant and equipment by examining the effect of expenditures made in the past five to seven years on revenue and income. That is, he will try to see if there is a clear relationship between dollars spent and increased revenues and income.

This kind of analysis requires seasoned judgment and a firm command of the facts. One technique, which is used when the facts are available, is to compare the return on investment in new plant facilities with the return on investment in old plant facilities, restated at insurable values. This sometimes helps the analyst to estimate returns on projected plant expansion.

The balance sheet comes in for attention because of possible changes in the capitalization structure and its effect on income and dividends. Will any long-term debts mature in the near future? Will the debt be paid? Will it be replaced with new debt? How?

The answers to all the above questions lead the analyst to a final question. What is going to be left of the dollar income after plant, long-term debt, and working capital needs have been met? In short, what is the outlook for dividends? Thus, the analyst does more than grasp for a future earnings-per-share figure. He interprets income. His thoughts about the future possibilities for earnings and dividends are heavily influenced by his understanding of *dollar flows as they affect the earnings, dividends, and capital structure of a specific company.*

USE OF RATIOS IN INTERPRETATION

Ratios Do Not Provide Answers

Predicting the financial future of a corporation and how the stock market is likely to react is an immensely complex task. The financial ratios discussed in this chapter, although used in most investor appraisals of corporations, should be kept in perspective. Their computation is simple. The interpretation of their significance and meaning is difficult, because they offer only clues. Ratios scratch surfaces and raise questions;

they rarely yield answers. The core of an analyst's finding lies beneath the ratios. His work requires an intimate grasp of the interrelationships of the economy, the industry, and the company, and of changes within the company. Consequently, financial analysts in banks, brokerage houses, and other institutions tend to specialize. There are oil experts, food chain experts, utility experts, railroad experts, mining experts, and so forth. These individuals are usually walking encyclopedias on the industry. Ratios are only a possible starting point for their evaluations, and ratios are fused with many other factors which affect decisions to buy, sell, or hold stocks.

No introduction to the analysis and interpretation of financial statements can be completely satisfying. The ratios are simple but their meaning may be elusive. The relative goodness or badness of a particular ratio depends on many interacting variables peculiar to a specific company at a specific time. In many instances, the question of whether a ratio is a favorable sign or an unfavorable sign must be answered with an unconsoling, "It depends."

Basic Data for Illustration: Ling-Temco-Vought

Exhibits 5-3, 5-4, and 5-5 provide the financial information on Ling-Temco-Vought, Inc. (sometimes abbreviated LTV) that we will use to demonstrate computations of the popular financial ratios. We will see as we proceed through various computations that the ratios are only one phase of a complete analysis.

Ling-Temco-Vought's sales in 1963 are summarized in Exhibit 5-1.

EXHIBIT 5-1

Product Line	Per Cent of Total Sales
Aeronautics	36
Electronics	33
Missiles and space	24
Other	7

Prime contracts with and subcontracts for United States government agencies accounted for 87 per cent of 1963 sales.

Unfortunately, the company's annual report for 1963 does not contain a statement of sources and application of funds. Moreover, the Change column in Exhibit 5-3 was not included. The complicated financial decisions, the sale and leaseback transactions (see the Note to Exhibit 5-3), and related matters should have been neatly summarized in a funds statement. Without it, the analyst must sift through scattered information to prepare a crude "where-got, where-gone" summary. Exhibit 5-2 is such a picture of the changes in balance sheet items:

EXHIBIT 5-2

(In millions of dollars)

Increases in working capital:		
Decrease in property, plant, and equipment	$14.7	
Increase in stockholders' equity	7.9	$22.6
Decreases in working capital:		
Decrease in long-term debt	$29.6	
Increase in long-term investments	1.2	30.8
Net decrease in working capital		$ 8.2

Such a makeshift analysis buries the details of many transactions that might provide insight, but at least it demonstrates that the company made a major effort to reduce long-term debt by using funds provided by operations and by the liquidation of plant and equipment. The company's failure to reveal the details of the sale and leaseback is disappointing.

Operating Performance

The most important measure of over-all accomplishment is the rate of return on invested capital:

$$\text{Rate of return on investment} = \frac{\text{Income}}{\text{Invested capital}} \qquad (1)$$

On the surface, this measure is straightforward, but its ingredients may differ according to the purpose it is to serve. What is Invested Capital, the denominator of the ratio? What income figure is appropriate?

Management functions may usefully be divided into *operating* (i.e., utilizing a given set of assets) and *financing* (i.e., obtaining the needed capital). The best managements perform both functions superbly. However, some companies are marked by superior operating management and inferior financial management, or vice versa.

The measurement of the effectiveness of operations (i.e., how assets are employed) should not be influenced by the management's financial decisions (i.e., how assets are obtained). Operating performance is best measured by the rate of return on total assets:

$$\text{Rate of return on total assets} = \frac{\text{Net operating income before interest expense and income taxes}}{\text{Average total assets available}} \qquad (2)$$

The right-hand side of Eq. (2) consists, in turn, of two important ratios:

$$\frac{\text{Net operating income before interest expense and income taxes}}{\text{Average total assets available}} = \frac{\text{Net income before interest expense and income taxes}}{\text{Sales}} \times \frac{\text{Sales}}{\text{Average total assets available}} \qquad (3)$$

EXHIBIT 5-3

LING-TEMCO-VOUGHT, INC.
Consolidated Balance Sheets*
As of Dec. 31
(In millions of dollars)

Assets	1963	1962	Change
Current assets:			
Cash and U.S. government securities	$ 12.1	$ 9.8	
Notes and accounts receivable	23.2	28.8	
Unreimbursed costs and fees under cost-plus contracts	{ 26.5	{ 33.7	
Inventories	{ 43.9	{ 43.6	
Prepaid expenses	1.1	.8	
Total current assets	$106.8	$116.7	$ −9.9
Long-term investments in unconsolidated subsidiaries	$ 13.2	$ 12.0	+1.2
Property, plant, and equipment, net of accumulated depreciation	$ 20.8	$ 35.5	−14.7
Total assets	$140.8	$164.2	$−23.4
Equities			
Current liabilities:			
Notes payable to banks	$ 26.8	$ 39.0	
Accounts payable	27.5	17.4	
Accrued wages, interest, etc.	12.3	14.0	
Income taxes payable	2.1	—	
Total current liabilities	$ 68.7	$ 70.4	$ −1.7
Long-term debt (mostly debentures)	$ 34.6	$ 64.2	−29.6
Stockholders' equity:			
Preferred stock, 150,000 shares, $30 par value; liquidating value is $31.50, dividend rate is $1.35 per share	$ 4.5	$ 4.5	
Common stock, 2,800,000 shares, and capital surplus	7.3	7.3	
Retained earnings	25.7	17.8	
Total stockholders' equity	$ 37.5	$ 29.6	+7.9
Commitments and contingencies (see Note)			
Total equities	$140.8	$164.2	$−23.4

* The financial statements in this and in Exhibits 5-4 and 5-5 have been slightly modified to bring out certain points.

Note: The annual report contains a long footnote about possible liabilities in relation to government price renegotiations. Notice the decrease in fixed assets. In December, 1963, machinery and equipment were sold and leased back, under two leases, for periods of five and ten years. Proceeds were applied to the redemption of long-term debt. The annual minimum rental obligations on these and other facilities are approximately $4,700,000 in 1964, between $4,300,000 and $3,900,000 for the next four years, and between $1,500,000 and $1,400,000 for the succeeding five years.

Using Exhibits 5-3 and 5-4, we may compute the following 1963 results for LTV:

$$\frac{15.0}{1/2(164.2 + 140.8)} = \frac{15.0}{331.3} \times \frac{331.3}{152.5}$$

The right-hand terms in Eq. (3) are often called the *operating income ratio* and the *total asset turnover*, respectively. Eq. (3) may be re-expressed:

Rate of return on total assets = Operating income ratio × Total asset turnover

$$9.9\% = 4.5\% \times 2.2$$

(4)

Note, too, that the ratios used to evaluate operating performance exclude the extraordinary $900,000 charge against income because it is

EXHIBIT 5-4

LING-TEMCO-VOUGHT, INC.
Consolidated Income Statements
As of Dec. 31
(In millions of dollars)

	1963	1962
Net sales	$331.3	$326.0
Cost of goods sold (approximated)	$250.0	$240.0
Research and development	13.6	9.6
Other operating expenses	47.0	56.2
Depreciation	5.7	5.7
Total operating expenses	$316.3	$311.5
Net income from operations	$ 15.0	$ 14.5
Interest expense	4.6	5.8
Net income before income taxes	$ 10.4	$ 8.7
Income taxes (after deducting loss carried forward)	3.3	—
Net income before extraordinary charge	$ 7.1	$ 8.7
Extraordinary charge for loss on notes receivable related to discontinued operations, net of specific income tax deductibility effect ($1.8 loss minus savings in income taxes)	.9	—
Net income	$ 6.2	$ 8.7

	Dividends		
	Total	*Per Share*	*Shares Outstanding*
Preferred	$202,500	$1.350	150,000
Common	350,000	.125	2,800,000

EXHIBIT 5-5

LING-TEMCO-VOUGHT, INC.
Comparative Statistics for Seven Years (1957 through 1963)
(In millions of dollars)

	1957	*1958*	*1959*	*1960*	*1961*	*1962*	*1963*
Sales	$4.0	$6.9	$48.1	$148.4	$192.8	$326.0	$331.3
Net income (loss)							
Before taxes	.6	.4	3.1	5.7	(14.5)	8.7	10.4
After taxes	.3	.2	1.9	3.0	(13.0)	8.7	6.2*
Earnings, per common share	.35	.21	1.13	1.20	(4.74)	3.03	2.14*
Stockholders' equity	1.4	2.7	9.8	28.5	17.9	29.6	37.5
Return on stockholders' equity, after taxes	22%	8%	20%	10%	—	30%	17%

* After extraordinary charge of $900,000, or $.32 per share.
Source: *1963 Annual Report.*

regarded as a nonrecurring item which does not reflect normal performance.

A scrutiny of Eq. (4) shows that there are two basic factors in profit-making: operating margin percentages and turnover. An improvement in either will, by itself, increase the rate of return on total assets. This phase of performance measurement is discussed fully in Chapter 12.

The ratios used in this chapter can also be computed on the basis of figures after taxes. However, the peculiarities of the income tax laws may sometimes distort results—for example, the tax rate may change, or losses carried back or forward might eliminate the tax in certain years. Ling-Temco-Vought suffered a staggering loss in 1961 (Exhibit 5-5) which eliminated income taxes in 1962 and reduced the 1963 tax rate from an estimated 52 per cent to under 32 per cent.

Trading on the Equity

Another measure of invested capital is stockholders' equity. The rate of return may be computed after taxes or, as in Eq. (5), before taxes:

$$\text{Rate of return on stockholders' equity} = \frac{\text{Net income, after interest, but before income taxes}}{\text{Average total stockholders' equity}} \quad (5)$$

$$\text{For LTV, 1963} = \frac{10.4}{1/2(37.5 + 29.6)} = 31\%$$

This ratio centers attention on the ultimate rate of return being earned by the business owners. When liabilities exist, the rate of return on total assets available will differ from that on stockholders' equity. LTV's return in 1963 was 9.8 per cent on total assets and 31 per cent on total stockholders' equity.

Equation (5) can be refined to compute the rate of return on *common* stockholders' equity before or, as in Exhibit 5-5, after taxes. Before taxes:

$$\begin{array}{c}\text{Rate of return} \\ \text{on common stock}\end{array} = \frac{\text{Net income after interest and preferred dividends, but before income taxes}}{\text{Average equity of holders of common stock}} \quad (6)$$

Is this rate of return higher or lower than the 31 per cent previously computed in Eq. (5)? It is higher, because the holders of preferred shares are entitled to a limited return based on the preferred dividend rate. It would be lower if the rate earned on total stockholders' equity was less than the preferred dividend rate.

Trading on the equity, which is also referred to as "using leverage," means using borrowed money at fixed interest rates in the hope of enhancing the rate of return on stockholders' equity. LTV fared well in 1963 by trading on the equity; it earned 31 per cent on stockholders' equity.

EXHIBIT 5-6

Trading on the Equity Effects of Debt on Rates of Return
(In thousands of dollars)

| | | *Equities* | | | | | *Return on Invested Capital* | |
	Assets	*Bonds Payable*	*Stock- holders' Equity*	*Income Before Interest*	*5% Interest*	*Net Income*	*Assets*	*Equity*
Year 1								
Co. *A*	$80,000	$30,000	$50,000	$12,000	$1,500	$10,500	15.0%	21.0%
Co. *B*	80,000	—	80,000	12,000	—	12,000	15.0	15.0
Year 2								
Co. *A*	80,000	30,000	50,000	4,000	1,500	2,500	5.0	5.0
Co. *B*	80,000	—	80,000	4,000	—	4,000	5.0	5.0
Year 3								
Co. *A*	80,000	30,000	50,000	2,000	1,500	500	2.5	1.0
Co. *B*	80,000	—	80,000	2,000	—	2,000	2.5	2.5

Exhibit 5-6, regarding hypothetical companies, shows that results differ, depending on whether the version of invested capital used is total assets or stockholders' equity. Borrowing is a two-edged sword. In Year 1, Co. *A* paid 5 per cent for the use of $30,000,000, which in turn earned 15 per cent. This method of financing benefited the stockholders handsomely, resulting in an ultimate return on equity of 21 per cent, compared with the 15 per cent earned by debt-free Co. *B*.

In Year 3, the picture is reversed. When a company is unable to earn at least the interest rate on the funds it borrows, the return on equity will be lower than for the debt-free company.

Obviously, the more stable the business, the less dangerous it is to trade on the equity. Moreover, the *prudent* use of debt is part of intelligent financial management. Managers who brag about having no long-term debt may not be obtaining the maximum return on equity. On the other hand, too much debt can cause financial disaster when operations become unprofitable.

Common Stock Statistics

Because stock market prices are quoted on a per-share basis, many of the popular ratios are expressed per share (and after taxes). Some of the more important of these ratios follow:

$$\text{Earnings per share of common stock} = \frac{\text{Net income} - \text{Preferred dividends}}{\text{Number of shares outstanding}} \quad (7)$$

$$\text{For LTV, 1963, before extraordinary charge} = \frac{\$7,100,000 - \$202,500}{2,800,000} = \$2.46$$

For LTV, 1963, after extraordinary charge $= \dfrac{\$6{,}200{,}000 - \$202{,}500}{2{,}800{,}000} = \$2.14$

$$\text{Price-earnings ratio} = \frac{\text{Average market price per share of common stock}}{\text{Earnings per share of common stock}} \qquad (8)$$

For LTV, 1963 $\qquad\qquad = \dfrac{\$15.00}{\$2.14} = 7 \text{ times}$

$$\text{Dividends per share of common stock} = \frac{\text{Common dividends}}{\text{Number of shares outstanding}} \qquad (9)$$

For LTV, 1963 $\qquad\qquad = \dfrac{\$350{,}000}{2{,}800{,}000} = \$.125$

$$\text{Dividend payout ratio} = \frac{\text{Common dividends per share}}{\text{Earnings per share of common stock}} \qquad (10)$$

For LTV, 1963 $\qquad\qquad = \dfrac{\$.125}{\$2.14} = 5.8\%$

$$\text{Dividend yield ratio} = \frac{\text{Common dividends per share}}{\text{Average market price per share of common stock}} \qquad (11)$$

For LTV, 1963 $\qquad\qquad = \dfrac{\$.125}{\$15.00} = .8\%$

The above ratios focus on net income and dividends per share—by far the two factors which most influence investors. When earnings are materially affected by an extraordinary charge, they are reported both before and after the extraordinary charge [Eq. (7)]. Equation (8), the price-earnings ratio (sometimes called an "earnings multiplier") generally measures how much the investing public is willing to pay for the company's prospects for earning. Note especially that the price-earnings ratio is a consensus of the market place. This earnings multipler may differ considerably for two companies within the same industry. It may also change for the same company through the years. For example, the average price-earnings ratio in the period from 1950 to 1954, for International Nickel, was 10.4; in the period from 1960 to 1964, it was 20.1. Glamour stocks have astronomical ratios. Xerox's price-earnings ratio in July, 1964, was 81.9. In general, a high price-earnings ratio indicates that investors are optimistic about the prospective stability and growth of the company's net income. Investors are apparently hesitant to award a high earnings multiplier to LTV, probably because of the severity of the 1961 loss, the heavy trading on the equity, and the notorious instability of earnings in an industry that depends largely on government contracts.

A study of the dividend payout ratio through the years gives concrete evidence that dividend polices are affected by fluctuations in a company's net income. The dividend yield ratio may be of particular importance to investors in common stock who seek regular cash returns on their investments. For example, an investor who favors high current returns would not buy stock in growth companies. Growth companies have conservative dividend policies because they are using their income to help finance expansion. For example, Xerox's yield in mid-1964 was 0.4 per cent, whereas American Motors' was 7.8 per cent.

Past statistics are not always a reliable way of appraising dividend policy. It is more assuring to obtain an explicit current statement from a company's board of directors. For instance, in February, 1964, LTV's board established an annual dividend, on common stock, of 50¢ per share. Therefore, the indicated yield in 1964 would be recomputed at 3.33 per cent ($.50 ÷ $15.00).

Another oft-quoted statistic is *book value:*

$$\text{Book value per share of common stock} = \frac{\text{Stockholders' equity} - \text{Liquidating value of preferred stock}}{\text{Number of common shares outstanding}} \quad (12)$$

$$\text{For LTV, 1963} = \frac{\$37,500,000 - (150,000 \times \$31.50)}{2,800,000} = \$11.70$$

The usefulness of this computation is highly questionable, except in the cases of investment companies. Supposedly, if a stock's market price is below its book value, the stock is attractively priced. The trouble is that market prices are geared to forecasted earnings and dividends—not to book values, which are based on balance sheet values. Consequently, some companies may perpetually have market prices in excess of book values, and vice versa. Book value may, however, be pertinent when companies have heavy investments in liquid assets and are contemplating liquidation.

Senior Securities and Safety

Long-term bonds and preferred stocks are sometimes called senior securities. Investors who buy senior securities want assurance that future operations will easily provide funds sufficient to pay bond interest, make repayments of principal on bonds, and pay dividends on preferred stock. Senior securities often have protective provisions, such as mortgage liens on real estate or restrictions on dividend payments to holders of common stock, but these are of minor importance compared with prospective earnings. Bondholders don't want the trouble and inconvenience of foreclosure; they would rather receive a steady stream of interest and repayments of principal. The guiding rule regarding investments in senior securities is to look to *earnings coverage,* not to liens or legal restrictions on common stock dividends, for protection. The presence of restrictive clauses in bond or preferred stock agreements is secondary; sole reliance on them as justification for investment is foolhardy.

Following are the key ratios for senior securities:

$$\text{Preferred dividend coverage} = \frac{\text{Net income after income taxes}}{\text{Preferred dividend requirement}} \quad (13)$$

$$\text{For LTV, 1963} \qquad = \frac{\$6,200,000}{\$202,500} = 31 \text{ times}$$

$$\text{Bond interest coverage} = \frac{\text{Net income before interest and income taxes}}{\text{Bond interest}} \quad (14)$$

$$\text{For LTV, 1963} \qquad = \frac{\$15.0}{\$4.6} = 3.3 \text{ times}$$

$$\text{Debt service coverage} = \frac{\text{Net income before interest and income taxes}}{\text{Bond interest} + \text{Sinking fund or other yearly debt repayment requirements}} \quad (15)$$

$$\text{For LTV, 1963} \qquad = \frac{\$15.0}{\$4.6 + 0^*} = 3.3 \text{ times}$$

* As far as can be gleaned from LTV's Annual Report.

$$\text{Total fixed charge coverage} = \frac{\text{Net income before fixed charges and income taxes}}{\text{All fixed charges including rent, interest, and other cash charges that would continue regardless of a drastic curtailment of operations}} \quad (16)$$

For LTV, 1963 = Information unavailable from Annual Report

The rule of thumb for adequate safety of an industrial bond is that the interest charges should be earned at least five times in the *poorest* year in the span of seven to ten years which is under review.[1]

Sale and Leaseback

By any standard, LTV senior securities are speculative. The Note to Exhibit 5-3 described a sale and leaseback that ostensibly reduced the company's debt. However, as the Note indicates, LTV is obligated for high rentals on long-term leases. Many accountants and analysts would prefer to estimate the present value of the obligations under the lease and show them as a long-term liability, showing the corresponding leasehold as an asset. This could change the balance sheet dramatically. As it is, the current balance sheet does not show the amount of the financial obligation under leases.

In a sense, the sale and leaseback transaction helped LTV to replace

---

[1] B. Graham, S. L. Dodd, and S. Cottle, *Security Analysis* (New York: McGraw-Hill Book Company, 1962), p. 348.

visible debt (i.e., long-term debentures) with invisible debt (i.e., long-term leases that are not capitalized on the balance sheet). Perceptive analysts would recast the balance sheet and recompute interest coverage [See Eq. (14)] by broadening the computation to include all fixed charges such as interest and rent.

Capital Structure

The foregoing remarks are not intended as criticism of LTV's management. Whether their heavy trading on the equity is good or bad depends on whether you are a creditor or a stockholder and on whether you are willing to risk more for higher prospective returns. The capital structure, using balance sheet figures, is shown in Exhibit 5-7.

EXHIBIT 5-7

Long-term debt	$34,600,000	48.0%
Preferred stock, at liquidating value	4,725,000	6.5
Common stockholders' equity	32,775,000	45.5
	$72,100,000	100.0%

The long-term debt is understated because the obligations under the leases are not shown. An investor looking for bonds with ample safety would be unenthusiastic about LTV bonds. A common stockholder, however, may be highly pleased with management's avid use of debt, because it enriches his rate of return far beyond that which would be made possible with a lighter use of credit.

Short-term Credit Analysis

Although all investors are interested in any clues that may yield insights into the operating and financial outlook for a company, the short-term lender is naturally more concerned with immediate prospects than with whether bonds due in 2010 will be paid. The direct way for him to obtain his answers is from a *budgeted statement of cash receipts and disbursements* (discussed in Chapter 6). The indirect way is to rely on the following ratios:

$$\text{Current ratio} = \frac{\text{Current assets}}{\text{Current liabilities}} \tag{17}$$

$$\text{For LTV, 1963} \qquad = \frac{106.8}{68.7} = 1.55 \text{ to } 1$$

$$\begin{array}{c} \text{Acid-test ratio} \\ \text{or} \\ \text{Quick ratio} \end{array} = \frac{\text{Cash} + \text{Receivables} + \text{Short-term investments}}{\text{Current liabilities}} \tag{18}$$

For LTV, 1963 $\qquad = \dfrac{12.1 + 23.2}{68.7} = .51$ to 1

$$\text{Inventory turnover} = \frac{\text{Cost of goods sold}}{\text{Average inventory}} \qquad (19)$$

For LTV, 1963 $\qquad = \dfrac{250}{1/2(26.5 + 43.9 + 33.7 + 43.6)} = 3.4$ times

per year, or average supply of $\dfrac{365 \text{ days}}{3.4}$, or 107 days

$$\text{Average collection period} = \frac{\text{Average accounts receivable}}{\text{Sales on account}} \times 365 \, (\text{or } 360) \text{ days} \quad (20)$$

For LTV, 1963 $\qquad = \dfrac{1/2(23.2 + 28.8)}{331.3} \times 365 = 29$ days

The current ratio [Eq. (17)], although it is probably as widely used as any ratio, is subject to many criticisms. For example, a high current ratio may be due to increases in inventories that have not been selling well. A low current ratio may be traceable to a high current liability for income taxes because of a prosperous year. An increase in the current ratio does not necessarily mean that the business is currently doing well, or vice versa. In other words, changes in current ratios are difficult to interpret.

The acid-test ratio [Eq. (18)], or quick ratio, attempts to show the ability of the company to pay its current liabilities without having to liquidate its inventory. The time-honored rules of thumb are that a company is below standard (1) if its quick ratio is not at least 1 to 1 and (2) if its current ratio is not at least 2 to 1. By now you are probably not surprised to learn that LTV's current and quick ratios do not meet these criteria. These rules of thumb are, of course, subject to countless exceptions, depending on a specific industry's or company's financial picture.

Inventory turnover (the number of times a given amount of stock is sold in a year), computed for classes of inventory, is an extremely useful technique for discovering slow-moving items, for comparing present with past performance, and for spotting possible pricing problems. All these factors are related to the gross profit associated with each turnover. The higher the turnover without price changes, for example, the greater the net income in that period. Turnover standards also differ from industry to industry. Turnovers are faster in grocery stores than in jewelry stores, for example, and turnover traditionally receives more attention in retail than in manufacturing companies.

The average collection period is a crude indicator of how well the credit terms are being enforced. The shorter the collection period, the better the quality of the receivables. On the other hand, too stringent credit terms may result in the loss of credit sales and thus may adversely affect profits. Again, variations from rule-of-thumb ratios may mean only that a company performs differently, not less effectively. LTV receivables apparently are collected smoothly: A 28-day collection period, when dealing mostly with United States disbursement agencies, is satisfactory.

Interval Measure

G. Sorter and G. Benston[2] have suggested a better measure of the current debt-paying ability of a company, the interval measure:

$$\text{Interval measure} = \frac{\text{Cash} + \text{Receivables} + \text{Marketable securities}}{\text{Year's cash expenses}}$$
$$\times 365 \text{ (or 360) days} \quad (21)$$

$$\text{For LTV, 1963} \quad = \frac{\$12.1 + \$23.2}{\$316.3 + \$4.6 + \$3.3} \times 365 = 39 \text{ days}$$

This is a crude statement of the concept, but the basic aim is to show the number of days (39, in the case of LTV) that normal operations could be continued, without additional financing, if there were a complete cessation of revenues. Sorter and Benston maintain that quick assets are held as a buffer against the uncertain future flow of funds, and that the current ratio and the quick ratio do not measure the debt-paying ability of the firm. For instance, assume the following current ratio:

$$\text{Current ratio} = \frac{\text{Current assets}}{\text{Current liabilities}} = \frac{\$150,000}{\$100,000} = 1.5 \text{ to } 1 \quad (17)$$

If the company pays $50,000 of accounts payable, its current ratio will increase to 2 to 1 ($100,000 ÷ $50,000). Yet no real change in debt-paying ability has occurred.

CHANGING PRICE LEVELS

Deficiencies of Historical Costs

Accountants in the United States and Canada use the dollar as their measuring rod. However, a 1960 dollar had a different purchasing power than a 1940 dollar, and financial statements, particularly in the capital goods industries, are conglomerations of different dollars. Critics have been disturbed by the defects of the dollar as a yardstick and have suggested modifications of accounting and financial reporting to compensate

---

[2] G. Sorter and G. Benston, "Appraising the Defensive Position of a Firm: The Interval Measure," *Accounting Review*, October, 1960, pp. 633-640.

for the effects of changing price levels. Widely varying remedies have been suggested, from sweeping overhauls of fundamental approaches to adamant adherence to the *status quo*.

If the price level remained perfectly stable, net income would be a meaningful mirror of over-all changes in physical resources and purchasing power (e.g., cash, inventory, production capacity). In practice, reported net income is often the result of equating 19x1 dollars with 19x9 dollars. When purchasing power is declining over the long run, a company cannot pay out in dividends an amount equal to net income without eroding its stock of physical assets. An increase in reported net income, thus, may not always indicate enhancement of distributable assets.

The price level dispute becomes most vivid in fixed asset accounting. It is self-evident that, in capital goods industries, depreciation is almost always significant. And even when depreciation is but a small fraction of total expenses, it may be an important figure in comparison to net income. Those who argue against using historical cost as a basis for recording the depreciation of fixed assets usually maintain that depreciation based on the historical cost of a plant built ten or twenty years ago is an understatement of current expenses and an overstatement of current net income. The extent of the error is the difference between the depreciation computed on the basis of present value and depreciation computed on the basis of historical acquisition cost.

The two leading approaches to departure from historical cost as a basis for determining income are: (1) that replacement costs should be charged against revenue; or (2) that all historical costs which are to be matched against revenue should be adjusted on some common dollar basis, so that all revenue and all expenses can be expressed in dollars of the same (usually current) purchasing power. The proponents of the second approach do not agree about whether general price indexes (e.g., a cost-of-living index) or specific price indexes (e.g., a construction index or an index for a particular raw material) should be used in adjusting historical dollar costs. Many who favor general price level indexes claim that such adjustments do not represent a departure from historical costs; the adjusted figures *are* historical costs, expressed in common dollars.

Exhibits 5-8 and 5-9 show how general price level adjustments affected the financial statements of the Indiana Telephone Corp. Note that Net Income in 1961 (Exhibit 5-8) was adjusted downward by $154,497—from $475,009 (Column *A*) to $320,512 (Column *B*)—when current dollars were used. Note also that the net Telephone Plant account in Exhibit 5-9 was adjusted upward—from $8,042,156 to $9,873,837—on the same basis. Finally, note that the adjustments are confined to depreciation and fixed assets and that they are adjustments to a general, rather than to a specific, price level (i.e., a general wholesale price index, rather than a specific plant construction index, was used).

EXHIBIT 5-8

INDIANA TELEPHONE CORP.
Comparative Income Statements

	1960		1961	
	Column A	*Column B*	*Column A*	*Column B*
Revenues				
Local service	$2,393,183.76	$2,393,183.76	$2,517,535.04	$2,517,535.04
Toll service	1,245,447.11	1,245,447.11	1,324,400.63	1,324,400.63
Miscellaneous	133,458.52	133,458.52	134,874.69	134,874.69
Less: Provision for uncollectibles	14,168.49	14,168.49	15,650.54	15,650.54
Total revenues, net	$3,757,920.90	$3,757,920.90	$3,961,159.82	$3,961,159.82
Expenses				
Estimated inroads on total plant result from current wear and tear, decay, obsolescence, etc. (Note 1)	$ 471,624.51	$ 593,798.84	$ 501,821.66	$ 656,318.47
Maintenance (Note 4)	430,676.23	430,676.23	525,196.33	525,196.33
Traffic	846,965.78	846,965.78	927,321.16	927,321.16
Commercial	224,250.40	224,250.40	255,645.54	255,645.54
General office salaries and expenses	127,833.79	127,833.79	194,460.22	194,460.22
Other operating expenses	100,853.48	100,853.48	134,370.52	134,370.52
Total	$2,202,204.19	$2,324,378.52	$2,538,815.43	$2,693,312.24
Taxes				
State and local property	$ 189,092.64	$ 189,092.64	$ 201,605.94	$ 201,605.94
Indiana gross income	48,940.44	48,940.44	51,459.82	51,459.82
Social security	55,272.51	55,272.51	61,662.32	61,662.32
Federal income	589,834.26	589,834.26	493,985.99	493,985.99
Total taxes	$ 883,139.85	$ 883,139.85	$ 808,714.07	$ 808,714.07
Total expenses	$3,085,344.04	$3,207,518.37	$3,347,529.50	$3,502,026.31
Net operating income (Note 2)	$ 672,576.86	$ 550,402.53	$ 613,630.32	$ 459,133.51
Add: Other income, net	23,666.34	23,666.34	18,190.17	18,190.17
Income available for fixed charges	$ 696,243.20	$ 574,068.87	$ 631,820.49	$ 477,323.68
Deduct: fixed charges:				
Interest on funded debt	$ 141,312.49	$ 141,312.49	$ 148,770.88	$ 148,770.88
Other fixed charges	5,263.70	5,263.70	8,039.83	8,039.83
Total fixed charges	$ 146,576.19	$ 146,576.19	$ 156,810.71	$ 156,810.71
Net income (Note 1)	$ 549,667.01	$ 427,492.68	$ 475,009.78	$ 320,512.97
Deduct: Preferred stock dividends	61,472.59	61,472.59	60,671.20	60,671.20
Net income applicable to common stock	$ 488,194.42	$ 366,020.09	$ 414,338.58	$ 259,841.77
Deduct: Common stock dividends	—	—	328,329.71	328,329.71
Net income after dividends	$ 488,194.42	$ 366,020.09	$ 86,008.87	($ 68,487.94)
Total number of stations in service at end of year	40,491	40,491	42,771	42,771

( ) *denotes red figure.*

The accompanying Notes to Financial Statements are an integral part of these Income Statements. [Not presented here.—*Au.*]

The CPA firm of Herdrich, Boggs and Co. rendered the following professional opinion on the Indiana Telephone statements:

> In our opinion the accompanying financial statements shown under Columns A present fairly the financial position of the Company as of December 31, 1961, and the results of its operations for the year then ended, in conformity with generally accepted accounting methods applied in a basis consistent with that of the preceding year.

EXHIBIT 5-9

INDIANA TELEPHONE CORP.
Balance Sheets
Dec. 31, 1961

Assets

	Column A	Column B
Telephone plant including construction in progress (Note 1)	$11,661,053.53	$14,683,370.59
Less: Estimated inroads on total plant resulting from accumulated wear and tear, decay, obsolescence, etc.	3,618,897.28	4,809,533.85
	$ 8,042,156.25	$ 9,873,836.74
Material and supplies	$ 164,941.54	$ 164,941.54
Other physical property and investments	$ 61,128.15	$ 61,128.15
Current assets		
Cash and special deposits	$ 408,064.00	$ 408,064.00
Temporary cash investments, at cost plus accrued interest receivable	844,677.08	844,677.08
Accounts and notes receivable, net	330,926.98	330,926.98
	$ 1,583,668.06	$ 1,583,668.06
Prepayments and deferred charges	$ 94,054.84	$ 94,054.84
	$ 9,945,948.84	$11,777,629.33

Stockholders' equity and liabilities

	Column A	Column B
Stockholders' equity		
Common stock; no par value; stated value $10 per share; 250,000 shares authorized. 206,605 shares issued, of which 1,818 shares are held in treasury	$ 2,047,870.00	$ 2,047,870.00
Capital surplus	514,369.20	514,369.20
Capital adjustment (resulting from conversion of historical cost to current dollars) charged to: (Note 1)		
Income, 19 4 to 1961, inclusive	—	932,414.63
Telephone plant, to be charged to income in future periods	—	1,831,680.49
Earned surplus	1,040,085.77	107,671.14
Less: Stock discount and expense	75,582.48	75,582.48
	$ 3,526,742.49	$ 5,358,422.98
Cumulative Preferred Stock (Note 3)	1,198,500.00	1,198,500.00
	$ 4,725,242.49	$ 6,556,922.98
First mortgage sinking fund bonds: Less current sinking fund payments (Note 3)	$ 4,244,000.00	$ 4,244,000.00
Current liabilities		
Sinking fund payments, bonds and preferred stock	$ 54,000.00	$ 54,000.00
Accounts payable	167,891.37	167,891.37
Dividends payable	97,023.05	97,023.05
Federal income tax payable	277,985.99	277,985.99
Other	336,652.17	336,652.17
	$ 933,552.58	$ 933,552.58
Other deferred credits	$ 43,153.77	$ 43,153.77
	$ 9,945,948.84	$11,777,629.33

The accompanying Notes to Financial Statements are an integral part of these Balance Sheets. [Not presented here.—*Au.*]

In our opinion, however, the accompanying financial statements shown under Columns B more fairly present the financial position of the Company and its results of operations since recognition has been given to variations in the purchasing power of the dollar on the basis of a general wholesale price index of all commodities other than farm or foods. . . .[3]

[3] Indiana Telephone Corp., *Annual Report,* 1961.

Another illustration has been provided by Ralph C. Jones,[4] who summarized (Exhibit 5-10) the adjustments that would be made in Armstrong Cork Co.'s financial statement by the use of uniform purchasing power, as measured by a general index of prices:

EXHIBIT 5-10

ARMSTRONG CORK CO.

1941-1951	Published Statements	Adjusted Statements
Earning rate on average equity of stockholders	8.8%	4.5%
Net earnings	$92 million	$59 million
Retained earnings	$39.5 million	$6.5 million
Income taxes	47% of net income	58% of net income
Dividends	56% of net income	89% of net income
1951		
Total equity of stockholders, Dec. 31, 1951	$110 million	$137 million
Working capital in 1951	59% greater than 1941	3% less than in 1941

At this time, none of the professional accounting organizations in the United States has officially advocated departures from the historical cost basis. They believe that any adjusted dollar statements should be supplementary to the conventional financial statements. Societies of professional financial analysts have not been as concerned with the need for price level adjustments as with the need for better ways of *disclosing* the historical dollar information which will aid them in making comparisons and predictions.

Mechanics of Adjusting for Price Level Changes

There are two major ways of adjusting for price changes. One way, illustrated by the Indiana Telephone Corp. exhibits, is to express all data in terms of current dollars. Another way is to select a base year and express all data in terms of that year. To illustrate, assume that you have purchased at par all the capital stock of the Handi Co., a service firm. The trial balance on the purchase date, Jan. 1, 19x6, was as follows:

---

[4] *Price Level Changes and Financial Statements: Case Studies of Four Companies* (Iowa City, Iowa: American Accounting Association, 1955), p. 67. For a thorough analysis of price-level problems, see *Reporting the Financial Effects of Price Level Changes,* the American Institute of Certified Public Accountants, Accounting Research Study No. 6.

Cash and receivables	$130,000	
Building	100,000	
Depreciation accumulated on building		$ 16,000
Equipment	70,000	
Depreciation accumulated on equipment		14,000
Land	20,000	
Current liabilities		90,000
Capital stock, $10 par value		200,000
	$320,000	$320,000

Balances in selected accounts, on Dec. 31 of each of the next three years were as follows:

	19x6	19x7	19x8
Sales	$100,000	$110,000	$132,000
Operating expenses, exclusive of depreciation	80,000	90,000	105,600

The building was erected in early 19x2 at a cost of $100,000, and had an estimated life of twenty-five years. The price level at that time was 60 per cent of the 19x6 price level.

The equipment was acquired in 19x4 at a cost of $80,000, and had an estimated life of ten years. The price level at that time was 80 per cent of the 19x6 price level.

The 19x7 price level was 20 per cent above the 19x6 price level, and the 19x8 price level was 10 per cent above the 19x7 level.

Required:

Using the 19x6 price level as the base year, compute the 19x8 net income on (1) a historical cost basis and (2) the basis of an adjusted price level. Assume straight line depreciation. Assume that all changes in the price level occur at the beginning of each year.

SOLUTION

HANDI CO.
Income Statement
For Year Ending Dec. 31, 19x8

	Unadjusted	Index of Adjustment	Adjusted for Price Levels
Sales	$132,000	100/132	$100,000
Less:			
Operating expenses	$105,600	100/132	$ 80,000
Depreciation on building	4,000	100/60	6,667
Depreciation on equipment	7,000	100/80	8,750
Total expenses	$116,600		$ 95,417
Net income	$ 15,400		$ 4,583

Note that the increase in sales is attributable to changes in prices rather than to changes in volume, which is the same as in 19x6. In terms of 19x6 dollars, the sales and operating expenses are the same in 19x8 as in 19x6.

The Funds-flow Approach to the Income Statement

The analyst has found that a funds-flow approach helps him to interpret net income. The analyst's funds-flow approach is tied in with his attitude toward depreciation. Depreciation may be viewed in at least two different ways. Accountants view it as a systematic and rational allocation to operations of the cost of fixed assets. In contrast, a financial analyst looks upon depreciation as that portion of incoming funds from customers which is, or should be, devoted to new expenditures for fixed assets or to retirements of long-term debt that arose from past outlays for fixed assets.

The funds-flow approach to the income statement may be briefly described as follows. The revenue from customers represents total current dollars provided by operations. Current expenses represent outlays in current dollars (with some exceptions, e.g., when prices of raw materials are fluctuating wildly and Fifo inventory methods are being used). After the current expenses are met, "what's left" of revenue (of current dollars) is commonly called *funds provided by operations* or, less accurately, *cash flow*. A part of the funds provided by operations is considered to be the recovery of past outlays for fixed assets. This recovery (depreciation) is, or should be, devoted to paying off the long-term debt which arose from prior expenditures, or else applied to maintaining or enhancing physical capacity. Thus depreciation is considered to be something special which is related to outlays for fixed assets. The final difference (the residual difference) may be used in a variety of ways, such as for dividends, plant expansion, more working capital or payment of long-term debts.

The analyst's approach emphasizes *current* dollars. Nevertheless, the funds-flow approach to the income statement does not mean that the analyst is ignoring the value of the dollar. The intelligent investor realizes, when purchasing power is declining, that reported earnings are not distributable earnings. He is aware that replacement of productive facilities requires more dollars than are being "generated" by depreciation charges. He deems depreciation to be inadequate if the price level has changed enough to make depreciation allowances insufficient to meet demands for replacement of fixed assets. The analyst takes price level changes into account by relating requirements for capital expenditure—past and future—to funds available.

Management must deal with *assets*, not with net income, an abstraction. Net income reflects increments in net assets. A realistic interpretation of income relates it to dividends, replacement of fixed assets, retirement of long-term debt, and plans for diversification and expansion.

The increased emphasis on funds provided by operations aids in the interpretation of reported net income. Both concepts—net income and funds provided by operations—are important; taken together, they reveal a story that neither divulges separately.

Management works with current dollars. It obtains current dollars, and it meets its immediate expenses with current dollars. The only real measure of purchasing power is what is acquired with what is spent at the time it is spent. If management delays spending, then the analyst may conjecture about the opportunity costs of not spending. The real test of financial decisions must wait until the future becomes the past.

Funds flow analysis is not the cure-all for the very real problems created by the eroding dollar. But then, neither is adjustment to statements by using index numbers. Coupled with index-number adjustments, funds flow analysis may be a definite aid in the interpretation of income and in the analysis of an entire enterprise.

ACCOUNTING PRACTICES AND STATEMENT ANALYSIS

From Chapters 2 and 3, we learned that there are a wide variety of generally accepted accounting practices. Intelligent analysis of financial statements requires a comprehension of the vagaries of the accounting

EXHIBIT 5-11

Summary of Accounting Practices Shown in Exhibit 5-12

Col.	Co. A	Co. B
2.	Uses Lifo (last in, first out) for pricing inventory	Uses Fifo (first in, first out)
3.	Uses accelerated depreciation for book and tax purposes	Uses straight-line depreciation
4.*	Charges research as current expense	Capitalizes and amortizes research over five-year period
5.†	Funds, a total of the current pension costs (i.e., deposits money with a trustee) current service and amortization of past service	Funds only the present value of pensions vested
6.	Pays incentive bonuses to officers in cash	Grants stock options instead of paying cash bonuses
7.	Credits gains (net of income taxes levied on such gains) directly to retained earnings (or treats them as special credits below net income)	Includes such gains (net of income taxes levied on such gains) in income

* If research costs remain at the same level, the difference disappears after five years. The difference of $80,000 in the chart is in the first year, where Co. A expenses $100,000, and Co. B capitalizes the $100,000 but amortizes one-fifth.

† Difference in pension charges might also arise when, as did U.S. Steel in 1958, management decides that current contributions can be reduced or omitted because of excess funding in prior years and/or increased earnings of the fund or the rise in market value of the investments.

EXHIBIT 5-12

Accounting Magic: All "in Conformity with Generally Accepted Accounting Principles"

Co. B's Profits Are Higher because of* (Columns 2 through 7)

	Co. A Col. 1	Use of Fifo in Pricing Inventory Col. 2	Use of Straight Line Depreciation Col. 3	Deferring Research Costs Over 5 Years Col. 4	Funding Only the Pensions Vested Col. 5	Use of Stock Options for Incentive Col. 6	Including Capital Gain in Income Col. 7	Co. B Col. 8
Sales in units	100,000 units $100 each							100,000 units $100 each
Sales in dollars	$10,000,000							$10,000,000
Costs and expenses:								
Cost of goods sold	$ 6,000,000							$ 6,000,000
Selling, general, and administrative	1,500,000							1,500,000
Lifo inventory reserve	400,000	$(400,000)†						—
Depreciation	400,000		$(100,000)					300,000
Research costs	100,000			$(80,000)				20,000
Pension costs	200,000				$(150,000)			50,000
Officers' compensation								
Base salaries	200,000							200,000
Bonuses	200,000					$(200,000)		—
Total costs and expenses	$ 9,000,000	$(400,000)	$(100,000)	$(80,000)	$(150,000)	$(200,000)		$ 8,070,000
Profit before income taxes	$ 1,000,000	$ 400,000	$ 100,000	$ 80,000	$ 150,000	$ 200,000		$ 1,930,000
Income taxes	520,000	208,000	52,000	42,000	78,000	104,000		1,004,000
	$ 480,000	$ 192,000	$ 48,000	$ 38,000	$ 72,000	$ 96,000		$ 926,000
Gain on sale of property (net of income tax)	—					—	$150,000	150,000
Net profit reported	$ 480,000	$ 192,000	$ 48,000	$ 38,000	$ 72,000	$ 96,000	$150,000	$ 1,076,000
Per share on 600,000 shares	$ .80	$ .32	$ .08	$ .06	$ .12	$ .16	$ .25	$ 1.79
Market value at:								
10 times earnings	$ 8.00	$3.20	$ .80	$ .63	$1.20	$1.60	$2.50	$17.93
12 times earnings	$ 9.60	$3.84	$ .96	$ .76	$1.44	$1.92	$3.00	$21.52
15 times earnings	$12.00	$4.80	$1.20	$ .95	$1.80	$2.40	$3.75	$26.90

* See explanation of Columns 2 through 7 in Exhibit 5-11.
† ( ) Denotes deduction.
SOURCE: Leonard Spacek, "Business Success Requires an Understanding of Unsolved Problems of Accounting and Financial Reporting," an Address delivered on Sept. 25, 1959.

process. If companies within an industry are to be compared, their individual statements must first be placed on a uniform basis.

Leonard Spacek has succinctly demonstrated some of the analytical difficulties in Exhibit 5-12, which is a comparison of the income statements of two companies with identical operations but different accounting methods. The differences, as summarized by Spacek, are shown in Exhibit 5-11.

Perhaps, in the coming years, accounting measurements will become better standardized and identical operations will be reported in more nearly identical figures. In the meantime, accountants and corporate executives should view increased disclosure and amplified description as the most pressing needs in financial reporting. These needs must be met if the investor is to have sufficient data for making his own comparisons among companies.

SUMMARY

Managers and investors are the two major uses of financial statements. Their interests often overlap. In this chapter the investor's use of financial statements was stressed; management's use is stressed throughout the remainder of the book.

The major representative of the investor is the professional financial analyst. His major tasks are comparison and prediction. He has many sources of information, but the one he most universally uses is the corporate annual report.

There are many aids to the intelligent analysis of statements. Financial ratios provide clues and uncover areas that deserve further scrutiny. They do not, by themselves, provide answers.

Above all, financial analysts want to assess future earnings and dividend-paying prospects. If analysts are investigating senior securities, they are concerned with the adequacy with which earnings cover interest payments and related yearly cash requirements. Short-term creditors are less interested in long-run earning power. They want to know the immediate outlook for smooth payment.

The comparison of industries, companies, and year-to-year performance is hampered by the insidious effects of changing price levels and by the wide variety of acceptable accounting practices. Financial analysts are much more concerned with ample disclosure than with possible index number adjustments which reflect changing price levels. They want more information about: sales, by product lines; leases; research activities; depreciation methods; foreign operations; inventory methods; variable and fixed cost behavior patterns (see Chapters 7 and 8), criteria for capital expenditure (see Chapter 14); and sources and applications of funds.

PROBLEM

You are given the following financial statements:

THE GREEN CO.
Balance Sheet
(In thousands of dollars)

	Dec. 31	
Assets	*19x1*	*19x0*
Current assets:		
Cash	$ 2,600	$ 2,200
Marketable securities	600	600
Receivables, net	5,300	5,100
Inventories at cost	14,600	14,400
Prepayments	600	600
Total current assets	$23,700	$22,900
Fixed assets:		
Land	$ 300	$ 300
Buildings and equipment, net	7,000	5,800
Total fixed assets	$ 7,300	$ 6,100
Total assets	$31,000	$29,000
Equities		
Current liabilities:		
Notes payable	$ 3,900	$ 2,800
Accounts payable	3,200	2,400
Accrued expenses	1,600	1,700
Income taxes payable	500	400
Total current liabilities	$ 9,200	$ 7,300
5 per cent bonds payable	$ 4,000	$ 4,000
Stockholders' equity:		
Preferred stock, 6 per cent, $100 par value, $100 liquidating value	$ 1,600	$ 1,600
Common stock, $10 par value	2,000	2,000
Premium on common stock	1,000	1,000
Retained earnings	13,000	12,900
Reserve for contingencies	200	200
Total stockholders' equity	$17,300	$17,700
Total equities	$31,000	$29,000

THE GREEN CO.
Statement of Income and Reconciliation of Retained Earnings
For the Year Ending Dec. 31, 19x1
(In thousands of dollars)

			Per Cent
Sales		$50,000	100.0
Cost of goods sold		40,000	80.0
Gross profit on sales		$10,000	20.0
Other operating expenses:			
Selling expenses	$4,600		
Administrative expenses	2,000		
Depreciation	1,000	7,600	15.2
Net operating income		$ 2,400	4.8
Interest expense		400	.8
Net income before income taxes		$ 2,000	4.0
Income taxes		1,000	2.0
Net income after income taxes		$ 1,000	2.0
Dividends on preferred stock		96	
Net income for holders of common stock		$ 904	
Dividends on common stock		804	
Net income retained		$ 100	
Retained earnings, Dec. 31, 19x0		12,900	
Retained earnings, Dec. 31, 19x1		$13,000	

Required:

Compute the

1. Rate of return on total assets.
2. Rate of return (after taxes) on total stockholders' equity.
3. Rate of return (after taxes) on equity of holders of common stock.
4. Earnings per share of common stock.
5. Book value per share of common stock.
6. Number of times that bond interest was earned.
7. Number of times that all interest was earned.
8. Number of times that preferred dividends were earned.
9. Current ratio.
10. Acid-test or quick ratio.
11. The rate of inventory turnover.
12. The average collection period of accounts receivable.

SOLUTION

1. *8%*: $$\frac{\text{Net operating income}}{\text{Average total assets}} = \frac{\$2,400,000}{1/2(\$31,000,000 + \$29,000,000)}$$

2. *5.6%*: $$\frac{\text{Net income after taxes}}{\substack{\text{Average total stockholders'}\\ \text{equity}}} = \frac{\$1,000,000}{1/2(\$17,800,000 + \$17,700,000)}$$

3. *5.65%:* $\dfrac{\text{Net income} - \text{Preferred}}{\begin{array}{c}\text{after taxes} \quad \text{dividends}\\[2pt]\text{Average total} \quad \text{Liquidating}\\ \text{stockholders'} - \text{value of pre-}\\ \text{equity} \quad \text{ferred equity}\end{array}} = \dfrac{\$1{,}000{,}000 - \$96{,}000}{\$17{,}750{,}000 - \$1{,}600{,}000}$

4. *$4.52:* $\dfrac{\begin{array}{c}\text{Net income} - \text{Preferred}\\ \text{after taxes} \quad \text{dividends}\end{array}}{\begin{array}{c}\text{Number of common shares}\\ \text{outstanding}\end{array}} = \dfrac{\$904{,}000}{200{,}000}$

5. *$81:* $\dfrac{\begin{array}{c}\text{Total} \quad\quad \text{Liquidating}\\ \text{stockholders'} - \text{value of pre-}\\ \text{equity} \quad\quad \text{ferred equity}\end{array}}{\begin{array}{c}\text{Number of common shares}\\ \text{outstanding}\end{array}} = \dfrac{\$17{,}800{,}000 - \$1{,}600{,}000}{200{,}000}$

6. *12 times:* $\dfrac{\begin{array}{c}\text{Net income before interest and}\\ \text{taxes}\end{array}}{\text{Bond interest}} = \dfrac{\$2{,}400{,}000}{5\% \text{ of } \$4{,}000{,}000}$

7. *6 times:* $\dfrac{\begin{array}{c}\text{Net income before interest and}\\ \text{taxes}\end{array}}{\text{Total interest}} = \dfrac{\$2{,}400{,}000}{\$400{,}000}$

8. *10 times:* $\dfrac{\text{Net income after taxes}}{\text{Preferred dividend}} = \dfrac{\$1{,}000{,}000}{\$96{,}000}$

9. *2.58 to 1:* $\dfrac{\text{Current assets}}{\text{Current liabilities}} = \dfrac{\$23{,}700{,}000}{\$9{,}200{,}000}$

10. *.92 to 1:* $\dfrac{\begin{array}{c}\text{Cash} + \text{Marketable securities}\\ + \text{Receivables}\end{array}}{\text{Current liabilities}} = \dfrac{\$8{,}500{,}000}{\$9{,}200{,}000}$

11. *2.76 times:* $\dfrac{\text{Cost of goods sold}}{\text{Average inventory}} = \dfrac{\$40{,}000{,}000}{1/2(\$14{,}600{,}000 + \$14{,}400{,}000)}$

12. *38 days:* $\dfrac{\text{Average receivables}}{\begin{array}{c}\text{Sales (assumed all}\\ \text{on account)}\end{array}} \times 365 = \dfrac{\$5{,}200{,}000}{\$50{,}000{,}000} \times 365$

ASSIGNMENT MATERIAL

ESSENTIAL ASSIGNMENT MATERIAL

5-1. *Computation of financial ratios.* You are given the following financial statements.

THE MAXIM CO.
Balance Sheet
(In thousands of dollars)

	Dec. 31	
Assets	*19x2*	*19x1*
Current assets:		
Cash	$ 1,000	$ 1,000
Marketable securities	—	1,000
Receivables, net	5,000	4,000
Inventories at cost	12,000	9,000
Prepayments	1,000	1,000
Total current assets	$19,000	$16,000
Fixed assets, net	22,000	23,000
Total assets	$41,000	$39,000
Equities		
Current liabilities:		
Accounts payable	$10,000	$ 6,000
Accrued expenses	500	500
Income taxes payable	1,500	1,500
Total current liabilities	$12,000	$ 8,000
4 per cent bonds payable	$10,000	$10,000
Stockholders' equity:		
Preferred stock, 6 per cent, par value and		
liquidating value are $100 per share	$ 5,000	$ 5,000
Common stock, $10 par value	8,000	8,000
Premium on common stock	4,000	4,000
Retained earnings	1,000	3,000
Reserve for plant expansion	1,000	1,000
Total stockholders' equity	$19,000	$21,000
Total equities	$41,000	$39,000

THE MAXIM CO.
Statement of Income and Reconciliation of Retained Earnings
For the Year Ended Dec. 31, 19x2
(In thousands of dollars)

Sales (all on credit)		$40,000
Cost of goods sold		30,100
Gross profit on sales		$ 9,900
Other operating expenses:		
Selling expenses	$ 5,000	
Administrative expenses	2,000	
Depreciation	1,000	8,000
Net operating income		$ 1,900
Interest expense		400
Net income before income taxes		$ 1,500
Income taxes		700
Net income after income taxes		$ 800
Dividends on preferred stock		300
Net income for common stockholders		$ 500
Dividends on common stock		2,500
Net income retained		$ (2,000)
Retained earnings, Dec. 31, 19x1		3,000
Retained earnings, Dec. 31, 19x2		$ 1,000

Required:

Compute the following for the 19x2 financial statements:

1. Rate of return on total assets.
2. Rate of return, after taxes, on total stockholders' equity.
3. Rate of return, after taxes, on common stockholders' equity.

4. Earnings per share of common stock.
5. Book value per share of common stock.
6. Number of times bond interest earned.
7. Number of times preferred dividends earned.
8. Current ratio.
9. Acid-test or quick ratio.
10. Inventory turnover.
11. Average collection period of receivables outstanding.

5-2. *Effects of transactions on financial statements.* For each of the following numbered items you are to select the lettered transaction which indicates its effect on the corporation's financial statements. If a transaction has more than one effect, list all applicable letters. Assume that the total current assets exceed the total current liabilities both before and after every transaction described.

Numbered Transactions

1. The appropriation of retained earnings as a reserve for contingencies.
2. Declaration of a cash dividend on common stock, payable one month hence.
3. Payment of dividend in (2).
4. Failure to declare the regular dividend on cumulative preferred stock.
5. Issue of new shares in a three-for-one split of the common stock.
6. Issuance of additional common shares as a stock dividend.
7. Sale and leaseback of factory building at a selling price which substantially exceeds the book value.
8. The destruction of a building by fire. Insurance proceeds, collected immediately, slightly exceed book value.
9. Payment of trade account payable.
10. Purchase of inventory on open account.
11. Collection of account receivable.
12. Sale on account (ignore related cost of goods sold).

Lettered Effects

a. Increases current ratio.
b. Decreases current ratio.
c. Increases net working capital.
d. Decreases net working capital.
e. Increases total stockholders' equity.
f. Decreases total stockholders' equity.
g. Increases the book value per share of common stock.
h. Decreases the book value per share of common stock.
i. Increases total retained earnings.
j. Decreases total retained earnings.

5-3. *Analysis of financial statements: multiple choice.* (Prepared by David Green, Jr. Problem 5-27 may be substituted for this problem. See Note preceding Problem 5-4.)

STANDARD OIL CO. OF N.J.
Consolidated Statement of Financial Position
Dec. 31, 19x9-19x8

	19x9	*19x8*
Current Assets		
Cash	$ 202,168,412	$ 193,152,886
Marketable securities (at lower of cost or market)	351,388,630	222,708,131
Acceptances, notes, and accounts receivable, less estimated doubtful accounts	271,166,567	327,486,271
Inventories:		
Crude oil (at first-in, first-out cost)	217,162,569	218,630,259
Other merchandise	25,848,900	28,507,860
Materials and supplies	178,947,209	193,802,944
Total current assets	$1,246,682,287	$1,184,288,351
Less: Current Liabilities		
Accounts payable and accrued liabilities	$ 270,511,742	$ 316,491,216
Long-term debt due within one year	3,840,302	2,434,121
Estimated income taxes payable	125,065,639	205,524,288
Total current liabilities	$ 399,417,683	$ 524.449,625
Working capital	$ 847,264,604	$ 659,838,726
Investments		
Stocks of companies, owned over 50 per cent, in Europe and North Africa (at cost or less), and net amounts receivable	$ 220,393,056	$ 231,045,092
Other investments and long-term receivables, less estimated losses	231,403,015	215,537,122
Property, Plant, and Equipment (at original cost), less depreciation, depletion, and amortization	2,085,721,726	1,858,675,283
Other Assets		
Special deposits and funds	6,227,652	12,000,766
Patents, copyrights, and goodwill, less amortization	1,648,747	1,658,846
Prepaid and deferred charges	23,968,178	22,837,888
Total assets, less current liabilities	$3,416,626,978	$3,001,593,723
Deductions		
Funded and other long-term indebtedness	$ 475,710,293	$ 225,097,887
Deferred credits	7,134,574	21,105,188
Reserve for possible losses on foreign investments	105,000,000	105,000,000
Annuity, insurance, and other reserves	150,508,097	141,232,963
Equity of minority stockholders in affiliated companies	351,032,285	344,056,338
Stockholders' equity	$2,327,241,729	$2,165,101,347
Stockholders' Equity		
Capital:		
Standard Oil Co. of N.J., parent co.		
Stock issued	$ 754,584,861	$ 734,635,877
Amount in excess of par value	145,581,099	112,068,997
Excess of assets (over cost) of consolidated companies acquired	38,871,101	39,150,495
Earnings reinvested and employed in business		
Standard Oil Co. of N.J., parent co.	293,231,236	281,975,892
Other companies, consolidated	1,094,973,432	997,270,086
	$2,327,241,729	$2,165,101,347

Required:

Questions (1) through (13) refer to the balance sheets given for the Standard Oil Co. You are to use *exclusively* the information on these balance sheets in selecting your responses. Any other information which you have—of this company, the industry, or the general business picture—should not influence your answer. Accept these financial statements as being correctly prepared and in proper order.

For the following Questions (1) through (13), select answer *a, b, c, d,* or *e.*

a. True, without reservation.

b. Probably true, but additional information is needed to eliminate any reservation.

c. False, without reservation.

d. Probably false, but additional information is needed to eliminate any reservation.

e. The data are insufficient to indicate the probable truth or falsity of the statement.

Questions for Standard Oil Co.

(1) 19x9 prices of property, plant, and equipment items were double the level of 1939; therefore, the real value of property, plant, and equipment on Dec. 31, 19x9, is $4,171,443,452.

(2) Stocks of companies owned in Europe and North Africa would, if liquidated on Dec. 31, 19x9, have brought approximately $220,393,056.

(3) Since prices of crude oil have risen, the physical inventory of crude oil was smaller on Dec. 31, 19x9, than on Dec. 31, 19x8.

(4) The management continues to believe that it might incur losses on its foreign investments.

(5) The company charges receivables to bad debts expense as they actually prove uncollectible.

(6) The increase, during the year 19x9, in the amount at which marketable securities are carried was due in part to market appreciation.

(7) The total equities of the company on Dec. 31, 19x9, amounted to $2,726,659,412.

(8) The stockholders of Standard Oil Co. of N.J. contributed no more than $900,165,960 in cash or other assets for their stock.

(9) The company disbursed at least $2,434,121 to retire long-term debt in 19x9.

(10) The company offers no discounts on sales to its customers.

(11) The cost of additions to property, plant, and equipment during 19x9 was $227,046,443.

(12) Taxable net income for 19x9 was less than for 19x8. (The income tax rates remained constant through the two years.)

(13) Total cost of materials and supplies used in 19x9 exceeded the purchases of those items for the year.

ADDITIONAL ASSIGNMENT MATERIAL

Note: Several multiple choice problems are included. Problems 5-23, 5-24, and 5-25 deal with the difficulties of measuring changes in price levels. Problem 5-27 may be substituted for Problem 5-3. Both are multiple-choice problems and may be loosely described as "multiple-choice cases," because they deal with "real-life" company data. Both generate active classroom discussion. Students tend to disagree about specific answers, but they tend to agree that Problems 5-3 and 5-27 have positive educational value.

5-4. What are the major analytical tasks of internal and external users of financial statements?

5-5. What is the financial analyst's most important single source of financial information?

5-6. What are some of the items in the income statement which most interest the analyst?

5-7. What sections of the balance sheet are of major interest to him?

5-8. What questions do the analysts attempt to answer when examining revenues and expenses?

5-9. How does the analyst approach depreciation?

5-10. "Ratios are mechanical and incomplete." Explain.

5-11. "Trading on the equity means exchanging bonds for stock." Do you agree? Explain.

5-12. "Borrowing is a two-edged sword." Do you agree? Explain.

5-13. "Senior securities are all those issued before 1940." Do you agree? Explain.

5-14. What is the guiding rule for investing in senior securities?

5-15. "Sale and leasing back entails invisible debt." Explain.

5-16. "The objective of credit management is to avoid credit losses." Do you agree? Explain.

5-17. What is the argument for departing from the use of historical cost as a basis of recording depreciation of fixed assets?

5-18. "Depreciation may be viewed in at least two different ways." Explain.

5-19. What are the most pressing problems of financial reporting?

5-20. *Financial ratios: multiple choice.* (CPA Adapted.) The transactions listed below relate to Jekyll Chemicals, Inc. You are to assume that, on the date on which each of the transactions occurred, the corporation's accounts showed only common stock ($100 par value) outstanding, a current ratio of 2.5 to 1, and a substantial net income for the year to date (before giving effect to the transaction concerned). On that date the book value, per share of stock, was $146.48.

Each numbered transaction *is to be considered completely independently of all the others,* and your answer should be based on the effect of that transaction alone. Assume that all numbered transactions occurred during 19x7 and that the amount involved in each case is sufficiently material to distort reported net income, if it were *improperly* included in the determination of net income. Assume further that each transaction was recorded in accordance with generally accepted accounting principles and, where appropriate, in conformity with the *current operating concept* of the income statement.

Required:

For each of the numbered transactions you are to decide whether it:

a. Increased the corporation's 19x7 net income.
b. Decreased the corporation's 19x7 net income.
c. Increased the corporation's total retained earnings *directly* (i.e., *not* via net income).
d. Decreased the corporation's total retained earnings *directly*.
e. Increased the corporation's current ratio.
f. Decreased the corporation's current ratio.
g. Increased each stockholder's total *owner's equity*.
h. Decreased each stockholder's total *owner's equity*.
i. Increased each stockholder's equity *per share* of stock.
j. Decreased each stockholder's equity *per share* of stock.
k. Had none of the above effects.

Answer by selecting as many letters as you deem appropriate to reflect the effect(s) of each transaction as of the date of the transaction.

TRANSACTIONS

(1) Treasury stock, which had been repurchased at and carried at $102 per share, was issued as a stock dividend. In connection with this distribution, the board of directors of Jekyll Chemicals, Inc. authorized a transfer from retained earnings to permanent capital. The amount of the transfer was equal to the aggregate market value ($104 per share) of the shares issued. No entries relating to this dividend have been made previously.

(2) In January, the board directed the write-off of certain patent rights which had suddenly and unexpectedly become worthless.

(3) The corporation wrote off a *portion* of the unamortized discount and issue expense applicable to bonds which it refinanced in 19x7. It intends to amortize the remainder over the next seven years, the remaining life of the new issue, although the bonds would have had twelve more years to run had they not been refunded.

(4) Treasury stock, originally repurchased and carried at $101 per share, was sold for cash at $103.50 per share.

(5) The corporation sold, at a profit, land and a building which had been idle for some time. Under the terms of the sale, the corporation immediately received a portion of the sales price in cash. The balance is to mature at six-month intervals.

(6) The board of directors authorized the writing-up of certain fixed assets, to values established by a competent appraisal.

(7) The corporation called in all its outstanding shares of stock and exchanged them for new shares on a 2 for 1 basis, at the same time reducing the par value to $50 per share.

(8) The corporation paid a cash dividend, the declaration of which had previously been recorded in the accounts.

(9) Litigation involving Jekyll Chemicals, Inc., as defendant, was settled in the corporation's favor, with the plaintiff paying all court costs and legal fees. In 19x6, the corporation had appropriated retained earnings for a special contingency reserve for this court action, and the board directs abolition of the reserve.

(10) The corporation received a check from the company which insures it against theft of trucks. No entries concerning the theft have been made. The proceeds reduce, but do not completely cover, the loss.

5-21. *Analysis of financial statements: multiple choice.* (CPA Adapted.)

a. For each of the following numbered items you are to select the lettered item which indicates its effect on the corporation's statements. Using an answer sheet, indicate your choice by printing the letter identifying the effect which you select. If there is no appropriate response among the effects listed, leave the item blank. If more than one effect is applicable to a particular item, be sure to list all applicable letters. (Assume that the state statutes do not permit declaration of non-liquidating dividends except from earnings.)

Item

(1) Declaration of a cash dividend due in one month on noncumulative preferred stock.

(2) Declaration and payment of an ordinary stock dividend.

(3) Receipt of a cash dividend, not previously recorded, on stock of another corporation.

(4) Passing of a dividend on cumulative preferred stocks.

(5) Receipt of preferred shares as a dividend on stock held as a temporary investment. This was not a regularly recurring dividend.

(6) Payment of dividend mentioned in (1).

(7) Issue of new common shares in a five-for-one stock split.

Effect

(a) Reduces working capital.

(b) Increases working capital.

(c) Reduces current ratio.

(d) Increases current ratio.

(e) Reduces the dollar amount of total capital stock.

(f) Increases the dollar amount of total capital stock.

(g) Reduces total retained earnings.

(h) Increases total retained earnings.

(s) Reduces equity per share of common stock.

(t) Reduces equity of each common stockholder.

b. The following partially condensed financial statements are to be used in computing Items (1) through (8), below.

X CORP.
Balance Sheet, December 31, 19x2

Cash	$ 63,000
Trade receivables, less estimated uncollectibles of $12,000	238,000
Inventories	170,000
Prepaid expenses	7,000
Property and equipment, cost less $182,000 charged to operation to date	390,000
Other assets	13,000
	$881,000
Accounts and notes payable, trade	$ 98,000
Accrued liabilities	17,000
Estimated federal income tax liability	18,000
First mortgage, 4 per cent bonds, due in 19x9	150,000
$7 preferred stock, no par value (entitled to $110 per share in liquidation); authorized, 1,000 shares; in treasury, 400 shares; outstanding, 600 shares	108,000
Common stock, no par value; authorized, 100,000 shares; issued and out-standing, 10,000 shares stated at a nominal value of $10 per share	100,000
Excess of amounts paid in for common stock over stated values	242,000
Reserve for plant expansion	50,000
Reserve for contingencies	50,000
Retained earnings	95,000
Cost of 400 shares of treasury stock	(47,000)
	$881,000

Notes: Working capital as of Dec. 31, 19x1 was $205,000; trade receivables as of Dec. 31, 19x1 were $220,000 gross, $206,000 net; dividends for 19x2 have been declared and paid; there has been no change in amount of bonds outstanding during 19x2.

X CORP.
Income Statement
Year Ending Dec. 31, 19x2

	Cash	*Charge*	*Total*
Gross sales	$116,000	$876,000	$992,000
Less: Discounts	$ 3,000	$ 12,000	$ 15,000
Returns and allowances	1,000	6,000	7,000
	$ 4,000	$ 18,000	$ 22,000
Net sales	$112,000	$858,000	$970,000
Cost of sales:			
Inventory of finished goods, Jan. 1		$ 92,000	
Cost of goods manufactured		680,000	
Inventory of finished goods, Dec. 31		(100,000)	$672,000
Gross profit on sales			$298,000
Selling expenses		$173,000	
General expenses		70,000	243,000
Net profit on operations			$ 55,000
Other additions and deductions, net			3,000
Net income before federal income tax			$ 58,000
Federal income tax, estimated			18,000
Net income			$ 40,000

Required:

From the X Corp. financial statements, compute the following Items (1) through (8). Select the best answer from Columns *a* through *e* and write the letter you have selected next to the Item number.

Items to Be Computed	Approximate Answers				
	(a)	(b)	(c)	(d)	(e)
(1) Acid-test ratio	3.2:1	2.3:1	2.9:1	2.4:1	3.07:1
(2) Average number of days' charge sales uncollected	89	94	35	100	105
(3) Average finished goods turnover	7	10.1	10.3	9.7	6.7
(4) Number of times bond interest was earned (before taxes)	6⅔	10⅔	7⅔	9⅔	20⅓
(5) Number of times preferred dividend was earned	5.71	8.3	13.8	9.52	8.52
(6) Earnings per share of common stock	$4.00	$3.30	$3.58	$5.10	$5.38
(7) Book value per share of common stock	$33.80	$35.00	$49.80	$48.80	$53.20
(8) Current ratio	3.6:1	1:2.7	2.7:1	4.2:1	1:3.6

5-22. *Various asset valuation bases.* Assets may be valued at market or realizable value, at original cost or depreciated cost, and at appraised value. Briefly present the argument in behalf of each of these valuation bases. How do each of these bases relate to the going concern concept?

5-23. *Price indexes and financial statements.* (CPA Adapted.)

a. In considering the merits of using price indexes for the purpose of converting the accounting data as reflected in the conventional historical cost accounts, some people have suggested that these price-level adjustments should be confined to the fixed assets and related depreciation. What can be said in favor of such a proposal? Against it?

b. The price index rose from 125 to 175 during the previous year, and from 175 to 225 during the current year. The dollar sales during the previous year were $240,000 and, during the current year, were $300,000.

(1) For comparative income statement purposes, you are to convert the sales figures for both years to the price level existing at the end of the current year. You are to assume that sales were made uniformly throughout both years, and that the change in price level was also uniform.

(2) What additional information is revealed by a comparison of the converted figures? How do you interpret them?

5-24. *General versus specific price indexes.* (CPA Adapted.) There has been a good deal of criticism of the traditional historical cost records and the data which they reflect, especially during times of inflation. In order to assist in the interpretation of accounting reports as normally prepared, many accountants have suggested that the recorded cost data be first utilized in the preparation of the conventional financial statements, and that, as a supplementary technique, these statements then be converted into dollars having a uniform purchasing power through the application of price indexes to the recorded dollar amounts. There has been some considerable difference of opinion among these accountants as to whether to use a general price index, such as the wholesale commodity price index or the cost-of-living index, or, on the other hand, to use a more specific price index that is more applicable to the industry involved, or to the particular items being converted (for instance, using a construction index for the conversion of plant and equipment items, or using a special price index constructed for a specific industry).

Give arguments in favor of and against each of these two types of indexes.

5-25. *Investment: price level adjustments.* (CPA Adapted.) To obtain a more realistic appraisal of his investment, Martin Arnett, your client, has asked you to adjust certain financial data of The Glo-Bright Co. for price level changes. On Jan. 1, 19x9, he invested $50,000 in The Glo-Bright Co. in return for 10,000 shares of common stock. Immediately after his investment, the trial balance appeared as follows:

	Debit	Credit
Cash and receivables	$ 65,200	
Merchandise inventory	4,000	
Building	50,000	
Accumulated depreciation on building		$ 8,000
Equipment	36,000	
Accumulated depreciation on equipment		7,200
Land	10,000	
Current liabilities		50,000
Capital stock, $5 par value		100,000
	$165,200	$165,200

Balances in certain selected accounts, as of Dec. 31 of each of the next three years were as follows:

	19x9	19x0	19x1
Sales	$39,650	$39,000	$42,350
Inventory	4,500	5,600	5,347
Purchases	14,475	16,350	18,150
Operating expenses (excluding depreciation)	10,050	9,050	9,075

Assume the 19x9 price level as the base year and assume that all changes in the price level take place at the beginning of each year. Further assume that the 19x0 price level is 10 per cent above the 19x9 price level and that the 19x1 price level is 10 per cent above the 19x0 level.

The building was constructed in 19x5 at a cost of $50,000, and had an estimated life of 25 years. The price level at that time was 80 per cent of the 19x9 price level.

The equipment was purchased in 19x7 at a cost of $36,000, and had an estimated life of 10 years. The price level at that time was 90 per cent of the 19x9 price level.

The Lifo method of inventory valuation is used. The original inventory was acquired the year the building was constructed and was maintained at a constant $4,000 until 19x9. In 19x9, a gradual buildup of the inventory was begun in anticipation of an increase in the volume of business.

Arnett considers the return on his investment as the dividend he actually receives. In 19x1 Glo-Bright paid cash dividends in the amount of $8,000.

On July 1, 19x0 there was a reverse stock split-up of Glo-Bright stock in the ratio of 1 for 10.

Required:

a. Compute the 19x1 earnings per share of common stock, in terms of 19x9 dollars.

b. Compute the percentage return on investment for 19x9 and 19x1, in terms of 19x9 dollars.

5-26. *Financial ratios, inventories, costing.* (CPA Adapted.) In the cases cited below, five different conditions are possible when X is compared with Y. These possibilities are as follows:

a. X equals Y.

b. X is greater than Y.

c. X is less than Y.

d. X is equal to or greater than Y.

e. X is equal to or less than Y.

Required:

Show the relationship between X and Y for each of the following independent statements [Questions (1) through (9)].

An example of the manner in which the questions should be answered is shown in the following illustration:

Question	Answer
(0) The Effee Co. declared a cash dividend. Compare the amount of the stockholders' equity before the declaration of the cash dividend (X) with the amount of the stockholders' equity after the payment of the cash dividend (Y).	b

(1) The working capital ratio of the Zeno Co. is 2 to 1. If cash is used to pay a current liability, compare the ratio before payment (X) with the ratio after payment of the current liability (Y).

(2) The Zeno Co. has written off an uncollectible account against the allowance account. Compare the working capital ratio before the write-off (X) with the ratio after the write-off (Y).

(3) The cash sale of a fixed asset has resulted in a loss. Compare the working capital ratio before the sale (X) with the ratio after the sale (Y).

(4) The authorized capital stock of the K Corp. consisted of one million shares of $5 par value common, of which 800,000 shares were issued and outstanding. The balance in the retained earnings account was $1,260,000. A 10 per cent stock dividend was declared and issued when the market value of the stock was $7.50 per share. Compare the total net worth before the issuance of the stock dividend (X) with the total net worth after the issuance of the stock dividend (Y).

(5) Prices have been rising steadily; physical turnover of goods has occurred approximately four times in the last year. Compare the ending inventory computed by the Lifo method (X) with the same ending inventory computed by the moving-average method (Y).

(6) "Cost or market, whichever is lower," may be applied to the inventory as a whole [procedure (a)] or to categories of inventory items [procedure (b)]. Compare the reported value of inventory when procedure (a) is used (X) with the reported value of inventory when procedure (b) is used (Y).

(7) Prices have been rising steadily; physical turnover of goods has occurred five times in the last year. Compare unit prices of ending inventory items at moving-average pricing (X) with those at weighted-average pricing (Y).

(8) The following data concerning the sales and collections of Co. *A* and Co. *B* were compiled from their records. Compare the average collection period of Co. *A*'s accounts receivable (*X*) with that of Co. *B* (*Y*).

	Co. A	Co. B
Sales	$245,000	$90,000
Accounts receivable, Jan. 1	20,000	4,000
Accounts receivable, Dec. 31	15,000	8,000

(9) The following data concerning Co. *A* and Co. *B* were compiled from their records. Compare Co. *A*'s inventory turnover (*X*) with that of Co. *B* (*Y*).

	Co. A	Co. B
Sales	$100,000	$400,000
Gross profit percentage:		
Based on cost price	25	
Based on selling price		30
Initial inventory	30,000	160,000
Ending inventory	34,000	90,000

5-27. *Financial analysis: multiple choice.* (Prepared by David Green, Jr.)

THE OIL CO. OF CALIFORNIA
Consolidated Financial Position

	Dec. 31	
Current Assets	*19x9*	*19x8*
Cash in banks and on hand	$ 16,736,501	$ 22,126,407
U.S. Government securities (at cost, which is below market)	14,168,267	308,569
Marketable securities (at cost, which is below market)	1,202,697	2,118,406
	$ 32,107,465	$ 24,553,382
Accounts and notes receivable, less allowance of $385,007 and $409,722, respectively, for uncollectible accounts	$ 25,324,924	$ 25,869,068
Inventories:		
Crude oil	4,437,762	5,989,870
Petroleum products (at first-in, first-out cost)	22,785,488	19,351,417
Materials and supplies	2,087,598	3,269,241
Total current assets	$ 86,743,237	$ 79,032,978
Less: Current Liabilities		
Amounts payable for oil purchases, lessors' royalties, employees' wages, construction projects, material and supplies, utilities, etc.	$ 15,464,937	$ 15,790,355
Motor fuel and other sales and excise taxes collected from customers for governmental agencies	3,382,528	2,841,330
Dividend payable on common shares	2,633,135	2,916,419
Interest accrued on long-term debt	290,903	92,292
Portion of debentures to be retired within one year, as required by sinking fund provisions	300,000	200,000
Amounts payable for property and miscellaneous taxes	2,813,722	2,487,388
Amounts provided for estimated federal and other income taxes	3,187,049	7,075,658
Total current liabilities	$ 28,072,274	$ 31,403,442
Working capital	$ 58,670,963	$ 47,629,536

THE OIL CO. OF CALIFORNIA
Consolidated Financial Position (cont'd)

	Dec. 31	
Properties	*19x9*	*19x8*
Gross investment in oil lands and wells, pipe lines, tankships, refineries, marketing facilities, etc.	$503,631,629	$431,124,879
Less: Related accumulated charges for depletion and depreciation, etc., representing exhaustion of oil properties, wear and tear on facilities, and obsolescence	254,259,360	234,525,287
Net investment in properties	$249,372,269	$196,599,592
Other Assets		
Investment in capital stocks of, and advances ($2,000,000 on Dec. 31, 19x9) to, controlled companies	$ 5,313,593	$ 3,378,569
Investment in other securities (at cost); long-term receivables; and royalty and other advances	3,717,823	2,109,782
	$ 9,031,416	$ 5,488,351
Less: Allowance for losses	2,565,056	1,965,056
	$ 6,466,360	$ 3,523,295
Proceeds from 2.80 per cent promissory note invested in U.S. Government securities (transferred to current assets in 19x9)		$ 14,907,433
Taxes and insurance paid in advance	$ 2,941,794	2,778,764
Other prepaid expense and deferred charges	2,023,837	1,573,841
Total other assets	$ 11,431,991	$ 22,783,333
Total working capital, properties, and other assets	$319,475,223	$267,012,461
Less: Long-term debt outstanding, after deducting amounts to be retired within one year (see current liabilities)		
2.75 per cent promissory notes, due 19x5 to 19x4	$ 40,000,000	
2.80 per cent promissory notes, due 19x3 to 19x2	15,000,000	$ 15,000,000
2.75 per cent debentures, due 19x1 to 19x0	24,700,000	25,000,000
3 per cent debentures, maturing 19x7 (redeemed in 19x9)		14,400,000
Total long-term debt	$ 79,700,000	$ 54,400,000
Reserve for self-insurance	1,670,512	1,508,259
Total long-term debt and reserve	$ 81,370,512	$ 55,908,259
Shareholders' Ownership, consisting of outstanding preferred and common shares; premium from sale, and credit arising from retirement of, capital stock; and net income retained in business	$238,104,711	$211,104,202

Required:

Questions (1) through (12) refer to the accompanying balance sheets for The Oil Co. of California. You are to use exclusively the information on these balance sheets in selecting your responses. Any information which you have— of this company, the industry, or the general business picture—should not influence your answer. Accept these financial statements as being correctly prepared and in proper order.

For the following Questions (1) through (12), select answer *a*, *b*, *c*, *d*, or *e*

a. True, without reservation.

b. Probably true, but additional information is needed to eliminate any reservation.

c. False, without reservation.

d. Probably false, but additional information is needed to eliminate any reservations.

e. The data are *insufficient* to indicate the probable truth or falsity of the statement.

Questions for The Oil Co. of California

(1) During the year 19x9, the company acquired U.S. Government securities at a cost of at least $13,859,698.

(2) Market price appreciation of $113,278 in marketable securities was taken into income in 19x9.

(3) Dollar purchases of materials and supplies in 19x9 exceeded the dollar amounts of these items used during the year.

(4) The company anticipated serious declines in the market prices of crude oil and petroleum products in the coming year, 19x0.

(5) The company charges receivables to bad debts as they actually prove uncollectible.

(6) The current ratio, on Dec. 31, 19x9, was 3.1 to 1.

(7) The amount of notes and bonds retired during 19x9 was $14,700,000.

(8) Some of the company's long-term debt has interest payment dates other than Dec. 31.

(9) Investments in capital stocks of controlled companies in the amount of $64,976 were charged to the Allowance for Losses account in 19x9.

(10) Total assets, on Dec. 31, 19x9, amounted to $319,475,223.

(11) On Dec. 31, 19x9, the company had funds of $1,670,512 segregated to take care of the replacement of noninsured properties.

(12) The number of shares of common stock outstanding was decreased during 19x9.

PART TWO

The Core of Accounting for Planning and Control

CHAPTER 6

The Master Budget: Planning for Profit

ACCOUNTING FOR EXTERNAL REPORTING IS MOSTLY CONCERNED with the stewardship or custodial responsibilities of management. That is, the usual financial statements attempt to show what has been done, rather than what will be done. Predictions are seldom incorporated into formal public reports, primarily because the introduction of necessarily less objective material might undermine confidence in the entire reporting process.

However, management—and many investors and bank loan officers—have become increasingly aware of the merits of formal business plans. This chapter provides a condensed review of basic accounting, because the over-all business plan—the master budget—is essentially nothing more than the preparation of the familiar major financial statements. The major technical difference is that the accountant is dealing with expected future data rather than with historical data. There is, however, a major philosophical difference. The advocates of budgeting maintain that the process of preparing the budget forces executives to become more effective administrators. Budgeting puts planning where it belongs—in the forefront of the manager's mind.

This chapter is a bird's-eye view of planning for the organization as a whole. We will see that planning requires all the functions of a business to blend together. We will see the importance of an accurate sales forecast. Most of all, we should begin to appreciate why budgeting is helpful. Budgeting is primarily attention-directing because it helps managers to focus on operating or financial problems early enough for effective planning or action.

CHARACTERISTICS OF BUDGETS

Definition of Budget

A budget is a formal quantitative expression of management plans. The master budget summarizes the goals of all phases of a company—sales, production, distribution, and finance. It depicts targets for sales, production, net income, and cash position, and for any other objective that management specifies. The master budget usually consists of a statement of expected future income, a balance sheet, a statement of cash receipts and disbursements, and supporting schedules. These statements are the culmination of the budgetary process—a detailed, rigorous look at the organization's future.

Advantages of Budgets

Many skeptics who have never used budgets are quick to state, "I suppose budgeting is okay for the other fellow's business, but *my* business is different. There are too many uncertainties and complications to make budgeting worthwhile for me." Perhaps the best way to combat such a short-sighted attitude is to name others in the same industry who are zealous about budgeting and who, inevitably, are among the industry's leaders. An organization which adopts formal budgeting usually becomes rapidly convinced of its helpfulness and would not consider regressing to its old-fashioned, nonbudgeting days. The benefits of budgeting almost always clearly outweigh the cost and the effort.

Some managers contend that the uncertainties which plague their business make budgeting impractical. But the same managers, when prodded for details, usually reveal that they are planning incessantly. Some kind of budget program is bound to be useful to any organization, regardless of its size or its uncertainties.

The major benefits of budgeting may be enumerated as follows:

1. Budgeting, by formalizing their *planning* responsibilities, compels managers to think ahead.
2. Budgeting provides definite expectations that are the best framework for judging subsequent performance.
3. Budgeting aids managers to coordinate their efforts, so that the objectives of the organization as a whole harmonize with the objectives of its parts.

Formalization of Planning

The principal advantage of budgeting is probably that it forces managers to think ahead—to anticipate and prepare for changing conditions. The budgeting process makes planning an explicit management responsibility. Too often, managers operate from day to day, extinguishing one business brush fire after the other. There simply is not time for any tough-minded thinking about anything beyond the next day's problems. Planning takes a back seat or is actually obliterated by workaday pressures.

The trouble with the day-to-day approach to managing an organization is that objectives are never crystallized. Without goals, company operations lack direction, problems are not foreseen, and results are hard to interpret. Advocates of budgeting maintain that most business emergencies can be avoided by careful planning.

Expectations as a Framework for Judging Performance

As a basis for judging actual results, budgeted performance is generally regarded as being better than past performance. The news that a company had sales of $10 million this year, as compared with $8 million the previous year, may or may not indicate that the company has achieved maximum success. Perhaps sales should have been $11 million this year. The major drawback of using historical data for judging performance is that inefficiencies may be buried in the past performance. Moreover, the usefulness of comparisons with the past is also limited by intervening changes in economic conditions, technology, competitive maneuvers, personnel, etc.

Another benefit of budgeting is that key personnel are informed of what is expected of them. Nobody likes to drift along, not knowing what his boss anticipates.

Coordination and Communication

Coordination is the meshing and balancing of all the organization's resources, so that the over-all objectives are attained—so that the interests of the individual manager harmonize with the interests of the organization as a whole. The budget is the means for communicating over-all objectives and for blending the objectives of all departments.

Coordination requires, for example, that purchasing officers integrate their plans with production requirements, and that production officers use the sales budget to help them anticipate and plan for the manpower and plant facilities they will use. The budgetary process obliges executives to visualize the relationship of their departments to other departments, and to the company as a whole.

Middle management's attitude toward budgets will be heavily influenced by the attitude of top management. The chief executive must support budgeting wholeheartedly if a budgetary program is to achieve maximum benefits.

HUMAN RELATIONS

The ability to adhere to a budget is often an important factor in judging a manager's performance. Naturally, budgets are usually not the most popular feature of a manager's business life. Budgets pinpoint a manager's performance and direct his superior's attention to trouble spots. Few individuals are ecstatic about any techniques used by the boss to check their performance. So budgets are commonly regarded as embodiments of nickel-nursing, restrictive, negative top management attitudes.

These misconceptions can be overcome by persuasive education and salesmanship. The budget is not a repulsive technique for harassing the employee. Properly used, it is of positive aid in setting standards of performance, in motivating toward goals, in metering results, and in directing attention to the areas that need investigation. The budget is inanimate. Its administration, however, is a delicate task because everyone it affects must understand and accept the notion that the budget is primarily designed to help, not hinder.

The supreme importance of the human aspects of budgeting cannot be overemphasized. Too often, top management and its accountants are overly concerned with the mechanics of budgets. The effectiveness of any budgeting system depends directly on whether the managers it affects understand it and accept it. Ideally, managers should be cooperative and cost-conscious.

A budget is not a cure-all for existing organizational ills. A budget will not solve the problems created by a bumbling management or a faulty information system. The budget is a device whose value depends on its being administered astutely in conjunction with an information system that is tuned to a coordinated organization.

TYPES OF BUDGETS

Time Span

The planning horizon for budgeting may vary from a year or less to many years, depending on budget objectives and on the uncertainties involved. Long-range budgets, called *capital budgets,* are often prepared for particular projects such as equipment purchases, locations of plant, and additions of product lines. *Master budgets,* which consolidate an organization's over-all plans, are usually prepared on an annual basis.

The annual budget may be subdivided on a month-to-month basis, or perhaps on a monthly basis for the first quarter and on a quarterly basis for the three remaining quarters.

Continuous budgets are increasingly used. These budgets perpetually add a month in the future as the month just ended is dropped. Continuous budgets are desirable because they compel managers to think specifically about the forthcoming twelve months and thus maintain a stable planning horizon.

Classification of Budgets

The terms used to describe assorted budget schedules vary from company to company. Sometimes budgets are called *pro forma* statements because they are forecasted financial statements.

Budgets, accompanied by subsidiary schedules, may be classified as follows:

1. Master budget.   Budgeted Income Statement
   a. Operating budget.
      (1) Sales budget.
      (2) Production budget.
         (*a*) Materials used and material purchases.
         (*b*) Direct labor.
         (*c*) Indirect manufacturing overhead.
         (*d*) Changes in inventory levels.
      (3) Cost-of-goods-sold budget.
      (4) Selling expense budget.
      (5) Administrative expense budget.
   b. Financial budget.
      (1) Cash budget: cash receipts and disbursements.
      (2) Budgeted balance sheet.
      (3) Budgeted statement of sources and applications of funds (net working capital).
2. Special budget reports.
   a. Performance reports (comparisons of results with plans).
   b. Capital budgets (long-range expectations for specific projects).

THE PREPARATION OF A MASTER BUDGET

Try to prepare the budget schedules required for the solution of this problem. Use the basic steps described after the problem.

PROBLEM

The *R* Co. is a retailer of a wide variety of household items. The company rents a number of retail stores and also has a local door-to-door sales force.

The *R* Co.'s newly hired accountant has persuaded the management to prepare a budget, in order to aid financial and operating decisions. Because this is the company's first attempt at formal budgeting, the planning horizon is only four months, April through July. In the past, sales have increased during the spring season. Collections lag behind and cash is needed for purchases, wages, and other operating outlays. In the past, the company has met this cash squeeze with the help of six-month loans from banks.

Exhibit 6-1 is the closing balance sheet for the fiscal year just ended.

EXHIBIT 6-1

R CO.
Balance Sheet
Mar. 31, 19x1

Assets

Current assets:		
Cash	$10,000	
Accounts receivable, net (.4 × March sales of $40,000)	16,000	
Merchandise inventory, $20,000 + .8 (.7 × April sales of $50,000)	48,000	
Unexpired insurance	1,800	$ 75,800
Fixed assets:		
Equipment, fixtures, and other	$37,000	
Accumulated depreciation	12,800	24,200
Total assets		$100,000

Equities

Current liabilities:		
Accounts payable (.5 × March purchases of $33,600)	$16,800	
Accrued wages and commissions payable ($1,250 + $3,000)	4,250	$ 21,050
Owners' equity		78,950
Total equities		$100,000

Sales in March were $40,000. Monthly sales are forecasted as follows:

April	$50,000	June	$60,000	August	$40,000
May	$80,000	July	$50,000		

Sales consist of 60 per cent cash and 40 per cent credit. All credit accounts are collected in the month following the sales. The accounts receivable on Mar. 31 represent credit sales made in March (40 per cent of $40,000). Bad debts are negligible and may be ignored.

At the end of any month, the *R* Co. wishes to maintain a basic inventory of $20,000 plus 80 per cent of the cost of goods to be sold in the following month. The merchandise cost of goods sold averages 70 per cent of sales. Therefore, the inventory, on Mar. 31, is $20,000 + .8 (.7 × April sales of $50,000) = $20,000 + $28,000 = $48,000. The purchase terms available to the *R* Co. are net, 30 days. 50 per cent of a given month's purchases is paid during that month and 50 per cent during the following month.

Wages and commissions are paid semimonthly, half a month after they are earned. They are divided into two portions: monthly fixed wages of $2,500 and commissions equal to 15 per cent of sales, which are uniform throughout each month. Therefore, the Mar. 31 balance of Accrued Wages and Commissions Payable consists of $(.5 \times \$2,500) + .5$ $(.15 \times \$40,-000) = \$1,250 + \$3,000 = \$4,250$. This $4,250 will be paid on April 15. A delivery truck will be purchased for $3,000 cash in April.

Other monthly expenses are:

Miscellaneous expenses	5 per cent of sales, paid as incurred
Rent	$2,000, paid as incurred
Insurance	$200
Depreciation, including new truck	$500

The company desires to maintain a minimum cash balance of $10,000 at the end of each month. Money can be borrowed or repaid in multiples of $1,000, at an interest rate of 6 per cent per annum. Management does not want to borrow any more cash than necessary and wants to repay as promptly as possible. Interest is computed and paid when the principal is repaid. Assume that borrowing takes place at the beginning, and repayment at the end, of the months in question.

Required:

1. Using the data given, prepare the following detailed schedules:
   a. Sales forecast.
   b. Cash collections from customers.
   c. Purchases.
   d. Disbursements for purchases.
   e. Wages and commissions.
   f. Disbursements for wages and commissions.
2. Using the data given and the schedules you have prepared, prepare a master budget with the following major statements:
   a. Budgeted income statement for four months ending July 31, 19x1.
   b. Budgeted statement of cash receipts and disbursements by months, including details of borrowings, repayments, and interest.
   c. Budgeted balance sheet as of July 31, 19x1.

For consistency with the numbering scheme used in this book, label your major exhibits 6-2, 6-3, and 6-4, respectively. Note that Schedules *a, c,* and *e* will be needed to prepare Exhibit 6-2, and Schedules *b, d,* and *f* will be needed to prepare Exhibit 6-3.

Basic Steps in Preparing Master Budget

The basic steps in preparing budgeted financial statements follow. Use the steps to prepare your own schedules. Then examine the schedules in the Solution.

Step 1. The Sales Forecast (Schedule *a*) is the starting point for budgeting, because inventory levels, purchases, and operating expenses are generally geared to the rate of sales activity.

Step 2. After sales are budgeted, the purchases budget (Schedule *c*) may be prepared. The total merchandise needed will be the sum of the desired ending inventory plus the amount needed to fulfill current demand. The total need will be partially met by the beginning inventory; the remainder must come from current purchases. Therefore, purchases are computed as follows: Purchases = Desired ending inventory + Cost of goods sold − Beginning inventory.

Step 3. The budgeting of operating expenses is dependent on various factors. Many operating expenses are directly influenced by month-to-month fluctuations in sales volume. Examples are sales commissions and delivery expenses. Other expenses are not directly influenced (e.g., rent, insurance, depreciation, certain types of payroll). In this solution, Schedule *e* should be prepared for wages and commissions. The other operating expenses may be entered directly in the pertinent major exhibits.

Step 4. Steps *1* through *3* will provide enough information for a budgeted income statement (Exhibit 6-2).

Step 5. Cash budget (Exhibit 6-3). Estimate the month-to-month effects on the cash position of the level of operations outlined in Exhibit 6-2.

The illustrative cash budget shows the pattern of short-term, self-liquidating financing. Seasonal peaks often result in heavy drains on cash, for merchandise and operating expenses, before the sales are made and the cash is collected from customers. The resulting loan is self-liquidating—that is, the borrowed money is used to acquire merchandise for sale, and the proceeds from the sale are used to repay the loan. This working capital cycle moves from cash to inventory to receivables and back to cash.

Cash budgets help management to avoid having unnecessary, idle cash, on the one hand, and unnecessary, nerve-wracking cash deficiencies, on the other. An astutely mapped financing program keeps cash balances in reasonable relation to needs.

The cash budget (budgeted statement of cash receipts and disbursements, Exhibit 6-3) has the following major sections:

w. The beginning cash balance plus cash receipts yield the total cash available for needs, before financing. Cash receipts depend on collections from customers and cash sales (Schedule *b*) and on other operating sources such as miscellaneous rental income. Studies of the collectibility of accounts receivable are a prerequisite to accurate forecasting. Key factors include bad debt experience and average time lag between sales and collections.

x. Cash Disbursements:
   (1) Purchases depend on the credit terms extended by suppliers and the bill-paying habits of the buyer (Schedule *d*).
   (2) Payroll depends on wage, salary, or commission terms and on payroll dates (Schedule *f*).
   (3) Other costs and expenses depend on timing and credit terms. *Note that depreciation does not entail a cash outlay.*

EXHIBIT 6-2

R CO.
Budgeted Income Statement
For the Four Months Ending July 31, 19x1

		Data	*Source of Data*
Sales		$240,000	Schedule *a*
Cost of goods sold		168,000	Schedule *c*
Gross margin		$ 72,000	
Operating expenses:			
Wages and commissions	$46,000		Schedule *e*
Rent	8,000		Exhibit 6-3
Miscellaneous expenses	12,000		Exhibit 6-3
Insurance	800		Given
Depreciation	2,000	68,800	Given
Net income from operations		$ 3,200	
Interest expense		220	Exhibit 6-3
Net income		$ 2,980	

EXHIBIT 6-3

R CO.
Budgeted Statement of Cash Receipts and Disbursements
For the Four Months Ending July 31, 19x1

		April	*May*	*June*	*July*
	Cash balance, beginning	$10,000	$10,550	$10,990	$10,240
	Cash receipts:				
	Collections from customers (Schedule *b*)	46,000	68,000	68,000	54,000
*w.**	Total cash available for needs, before financing	56,000	78,550	78,990	64,240
	Cash disbursements:				
	Merchandise (Schedule *d*)	42,700	48,300	40,600	32,900
	Wages and commissions (Schedule *f*)	9,250	12,250	13,000	10,750
	Miscellaneous expenses, 5 per cent of sales	2,500	4,000	3,000	2,500
	Rent	2,000	2,000	2,000	2,000
	Truck purchase	3,000	—	—	—
x.	Total disbursements	59,450	66,550	58,600	48,150
	Minimum cash balance desired	10,000	10,000	10,000	10,000
	Total cash needed	69,450	76,550	68,600	58,150
	Excess (or deficiency)	(13,450)†	2,000	10,390	6,090
	Financing:				
	Borrowings (at beginning)	14,000			
	Repayments (at end)	—	(1,000)	(10,000)	(3,000)
	Interest (at 6 per cent per annum)	—	(10)	(150)	(60)
y.	Total effects of financing	14,000	(1,010)‡	(10,150)	(3,060)
z.	Cash balance, ending (*w + y − x*)	$10,550	$10,990	$10,240	$13,030

Note: Expired insurance and depreciation do not entail cash outlays.

* Letters are keyed to Step 5, described in the text.
† ( ) indicates deficiency.
‡ $2,000 is not repaid here because the repayment, plus interest of $20, would result in an ending cash balance of $9,980, which—strictly interpreted—is insufficient.

(4) Other disbursements include purchases of fixed assets, long-term investments, installment payments on purchases.

y. Financing requirements depend on how the total cash available w compares with the total cash needed. Needs include the disbursements x plus the ending cash balance z desired. The financing plans will depend on the relationship of cash available to cash sought. If there is an excess, loans may be repaid or temporary investments made. The pertinent outlays for interest expenses are usually contained in this section of the cash budget.

z. The ending cash balance $z = w + y - x$. Financing y may have a positive (borrowing) or a negative (repayment) effect on the cash balance.

Step 6. Budgeted Balance Sheet (Exhibit 6-4): Each item is projected in the light of the details of the business plan as expressed in the previous schedules. For example, Unexpired Insurance is $1,800 (the balance on Mar. 31) minus $800 (i.e., 200 × 4 months), or $1,000.

Solution

	March	April	May	June	July	Apr.-Jul. Total
Schedule *a: Sales Forecast*						
Credit sales, 40 per cent	$16,000	$20,000	$ 32,000	$24,000	$20,000	
Cash sales, 60 per cent	24,000	30,000	48,000	36,000	30,000	
Total sales, 100 per cent	$40,000	$50,000	$ 80,000	$60,000	$50,000	$240,000
Schedule *b: Cash Collections*						
Cash sales this month		$30,000	$ 48,000	$36,000	$30,000	
100 per cent of last month's credit sales		16,000	20,000	32,000	24,000	
Total collections		$46,000	$ 68,000	$68,000	$54,000	

	March	April	May	June	July	Apr.-Jul. Total
Schedule *c: Purchases*						
Ending inventory	$48,000	$64,800	$ 53,600	$48,000	$42,400	
Cost of goods sold	28,000	35,000	56,000	42,000	35,000	$168,000
Total needed	$76,000	$99,800	$109,600	$90,000	$77,400	
Beginning inventory	42,400*	48,000	64,800	53,600	48,000	
Purchases	$33,600	$51,800	$ 44,800	$36,400	$29,400	
Schedule *d: Disbursements for Purchases*						
50 per cent of last month's purchases		$16,800	$ 25,900	$22,400	$18,200	
50 per cent of this month's purchases		25,900	22,400	18,200	14,700	
Disbursements for merchandise		$42,700	$ 48,300	$40,600	$32,900	

handwritten margin note: CofGS / Beg Inv. / Purch. / End. Inv

* $20,000 + .8 (.7 × March sales of $40,000) = $20,000 + $22,400 = $42,400.

	March	April	May	June	July	Apr.-Jul. Total
Schedule *e: Wages and Commissions*						
Wages, all fixed	$ 2,500	$ 2,500	$ 2,500	$ 2,500	$ 2,500	
Commissions (15 per cent of current month's sales)	6,000	7,500	12,000	9,000	7,500	
Total	$ 8,500	$10,000	$ 14,500	$11,500	$10,000	$ 46,000

	April	*May*	*June*	*July*
Schedule *f: Disbursements for Wages and Commissions*				
50 per cent of last month's expenses	$ 4,250	$ 5,000	$ 7,250	$ 5,750
50 per cent of this month's expenses	5,000	7,250	5,750	5,000
	$ 9,250	$ 12,250	$13,000	$10,750

EXHIBIT 6-4

R CO.
Budgeted Balance Sheet
July 31, 19x1

Assets

Current assets:		
Cash (Exhibit 6-3)	$13,030	
Accounts receivable (.40 × July sales of $50,000)	20,000	
Merchandise inventory (Schedule c)	42,400	
Unexpired insurance ($1,800 old balance − $800 expired)	1,000	$ 76,430
Fixed assets:		
Equipment, fixtures, and other ($37,000 + truck, $3,000)	$40,000	
Accumulated depreciation ($12,800 + $2,000 depreciation)	14,800	25,200
Total assets		$101,630

Equities

Current liabilities:		
Accounts payable (.5 × July purchases of $29,400)	$14,700	
Accrued wages and commissions payable ($1,250 + $3,750)	5,000	$ 19,700
Owners' equity ($78,950 + $2,980 net income)		81,930
Total equities		$101,630

Note: Beginning balances were used as a start for the computations of Unexpired Insurance, Fixed Assets, and Owners' Equity.

THE DIFFICULTIES OF SALES FORECASTING

The sales forecast is the foundation of the entire master budget. The accuracy of estimated production schedules and of cost to be incurred depends on the detail and accuracy, in dollars and in units, of the forecasted sales.

The sales forecast is usually prepared under the direction of the top sales executive. All of the following factors are important: (1) past patterns of sales; (2) the estimates made by the sales force; (3) general economic and competitive conditions; (4) specific interrelationships of sales and economic indicators, such as gross national product or industrial production indexes; (5) changes in prices; (6) market research studies; and (7) advertising and sales promotion plans.

Sales forecasting is still somewhat mystical, but its procedures are becoming more formal and are being viewed more seriously because of the intensity of competitive pressures. Although this book does not encompass a detailed discussion of the preparation of the sales budget, the importance of an accurate sales forecast cannot be overstressed.

SUMMARY

The master budget expresses management's over-all operating and financing plan. It outlines company objectives and steps in achieving them. The budgetary process compels managers to think ahead and to prepare for changing conditions. Budgets are aids in setting standards of performance, motivating personnel toward goals, measuring results, and directing attention to the areas that most need investigation.

The human factors in budgeting are more important than the mechanics. Top management must support a budgetary program wholeheartedly. The job of educating personnel and selling them on the budget is everlasting, but essential, if those who are affected by the budget are to understand it and accept it.

The cornerstone of the budget is the sales forecast. All current operating and financial planning are generally tied to the volume of sales.

SUMMARY PROBLEM FOR YOUR REVIEW

PROBLEM

Before attempting to solve the homework problems, review the illustration in this chapter.

SUGGESTED READINGS

Heiser, H., *Budgeting: Principles and Practice.* New York: The Ronald Press Co., 1959.

Knight, D., and E. Weinwurm, *Managerial Budgeting.* New York: The Macmillan Company, 1964.

Welsch, G., *Budgeting: Profit Planning and Control,* 2nd ed. Englewood Cliffs, N.J.: Prentice-Hall, Inc., 1964.

ASSIGNMENT MATERIAL

ESSENTIAL ASSIGNMENT MATERIAL

6-1. *Terminology.* Define: master budget; continuous budget; *pro forma* statements; cash budget

6-2. *Importance of sales forecast.* A retail department of a local chain of department stores sells a plain and a fancy pound box of hard candy. The candy is purchased in bulk from a local candy manufacturer, and two types of pound containers are purchased from a local container manufacturer. The store clerks use a back room for packaging the candy, as the need arises. Purchasing and selling prices have been stable, and no price changes are anticipated.

It is near the end of October. Orders must be placed today for delivery by Nov. 1. These orders are to provide sufficient stock to last through the Christmas season.

Federal Reserve statistics for the local area show retail department store sales to be 2 per cent over last year, for the period Jan. 1-Sept. 30. The store's top management anticipates an increase of 1 per cent in dollar sales of ordinary items and of 10 per cent in dollar sales of luxury items this year, as compared with last year.

Other data:

	Last Year		This Year	
	November	December	Inventory Oct. 31	Target Inventory Dec. 31
Selling price per pound, $1.50 fancy and $1.00 plain				
Pounds sold:				
Plain	4,000	7,000		
Fancy	4,000	12,000		
Pounds			1,000	600
Number of containers:				
Plain			200	100
Fancy			500	100
Purchase costs:				
Candy, per pound $.40				
Container, plain $.05				
Container, fancy $.20				

Required:

1. Budgeted sales of plain candy, in pounds and in total dollars, for November and December.
2. Budgeted sales of fancy candy, in pounds and in total dollars, for November and December. 4080   12,240 lbs. $4400 $13,200
3. Pounds and total cost of needed candy purchases.
4. Number and total cost of needed plain containers. Nov. 4080 boxes $20400
   Dec. 7140 $357.00
5. Number and total cost of needed fancy containers. NOV 4080
   DEC 12240 $2448.00

6-3. *Prepare master budget.* The Cello Co. wants a master budget for the next three months. It desires an ending minimum cash balance of $4,000 each month. Sales are forecasted at average selling prices of $4 per unit. Inventories are supposed to equal 125 per cent of the next month's sales in units, except for the end of March. The Mar. 31 inventory in units should be 75 per cent of the next month's sales. Merchandise costs are $2 per unit. Purchases during any given month are paid in full during the following month. All sales are on credit, payable within 30 days, but experience has shown that 40 per cent of current sales are collected in the current month, 40 per cent in the next month, and 20 per cent in the month thereafter. Bad debts are negligible.

Monthly operating expenses are as follows:

Wages and salaries	$12,000
Insurance expired	100
Depreciation	100
Miscellaneous	2,000
Rent	100 + 10 per cent of sales

Cash dividends of $1,000 are to be paid quarterly, beginning Jan. 15, and are declared on the fifteenth of the previous month. All operating expenses are paid as incurred, except insurance, depreciation, and rent. Rent of $100 is paid at the beginning of each month, and the additional 10 per cent of sales is paid quarterly on the tenth of the month following the quarter. The next settlement is due Jan. 10.

The company plans to buy some new fixtures, for $2,000 cash, in March.

Money can be borrowed or repaid in multiples of $500, at an interest rate of 6 per cent per annum. Management wants to minimize borrowing and repay rapidly. Interest is computed and paid when the principal is repaid. Assume that borrowing takes place at the beginning, and repayments at the end, of the months in question. Money is never borrowed at the beginning and repaid at the end of the *same* month. Compute interest to the nearest dollar.

Assets as of Dec. 31:		*Liabilities as of Dec. 31:*	
Cash	$ 4,000	Accounts payable (merchandise)	$28,750
Accounts receivable	16,000	Dividends payable	1,000
Inventory	31,250	Rent payable	7,000
Unexpired insurance	1,200		$36,750
Fixed assets, net	10,000		
	$62,450		

Recent and forecasted sales:

October	$30,000	December	$20,000	February	$60,000	April	$36,000
November	20,000	January	50,000	March	30,000		

Required:

Prepare a master budget, including supporting schedules.

ADDITIONAL ASSIGNMENT MATERIAL

Note: Problems 6-18 and 6-20 stress the difficulties of sales forecasting. Problem 6-22 is a summary of cash budgeting; it requires 40 to 60 minutes of solution time.

6-4. Describe the contents of the master budget.

6-5. What are the major benefits of budgeting?

6-6. Why is budgeted performance better than past performance, as a basis for judging actual results?

6-7. What is coordination?

6-8. "Education and salesmanship are key features of budgeting." Explain.

6-9. "Capital budgets are plans for managing long-term debt and common stock." Do you agree? Explain.

6-10. "*Pro forma* statements are those statements prepared in conjunction with continuous budgets." Do you agree? Explain.

6-11. What is the difference between an operating budget and a financial budget?

6-12. Why is the sales forecast the starting point for budgeting?

6-13. What is a self-liquidating loan?

6-14. What is the principal objective of a cash budget?

6-15. What factors influence the sales forecast?

6-16. "There are too many uncertainties and complications to make budgeting worthwhile in my business." Do you agree? Explain.

6-17. What is the major technical difference between historical and budgeted financial statements?

6-18. *Sales quotas and budgets.* For the past few years the Windal Co. has budgeted sales in its various territories. In addition, the company sets ambitious target quota volumes, despite the fact that actual performance will not meet the quotas assigned.

For the coming year, the following budget has been formulated for Districts *A* and *B*.

	District A	District B
Gross sales	$5,000,000	$8,000,000
Returns and allowances	$ 100,000	$ 120,000
Sales discounts (not cash discounts)	250,000	480,000
Freight-out allowance*	250,000	80,000
Total deductions	$ 600,000	$ 680,000
Net sales	$4,400,000	$7,320,000

* Windal's plants are located in the center of each district, but local competitors' plants have freight advantages that Windal must allow for in setting competitive prices.

The *quotas* for *net sales* in District *A* and District *B* have been set at $5,000,000 and $8,000,000, respectively.

Required:

1. Use the given data as a basis for describing the principal differences in selling in Districts *A* and *B*.

2. What figures should be used for formulating the master financial budget? Why?

3. Evaluate the Windal method of setting quotas. Why doesn't Windal simply use currently attainable net sales as a quota?

6-19. *Cash forecast; loan commitment.* (CPA Adapted.) The Loading Co. is planning to construct a two-unit facility for the loading of iron ore into ships. On or before Jan. 1, 19x1, the stockholders will invest $100,000 in the company's capital stock to provide its initial working capital. To finance the construction program (the total planned cost of which is $1,800,000), the company will obtain a commitment from a lending organization for a loan of $1,800,000. This loan is to be secured by a ten-year mortgage note, bearing interest at 5 per cent per year on the unpaid balance. The principal amount of the loan is to be repaid in equal semiannual installments of $100,000, beginning June 30, 19x2.

Inasmuch as the proceeds of the loan will be required only as construction work progresses, the company has agreed to pay a commitment fee, beginning Jan. 1, 19x1 equal to 1 per cent per year of the unused portion of the loan commitment. This fee is payable at the time amounts are "drawn-down," except at the time of the first "draw-down."

Work on the construction of the facility will commence in the fall of 19x0. The first payment to the contractor will be due on Jan. 1, 19x1, at which time the commitment and loan agreement will become effective and the company will make its first "draw-down," for payment to the contractor, in the amount of $800,000. As construction progresses, additional payments will be made to the contractors by "drawing-down" the remaining loan proceeds as follows (it is assumed that payment to the contractors will be made on the same dates as the loan proceeds are "drawn-down"):

Apr. 1, 19x1	$500,000
July 1, 19x1	300,000
Dec. 31, 19x1	100,000
Apr. 1, 19x2	100,000

Because of weather conditions, the facility can operate only from Apr. 1 through Nov. 30 of each year. The construction program will permit the completion of the first of the two plant units (capable of handling 5,000,000 tons) in time for its use during the 19x1 shipping season. The second unit (capable of handling an additional 3,000,000 tons) will be completed in time for the 19x2 season. It is expected that 5,000,000 tons will be handled by the facility during the 19x1 season; thereafter, the tonnage handled is expected to increase in each subsequent year by 300,000 tons, until a level of 6,500,000 tons is reached.

The company's revenues will be derived by charging the consignees of the ore for its services at a fixed rate per ton loaded. Billing terms will be net, ten days. Based upon past experience with similar facilities elsewhere, it is expected that the Loading Co.'s operating profit should average $.04 per ton, before charges for interest, finance charges, and $.03 depreciation per ton.

Required:

A cash forecast for each of three calendar years, starting with 19x1, to demonstrate the sufficiency of cash, to be obtained from (*a*) the sale of capital stock, (*b*) "draw-downs" on the loan, and (*c*) amount to be produced by the operating facility, to cover payments to the contractor and on the debt principal and interest.

6-20. *Sales forecasting.* In each of the following diagrams *a* through *e*, the dollar value of a sales order is contrasted with the quantity of product or service sold. Assume a single product in each case.

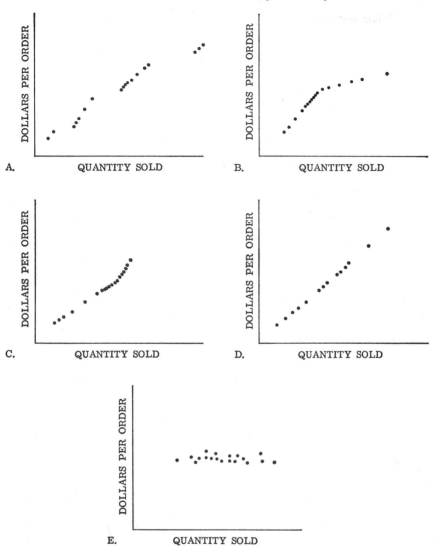

Required:

(1) What pricing policy is reflected by these order patterns (assuming all customers are rational)?

(2) Why are these patterns relevant to a sales forecast?

6-21. *Sales and purchases budgets; retail candy store.* The West Side Candy Shop is computing the purchases it must make for next week's sales. The store sells candy in boxes of three different sizes (one pound, two pounds, and three pounds) and in three different arrangements (soft centers, hard centers, and an assortment half of the total weight being soft centers and half hard centers). Sales are expected to be identical to last's week's, when

22,500 soft-center candies and 9,000 hard-center candies were sold. Last week's sales, in boxes, were as follows:

Size of Box	Percentage of Total Boxes Sold
3 lb.	10
2 lb.	30
1 lb.	60
	100%

The number of boxes of soft-center candy sold was exactly twice the number sold of either hard center boxes or assortment boxes for each size box.

Other data:

	Present Inventory (This Friday)	Target Inventory (Next Friday)
Number of Containers:		
3 lb.	50	20
2 lb.	100	60
1 lb.	275	120
Lbs. of Candy:		
Soft centers	400	300
Hard centers	125	150

	Purchase Costs	
Soft centers	$.70 per lb.	(60 soft centers)
Hard centers	.60 per lb.	(40 hard centers)
Containers:		
3 lb.	.30 each	
2 lb.	.20 each	
1 lb.	.10 each	

Price Schedule

	Arrangement		
Size of Box	Soft Centers	Hard Centers	Assortment
3 lb.	$3.00	$2.40	$2.70
2 lb.	2.00	1.60	1.80
1 lb.	1.00	.80	.90

Required:

1. Pounds and total cost of soft-center candies to be purchased.
2. Pounds and total cost of hard-center candies to be purchased.
3. Budgeted total sales in dollars, for next week.
4. Number and total cost of each size of containers to be purchased.

6-22. *Cash budget.* Prepare a statement of estimated cash receipts and disbursements for October 19x2, for the Spahn Co., which sells one product.

On Oct. 1, 19x2, part of the trial balance showed:

Cash	$ 6,000	
Accounts receivable	19,500	
Allowance for bad debts		$2,400
Merchandise inventory	12,000	
Accounts payable, merchandise		9,000

The company's purchases are payable within ten days. Assume that one-third of the purchases of any month are due and paid for in the following month.

The unit invoice cost of the merchandise purchased is $10. At the end of each month it is desired to have an inventory equal in units to 50 per cent of the following month's sales in units.

Sales terms include a 1 per cent discount if payment is made by the end of the calendar month. Past experience indicates that 60 per cent of the billings will be collected during the month of the sale, 30 per cent in the following calendar month, 6 per cent in the next following calendar month. 4 per cent will be uncollectible. The company's fiscal year begins Aug. 1.

Unit selling price	$ 15
August actual sales	15,000
September actual sales	45,000
October estimated sales	36,000
November estimated sales	27,000
Total sales expected in the fiscal year	$450,000

Exclusive of bad debts, total budgeted selling and general administrative expenses for the fiscal year are estimated at $58,500, of which $21,000 is fixed expense (inclusive of a $9,000 annual depreciation charge). These fixed expenses are incurred uniformly throughout the year. The balance of the selling and general administrative expenses vary with sales. Expenses are paid as incurred.

CHAPTER 7

Cost Behavior: Volume-Profit Relationships

IN THE PREVIOUS CHAPTER, WE SAW THAT PLANNING ENTAILS the selection of an organization's profit objective and the mapping of the ways to reach that objective. The importance of an accurate sales forecast was stressed because the over-all master plan is built upon contemplated volume levels.

But what if the planned-for sales are not achieved? What will be the impact of different sales volumes on net income? On financial needs? Furthermore, suppose costs change. This can also affect net income. Managers must know how an assortment of costs behave as the volume of sales expands or contracts. The study of the interrelationships of sales, costs, and net income is usually called cost-volume-profit analysis.

Cost-volume-profit analysis provides attention-directing and problem-solving background for important planning decisions such as selecting distribution channels, pricing, special promotions, and personnel hiring. "Know your costs" is an essential theme for any manager. And cost-volume-profit analysis helps to direct managerial attention to important problems and paves the way to their solution.

SOME COST TERMS

Unit Costs and Total Costs

The total bill for a senior class dance may be estimated at $400; but the bill is much more meaningful to the class members when it is stated as an amount per couple or per person. If 200 students attend, the unit cost is $2 per person; if 50 attend, the unit cost becomes $8 per person. The unit cost will determine the price—perhaps even the decision whether to hold the dance at all—because the total cost will be the same no matter how many students buy tickets. But this $400 total cost is difficult for the class members to interpret unless it is tied to some measure of volume (activity) that represents utilization. The division of a total cost by the number of times it will be utilized (in terms of units of activity or volume) yields the unit cost.

Generally, *unit costs should be expressed in terms most meaningful to the individuals who are responsible for incurring the costs.* The unit is not always a physical product; the unit (i.e., the base of the fraction) should be the definable statistic of volume or activity which is most closely correlated with the behavior of the cost. The base, or unit, will differ—it might be the number of orders processed, the number of lines billed in a billing department, the number of admissions to a theater, the number of pounds handled in a warehouse, the hours of labor worked in an assembly department, the number of rides in an amusement park, the seat-miles on an airline, or the dollar sales in a variety store.

Variable Costs

If Watkins Products pays its door-to-door salesmen a 40 per cent straight commission, then the total cost of sales commissions should be 40 per cent of the sales dollars. If a garden shop buys bags of weed killer at $2 each, then the total cost of weed killer should be $2 times the number of bags. These are variable costs. They are uniform *per unit*, but their total fluctuates in direct proportion to the total of the related activity or volume. These relationships are depicted graphically in Exhibit 7-1. The cost of most merchandise, materials, parts, and supplies, of many types of labor, and of commissions is variable.

Fixed Costs

If a manufacturer of picture tubes for color television rents a factory for $100,000 per year, then the unit cost of rent applicable to each tube will depend on the total number of tubes produced. If 100,000 tubes are produced, the unit cost will be $1; if 50,000 tubes are produced, $2. This

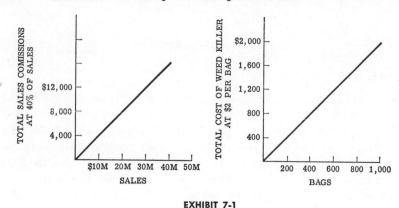

EXHIBIT 7-1

Variable Cost Behavior

is an example of a fixed cost, a cost which—like the cost of the senior dance—does not change in total but becomes progressively smaller on a *per unit* basis as volume increases. Real estate taxes, real estate insurance, many executive salaries, and most depreciation charges are fixed costs.

Relevant Range

A fixed cost is fixed only in relationship to a given period of time—the budget period—and a given, though wide, range of activity called the relevant range. Fixed costs may change from budget year to budget year solely because of changes in insurance and property tax rates, executive salary levels, or rent levels. But these items are highly unlikely to change within a given year. In addition, the total budgeted fixed costs may be formulated on the basis of an expected activity level (i.e., volume), say, within a relevant planning range of 40,000 to 85,000 units of production per month. However, operations on either side of the range will result in major salary adjustments or in the layoff or hiring of personnel. In Exhibit 7-2, the total monthly fixed cost within the relevant range is $100,-000. If operations fell below 40,000 units, changes in personnel and salaries would slash fixed costs to $60,000. If operations rose above 85,000 units, increases in personnel and salaries would raise fixed costs to $110,000.

These assumptions—a given time period and a given range—are shown graphically at the top of Exhibit 7-2. The possibility that operations will be outside the relevant range is usually remote. Therefore, the three-level refinement at the top of Exhibit 7-2 is usually not graphed. A single horizontal line is usually extended throughout the plotted activity levels, as at the bottom of the exhibit.

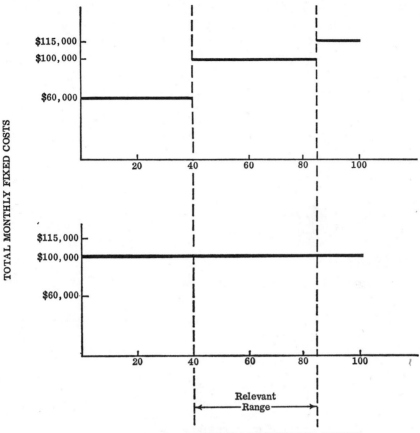

ACTIVITY IN THOUSANDS OF UNITS PER MONTH

EXHIBIT 7-2

Fixed Costs and the Relevant Range

Some Simplifying Assumptions

Nearly every organization has some variable costs and some fixed costs. As you may suspect, it is often difficult to classify a cost as exactly variable or exactly fixed. We shall investigate this problem in the next chapter; for now, we shall assume that any cost may be classified as either variable or fixed.

ILLUSTRATION OF COST-VOLUME-PROFIT ANALYSIS

The following situation will be used to demonstrate the techniques and analytical power of cost-volume-profit analysis. This problem is based on the actual analysis used by a Midwestern company in locating outlets.

A chain of gasoline stations which sell premium gasoline only is centrally owned. The stations are rented. The decision at hand is the desirability of opening another station which would have the following revenue and expense relationships:

	Per Gallon	Per Cent of Sales
Sales price	$ .30	100
Cost of gasoline, including taxes and delivery	.24	80
Gross profit (also the contribution margin in this case)	$ .06	20
Monthly fixed expenses:		
Rent	$ 600	
Electricity for 24-hour operation	150	
Wages, 7 men @ $72 per week	2,184	
Payroll fringe costs	175	
Other fixed costs	491	
Total fixed costs	$3,600	

Required:

1. Express the monthly break-even point in number of gallons and in dollar sales.
2. Graph the cost-volume-profit relationships in Question 1.
3. If the rent were doubled, what would be the monthly break-even point:
   a. In number of gallons?
   b. In dollar sales?
4. Assume that rent is unchanged.
   a. If the station manager is paid 1¢ per gallon as commission, what is the monthly break-even point in number of gallons? In dollar sales?
   b. If the selling price fell from 30¢ to 29¢, and the original variable expenses were unchanged, what is the monthly break-even point, in number of gallons? In dollar sales?
5. Refer to the original data. If the company considered $480 per month the minimum acceptable net income, how many gallons would have to be sold to warrant the opening of the station? Convert your answer into dollar sales.
6. Refer to the original data. Management is trying to decide whether a 24-hour operation is desirable. The closing of the station from 11:00 P.M. to 7:00 A.M. would reduce electricity costs by $70, and payroll and payroll fringe costs (one man) by $350. However, monthly sales would decline by 10,000 gallons. Should the 24-hour operation be continued? Assume that current sales on a 24-hour basis are:
   a. 62,000 gallons.
   b. 90,000 gallons.

1. Break-even Point—Two Techniques

The study of cost-volume-profit relationships is often called *break-even analysis.* The latter is a misnomer because the break-even point —the point of zero net income—is often only incidental to the planning decision at hand. Still, knowledge of the break-even point provides insights into the possible riskiness of certain courses of action.

There are three basic techniques for computing a break-even point: equation, unit contribution, and graphical. The graphical technique is shown in the solution to Question 2.

a. *Equation technique.* This is the most general approach, the one that may be adapted to any conceivable cost-volume-profit situation. You are familiar with a typical income statement. Any income statement can be expressed in equation form, as follows:

Sales = Variable expenses + Fixed expenses + Net profit   (1)
Let X = Number of gallons to be sold to break even
Then $\$.30X = \$.24X + \$3,600 + 0$
$\$.06X = \$3,600 + 0$

$$X = \frac{\$3,600 + 0}{\$.06}$$

$X = 60,000$ gallons

The same equation may be used to obtain the sales in dollars:

Let X = Sales in dollars needed to break even
$X = .80X + \$3,600$
$.20X = \$3,600 + 0$

$$X = \frac{\$3,600 + 0}{.20}$$

$X = \$18,000$

b. *Unit contribution technique.* If algebra is not one of your strong points, you may prefer to approach cost-volume-profit relationships in the following common-sense arithmetic manner. Every unit sold generates a *contribution margin* or *marginal income,* which is the excess of the sales price over the *variable* expenses pertaining to the unit in question:

Unit sales price	$.30
Unit variable expenses	.24
Unit contribution margin to fixed expenses and net profit	$.06

The $.06 unit contribution is divided into total fixed expenses plus a target net profit to obtain the number of units which must be sold to break even: $(\$3,600 + 0) \div \$.06 = 60,000$ units.
The computation in terms of dollar sales is similar:

Sales price	100%
Variable cost as a percentage of dollar sales	80%
Contribution margin ratio	20%

Therefore, 20 per cent of each sales dollar is the amount available for the recovery of fixed expenses and the making of net profit: ($3,600 + 0) ÷ .20 = $18,000 sales needed to break even.

Of course, the dollar sales answer *in this case* could be obtained in shortcut fashion by multiplying 60,000 gallons by $.30, which also yields the break-even dollar sales of $18,000. However, you should study the equation method of getting answers in dollars, because often no information on the number of units is given. Most companies sell more than one product, and the over-all break-even point is often expressed in sales dollars because of the variety of product lines. For example, although radios and television sets cannot be meaningfully added, their sales prices provide an automatic common denominator.

c. *Relationship of two techniques.* Reflect on the relationship of the equation technique and the unit contribution technique. The unit contribution technique is merely a shortcut version of the equation technique. Look at the second-last line in the solutions to Equation (1). They read:

Target Volume

In Units	*In Dollars*
$.06X = \$3,600 + 0$	$.20X = \$3,600 + 0$
$X = \dfrac{\$3,600 + 0}{\$.06}$	$X = \dfrac{\$3,600 + 0}{.20}$

SHORTCUT FORMULAS

This gives us the shortcut general formulas:

$$\text{Target volume in units} = \frac{\text{Fixed expenses} + \text{Net profit}}{\text{Contribution margin per unit}} \quad (2)$$

$$\text{Target volume in dollars} = \frac{\text{Fixed expenses} + \text{Net profit}}{\text{Contribution margin ratio}} \quad (3)$$

Which should you use, the equation or the unit contribution technique? Use either; the choice is a matter of personal preference.

2. Graphical Technique

The relationships in this problem may be depicted on a graph. The break-even point is represented by the intersection of the sales line and the total expenses line in Exhibits 7-3 and 7-4.

Exhibit 7-4 was constructed by using a sales line and a total expenses line that combined variable and fixed expenses. The procedure (see Exhibit 7-3) is as follows:

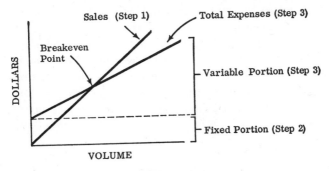

EXHIBIT 7-3

Cost-Volume-Profit Graph

Step 1. Plot the revenue (i.e., Sales) line.

Step 2. Determine where the line showing the Fixed Portion of expenses should intersect the vertical axis. Insert a dashed horizontal line to represent fixed expenses.

Step 3. Determine the Variable Portion of expenses at any single level of activity other than zero. Plot this on top of the fixed expenses. Draw a line between this point and the fixed cost intercept of the vertical axis. This is the Total Expenses line.

Exhibit 7-4 is the complete break-even chart. The break-even point is only one facet of this cost-volume-profit chart, which shows the profit or loss at any rate of activity. At any given volume, the vertical

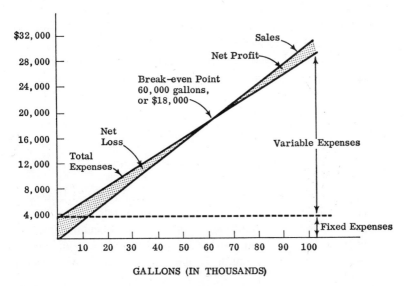

EXHIBIT 7-4

Complete Cost-Volume-Profit Chart

distance between the sales line and the total expenses line measures the net income or net loss.

The chart portrays only one of a number of methods for picturing cost-volume-profit variable expenses relationships. The chart often has educational advantages because it shows potential profits over a wide range of volume more easily than numerical exhibits. Whether graphs or other types of exhibits are used depends largely on management's preference.

3. Changes in Fixed Expenses

Reread and try to answer Question 3 before reading on.

The fixed expenses would increase from $3,600 to $4,200. Then:

$$\text{Target volume in units} = \frac{\text{Fixed expenses} + \text{Net profit}}{\text{Contribution margin per unit}} = \frac{\$4,200}{\$.06} = 70,000 \text{ gallons} \qquad (2)$$

$$\text{Target volume in dollars} = \frac{\text{Fixed expenses} + \text{Net profit}}{\text{Contribution margin ratio}} = \frac{\$4,200}{.20} = \$21,000 \qquad (3)$$

Note that a one-sixth increase in fixed expenses altered the break-even point by one-sixth: from 60,000 to 70,000 gallons and from $18,000 to $21,000.

4. Changes in Contribution Margin per Unit

Reread and try to answer Question 4 before reading on.

a. The variable expenses would be $.25, the unit contribution margin would be $.05, and the contribution margin ratio would be 16.67 per cent ($.05 ÷ $.30).

The original fixed expenses of $3,600 would be unaffected, but the denominators are changed as compared with the denominators used in the Solutions to Questions 1 and 3. Thus:

$$\text{Break-even point in units} = \frac{\$3,600}{\$.05} = 72,000 \text{ gallons} \qquad (2)$$

$$\text{Break-even point in dollars} = \frac{\$3,600}{.1667} = \$21,600 \qquad (3)$$

b. A change in unit contribution margin could also be caused by a change in selling price. If the selling price fell from $.30 to $.29, and the original variable expenses were unchanged, the unit contribution would still be $.05 (i.e., $.29 − $.24) and the break-even point would remain 72,000 gallons. However, the break-even point in dollars would change, because the selling price and contribution margin ratio change: the contribution margin ratio would be 17.24 + per cent ($.05 ÷ $.29). The break-even point, in dollars, would be 72,000 gallons × $.29, or $20,880, using the formula:

$$\text{Break-even point in dollars} = \frac{\$3,600}{.1724+} = \$20,880 \qquad (3)$$

5. Target Net Profit and an Incremental Approach

If the company considered $480 per month as the minimum acceptable net income, how many gallons would have to be sold to warrant the opening of the new station? What is your answer in terms of sales dollars?

$$\begin{matrix}\text{Target sales} \\ \text{volume} \\ \text{in units}\end{matrix} = \frac{\text{Fixed expenses} + \text{Net profit}}{\text{Contribution margin per unit}} = \frac{\$3,600 + \$480}{\$.06} = 68,000 \text{ gallons} \quad (2)$$

Another way of getting the same answer is to use your knowledge of the break-even point and adopt an incremental approach. If 60,000 gallons is the break-even point, all fixed expenses would be recovered at that volume. Therefore, every gallon beyond 60,000 would represent a unit contribution to *net profit* of $.06. If $480 were the target net profit, $480 ÷ $.06 would show that the target volume must exceed the break-even volume by 8,000 gallons.

The answer, in terms of dollar sales, can then be computed by multiplying 68,000 gallons by $.30, or by using the formula:

$$\begin{matrix}\text{Target sales} \\ \text{volume} \\ \text{in dollars}\end{matrix} = \frac{\text{Fixed expenses} + \text{Net profit}}{\text{Contribution margin ratio}} = \frac{\$3,600 + \$480}{\$.20} = \$20,400 \quad (2)$$

In the alternative incremental approach, the break-even point, $18,000, is a frame of reference. Every sales dollar beyond that point contributes $.20 to net profit. Divide $480 by $.20. The dollar sales must exceed the break-even volume by $2,400 to produce a net profit of $480.

6. Multiple Changes in the Key Factors

Reread and try to answer Question 6 before reading on.

First, whether 62,000 or 90,000 gallons are being sold is irrelevant to the decision at hand. The analysis of this situation consists of constructing and solving equations for conditions that prevail under either alternative and selecting the volume level that yields the highest net profit. However, the incremental approach is much quicker. What is the essence of this decision? We are asking whether the prospective savings in cost exceed the prospective loss in contribution margin:

Lost contribution margin, 10,000 gallons @ $.06 $600
Savings in fixed expenses   420
Prospective decline in net income $180

Regardless of the current volume level, whether it be 62,000 or 90,000 gallons, the closing of our station from 11:00 P.M. to 7:00 A.M., assuming that the prediction that sales will decline by 10,000 gallons is accurate, will decrease the profit by $180:

	Decline from 62,000 to 52,000 gallons		*Decline from 90,000 to 80,000 gallons*	
Gallons	62,000	52,000	90,000	80,000
Sales	$18,600	$15,600	$27,000	$24,000
Variable expenses	14,880	12,480	21,600	19,200
Contribution margin	$ 3,720	$ 3,120	$ 5,400	$ 4,800
Fixed expenses	3,600	3,180	3,600	3,180
Net income	$ 120	$ (60)	$ 1,800	$ 1,620
Change in net income		($180)		($180)

USES AND LIMITATIONS OF COST-VOLUME ANALYSIS

Optimum Combination of Factors

The analysis of cost-volume-profit relationships is one of management's paramount responsibilities. The knowledge of patterns of cost behavior offers insights valuable in planning and controlling short- and long-run operations. This is a major theme of this book, so we should regard the current material as introductory. Our purpose in this chapter is to provide perspective, rather than to impart an intimate knowledge of the niceties of cost behavior.

The example of the gasoline station demonstrated some valuable applications of cost-volume-profit analysis. One of management's principal duties is to discover the most profitable combination of the variable and fixed cost factors. For example, a sales force may be expanded to reach markets directly, instead of through wholesalers, thereby increasing unit sales prices. Or automated machinery may be purchased, to reduce labor cost per unit. On the other hand, it may be wise to reduce fixed costs in order to obtain a more favorable combination. Thus, direct selling by a salaried sales force may be supplanted by the use of manufacturers' agents.

The quest for flexibility is also unending. Ideally, perhaps, the best combination consists of no fixed costs, fantastically high selling prices, tiny variable costs, and unlimited potential sales volume. The least desirable combination consists of high fixed costs, low selling prices, high variable costs, and limited potential sales volume. Most businesses are somewhere between these poles.

Generally, companies which spend heavily for advertising have high contribution margins (e.g., cigarette and cosmetic companies). Companies with low advertising and sales promotion outlays do not usually have high contribution margins (e.g., manufacturers of industrial equipment). The size of the contribution margin influences such outlays. Obviously, a company with a volume of 100,000 units and a contribution margin of $.10 per unit is not going to risk the same promotional outlay to obtain, say, a 10 per cent increase in volume as a company with a contribution margin of $.90 per unit.

Therefore, when the contribution margin ratio is low, great increases in volume are necessary before noticeable increases in net profits can occur. As sales exceed the break-even point, a high contribution margin ratio increases profits faster than a small contribution margin ratio.

Limiting Assumptions

The notion of *relevant range,* which was introduced when fixed costs were discussed, is applicable to the entire break-even chart. Almost all break-even charts have lines extending back to the vertical axis. This is misleading, because the relationships depicted in such graphs are valid only within the relevant range that underlies the construction of the graph. Exhibit 7-5(a), a modification of the conventional break-even

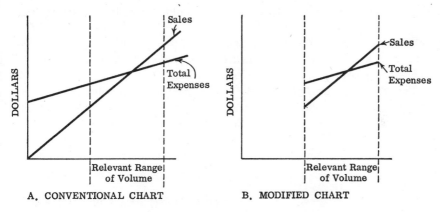

A. CONVENTIONAL CHART   B. MODIFIED CHART

EXHIBIT 7-5

Conventional and Modified Break-even Charts

chart (Exhibit 7-5(b)) partially demonstrates the multitude of assumptions that must be made in constructing the typical break-even chart.

Some of these assumptions are:

1. The behavior of revenues and expenses is accurately portrayed and is linear over the relevant range. The principal difference between the accountant's break-even chart and the economist's are: (*a*) The accountant's sales line is drawn on the assumption that prices do not change with production or sales, and the economist assumes that price changes may be

needed to spur sales; (*b*) the accountant usually assumes a constant variable expense per unit, and the economist assumes that variable expense changes with production.

2. Expenses may be classified into variable and fixed categories. Total variable expenses vary directly with volume. Total fixed expenses do not change with volume.
3. Efficiency and productivity will be unchanged.
4. Sales mix will be constant. The *sales mix* is the relative combination of quantities of a variety of company products that compose total sales.
5. The difference in inventory level at the beginning and at the end of a period is insignificant. (The impact of inventory changes on cost-volume-profit analysis is discussed in Chapter 15).

SUMMARY

An understanding of cost behavior patterns and cost-volume-profit relationships can deepen a manager's comprehension and can guide his decisions.

Variable costs and fixed costs have contrasting behavior patterns. Their relationship to sales, volume, and net income is probably best seen on a cost-volume-profit chart. However, the chart should be used with great care. The portrayal of all profit-influencing factors on such a chart entails many assumptions that may hold over only a relatively narrow range of volume. As a tool, the chart may be compared to a meat-ax rather than to a surgeon's scalpel. Cost-volume-profit analysis, as depicted on a chart, is a framework for analysis, a vehicle for appraising over-all performance, and a planning device.

The assumptions that underlie typical cost-volume-profit analysis are static. A change in one assumption (e.g., total fixed costs or the unit price of raw materials) will affect all the cost-volume-profit relationships on a given chart. The static nature of these assumptions should always be remembered by the managers who use this valuable analytical technique.

SUMMARY PROBLEM FOR YOUR REVIEW

PROBLEM

The income statement of Wiley Mitchell Co. is summarized as follows:

Net revenue	$800,000
Less: Expenses, including $400,000 of fixed expenses	880,000
Net loss	$ (80,000)

The manager believes that an increase of $200,000 in advertising outlays will increase sales substantially. His plan was approved by the chairman of the board.

Required:

a. At what sales volume will the company break even?
b. What sales volume will result in a net profit of $40,000?

SOLUTION

(*a*) Note that all data are expressed in dollars. No unit data are given. Most companies have many products, so the over-all break-even analysis deals with dollar sales, not units. The variable expenses are $880,000 − $400,000, or $480,000. The variable expense ratio is $480,000 ÷ $800,000, or .60. Therefore, the contribution margin ratio is .40.

$$\text{Let } S = \text{Break-even sales, in dollars}$$
$$\text{Then } S = \text{Variable expenses} + \text{Fixed expenses} + \text{Net profit} \quad (1)$$
$$S = .60S + (\$400,000 + \$200,000) + 0$$
$$.40S = \$600,000 + 0$$

$$S = \frac{\$600,000 + 0}{.40} = \frac{\text{Fixed expenses} + \text{Target net profit}}{\text{Contribution margin ratio}} \quad (3)$$

$$S = \$1,500,000$$

(*b*) $$\text{Required sales} = \frac{\text{Fixed expenses} + \text{Target net profit}}{\text{Contribution margin ratio}} \quad (3)$$

$$\text{Then Required sales} = \frac{\$600,000 + \$40,000}{.40} = \frac{\$640,000}{.40}$$

$$\text{Required sales} = \$1,600,000$$

Alternatively, we can use an incremental approach and reason that all dollar sales beyond the $1,500,000 break-even point will result in a 40 per cent contribution to net profit. Divide $40,000 by .40. Sales must be $100,000 beyond the $1,500,000 break-even point in order to produce a net profit of $40,000.

SUGGESTED READINGS

Much has been written on this subject. Therefore, the following suggestions are only a sampling. The National Association of Accountants' pamphlet is particularly valuable. The two books contain helpful analysis and description of cost-volume profit relationships.

The Analysis of Cost-Volume-Profit Relationships. National Association of Accountants. New York, 1950.

Tse, J., *Profit Planning Through Volume-Cost Analysis.* New York: The Macmillan Company, 1960.

Welsch, G., *Budgeting: Profit-planning and Control* (2nd ed.). Englewood Cliffs, N.J.: Prentice-Hall, Inc., 1964.

ESSENTIAL ASSIGNMENT MATERIAL

7-1. *Terminology.* Define: fixed cost; relevant range; contribution margin; marginal income; and variable cost.

7-2. *Cost-volume-profits and vending machines.* The Vendit Co. operates and services cigarette vending machines located in restaurants, gas stations, factories, etc. The vending machines are rented from the manufacturer. In addition, Vendit must rent the space occupied by its machines. The following expense and revenue relationships pertain to a contemplated expansion program of 20 machines.

Fixed monthly expenses:

Machine rental: 20 machines @ $26.75	$ 535
Space rental: 20 locations @ $14.40	288
Wages to service the additional 20 machines: 1 man @ $90 per week	390
Payroll fringe costs: 10 per cent	39
Other fixed costs	44
Total monthly fixed costs	$1,296

Gross profit data:

	Per Package	Per $100 of Sales
Selling price	$ .30	100%
Cost of cigarettes	.21	70%
Gross profit (Contribution margin in this case)	$ .09	30%

Required:

These questions relate to the above data unless otherwise noted. Consider each question independently.

1. What is the monthly break-even point in dollar sales? In number of packages?
2. If 20,000 packages were sold, what would be the company's net margin?
3. If the space rental were doubled, what would be the monthly break-even point in dollar sales? In number of packages?
4. If, in addition to the fixed rent, the vending machine manufacturer is also paid 1¢ per package sold, what is the monthly break-even point in dollar sales? In number of packages? Refer to the original data.
5. If, in addition to the fixed rent, the machine manufacturer is paid 1¢ for each package sold in excess of the break-even point, what would be Vendit's net margin be if 20,000 packages were sold? Refer to the original data.

7-3. *Exercises in cost-volume-profit relationships.* The Bauer Co. manufactures plastic dishpans for kitchen use. Following is the budget data for next year:

Sales	500,000 units
Selling price	$1 per unit
Fixed expenses	$60,000
Variable expenses	$.80 per unit

Required:

Compute the new profit for each of the following changes. Consider each case independently.

a. A $.10 increase in selling price.

b. A $.10 decrease in selling price.

c. A 12 per cent increase in sales volume.

d. A 12 per cent decrease in sales volume.

e. A $.05 increase in variable expenses per unit.

f. A $.05 decrease in variable expenses per unit.

g. A 10 per cent increase in fixed expenses.

h. A 10 per cent decrease in fixed expenses.

i. A 12 per cent decrease in sales volume and a $.10 increase in selling price.

j. A decrease of $.05 per unit in variable expenses and a $.10 decrease in selling price.

k. A 10 per cent increase in fixed expenses and a 12 per cent increase in sales volume.

l. An increase of $.05 per unit in variable expenses and a $.10 decrease in selling price.

7-4. *Fixed, variable, and unit costs.*

1. Kohlmeier Engineering Consultants has a substantial year-to-year fluctuation in billings. Top management has the following policy regarding the employment of key personnel and staff engineers:

Number of Engineers	Engineers' Salaries	Gross Annual Billings
4	$60,000	$100,000 or less
5	$70,000	$100,001-$200,000
6	$80,000	$200,001 or more

For the past four years, gross annual billings have fluctuated between $120,000 and $180,000. You are preparing a budget for the coming year. Expectations are that gross billings will be between $165,000 and $185,000. What amount should be budgeted for engineers' salaries? Graph the relationships on an annual basis using:

a. Refined analysis.

b. The analysis that would be shown in practice.

Indicate the relevant range on each graph. You need not use graph paper; simply approximate the graphical relationships.

2. Do you agree with the following? Why, or why not? Be specific.

As I understand it, costs like the manufacturing vice-president's salary are variable because the more you produce, the less your unit cost. In contrast, costs like lumber in a furniture factory are fixed because, say, each dining room table made should contain approximately the same amount of lumber and hence bear the same unit cost.

ADDITIONAL ASSIGNMENT MATERIAL

Note: Problems 7-15 and 7-22 are probably the most unusual. Problem 7-15 deals with the relationships between price changes and volume. Problem 7-22 deals with the sales mix.

7-5. What is meant by unit cost?

7-6. Distinguish between variable and fixed costs.

7-7. Why is "break-even analysis" a misnomer?

7-8. Distinguish between the equation technique and the unit contribution technique.

7-9. What is the difference between conventional and modified break-even charts?

7-10. What are the principal differences between the accountant's and the economist's break-even charts?

7-11. What is sales mix?

7-12. What is the general guide for expressing unit costs?

7-13. What is meant by an optimum combination of factors?

7-14. *Cost-volume-profit relationships.* The Alpha Beta Gamma Fraternity has been charging a house bill of $110 a month and wishes to do so next year. The variable expense per member per month is $70. The fixed expenses of running the fraternity house are $1,240 per month.

The fraternity house holds thirty members. If there are more members than thirty, the fraternity can rent apartments at $100 per month. Each apartment can hold three persons. The variable expense per person living in an apartment is also $70.

Required:

How many members should the fraternity plan to have next year in order to break even?

7-15. *Cost-volume-profit and demand relationships.* The Ajax Metal Co. is the only supplier of a rare metal. Ajax can influence the amount of the product which it sells by manipulating the price. Market studies show that the number of pounds of metal which can be sold at a price of p dollars per pound is $10,000 \div p$. The variable costs of sales are $1 per pound, regardless of the level of output. Fixed expenses are $6,000.

Required:

1. At what price will the company have zero net income?

2. What is the profit when the price is $4 per pound?

3. What price should the company set to make a profit of $2,000?

7-16. *Cost-volume-profit relationships and a dog track.* The Multnomah Kennel Club is a dog-racing track. Its revenue is derived mainly from attendance and a fixed percentage of the pari-mutuel betting. Its expenses for a 90-day season are:

Wages of cashiers and ticket takers	$150,000
Commissioner's salary	20,000
Maintenance (repairs, etc.)	20,000
Utilities	30,000
Other expenses (depreciation, insurance, advertising, etc.)	100,000
Purses: Total prizes paid to winning racers	810,000

The track made a contract with the Auto Parking Association to park the cars. Auto Parking charged the track 15¢ per car. A survey revealed that on the average three persons arrived in each car and that there were no other means of transportation except by private automobiles.

The track's sources of revenue are:

Rights for concession and vending	$50,000
Admission charge	25¢ per person
Percentage of bets placed	10%

Required:

1. Assuming that each person bets $25 a night:
   (a) How many persons have to be admitted for the track to break even for the season?
   (b) What is the total contribution margin at the break-even point?
   (c) If the desired profit for the year is $540,000, how many people would have to attend?

2. If a policy of free admission brought a 10 per cent increase in attendance, what would be the new level of profit? Assume that the previous level of attendance was 600,000 people.

3. If the purses were doubled in an attempt to attract better dogs and thus increase attendance, what would be the new break-even point? Refer to the original data and assume that each person bets $25 a night.

7-17. *Cost-volume-profit analysis and barbering.* Sidney's Barber Shop has five barbers. (Sidney is not one of them.) Each barber is paid $3 per hour and works a 40-hour week and a 50-week year. Depreciation on store fixtures is $500 annually and depreciation on equipment is $1,000 annually. Rent is $100 per month. Since the shop is located in the area of a large Midwestern university and the clientele is almost exclusively students, the only service performed is the giving of haircuts, the unit price of which is $2.

Required:

1. Contribution margin, per haircut.
2. Annual break-even point, in number of haircuts.
3. What will be net income if 20,000 haircuts are given?
4. Suppose the landlord decides to revise the monthly rent to $95 + 10¢ per haircut. What is the new contribution margin, per haircut? What is the annual break-even point (in number of haircuts)?
5. Ignore (3) and (4), and assume that the barbers cease to be paid by the hour but receive a 50 per cent commission for each haircut. What is the new contribution margin per haircut? The annual break-even point (in number of haircuts)?

7-18. *Cost-volume-profit relationships and vending machines.* The Valet-Vendor Vending Co. operates and services vending machines located in theaters, restaurants, factories, airports, etc. The machines sell razors, toothbrushes, fingernail clippers, handkerchiefs, and combs. The machines are purchased from the manufacturer at a cost of $300 each and have a useful life of five years. They have no disposal value. The company rents the space occupied by the machines for 10 per cent of gross sales. The following expense and revenue relationships pertain to a contemplated expansion program of ten machines.

		Per Unit
Selling price		$.50
Cost of item	$.28	
Rental commission	.05	.33
Contribution margin		$.17
Yearly fixed expenses:		
Depreciation on machines		$ 600
Wages (1 man @ $390 per month)		4,680
Other fixed costs		120
Total fixed costs		$5,400

Required:

Consider each question independently.

1. What is the monthly break-even point, in dollar sales? In number of units?
2. If the company sold 5,000 units per month, what would the net income be?
3. If the rental commission were doubled, what would be the monthly break-even point, in dollar sales? In number of units?
4. If, in addition to the rental commission, the building owners are also paid $60 per year as a fixed rent, what is the monthly break-even point in dollar sales? In number of units? Refer to the original data.
5. If, in addition to the rental commission, the building owners are paid 1¢ per unit sold in excess of the break-even point, how many units would the company have to sell to have a net margin of $160 per month? Refer to the original data.

7-19. *Adding a product to the sales mix.* Jiminy's Greenlawn Tap, a pub located in a college community, serves as a gathering place for the university's more social scholars. Jiminy sells beer on draft and all brands of bottled beer at a contribution margin of 15¢ a beer.

Jiminy is considering also selling hamburgers. His reasons are twofold. First, sandwiches would attract daytime customers. A hamburger and a beer are a quick lunch. Second, he has to meet competition from other local bars, some of which provide more extensive menus.

Jiminy owns an old stove and refrigerator. The stove is valued at $250, the refrigerator at $50. They can be put into working condition at a negligible cost, but at the end of one year, they will not be worth the repairs they will need.

Selling Price	30¢ per hamburger
Monthly fixed expenses:	
Wages, additional man as cook	$320
Depreciation on stove and refrigerator	25
Total	$345

Variable expenses per hamburger:	
Rolls	3¢
Meat @ 70¢ per lb. (7 hamburgers per pound)	10¢
Other	2¢
Total	15¢

Required:

For all questions, assume a thirty-day month.

1. What are the monthly and daily break-even points, in number of hamburgers?
2. What are the monthly and daily break-even points, in dollar sales?
3. At the end of two months, Jiminy finds he has sold 3,600 hamburgers. What is his net profit margin per month on hamburgers?
4. Jiminy thinks that at least thirty extra beers are sold per day because he has these hamburgers available. This means that thirty extra people come to the bar or that thirty buy an extra beer because they are attracted by the hamburgers. How does this affect Jiminy's monthly income?

7-20. *Hospital cost-volume-profit relationships.* Dr. Brown and Dr. Black, the two radiologists of the San Susi Hospital, have submitted the following costs for operating the Department of Radiology:

Radiologists' salary	30% of gross receipts
Technicians' and clerical salaries	$70,000
Supplies (fixed)	80,000
Depreciation	60,000

This year the department processed 65,000 films with three 200-milli-ampere X-ray machines. (Their original cost was $200,000 each, their life ten years.) For these processed films, the average charge was $6. The 65,000 films represent maximum volume possible with the present equipment.

Drs. Brown and Black have submitted a request for two new 300-milli-ampere X-ray machines. (Their cost will be $250,000 each, their life ten years.) They will increase the capacity of the department by 35,000 films per year. Because of their special attachments (i.e., fluoroscopes) it will be possible to take more intricate films, for which a higher charge will be made. The average charge to the patient for each of these additional 35,000 films is estimated at $10. In order to operate the new machines, two highly trained technicians must be hired at an annual salary of $7,500 per year. The added capacity will increase the cost of supplies by $20,000.

Required:

1. Determine the break-even point in films for the three 200-milliampere X-ray machines. How much do they contribute to the hospital's over-all profits?
2. Determine the break-even point if the two new 300-milliampere X-ray machines are added to the department. How much will be contributed to the hospital's over-all profit, assuming they are operated at maximum volume?

7-21. *Concessionaire operations at baseball parks.* The Hammy Bear Beer Distributing Co. handles the beer concessions at both the local Sweat Sox and Cubbie baseball parks. Weather reports and the Farmers Almanac forecast unseasonably warm weather for the next month. The company, sensing a potential increase in normal monthly beer sales, has taken the necessary action in order to prepare and be ready to take advantage of this opportunity to increase sales. They have scheduled another delivery truck to deliver the additional volume of beer. The only other adjustment needed was the addition of 20 additional vendors to hawk their liquid refreshment in the stands. Because the schedule is such that at no time do both teams play at home at the same time, this crew of vendors works at both parks.

The company has to go to an agency called the Sportsmans Syndicate for their vendors, because this agency has a monopoly on supplying service personnel to the parks. It costs Hammy $400 per vendor per month to obtain the right to employ these vendors. He usually employs 30 vendors. The Hammy Company also pays each vendor a commission of 20 per cent of gross sales. The company also has to pay the owners of each ball park $1,500 a month for the privilege of carrying on their business in the ball parks. Other fixed costs incurred monthly by the Hammy Company total $1,000. The cost of a case of 24 bottles of beer, to the Hammy Company, is $3.00. Its selling price at the ball parks is 50¢ a bottle.

Required:

1. What is the Hammy Co.'s break-even point in dollars? In cases? In bottles?
2. If gross sales next month are 10,000 cases, what is the company's net margin?
3. The company is considering paying each vendor $220 per month, plus 10 per cent commission, instead of the usual payment plan of 20 per cent commission. Compare the break-even points, in cases, for the two payment plans, and explain why one is higher than the other.

7-22. *Cost-volume-profit chart and sales mix.* A firm sells two products, A and B, at unit prices of $9.24 and $7.69, respectively. The sales of A and B are simultaneous, and always in a 1 to 4 ratio. The over-all contribution margin ratio is 40 per cent, and the break-even point is 15,000 units.

Required:

1. Given the above conditions, what are the dollar amounts appropriate to points x, y, and z in the graph?

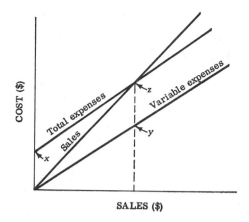

2. How many units, in total together, of *A* and *B* must be sold in order to arrive at a profit of $24,000 if:
   a. The selling prices now prevailing are maintained.
   b. By incurring some extra shipping and sales commission costs, the company can boost volume. The incidence of these costs would be an extra $1.24 per unit for each unit of product *A* sold in excess of 3,000 per year and an extra $.69 per unit for each unit of product *B* sold in excess of 12,000 units per year.
3. Assume that the break-even point is 15,000 units under either Plan 2(a) or Plan 2(b). Beyond the break-even point, the total units sold under Plan 2(b) will exceed the total under Plan 2(a) by 40 per cent. Which pricing plan is more profitable, 2a or 2b? Show computations.

7-23. Electromagic Co., an appliance dealer, has always sold its merchandise through four company-operated stores. Last year sales were $1 million and net profit was 8 per cent of sales. Fixed costs were $170,000.

As a result of shifting population and increased competition, the four locations have become less desirable. Electromagic is considering eliminating its retail stores in favor of door-to-door selling. It is estimated that sales would increase by 25 per cent and net profit by $30,000. Fixed costs would decrease by $80,000 because operations would be moved to a low-rent warehouse.

Required:

1. What was the break-even point under the old situation?
2. What will be the break-even point under the proposed situation?
3. What dollar sales volume must be obtained under the proposed plan to make as much profit as last year?

7-24. *Retailing in a shopping center.* George Pedi has operated a neighborhood shoe store in the same location for the past 20 years. Business is very steady. Rent is $1,000 a month. Last year's income statement was as follows:

Sales		$100,000
Cost of goods sold		50,000
Gross margin		$ 50,000
Operating expenses		
Variable	$11,000	
Fixed	32,000	43,000
Net income		$ 7,000

George has the opportunity to move into substantially larger quarters in a large shopping center that is being established in the same general area. He figures that fixed expenses, excluding rent, will increase by $5,000 a year if the move is made. Variable expenses and cost of goods sold would remain at the present percentage of sales. A two-year lease for the new location would have to be signed, with the following provisions:

a. Base rent of $500 monthly, plus

b. 6 per cent of sales through $175,000 and 8 per cent of sales over $175,000, plus

c. Contribution to maintenance and promotion overhead of $2,000 yearly plus 1 per cent of sales volume in excess of $50,000.

Required:

From the data given,

1. What would George's profit be if his volume of sales totaled $100,000? $200,000?

2. What would be the volume needed to make the same net income as last year?

3. What is the most crucial single factor that will influence George's decision?

7-25. *The case of the advertising agency.* Three advertising men, Smith, Cummings, and Combs, have formed an agency in which they are to be equal stockholders. The new agency advises its customers on the media for their ads and submits copy, layout, and rough design for approval. The Smith, Cummings, and Combs Agency charges the standard 15 per cent of media billings for their services. For example, an advertisement that is billed by *Life* magazine for $10,000 would be subject to a 15 per cent agency commission. The agency would be billed by *Life*, would pay $8,500, and in turn would bill the client for the full $10,000. Total charges to customers include:

Billings (media costs, including 15 per cent agency commission)		xxx
Production charges (work done outside the agency)		
Finished art work	xx	
Typesetting	xx	
Engraving	xx	xxx
Total charges		xxx

To help serve the nucleus of customers who have followed the owners from their previous employments, two account executives are hired. The two, Brand and Reed, are each paid $4,000 per year plus three-fourths of 1 per cent of all the agency's media billings. Brand, Reed, and the three owners entertain the agency's clients at a fishing lodge maintained, for that purpose, at an annual cost of $900. In addition, the agency pays $1,400 annually for memberships in clubs where clients are entertained. Other annual costs are:

Office rent	$ 4,800
Subscriptions to readership surveys and service publications	470
Clerical and administrative expenses	14,500
Production chief's salary	8,700
Copywriters' salary (2 @ $9,400)	18,800
Property tax and insurance	480
Salaries of Smith, Cummings, and Combs	81,000

Required:

1. What media billings are needed to break even?
2. Smith, Cummings, and Combs believe they can expand their services and profits if they set up their own art department. The art department would use a converted storage room adjacent to the offices. Rent would be $75 a month, and insurance and property tax would be another $30 per annum. For $130 annually, a messenger service would ferry art work between agency and clients. Materials are expected to cost 1 per cent of art work charges. The partners agree to charge $6 per hour for work done in the art department.
   (a) Cummings estimates that the art break-even point is billings of $14,454. How much per hour does he plan to pay the artists?
   (b) Smith has determined that art work billings of $25,914 will yield a profit of $3,000, with a contribution margin ratio of .157. How much per hour does Smith plan to pay the artists?

CHAPTER 8

Cost Behavior:
A Closer
Look

ACCOUNTANTS AND OPERATING MANAGERS HAVE DISCOVERED that the most important single aspect of intelligent attention directing and problem solving is the knowledge of cost behavior patterns and influences. We shall now pursue the overview that we obtained in the previous chapter by examining the types of cost behavior in more detail. We shall study the major factors which influence cost incurrence. We shall also consider some techniques for detecting cost behavior. In order to develop an expectation of what costs should be, it is first necessary to study the behavior of individual costs. If a behavior pattern can be delineated, then a useful plan may be formulated. Although there are no pat answers in this area, there are useful and practical approaches to cost behavior.

All the definitions in this chapter assume the existence of a given, wide range of probable activity levels, called the *relevant range,* and of a given budget period, usually a year. The notion of variable and fixed costs will be retained, but we shall begin by examining each category in some detail.

TYPES OF VARIABLE COSTS

Examples of Variable Costs

Variable costs are those which are expected to fluctuate, in total, directly in proportion to sales, production volume, or *other measure of activity*. The last is emphasized because some items may be variable, but may lead or lag in relation to production or sales. For example, the number of service calls on product warranties will be a volume measure of that activity, but the volume of service calls in a given period may have no relation to the sales or production during the same period. Still, the cost of service calls is regarded as variable.

The classification of variable costs will depend on the type of organization. A few of the more commonly encountered variable items are:

Retailer or Wholesaler	*Manufacturer*

Merchandise cost of goods sold, including freight in	Manufacturing costs:
	   Prime costs
	     Direct material [1] [*]
	     Direct labor [2]
	   Variable indirect manufacturing costs (sometimes called variable factory overhead) [3a]
	     Power
	     Supplies
	     Rework labor
	     Idle time
	     Oiling and cleaning
	     Some repairs and maintenance

Selling and administrative costs:
   Sales commissions
   Shipping or delivery expenses
   Packaging supplies
   Warranty service
   Clerical costs
	Selling and administrative costs:
	   Same as retailer or wholesaler

[*] Reference numbers are keyed to the numbered items which are discussed in the next section.

Explanation of Variable Manufacturing Costs

Manufacturing cost terminology is specialized, so let us examine the terms carefully. There are three major elements in the cost of a manufactured product:

1. *Direct material.* This includes all raw material which is an integral part of the finished goods and which may be conveniently assigned to specific physical units (e.g., sheet steel, subassemblies). These materials are usually specified on a list of materials or on a blueprint. Certain minor materials, such as glue or nails, may be considered supplies or indirect material, rather than direct material, because of the impractical-

ity of tracing such items to specific physical units of product. They are usually included in indirect manufacturing costs.

The word "direct" as used in cost accounting differs considerably from company to company. In deciding whether any manufacturing cost is direct or indirect, we will find it helpful to assume "job order" manufacturing, where batches of unique goods are produced (e.g., furniture, jewelry, printing).

2. *Direct labor.* This includes all labor which is obviously related to and easily traceable to a specific product (e.g., the labor of machine operators and assemblers). This type of labor is usually specified on a Master Operations List or Routing sheet (Exhibit 8-1). Much labor (e.g.,

---

MASTER OPERATIONS LIST

Part name ___Fuel pump body with bushings___   Part number ___B-489___

Stock specifications___Grey iron casting___   Standard quantity ___200___

Operation Number	Department Number	Standard Time Allowed in Minutes		Description of Operation
		Setup	Operation Per Unit	
20	27	90	10.2	Drill, bore, face, chamfer and ream
25	29	18	.7	Face and chamfer hub
30	29	12	1.5	Mill eng. fit pad
35	31	18	8.0	Drill and tap complete
40	29	12	1.5	Mill clearance
45	29	-	1.8	Clean and grind hose connection
50	29	12	2.3	Press in 2 bushings G-98 and face flange on mandrel
	13			Inspect
	21			To stockroom

EXHIBIT 8-1

Master Operations List or Routing

---

of material handlers, janitors, and plant guards) is considered indirect labor because of the difficulty or impracticality of assigning the cost of their work to specific physical units. Their wages are therefore included in indirect' manufacturing costs.

The two elements—direct material and direct labor—are often combined in cost terminology and called *prime costs*.

3. *Indirect manufacturing costs*. This includes all manufacturing costs other than direct material and direct labor. Other terms used to describe this category are: *factory overhead, factory burden, manufacturing overhead*, and *manufacturing expenses*. There are two major types of indirect manufacturing costs:

    a. Variable factory overhead. The two principal examples are supplies and most indirect labor. Whether the cost of a specific category of indirect labor is variable or fixed depends on its behavior in a given company. In this book, unless we specify otherwise, indirect labor will be considered a variable rather than a fixed cost.

    b. Fixed factory overhead. Examples are supervisory salaries, property taxes, rent, insurance, and depreciation. Such costs are discussed later in the chapter, under the heading Types of Fixed Costs.

Admittedly, the area of manufacturing costs contains a thicket of new terms. One of your main tasks, in studying this chapter, is to assimilate these terms. At the moment, note particularly that the total *variable* manufacturing costs usually include the following: direct material; direct labor; and *variable indirect* manufacturing costs.

Subdivisions of Labor Costs

The terminology for labor costs is usually the most confusing. Each organization seems to develop its own interpretation of various labor cost classifications. We shall begin by considering some commonly encountered labor cost terminology.

For our purposes, we shall categorize the terminology as follows:

Direct labor (already defined)
Indirect labor:
        Fork-lift truck operators (internal handling of materials)
        Janitors
        Plant guards
        Rework labor (time spent by direct laborers redoing spoiled work)
        Overtime premium paid to *all* factory workers
        Idle time
Payroll fringe costs

All factory labor costs, other than those for direct labor, are usually classified as *indirect labor costs,* a major component of indirect manufacturing costs. The term "indirect labor" is usually broken down into many subsidiary classifications. The wages of fork-lift truck operators are generally not commingled with janitors' salaries, for example, although both are regarded as indirect labor.

Costs are classified in a detailed fashion primarily in the attempt to associate a specific cost with its specific cause, or reason for incurrence. Two classes of indirect labor need special mention. *Overtime premium* paid to *all* factory workers is usually considered a part of overhead. If a lathe operator earns $3 per hour for straight time, and time and one-half for overtime, his *premium* is $1.50 per overtime hour. If he works 44 hours, including 4 overtime hours, in one week, his gross earnings would be classified as follows:

Direct labor: 44 hours × $3	$132
Overtime premium (factory overhead): 4 hours × $1.50	6
Total earnings	$138

Why is overtime premium considered an indirect cost rather than direct? After all, it can usually be traced to specific batches of work. It is usually not considered a direct charge because the scheduling of production jobs is generally random. For example, assume that Jobs No. 1 through 5 are scheduled for a specific work-day of ten hours, including two overtime hours. Each job requires two hours. Should the job scheduled during hours 9 and 10 be assigned the overtime premium? Or should the premium be prorated over all the jobs? The latter approach does not penalize a particular batch of work solely because it happened to be worked on during the overtime hours. Instead, the overtime premium is considered to be attributable to the heavy over-all volume of work and its cost is thus regarded as factory overhead.

Another subsidiary classification of indirect labor costs is *idle time*. This cost typically represents wages paid for unproductive time caused by machine breakdowns, material shortages, sloppy production scheduling, and the like. For example, if the same lathe operator's machine broke down for 3 hours during the week, his earnings would be classified as follows:

Direct labor: 41 hours × $3	$123
Overtime premium (factory overhead): 4 hours × $1.50	6
Idle time (factory overhead): 3 hours × $3	9
Total earnings	$138

The classification of factory *payroll fringe costs* (e.g., employer contributions to social security, life insurance, health insurance, pensions, and miscellaneous other employee benefits) differs from company to company. In most companies, these are classified as indirect manufacturing costs. In some companies, however, the fringe benefits related to direct labor are charged as an additional direct labor cost. For instance, a direct laborer, such as a lathe operator whose gross wages are computed on the basis of $3 an hour; may enjoy payroll fringe benefits totaling, say, 75¢ per hour. Most companies tend to classify the $3 as direct labor cost and the 75¢ as factory overhead. Other companies classify the entire $3.75 as direct labor cost.

Explanation of Behavior of Variable Overhead Costs: Step Costs

Variable overhead costs are those factory overhead, selling overhead, and administrative overhead costs that, according to the budget, are expected to vary with some measure of activity, though not necessarily in direct relationship to sales or production volume. As we explained in the earlier definition of variable costs, they may lead or lag behind production or sales.

Many of these costs are not readily divisible into small units, and they do not all behave in the same way. For example, raw materials may be purchased in the exact quantities needed. In contrast, clerical help may represent a variable cost that increases or decreases in steps. Excess raw materials can be stored for future use. In contrast, excess clerical help cannot be stored for future use; clerical services are either efficiently utilized or lost as the clock ticks away the workday.

Step-variable costs are costs which change abruptly at intervals of activity because their acquisition comes in indivisible chunks. Although one extra unit of raw material can usually be ordered as needed, at a small incremental cost, the hiring of one more clerk assumes that there will be a prolonged need for the clerk's full-time efforts. Furthermore, the need for a unit of raw material is easy to determine, while measurement of office and other indirect labor is more difficult. In practice, secretaries, billing clerks, and stock boys are often subject to uneven work pressures. They may be able to work intensively or leisurely for long spans of time.

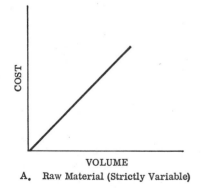

A. Raw Material (Strictly Variable)

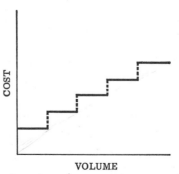

B. Clerical Services (Step-Variable)

EXHIBIT 8-2

Variable Cost Behavior

The graphs in Exhibit 8-2 show the difference between strict linear variability and step variability of costs. The ideal objective in the planning and control of step costs is to attain activity or utilization at the highest volume for any given step. This will achieve maximum returns for each dollar spent because the services involved will be fully utilized and their unit cost will be least.

Assumption of Strict Linearity

Management usually views costs as being variable when they vary directly with volume or when it is hoped that they may so vary. For practical budgeting purposes, costs do not have to vary in strictly linear fashion [as in Exhibit 8-2(a)] in order to be regarded as variable. Step-variable costs [Exhibit 8-2(b)] have already been discussed. Costs may

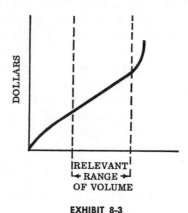

EXHIBIT 8-3

Variable Cost Behavior, Curvilinear

also vary in curvilinear fashion, which economists often rightly portray as behaving differently at low and high volumes of activity. The accountant usually takes a straight-line approach because he assumes that the curve is *straight within the relevant range of activity* (see Exhibit 8-3).

TYPES OF FIXED COSTS

Fixed Costs Are Capacity Costs

As industry becomes more automated, and as companies become more strongly committed to stable employment, the likelihood is great that most companies will endure a higher proportion of sticky, unresponsive fixed costs as compared with flexible, responsive variable costs. Fixed costs are those which are not expected to change in total within the current budget year, regardless of fluctuations in the volume of activity.

The fixed nature of costs must always be evaluated in relation to given conditions or plans, because all costs vary in the long run. In general, however, few day-to-day or month-to-month decisions affect fixed costs, so that an organization's performance is somewhat locked in by far-reaching decisions concerning fixed costs. That is why the *planning* process is so crucial.

Fixed costs affect the operating facilities and the organization which can produce and sell. These costs have been called *capacity costs*, because the outlays for plant, equipment, key personnel, research facilities, and advertising programs have all been incurred by management in order to maintain a capability for sustaining a planned volume of activity.

Committed and Programmed Fixed Costs

Fixed costs can be subdivided in many ways. For planning and control, committed and programmed fixed costs are useful classifications.

Committed costs consist largely of those fixed costs which arise from *essential* the possession of plant, of equipment, and of a basic organization. Examples are depreciation, property taxes, rent, insurance, and the salaries of key personnel. These costs are affected primarily by long-run sales forecasts that, in turn, indicate the long-run capacity needs.

The behavior of committed costs may best be viewed by assuming a zero volume of activity in an enterprise which fully expects to resume normal activity (e.g., during a strike or a shortage of material that forces a complete shut-down of activity). The committed costs are all those organization and plant costs which continue to be incurred and which cannot be reduced without injuring the organization's competence to meet long-range goals.

Programmed costs (sometimes called *managed costs*) are fixed costs *nonessential* which arise from periodic (usually yearly) appropriation decisions which directly reflect top management policies. Programmed costs may have no particular relation to volume of activity. Examples are research and development, advertising, sales promotion, donations, management consulting fees, and many employee training programs. Conceivably, these costs could be reduced almost entirely for a given year in dire times, while the committed costs would be much more difficult to reduce.

Programmed costs are decided upon by management at the start of the budget period. Goals are selected, the means for their attainment are chosen, the maximum expense to be incurred is specified, and the total amount to be spent is appropriated. For example, a company may appropriate $5 million for an advertising campaign. The company's advertising agency is unlikely to exceed that amount, nor is it likely to spend much less than $5 million in trying to attain the company goals.

The size of fixed costs is influenced by long-run marketing considerations, by technology, and by the methods and philosophies of management. Examples of the last include sales salaries versus sales commissions and one-shift versus two-shift operations. Generally, a heavier proportion of fixed to variable costs reduces management's ability to respond to short-run changes in economic conditions and opportunities. On the other hand, an inability or unwillingness to incur fixed costs reveals an aversion to risk that will shut out a company from potentially profitable ventures. The launching of new products and new business often entails exceedingly large fixed costs for research, advertising, equipment, and so forth.

MIXED COSTS

Nature of Mixed Costs

As the name implies, a mixed cost has both fixed and variable elements (see Exhibit 8-4). The fixed element represents the minimum cost of supplying a service. The variable element is that portion of the mixed cost which is influenced by changes in activity (e.g., repairs, power, and some clerical costs).

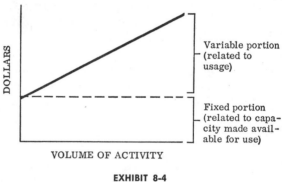

EXHIBIT 8-4

Mixed Cost

Ideally, there should be no accounts for mixed costs. All such costs should be subdivided into two accounts, one for the variable portion and one for the fixed portion. In practice, these distinctions are rarely made in the recording process, because of the difficulty of analyzing day-to-day cost data into variable and fixed sections. Costs like power, indirect labor, repairs, and maintenance are generally accounted for in total. It is generally very difficult to decide, as such costs are incurred, whether a particular invoice or work ticket represents a variable or fixed item. Moreover, even if it were possible to make such distinctions, the advantages might not be worth the additional clerical effort and costs. Whenever cost classifications are too refined, the perpetual problem of getting accurate source documents is intensified.

In sum, mixed costs are merely a blend of two unlike cost behavior patterns; they do not entail new conceptual approaches. Anybody who obtains a working knowledge of the planning and controlling of variable and fixed costs, separately, can adapt to a mixed cost situation when necessary.

Budgeting Mixed Costs

How should mixed costs be budgeted? Ideally, of course, their variable and fixed elements should be isolated and budgeted separately. One widely practiced method is a budget formula which contains both a fixed and a variable element. For example, repairs for delivery trucks might be budgeted at $15 per month plus 1¢ per mile.

The estimation of mixed cost behavior patterns preferably should begin with a scatter chart of past cost levels, a graph on which dots are plotted to show various historical costs. A line is fitted to the points, either visually or by the statistical method of least squares (described in the Appendix to this chapter). The intersection of the line with the vertical axis indicates the amount of the fixed-cost component.

A simplified version of the scatter chart is the *high-low two-point method.* Although this method is probably too simple for wide use, it illustrates the utility of studying past cost behavior patterns.

The High-low Two-point Method of Estimating Mixed Costs (Exhibit 8-5) requires the plotting of two points, representing the highest cost and the lowest cost, respectively, over the contemplated relevant range.

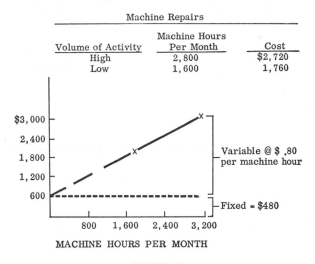

Machine Repairs

Volume of Activity	Machine Hours Per Month	Cost
High	2,800	$2,720
Low	1,600	1,760

MACHINE HOURS PER MONTH

EXHIBIT 8-5

High-low Two-point Method of Estimating Mixed Costs

A solid line is used to connect the high point and the low point. This line is extended back to intersect the vertical axis at the height at which the fixed portion of the cost has been plotted ($480 in Exhibit 8-5). The slope, or rate of change, of the line (80¢ per machine hour) represents the variable portion of the mixed cost. Thus, the formula that depicts the behavior of this mixed cost is $480 per month plus 80¢ per machine hour.

The same results could be computed by using the following algebraic technique:

$$\text{Variable rate} = \frac{\text{Change in mixed cost}}{\text{Change in machine hours}}$$

$$= \frac{\$2,720 - \$1,760}{2,800 - 1,600} = \frac{\$960}{1,200} = \$.80 \text{ per machine hour} \quad (1)$$

Fixed overhead component
$$= \text{Total mixed cost less variable component} \quad (2)$$

At 1,600-hour level of activity:
$$= \$1,760 - \$.80(1,600) = \$1,760 - \$1,280 = \$480$$

At 2,800-hour level of activity:
$$= \$2,720 - \$.80(2,800) = \$2,720 - \$2,240 = \$480$$

$$\text{Cost formula} = \$480 \text{ per month plus } \$.80 \text{ per machine hour.} \quad (3)$$

Such cost formulas are only the first step in the budgetary process. The budgeted figures are expected *future* data, so cost formulas must be altered to reflect anticipated changes in prices, efficiency, technology, and other influential factors.

COMPARISON OF CONTRIBUTION APPROACH WITH TRADITIONAL APPROACH

The emphasis on the importance of cost behavior patterns to the planning and controlling of costs differs from the traditional emphasis on product and functional costing. When cost behavior patterns are the focus, financial statements are based on a contribution approach (in which costs are classified according to whether they are variable or fixed) rather than on the traditional functional approach (in which costs are classified according to whether they are related to the manufacturing, selling, or administrative function). Exhibit 8-6 shows the difference in outline form.

EXHIBIT 8-6

Contribution Approach		*Traditional (Functional) Approach*	
Sales	xxx	Sales	xxx
Less variable expenses	xxx	Less manufacturing cost of goods sold	xxx
Contribution margin	xxx	Gross profit	xxx
Less fixed expenses	xxx	Less selling and administrative expenses	xxx
Net operating income	xxx	Net operating income	xxx

Exhibit 8-7 shows how the same data can be used to prepare two different financial statements, according to the approach used. Variable and fixed subclassifications are shown in the Schedules of Indirect Manufacturing Costs (Exhibit 8-8) in order to facilitate comparison. In practice, such labeling is rare.

EXHIBIT 8-7

Comparison of Contribution Approach with Traditional Approach

SAMSON CO.		
Contribution Income Statement		
For the Year Ending Dec. 31, 19x2		
(In thousands of dollars)		

Sales		$20,000
Less variable expenses:		
Direct material	$ 7,000	
Direct labor	4,000	
Variable indirect manufacturing (Schedule 1)	1,000	
Total variable manufacturing cost of sales	$12,000	
Variable selling expenses	1,000	
Variable administrative expenses	100	
Total variable expenses		13,100
Contribution margin		$ 6,900
Less programmed fixed expenses:		
Manufacturing (Schedule 2)	$ 300	
Selling	1,900	
Administrative	700	$ 2,900
Less committed fixed expenses:		
Manufacturing (Schedule 3)	$2,700	
Selling	100	
Administrative	200	3,000	5,900
Net operating income		$ 1,000

SAMSON CO.		
"Traditional" Income Statement		
For the Year Ending Dec. 31, 19x2		
(In thousands of dollars)		

Sales		$20,000
Less manufacturing cost of goods sold:		
Direct material	$7,000	
Direct labor	4,000	
Indirect manufacturing costs (Schedule 1—total)	4,000	15,000
Gross profit		$ 5,000
Selling expenses (detailed)	$3,000	
Administrative expenses (detailed)	1,000	
Total selling and administrative expenses		4,000
Net operating income		$ 1,000

EXHIBIT 8-8

SAMSON CO.

Schedules of Indirect Manufacturing Costs

For the Year Ending Dec. 31, 19x2

(In thousands of dollars)

Schedule 1: Variable Costs		
Supplies (lubricants, expendable tools, coolants, sandpaper)	$150	
Indirect labor (material transfer, idle time, setup costs)	700	
Repairs	100	
Power	50	$1,000
Schedule 2: Programmed Costs non essential		
Foremen's salaries	$200	
Employee training	90	
Factory picnic and holiday party	10	300
Schedule 3: Committed Costs essential		
Supervisory salaries, except foremen's salaries	$ 700	
Depreciation, plant and equipment	1,800	
Property taxes	150	
Insurance	50	2,700
Total indirect manufacturing costs		$4,000

The contribution approach facilitates cost-volume-profit analysis and focuses on the information pertinent to appraisals of performance. It is also more likely to supply data which are relevant to special decisions, such as pricing, dropping or adding products, advertising and promoting specific products, and selecting distribution channels. The traditional income statement fails to distinguish the items that are crucial to wise planning and control. These points will be pursued further in the following chapters.

SUMMARY

The most important aspect of intelligent cost planning and control is an understanding of cost behavior patterns and influences. The behavior pattern of costs may be described as *variable* or *fixed*. Variable costs may be subdivided into strictly variable and step-variable categories. Fixed costs may be subdivided into committed and programmed categories. Mixed costs contain both variable and fixed elements.

Variable costs are those which are expected to fluctuate, in total, in proportion to sales, production, or other measure of activity. Included in this category are variable manufacturing costs: direct material; direct labor; and *variable* factory overhead. Step-variable costs are not strictly variable. They change abruptly at intervals of activity because they are incurred in indivisible chunks.

Fixed costs are those which are not expected to change in total within the current budget year, regardless of fluctuations in the volume of activity. Their incurrence provides capacity to produce and sell. Committed costs largely consist of those fixed costs arising from the possession of plant, equipment, and a basic organization. Programmed costs (sometimes called managed costs) are those fixed costs which arise from periodic appropriation decisions which directly reflect top management policies. The amount of fixed costs is affected by long-range marketing factors, by technology, and by the methods and philosophies of top management.

The contribution approach to presenting an income statement emphasizes those cost behavior patterns which should influence management appraisals and decisions.

Many new terms were introduced in this chapter. You should review them to make sure you know their exact meanings.

SUMMARY PROBLEMS FOR YOUR REVIEW

PROBLEMS

1. The following information is from the records of the Levander Co. for the year ending Dec. 31, 19x2. There were no beginning or ending inventories.

Sales	$10,000,000	Long-term rent, factory	$ 100,000
Sales commissions	500,000	Factory superintendent's salary	30,000
Advertising	200,000	Foremen's salaries	100,000
Shipping expenses	300,000	Direct material	4,000,000
Administrative executive		Direct labor	2,000,000
salaries	100,000	Cutting bits	60,000
Administrative clerical		Factory methods research	40,000
salaries (variable)	400,000	Abrasives for machining	100,000
Fire insurance on equipment	2,000	Indirect labor	800,000
Property taxes on equipment	10,000	Depreciation on equipment	300,000

Prepare a "traditional" income statement and a contribution income statement. If you are in doubt about any cost behavior pattern, decide on the basis of whether the total cost in question will fluctuate substantially over a wide range of volume.

2. The Delite Co. has its own power plant. All costs related to the production of power have been charged to a single account, Power, which is a mixture of variable and fixed costs. We know that the total cost for power was $24,000 in one month and $28,000 in another month. Total machine hours in those months were 120,000 and 160,000, respectively. Express the cost behavior pattern of the Power account in formula form.

SOLUTIONS

1.

LEVANDER CO.
Contribution Income Statement
For the Year Ending Dec. 31, 19x2
(In thousands of dollars)

Sales			$10,000
Less variable expenses:			
Direct material		$4,000	
Direct labor		2,000	
Variable indirect manufacturing costs (1)*		960	
Total variable manufacturing cost of sales		$ 6,960	
Variable selling expenses			
Sales commissions	$500		
Shipping expenses	300	800	
Variable clerical salaries		400	
Total variable expenses			8,160
Contribution margin			$ 1,840
Less programmed fixed expenses:			
Manufacturing (2)	$140		
Selling (advertising)	200	$ 340	
Less committed fixed expenses:			
Manufacturing (3)	$442		
Administrative—executive salaries	100	542	
Total fixed expenses			882
Net operating income			$ 958

*Keyed to accompanying schedules.

LEVANDER CO.
"Traditional" Income Statement
For the Year Ending Dec. 31, 19x2
(In thousands of dollars)

Sales			$10,000
Less manufacturing cost of goods sold:			
Direct material		$4,000	
Direct labor		2,000	
Indirect manufacturing costs (from schedules)		1,542	7,542
Gross profit			$ 2,458
Selling expenses:			
Sales commissions	$500		
Advertising	200		
Shipping expenses	300	$1,000	
Administrative expenses:			
Executive salaries	$100		
Clerical salaries	400	500	1,500
Net operating income			$ 958

LEVANDER CO.
Indirect Manufacturing Costs
For the Year Ending Dec. 31, 19x2
(In thousands of dollars)

Schedule 1: Variable Costs		
Cutting bits	$ 60	
Abrasives for machining	100	
Indirect labor	800	$ 960
Schedule 2: Programmed Costs		
Foremen's salaries	$100	
Factory methods research	40	140
Schedule 3: Committed Costs		
Long-term rent, factory	$100	
Fire insurance on equipment	2	
Property taxes on equipment	10	
Depreciation on equipment	300	
Factory superintendent's salary	30	442
Total indirect manufacturing costs		$1,542

2. $$\text{Variable rate} = \frac{\text{Change in mixed cost}}{\text{Change in volume}}$$

$$= \frac{\$28,000 - \$24,000}{160,000 - 120,000} = \frac{\$4,000}{40,000} = \$.10 \text{ per machine hour}$$

Fixed component = Total mixed cost less variable component
At 160,000-hour level = $28,000 − $.10(160,000) = $12,000

Or, at 120,000-hour level = $24,000 − $.10(120,000) = $12,000
Cost formula = $12,000 per month + $.10 per machine hour

SUGGESTED READINGS

Beyer, R., *Profitability Accounting for Panning and Control.* New York: The Ronald Press Company, 1963.

Separating and Using Costs as Fixed and Variable, National Association of Accountants, Accounting Practice Report No. 10. New York, June, 1960.

APPENDIX

Method of Least Squares

The method of least squares is the most accurate device for formulating the past behavior of a mixed cost. A scatter diagram is prepared, to see whether a straight-line relationship exists between the mixed cost and the activity measure.

The line itself is not plotted visually, however; it is located by means of two simultaneous linear equations:

$$\Sigma XY = a\Sigma X + b\Sigma X^2 \qquad (1)$$

$$\Sigma Y = na + b\Sigma X \qquad (2)$$

where a is the fixed component; b is the variable cost rate; X is the activity measure; Y is the mixed cost; n is the number of observations; and Σ means summation.

EXHIBIT 8-9

Least-squares Computation of Budget Formula for Mixed Cost

Month	Machine Hours X	Total Mixed Cost Y	XY	X²
1	22	$ 23	$ 506	484
2	23	25	575	529
3	19	20	380	361
4	12	20	240	144
5	12	20	240	144
6	9	15	135	81
7	7	14	98	49
8	11	14	154	121
9	14	16	224	196
	129	$167	$2,552	2,109

SOURCE: Adapted from *Separating and Using Costs As Fixed and Variable*, N.A.A., *Bulletin*, Accounting Practice Report No. 10 (New York, June, 1960), p. 13. For a more thorough explanation, see any basic text in statistics.

For example, assume that nine monthly observations of power costs are to be used as a basis for developing a budget formula. A scatter diagram indicates a mixed cost behavior in the form $Y = a + bX$. Computation of the budget formula by the method of least squares is shown in Exhibit 8-9. The answer is: Total cost $9.82 per month + 60.9¢ per machine hour.

Substitute the values from Exhibit 8-9 into Eqs. (1) and (2):

	$2552 = 129a + 2109b	(1)
	$ 167 = 9a + 129b	(2)
Multiply Eq. (1) by 3	$7656 = 387a + 6327b	
Multiply Eq. (2) by 43	$7181 = 387a + 5547b	
Subtract:	$ 475 = 7806b	
	b = $.609	
Substitute $.609 for b in Eq. (2)	$ 167 = 9a + 129($.609)	
	a = $9.82	

Therefore, fixed cost is $9.82 and variable cost is 60.9 cents per machine hour.

ESSENTIAL ASSIGNMENT MATERIAL

8-1. *Terminology.* Define: direct material; direct labor; idle time; overtime premium; indirect labor; prime costs; indirect manufacturing costs; factory overhead; factory burden; manufacturing overhead; manufacturing expenses; step-variable costs; capacity costs; committed costs; programmed costs; managed costs; mixed cost; and contribution approach.

8-2. *Contribution and traditional income statements.* The Matrix Corp. was incorporated on Jan. 1, 19x1. The controller has given you the following information pertaining to the company's operations for the year ending Dec. 31, 19x1. There are no ending inventories. During a discussion with the sales manager, he informs you that the company's ten salesmen are paid a base salary of $3,000 each, plus 2 per cent of their sales.

Sales	$3,000,000	Salesmen's compensation	$ 90,000
Training program, factory	50,000	Advertising and promotion	150,000
Direct material	1,000,000	Direct labor	750,000
Shipping expense (a selling		Manufacturing manager's salary	25,000
expense)	36,000	Indirect labor	200,000
Administrative and clerical		Engineering consultants on	
salaries (variable)	28,000	factory operations	70,000
Depreciation, factory	90,000	Foremen's salaries	125,000
Miscellaneous factory supplies	10,000	Rental of factory equipment	
Time and motion studies of		on long-term lease	75,000
factory operations	12,000	Property taxes on factory	18,000
Administrative executive		Fire insurance on factory	4,000
salaries	135,000		

Required:

Prepare a traditional income statement and a contribution income statement for the Matrix Corp. for the year ending Dec. 31, 19x1. Include a separate schedule of indirect manufacturing costs.

8-3. *Variable costs and fixed costs; manufacturing and other costs.* For each of the numbered items, choose the appropriate classification for a job-order manufacturing company (e.g., custom furniture, job printing). If in doubt about whether the cost behavior is basically variable or fixed, decide on the basis of whether the total cost will fluctuate substantially over a wide range of volume. Most items have two answers from among the following possibilities:

    a. Variable cost   *e.* Manufacturing costs, direct
    b. Fixed cost   *f.* Manufacturing costs, indirect
    c. General and administrative cost   *g.* Other (specify)
    d. Selling cost

Sample answers

Direct material.	*a, e*
President's salary.	*b, c*
Bond interest expense.	*b, g* (financial expense)

Items for your consideration:

1. Sandpaper. a , f
2. Supervisory salaries, production control. b , ⌀ f
3. Supervisory salaries, assembly department. b , ⌀ f
4. Supervisory salaries, factory storeroom. b , ⌀ f
5. Company picnic costs. b , g
6. Overtime premium, punch press. a , f
7. Idle time, assembly. a , f
8. Freight out. a , f
9. Property taxes. b , g (Committed Costs)
10. Factory power for machines. a , g (mixed costs)
11. Salesmen's commissions. b , g ⟩ d
12. Salesmen's salaries. b , g ⟩ Programmed Costs b , d
13. Welding supplies. a , f
14. Fire loss. g   Cost on loss (unusual loss)
15. Paint for finished products. a , f
16. Heat and air-conditioning, factory. f , g   b , f
17. Material-handling labor, punch press. b , t   a , f
18. Straight line depreciation, salesmen's automobiles. b , g (Committed Costs) Programmed

(handwritten left margin:) should be rough committed costs   Programmed Cost

8-4. *Classification of cost behavior.* Identify the following as (*a*) strictly variable costs; (*b*) committed costs; (*c*) programmed costs; (*d*) mixed costs; (*e*) step-variable costs.

More than one letter can be used in an answer. If in doubt, write a short explanation of why doubt exists.

1. Straight-line depreciation on a building. b
2. Fork-lift truck operators' wages. One operator is needed for every 5,000 tons of steel sold monthly by a steel warehouse.   d
3. Property taxes on plant and equipment. b
4. Advertising costs. c
5. Research costs. c
6. Total rental costs of salesmen's automobiles. Charge is a flat $60 per month plus 5¢ per mile.   d
7. Salesmen's total compensation, including salaries and commissions. d
8. Total repairs and maintenance. a
9. Foremen's salaries. A new foreman is added for every ten workers employed.   c
10. Management consulting costs.   e
11. Public accounting fees.   e
12. Management training costs. c

8-5. *Division of mixed costs into variable and fixed components.* The president and the controller of the Dopuch Transformer Co. have agreed that refinement of the company cost classifications will aid planning and control decisions. They have asked you to approximate the fundamental variable and fixed cost behavior of repairs and maintenance from the following:

Monthly Activity in Direct Labor Hours	Monthly Repair and Maintenance Costs Incurred
3,000	$1,700
5,000	2,300

8-6. *Case study of cost-volume-profit relationships; analysis of financial statements.* The Rummy Co. is a processor of a Bacardi-mix concentrate. Sales are made principally to liquor distributors throughout the country.

The company's income statements for the past year and the coming year are being analyzed by top management.

RUMMY CO.
Income Statements

	For the Year 19x1 Just Ended		For the Year 19x2 Tentative Budget	
Sales, 1,500,000 gallons in 19x1		$900,000		$1,000,000
Cost of goods sold:				
Direct material 30%	$450,000		$495,000	
Direct labor 6%	90,000		99,000	
Factory overhead:				
Variable 1.2%	18,000		19,800	
Fixed	50,000	608,000	50,000	663,800
Gross margin		$292,000		$ 336,200
Selling expenses:				
Variable:				
Sales commissions (based on dollar sales) 3%	$ 45,000		$ 50,000	
Shipping and other 6%	90,000		99,000	
Fixed: Salaries, Advertising, etc.	110,000		138,000	
Administrative expenses:				
Variable 0.8%	12,000		13,200	
Fixed	40,000	297,000	40,000	340,200
Net income		$—5,000		$ —4,000

Handwritten annotations: 1,500,000 / 450,000 etc.

Required:

Consider each requirement independently.

1. The president has just returned from a management conference at a local university, where he heard an accounting professor criticize conventional income statements. The professor had asserted that knowledge of cost behavior patterns was of key importance in determining managerial strategies. The president now feels that the income statement should be recast to harmonize with cost-volume-profit analysis. That is, the statement should have three major sections: sales; variable costs; and fixed costs. Using the 19x1 data, prepare such a statement, showing the contribution margin as well as net income.

2. Comment on the changes in each item in the income statement. What are the most likely causes for each increase? Assume that unit costs of direct material will not change during 19x2.

3. The president is unimpressed with the 19x2 budget: "We need to take a fresh look in order to begin moving toward profitable operations. Let's tear up the 19x2 budget, concentrate on 19x1 results, and prepare a new comparative 19x2 budget under each of the following assumptions:

   a. A 5 per cent average price cut will increase unit sales by 20 per cent.
   b. A 5 per cent average price increase will decrease unit sales by 10 per cent.
   c. A sales commission rate of 10 per cent and a $3\frac{1}{3}$ per cent price increase will boost unit sales by 10 per cent."

Prepare the budgets for 19x2, using a contribution margin format and three columns. Assume that there are no changes in fixed costs.

4. The advertising manager maintains that the advertising budget should be increased by $100,000 and that prices should be increased by 10 per cent. Resulting unit sales will soar by 25 per cent. What would be the expected net income under such circumstances?   *$50,625*

5. A nearby distillery has offered to buy 300,000 gallons in 19x2, if the unit price is low enough. The Rummy Co. would not have to incur sales commissions or shipping costs on this special order. Rummy's regular business would be undisturbed. Assuming that 19x2's regular operations will be exactly like 19x1's, what unit price should be quoted in order for the Rummy Co. to earn a net income of $5,000 in 19x2?

6. The company chemist wants to add a special ingredient, an exotic flavoring that will add $.02 per gallon to the Bacardi-mix costs. He also wants to replace the ordinary grenadine now used, which costs $.03 per gallon of mix, with a more exquisite type costing $.04 a gallon. Assuming no other changes in cost behavior, how many units must be sold to earn a net income of $5,000 in 19x2?

ADDITIONAL ASSIGNMENT MATERIAL

Note: These problems explore the effects of various revenue and cost behavior patterns.

8-7. Distinguish between prime costs and direct material.

8-8. "Glue or nails become an integral part of the finished product, so they would be direct material." Do you agree? Explain.

8-9. Why are fixed costs also called capacity costs?

8-10. How do committed costs differ from programmed costs?

8-11. How do the methods and philosophies of management affect cost behavior?

8-12. "Ideally, there should be no accounts for mixed costs." Explain.

8-13. Describe how mixed costs are budgeted.

8-14. What is the advantage of the contribution approach as compared to the traditional approach?

8-15. "Variable costs are those that should fluctuate directly in proportion to sales." Do you agree? Explain.

8-16. How do the basic behavior of the cost of raw materials and the cost of clerical services differ?

8-17. "For practical budgeting purposes, costs do not have to be strictly variable in order to be regarded as variable." Explain.

8-18. "The objective in controlling step costs is to attain activity at the highest volume for any given step." Explain.

8-19. What is the primary determinant of the level of committed costs?

8-20. What is the primary determinant of the level of programmed costs?

8-21. *Identifying cost behavior patterns.* At a seminar, a cost accountant spoke on the classification of different kinds of cost behavior.

Mr. Dipple, a hospital administrator who heard the lecture, identified several hospital costs and classified them. After his classification, Mr. Dipple presented you with the following list of costs and asked you to classify their behavior as one of the following: variable; step-variable; mixed; programmed; cr committed:

1. Straight line depreciation of operating room equipment.
2. Costs incurred by Dr. X. Cise in cancer research.
3. Costs of services of Better-run Hospital Consultant Firm.
4. Repairs made on hospital furniture.
5. Nursing supervisors' salaries (a supervisor is added for each 45 nursing personnel).
6. Leasing costs of X-ray equipment ($7,500 a year plus $.015 per film).
7. Training costs of an administrative resident.
8. Blue Cross insurance for all full-time employees.

8-22. *Mixed costs.* The Avers Corp. charges maintenance and minor repairs to the same account. During the past five years, the maximum repair and maintenance expense incurred was $50,450, and this maximum occurred during a year in which 210,000 machine hours were logged. The minimum during this period was $46,100, during a year in which 180,000 hours were logged.

Required:

1. What is the formula for the repair and maintenance expense?
2. If the machine utilization forecast for the next year is 200,000 hours, what expense for repair and maintenance do you predict?

8-23. *Cost behavior and estimates of net income.* The Korifax Co. president shows you the following data:

	19x3	19x2	19x1
Dollar sales	$92,000 (estimated)	$100,000	$80,000
Total expenses	?	90,000	75,000

Basic revenue and cost behavior patterns have not changed during the past three years. The president knows little about cost-volume-profit relationships, and he asks for your estimate of *net income* for 19x3, based solely on the given data.

8-24. *Separation of hospital X-ray mixed costs into variable and fixed components.* A staff meeting has been called at the Hugh G. Dephicit Memorial Hospital by the new administrator, Buck Saver. Mr. Saver has examined the income statement and is particularly interested in the X-ray department. The chief radiologist, Dr. I. C. Throoyou, has demanded an increase in prices to cover the increased repair costs because of the opening of an outpatient clinic. He claims it is costing more per X-ray for this expense.

Mr. Saver asks the controller, Mr. Adam Upp, to approximate the fundamental variable and fixed cost behavior of repairs and maintenance for the X-ray department and to prepare a graphic report he can present to Dr. Throoyou. Data for the relevant range follow:

	X-rays per Month	Monthly Repair and Maintenance Cost Incurred
Low volume	6,000	$3,400
High volume	10,000	5,400

As the controller, prepare the requested information.

8-25. *Method of least squares and sales forecasts.* (SICA Adapted.) The Progressive Co. Ltd., has recorded the following sales since its inception in 19x2:

19m2	$ 10,000
19m3	20,000
19m4	30,000
19m5	45,000
19m6	70,000
19m7	90,000
19m8	125,000
19m9	150,000
19n0	180,000
19n1	220,000
19n2	270,000

Required:

a. By the method of least squares calculate 19n3 sales.

b. If the directors have determined from an outside consultant that the cyclical factor in 19n4 will cause sales to be 10 per cent above the forecast trend, what will they amount to?

8-26. *The impact of wage incentives on cost-volume-profit relationships.* The Weber Co. manufactures widgets. The present method of wage payment is straight salary. That is, the workers' salaries are independent of production, effort, etc. All labor costs are fixed within the relevant range of output. The selling price is $20 per unit. The yearly costs are as follows:

Fixed:	
Direct labor	$10,000
Indirect labor	5,000
Fixed overhead	5,000
Variable:	
Direct materials	$10 per unit
Variable overhead	2 per unit

Some industrial engineers hired by the president, Mr. Arnold R. Weber, to devise methods of increasing worker productivity, have suggested that a wage incentive plan be introduced. This plan would cover only the direct labor, not the indirect labor. The objective is to provide motivation for the workers to increase their output and thereby lower unit costs. A straight piecework system is proposed, with the workers (i.e., direct labor) being paid $4 per unit produced rather than a total of $10,000 per year. The fixed costs of administering the wage incentive system (setting and maintaining standards, calculating wages, etc.) will be $2,000 per year. The yearly costs, then, under the new system will be as follows:

Fixed:	
Indirect labor	$5,000.
Fixed miscellaneous overhead	5,000
Costs of administration of incentive plan	2,000
Variable:	
Direct materials	$10 per unit
Variable overhead	2 per unit
Direct labor	4 per unit

Required:

1. Under the old (i.e., salary) system, what is the break-even point in units? How many units must be sold for the firm to make a net profit of $1,000?
2. Under the new incentive system, what is the break-even point in units? How many units must be sold to make a net profit of $1,000?
3. Mr. Weber wants to know whether or not he should adopt the incentive plan. He is now making a net profit of $1,000 per year and will not use the new plan unless he can at least equal this. If the wage incentive system results in increased production, he is sure that he can sell the added production without lowering his price. After investigating some data on the impact of wage incentives on production in situations similar to the Weber Company, Mr. Weber decides that the incentive plan will increase production by 25 per cent. Should he introduce the wage incentive plan or continue with the salary system?

8-27. *Cost behavior patterns and planning.* The Diller Co. has the following cost behavior patterns:

Production range in units	0-5,000	5,001-10,000	10,001-15,000	15,001-20,000
Nonvariable costs	$150,000	$220,000	$250,000	$270,000

Maximum production capacity is 20,000 units per year. Variable costs per unit are $30 at all production levels.

Required:

Each situation described below is to be considered independently.

1. Production and sales are expected to be 11,000 units for the year. The sales price is $50 per unit. How many additional units need to be sold, in an unrelated market, at $40 per unit to show a total over-all net income of $8,000 for the year?
2. The company has orders for 23,000 units at $50. If the company desires to make a minimum over-all net income of $148,000 on these 23,000 units, what unit purchase price would it be willing to pay to a subcontractor for 3,000 units? Assume that the subcontractor would act as Diller's agent and deliver the units to customers directly and bear all related costs of manufacture, delivery, etc. The customers, however, would pay Diller directly as goods are delivered.
3. Production is currently expected to be 7,000 units for the year at a selling price of $50. By how much may advertising or special promotion costs be increased to bring production up to 14,500 units and still earn a total net income of four per cent of dollar sales?
4. Net income is currently $125,000. Nonvariable costs are $250,000. However, competitive pressures are mounting. A 5 per cent decrease in price will not affect sales volume, but will decrease net income by $37,500. What is the present volume, in units? Refer to the original data.

CHAPTER 9

Standards
and Flexible Budgets
for Control

NOW THAT WE ARE FAMILIAR WITH VARIOUS PATTERNS OF COST behavior, we may fruitfully examine some major attention-directing techniques for planning and controlling individual costs.

We can see that managers make two major types of decisions in the planning and controlling of costs: *price* decisions and *quantity* decisions. That is, material and human resources are supposed to be obtained at the lowest possible price which is consistent with quality and other long-run objectives. Once obtained, the resources should be utilized effectively. These resources are *inputs;* they should be used efficiently to produce the maximum possible good *output.*

In this chapter we will discuss the standards and budgets used in attention directing for the control of variable costs.

NEED FOR STANDARDS AND FORECASTING

Role of Past Experience

As we have already seen (Chapter 8), the study of past behavior patterns is a basic step in formulating an expected or budgeted cost. Such study yields knowledge of the cost's essential nature and permits its classification as strictly variable, step-variable, programmed, committed, or mixed.

209

Although the study of past cost behavior is a useful starting point, a budgeted cost should not be merely an extension of past experience. Inefficiencies may be reflected in prior costs. Changes in technology, equipment, and methods also limit the usefulness of comparisons with the past. Also, performance should be judged in relation to some currently attainable goal, one that may be reached by skilled, diligent, superior effort. *Concern with the past is justified only insofar as it helps prediction.* Management wishes to plan what costs should be, not what costs have been.

Role of Other Information: Work Measurement

Two major sources for preparing cost budgets are: (1) discussions with the managers affected; and (2) industrial engineering, including measurement of work. Work measurement entails the careful analysis of a task, its size, the methods which are used in its performance, and the efficiency with which it is performed. The work load is expressed in *control factor units,* which are used in formulating the budget. For example, the control factor units in a payroll department might include operations performed on time cards, on notices of change in the labor rate, on notices of employee promotion, on new employment and termination reports, and on routine monthly reports. All of these would be weighted. The estimated work load would then be used as a basis for determining the required labor force and budgetary allowance.

Role of the Accountant

The standard-setting and budget-setting process in an organization should be, primarily, the responsibility of the line personnel directly involved. The relative tightness of the budget should be the result of face-to-face discussion and bargaining between the manager and his immediate superior. The budgetary accountants, the industrial engineers, and the market researchers should extend all desired technical assistance and advice, but the final decisions should not be theirs. The line manager is the person who is supposed to accept and live with the budget or standard.

TYPES OF STANDARDS OR BUDGETS

Current Attainability: The Most Widely Used Standard

What standard of expected performance should be used? Should it be so severe that it is rarely, if ever, attained? Should it be attainable 50 per cent of the time? 80 per cent? 20 per cent? Individuals who have worked a lifetime in setting standards for performance cannot agree, so we must conclude that there are no universal answers to these questions.

Two types of standards deserve mention here. *Ideal standards* are expressions of absolute perfection. No provision is made for shrinkage, spoilage, machine breakdowns, and the like. Those who favor this approach maintain that the resulting unfavorable variances will constantly remind managers of the perpetual need for improvement in all phases of operations. These standards are not widely used, however, because they have an adverse effect on employee motivation. Employees tend to ignore unreasonable goals.

Currently attainable standards are those that can be achieved by *very efficient* operations. Expectations are set high enough so that employees regard their fulfillment as possible, though perhaps not probable. Allowances are made for normal shrinkage, waste, and machine breakdowns. Variances tend to be unfavorable, but managers accept the standards as being reasonable goals.

The major reasons for using currently attainable standards are:

1. The resulting standard costs serve multiple purposes. For example, the same cost may be used for cash budgeting, for inventory valuation, and for budgeting departmental performance. In contrast, ideal standards cannot be used *per se* for cash budgeting, because financial planning will be thrown off.
2. The desirable motivational impact on employees. The standard represents reasonable future performance, not fanciful ideal goals or antiquated goals geared to past performance.

Difference Between Standards and Budgets

What is the difference between a standard amount and a budget amount? If standards are currently attainable, as they are assumed to be in this book, there is no conceptual difference. The term *standard cost,* as it is most widely used, is a unit concept; that is, the standard cost of material per unit is, say, $1. The term *budgeted cost,* as it is most widely used, is a total concept; that is, the budgeted cost of material is $10,000 if 10,000 units are to be produced at a standard cost of $1 per unit. It may be helpful to think of a standard as a budget for the production of a single unit. In many companies, the terms "budgeted performance" and "standard performance" are used interchangeably.

In practice, direct material and direct labor are said to be controlled with the help of *standard costs*, while all other costs are usually said to be controlled with the help of *departmental overhead budgets*. This distinction probably arose because of different timing and control techniques for various costs. Direct material and direct labor are generally relatively costly, and are easily identifiable for control purposes. Therefore, techniques for planning and controlling these costs are relatively refined. Overhead costs are combinations of many individual items, none of which justifies an elaborate control system. In consequence, use of direct material may be closely watched on an hourly basis; direct labor, on a daily basis; and factory overhead, on a weekly or monthly basis.

All of this leads to the following straightforward approach (using assumed figures), which we will pursue throughout the remainder of this book. The standard is a *unit* idea; the *budget is a total* idea:

	Standards	Budget for 10,000 units and 10,000 hours
Direct material	$1 per unit	$10,000
Direct labor	$4 per hour	40,000
Factory overhead (detailed)*		20,000
Selling expenses (detailed)*		15,000
Administrative expenses (detailed)*		5,000

* For planning and control, these individual detailed costs are not usually expressed as a standard cost per unit, though there are exceptions.

If standards are not currently attainable because they are ideal or out-dated, the amount budgeted for financial (cash) planning purposes has to differ from the standard. Otherwise, projected income and cash disbursements will be forecasted incorrectly. In such cases, ideal or outdated standards may be used for compiling performance reports, but expected variances are stipulated in the master budget for financial planning. For example, if unusually strict labor standards are used, the standard cost per finished unit may be $1 despite the fact that top management anticipates an unfavorable performance variance of $.10 per unit. In the master budget, the total labor costs would be $1.10 per unit: $1 plus an expected variance of $.10.

PRICE VARIANCES

Need for Price Variances

In most companies, the *acquisition* of materials or merchandise entails different control decisions than their *use*. The purchasing executive of a manufacturing company worries about getting raw materials at favorable prices, while the production executive concentrates on using them efficiently. The merchandise manager of a large grocery company will be responsible for skillful buying of foodstuffs, but the store manager will be responsible for their sale and for minimizing losses from shrinkage, shoplifting, and the like.

The assessment of performance is facilitated by separating the items which are subject to the manager's direct influence from those which are not. The general approach is to separate *price* (i.e., *rate*) factors from *quantity* (i.e., *usage, efficiency*) factors. Price factors are subject to less immediate control than quantity factors, principally because of external forces, such as general economic conditions and unforeseeable price changes. Even when price factors are regarded as outside of company control, it is still desirable to isolate them and so keep them out of performance reports dealing with the efficient usage of the goods or services in question. When one executive is responsible for *prices* and the other for *usage*, each will be evaluated with a measuring stick that is not polluted by uncontrollable factors.

Purchases of Merchandise or Raw Materials

The buyers in retail stores and the purchasing executives in wholesale and manufacturing companies usually plan their purchases in accordance with forthcoming demand. Their objective is to obtain the correct number of items, of the appropriate quality, at the right time and at the right price. Unsatisfactory performance can usually be traced to failure to meet one or more of these requirements (e.g., an incorrect number of items might be ordered, the quality might be inferior, or the unit price might be high).

The most common example is acquisition at a price not equal to the standard price. (Ordinarily, the purchasing agent is given little discretion over the quantities to be purchased, though in exceptional circumstances he may have permission to buy a huge lot at a bargain price.) A performance report for a purchasing department using standard prices might include the following:

Actual Quantity	Type	Actual Price	Standard Price	Total Actual	Total Budgeted	Purchase Price Variance
1,000 lbs.	Material *A*	$1.10	$1.00	$1,100	$1,000	$100 (Unfavorable)
500 sq. ft.	Material *B*	3.70	4.00	1,850	2,000	150 (Favorable)

The price variance may be defined as the *difference in unit price* multiplied by the *actual quantity*. In the case of Material *A*: ($1.10 − $1.00) × 1,000 lbs. = $100, unfavorable.

How do we decide whether a variance is favorable or unfavorable? When actual costs exceed standard costs, the variance is unfavorable; when actual costs are less than standard costs, the variance is favorable.

What do the purchasing officer and his superior *do* with this information? First, we should recognize that the variances are only a starting point, a clue for investigation. Most variances have to be analyzed if their underlying causes are to be discovered. Second, from the viewpoint of control, these variances should be measured as soon as possible. The longer the delay, the staler the data and the fewer the opportunities for corrections. In some companies, price variances are computed when the original purchase order is sent to the supplier; in others, the most feasible time for measuring is upon receipt of the supplier's invoice.

The responsibility for price variances usually rests with the purchasing officer. Price variances are often regarded as a measure of forecasting ability rather than of failure to buy at specified prices. Some control over the price variance is obtainable by getting many quotations, buying in economical lots, taking advantage of cash discounts, and selecting the most economical means of delivery.

Failure to meet price standards may result from a sudden rush of sales orders or from unanticipated changes in production schedules, which in turn may require the purchasing officer to buy at uneconomical prices or to request delivery by air freight. In such cases, the responsibility may rest with the sales manager or the head of production scheduling, rather than with the purchasing officer.

Labor Price Variances

Price variances for labor are usually called *rate variances*. In most companies, because of union contracts or other predictable factors, labor rates can be foreseen with much greater accuracy than prices of materials. Therefore, rate variances tend to be relatively insignificant.

As we mentioned in Chapter 8, labor, unlike material and supplies, cannot ordinarily be stored for later use. The acquisition and use of labor occurs simultaneously. For these reasons, labor rate variances are usually charged to the same manager who is in charge of labor *usage*.

Labor rate variances may be traceable to faulty predictions of the labor rates. However, the more likely causes include: (1) the use of a single average standard labor rate for a given operation that is, in fact, performed by individuals earning slightly different rates because of seniority; (2) the assignment of a man with the wrong rate for a given operation; and (3) the payment of hourly rates, instead of prescribed piece rates, because of low productivity.

QUANTITY VARIANCES

Computational Technique

The quantity, or *usage*, variance is computed by multiplying the standard price by the difference between the quantity of material used and the quantity of material allowed for the number of units produced. The general approach is probably best exemplified by the control of direct materials in standard cost systems. The performance of the production department manager is usually judged by a *standard formula* or by a Bill of Materials (Exhibit 9-1). This is a specification of the quantities allowed—the physical needs for manufacturing a given amount.

Let us consider an example. Assume that 10,000 units of a particular item were produced. Suppose that the standard direct material allowance is two pounds per unit, at a unit cost of $2. Actually, 21,000 pounds of materials (input) were used to produce the 10,000 units (output). The variance would be:

Quantity variance = Difference in pounds × Standard price   (1)
= (21,000 − 20,000) × $2.00 = $2,000 unfavorable

Similarly, assume that it is supposed to take four direct labor hours to produce one unit, and that the standard hourly labor cost is $3. 41,000 hours (input) were used to produce the 10,000 units. The variance would be:

Efficiency variance = Difference in hours × Standard rate   (2)
= (41,000 actual hours − 40,000 standard hours) × $3
= $3,000, unfavorable

Standard Bill of Material		
Assembly No. 4xy Description: Card table		
Part Number	Quantity	Description
A 403	4	Steel Legs
A 501	1	Table top
P 42	16 sq. ft.	Plastic cover
P 48	6 oz.	Adhesive
B 5	1	Bolt kit

EXHIBIT 9-1

Standard Bill of Materials

Causes for Variances

Again, what does the manager *do* with the variances? He seeks explanations for their existence. Common causes of quantity variances include: improper handling; inferior quality of material; poor workmanship; changes in methods; new workmen; slow machines; broken cutting tools; and faulty blueprints.

The key questions in the analysis and follow-up of variances are: *Why* do we have this particular variance? What will we *do* with it? If practical use cannot be made of the variance figure, it should not be computed.

Control Procedures

There are many ways of systematizing the control of quantity variances. One popular way is to issue direct material only in response to a

Standard Bill of Materials (Exhibit 9-1), which states the amount of material that should be needed to produce a specified number of acceptable units. As manufacturing proceeds, additional material may be obtained only by submitting a special *excess materials requisition*. From the latter, the material usage variance is compiled.

Labor time variances are usually carefully followed by foremen, who scrutinize work tickets. These coded tickets may have a number showing the department, another number showing the particular operation (e.g., the work-step like milling, boring, grinding), and another number showing the cause of the variance.

Mutual Price and Quantity Effects

The usual breakdown of variances into price and quantity is not theoretically perfect because there may be a small mutual price-quantity effect. A production foreman and a purchasing agent might argue over the following situation. The direct material standard is 1,000 pounds @ $1, to produce 1,000 good finished units. The performance report shows the use of 1,150 pounds @ $1.20, to produce 1,000 good finished units.

The ordinary analysis of variances would appear as follows:

Actual quantity × Actual price or 1,150 × $1.20 =			$1,380
Price variance	= Difference in price × Actual pounds		
	= ($1.20 − $1) × 1,150 =	$230 *U*	
Quantity variance	= Difference in quantity × Standard price		
	= (1,150 − 1,000) × $1 =	150 *U*	
Total variance explained			380 *U*
Standard quantity allowed for units produced × Standard price			
	= 1,000 × $1 =		$1,000

The small area in the upper right-hand corner of the graphic analysis (Exhibit 9-2) is the area of controversy. The purchasing officer might readily accept responsibility for the price variance on the 1,000 pounds in the standard allowance, but he might claim that the extra $30 which is buried in his $230 total variance is more properly attributable to the production foreman. After all, if the foreman had produced in accordance with the standard, the extra 150 pounds would not have been needed. But this distinction is not often made, simply because it usually involves a small sum. However, we should be aware that the conventional variance analysis, which includes the joint price-quantity variance ($30, in this case) as a part of an over-all price variance, has logical deficiencies.

In practice, the quantity variance is considered much more important than the price variance, because the manager can exert more direct influence over the quantity variance. Consequently, the performance report on quantity should minimize the possibility of the production manager's criticisms of any accounting or measurement methods. Joint price-quantity

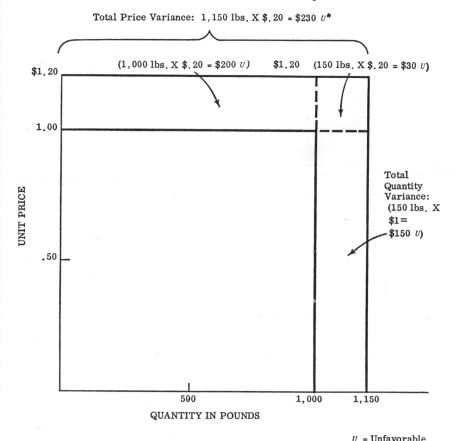

Total Price Variance: 1,150 lbs. X $.20 = $230 U^*

(1,000 lbs. X $.20 = $200 U) $1.20   (150 lbs. X $.20 = $30 U)

$1.20

1.00

UNIT PRICE

.50

Total
Quantity
Variance:
(150 lbs. X
$1=
$150 U)

500   1,000   1,150

QUANTITY IN POUNDS

U = Unfavorable

EXHIBIT 9-2

Graphic Analysis of Variances

variance is less likely to cause arguments if it is buried in the total price
variance than if it is buried in the quantity variance.

FLEXIBLE BUDGETS

Modification of Techniques for Overhead Items

In our discussion of direct material and direct labor, we have emphasized the necessity of fixing responsibility, of setting standards, and of
measuring performance against the standards. Special source documents,
such as excess material requisitions and work tickets for excessive time, are
used as a basis for collecting variances. Similar ideas underlie the control
of other costs in the organization. Two basic questions must be asked in

approaching the control of all costs: How do individual costs behave? Who is responsible for their control?

In this section, we will continue our study of individual cost behavior, with special emphasis on flexible departmental overhead budgets. The problem of fixing responsibility, which is approached through so-called responsibility accounting systems and reports, is discussed in Chapter 11.

Every organization has individual items of cost that are relatively huge. In a wholesaling or retailing business, the purchase cost of merchandise is usually the most important item. In a manufacturing business, the costs of direct materials and direct labor are usually both important. The distinct importance of such individual items generates elaborate formal techniques for controlling them.

Other costs, usually classified as manufacturing, selling, or administrative overhead, must also be planned and controlled. However, the techniques differ because: (1) the size of individual overhead costs does not usually warrant elaborate individual control systems; (2) the various items are the responsibility of different individuals; and (3) the individual costs differ considerably.

Characteristics of Flexible Budgets

As a general term, the word "budget" embraces any formalized quantitative plan. The budget may include all of the organization's activities—cash planning, production scheduling, and the purchases of paper clips. The term "flexible budget," often called variable budget, usually refers to overhead costs only. (Some manufacturing companies, however, also include total direct material and total direct labor in their flexible budgets.) The important point is not what items are included or excluded from a particular flexible budget; rather, it is the flexibility which is built into the technique.

"Flexible" is the key word. All other budgets have two characteristics: (1) They are usually prepared for *one* target level of activity. A typical budget is a single plan encompassing sales, production, and cash figures required to meet a target volume of, say, 1,000,000 units. (2) They are a *static* basis for comparison. All results are compared with the original plan, regardless of changes in ensuing conditions—even *if* for example, the volume of production turns out to be 1,100,000 units instead of the original 1,000,000.

In contrast, flexible budgets have the following distinguishing features:

1. They are prepared for a *range of activity* rather than for a single level.
2. They provide a *dynamic* basis for comparison because they are automatically geared to changes in the level of volume. In other words, the flexible budget approach says, "You tell me what your activity level was during the past month, and I'll provide a budget that specifies what costs *should have been*. I'll go to my flexible budget toolbag and tailor a budget to the particular volume—after the fact."

Comparison of Static and Flexible Budgets

Consider the following condensed example. The planned level of activity for a machining department, expressed in finished units of production, is 5,000 for the next month. Exhibit 9-3 is the budget for the variable overhead items.

EXHIBIT 9-3

Machining Department
Static Budget, Variable Overhead
For the Month of June, 19x1

Units to be produced	5,000
Variable overhead:	
Indirect labor	$2,100
Supplies	500
Repairs	400
Total	$3,000

Assume that June has ended. The units produced were only 4,700, principally because of a work stoppage caused by storm. Exhibit 9-4 is the performance report which would be prepared under a static budget approach.

EXHIBIT 9-4

Performance Report

	Actual	*Budget*	*Variance*
Units produced	4,700	5,000	300 *U*
Indirect labor	$2,080	$2,100	$ 20 *F*
Supplies	480	500	20 *F*
Repairs	400	400	—
	$2,960	$3,000	$ 40 *F*

The foreman of this department has two major obligations: (1) to meet his production schedules; and (2) to produce any given output efficiently. These two obligations can and should be separated in judging his performance. The trouble with the static budget is that it fails to distinguish between these two facets of a manager's performance.

The idea of comparing performance at one activity level with a plan that was developed at some other activity level is nonsense from a *control* viewpoint, from the viewpoint of judging how efficiently a manager has produced any given output. However, such a comparison may be pertinent in judging how well a manager has adhered to a single objective, the meeting of a target production schedule. The foreman and his superiors may wish to know about the top line in Exhibit 9-4, which contains the information that production was only 4,700, rather than 5,000, units. The use of a static budget for this purpose provides helpful information. However, the use of a 5,000-unit budget for judging how efficiently (on the next three lines of the report) the given output of **4,700** units was produced is an example of using a good tool for the wrong purpose.

Basic Approach of the Flexible Budget

The flexible budget approach is based on an adequate knowledge of cost behavior patterns. It is essentially a means for constructing a budget tailored to *any* level of activity within the relevant range. In some companies using a flexible budget technique, the budget would resemble Exhibit 9-5.

EXHIBIT 9-5

Machining Department
Flexible Budget, Variable Overhead
For the Month of June, 19x1

	*Budget Formula**	*Various Levels of Activity*			
Units produced		4,600	4,800	5,000	5,200
Indirect labor	42¢ per unit	$1,932	$2,016	$2,100	$2,184
Supplies	10¢ per unit	460	480	500	520
Repairs	8¢ per unit	368	384	400	416
Total variable overhead	60¢ per unit	$2,760	$2,880	$3,000	$3,120

* The budget formulas used in this chapter assume strictly variable behavior. Flexible budgets often can encompass mixed costs also. The budgeting technique for mixed costs was described in Chapter 8.

Note that the budget would not necessarily have to be shown for the 4,600 to 5,200 activity levels. The essential ingredient is the budget formula, which may be used in constructing a total budget for any given activity level within the relevant range. For example, the performance report prepared at the *end* of June (Exhibit 9-6) shows the application of the budget formula to the 4,700-unit level of activity.

EXHIBIT 9-6

Machining Department
Performance Report
For the Month of June, 19x1

	Actual	*Budget*	*Variance*	*Explanation*
Units produced	4,700	4,700	—	—
Indirect labor	$2,080	$1,974	$106 *U*	Idle time due to storm
Supplies	480	470	10 *U*	None offered
Repairs	400	376	24 *U*	Extra repairs due to storm
Total variable overhead	$2,960	$2,820	$140 U	

This report shows unfavorable variances, in contrast to the favorable variances in the performance report prepared under the static budget (Exhibit 9-4). Unfavorable variances do not always indicate inefficiency. In this case, the unfavorable performance is largely traceable to outside influences—the storm. Random influences will always affect variances to some extent. However, it should be evident that the flexible budget presents a more meaningful comparison of the foreman's day-to-day overhead cost control, because the level of activity underlying the comparison is the same. On the other hand, the flexible budget does not directly report the foreman's deviation from his production schedule. The ideal combination, therefore, is a flexible budget for measuring efficient use of input factors, accompanied by information, perhaps expressed in units only, about the manager's ability to meet any single production schedule (or, in the case of a sales manager, any single sales target).

Terminology and Flexible Budgets

In this book, the term "flexible budgets" will relate to *variable costs* only. Since fixed costs will not change, in total, as activity fluctuates within a relevant range, static budgets are adequate for planning and controlling fixed costs. We shall examine the problem of controlling fixed costs more closely in Chapter 10.

In many organizations, no distinctions are made between variable and fixed costs in overhead budgeting. The resulting flexible budgets will be influenced by both variable and fixed cost behavior. The part representing fixed costs is really a static budget. In other words, although the flexible budget totals will be different at each level of activity, their behavior will be *mixed* (i.e., will consist of a static fixed portion per month plus a dynamic variable portion geared to fluctuations in activity) rather than *strictly variable*, as we assume in this text.

RECAPITULATION OF CONTROL OF VARIABLE COSTS

Similarity of Approach

At this point let us examine the similarity in approach to the control of all variable costs: direct material; direct labor; and variable manufacturing, selling or administrative overhead. Two types of variances are distinguished: (1) price, rate, or spending; and (2) quantity, efficiency, or usage. A thorough analysis rests on the three key figures shown in Exhibit 9-7.

EXHIBIT 9-7

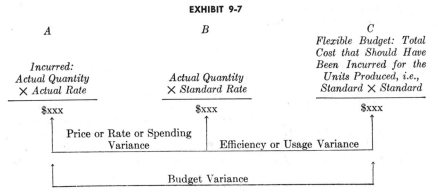

The meaning and significance of price and efficiency variances in relation to direct material costs and direct labor costs were discussed in the previous section. Now we shall study the meaning of the spending and efficiency variances in relation to variable overhead costs.

Spending and Efficiency Variances

Assume that a department produces 7,000 units. The standard direct labor time per unit is two hours. The hourly labor rate is $4. The variable overhead rate per hour is $1.50, computed as follows:

Actual Costs Incurred		Budget Formula per Standard Direct Labor Hour
$11,100	Labor to transport materials internally	$ .80
3,550	Idle time	.20
2,500	Clean-up time	.15
800	Other indirect labor	.05
3,100	Lubricants and coolants	.20
1,600	Polishing supplies	.10
$22,650	Total variable overhead	$1.50

The actual direct labor time needed for production was 15,000 hours. The actual average labor rate was $4.10.

See if you can satisfy the requirements before studying the solution to questions 1 and 2 (Exhibit 9-8) and the solution to question 3, which is discussed in the next paragraph. Exhibit 9-8 is an extremely important exhibit. The format of the Summary Explanations at the bottom of the exhibit is particularly helpful in variance analysis.

Required:

1. Prepare a detailed performance report, with two major sections: direct labor and variable overhead.
2. Prepare a summary analysis of direct labor rate variance, direct labor efficiency variance, variable overhead spending variance, and variable overhead efficiency variance.
3. Explain the similarities and differences between the direct labor and the variable overhead variances.

SOLUTION

1. and 2. See Exhibit 9-8.
3. *The limitation of analyses of variances should be stressed. The only way to discover why variable overhead performance did not agree with the budget* is to investigate possible causes, *item* by *item*, from Labor to Transport Material through Polishing Supplies. However, the summary analysis helps us to find out what to look for in a more detailed investigation.

   The subdivision (in Exhibit 9-8) of the budget variance for variable overhead into *spending variance* and *efficiency variance* is similar to the

EXHIBIT 9-8

Analysis of Direct Labor and Variable Overhead Variances
Department Performance Report
Direct Labor and Variable Overhead

Actual Hours   15,000
Standard Hours Allowed   14,000
Excess Hours   1,000

	Actual Costs Incurred	Budget Based on 14,000 Standard Direct Labor Hours Allowed for 7,000 Units (Standard × Standard)	Total Budget Variance to be Explained
Direct labor	$61,500	$56,000	$5,500 U
Variable overhead:			
Labor to transfer materials within the factory	$11,100	$11,200	$ 100 F
Idle time	3,550	2,800	750 U
Clean-up time	2,500	2,100	400 U
Other indirect labor	800	700	100 U
Lubricants and coolants	3,100	2,800	300 U
Polishing materials	1,600	1,400	200 U
Total variable overhead	$22,650	$21,000	$1,650 U

Summary Explanation:

Direct Labor

A	B	C
Incurred: Actual Quantity × Actual Rate	Actual Quantity × Standard Rate	Flexible Budget: Standard Rate × Standard Hours Allowed
(15,000 hrs. × $4.10)	(15,000 hrs. × $4)	(14,000 hrs. × $4)
$61,500	$60,000	$56,000

15,000 hrs. × ($4.10 − $4) = Rate variance, $1,500 U

(15,000 hrs. − 14,000 hrs.) × $4 = Efficiency variance, $4,000 U

Total budget variance $5,500 U

Variable Overhead

(15,000 hrs. × average rate of $1.51)	(15,000 hrs. × $1.50)	(14,000 hrs. × $1.50)
$22,650	$22,500	$21,000

15,000 hrs. × ($1.51 − $1.50) = Spending variance, $150 U

(15,000 hrs. − 14,000 hrs.) × $1.50 = Efficiency variance, $1,500 U

Total budget variance $1,650 U

split of the total direct labor variance into *rate variance* and *efficiency variance.*

The efficiency variance for overhead is a measure of the extra overhead costs (or savings) incurred solely because direct labor usage exceeded (or was less than) the standard direct labor hours allowed. Because variable overhead is often most closely related to labor time, fluctuations in overhead costs should correspond with variances in labor time.

Overhead efficiency variance =
(Actual hours − Standard hours allowed) × Overhead rate

Note the similarity between the efficiency variances for direct labor and for variable overhead. Both are differences between actual hours and standard hours allowed multiplied by a standard rate.

The spending variance is similar to the labor rate variance, but its causal factors encompass more than price changes alone. Other causes include: poor budget estimates for one or more individual overhead items; variation in attention to and control of individual costs; and erratic behavior of individual overhead items that have been squeezed for convenience into a budget formula with only one base (i.e., hours of labor). The cost of labor for transporting materials, for example, may be closely related to the number of units started during a period and have nothing directly to do with the standard direct labor hours worked.

How Should Activity Be Measured?

So far we have been expressing measures of activity or volume in convenient terms. In practice, the measurement of volume is not so easy, except in the rare instance of a department which produces only one uniform product. When there are a variety of products or operations, the following criteria should be of help in selecting a measure of volume:

1. *Cause of cost fluctuation.* An individual cost should be related to some activity that causes that cost to vary. Common measures include hours of labor, machine hours, weight of materials handled, miles traveled, number of calls made by salesmen, number of beds in a hospital, number of lines billed, number of credit investigations, and so forth.

2. *Adequacy of control over base.* The common denominator which serves as a measure of activity must be under adequate control. *Because it is not affected by variations in performance, the standard direct labor hours allowance for units produced is a better measure of volume than actual direct labor hours.* A department head should not enjoy a more generous budget allowance because of his inefficiency, which would increase both the actual hours and his budget—if the budget were based on actual hours instead of standard hours allowed.

If standard allowances are developed for all the factors of production, one factor may be tied to the other so that all factors may be related to a common base. For example, if it takes one pound of direct material, one grinding wheel, one machine hour, and one direct labor hour to produce one finished unit, usage may be related to the standard direct labor hour as follows: If 1,000 standard direct labor hours are used, the use of 1,000 units of each of the other factors may be anticipated. These relationships may be expedient and meaningful even though use of grinding wheels, repairs, and the like is most closely related to finished units produced.

To summarize, an index of activity based on actual hours fluctuates with efficiency; it is not a uniform common denominator. The use of standard hours or of some base built on standard hours (e.g., standard direct labor dollars) causes the cost variations due to inefficient usage of the budget base factor to appear as variances.

3. *Independence of activity unit.* The activity unit should not be greatly affected by variable factors other than volume. For example, the use of total direct labor dollars or total dollar sales, as a measure of volume, is subject to the basic weakness of being changeable by labor rate or price fluctuations. The use of machine hours or labor hours eliminates the unwanted influence of fluctuations in the purchasing power of the dollar. Then, if physical volume does not change, a change in wage rates does not necessarily mean a change in other costs. The effects of price changes should not affect the unit with which activity is measured; this is usually accomplished by using standard wage rates or uniform sales prices.

Standard labor costs (labor hours × standard hourly rates) and standard sales dollars (units × selling prices) are frequently used in place of labor hours or physical units *because they accurately reflect changes in physical volume without requiring the computation of labor hours or the weighted averages of a variety of physical units.*

4. *Ease of Understanding.* Units for the measurement of activity should be easily understandable and should be obtainable at minimum clerical expense. Complicated indexes are undesirable.

The Question of Accuracy

Much of the literature on standard costs and budgets conveys the impression that they are always based on elaborate engineering studies and rigorous specifications. Less scientific standards also provide a forceful way of presenting information that will stimulate corrective action. An accounting system is effective when it routinely focuses management's eyes on the areas that warrant investigation. The accuracy of standards and budgets is not as basic to successful management control as the more fundamental notion—that of the relevance of using some predetermined targets as a means of implementing management by exception.

SUMMARY

Management is best aided by carefully prepared standards and budgets representing what *should be* accomplished. These standards should be based on material specifications and on work measurement, rather than on past performance, because the latter too often conceals past inefficiencies.

Currently attainable standards are the most widely used because they have the most desirable motivational impact and because they may be used for a variety of accounting purposes, including financial planning, as well as for monitoring departmental performance.

When standards are currently attainable, there is no logical difference between standards and budgets. A standard is a *unit* concept, while a budget is a *total* concept. In a sense, the standard is the budget for one unit.

The assessment of performance is aided by a comparison of actual results with budgeted expectations. The resulting variances are often divided into price and quantity factors. In practice, the quantity (usage or efficiency) factors are more important because they are subject to more direct management influence than prices of materials or wages.

There is a similarity in approach to the control of all costs that are regarded as strictly variable. The *price* (rate or spending) variance is the *difference in price* × *actual quantity*. The *quantity* (usage or efficiency) variance is the *difference in quantity* × *standard price*.

Variances raise questions; they don't provide answers. The analysis and follow-up of variances are the keys to successful management control. Variances provide clues, jog memories, and open pertinent avenues for management investigation. If managers do not do anything with the performance variances, then either the reporting system needs overhauling or the managers need educating and selling.

Standard bills of material, excess material requisitions, special tickets for extra work, and master operations lists (Exhibit 8-1) are documents that aid control.

Flexible budgets are geared to changing levels of activity rather than to a single, static level. They are used particularly for manufacturing, selling, and administrative department overhead control. They are based on careful studies of variable cost behavior patterns. Consequently, flexible budgets may be tailored to a particular volume—before or after the fact.

Flexible budgets tell how much cost *should have been* incurred for any level of output, which is usually expressed either in product units or standard direct labor hours. Flexible budgets provide a basis for measuring departmental overhead control but do not, in themselves, measure a manager's ability to meet a given production schedule.

In this book, *flexible budgets* are based on variable costs only. Fixed costs are not included in the flexible budget. (They are controlled separately, as we will see in Chapter 10). In practice, this terminology is not uniformly used.

Because it is a figure not affected by variations in performance, the standard direct labor hours allowed is a better yardstick than actual direct labor hours for measuring volume or activity.

SUMMARY PROBLEM FOR YOUR REVIEW

PROBLEM

The Didgid Co. uses standard costs to control its direct material and direct labor costs. The purchasing agent is responsible for material price variances, and the production manager is responsible for material usage variances, direct labor rate and efficiency variances, and variable manufacturing overhead spending and efficiency variances.

Operating data for the past week are summarized as follows:

Finished units produced: 5,000.

Direct material: Purchases, 10,000 lbs. @ $1.50. Standard price, $1.60 per lb. Used, 5,400 lbs. Standard allowed per unit produced, 1 lb.

Direct labor: Actual costs, 8,000 hours @ $3.05, or $24,400.
Standard allowed per good unit produced, 1½ hours.
Standard rate per direct labor hour $3.

Variable manufacturing overhead: Actual costs, $8,800. Budget formula is $1 per standard direct labor hour.

Required:

1. Material purchase price variance; material quantity variance; direct labor rate variance; direct labor efficiency variance; variable manufacturing overhead spending and efficiency variances.
2. *a.* What is the budget allowance for direct labor?
   b. Would it be any different if production were 6,000 good units?

SOLUTION

1. The format of the solution (Exhibit 9-9) may seem awkward at first, but you will find, upon review, that it provides perspective on the analysis of variances.

EXHIBIT 9-9

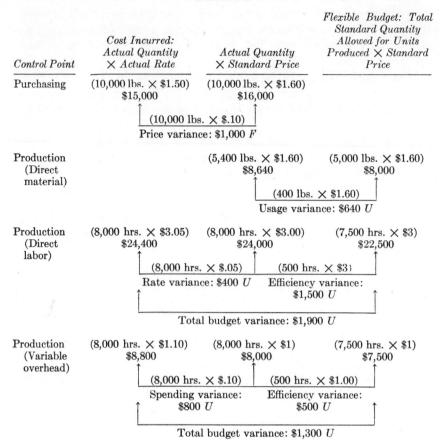

Control Point	Cost Incurred: Actual Quantity × Actual Rate	Actual Quantity × Standard Price	Flexible Budget: Total Standard Quantity Allowed for Units Produced × Standard Price
Purchasing	(10,000 lbs. × $1.50) $15,000	(10,000 lbs. × $1.60) $16,000	
		(10,000 lbs. × $.10) Price variance: $1,000 F	
Production (Direct material)		(5,400 lbs. × $1.60) $8,640	(5,000 lbs. × $1.60) $8,000
		(400 lbs. × $1.60) Usage variance: $640 U	
Production (Direct labor)	(8,000 hrs. × $3.05) $24,400	(8,000 hrs. × $3.00) $24,000	(7,500 hrs. × $3) $22,500
	(8,000 hrs. × $.05) Rate variance: $400 U	(500 hrs. × $3) Efficiency variance: $1,500 U	
	Total budget variance: $1,900 U		
Production (Variable overhead)	(8,000 hrs. × $1.10) $8,800	(8,000 hrs. × $1) $8,000	(7,500 hrs. × $1) $7,500
	(8,000 hrs. × $.10) Spending variance: $800 U	(500 hrs. × $1.00) Efficiency variance: $500 U	
	Total budget variance: $1,300 U		

2. The flexible budget allowance for any variable cost is the *same as* (is equal to) the total standard quantity allowed for the good units produced × the standard price.

   The budget allowance under standard costing for variable costs will always depend on *output,* the units produced. Therefore, the budgetary allowance for 5,000 units is, as shown above, 5,000 units × 1½ hours × $3 = $22,500. For 6,000 units, the budgetary allowance would be 6,000 units × 1½ hours × $3 = $27,000. Note again that a budget can be established *after the fact*—after the number of good units produced is known—under a standard cost system.

SUGGESTED READINGS

Bennett, C., *Standard Costs: How They Serve Modern Management.* Englewood Cliffs, N.J.: Prentice-Hall, Inc., 1957.

Beyer, R., *Profitability Accounting for Planning and Control*. New York: The Ronald Press Company, 1963. Especially strong in the area of flexible budgeting.

Gillespie, C., *Standard and Direct Costing*. Englewood Cliffs, N.J.: Prentice-Hall, Inc., 1962.

Henrici, S., *Standard Costs for Manufacturing*, 3rd ed. New York: McGraw-Hill Book Company, 1960.

How Standard Costs Are Being Used Currently, New York: National Association of Accountants, 1950.

ASSIGNMENT MATERIAL

ESSENTIAL ASSIGNMENT MATERIAL

9-1. *Terminology.* Define: currently attainable standards; standard cost; price variance; rate variance; bill of materials; quantity variance; usage variance; flexible budget; variable budget; static budget; spending variance; efficiency variance; excess material requisitions; and master operations lists.

9-2. *Comprehensive problem in standards and budgets.* The Wentworth Co. uses standard costs and flexible budgets to help control its costs of direct material, direct labor, and variable manufacturing overhead. All variances are regarded as the responsibility of the production manager, except that material price variances are attributable to the purchasing manager.

Operating data for the month of June, in which 8,000 finished units were produced, are summarized as follows.

Purchases of direct material: 12,000 lbs. @ $1.70, which is $.20 below the standard price.

Usage of direct material: 8,500 lbs. The standard allowance per finished unit is one lb.

Direct labor: Standard rate is $4 hourly. Standard time allowance per unit is 2 hours. Actual cost was $69,700. Actual hourly rates averaged $4.10.

Variable manufacturing overhead: Budget formula is $1.20 per standard direct labor hour. Actual costs, $20,000.

Required:

1. Material purchase price variance — Direct labor efficiency variance
   Material usage variance — Variable manufacturing overhead
   Direct labor rate variance — spending, efficiency, and budget variances

2. Although the term "flexible budget" is commonly linked only with overhead items, it can also embrace direct material and direct labor. In this problem, what is the budget allowance for direct labor? Would it be different if production were 7,000 units?

9-3. *Similarity of direct labor and variable overhead variances.* The Clax Co. has had great difficulty controlling costs during the past three years. Last month, a standard cost and flexible budget system was installed. A condensation of results for a department follows:

	Expected Behavior per Standard Direct Labor Hour	Total Budget Variance
Lubricants	$ .30	$200 F
Other supplies	.20	150 U
Rework	.40	300 U
Other indirect labor	.50	300 U
Total variable overhead	$1.40	$550 U

F = Favorable
U = Unfavorable

The department had initially planned to manufacture 6,000 units in 4,000 standard direct labor hours. However, material shortage and a heat wave resulted in the production of 5,400 units in 3,900 actual direct labor hours. The standard wage rate is $3.50 per hour, which was $.20 higher than the actual average hourly rate.

Required:

1. A detailed performance report with two major sections: direct labor and variable overhead.

2. Summary analysis of rate and efficiency variances for direct labor and spending and efficiency variances for variable overhead.

3. Explain the similarities and differences between the direct labor and variable overhead variances. What are some of the likely causes of the detailed spending variances?

ADDITIONAL ASSIGNMENT MATERIAL

Problems 9-21 through 9-24 provide additional practice in the analysis of variances. Problems 9-26 and 9-27 require a close examination of flexible budgeting.

9-4. "Direct material and direct labor may be included in a flexible budget." Do you agree? Explain.

9-5. Distinguish between input and output.

9-6. Why should a budgeted cost not be merely an extension of past experience?

9-7. Distinguish between ideal and currently attainable standards.

9-8. What is the difference between a standard amount and a budget amount?

9-9. What are expected variances?

9-10. "Price variances should be computed even if prices are regarded as outside of company control." Do you agree? Explain.

9-11. "Failure to meet price standards is the responsibility of the purchasing officer." Do you agree? Explain.

9-12. Why do labor rate variances tend to be insignificant?

9-13. What are the key questions in the analysis and follow-up of variances?

9-14. What are some common causes of quantity variances?

9-15. Why is the joint price-quantity variance buried in the price variance rather than in the quantity variance?

9-16. What two basic questions must be asked in approaching the control of all costs?

9-17. Why do the techniques for controlling overhead differ from those for controlling direct material and direct labor?

9-18. "The flex in the flexible budget relates solely to variable costs." Do you agree? Explain.

9-19. How does the overhead spending variance differ from the labor rate variance?

9-20. Why are standard hours superior to actual hours as an index of activity?

9-21. *Prepare performance report for variable overhead.* The variable overhead items for the lathe department of Sloan Co. include:

	Budget Amount per Standard Labor Hour
Machine setup	$0.35
Material handling	0.20
Inspection	0.20
Idle time	not allowed
Lubricants	0.15
Miscellaneous supplies	0.30
Total budget formula	$1.20

Actual variable overhead incurred during January, 19x4 is:

Machine setup	$ 375
Material handling	200
Inspection	250
Idle time	50
Lubricants	140
Miscellaneous supplies	380
Total	$1,395

Standard hours allowed for work done were 1,000. Actual hours required were 1,100.

Required:

1. Prepare a performance report.
2. Prepare a summary analysis of the spending and efficiency variances for variable overhead.

9-22. *Comprehensive, straightforward problem on standard cost system.* The Flagon Co. uses a standard cost system. The month's data regarding its lone product follow:

Variable overhead budgeted at $.90 per hour
Standard direct labor cost: $4 per hour
Standard material cost: $1 per pound
Standard pounds of material in a finished unit: 3
Standard direct labor hours per finished unit: 5
Material purchased (10,000 lbs.): $9,500
Material used: 6,700 lbs.
Direct labor costs incurred (11,000 hours): $41,800
Variable overhead costs incurred: $9,500
Finished units produced: 2,000

Required:

Prepare schedules of all variable cost variances, using the approach described in this chapter.

9-23. *Variance analysis.* The Laxer Co. uses a standard cost system and a flexible budget. At a normal level of activity of 12,000 finished units and 36,000 standard direct labor hours, the following standard variable costs would be applied to production:

Direct material	$144,000
Direct labor	108,000
Factory variable overhead	18,000
	$270,000

During August, 38,800 direct labor hours were actually needed to produce a total of 13,000 finished units. The actual costs of this production included $120,280 for direct labor and $19,700 for variable overhead.

Required:

1. Standard variable cost per finished unit.
2. Direct labor rate and efficiency variances.
3. Variable overhead spending and efficiency variances.

9-24. *Routine analysis of variances.* The Emblen Co. makes only one product, called Unknown X. The standard variable costs for one unit are:

EMBLEN CO.

Standard Cost Sheet
Unknown X

Direct material: 1 unit @ $.50	$0.50
Direct labor: 1 hour @ $2	2.00
Variable overhead: 1 hour @ $1.50	1.50
Total variable costs per unit	$4.00

There are no initial inventories. Production for the month of June was 10,000 units. The costs for this production are as follows:

Materials purchased: 15,000 units @ $.40	$ 6,000
Materials used: 11,000 units	
Direct labor: 9,000 hours @ $2.10	18,900
Variable overhead incurred	16,000

The overhead rate is based on direct labor hours.

Compute the following variances from the standard and designate them as favorable or unfavorable.

1. Materials purchase price.
2. Materials usage.
3. (a) Direct labor rate;
   (b) Direct labor efficiency.

4. (a) Variable overhead spending variance;
   (b) Variable overhead efficiency variance.

9-25. *Flexible budgets and the income statement; mixed costs.* (SICA Adapted.)
The Harrison Co. Ltd. manufactures and distributes a single product. The
company has prepared a flexible budget for the fiscal year, ending June 30,
19x0, that forecasts the following income and costs at the maximum and
minimum levels of activity:

	Maximum Level	Minimum Level
Production	*8,000 units*	*6,000 units*
Manufacturing costs		
Material	$ 80,000	$ 60,000
Direct labor	64,000	48,000
Manufacturing expense:		
Indirect labor	20,000	16,000
Supplies expense	10,000	7,600
Depreciation expense	6,800	6,800
Other expenses	7,200	5,600
Total manufacturing costs	$188,000	$144,000
Sales		
8,000 units	$320,000	
6,000 units		$240,000
Selling expenses		
Sales salaries	$ 33,600	$ 28,000
Sales commissions	16,000	12,000
Advertising expense	13,600	11,200
Traveling expenses	6,000	6,000
Other expenses	4,800	4,000
Total selling expenses	$ 74,000	$ 61,200
Administrative expenses		
Administrative salaries	$ 16,000	$ 14,000
Directors' fees	6,000	6,000
Other expenses	6,000	4,800
Total administrative expenses	$ 28,000	$ 24,800
Net profit	$ 30,000	$ 10,000

During the year ending June 30, 19x0, 6,400 units were made and sold for
$256,000. Actual costs for the year were:

Material	$67,200
Indirect labor	16,000
Depreciation expense	6,800
Sales salaries	29,200
Advertising expense	11,000
Other selling expenses	4,320
Directors' fees	6,000
Direct labor	49,600
Supplies expense	9,800
Other manufacturing expenses	6,400
Sales commissions	12,800
Traveling expenses	6,480
Administrative salaries	14,600
Other administrative expenses	5,200

Required:

1. Using the forecasted figures as a basis, prepare a statement showing budgeted cost allowances for the actual level of activity. Compare budgeted and actual expenditures, showing clearly any favorable or unfavorable variances.
2. Calculate the break-even point for this business on the basis of the flexible budget.

9-26. *Flexible and static budgets.* The Bentley Co. executives have had trouble interpreting operating performance for a number of years. The company has used a budget based on detailed expectations for the forthcoming quarter. For example, the condensed performance report for a recent quarter for assembly department overhead was:

	Budget	Actual	Variance
Units of production	100,000	95,000	
Variable:			
Idle time	$10,000	$ 9,800	$200 *F*
Rework	20,000	19,900	100 *F*
Other indirect labor	40,000	39,500	500 *F*
Supplies	10,000	9,900	100 *F*
Total variable overhead	$80,000	$79,100	$900 *F*
Fixed:			
Supervision	$10,000	$10,000	—
Factory rent	1,000	1,000	—
Depreciation on equipment	1,000	1,000	—
Total fixed overhead	$12,000	$12,000	—
Total overhead	$92,000	$91,100	$900 *F*

The department head was proud of his favorable performance report, but the factory superintendent was unhappy and commented: "I can see some merit in comparing actual performance with budgeted performance, in the sense that we can see whether actual volume coincided with our best guess for budget purposes. But I can't see how this performance report helps me evaluate the day-to-day control performance of the department head."

Required:

1. Prepare a performance report that might provide the superintendent with better insight into the department head's performance.
2. Prepare a columnar flexible budget at 90,000, 100,000 and 110,000-unit levels of volume. Have your budget include both variable and fixed costs, even though the chapter confined flexible budgets to variable costs only.
3. Express (2) in formula form.
4. In light of requirements (1) through (3), evaluate the contention that performance reports should be confined to variable overhead items only.

9-27. *Spending and efficiency variances and selection of standard or actual hours as a volume base.*

1. Refer to Problem 9-26. Assume that a standard cost system is in use. The standard direct labor time allowed to complete one unit is two hours. The standard direct labor rate is $3.50 per hour. The total actual direct labor costs incurred were $663,000 for 195,000 hours. Compute:

(1) Direct labor *rate* and *efficiency* variances.

(2) Total variable overhead *spending* and *efficiency* variances. Show your work.

2. The analysis in Requirement (1) assumed that the budget allowance for variable overhead was based on the standard hours allowed for the units produced. Repeat your analysis in part (1) for direct labor and variable overhead, but assume that the budget allowance is based solely on the 195,000 actual hours worked. What would be the budget variance for direct labor and variable overhead? Could it be subdivided for further analysis? Why are budget allowances based on standard hours allowed for units produced superior to budget allowances based on actual hours worked (input)?

9-28. *Review problem on standards and flexible budgets; answers provided.* The Alphonse Company makes a variety of leather goods. It uses standard costs and a flexible budget to aid planning and control. Budgeted variable overhead at a 60,000 direct-labor-hour level is $36,000.

During April the company had an unfavorable variable overhead efficiency variance of $1,200. Material purchases were $322,500. Actual direct labor costs incurred were $187,600. The direct labor efficiency variance was $6,000 unfavorable. The actual average wage rate was $.20 lower than the average standard wage rate.

The company uses a variable overhead rate of 20 per cent of standard direct labor *cost* for flexible budgeting purposes. Actual variable overhead for the month was $41,000.

Required:

Use U or F to indicate whether requested variances are favorable or unfavorable.

1. Standard direct labor cost per hour.
2. Actual direct labor hours worked.
3. Total direct labor rate variance.
4. Total flexible budget for direct labor costs.
5. Total direct labor variance.
6. Variable overhead spending variance in total.

Answers to Problem 9-28:

1. $3.00. The variable overhead rate is $.60, obtained by dividing $36,000 by 60,000 hours. Therefore, the direct labor rate must be $.60 ÷ .20 = $3.00.
2. 67,000 hours. Actual costs, $187,600 ÷ ($3.00 − $.20) = 67,000 hours.
3. $13,400 F. 67,000 actual hours × $.20 = $13,400.
4. $195,000. Efficiency variance was $6,000, unfavorable. Therefore, excess hours must have been $6,000 ÷ $3.00 = 2,000. Consequently, standard hours allowed must be 67,000 − 2,000 = 65,000. Flexible budget = 65,000 × $3.00 = $195,000.
5. $7,400 F. $195,000 − $187,600 = $7,400 F; or $13,400 F − $6,000 U = $7,400 F.
6. $800 U. Flexible budget = 65,000 × $.60 = $39,000. Total variance = $41,000 − $39,000 = $2,000 U. Spending variance = $2,000 − $1,200 efficiency variance = $800 U.

CHAPTER 10

Control of Fixed Costs: Programmed and Committed Costs

ADVANCES IN AUTOMATION, INCREASES IN TECHNICAL SPECIALI-zation, and pressures toward stable employment have had a substantial effect on the cost behavior patterns of organizations. More costs are tending to become fixed. In this chapter, we shall investigate the techniques for controlling fixed costs.

Fixed costs provide *capacity* for manufacturing, sales, administration, and research. They often entail relatively heavy sums and long spans of time. Hence, decisions regarding fixed costs are far-reaching and usually have sizable short-run and long-run effects. The implications for managers are twofold: First, *planning* techniques are crucial. Second, once acquired, the capacity should be *utilized* as fully as possible—provided, of course, that the increase in revenue exceeds the increase in costs as volume increases.

The planning of long-range commitments for plant and equipment, new products, and the like often involves discounted cash flow techniques. We shall discuss this type of problem solving in detail in Chapter 14. In this chapter, we shall concentrate on the planning of programmed costs and the utilization of capacity already on hand. The emphasis will be on attention directing.

236

PROGRAMMED COSTS

Difficulties of Measurement

As we defined them in Chapter 8, programmed costs, also called managed costs, are those fixed costs which arise from periodic appropriation decisions that directly reflect top management policies. Programmed costs are an assortment of manufacturing, selling, administrative, and research items. Like committed costs, they should be carefully planned and fully utilized if net income is to be maximized. Unlike committed costs, they can be influenced more easily from period to period. It is also harder to measure the utilization of programmed costs, principally because the results of services like creative personnel, advertising, research, and training programs are much more difficult to isolate and quantify than the results of utilizing plant and equipment to make products.

Lump-sum appropriations for advertising, research, training, public relations, sales promotion, donations, size of sales and engineering force, and the like, are usually made annually. In the give-and-take of the process of preparing the master budget, the programmed costs are the most likely to be revised.

Organizational objectives determine programmed costs. For example, a large portion of programmed costs may consist of salaries for salesmen, accountants, clerks, and engineers. Some managements may hire and fire more quickly than others, thus exercising *short-run* cost control. Other managements may believe that such short-run benefits are outweighed by the long-run difficulties of attracting and retaining top-flight talent. The latter tend to have proportionally higher programmed costs and lower variable costs; the former tend to have proportionally lower programmed costs and higher variable costs.

The behavior of some programmed costs is easy to delineate. Advertising, research, donations, and training programs, for example, are usually formulated with certain objectives in mind. Total costs are then estimated, and requests are made to higher management for an appropriation, an authorization to spend up to a specified dollar ceiling. The execution of such projects is measured by comparing total expenditures with the appropriation. Because the tendency is to spend the entire appropriation, the resulting dollar variances are generally trivial. But planning is far more important than this kind of day-to-day control. The perfect execution of an advertising program—in the sense that the full amount authorized was spent in the specified media at the predetermined times—will be fruitless if the advertisements are unimaginative and lifeless and if they reach the wrong audience.

Because nonmanufacturing costs are predominantly composed of programmed costs, we shall concentrate on marketing and administrative costs for the bulk of the remaining discussion in this section.

Comparison of Marketing and Manufacturing Costs

The marketing function embraces all nonmanufacturing activities aimed directly at obtaining and filling orders. Marketing has often been described as a combination of order-getting and order-filling activities. *Order-getting* is the attainment of a desired sales volume and mix. It is the art of landing the order through advertising, promoting, and selling. *Order-filling* includes warehousing, packing, shipping, billing, and credit and collection. Many order-getting and order-filling costs may be variable; however, some are programmed.

The fundamental concepts of planning and control are as applicable to marketing as to manufacturing. Budgets, standards, performance reports, investigation of variances, and the like are used in all business operations.

Accounting techniques for planning and control were initially developed for manufacturing rather than for marketing. This occurred because manufacturing input and output are easier to classify and measure. The measurement of direct material and direct labor consumed, and of various parts and products produced, is straightforward. The measurement of the efforts (input) of advertising and salesmen and of the effectiveness (output) of advertising and salesmen is often difficult.

Formal planning and control techniques seem more meaningful when facilities are fixed, routine is entrenched, and external influences are small. They have traditionally been less meaningful when external influences are overwhelming, when many short-run alternatives exist, and when courses of action (and cost incurrence) are heavily influenced by management's opinions or hunches. For example, decisions about marketing are complicated by such interacting factors as product mix, design, types of outlets, pricing, advertising, competition, customer reaction, and general economic conditions.

Marketing managers are becoming increasingly aware that traditional guesses, hunches, and reliance on generalized rules of thumb are no longer enough. Detailed accumulation and analysis of data, including budgets and standards, help identify the products, territories, distribution channels, order-sizes, divisions, departments, and employees most in need of attention. The use of management accounting in marketing is bound to increase because it can yield fruitful insights at little cost.

A successful marketing operation obtains the highest possible contribution to profits over the long run. Note that the objective is contribution to profits, not merely increasing sales or decreasing expenses. That is why marketing executives should know cost-volume-profit relationships. That is why the contribution approach to analysis of marketing performance is superior to other approaches, which fail to distinguish the vital influence of various cost behavior patterns.

General Characteristics of Order-getting Costs

The outstanding characteristic of order-getting costs is that they are generally incurred to obtain sales, rather than being a result of sales. For the most part they are programmed costs.

Day-to-day control has little influence on over-all order-getting costs (input). However, day-to-day control may have a considerable impact on the effectiveness of the costs—the quantity and quality of the sales volume obtained (output). The analysis of order-getting costs usually has a central purpose: the shifting or concentration of efforts and resources toward the most profitable course of action.

Sales performance, or output, is influenced by many variables whose independent effects are difficult to isolate—for example, the inter-linking of advertising with other sales efforts, the action of competitors, general business conditions, the personalities of salesmen and of customers, and the short- and long-run effects of order-getting activities.

The difficulties of measurement become more imposing as advertising becomes more general and selling more personal. Still, the efforts and results involved in some order-getting activities are subject to specific measurement. Certain retail and wholesale selling duties, for example, are more akin to order-filling than to order-getting. Direct-mail advertisements may be evaluated in several specific ways—by their relative effectiveness in different publications, at various times, in various sizes, and in various forms.

The effectiveness of advertising is usually measured by the advertising or market research department. The ideal measure is the variation in net sales as advertising and promotion expenditures are varied. However, the unreliability of such measurements is widely recognized. It is difficult to establish a cause-and-effect relationship between advertising and sales, and conventional accounting tools are not too helpful. However, promising statistical and mathematical approaches have been developed in the field called operations research.

Budgeting Order-getting Costs: Influential Factors

The programming of order-getting costs is affected by the following factors: (1) past experience; (2) general economic conditions; (3) behavior of competitors; (4) new specific objectives; (5) market research and tests; (6) whims of the president; and (7) the maximum that may be spent in light of desired profits.

The last point (7) illustrates the circularity of advertising and sales.

For example, a large soap company introduces new products which are similar to old products, so that experience with old products may be used as a guide. Basically, a forecast is prepared as follows:

Sales potential		xx
Manufacturing and other costs	xx	
Desired profit	xx	xx
Remainder available for advertising		xx

(handwritten annotations: a bracket grouping "Sales potential" with arrow; "subtract" pointing to the grouped "Manufacturing and other costs / Desired profit")

If the remainder is sufficient for the advertising necessary to attain the sales potential, the new product is introduced.

Measuring Effectiveness: Salesmen's Performance

The fundamental gauge of a salesman's effectiveness is his long-run contribution to net profit. Salesmen should not only know the characteristics of their products; they should also know the relative profitability of the various products. For example, consider a company which sells welding equipment. Lorner is the salesman who consistently attains the highest dollar sales. Karnes is the salesman who ranks third out of seven in sales volume, but he is regarded as the most valuable salesman. Why? Because Karnes allots the bulk of his time to getting orders that provide a minimum of follow-up and a maximum contribution to profit. In contrast, Lorner quotes the lowest possible prices, incurs large travel and entertainment costs, and makes unrealistic delivery promises. His orders require more follow-up and generate more confusion than any other salesman's.

EXHIBIT 10-1

Salesmen's Performance Report
For the Quarter Ending June 30, 19x1

	Lorner	Karnes
Sales	$100,000	$70,000
Travel expenses (hotel, meals, etc.)	$ 1,400	$ 1,000
Entertainment	300	200
Automobile	400	350
Extra direct charges for special handling, delivery, etc.	1,800	200
Cost of goods sold	80,000	49,000
Total charges	$ 83,900	$50,750
Sales, less above charges (profit contribution)	$ 16,100	$19,250
Alternative One: Commission Based on Sales Volume		
Sales	$100,000	$70,000
Commission, assumed rate, 4.15 per cent	4,150	2,905
Alternative Two: Commission Based on Contribution to Profit		
Contribution to profit	$ 16,100	$19,250
Commission, assumed rate, 20 per cent	3,220	3,850

Exhibit 10-1 is a comparison of the performance of the two salesmen. We make the special assumption that these two have comparable territories and potential sales: otherwise the expectations could not be the same for each man. Note that Lorner's performance appears better than Karnes' under the commonly used measurement, volume of sales. However, Karnes' performance is clearly better when measured as contribution to profit.

Order-filling Costs and Administrative Costs: Work Measurement

Order-filling costs include costs for warehousing, packing, shipping, billing, and credit and collection. They are much more akin to manufacturing costs than are order-getting costs. Standards for certain order-filling activities, such as truck loading or truck driving, may have to be less refined than for such manufacturing activities as assembly work, but they still provide the best available formal tool for planning and control.

Companies with heavy order-filling activities and clerical and administrative costs have used work measurement techniques as a basis for formulating standards. This is an extension of the control philosophy that originated in the factory. The general idea is that permanent improvement in any performance is impossible unless "scientific" measurement is used to specify the time required for the job.

Work measurement is a detailed analysis of the order-filling or clerical operation. Its objective is to determine the workload in an operation and the number of workers needed to perform that work efficiently. The techniques used include time and motion study, observation of a random sample of the work (i.e., work sampling) and the estimation, by a work measurement analyst and a line supervisor, of the amount of time required for the work (i.e., time analysis).

Budgeting of Clerical Costs: A Comparison of the Variable Cost Approach and the Programmed Cost Approach

As we mentioned in Chapter 8, clerical costs are step-variable costs which may be budgeted flexibly along with strict variable costs.

Although techniques of work measurement have been increasingly applied to clerical tasks, the vast majority of organizations use more informal budgeting techniques which amount to regarding such costs as programmed costs. This reflects the philosophy that budgets are best related to currently attainable, rather than to ideal, performance. A comparison of the two approaches will be facilitated by the following example.

Assume that ten payroll clerks are employed, and that each clerk's operating efficiency *should be* the processing of the pay records of 500 employees per month. In the month of June, 4,700 individuals' pay records were processed by these ten clerks. Each clerk earns $600 per month. The variances shown by the variable cost approach and the programmed cost approach are tabulated below and graphed in Exhibit 10-2.

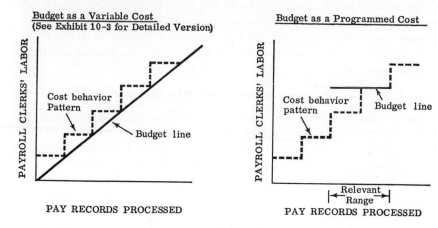

	Budget as a Variable Cost (Ideal)	Budget as a Programmed Cost (Currently Attainable)
Actual cost incurred	$6,000	$6,000
Budget allowance	5,640*	6,000
Variance	360 U	0

management proagative variance

* Rate = $6,000 ÷ 5,000 records or $1.20 per record; total = 4,700 records @ $1.20 = $5,640.

The Variable Cost Approach: Ideal Standards

The step-variable cost approach to this situation is to base the budget formula on the unit cost of the individual pay record processed— $600 ÷ 500 records, or $1.20. Therefore, the budget allowance for payroll clerk labor would be $1.20 × 4,700, or $5,640. Assume that the ten employees worked throughout the month. The following performance report would be prepared:

	Actual Cost	Flexible Budget: Total Standard Quantity Allowed for Good Units Produced	Budget Variance
Payroll clerk labor	(10 × $600) $6,000	(4,700 × $1.20) $5,640	$360 U

A graphic representation of what has occurred (Exhibit 10-3) may yield insight.

Essentially, two decisions must be made in this operation. The first is a programming decision. How many clerks do we need? How flexible should we be? How divisible is the task? Should we use part-time help? Should we hire and fire as the volume of work fluctuates? The implication of these questions is that once the hiring decision is made, the total costs incurred can be predicted easily—$6,000 in our example.

The second decision concentrates on day-to-day control, on how effectively the given resources are being utilized. The work measurement approach is an explicit and formal attempt to measure the utilization of resources by:

1. Assuming a strictly variable budget and the complete divisibility of the workload into small units. Note that the budget line on the graph in Exhibit 10-3 is strictly variable, despite the fact that the costs are really incurred in steps.

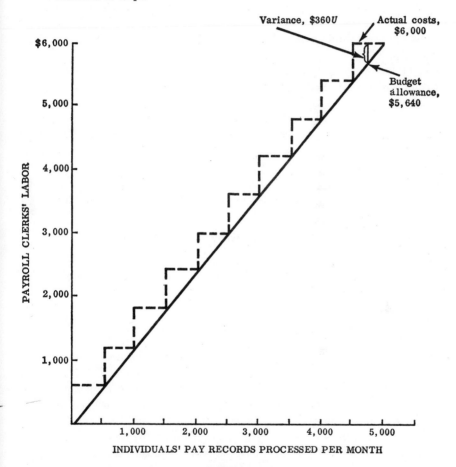

EXHIBIT 10-3

Step-Variable Costs and Variances

2. Generating a budget variance that assumes a comparison of actual costs with an ideal standard—the cost that would be incurred if payroll clerk labor could be turned on and off like a faucet. In this case, the variance of

$360 informs management that there was overstaffing (that is, the tenth step was only partially utilized). The workload capability was 5,000 pay records, not the 4,700 actually processed. $360 is the extra cost that resulted from operating in a way which does not attain the lowest possible cost, even though this may not be the result of a conscious decision but merely the effect of producing the volume which satisfies the monthly changes in demand. Robert Beyer writes that such a variance points out "an area in which the managers should be alert for cost reduction opportunities, since alternatives may be available." [1] Such an approach provides a measure ($360) of the amount that management is currently investing to provide stability in the workforce.

Admittedly, work measurement of order-filling and clerical administrative activities is not widespread. However, advocates of work measurement maintain that such an approach is the only reliable way to satisfy management's desire to plan and control such costs. The use of a tight budget based on ideal standards generates variances that upon investigation will reveal either or both of the following: (1) ineffective use or under-utilization of available personnel (for instance, perhaps 5,000 individual payroll records had to be processed, and other clerks or supervisors had to pitch in to get all the work done) ; (2) the cost of a managerial policy of deliberately retaining personnel to service long-run needs even though the volume of the current workload is insufficient (for instance, the maximum work available for payroll clerical labor may be 4,700 individual payroll records and the individual work may have been performed with complete efficiency).

The Programmed Cost Approach: Currently Attainable Standards

Work measurement techniques are not used in the vast majority of organizations. Consequently, the tendency is to rely on the experience of the department head and his superior for judging the size of the workforce needed to carry out the department's functions. There is a genuine reluctance to overhire because there is a corresponding slowness in discharging or laying off people when volume slackens. As a result, temporary peak loads are often met by hiring temporary workers or by having the regular employees work overtime.

In most cases, the relevant range of activity during the budget period can be predicted with assurance, and the work force needed for the marketing and administrative functions can be readily determined. If management refuses, consciously or unconsciously, to rigidly control costs in accordance with short-run fluctuations in activity, these costs become programmed. That is, their total amount is relatively fixed and unresponsive to short-run variations in volume.

Hence, there is a conflict between common practice and the objective of work measurement, which is to treat most costs as variable and so subject them to short-range management control. The moral is that man-

---

[1] *Profitability Accounting for Planning and Control* (New York: The Ronald Press Company, 1963), p. 162.

agement's attitudes and its planning and controlling decisions often determine whether a cost is fixed or variable. A change in policy can transform a fixed cost into a variable cost, and vice versa.

Moreover, management may regard a cost as programmed for *cash planning purposes* in the preparation of the master budget but may use the variable cost approach for *control purposes* in the preparation of flexible budgets for performance evaluation. These two views may be reconciled within the same over-all system. In our example, a master budget conceivably could include the following item:

Payroll clerk labor:

Flexible budget allowance for control	**$5,640**
Expected flexible budget variance (due to deliberate over-staffing)	360
Total budget variance for cash planning	$6,000

The common impression, which is reinforced by work measurement approaches, is that control should be constantly exerted to be effective. However, the National Association of Accountants comments:

> In one company, where considerable study had been devoted to determining how costs ought to be affected by volume changes, it was concluded that certain costs (e.g., maintenance) which management had attempted to control with current volume could better be controlled as managed [i.e., programmed] capacity costs. While this conclusion was contrary to management's impression that it was desirable to control costs with current volume wherever possible, trials showed savings when all relevant factors including quality and reliability of services were included in the comparison.[2]

Follow-up of Programmed Costs

Thus, we see that control may be exercised: (1) in the commonly accepted sense of the day-to-day follow-up that is associated with variable costs; and (2) in the special sense of periodically evaluating an expenditure, relating it to the objectives sought, and carefully planning the total amount of the cost for the ensuing period. The latter approach does not mean that day-to-day follow-up is neglected; follow-up is necessary to see that the resources made available are being used fully and effectively. It does mean that perceptive planning is stressed and that daily control is deemphasized. Reliance is placed more on hiring capable people and less on frequent checking up.

The practical effects of the programmed cost approach are that the budgeted costs and the actual costs tend to be very close, so that resulting budget variances are small. Follow-ups to see that the available resources are being fully and effectively utilized are regarded as the managers' responsibility, a duty that can be achieved by face-to-face control and by records of physical quantities (e.g., pounds handled per

---

[2] *Accounting for Costs of Capacity*, National Association of Accountants, Research Report No. 39 (New York, 1963), p. 13.

day in a warehouse, pieces mailed per hour in a mailing room) that do not have to be formally integrated into the accounting records in dollar terms.

COMMITTED COSTS

Committed costs are the stickiest of the fixed costs, because they tend to be the least affected by month-to-month and year-to-year decisions. They predominantly relate to buildings and equipment—depreciation, rentals, insurance, and property taxes. The salaries of the supervisory and other highly prized personnel that would be kept on the payroll at zero activity levels are also committed costs. Decisions in this area are often made only after careful weighing of alternatives by several key executives.

In planning, the focus is on the impact of these costs over a number of years. Such planning usually requires tailoring the capacity to future demand for the organization's products in the most economical manner. For example, should the store be 50,000 square feet, or 80,000, or 100,-000? Should the gasoline station have one, or two, or more stalls for servicing automobiles? Such decisions usually involve selecting the point of optimal trade-off. That is, constructing excess capacity now may save costs in the long run, because construction costs per square foot may be much higher later. On the other hand, if the forecasted demand never develops, the organization may own facilities which are unnecessarily idle.

These decisions regarding capital expenditures are generally shown in an annual budget called the *capital budget* or *capital spending budget*. As you recall, the *master budget* is based primarily on the annual sales forecast, the cornerstone of budgeting. Similarly, all capital spending decisions are ultimately based on long-range sales forecasts.

Utilization Does Not Affect Total Committed Costs

Once buildings are erected and equipment is installed, little can be done in day-to-day operations to affect the *total level* of committed costs. From a control standpoint, the objective is usually to increase current utilization of facilities because this will ordinarily increase net income.

There is another aspect to the control problem, however. A follow-up, or audit, is needed to find out how well the ensuing utilization harmonizes with the plan that authorized the facilities in the first place. The latter approach helps management to evaluate the wisdom of its past long-range plans and, in turn, should improve the quality of future plans.

Consider the following oversimplified example, which will be the basis for our discussion throughout the remainder of this chapter:

Top management decided to build a plant that can produce up to 100,000 units of a product per year. The forecasted demand averaged 80,000 units per year over a planning horizon of twelve years. The bigger plant was constructed because management decided that this was the most economical way to be ready for seasonal, cyclical, and trend factors that are likely to require a 100,000-unit per year capacity at certain times. The sales forecast used in a master budget for the current year was 82,000 units. Orders actually obtained and scheduled were for 74,000 units.

Long-Run Planning Capacity

Long-run planning capacity, or *normal capacity,* is the rate of activity needed to meet average sales demand over a period long enough to encompass seasonal and cyclical fluctuations (80,000 units in our example). It is usually somewhere between 75 and 90 per cent of practical capacity. It is the volume which is used as a basis for long-range plans, and depends on the time span selected, the forecasts made for each year, and the weighting of these forecasts. In our example, a comparison of the 82,000-unit master budget sales forecast capacity with the 80,000-unit long-run planning capacity might be the best basis for auditing long-range planning. The pertinent comparison is a particular year's master budgeted activity with that year's activity level used in the original authorization for the acquisition of the facilities. This comparison may be done project by project. *It need not be integrated in the over-all information system on a routine basis.* Moreover, attempting to use "normal capacity" as a reference point for judging current performance is an example of misusing a long-range measure for a short-range purpose.

SHORT-RANGE PLANNING AND CONTROL OF CAPACITY

Measuring Capacity

There are many ways to measure and value capacity. The relevance of a particular measure, of course, depends on its purpose. What information about capacity should help management in planning and controlling operations? The analytical framework in Exhibit 10-4, which will be explained more fully in the subsequent paragraphs, is useful.

We shall use Exhibit 10-4 to help formulate the following definitions of capacity:

Practical capacity, or *practical attainable capacity* (Column 1, Exhibit 10-4), is the maximum level at which the plant or department can realistically operate (100,000 units in our example). Practical capacity is ideal capacity less allowances for unavoidable interruptions. The following is a description of one company's approach to the measurement of capacity.

. . . practical attainable *hourly* capacity is developed by one company. Daily, monthy, and annual capacity is determined by multiplying the number of working hours in these periods by the practical attainable hourly capacity. Additional allowances are made for events which occur during a day, month, or year, but not hourly. For example, an allowance may be required for cleaning up equipment at the end of each day and for model change-over

EXHIBIT 10-4

Summary Framework for Analyzing Utilization of Capacity

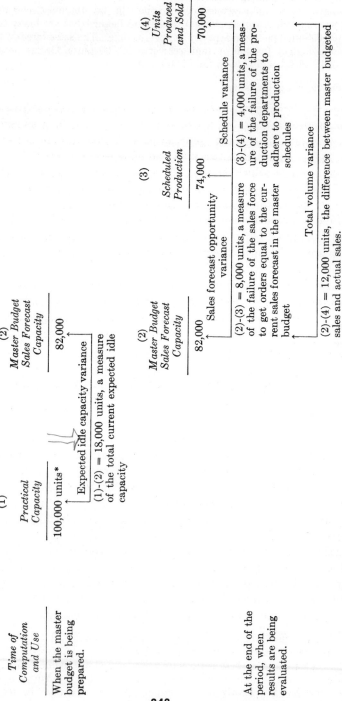

Time of Computation and Use

When the master budget is being prepared.

	(1) Practical Capacity	(2) Master Budget Sales Forecast Capacity
	100,000 units*	82,000

Expected idle capacity variance

(1)-(2) = 18,000 units, a measure of the total current expected idle capacity

At the end of the period, when results are being evaluated.

	(2) Master Budget Sales Forecast Capacity	(3) Scheduled Production	(4) Units Produced and Sold
	82,000	74,000	70,000

Sales forecast opportunity variance

(2)-(3) = 8,000 units, a measure of the failure of the sales force to get orders equal to the current sales forecast in the master budget

Schedule variance

(3)-(4) = 4,000 units, a measure of the failure of the production departments to adhere to production schedules

Total volume variance

(2)-(4) = 12,000 units, the difference between master budgeted sales and actual sales.

* Units could also be expressed in standard direct labor hours. For example, if the standard time allowance were one direct labor hour, practical capacity could be expressed as 100,000 standard hours.

time once a year. Industry practice and current management policy determines the number of shifts, number of hours worked per week, holidays, reserve capacity provided for contingencies and other allowances entering into the number of working hours per period. It may be noted that this company measures annual practical attainable capacity both with and without use of premium wage time. Thus management knows how much additional production can be obtained by use of premium wage rate time.[3]

Master budget sales forecast capacity (Column 2, Exhibit 10-4) is that rate of activity employed in formulating the master budget for the period. It may be any percentage of practical capacity, depending on the outlook for the period. In this example, it is 82,000 units.

Scheduled production (Column 3, Exhibit 10-4) is that rate of activity assigned for production in the current period (74,000 units in this case). Scheduled production does not necessarily coincide with the master sales forecast, because the sales department may be unable to sell the budgeted number of 82,000.[4]

Units produced and sold (Column 4, Exhibit 10-4) is self-explanatory, 70,000 units in this case.

The Measuring Unit and Percentage of Capacity

In the previous chapter, we discussed the various ways of measuring volume or activity. Any one of these, such as finished units produced, standard direct labor hours, or machine hours, may be used to measure capacity. Often, particularly when there is a wide variety of products, volume is expressed in percentages rather than in units. In our example, the practical capacity of 100,000 units may be expressed as 100 per cent capacity; the long-run planning capacity of 80,000 units as 80 per cent of capacity; the master sales forecast capacity of 82,000 units as 82 per cent of capacity; and the scheduled production as 74 per cent of capacity.

Expected Idle Capacity Variance

The *expected idle capacity variance* (Column 1 minus Column 2, Exhibit 10-4) should be computed when the original master budget is prepared. Management may then (a) obtain a specific measure of antici-

---

[3] *Ibid.,* p. 22.

[4] For simplicity, we shall assume throughout the subsequent discussion that all orders received are immediately scheduled and that production occurs immediately upon being scheduled—in other words, that there are no lags between orders, schedules, and expected production. In this way, we will not have to bother making some of the typical technical adjustments in the analysis of variances caused, e.g., by an order being booked in November, scheduled in February, and produced in April. These adjustments are not difficult to construct for a particular company, but they do interject confusion in an introduction to the analysis of variances. Moreover, we also assume that all units currently produced are currently sold; that is, there are no changes in inventory levels.

pated idle capacity early enough to (b) adjust plans in light of the possible uses for the expected idle capacity.

The responsibility for such a variance may be partially attributed to the sales department for inability to penetrate all possible market potential and partially attributable to the managers who may have deliberately or foolishly overbuilt facilities to meet future demand. Other possible explanations may include general economic conditions or particular competitive circumstances.

Note the difference in timing. Practical capacity becomes important in the course of preparing the master budget. At the end of the period, however, the master budgeted sales forecast is the key to the evaluation of results.

Total Volume Variance

Measurements designed to follow up various versions of capacity may serve various purposes. To continue our example, assume that production for the current year is 70,000 units, although current production schedules called for 74,000 units. What measures would interest management?

Variances should help pin down responsibility. Exhibit 10-4 shows a total volume variance (Column 2-Column 4), the over-all difference between budgeted sales and actual sales. In turn, this volume variance is sub-divided into the *schedule variance* (Column 3-Column 4), which is usually the responsibility of the production manager; and the *sales forecast opportunity variance* (Column 2-Column 3), which, to the extent that it can be assigned, is usually the responsibility of the sales manager. The approach to control of the utilization of capacity is summarized in Exhibit 10-4.

Schedule Variance

In our illustration, the *most important* current information is the 4,000-unit deviation from scheduled production. The ability to meet production schedules results from a mutuality of effort by the production planning and control department and the producing departments. Common reasons for failure to meet schedules include: (1) poor direction of operations by factory supervisors; (2) operating inefficiencies caused by untrained workmen, faulty machines, or inferior raw material; (3) lack of raw material or parts; and (4) careless scheduling by production planners. These reasons may be lumped together as possible explanations for a schedule variance.

Failure to meet a schedule results in an unfavorable schedule variance. This is the most commonly encountered situation. However, it may happen that actual production exceeds scheduled production. Technically, such a variance would be favorable. But all unusual variances are supposed to be investigated, and the findings may or may not substantiate a favorable label, in the layman's sense of the word. Unwanted excess production sometimes occurs because production schedules are not understood.

The usual cause of most schedule variances is labor's inability to meet currently attainable standards. Assume, in our example, that the standard time allowance per unit is one direct labor hour. Assume, further, that 74,000 actual direct labor hours were used but that labor inefficiencies resulted in the production of only 70,000 good units. Clearly, the entire schedule variance would be attributable to inefficient labor rather than to faulty scheduling or something else. However, it should be emphasized that variances in variable cost performance are not necessarily related to the schedule variance.

The schedule variance is the most crucial in everyday operating situations because it helps pinpoint the responsibility of operating managers to meet production schedules. The efficiency of the operating workmen is monitored with the aid of standards and budgets for the variable cost factors. The measure of ability to *meet production schedules* is metered by the difference between scheduled production and units produced.

Sales Forecast Opportunity Variance

The 8,000-unit deviation [Exhibit 10-4] from the Master Budget Sales Forecast Capacity (82,000 units, less 74,000 units scheduled) is an indication of lost sales opportunities, a measure that is primarily traceable to the sales arm of the organization. This sales forecast opportunity variance should be computed on a routine basis, because it integrates the master budget with the actual results and helps explain the differences between expectations and results.

Somewhere in the reporting scheme, management will probably want an explanation of why the target net income in the master budget was not achieved. A principal cause, of course, is the failure to attain the target volume, and the best measure of this is the sales forecast opportunity variance. This point is illustrated in this chapter's Summary Problem for Your Review.

The master budget sales forecast capacity, rather than practical capacity, is more germane to the evaluation of current results. Managers, particularly the sales executives, feel much more obligated to reach the master budget sales forecast, which should have been conscientiously set in relation to the maximum opportunities for sales in the current period. To have any meaning, an opportunity variance must reflect the existence of bona fide opportunities to sell. Consequently, on the operating firing line, the sales forecast opportunity variance is much more meaningful than a variance related to practical capacity. For example, a practical capacity variance could be computed by subtracting Column (3) from Column (1) in Exhibit 10-4. But this would blend two unlike items: the sales forecast opportunity variance plus the expected idle capacity variance.

Expressing Variances in Dollars Rather than in Physical Units

Our study of cost-volume-profit relationships revealed that once a certain capacity is provided, the addition of one unit of product to sales will increase net income by the unit selling price less the unit variable cost. Capacity costs are unaffected by changes in volume, so underutilization of capacity represents a lost opportunity to increase net income by the contribution margin associated with the unsold capacity.

For two reasons, we have deliberately avoided expressing capacity variance in dollars terms. First, it is often unnecessary and confusing to express control measures in dollars when the operating personnel being judged think in physical terms only. In general, measurement should be expressed in terms easily understood by the individuals affected. Second, the dollar basis most often used to measure capacity variances has little economic significance. It represents an attempt to apply to the control of *fixed costs*, control techniques well-suited to *variable costs*. The two costs behave differently, and their control should be different. The latter point is explored more fully in the Appendix to this chapter.

What is the best way to measure the cost of unutilized capacity? The total fixed costs will be the same, whether production is 70,000 or 82,000 units. Therefore, unutilized capacity will not affect short-run operating costs as they are ordinarily recorded by accountants. However, from an economic viewpoint, there is an opportunity cost, consisting of the foregone contribution to profit of the units which were not produced. This opportunity variance may be largely academic, particularly if the sales force has done everything possible to market the product and if there is no alternate use for the idle facilities (e.g., doing subcontracting work for some other manufacturer).

In our example, assume a sales price of $12 less variable costs per unit of $10, so that the unit contribution margin is $2. The variances are expressed in dollars in Exhibit 10-5.

EXHIBIT 10-5

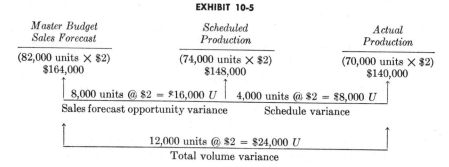

Master Budget Sales Forecast	*Scheduled Production*	*Actual Production*
(82,000 units × $2) $164,000	(74,000 units × $2) $148,000	(70,000 units × $2) $140,000

8,000 units @ $2 = $16,000 *U*   4,000 units @ $2 = $8,000 *U*

Sales forecast opportunity variance   Schedule variance

12,000 units @ $2 = $24,000 *U*

Total volume variance

This analysis dovetails well with the income statement in the master budget, which is compared with actual results in Exhibit 10-6.

EXHIBIT 10-6

Budget and Actual Income

	Budget: 82,000 Units	Actual: 70,000 Units	Variance
Sales, @ $12	$984,000	$840,000	
Variable costs, @ $10	820,000	700,000	
Contribution margin, @ $2	$164,000	$140,000	$24,000 U
Fixed costs	139,000	139,000	—
Net income	$ 25,000	$ 1,000	$24,000 U*

* *Explanation of variance:* Failure to reach volume level originally budgeted (see tabulation which follows) resulted in inability to obtain the contribution margin originally budgeted.

Sales department failed to obtain enough orders:
(82,000 units budgeted — 74,000 units scheduled for production)
$\times$ $2 = Sales forecast opportunity variance $16,000
Production departments failed to meet production schedules,
(74,000 units scheduled — 70,000 units produced and sold)
$\times$ $2 = Schedule variance,   8,000
Total volume variance, which *in this case* wholly explains the difference
in net income $24,000

Opportunity cost may be an especially pertinent notion when the master budget sales forecast is hovering near practical capacity. For example, production might be budgeted and scheduled at the practical capacity level of 100,000 standard direct labor hours, but inefficiencies might result in only 97,000 units being produced. The economic impact of this schedule variance is best measured by the lost contribution margin per hour times the difference between the 100,000 actual hours and the 97,000 standard direct hours allowed for the 97,000 good units produced.

For clarity, we have simplified our discussion in two major ways: First, most companies have more than one product. In such cases, the same fundamental analysis is conducted on a product-by-product basis. Second, a uniform unit contribution margin was assumed. In many cases, of course, increases in volume may be attained only by reducing unit prices. In these instances, the dollar measure of the opportunity variance has to be adjusted.

SUMMARY

Costs may be classified in many ways, but classification by behavior patterns and by responsibility are the most valuable to management planning and control. The classification of cost behavior can be a very detailed one. For our purposes, however, any cost may be viewed as belonging in one of the following categories.

Behavior Pattern	*Key Planning and Control Techniques*
Variable	Standards and flexible budgets.
Fixed	Periodic (i.e., yearly) static budgets reached by explicit management decisions.
Programmed (Managed)	Periodic (i.e., yearly) appropriations for the ensuing period. The classification of a cost as variable or programmed often reflects management policy rather than an inherent characteristic of the cost.
Committed	Periodic decisions that usually involve relatively large capital outlays affecting operations over a long period of time. These appear as committed costs in the periodic operating budgets. *Planning* decisions hinge on discounted cash flow techniques, which are discussed in Chapter 14.
Variances and Fixed costs	The *control* aspect depends on follow-up to see that *utilization* of existing facilities and resources is in accordance with short-term master budget forecasts and with long-run plans. Utilization can be measured in physical rather than in dollar terms. If dollar measures are used, they should be based on lost contribution margins rather than on unitized historical fixed costs. For an elaboration of the latter point, see the Appendix to this chapter.

SUMMARY PROBLEM FOR YOUR REVIEW

PROBLEM

The Gannon Co. based its master budget for 19x2 on an expected sales volume of 110,000 units, at an average unit selling price of $25. Costs were expected to be:

Variable Costs per Unit		*Total Fixed Costs*	
Direct materials	$ 9.00	Programmed and committed	
Direct labor	5.00	costs:	
Factory overhead	1.00	Manufacturing	$600,000
Order-filling	.75	Nonmanufacturing	250,000
Administrative	.25	Total static budget	$850,000
Total variable costs per unit	$16.00		

Standard costs and flexible budgets were used for variable cost control. Practical capacity is 130,000 units. There were no beginning or ending inventories. During 19x2, 97,000 units were produced and sold. The only variances were an unfavorable direct labor ($15,000) efficiency variance and variable factory overhead ($3,000).

Required:

1. Prepare a two-column income statement for 19x2 comparing the master budget figures with the actual results. At the bottom, present a short explanation of why the net income of the master budget was not attained.

2. Suppose that production for the year was 3,000 units less than scheduled. That is, sales orders were for 100,000 units but inefficiency prevented schedules from being met.

a. What is the schedule variance, in units?

b. What is the sales forecast opportunity variance, in units?

3. Quantify the variances in Question 2, *a* and *b,* using lost contribution margin per unit.

4. *a.* The programmed costs had no variances. Why?

    b. Does this mean that control has been achieved? Why?

5. What is the amount of the expected idle capacity opportunity variance? What is its meaning?

SOLUTION

1.

	Master Budget: 110,000 units	Actual Results: 97,000 units	Variance
Sales @ $25	$2,750,000	$2,425,000	
Variable costs:			
Direct material, @ $9	$ 990,000	$ 873,000	
Direct labor, @ $5	550,000	485,000	
Factory overhead, @ $1	110,000	97,000	
Order-filling, @ $.75	82,500	72,750	
Administrative expenses, @ $.25	27,500	24,250	
Total variable costs at standard, $16	$1,760,000	$1,552,000	
Contribution margin at standard, $9	$ 990,000	$ 873,000	$117,000 *U*
Less unfavorable variable cost variances:			
Direct labor efficiency $15,000			
Variable factory overhead efficiency 3,000	—	18,000	18,000 *U*
Contribution margin, after variable cost variances	$ 990,000	$ 855,000	$135,000 *U*
Fixed costs:			
Manufacturing $600,000			
Nonmanufacturing 250,000	850,000	850,000	
Net income	$ 140,000	$ 5,000	$135,000 *U**

* Explanation of variance:

Efficiency variances	$ 18,000 *U*
Volume variance (explained more fully in Solution to Questions 2 and 3)	
Failure to reach volume level originally budgeted resulted in the lack of contribution margin, (110,000 units − 97,000 units) × $9	117,000 *U*
Unfavorable variance explained	$135,000 *U*

2.

Master Budget Sales Forecast Capacity	Scheduled Production	Actual Production
110,000 units	100,000 units	97,000 units

Sales forecast opportunity variance, 10,000 *U*   Schedule variance, 3,000 *U*

Total volume variance, 13,000 *U*

3.

(110,000 units @ \$9)	(100,000 units @ \$9)	(97,000 units @ \$9)
\$990,000	\$900,000	\$873,000

10,000 units @ \$9 = \$90,000 U ┊ 3,000 units @ \$9 = \$27,000 U

Sales forecast opportunity variance   Schedule variance

Total volume variance: \$117,000 U

4. *a.* Most programmed costs are *appropriated.* Authorization is given to spend up to a specified amount. The tendency is to spend the total appropriation, so the resulting dollar variances are generally trivial.

   b. In the commonly accepted sense, control has been achieved because actual costs and budgeted costs are identical. In another sense, control is achieved only if all available resources have been used fully and effectively. Unless techniques to measure utilization and effectiveness can be developed, the control is largely dependent on hiring qualified personnel and checking up in only a general way.

5. Above all, variances should be tailored to the particular needs of management. For example, *when the original master budget is prepared,* management may prefer to:

   (1) Compare the potential contribution margin at the two capacity levels:

Practical capacity, 130,000 units × \$9	\$1,170,000
Master budget sales forecast capacity, 110,000 units × \$9	990,000
Difference, 20,000 units × \$9, expected idle capacity variance	\$ 180,000

   (2) Adjust plans in light of possible uses for the expected idle capacity.

   Note the difference in timing. Practical capacity becomes important in the course of preparing the master budget. At the end of the period, however, the master budgeted sales forecast is the key to the evaluation of results.

   This variance means that if Gannon Company could fully utilize its practical capacity at normal selling prices, its expected net income would be \$180,000 greater than budgeted in 19x2. Note, too, that such a measure assumes no change in fixed costs over the entire range of volume.

APPENDIX

Unitizing Historical Fixed Costs for Measuring Capacity Variances

In current practice, there is a tendency to apply dollar measures to the utilization of capacity that have no particular significance to the management problem at hand. Let us use the same example we used in Chapter 10. Suppose that, of the \$139,000 total fixed costs, \$100,000 represents the committed costs plus the programmed *manufacturing* costs. The accountant would relate the \$100,000 to the number of units, to get a predetermined unit cost. He might select from several possible rates. Let us consider two:

Alternative *A*—Practical capacity as a base:

$$\text{Unit cost} = \frac{\text{Total fixed manufacturing costs}}{\text{Practical capacity}} = \frac{\$100,000}{100,000 \text{ units}} = \$1 \text{ per unit}$$

Alternative *B*—Master budget sales forecast capacity as a base:

$$\text{Unit cost} = \frac{\text{Total fixed manufacturing costs}}{\text{Master budget sales forecast capacity}} = \frac{\$100,000}{82,000 \text{ units}} = \$1.22 \text{ per unit}$$

The accountant uses one of these unit costs for costing the product and for measuring capacity variances. There are drawbacks to using the historical cost in management planning and control, as an analysis of the above alternatives will show.

Let us compare the dollar results of using the above two historical unit costs:

Alternative *A*: Use a historical cost unitized at $1 per unit.

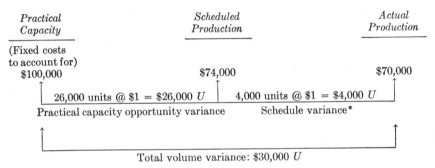

* Due to ineffective utilization of facilities.

Alternative *B*: Use a historical cost unitized at $1.22 per unit.

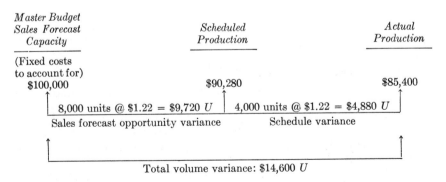

Now let us analyze the alternatives.

1. The unit cost is affected by the denominator selected. The use of practical capacity as a denominator results in one unit cost; the use of the master

budget sales forecast capacity as a denominator results in another unit cost.

2. The attempt to unitize *fixed costs* in the same way as *variable costs* are unitized is artificial. Fixed costs do not behave in the same way, nor can they be controlled in the same way. Fixed costs are simply not divisible like variable costs; they come in big gobs and they are related to providing big chunks of sales or production capacity, rather than to producing a single unit of product.

3. The unit measure has no direct economic significance. It is conceptually inferior to the notion of lost contribution margin per unit. Unlike variable costs, total fixed costs do not change as production or sales fluctuate. Fixed cost incurrence often entails lump-sum outlays based on a pattern of expected recoupment. But ineffective utilization of existing facilities has no bearing on the amount of fixed costs currently incurred. The economic effects of the inability to reach target volume levels are directly measured by lost contribution margins, even though these often are approximations. The historical cost approach fails to emphasize the useful distinction between *fixed cost incurrence,* on the one hand, and the objective of *maximizing the total contribution margin,* on the other hand. These are separable management problems, and the utilization of existing capacity is more closely related to the latter.

4. An example of the attempt to analyze variable costs and fixed costs in a parallel manner is the computation of an efficiency variance for fixed overhead:

Efficiency variance
= (Actual hours − Standard hours allowed) × Hourly fixed overhead rate

But the resulting variance should be distinguished sharply from the efficiency variances for material, labor, and variable overhead, because efficient usage of these three factors can affect actual cost, whereas short-run fixed overhead cost is not affected by efficiency. Moreover, the managers responsible for inefficiency will be aware of its existence through reports on variable cost control, so there is little for management to gain from expressing ineffective utilization of fixed factory overhead costs in historical dollar terms.

ASSIGNMENT MATERIAL

ESSENTIAL ASSIGNMENT MATERIAL

10-1. *Terminology.* Define: committed costs; ideal capacity; theoretical capacity; practical capacity; practical attainable capacity; long-run planning capacity; normal capacity; master budget sales forecast capacity; scheduled production; schedule variance; sales forecast opportunity variance; programmed costs; managed costs; appropriation; order-getting cost; and order-filling cost.

10-2. *Clerical costs and the budgeting of variances.* The Bergeron Co. has many small accounts receivable. Work measurement of billing labor has shown that a billing clerk can process 2,000 customers' accounts per month. The company employs 30 billing clerks at an annual salary of $4,800 each.

Next year's outlook is for a decline in the number of customers, from 59,900 to 56,300 per month.

1. Assume that management has decided to continue to employ the 30 clerks despite the drop in billings. Show two approaches, the variable cost approach and the programmed cost approach, to the budgeting of billing labor. Show how the *performance report* for the year would appear under each approach.

2. Some managers favor using tight budgets as motivating devices for controlling operations. In these cases, the managers really expect an unfavorable variance and must allow, in financial planning, for such a variance so that adequate cash will be available as needed. What would be the budgeted variance, also sometimes called expected variance, in this instance?

3. Assume that the workers are reasonably efficient. (a) Interpret the budget variances under the variable cost approach and the programmed cost approach. (b) What should management do to exert better control over clerical costs?

10-3. *Capacity variances.* The Richer Co. makes a variety of products that result in standard contribution margins averaging 30 per cent of dollar sales and average unit selling prices of $8. Average productivity is three units per standard direct labor hour. The master budget for 19x1 had predicted sales of 500,000 units. Practical capacity is 550,000 units. 470,000 units were ordered and scheduled for production, but it took 156,000 actual direct labor hours to produce 460,000 units.

Fixed manufacturing costs were $700,000 and fixed nonmanufacturing costs were $300,000. There were no beginning or ending inventories.

The president was upset because the budgeted net income of $200,000 was not attained, particularly since the only budget variances were unfavorable variable cost efficiency variances amounting to merely $6,000.

1. What is the net income for the year?

2. Explain fully why the target net income was not achieved. Include a presentation of the total volume variance and schedule variance. Show computations.

10-4. *Review problem covering Chapters 9 and 10.* The master budgeted income statement for 19x2 for the Swanal Co. was:

Sales (1,000,000 units @ $3)		$3,000,000
Variable charges:		
Direct material @ $.50	$ 500,000	
Direct labor @ $1	1,000,000	
Variable factory overhead @ $.20	200,000	
Selling @ $.30	300,000	
Administrative @ $.10	100,000	2,100,000
Contribution margin @ $.90		$ 900,000
Fixed charges:		
Manufacturing	$ 300,000	
Other	500,000	800,000
Budgeted net income		$ 100,000

Results for 19x2 did not fulfill expectations. 950,000 units were ordered and scheduled for production but, because of year-end material shortages, only

940,000 units were produced. Average productivity was supposed to be four units per direct labor hour. Direct material price and usage variances totaled $30,000, unfavorable. Actual direct labor hours were 250,000. There was a favorable direct labor rate variance of $25,000. The variable overhead spending (rate) variance was $10,000, favorable. Variable overhead cost behavior was most closely related to fluctuations in direct labor hours.

Negotiations with tax assessors resulted in lower property taxes than anticipated. Fixed charges had a favorable budget variance of $15,000. Practical capacity is 1,250,000 units.

There were no beginning or ending inventories or variable selling and administrative cost variances.

Required:

1. Prepare a columnar income statement for 19x2 comparing budgeted and actual results. Briefly summarize why the target income was not achieved. (You may wish to answer the subsequent questions before completing this requirement.)
2. Quantify the following variances in dollars, and show your computations:
   a. Sales forecast opportunity variance.
   b. Schedule variance.
   c. Total volume variance.
   d. Expected idle capacity variance.
   e. Direct labor efficiency variance.
   f. Variable factory overhead efficiency variance.
   g. Variable factory overhead budget variance.
3. Is an unfavorable schedule variance always attributable to labor inefficiency? Why?

ADDITIONAL ASSIGNMENT MATERIAL

Note: Problems 10-20 through 10-24 deal mostly with programmed costs. Problems 10-25 through 10-28 concern utilization of capacity; 10-27 and 10-28 also cover the historical cost approach to capacity variances. Problem 10-29 relates the budgeting of wages to the over-all difficulties in the use of flexible budgets for measuring performance.

10-5. Why is the utilization of programmed costs harder to measure than the utilization of committed costs?
10-6. "Planning is far more important than day-to-day control of programmed costs." Do you agree? Explain.
10-7. Distinguish between order-getting and order-filling.
10-8. When are planning and control techniques most effective?
10-9. What is the central purpose of analyzing order-getting costs?
10-10. What is the best single gauge of a salesman's effectiveness?
10-11. What is work measurement?
10-12. Why are committed costs the stickiest of the fixed costs?
10-13. Distinguish between ideal capacity, practical capacity, and long-run planning capacity.

10-14. What is the most common method of judging the wisdom of a long-range plan?

10-15. Distinguish between the sales forecast opportunity variance, the schedule variance, and the volume variance.

10-16. Why is the sales forecast opportunity variance much more meaningful than the practical capacity opportunity variance?

10-17. Why is it artificial to unitize fixed costs?

10-18. "The fixed cost per unit is directly affected by the denominator selected." Do you agree? Explain.

10-19. "An unfavorable variance for programmed costs would measure the failure to spend the entire appropriation." Do you agree? Explain.

10-20. *Utilization of programmed cost: advertising.* Late in the year, the marketing manager of the Rockwater Corp., a multiplant corporation, is trying to decide between two alternative advertising programs, either of which will use all the $10,000 remaining in the advertising budget. The first alternative is estimated to increase the sales of product *A* (which is produced in Plant No. 1) by 6,200 units. It is estimated that the second alternative will produce a 4,000 unit increase in the sales of product *B* (which is produced in Plant No. 2). The following data pertain to products *A* and *B*. Neither plant is producing at close to practical capacity.

	Product A Plant No. 1	Product B Plant No. 2
Direct material, per unit	$ 4.50	$ 6.25
Direct labor, per unit	$ 2.00	$ 3.50
Other variable manufacturing costs, per unit	$ 1.00	$ 1.50
Total fixed manufacturing costs	$100,000	$100,000
Practical plant capacity, in units	100,000	80,000
Selling price, per unit	$ 10.00	$ 15.00

Required:

Would you recommend either advertising program to the marketing manager? If so, which one? Support your answer with adequate calculations.

10-21. *Salesmen's performance.* The Loebl Merchandising Co. has a number of salesmen who sell a variety of products. Jones and Smith have similar territories and have the following records for a recent period:

	Jones	Smith
Sales	$170,000	$200,000
Cost of goods sold	102,000	140,000
Travel expenses, excluding auto	1,000	1,000
Entertainment	1,000	1,500
Automobile	500	500
Sales returns and allowances	3,400	10,000

Prepare a report comparing the performance of Jones and Smith. If these men were to be paid a sales commission, which type of commission plan would you favor? Why?

10-22. *Programmed costs and advertising agencies.* A noted advertising agency had the following operating results:

	Year Ending Nov. 30 (In millions of dollars)	
	19x2	19x1
Space and mechanical billings	$45.7	$53.0
Space and mechanical cost	39.0	45.3
Agency commission	$ 6.7	$ 7.7
Expenses:		
Salaries	$ 4.4	$ 4.4
Profit sharing	.2	.4
Rent	.6	.6
Business promotion	.4	.4
Dues and subscriptions	.1	.1
Office expenses	.2	.2
Personnel and employment expenses	.1	.1
Telephone and telegraph	.2	.2
Insurance and taxes	.1	.1
Other expenses	.1	.3
Total expenses	$ 6.4	$ 6.8
Net income before income taxes	$ .3	$ .9

1. (a) What is the single important factor that brought about the decline in net income? Why?
   (b) What would net income probably have been if Space and Mechanical Billings had increased by 10 per cent? By 20 per cent? By 30 per cent? Decreased by 10 per cent? By 20 per cent? By 30 per cent?

   For your analysis, assume an agency commission of 14.6 per cent and operating expenses of $6.6 million, including profit sharing.

2. Plot a cost-volume-profit graph of the relationships you assumed in your answer to (1). What is the break-even point in dollar billings?

3. (a) What factors influence the size of the Agency Commission?
   (b) What factors influence total salaries expenses?

10-23. *Profit potential of a new product: advertising budget.* Auto Wax Co. has been in business for years. Past experience has shown that its new, self-polishing, diamond-lustre, sparkling-finish products have limited lives because of competition. The planning horizon for any new product is three years.

The board of directors is currently considering a truly revolutionary product. The consumer merely has to wash his car and use a spray can of wax that applies a long-lasting, glistening finish that should last for 60 to 90 days. No rags, buffers, or elbow grease are needed for dazzling results.

The board is somewhat hesitant about approving the product because the selling price per unit would have to be the highest ever—$3.50. The principal difficulty has been the high research and development costs of the spray can and the special nozzle. The chemical ingredients are such that the product can be applied only with the special spray can. The research engineers and chemists have invested $200,000 in the development and testing of the new product, and they believe that the product is now ready to market.

Pilot production runs have yielded the following cost estimates per unit:

Direct materials, excluding spray can	$ .30
Spray can and nozzle	.40
Direct labor and variable overhead	.10
Fixed manufacturing, selling, and administrative overhead	.30
Unit costs, before advertising and product development	$1.10

The marketing department believes that there is a sales potential of 1,000,000 cans per year at $3.50 per can, if the advertising budget is $2,500,000 for the first year and $1,500,000 for the next two years.

The board of directors will not approve any new product unless the prospective net income averages at least 10 per cent of dollar sales over the life of the product. The board's reasoning is based on the notion that the required investment consists of the first year's advertising budget, plus an average investment in plant and working capital of $800,000, plus $200,000 in product development and testing. Past experience has shown that 10 per cent of dollar sales yields approximately 10 per cent on invested capital.

Required:

Should the board of directors approve the marketing of the new prodduct? Why?

10-24. *Temporary versus permanent help.* The Central States Division of Lawrence's Famous Candies, Inc., is responsible for filling all orders, in an area comprising 15 Midwestern states, for the product, a high-grade candy which is retailed in many fine stores from coast to coast. The clerical work incidental to filling an order has traditionally been done by a staff of seven women who work a five-day week of eight hours per day. Their salary is $360 per month. State law prohibits hiring these women for more than 40 hours per week, so overtime is impossible. Assume, for simplicity, that each month consists of exactly 20 working days.

The division manager has noticed that the women are idle part of the day during certain parts of the year. He is considering reducing the permanent staff and hiring part-time help during peak periods. Womanpower, Inc., has quoted a price of $25 per day for part-time help (one-day minimum). The manager learns that the New York division hires some part-time help for the same duty, but with a slight loss of efficiency. Part-time help, he is told, can process only 35 orders a day, while permanent help can process 40 orders a day.

Sales fluctuate significantly from month to month, but not from year to year. Any fluctuation within a given month is so minor that it can be absorbed by a slight delay. For computational simplicity, the manager assumes that sales are constant throughout the month.

The month-to-month sales record, expressed in terms of orders filled, has been as follows for the past five years:

January	4,800	May	4,400	September	4,400
February	4,800	June	4,000	October	4,800
March	4,800	July	4,000	November	5,600
April	5,600	August	4,000	December	5,600

Required:

Should the division manager retain all seven clerks? If not, how many should he retain?

10-25. *Lost opportunities and operations near practical capacity.* The Vickers Co. has been enjoying heavy demand for its assorted products. In 19x2, practical capacity was 20,000 standard direct labor hours per month. In June, the master budget sales forecast and the work schedules called for full utilization of practical capacity, but a severe heat wave in the latter part of June hampered productivity. Although 20,000 actual hours were worked, good production, expressed in standard direct labor hours of work done, was only 18,500 hours.

The lost contribution margins on the products in question averaged $3 per unit. The average standard direct labor hours allowed per unit were four.

Required:

What was the volume variance in dollars? The sales forecast opportunity variance? The schedule variance?

10-26. *Master budget and capacity variance.* The Terry Co. manufactures men's sport jackets. The president of Terry feels that the sales forecast of 200,000 jackets included in the 19x4 master budget is much more meaningful as a basis for computing variances than is the practical plant capacity of 250,000 jackets. An analysis of unit variable costs and revenues revealed the following data:

> Average selling price: $17.50
> Direct material: 5 yards per jacket, @ $.90 a yard
> Direct labor: 3 hours, @ $2 an hour
> Other variable manufacturing costs: 25 per cent of direct labor
> Order-filling costs: $.25
> Salesmen's commissions: 10 per cent of selling price
> Variable administrative expense: $.50

The static budget for 19x4 called for $110,000 of programmed costs and $180,000 of committed costs. During 19x4, 230,000 jackets were ordered by customers and scheduled for production. Actual sales (deliveries) and production amounted to 220,000 jackets. Salesmen's commissions are based on actual sales, not orders.

Required:

1. Prepare an income statement for 19x4, using the contribution approach. Provide an explanation for the difference between actual net income and the net income forecast in the master budget.
2. What is the schedule variance in units? What is the sales forecast opportunity variance in units? Quantify these variances, using the contribution margin per unit.
3. (a) Substituting practical plant capacity for forecasted sales, compute a new lost sales opportunity variance in both units and dollars.
   (b) Do you agree with the president that variances are more meaningful when they are based on the sales forecast? State your reasons.
   (c) Is the schedule variance as computed in (2) affected by substituting practical plant capacity for forecasted sales?

10-27. *Comprehensive problem on capacity variances, including historical unit costs.* The Maximill Co. based the master budget for 19x1 on an expected sales volume of 100,000 units at an average selling price of $10 per unit. Variable costs per unit were expected to be: direct material, $3; direct labor, $2; factory overhead, $.70; order-filling, $.20 and administrative expenses, $.10. The static budget included $200,000 of programmed costs and $100,000 of committed costs.

During 19x1, 90,000 units were produced and sold. Unfavorable variances were $4,000 in direct labor efficiency and $1,400 in variable factory overhead efficiency. Standard costs and flexible budgets were used for variable cost control. Practical capacity is 105,000 units. There were no beginning or ending inventories.

Required:

1. Prepare an income statement for 19x1, using the contribution approach. At the bottom of your income statement, show a short explanation of why the net income of the master budget was not attained.
2. Assume that production for the year was 2,000 units less than scheduled. That is, sales orders were for 92,000 units but worker inefficiency prevented schedules from being met. What is the schedule variance in units? What is the master budget sales forecast opportunity variance in units?
3. Assume that $210,000 of the programmed and committed costs represent fixed indirect manufacturing overhead. Quantify the variances in (2), using:
   (a) Lost contribution margin per unit.
   (b) Historical fixed indirect manufacturing costs.
   Which answers provide more insight?
4. The programmed costs had no variances. Why? Does this mean that control has been achieved? Why?

10-28. *Capacity or volume variances: comprehensive problem including historical unit costs.* The Campo Co. makes a variety of products and had relatively heavy fixed manufacturing costs of $320,000 for the past year, 19x2. The products bring in standard contribution margins of 40 per cent of dollar sales. The average selling price is $5 per unit. The average productivity is two units per standard direct labor hour. Practical capacity is 400,000 units per year. The master budget for 19x2 was predicated on expected sales of 320,000 units. In 19x2, 300,000 units were scheduled for production, but it took 160,000 actual direct labor hours to produce 297,000 units. There were no beginning or ending inventories.

Required:

1. Expected idle capacity variance, sales forecast opportunity variance, and schedule variance expressed in (a) standard direct labor hours, (b) in lost contribution margins, and (c) in historical costs.
2. Standard direct labor rates averaged $3.50 per hour. What was the direct labor efficiency variance?
3. The variable factory overhead spending variance was $10,000, unfavorable. The budget formula for total variable overhead was 50¢ per unit of product. What was the variable overhead efficiency variance? Budget variance?
4. The company also had unfavorable direct material usage variances of $25,000. Fixed costs, other than fixed manufacturing costs, totaled $100,000. Prepare an income statement for 19x2, using the contribution approach. Briefly explain why the budgeted net income was not reached.

You need not subdivide the total standard variable costs into direct material, direct labor, and variable manufacturing overhead.

10-29. *Flexible budgets and wages.* The administrator of the Adams Hotel has established a budget for the laundry department. The department's equipment consists of a washer that can process 500 pounds an hour. For every 100 pounds of linen processed, soap costs of 15¢ and water costs of 5¢ are incurred. One man operates the laundry. He works eight hours daily, six days per week, at $2 per hour.

The depreciation on the machine is $1,950 per year. The budget drawn by the administrator calls for $100 of overhead to be charged to the laundry for every four-week period. When the budget was established, the administrator thought that the expenses for the normal volume of linen would be $802 for a four-week period, including fixed expenses.

During the last four weeks, the laundry processed 72,000 pounds of linen, and incurred $814 in expenses, of which $145 was for soap, and $35 was for water. The man in charge of the laundry says he is doing a good job, because the budget calls for expenses of $802, and he incurred only $814.

Required:

1. What volume of laundry did the administrator use for his $802 budget for the four-week period?
2. Prepare a performance report that will give the administrator a method for evaluating the laundry.

CHAPTER 11

Responsibility Accounting
and the Contribution Approach
to Cost Allocation

MANAGEMENT REPORTS MEASURE AND COMMUNICATE IMPOR-
tant information about objectives, plans, and performance.
We have investigated standards and budgets as key factors
in planning and control. Now we shall concentrate on another key factor: fixing responsibility.

Management accounting has developed score-keeping and
attention-directing techniques for helping management to
evaluate performance. In this chapter and the next, we shall
discuss the strengths and weaknesses of these techniques.
In this chapter we are concerned with responsibility accounting and the contribution approach to the difficult problems of cost allocation. These two modern techniques facilitate measurement of performance and the making of intelligent decisions.

RESPONSIBILITY ACCOUNTING

Characteristics of Responsibility Accounting

Individuals operate organizations. Any management accounting system, to be effective, must be designed around
the *responsibility centers of individual managers*. The accounting system must cohesively reflect the plans and
actions of all responsibility centers in the organization—

from the smallest to the biggest. This basic idea is being implemented on a wide scale in the form of so-called *responsibility accounting, profitability accounting,* or *activity accounting* systems.

The impact of the responsibility accounting approach is described in the following:

> The sales department requests a rush production. The plant scheduler argues that it will disrupt his production and cost a substantial though not clearly determined amount of money. The answer coming from sales is: "Do you want to take the responsibility of losing the X Company as a customer?" Of course the production scheduler does not want to take such a responsibility, and he gives up, but not before a heavy exchange of arguments and the accumulation of a substantial backlog of ill feeling. Analysis of the payroll in the assembly department, determining the costs involved in getting out rush orders, eliminated the cause for argument. Henceforth, any rush order was accepted with a smile by the production scheduler, who made sure that the extra cost would be duly recorded and charged to the sales department—"no questions asked." As a result, the tension created by rush orders disappeared completely; and, somehow, the number of rush orders requested by the sales department was progressively reduced to an insignificant level.[1]

Ideally, particular revenues and costs are recorded and automatically traced to the one individual in the organization who shoulders primary responsibility for the item. He is in the best position to evaluate and to influence a situation—to exert control. In practice, the diffusion of control throughout the organization complicates the task of collecting relevant data by responsibility centers. The organizational networks, the communication patterns, and the decision-making processes are complex —far too complex to yield either pat answers or an ideal management accounting system.

Illustration of Responsibility Accounting

The simplified organization chart in Exhibit 11-1 will be the basis for our illustration. We will concentrate on the manufacturing phase of the business. The lines of responsibility are easily seen in Exhibit 11-2, which is an over-all view of responsibility reporting. Starting with the supervisor of the machining department and working toward the top, we shall see how these reports may be integrated through three levels of responsibility.

Note, in Exhibit 11-3, that all direct material is charged at standard unit prices to the machining department only. The other producing departments do not include the same direct material in their budgets. In this way, the Lustre Co. incorporates direct material and direct labor, as well as the variable overhead items, in its departmental flexible

---

[1] Raymond Villers, "Control and Freedom in a Decentralized Company," *Harvard Business Review,* XXXII, No. 2 (Mar.-April, 1954), p. 95.

budgets. All of the variances shown may be subdivided for further analysis, either in these reports or in subsidiary reports.

Note that each of these three responsibility reports furnishes the department head with figures on only those items subject to his control. Irrelevant items (i.e., those not subject to his control) are removed from these performance reports. The department head concentrates on those things subject to his influence. He should not receive data which may clutter and confuse his thinking.

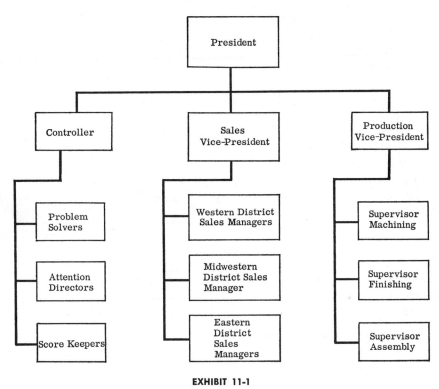

EXHIBIT 11-1

Lustre Co.: Simplified Organization Chart

Trace the $72,000 total from the Machining Department Report (Exhibit 11-3) to the Production Vice-president's Report (Exhibit 11-4). The Vice-president's report merely summarizes the reports of the three individuals under his jurisdiction. He may also want copies of the detailed statements of each supervisor responsible to him.

Trace the $116,000 total from the Production Vice-president's Report to the President's Report (Exhibit 11-5). His summary report includes data for his own office plus a summarization of the entire company's current cost control performance.

To simplify the illustration, only variable costs are shown in the ex-

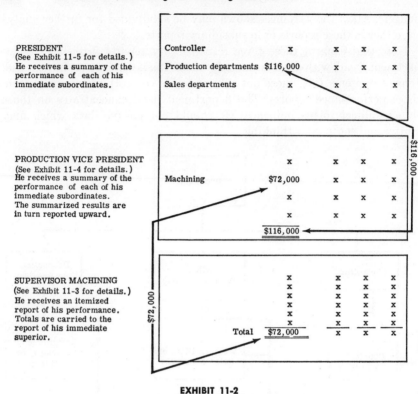

PRESIDENT
(See Exhibit 11-5 for details.)
He receives a summary of the performance of each of his immediate subordinates.

Controller	x	x	x	x
Production departments $116,000		x	x	x
Sales departments	x	x	x	x

PRODUCTION VICE PRESIDENT
(See Exhibit 11-4 for details.)
He receives a summary of the performance of each of his immediate subordinates.
The summarized results are in turn reported upward.

	x	x	x	x
Machining	$72,000	x	x	x
	x	x	x	x
	x	x	x	x
	$116,000			

SUPERVISOR MACHINING
(See Exhibit 11-3 for details.)
He receives an itemized report of his performance. Totals are carried to the report of his immediate superior.

$72,000

	x	x	x	x
	x	x	x	x
	x	x	x	x
	x	x	x	x
	x	x	x	x
Total	$72,000	x	x	x

$116,000

EXHIBIT 11-2

Responsibility Reporting at Various Management Levels

hibits. However, an individual manager may exert control over many programmed costs, which would also be included, separately labeled, in the responsibility short-run performance reports.

EXHIBIT 11-3

LUSTRE CO.
Machining Department
Supervisor's Monthly Responsibility Performance Report

	Flexible Budget		Variance: Favorable, (Unfavorable)	
	This Month	*Year to Date*	*This Month*	*Year to Date*
Direct material	$40,000	$140,000	$(1,000)	$ (4,000)
Direct labor	25,000	75,000	(2,000)	(7,000)
Setup	4,000	12,000	400	100
Rework	2,000	6,000	(200)	(300)
Supplies	200	600	(40)	(100)
Small tools	300	900	(50)	(100)
Other	500	1,500	(60)	(200)
Total variable costs	$72,000	$236,000	$(2,950)	$(11,600)

EXHIBIT 11-4

LUSTRE CO.
Production Vice-president
Monthly Responsibility Performance Report

	Flexible Budget		Variance: Favorable, (Unfavorable)	
	This Month	Year to Date	This Month	Year to Date
Vice-president's office	$ 9,000	$ 29,000	$(1,000)	$ (1,000)
Machining department	72,000	236,000	(2,950)	(11,600)
Finishing department	15,000	50,000	(2,000)	(3,000)
Assembly department	20,000	62,000	(3,000)	(5,000)
Total variable costs	$116,000	$377,000	$(8,950)	$(20,600)

EXHIBIT 11-5

LUSTRE CO.
President's Monthly Responsibility Performance Report

	Flexible Budget		Variance: Favorable, (Unfavorable)	
	This Month	Year to Date	This Month	Year to Date
President's office	$ 6,000	$ 20,000	$ 100	$ 400
Controller	4,000	13,000	(200)	(1,000)
Production vice-president	116,000	377,000	(8,950)	(20,600)
Sales vice-president	40,000	130,000	(1,000)	(4,000)
Total variable costs	$166,000	$540,000	$(10,050)	$(25,200)

CONTROLLABLE AND UNCONTROLLABLE COSTS: THE PRACTICAL DIFFICULTIES

Distinguishing Features of Controllability

Responsibility accounting has an innate appeal because it delineates a sphere of operations and supposedly distinguishes between controllable and uncontrollable costs. But, as in so many other attempts to classify things neatly (e.g., into variable and fixed costs), one finds that the distinctions are extremely difficult to make. So do not expect to obtain a crystal-clear, working concept of a controllable cost. Such a concept does not exist, except in the abstract.

Controllable costs are those which may be directly regulated at a given level of managerial authority. Put another way, controllable costs are those that are directly influenced by a *manager* within a *given time period*. Too often, people assume that variable costs are controllable and fixed costs are uncontrollable. Such thinking may lead to erroneous conclusions. For example, rent is uncontrollable by the assembly foreman, but it may be controllable by the executive vice-president, who may be assigned the responsibility of choosing plant facilities and of deciding whether to own or rent. Moreover, managers frequently have the option of trading off variable for fixed costs—for example, by purchasing labor-saving devices.

The distinction between controllability and uncontrollability also has a time dimension. Some accountants would maintain that rent is uncontrollable at any level of managerial supervision. This may be so, for any given year included in a long-term lease, but over the long run, top management must determine the commitments which are reflected in such accounts as rent, depreciation, and property taxes. The level of property taxes, for example, is sometimes subject to change by management negotiation with assessors and by control over inventory levels.

In the long run, all costs are subject to at least some degree of managerial control. Long-run costs are usually incurred with special care because they are generally large and irrevocable.

In summary, controllability is a matter of degree that is affected by two major factors: the managerial area of responsibility, and the time period in question. All costs are controllable, to some degree and by somebody, over the long run. In the short run, not as many costs are controllable, and those that are controllable are subject to various degrees of influence.

In a given situation, therefore, certain costs may be regarded as controllable and others as uncontrollable. This is a useful distinction in assigning responsibility for cost control. The budget for which a shop foreman is responsible should show only the costs that are considered under his control. Such items as rent and taxes would not appear on his budget; from his standpoint, these are uncontrollable costs.

Difficulties in Assigning Costs to Individual Managers

The fundamental idea that individuals should be charged only with costs subject to their control is conceptually appealing. Practically, however, there are difficulties.

Few, if any, elements of cost are the sole responsibility of one person. Some guides to deciding the appropriate costs to be charged to a person (i.e., responsibility center) are as follows:

1. If the person has authority over both the acquisition and the use of the service, he should be charged with the cost of such services.
2. If the person can significantly influence the amount of cost through his own action, he may be charged with such costs.
3. Even if the person cannot significantly influence the amount of cost through his own direct action, he may be charged with those elements with which the management desires him to be concerned, so that he will help to influence those who are responsible.[2]

[2] "Report of Committee on Cost Concepts and Standards," *Accounting Review*, April, 1956, p. 189.

The diffusion of control throughout the organization complicates the task of collecting data by responsibility centers. For example. material and supply *prices* may be influenced by the effectiveness of the purchasing officer, whereas material and supply *usage* may be most strongly influenced by the foremen. Another illustration would be the cost of operating a department which maintains and repairs machinery of producing departments. If the repair work is done under the supervision of the maintenance and repair foreman, the efficiency of the workmen is subject to his control. However, the total cost of repairs is also influenced by the day-to-day care given the machinery by the production workers.

A practical over-all guide for judging controllability is the following: Although more than one executive may regard a given cost as being within his control, *there is usually one officer in the whole organization who bears primary responsibility for control.* This is usually the executive who most closely supervises the day-to-day action which influences that cost. All costs which are controllable by him are also regarded as being controllable by his superior line executives.

Timing and Control

Control is exercised in the form of particular actions. An action, once taken, cannot be changed by subsequent events. Performance reports, which provide data for appraisal, call management's attention to situations that have not been "in control." Performance reports are control mechanisms, not because they help rectify past mistakes but because they spur management to prevent future mistakes. Thus, accounting for control is oriented to the future rather than to the past. Historical data are important only insofar as they help to predict performance or help managerial investigation so that control may be better maintained in the future.

CONTRIBUTION APPROACH TO COST ALLOCATION

Allocation is an Imposing Problem

The attempt to design an accounting system around responsibility centers for various products or territories has accentuated one of accounting's most imposing measurement problems—cost allocation. Kohler, in *A Dictionary for Accountants,* defines *allocate* as follows:

> . . . to charge an item or group of items of revenue or cost to one or more objects, activities, processes, operations, or products, in accordance with cost responsibilities, benefits received, or other readily identifiable measure of application or consumption.[3]

---

[3] Eric L. Kohler, *A Dictionary for Accountants,* 3rd ed. (Englewood Cliffs, N.J.: Prentice-Hall, Inc., 1963), p. 28.

The term usually implies the subdividing of a lump sum over two or more objects. In this section we will consider the applicability of the contribution approach to this pervasive problem.

Objectives of Allocation: The Segment

In order to guide his decisions, the manager needs information pertaining to a variety of objectives. He seeks the cost of *something:* a product; a group of products; a plant; a territory; a machine hour; a labor hour; an operating division; a customer; or an order. We shall call this something a segment, and define it as any line of activity or part of an organization for which a separate determination of costs and/or sales is wanted. For example, the Chevrolet division of General Motors Corp. is a segment; so is the truck division of Chevrolet. So is each type of Chevrolet, and so is each truck.

Because segment costs are very influential in decision making, they should be developed thoughtfully, and with particular regard to the *purpose* of the information being compiled. Among the purposes are: (1) evaluating the performance of an individual manager, a product or product group, a salesman, a territory, or a machine; (2) setting prices, selecting facilities, and making various project decisions; and (3) obtaining costs for inventory valuation and income determination. Inventory valuation and income determination are related primarily to external reporting and are discussed in Chapter 15. In this chapter, we shall concentrate on an over-all approach that will be adaptable to appraisals of performance, pricing, dropping or adding product lines, advertising and promoting specific products, subcontracting decisions, *and* to inventory valuation.

Exhibit 11-6, a Model Income Statement, by Segments, is an extremely important exhibit because it gives a bird's-eye view of a large part of management accounting. The overriding emphasis is on cost behavior patterns. The basic distinctions in cost behavior should be preserved in management reports and in cost allocations. Failure to maintain these distinctions is the biggest hindrance to progress and clarity in management accounting.

Revenue, Variable Costs, and Contribution Margins

The allocation of revenue and of variable costs is usually straightforward, because each item is directly and specifically identifiable with a given segment of activity. The Contribution Margin, Line (*a*) in Exhibit 11-6, is especially helpful for gauging the impact on net income of short-run changes in volume. Changes in net income may be quickly computed by multiplying the change in units by the unit contribution margin or by multiplying the increment in dollar sales by the contribution margin ratio.

The implications of these and other uses of the contribution margin are discussed at length in Chapter 13.

Separable Costs and Joint Costs

A *separable cost* is directly identifiable with a particular segment; a *joint cost* is common to all the segments in question and is not clearly or practically allocable except on some questionable basis. Examples of typical separable costs are advertising, product research and development, sales promotion, specific management consulting, and some supervisory costs. Examples of joint costs are the salaries of the president and other top officers, basic research and development, and some central corporate costs like public relations or corporate image advertising.

Programmed and committed costs may be separable or joint, *depending on the segments in question.* Moreover, there may be a limit to a given cost's separability. In Exhibit 11-6, a retail food company's outlay for a newspaper advertisement may easily be identified with a territorial branch in a territorial income statement. The cost of the advertisement may also be readily split between groceries, produce, and meats. However, allocating the cost between the stores is more questionable. Consequently, it may be unallocated in an income statement by stores.

Similarly, the salary of the branch meat merchandise manager may be directly identified with a breakdown of the branch's activities by product lines, but the same cost may be unallocable to individual stores.

Short-run Performance Margin and Programmed Costs

What version of income is most appropriate for judging the short-run performance of division managers or product managers? When it is interpreted in conjunction with the Contribution Margin, the Short-run Performance Margin, Line (b) in Exhibit 11-6, should be useful. Reliance solely on the contribution margin as a measure of short-run performance would be misleading, because programmed costs may influence variable costs. For example, outlays for maintenance, advertising, training, or management consulting may increase machine speeds, boost sales volume, or increase the productivity of labor.

Segment Margin and Net Income

The Segment Margin, Line (c) in Exhibit 11-6, is computed after deducting the Separable Committed Costs. It is probably the best single approximation of long-run segment profitability.

The Net Income before Income Taxes, Line (d) in Exhibit 11-6, is computed only for the company as a whole. No attempt is made to allocate any joint costs; therefore, net income is not computed by segments. This refusal to allocate joint costs is the most controversial aspect of the

EXHIBIT 11-6

The Contribution Approach: Model Income Statement, by Segments*
(In thousands of dollars)

	Retail Food Company as a Whole	Company Breakdown into Two Divisions		Possible Breakdown of Branch B Only				Possible Breakdown of Branch B, Meats Only		
		Branch A	Branch B	Not Allocated†	Groceries	Produce	Meats	Not Allocated†	Store 1	Store 2
Net sales	$4,000	$1,500	$2,500	—	$1,300	$300	$900	—	$600	$300
Variable costs:										
Cost of merchandise sold	$3,000	$1,100	$1,900	—	$1,000	$230	$670	—	$450	$220
Variable operating expenses	260	100	160	—	100	10	50	—	35	15
Total variable costs	$3,260	$1,200	$2,060	—	$1,100	$240	$720	—	$485	$235
(a) Contribution margin	$740	$300	$440	$20	$200	$60	$180	$30	$115	$65
Separable programmed costs	260	100	160	40	40	10	90	35	35	25
(b) Short-run performance margin	$480	$200	$280	$(20)	$160	$50	$90	$(30)	$80	$40
Separable committed costs	200	90	110	20	40	10	40	10	22	8
(c) Segment margin	$280	$110	$170	$(40)	$120	$40	$50	$(40)	$58	$32
Joint programmed and committed costs	100									
(d) Net income before income taxes	$80									

* Three different types of segments are illustrated here: branches, product lines, and stores. As you read across, you will note that the focus becomes narrower: from Branch A and B, to Branch B only, to Meats in Branch B only.

† Only those costs clearly identifiable to a product line should be allocated.

contribution approach to the income statement. Accountants and managers are used to the whole being completely broken down into neat parts that can be added up again to equal the whole. In traditional segment income statements, all costs are fully allocated so that the segments show final net incomes that can be summed to equal the net income for the company as a whole.

Of course, if for some reason management prefers a whole-equals-the-sum-of-its-parts net income statement, the joint costs may be allocated so that the segments show net income figures that will cross-add to equal the net income for the company as a whole. The important point is that the contribution approach distinguishes between various degrees of objectivity in cost allocations. As you read downward in Exhibit 11-6, you become less and less confident about the validity and accuracy of the cost allocations. A dozen independent accountants will be most likely to agree on how the variable costs should be allocated and least likely to agree on whether and how the joint costs should be allocated.

Reports by Product Lines and Sales Territories

The most widely used detailed operating statements are tabulated by product lines and by sales territories. The emphasis depends on the organization of the marketing function. Some companies have distinct product lines with separate sales forces and separate advertising programs, and their operating reports emphasize contributions by products. Other companies make a multitude of products that are promoted by brand-name advertising and which are all sold by the same salesmen. Their operating reports emphasize territorial or district sales and contributions to profit.

Some Guides to Allocation

The following general points should guide cost allocations:

1. The fundamental distinctions between cost behavior patterns should be preserved.
2. The exactness of the breakdown in classification by segments depends on the extent of the joint costs and the clerical costs. In general, the greater the detail, the more useful the cost allocation information. However, there is the corresponding danger—that too much detail encourages inaccurate initial record keeping. Costs which are really joint should not be allocated; but attempts to identify them with specific segments should be made before it is decided that the costs in question are really joint costs.

Allocation Bases: Weakness of Sales Dollars

In any good accounting system, the need for allocation is minimized by regarding as many costs as possible as direct charges. Allocations should be based on the factor most likely to affect the cost to be allocated. Some commonly used bases for allocation are shown in Exhibit 11-7.

EXHIBIT 11-7

Bases for Allocation of Costs to Territories

Cost to be Allocated	Allocation Base
Field salesmen	Direct
Central sales management	Budgeted sales; number of men; amount of time
Central administration	Unit rate for type of service, such as billing, printing, etc.
Central warehousing	Service used as measured by quantities handled
Central advertising costs	Projected sales volume
Advertising:	
Magazine	Circulation
Radio and television	Number of set owners
Samples	Territorial sales quota

A commonly, but wrongly, used basis for allocation is dollar sales. The costs of effort are independent of the results actually obtained, in the sense that the costs are programmed by management, not determined by sales. Moreover, the allocation of costs on the basis of dollar sales entails circular reasoning. That is, the costs per segment are determined by relative sales per segment. For example, examine the effects in the following situation (figures are in millions of dollars):

Year 1

Product	A	B	C		Total
Sales	$100	$100	$100	$300	(100%)
Costs allocated by dollar sales	$ 10	$ 10	$ 10	$ 30	(10%)

Assume that prices are raised on Products *A* and *B*. Their total dollar volume rises considerably. However, the direct costs and sales of Product *C* are not changed. The total costs to be allocated on the basis of dollar sales are also unchanged.

Year 2

Product	A	B	C		Total
Sales	$137.5	$137.5	$100.0	$375.0	(100%)
Costs allocated by dollar sales	$ 11.0	$ 11.0	$ 8.0	$ 30.0	(8%)

The ratio between the costs allocated on the basis of dollar sales and total sales was reduced, in the second year, to 8 per cent ($30 ÷ $375), as compared with 10 per cent ($30 ÷ $300) in the first year. This resulted in less cost being allocated to Product *C*, despite the fact that its unit volume and directly attributable costs were approximately the same as for the first year. The point is that the product which did the worst is relieved of costs without any reference to underlying causal relationships.

Advertising is a prime example of a cost that is typically allocated on the basis of dollar sales. Basing allocation on dollar sales *achieved* may be questionable, because the unsuccessful product or territory may be unjustifiably relieved of costs. However, there is some merit in basing allocation on *potential* sales or purchasing power available in a particular territory or for a particular product. For example, there would be a consistent relationship between the advertising costs and sales volume in each territory, if all territories were equally efficient. If, however, a manager has poor outlets or a weak sales staff, one of the indicators would be a high ratio of advertising to sales.

Functional Costing: Allocate with Care

Although costs should be allocated as far as possible, to facilitate decision making, there are definite limitations. Some well-known consultants and writers in this field have stressed a functional costing approach, i.e., the classification of costs by function (warehousing, delivery, billing, etc.). This objective is meritorious, but the approach taken is often downright misleading. Many proponents of functional costing are grimly determined to compute a unit cost for nearly any activity, without bothering to distinguish between variable and fixed behavior patterns. All of us are familiar with glib statements such as the following (taken from an actual report): "The cost summary discloses a unit cost of $.097 for handling commercial deposits, and this is made up of the following items (functions): teller $.0658, proof $.0057, and bookkeeping $.0256." The difficulty here is not caused by interest in the costs of performing various functions; it is that cost studies are too often focused on determining the exact cost of processing an order, of posting an invoice, or of making a sales call. Too often, the attempt involves flimsy assumptions concerning what costs are pertinent and what unit should be used as the base.

The data relating to costs and the data relating to units must be examined separately before the two are expressed as costs per unit. When costs and units are studied separately, the fundamental variable, mixed, or fixed behavior of each becomes evident, the importance of joint or common costs emerges, and the variations in cost which are not due to unit volume variations are revealed. The contribution approach seems more promising than functional unit costing.

SUMMARY

In this chapter, we have discussed the delineation of responsibility via the techniques of responsibility accounting and the contribution approach to cost allocation.

Short-run responsibility performance reports should focus on the items subject to the immediate control of the manager in question. Uncontrollable items should be omitted; if they are included, they should be distinctly labeled and not mixed with the controllable items.

The contribution approach to the income statement and to the problems of cost allocation is accounting's most effective method for helping management to evaluate performance and make decisions. Allocations are made with thoughtful regard for the *purpose* of the information being compiled. Various subdivisions of net income are drawn for different purposes. Contribution margins, short-run performance margins, and segment margins may be measured, in addition to net income. The contribution approach distinguishes sharply between various degrees of objectivity in cost allocations.

Allocations of fixed costs should be made in lump sums, when possible. Two widespread practices may produce misleading results: (1) functional unit costing without separation of variable and fixed components; and (2) using dollar sales as an allocation base when no cause-and-effect relationship can be established with assurance.

SUMMARY PROBLEMS FOR YOUR REVIEW

PROBLEMS

1. Review the section on the contribution approach to cost allocation, especially Exhibit 11-6.
2. The Lindhe Co. has a responsibility accounting system. Uncontrollable costs, such as insurance, property taxes, depreciation, and supervisory salaries, are excluded from the periodic performance reports. A summary of the performance of Departments *A* and *B* follows:

| | *Department* | | | |
| | *A* | | *B* | |
	Actual	*Budget*	*Actual*	*Budget*
Direct material	$ 70,000	$ 69,000	$150,000	$155,600
Direct labor	30,000	28,000	70,000	68,000
Supplies	2,000	2,600	3,200	4,000
Idle time	1,100	1,000	5,100	1,500
Rework	3,000	1,400	2,000	2,100
Overtime premium	800	—	2,000	—
Other indirect labor	4,000	4,200	6,700	6,800
	$110,900	$106,200	$239,000	$238,000

During the period reported, one of the important machines in Department *A* developed a misalignment that was not detected until the machine had been used for a considerable time. The product has an assembly-line production pattern, moving from Department *A* to Department *B*.

Required:

Explain the possible causes of the variations noted above in light of the information given here. Comment on the controllability of the cost elements.

SOLUTIONS

1. See Exhibit 11-6.
2. Neither department shows significant deviations from budget *totals*. However, the detailed items reveal clues for investigation. A major point here is that summary analysis often buries significant, but offsetting, variances.

   The high rework costs in Department *A* are probably due to the faulty machine. The idle time in Department *B* was probably spent waiting for goods reworked in Department *A*. The overtime premiums in both departments may have resulted from efforts to adhere to scheduled production requirements. For example, in Department *A* the rework cost was $1,600 in excess of budget; the overtime premium was $800 (50 per cent of $1,600). Therefore, the idle time and the overtime premium in Department *B* may not have been controllable by the head of that department. And this raises the possibility that these costs might more properly be charged to Department *A*.

   The notable savings in supplies in both departments are difficult to explain with the sketchy information we have. One possible explanation is an honest-to-goodness bearing down on the cost of supplies. Other possible explanations are faulty budget figures, errors in record keeping, or deliberate holding back of new orders for supplies in an effort to keep costs within the over-all budget.

   The direct material and direct labor performances are difficult to evaluate because no distinctions are available between prices or labor rates, on the one hand, and usage, on the other. We have no assurance that the direct material and direct labor figures shown are computed either at standard or at actual unit rates. The department heads probably have control over usage but not over prices or rates.

ASSIGNMENT MATERIAL

ESSENTIAL ASSIGNMENT MATERIAL

11-1. *Terminology.* Define: responsibility accounting; profitability accounting; activity accounting; controllable cost; segment; allocation; separable cost; joint cost; common cost; short-run performance margin; segment margin; and functional costing.

11-2. *Divisional contribution, performance, and segment margins.* The Williamson Co. has two separate operating divisions, *A* and *B*, each division producing only one product, *X* and *Y*, respectively. The divisions have a practical monthly capacity of 12,000 units. In order for either division to operate in excess of practical capacity, it would have to sustain an additional cost of $2.50 per extra unit. Sales are expected to remain constant. You have the following data available for the month of January, 19x6.

	Division	
	A	B
Sales	12,000 units	10,000 units
Selling price per unit	$10	$10

Cost Data

	Product	
	X	Y
Variable Costs, per Unit		
Material	$1.00	$1.50
Labor	1.00	1.50
Factory overhead	1.00	1.00
Selling and administrative	1.00	2.00

	Division	
	A	B
Fixed Costs, per Month		
Advertising	$10,000	$ 2,000
Engineering	5,000	2,000
Research	5,000	2,000
Manager's salary	1,000	1,000
Depreciation	12,000	4,000
Taxes and insurance	3,000	1,000
Joint (allocated here on an arbitrary basis)	11,000	8,000
Total	$47,000	$20,000

Required:

1. Prepare an income statement, by segments, for the month of January, 19x6, making sure to include contribution, short-run performance, and segment margins.

2. Assume that costs remain constant. If 1,000 additional units could be sold at $7 each, by each division, what would be the increase in the profits of each division and of the company as a whole?

11-3. *Cost allocations based on sales: effect of shift of sales mix.* The Zeff Co. allocates its sales manager's salary, national advertising, and miscellaneous selling and administration costs to its products in proportion to dollar sales. For example, in 19x1 the following allocations were made:

Product	X	Y	Z	Total
Sales	$2,000,000	$2,000,000	$1,000,000	$5,000,000
Cost allocated by dollar sales	180,000	180,000	90,000	450,000

Required:

1. Assume that the prices and dollar sales of Z double in 19x2 (because of special snob appeal), without any change in the total cost, $450,000. Assume that dollar sales are still the basis for allocation. What cost will be allocated to each product in 19x2?

2. Discuss the limitations of using dollar sales as a basis for cost allocation.

11-4. *Responsibility of purchasing agent.* Ajax Manufacturing Co. has received an order for 500 special parts which will require modifications of stock part No. 1739. There is a penalty clause on the order—$200 a day for every day delivery is late. It will cost the company $2 less per unit to purchase and process raw materials for the special part than to rework standard part No. 1739.

Mr. Smith, the purchasing agent, is responsible for securing the raw material in time to meet the scheduled delivery date. Mr. Smith placed the order and received an acceptable delivery date from his supplier. He checked up several times and did everything in his power to insure prompt delivery of the raw material.

On the delivery date specified by the supplier, Mr. Smith is notified that the raw material was damaged in packaging and will be delivered four days late. As a result, the special order will also be four days late. Consequently, an $800 penalty must be paid by Ajax Co.

What department should bear the $800 penalty? Why?

ADDITIONAL ASSIGNMENT MATERIAL

Note: In Problems 11-24 and 11-25, we explore the intricacies of cost allocation in greater depth. Problem 11-26 incorporates our previous study of cost behavior and emphasizes cost allocation.

11-5. "Collecting relevant data by responsibility centers is difficult." Why?

11-6. "Variable costs are controllable and fixed costs are uncontrollable." Do you agree? Explain.

11-7. "Managers may trade off variable for fixed costs." Give three examples.

11-8. What two major factors influence controllability?

11-9. Describe three guides to deciding how costs should be charged to a responsibility center.

11-10. "Material costs are controllable by a production department foreman." Do you agree? Explain.

11-11. Give examples of segments, as described in this chapter.

11-12. Distinguish between a separable cost and a joint (common) cost.

11-13. "The contribution margin is the best measure of short-run performance." Do you agree? Why?

11-14. What is the most controversial aspect of the contribution approach to cost allocation?

11-15. Give two guides to cost allocation.

11-16. "A commonly misused basis for allocation is dollar sales." Explain.

11-17. How should national advertising costs be allocated to territories?

11-18. What are the weaknesses of so-called functional costing?

11-19. *Cost-volume-profit relationships for two divisions: joint costs.* The Grose Co. has two separate operating divisions, *A* and *B*. Each division produces one product, *X* and *Y*, respectively. In the production of the two products *X* and *Y*, there are many similar manufacturing techniques. This gives rise to a $20,000 nonallocable joint variable cost. Other pertinent information for the year 19x6 is available and follows.

	Division	
	A	*B*
Sales	20,000 units	·20,000 units
Sales price per unit	$10	$10

Cost Data

	Product	
Variable Costs	X	Y
Material	$ 40,000	$ 20,000
Direct labor	20,000	10,000
Factory overhead	20,000	10,000
Sales commissions (based on sales dollars)	40,000	—

	Division	
Fixed Costs	*A*	*B*
Advertising	$ 10,000	$ 30,000
Engineering	10,000	20,000
Salesmen's salary	—	40,000
Manager's salary	20,000	10,000
Depreciation	10,000	20,000
Joint (allocation questionable)	10,000	20,000
Total costs	$180,000	$180,000

Required:

1. Prepare an income statement for the company and for the segments, making sure to show contribution, short-run performance, and segment margins.

2. Nelick Consulting Co. informs Mr. Grose that, if he cut prices in half for both X and Y, he could triple sales of both products with no additional fixed costs. Show the effects of this step by preparing another income statement. Comment.

11-20. *Segment margin and joint costs.* The Carson City Hospital has 400 beds. The beds are divided into two separate wings. All private (one-bed) rooms are located in one wing, and all semiprivate (two-bed) rooms are located in the other. During the past month, 30 days, occupancy was 90 per cent. All of the 260 private rooms were occupied each day.

The hospital charges $35 per bed per day for a private room, and $31 per bed per day for a semiprivate room.

	Private	*Semiprivate*
Variable costs per bed per day:		
Supplies	$ 1.25	$ 1.25
Wages	20.00	20.00
Administrative	1.75	.75
Department overhead	2.00	1.00
Total	$25.00	$23.00
Fixed costs per month:		
Physicians' salaries	$50,000	$15,000
Supervisor's salary	600	600
Insurance	300	100
Depreciation	10,000	7,000
Joint costs (allocation questionable)	20,000	2,120
Total	$80,900	$24,820

Required:

1. Find the number of patient days (a bed occupied for the entire month would represent 30 patient days) for the month in:
   (1) The private wing.
   (2) The semiprivate wing.
2. Construct an income statement showing the contribution margin and segment margin of each wing and the net income of the two wings together.
3. The administrator believes that if the hospital had charged $36 per bed per day for the private room and $31 per bed per day for the semiprivate, they would still have had 90 per cent occupancy. But he estimated that 10 per cent of the people with a private room would have taken a semiprivate room. How would changing the private room rate to $36 affect net income, assuming his estimate is correct?

11-21. *Accuracy of source documents and fixing responsibility.* Interdepartmental confusion in a printing company was described by Prof. George Shultz. A producing department's committee objected vigorously to the planning done by the scheduling department. Workmen complained that frequently they set up a job, only to discover that the paper they needed was unavailable. Though paper for other jobs was available, a switch was not desirable because setup time was too great. Since the complaint involved another department, the production department committee could not correct the situation. So they passed it upward to a top committee, which included the president.

The head of the scheduling department was naturally upset by this complaint and investigated the matter thoroughly in preparation for the meeting. The worker prepares a time slip for each job, showing the total elapsed time in terms of running time, delays, and so on. The scheduling department uses this information for production planning. The scheduling department head examined the file of these slips and found that extremely little delay was ascribed to insufficient paper.

At the meeting, he triumphantly produced his facts and maintained that the complaint was insignificant. Shultz reports that his disclosure was greeted with embarrassed silence. After a long half-minute, a worker said: "Those time slips are way off. We fill them out. We were told by the foreman that he would get in trouble if we showed delay time, so we usually add it to the running time. We've been doing it that way for years. We had no idea that you were using the slips as a basis for planning."

Required:

What are the implications, for the accountant, of the above incident? How may the trouble have been avoided? What was a likely reason for the attitude of the foreman toward the time-slip procedure?

11-22. *Responsibility accounting, profit centers, and the contribution approach.* Consider the following data for the year's operations of an automobile dealer:

Sales of vehicles	$2,000,000
Sales of parts and service	500,000

Cost of vehicle sales	1,600,000
Parts and service materials	150,000
Parts and service labor	200,000
Parts and service overhead	50,000
General dealership overhead	100,000
Advertising of vehicles	100,000
Sales commissions, vehicles	40,000
Sales salaries, vehicles	50,000

The president of the dealership has long regarded the markup on materials and labor for the parts and service activity as the amount which is supposed to cover all parts and service overhead plus all general overhead of the dealership. In other words, the parts and service department is viewed as a cost recovery operation, and the sales of vehicles as the income-producing activity.

Required:

1. Prepare a departmentalized operating statement that harmonizes with the views of the president.

2. Prepare an alternative operating statement that would reflect a different view of the dealership operations. Assume that $10,000 and $50,000 of the $100,000 general overhead can be allocated with confidence to the parts and service department and to sales of vehicles, respectively. The remaining $40,000 cannot be allocated except in some highly arbitrary manner.

3. Comment on the relative merits of approach (1) and (2).

11-23. *Departmental cost allocations and the contribution approach.* Impecunious Hospital has two income-producing departments, Laboratory and X-ray. The revenue derived from these departments must be sufficient to cover the total expenses of the hospital. It is desired that the hospital break even, that is, earn zero profit. In the past, average prices in each department have been set by marking up variable costs per unit of service by 200 per cent, to cover the costs incurred in departments which produce no income. It is customary to charge all supervisory and professional salaries to Administration, and all depreciation to Overhead.

The following data were available on Dec. 31, 19x1:

Laboratory tests performed	20,000 per year, @ $7.50		
X-ray pictures taken:	5,000 per year, @ $45.00		
Income statement:			
Revenue: Laboratory		$150,000	
X-ray		225,000	$375,000
Expenses: Laboratory	$ 50,000		
X-ray	75,000	$125,000	
Administration	$115,000		
Overhead	150,000	265,000	
Total expenses			390,000
Deficit			($ 15,000)

The director was interested in eliminating the deficit and presented the following analysis to the board of trustees:

	Laboratory	*X-ray*	*Total*
Revenue	$150,000	$225,000	$375,000
Expenses:			
Variable	$ 50,000	$ 75,000	$125,000
Apportioned*	212.000	53,000	265,000
Total expenses	$262,000	$128,000	$390.000
Net income	($112,000)	$ 97,000	($ 15.000)

* A total of 25,000 units of service was performed. 20,000 (80 per cent) were laboratory services, and 5,000 (20 per cent) were X-ray services.

$265,000 $265,000
.80   .20
$212,000 (Laboratory) $ 53.000 (X-ray)

He argued as follows: "Our losses are in the laboratory. We can't hope to make the department a paying one, but we can eliminate the over-all deficit by raising the average price for lab services by $.75."

The medical staff, however, objected on the grounds that this would raise Impecunious's charges above those of other hospitals in the area. After a prolonged, violent disagreement during which neither side would give in, the medical staff forced the administrator's resignation.

Max I. Mizer, a young university-trained administrator, has been hired for the job, and has prepared the following analysis of cost patterns:

Variable Cost per unit:

Laboratory		X-ray
$2.10	Wages	$ 6.40
.40	Supplies	4.75
–0–	Power	3.85
$2.50	Total	$15.00

Fixed Costs:

Depreciation:	Laboratory	$31,000
	X-ray	94,000
	Administration	25,000

Salaries:	Laboratory	1 pathologist, @ $16,000 per year
	X-ray	4 radiologists, @ $16,000 per year
	Administration	1 administrator, @ $20,000 per year and
		3 clerks, @ $5,000 per year

Max immediately saw the fallacy of charging all salaries to Administration and all depreciation to Overhead, realizing that direct fixed costs should be immediately charged to the department receiving the benefit. He decides that volume of services performed is a satisfactory base for allocation of Administrative expenses and that volume will be constant for the foreseeable future.

Required:

1. Prepare revised income statements for the fiscal year 19x1 for the two income-producing departments and for the hospital as a whole, using a contribution format and Max's new cost data.

2. Prepare income statements for 19x2, assuming that volume is constant but that *prices* are changed so that both income-producing departments, and the hospital, break even.

3. Comment on the old administrator's analysis of the situation and his presentation to the board. What criticisms do you have of his stand?

11-24. *Analysis of channels of distribution and territories.* The Schindler Co. has three sales districts which sell a single product. Its income statement for 19x1 contained the following data:

		District		
	Total	*A*	*B*	*C*
Sales: 100,000 units, @ $11	$1,100,000	$550,000	$330,000	$220,000
Cost of goods sold, including				
$100,000 of fixed factory overhead	500,000	250,000	150,000	100,000
Gross margin	$ 600,000	$300,000	$180,000	$120,000
Order-filling costs:				
Freight out	$ 68,000	$ 34,000	$ 20,400	$ 13,600
Shipping supplies	50,000	25,000	15,000	10,000
Packing and shipping labor	50,000	25,000	15,000	10,000
Total	$ 168,000	$ 84,000	$ 50,400	$ 33,600
Order-getting costs:				
Salesmen's salaries	$ 50,000	$ 50,000		
Salesmen's commissions	26,400		$ 26,400	
Agents' commissions	11,000			$ 11,000
Sales manager's salary	30,000	15,000	9,000	6,000
Advertising, local	80,000	40,000	24,000	16,000
Advertising, national	100,000	50,000	30,000	20,000
Total	$ 297,400	$155,000	$ 89,400	$ 53,000
Total marketing costs	$ 465,400	$239,000	$139,800	$ 86,600
Administrative expenses:				
Variable	$ 50,000	$ 25,000	$ 15,000	$ 10,000
Nonvariable	100,000	50,000	30,000	20,000
Total administrative expense	$ 150,000	$ 75,000	$ 45,000	$ 30,000
Total expenses	$ 615,400	$314,000	$184,800	$116,600
Net operating income	$ (15,400)	$(14,000)	$ (4,800)	$ 3,400

District *A* contains the company's only factory and central headquarters. This district employs five salaried salesmen.

District *B* is 200 to 400 miles from the factory. The district employs three salesmen on a commission basis and advertises weekly, locally.

District *C* is 400 to 600 miles from the factory. The district employs three manufacturers' agents. Local advertising costs are split fifty-fifty between the agents and the company. Cost per unit of advertising space is the same as in District *A*.

The following variable unit costs have been computed:

Freight out, per unit	$.50, $.70, and $1.10, for Districts *A*, *B*, and *C*, respectively
Shipping supplies, per unit	.50
Packing and shipping labor, per unit	.50
Variable administrative per sales order	2.00

District *A* had 17,000 orders; District *B*, 6,000; and District *C*, 2,000. Local advertising costs were $60,000, $15,000, and $5,000, for Districts *A*, *B*, and *C*, respectively.

Required:

1. Mr. Schindler asks you to recast the income statement in accordance with the contribution approach that he heard described at a recent sales convention. Assume that fixed manufacturing overhead, national advertising, the sales manager's salary, and nonvariable administrative expense are not allocated.

2. What is the net margin per order, in each district (territorial) segment? What clues for management investigation are generated by such a computation?

3. The salesmen in District *B* have suggested a saturation campaign in local newspaper advertising, to cost $30,000. How much must the sales volume in District *B* increase to justify such an additional investment?

4. Why does District *A* have the highest contribution margin percentage but the lowest district margin percentage?

5. On the basis of the given data, what courses of action seem most likely to improve profits? Should District *A* be dropped? Why?

11-25. *Product line and territorial income statements.* The Frumer Co. shows the following results for the year 19x1:

Sales	$1,000,000	100.0%
Manufacturing costs of goods sold	$ 675,000	67.5%
Selling and advertising*	22,000	22.0%
Administrative (all nonvariable)	35,000	3.5%
Total expenses	$ 930,000	93.0%
Net income before income taxes	$ 70,000	7.0%

* All nonvariable, except for $40,000 freight-out cost.

The sales manager has asked you to prepare statements that will help him assess the company efforts by product line and by territories. You have gathered the following information:

	Product			Territory		
	A	*B*	*C*	*North*	*Central*	*Eastern*
Sales*	25%	40%	35%			
Product *A*				50%	20%	30%
Product *B*				15%	70%	15%
Product *C*				14/35	8/35	13/35
Variable manufacturing and packaging costs†	68%	55%	60%			
Nonvariable separable costs:						
Manufacturing	15,000	14,000	21,000	(not allocated)		
Selling and advertising	40,000	18,000	42,000	48,000	32,000	40,000
Freight out	(not allocated)			13,000	9,000	18,000

Note. All items not directly allocated were considered joint or common costs.

* Per cent of company sales.
† Per cent of product sales.

Required:

1. Prepare a product-line income statement, showing the results for the company as a whole in the first column and the results for the three products in adjoining columns. Show a contribution margin and a product margin, as well as net income.
2. Repeat (1) on a territorial basis. Show a contribution margin and a territory margin.
3. Should salesmen's commissions be based on contribution margins, product margins, territorial margins, net income, or dollar sales? Explain.

11-26. *Evening college operations: revenue potential and cost allocation.* (Based on a situation described by Richard C. John.) The budget officer of a large university informed the dean of the Adult Education College that his operation was supposed to produce a revenue of $1,500 in excess of expenses. The dean's anticipated revenues are $49,500, from 1,650 enrollments. His total estimated costs are $48,000, including $19,800 of general programmed costs and committed costs. The dean classified his costs as follows:

a. *Direct event or course costs.* All costs that will be incurred if the specific event or course in question is held and that will be avoided if the course is not held. Examples: instructor's salary, specific promotional costs, rental of visual aid equipment.

b. *General programmed costs.* All costs that were fixed, in total, for a given period, in light of a general forecast of over-all enrollment or scope of activity. Examples are part-time clerical salaries, printings and mailings of general promotional literature, general space leasing, advertising, and supplies.

c. *Committed costs.* All costs that entail long-range obligations or responsibilities. Decisions about these costs usually involve a longer planning horizon than a single budget period. These costs are also fixed, in total, for a budget period. Examples are full-time administrative and clerical salaries.

Precious Stones, a new course, had been scheduled in response to some requests. The dean had hired a geology professor who was very distinguished in lapidary science. His salary for the course would be $300. Required audiovisual equipment would be rented for $60. The class was budgeted for an enrollment of 25 and was assigned to a room which would comfortably accommodate 60. Tuition for the course was $30. In addition, the college furnished a stone kit which was to be bought in the exact quantity needed, from a local supplier, at a special price of $4 per kit.

The dean had learned a little about cost-volume-profit relationships. His enthusiasm for this course diminished after he computed the following breakeven point:

Let X = Number of enrollments
Then   Tuition revenue = Direct event costs
$$+ \text{(General programmed costs + Committed costs)}$$
$$\$30X = \$300 + \$60 + \$4X + (25/1{,}650 \times \$19{,}800)$$
$$\$26X = \$360 + \$300$$
$$\$26X = \$660$$
$$X = 25+$$

He was unenthused about adding a course that would bring in $750 and cost $760.

Required:

1. Should the dean hold the class? Why or why not? Be specific. Show computations and assumptions that underlie your decision.
2. Show an alternate way of computing a break-even point.
3. What is probably the limiting, restricting, or scarce factor that is probably most crucial in most evening college operations? What is probably the key to the maximum financial performance of a particular course, assuming that the course will definitely be offered?
4. Sketch how the dean's operating statement would be constructed under the contribution approach.

CHAPTER 12

Motivation,
Accounting Systems,
and Measuring Divisional Performance

HOW DO YOU JUDGE THE EFFECTIVENESS, FOR PLANNING AND control, of an accounting system? Many checklists and criteria have been formulated through the years, but we shall dwell on motivation as the overriding consideration in formulating and using measurements of performance. Above all, the system and techniques used should encourage managers to act in harmony with the objectives of top management.

The directing of attention, the providing of clues, the raising of pertinent questions, the inducing of desired behavior—these are the principal tasks of accounting for the planning and controlling of operations. The basic questions that need answering are:

1. What are the objectives of the organization as a whole?
2. Who are the executives who are expected to seek such objectives? What are their spheres of responsibility?
3. What data can be provided to help them make individual decisions that will harmonize with, and spur them toward, over-all company goals?

We shall assume here that the answers to Question 1 are available. Profit is generally regarded as the prime objective. A discussion of organizational objectives (e.g., profit, growth, power, social service) is beyond the scope of this book. The answer to Question 2 lies in some form of responsibility accounting that reflects the executive's freedom to make decisions. This was discussed in Chapter 11.

In this chapter, we shall concentrate on Question 3. Three major topics are discussed: motivation and harmony of objectives; rate of return as a basis for judging divisional performance; and transfer pricing.

MOTIVATION AND HARMONY OF OBJECTIVES

Conflicts of Individual Goals and Top Management Goals

Perhaps the most important question to ask in judging the effectiveness of measurements of performance is whether they help personnel to act in harmony with over-all organization goals. It follows that managers and accountants must evaluate the influence of the accounting system on the motivations of individuals. Raymond Viller's account of the trouble caused by rush orders, cited on p. 268, shows how the accounting system can affect the behavior of executives.

The trouble is that conflicts arise between individual goals and top management goals. The following six questions should help to pinpoint possible weakness in the motivational influences of any given accounting system.

Overemphasis of One Facet

1. *Does the measurement system overemphasize one facet of operations?* The greatest danger is probably overemphasis of the rate of return on assets as a measure of efficiency. (This is discussed more fully later in the chapter.) General Electric Co., for example, has tried to avoid overemphasizing one measurement by stating that their divisional managers will be judged in relation to the following eight areas: (1) return on investment; (2) share of the market; (3) efficiency or productivity; (4) product leadership; (5) employee attitudes; (6) public responsibility; (7) personnel development; and (8) balance between short-range and long-range goals. The eighth area, in itself, demonstrates management's desire to avoid stressing any one facet.

An executive of a major U.S. corporation[1] described the following situation. Central headquarters ordered all plants to reduce their inventories of supplies from a 90-day to a 60-day level. Subsequently, the internal audit staff discovered two interesting developments. Two of the plant managers really rode herd on the inventory amounts and achieved the requested reduction. In the first plant, the employees threw the factory supplies out the back door. In the second plant, their consciences hurt. They did not throw the supplies out. Instead, they hid the items throughout the plant.

---

[1] Source withheld.

Sometimes top management's goals are faulty. *Time* magazine[2] reported the following incident in the Soviet economy. The Moscow Cable Co. decided to reduce copper wastage, and actually slashed waste by 60 per cent in a given year. But top management in the central government noticed that the company produced copper scrap worth only $40,000 instead of the $100,000 originally budgeted. The goals were so uncoordinated that the plant was fined $45,000 for not meeting the budget of $100,000 in scrap.

Short-run Optimization

2. *Does the measurement system encourage short-run gains to the detriment of long-run results?* There are many questionable ways to improve short-run performance. One can stint on repairs, quality control, or training. A manager may successfully exert pressure on employees for more productivity for short spurts of time, a technique which may have some unfavorable repercussions in the long run.

Fixing Responsibility

3. *Does the measurement system fail to delineate responsibility?* We have already discussed responsibility accounting (see Chapter 11). There can be no doubt that buck-passing is minimized when responsibility is unequivocally fixed.

Responsibility accounting should be extended as far down in the organization as possible. This means having sales clerks sign sales slips, having inspectors initial packing slips, and having workmen sign their time cards and requisitions.

Controllable and Uncontrollable Factors

4. *Does the measurement system fail to distinguish between controllable and uncontrollable factors?* This question was also discussed in Chapter 11. Essentially, it may not matter so much whether a particular department's report includes both the controllable items (e.g., short-run material waste) and the uncontrollable items (e.g., an allocation of the president's salary), although the weight of modern opinion favors excluding the uncontrollable items. Top management may feel that there is some psychological benefit in including the uncontrollable items because it creates an awareness of the whole organization and its costs. The important point is that the controllable and uncontrollable items should not be mixed together.

False Record Keeping

5. *Does the measurement system encourage false record keeping?* Perhaps the source documents are too complicated. Or perhaps the pressures

---

[2] *Time,* February 21, 1964.

are such that managers encourage their subordinates to record time erroneously or to tinker with scrap or usage reports.

For example, the maintenance crews of one telephone company regularly performed recurring short-term maintenance and repair work on various projects. At other times, the same crews would be concerned with huge construction projects—installing or building plant and equipment. The company had weekly reports on performance of the regular maintenance work, but had loose control over the construction projects. An investigation disclosed that the foremen were encouraging the workmen to boost the time on the construction projects and to understate the time on the regular maintenance projects. The foreman's performance on the latter always looked good. The situation was corrected when the emphasis on maintenance and construction was balanced so that both were currently budgeted and controlled.

Faulty Cost Analysis

6. *Does the measurement system engender faulty cost analysis?* The accounting system may lead managers into wrong decisions—regarding either evaluation of performance or selection among courses of action. In Chapter 11, we cited a situation in which central costs were allocated on the basis of dollar sales, with the result that the product that was making the greatest contribution to the organization was being saddled with the most cost, without regard to any possible cause-and-effect relationships. In Chapter 13, we illustrate similar analytical dangers which so often are attributable to the failure to distinguish between various cost behavior patterns.

The Means of Motivation

Although opinion is far from settled, most accountants and executives probably would agree with the following summary observations concerning motivation:

> Interview results show that a particular figure does not operate as a norm, in either a score-card or attention-directing sense, simply because the controller's department calls it a standard. It operates as a norm only to the extent that the executives and supervisors, whose activity it measures, accept it as a fair and attainable yardstick of their performance. Generally, operating executives were inclined to accept a standard to the extent that they were satisfied that the data were *accurately recorded,* that the standard level was *reasonably attainable,* and the variables it measured were *controllable* by them.[3]

The above quotation centers on criteria that are basic to management accounting:

---

[3] Simon *et al., Centralization vs. Decentralization in Organizing the Controller's Department* (New York: Controllership Foundation, Inc., 1954), p. 29.

1. Score keeping data should be accurate.

2. Budgets or standards should be understood and accepted as appropriate goals.

3. The items used to judge performance must be controllable by the recipient.

Importance of Accuracy: The Score-keeping Function

No accounting system can mean much if it is based on inaccurate data. The problem of having source documents reflect physical reality is immense and pervasive.

For example, Scharff [4] had a study made of the accuracy of time reporting in the shops of a large steel and alloy plate fabricator. Each workman reported his own time. The findings revealed that the time reported for any job could vary as much as 15 to 20 per cent from the time actually spent on it, without the discrepancy being detected by the foreman's checking of time cards at the end of the day or by other checks, such as comparing estimated with actual hours, and so forth. The two most glaring sources of error were, first, inadvertently charging time to the wrong job and, second, willfully charging time to another job when it was obvious that a given job was running over the estimated hours. In all, some 25 sources of error were identified.

Scharff believes that the accountant and the manager should be more sensitive to possible errors, more aware of the futility of trying to get time reported accurately in small increments, and more conscious of the natural tendency of individuals to report their activities so as to minimize their individual bother and maximize their personal showing.

Understanding and Acceptance of Goals: The Attention-directing Function

Score keeping is essential for cost accumulation; but attention directing is the key to augmenting management's appreciation of the accounting function. The accountant's staff role includes being an attention director (i.e., an interpreter and analyst) and a score keeper (i.e., an accumulator and reporter of costs—a policeman of sorts). However, these two roles often clash. The accounting department should therefore divorce attention directing from score keeping; otherwise, the day-to-day routine, the unending deadlines, and the insidious pressures of assembling cost data will shunt attention directing into the background and, most likely, into oblivion.

The attention-directing roles (e.g., explaining variances) should be occupied by capable, experienced accountants who, at least to some degree, can talk the line manager's language. The attention directors are the individuals who, by and large, establish the status of the controller's

---

[4] S. Scharff, "The Industrial Engineer and the Cost Accountant." *N.A.A. Bulletin,* LXII, No. 7 (March, 1961).

department in the company. Close, direct, and active contact between accountants and operating managers instill confidence in the reliability of the standards, budgets, and reports which are the measuring devices of performance.[5]

RATE OF RETURN FOR JUDGING DIVISIONAL PERFORMANCE

Profit Centers

The growth of decentralized operations has been accompanied by the development of accounting techniques for measuring the performance of individual managers. We have seen how responsibility accounting measures control performance by establishing responsibility centers for individual costs.

The basic ideas of responsibility accounting have been extended to encompass profit centers. A profit center is a segment of a business, usually called a division, that is responsible for both revenue and expenses. In effect, these divisions are regarded as independent businesses with a top manager who is ultimately responsible for revenue, expenses, and the resources (i.e., assets) which are utilized to sustain operations.

In the remainder of this chapter, we shall examine two measurement techniques that have especially facilitated the measurement of the performance of the profit centers of a business: (1) rate of return on assets; and (2) transfer pricing. Although both techniques have considerable conceptual appeal, each has practical limitations.

Turnover and Margins

The general concept of the rate of return on available assets is no different from the concept of the rate of return on required investment that has been used for years in the financial markets. The desirability of an investment depends largely on its prospective rate of return. If one borrower promises to pay 5 per cent interest for a loan of $1,000, and another, equally trustworthy, borrower promises to pay 6½ per cent, the latter investment is deemed more desirable. Similarly, if one manager can earn 5 per cent on his assets, and another manager can earn 9 per cent under comparable conditions, the latter manager is ordinarily deemed more efficient.

The major advantage of the rate-of-return technique is its focus on an often-neglected phase of management responsibility—the required investment in assets. For a given company at a given time, there is a best level of investment in any asset—whether it be cash, receivables, physical plant, or inventories. Cash balances, for example, may be too

---

[5] Simon *et al., op. cit.,* pp. 45-56.

large or too small. The principal cost of having too much cash is the sacrifice of possible earnings; idle cash earns nothing. The principal cost of having too little cash may be lost discounts on purchases or harm to one's credit standing. For every class of asset, then, there is an optimum level of investment which, along with optimum levels of investment in other assets, helps to maximize long-run profits.

The rate-of-return measure blends together all the major ingredients of operating management's responsibility. Rate of return is probably the best single measure of performance. It can be compared with the rates of return of other divisions and with opportunities elsewhere, within or outside the company.

Most managers are well aware of the importance of gross profit percentages and net operating profit percentages in relation to net sales. However, such percentages, considered by themselves, can be misleading. What counts is total dollar profits and the rate of return on available assets:

$$\text{Rate of return} = \text{Asset turnover} \times \text{Net margin percentage on sales}$$

$$\text{Rate of return} = \frac{\text{Sales}}{\text{Total available assets}} \times \frac{\text{Net operating income before interest and income taxes}}{\text{Sales}}$$

$$\text{Rate of return} = \frac{\text{Net operating income before interest and income taxes}}{\text{Total available assets}}$$

Concentrate on the components of these equations. If the objective is solely to maximize rate of return, any action is beneficial which: (1) increases sales; (2) decreases total available assets; or (3) decreases costs while holding the other two factors constant. In other words, turnover and margin percentages are the key factors. An improvement in either, without changing the other, will improve the rate of return on available assets.

General Analytical Uses

Top management may decide upon a 30 per cent rate of return as a target that will yield adequate rewards and yet not invite entry into the market by new competitors. How can this new return be achieved? The equations which follow summarize two approaches to the problem. All figures, other than percentages, are in millions of dollars.

	$\dfrac{\text{Sales}}{\text{Total assets available}}$	$\times$	$\dfrac{\text{Net operating income before interest and income taxes}}{\text{Sales}}$	$=$	Rate of return
Present outlook	$\dfrac{\$200}{\$50}$	$\times$	$\dfrac{\$14}{\$200}$		$= 14/50$, or 28%

Alternatives:

A: Increase margin
by reducing ex-
penses
$$\frac{\$200}{\$50} \times \frac{\$15}{\$200} = 15/50, \text{ or } 30\%$$

B: Decrease assets
$$\frac{\$200}{\$46.67} \times \frac{\$14}{\$200} = 14/46.67, \text{ or } 30\%$$

Alternative *A* demonstrates a popular way of improving performance. Margins may be increased by reducing expenses, as in this case, or by boosting selling prices.

Alternative *B* shows that controlling investments in assets may also improve performance. This means determining proper inventory levels, managing credit judiciously, and spending carefully on fixed assets. In other words, increasing the turnover of assets means obtaining the most in dollar sales for every dollar of assets. For example, having too much inventory is sometimes worse than having too little. Turnover decreases and goods deteriorate or become obsolete, thus dragging the rate of return downward.

The Investment Base: Available Assets

As a basis for measuring the efficiency of operating management, average total available assets is usually superior to alternative bases. Available assets are the total resources subject to the control of the manager being evaluated. Therefore, this base can differ within the segments of the same company. Just as there may be different costs for different purposes, there may be different rates of return for different purposes. For example, the available assets to a division may exclude cash, if the manager has no voice in its control. Yet the assets available to the company as a whole would include cash.

Another possible base is stockholders' equity. Such a base is important to the owners, but it is not so significant to the operating manager. He is usually concerned with the utilization of assets, not with the sources of assets. Business has two major management functions—operating and financing—and measurement of operating performance (how available assets are employed) should not be influenced by financing decisions (what sources of assets were selected). It would be unfair, for example, to use stockholders' equity as a basis for comparing the *operating* performance of two managers of similar companies, if one company is debt-free and the other debt-ridden.

Rates of return for the company as a whole are sometimes compared with those of other companies or with industry averages. For such comparisons to be valid, however, the assets of all the companies must first be put on the same basis. Some adjustments necessary to achieve comparability may include the capitalization of leased facilities and the exclusion of unlike products or divisions.[6]

The Measurement of Available Assets

The figure used for total available assets should be the average amount during the period under review. This average might be computed by summing the beginning and ending balances and dividing by two; in other instances, a moving or weighted average may be needed to achieve accuracy.

Should assets be measured at book value, net realizable value, or replacement cost? For internal purposes, there is no necessity to adhere to conventional accounting measures. Still, a National Association of Accountants' Study[7] showed that 18 of 28 companies surveyed value fixed assets at their net book value for gauging performance. The biggest advantage is that book values minimize confusion; results correspond with widely used measurements of operating performance and assets. But do they measure the economic sacrifices associated with the available assets? In many cases, the answer is negative. For example, the book values of fixed assets often differ from current replacement costs. Facilities used under long-term leases are usually not included in the list of assets. The variety of accounting methods for valuing inventories, research, depreciation, patents, market research, and advertising will have an important influence on the asset base.

The most troublesome item is fixed assets. The relative merits of using original cost (gross value) or net book value are discussed at length elsewhere[8] and will not be dwelled on here. Those who favor using gross assets claim that it facilitates comparisons among plants and divisions. If income decreases as a plant ages, the decline in earning power will be made evident, while the constantly decreasing net book value will reflect a possibly deceptive higher rate of return in later years. For this reason, du Pont and Monsanto use gross book value as a measure of their fixed assets when they compute rate of return.

In an orderly market, current replacement value is the proper basis for measuring a fixed asset (and its depreciation) for rate-of-return calculations. But the approximation of current replacement values of fixed assets is not always simple. Unless there is an active market, some price index may have to be used. Depreciation, on the other hand, should be based on engineering estimates. These two techniques are illustrated in the following table.

---

[6] For additional discussion of these ideas, see Chapter 5.

[7] *Return on Capital as a Guide to Managerial Decisions,* National Association of Accountants, Research Report No. 35 (New York, December, 1959).

[8] *Ibid.*

	Original Cost	Multiplier for Price Index	Current Value
Equipment	$50,000	1.40	$70,000
Accumulated depreciation	30,000		40,000
	$20,000		$30,000*

* Engineering estimate.

This approach may be somewhat more complicated than conventional accounting measurements. However, the year-to-year updating of such a system should not be too burdensome, particularly if the fixed assets are subdivided into broad classes.

Income and Rate of Return

The definition of income should be consistent with the definition of the investment base to which it is related. Thus, interest expense and income taxes are ordinarily excluded in computing incomes which are related to asset bases. Of course, interest expense and income taxes are deducted in computing income which is related to stockholders' equity bases. Non-recurring items are ordinarily excluded when current operating performance is to be evaluated.

Allocation of Assets to Segments

Allocations of sales, costs, and assets are needed to obtain rates of return by product lines, divisions, and plants. The corporate whole is split into individual parts as if each were a separate company with its own rate-of-return target. The rate-of-return technique is rarely used at lower levels, because managers at such levels do not have control over sales, costs, and assets.

The same difficulties that plague allocation of costs to departments beset allocation of assets to profit centers. Just as there is a danger in holding foremen to budgets which contain uncontrollable costs, there is a similar danger in holding managers to uncontrollable rate-of-return targets. Where the allocation of an asset (such as corporate cash or central office facilities) would be arbitrary, it is better not to allocate. Instead, a contribution approach, similar to that described in Chapter 11, should be taken. A performance margin (sales, less variable costs, less programmed fixed costs) should be related to those assets which are clearly assignable to a given division. The resulting rate of return will reflect short-run management performance. A segment margin (sales, less variable costs, less all fixed costs directly identifiable with a division) may be used as a basis for measuring long-run performance.

Commonly used bases for allocation, when assets are not directly identified with a specific division, include the following:

Asset Class	Possible Allocation Base
Corporate cash	Budgeted cash needs; No allocation
Receivables	Sales weighted by payment terms
Inventories	Forecasted sales or usage
Fixed assets	Usage of services in terms of long-run forecasts, area occupied, hours, or service unit

Rate-of-Return Targets Are Flexible

The imprecision of the rate-of-return tool has not necessarily resulted in its rejection. Companies often limit its use to broad segments, where the problems of allocating assets and expenses are not overwhelming. Furthermore, companies tend to emphasize changes in the rate of return, rather than the absolute rate. Overemphasis of high rates of return may actually hurt long-run profits, because too high a return invites new competition. A company may deliberately lower its rate of return in order to preserve or enhance its long-run share of the market.

The National Association of Accountants reported [9] the techniques used by one company which emphasizes *change* in rate of return. Each division's performance is compared with its own performance in a prior period, not with another division's performance. Therefore, available assets and allocation are comparable from one period to another. This company also keeps the rate-of-return technique in perspective by using other quantitative measures of performance, such as share of market, adherence to budgets or standards, employee turnover, sales volume, discovery of new products, and public relations.

Bonus Plans: Three Illustrations

Some companies have tied management bonuses directly into their rate-of-return system. The National Association of Accountants has described three bonus plans.[10] All three measure the net contribution to profit of the total of receivables, inventories, and fixed assets directly identified with a given division. A description of the plans follows:

Plan No. 1. A manufacturing company offers a twofold reward scale described hypothetically as follows:

Exceeding a Basic Target Return Set Separately for Each Division		Bettering the Rate of Return of the Previous Year	
Improvement Bracket	*Per Cent of Salary for Each Per Cent Increase Within Bracket*	*Improvement Bracket*	*Per Cent of Salary for Each Per Cent Increase Within Bracket*
to 15%	None	to 5%	1%
15% to 20%	1%	5% to 10%	2%
20% to 25%	2%	over 10%	3%
over 25%	3%		

---

[9] Ibid.

[10] *Experience With Return on Capital to Appraise Management Performance,* National Association of Accountants, Accounting Practice Report No. 14 (New York, February, 1962).

Three years of experience with this scheme has resulted in changing a net loss to a net profit and has led to a 40-per cent reduction in receivables, a 50-per cent reduction in inventories, and a 25-per cent reduction in fixed assets. Of course, improvement cannot be attributed to this scheme alone.

Plan No. 2. A lumber and building supply company with 12 outlets devised a decentralized plan that based the bonus on dollars of profits contribution in excess of a 6 per cent rate of return on investment:

	Branch A		*Branch B*	
Annual profits		$15,000		$15,000
Less 6 per cent of average				
Fixed assets	$30,000		$30,000	
Accounts receivable	25,000		5,000	
Inventories	45,000		35,000	
6 per cent of	$100,000	6,000	$70,000	4,200
Excess over 6 per cent of investment		$ 9,000		$10,800
Bonus to manager (10 per cent of excess)		$ 900		$ 1,080

The chief result of this plan was, once again, a pruning of slow-moving assets. The company's over-all return on stockholders' equity soared from 2 to 10 per cent.

Plan No. 3. A retail store division of a large corporation gave each shop manager an opportunity to earn all or part of a $1,000 annual bonus. A quota, based upon the potential of each store, was formulated in terms of rate of return on assets. If the quota is attained, the manager receives $100 of the bonus, plus $50 for each half per cent in excess of the quota, up to 9 per cent over quota, which would earn the full $1,000 bonus.

Results were that sales improved considerably and inventories were slashed substantially.

The Most Important Guide: Harmony of Goals

Earlier, we stressed the idea that accounting systems and techniques should be judged primarily by how successfully they induce managers to make decisions that harmonize with over-all organizational objectives. This motivational influence should be the overriding consideration that should guide management in deciding: (1) how assets should be allocated; (2) how the available assets should be measured; and (3) whether bonuses should be directly tied to quantitative measures of performance.

For example, the use of net assets as an investment base may prompt incorrect decisions by divisional management. If assets are replaced or scrapped before they are fully depreciated, the division may have to show a loss. Although such a loss may be irrelevant to the decision, it would affect the division's immediate profit and thus influence the division manager to make the wrong decision.[11]

The three illustrations of incentive bonuses which were described in the previous section have surface appeal, but they also have motivational dangers. Unless the system is extremely clear-cut and the manager somehow insulated from the temptations to manipulate it, there will be a strong, undesirable likelihood that the manager will be overly concerned with the accounting system and with making a good short-run showing to maximize his bonus. In general, no accounting system or technique should have the power, by itself, to focus the manager's attention on beating the system or improving his personal showing at the expense of over-all company goals. Put another way, the worth of an accounting technique can be judged by how well it helps to coordinate individual and company goals. Any accounting technique can be overused or misused, and any such overemphasis may boomerang and hinder the attainment of over-all goals.

The Time Span and Management Performance

An executive's performance should contribute to the maximization of profits, not for one quarter or for one year but over the long run. The focus should be on long-run earning power, not on short-run profits. Yet managers switch from one executive position to another over the years; they are typically appraised in terms of those short-run factors which tend to maximize long-run earnings potential. Managers are evaluated in terms of quantifiable performance and also performance which is difficult to measure (such as public relations or employee morale).

Rate of return wraps many quantifiable factors into one convenient package. Yet short-run maximization of rate of return may not provide the best measure of managerial efficiency in many cases. Profitability in one year may bear a direct relationship to profitability in the long run, but not necessarily. A division may increase sales by reducing quality, thus harming the corporate image. A manager might slash maintenance, reduce supervisory help, exert severe pressures for productivity, or neglect employee training. His division may show a high rate of return, but he deserves a low ranking.

In summary, rate of return, as a measure of efficiency, cannot stand alone. Short-run profitability is only one of the factors that contribute to a company's long-run objectives. Rate of return is a short-run concept, dealing only with the past quarter or year, whereas managerial efficiency can best be expressed in terms of the future results of present actions.

---

[11] For several examples of how division managers' interests can conflict with the interests of the company as a whole, see John Dearden, "Problem in Decentralized Profit Responsibility," *Harvard Business Review,* May-June, 1960, pp. 79-86.

TRANSFER PRICING

Intracompany Transfers

Goods and services are often exchanged between various company segments or profit centers. An integrated company may have an iron mine which supplies ore to a steel mill which, in turn, supplies steel to an assembly plant. Opponents of the profit-center approach maintain that the performance of all three of these divisions is best measured by standard costs and budgeting. Those who favor assigning profit responsibility to subdivisions of a business are often faced with the problem of pricing intracompany transfers so that each division shows sales, expenses, and profits. Transfer price has an important bearing on the profits of both the supplying and receiving units.

The accountant is embroiled in top management policy making because the accounting techniques used often will have direct impacts on the following: measuring performance of profit centers; measuring consequences of proposed changes in integration policy; formulating transfer pricing policies; and computing bonuses awarded for superior managerial performance.

Two basic alternatives have emerged for pricing intracompany transfers: some version of cost or some version of market.

Cost Basis

In the above example, the transfer of products on the basis of accumulated cost would show no returns for the mine or the steel mill, but the performance of the assembly plant would reflect the accumulated efficiencies or inefficiencies of other divisions not subject to the assembly manager's control. Transfer prices based on costs, or on cost plus some markup, may or may not be related to market prices. Moreover, transfer prices which insure recovery of costs often fail to provide an incentive to control costs. If pricing is not subjected to competitive comparisons at intermediate transfer points, excess costs are less likely to be discovered.

Despite the obvious limitations of the approach, transfer prices based on cost, or on cost plus some markup, are in common use. The main reason for its wide use is that it is understandable and convenient. Moreover, when it yields prices that, on the average, are reasonably close to market prices, it is justified because it is practical, convenient, clear, and fair.

Market Price Basis

When the market-price approach is used, the attempt is to transfer goods at a price equivalent to that prevailing in an outside market at the time of transfer, that is, at the price that the receiving division would have to pay outsiders. Put another way, the market-price approach is an attempt to approximate an arm's length, bargained, open-market price. The National Association of Accountants has described this method as follows:

> Internal procurement is expected where the company's products and services are superior or equal in design, quality, performance, and price, and when acceptable delivery schedules can be met. So long as these conditions are met, the receiving unit suffers no loss and the supplier unit's profit accrues to the company. Often the receiving division gains advantages such as better control over quality, assurance of continued supply, and prompt delivery.
>
> If a receiving unit finds that internal sources of supply are not competitive, policy calls for one of the following actions:
>
> a. It may purchase from an outside supplier after it has made a reasonable effort to bring the internal supplier unit's quotations and terms into line with those available outside.
>
> b. It is free to purchase outside, but must be prepared to justify its decision. Central executives usually review such actions and have an opportunity to take action where needed.
>
> Normally the right to buy outside is seldom used because the advantages of integration make interunit transfers preferable for both supplying and receiving units. However, companies interviewed stated that the policy had sometimes been instrumental in bringing to light the presence of excessive costs due to obsolete or poorly located facilities, inefficient management, lack of volume, or other causes.[12]

The usefulness of a market-price method is contingent on the availability of dependable market price quotations of other manufacturers. It is these prices which would be taken into account by parties dealing at arm's length as they establish the competitive price levels.

In sum, market prices establish the *ceiling* for transfer pricing. In many instances, a lower price may easily be justified, particularly when large purchases are made, when selling costs are less, or when an advantage is obtained through an exclusive supplier contract or through a cost-plus arrangement assuring profits in all cases. These situations lead to the notion of negotiated market prices.

Negotiated Market Prices

Special circumstances create difficulties in ascertaining a market price that is clearly relevant to a particular transfer-pricing situation. In addition to those situations described in the previous paragraph, a division sometimes provides a product that is unavailable from outsiders or that is not sold to outsiders (e.g., special parts or research). A price is then negotiated between the buying and selling divisions, or a company

---

[12] *Accounting for Intra-Company Transfers,* National Association of Accountants, Research Series No. 30 (New York, June, 1956), pp. 13-14.

formula may be used for determining the price. Negotiations may be time-consuming or inflammatory, and top management may have to serve as arbitrator.

When market prices are not available as a foundation for negotiations, the resultant transfer prices are artificial to a point which severely limits the significance of rate of return or other measures of performance. The whole idea of decentralization and of profit centers is based on the manager's freedom and independence. Unless he has alternatives, unless he can resort to buying and selling outside the company, his so-called profit center is artificial; it is essentially a cost center in a centralized company.

Coordination of Objectives

Company policies concerning transfer pricing should be carefully drawn so that the profitability of the divisions is sensibly measured and so that division managers' decisions will meet over-all company goals. The general rule of having supplying divisions meet all bona fide outside price competition (perhaps often adjusted downward for pertinent factors such as volume or selling cost) is most likely to permit division managers to act in harmony with over-all company objectives. The point is that orders should be kept within the corporate family as long as the market price or the synthetic market price is not less than the variable manufacturing costs. This rule assumes that internal facilities would otherwise be idle.

EXAMPLE

Process Division A makes a chemical that it sells to another processing division and, through regular market channels to outsiders. Operating details for a given period are as shown in Exhibit 12-1.

The manager of Division B has been offered a firm price of $\$.84$ by an outside supplier. The manager of Division A says that he cannot sell at

EXHIBIT 12-1
(In millions of dollars)

		Breakdown of Division A Operations			
		Sales to Process Division B		Sales to Outsiders	
Sales		100,000,000		200,000,000	
	$295	gallons @ $.95*	$95	gallons @ $1	$200
Variable costs @ $.60		100,000,000		200,000,000	
	$180	gallons @ $.60	$60	gallons @ $.60	$120
Fixed costs	75		25		50
Total costs	$255		$85		$170
Net operating income	$40		$10		$30

* The transfer price is the outside sales price, less selling and administrative expenses wholly applicable to outside business.

$.84, because no operating income can be earned. Of course, if he understood cost-volume-profit relationships, he would realize that the loss of 100,000,000 gallons in volume would entail foregoing a contribution margin of $.24 a gallon ($.84—$.60), a total of $24,000,000. Unless he can save on fixed costs or increase his other sales, or both, to make up the $24,000,000 drop in contribution, his best short-run alternative is to sell at 84¢. In the long run, he would try to reduce capacity, or find more profitable ways to use available capacity, or improve production techniques to the point where the lower price becomes more profitable.

To recapitulate, this example shows that the company as a whole will benefit if Division *A* sells to *B* at the lower price, even though the total operating income of Division *A* is reduced to $29,000,000. The $11,000,000 decline from $40,000,000 is the 11¢ reduction in the selling price of 100,000,000 gallons. If the facilities lie idle, Division *A*'s performance will be even worse, assuming that fixed costs cannot be decreased (Exhibit 12-2). Note that the difference in net operating income is $24,000,-000, the lost contribution margin. Note, too, that fixed costs remain the same under all these alternatives, and thus are completely irrelevant.

EXHIBIT 12-2
(In millions of dollars)

Total Division A *Performance*

	Alternative	
	Sell to B @ *$.84*	*Refuse to Sell to* B
Sales	$284	$200
Variable costs	$180	$120
Fixed costs	75	75
Total costs	$255	$195
Net operating income	$ 29	$ 5

Of course, the company as a whole will be hurt if Division *B* buys from the outsider (see Exhibit 12-3).

EXHIBIT 12-3
(In millions of dollars)

	Alternatives for the Company as a Whole	
	Buy from Outsider	*Keep Inside*
100,000,000 gallons @ $.84	$84	
100,000,000 gallons @ $.60		$60
Fixed costs (irrelevant assuming that they are unchanged)	—	—
Total variable costs	$84	$60

Thus, the disadvantage to the company as a whole from buying outside is $24,000,000, the difference in variable costs.

SUMMARY

Conceptually, the rate of return on available assets is the most attractive single measure of management efficiency. In practice, the measure has many limitations. No single measure is ever adequate. The rate of return should be used along with other measures such as budgets and standards, market shares, employee turnover, and the like. The *change* in these measures is often more significant than their absolute size.

Transfer pricing systems are needed if profit centers are to be established in companies whose divisions exchange goods and services. The transfer price must be some version of the market price to enable managers to make decisions that harmonize with over-all company objectives. The whole area of transfer pricing is filled with problems of human relations and the need for relevant data as a guide to pricing decisions and evaluation of performance. Transfer price policies must be workable in the sense that they neither impinge unduly on executive time nor interfere with over-all company goals.

Motivation is the overriding consideration that should influence management in formulating and using performance measures. Above all, the system and techniques should induce managers to act in ways that do not conflict with top management objectives.

SUMMARY PROBLEM FOR YOUR REVIEW

PROBLEM

You are given the following data regarding budgeted operations of a company division:

Average available assets:	
Receivables	$100,000
Inventories	300,000
Fixed assets, net	200,000
	$600,000
Fixed overhead	$200,000
Variable costs	$1 per unit
Desired rate of return on average available assets	25%
Expected volume	100,000 units

Required:

1. *a.* What average unit sales price is needed to obtain the desired rate of return on average available assets?

b. What would be the expected turnover of assets?

c. What would be the net income percentage on dollar sales?

2. a. What rate of return would be earned on available assets if sales volume is 120,000 units?

b. If sales volume is 80,000 units?

3. Assume that 30,000 units are to be sold to another division of the same company. The other division manager has balked at a tentative selling price of $4. He has offered $2.25, claiming that he can manufacture the units himself for that price. The manager of the selling division has examined his own data. He has decided that he could eliminate $40,000 of inventories, $60,000 of fixed assets, and $20,000 of fixed overhead if he did not sell to the other division. Should he sell for $2.25? Show computations.

SOLUTION

1. a. 25 per cent of $600,000 = $150,000 target net income.

Let X = Unit sales price

Dollar sales = Variable costs + Fixed costs + Net income

$100,000X = 100,000 \,(\$1) + \$200,000 + \$150,000$

$$X = \frac{\$450,000}{100,000} = \$4.50$$

b. Expected asset turnover $= \dfrac{\$450,000}{\$600,000} = .75$

c. Net income percentage on dollar sales $= \dfrac{\$150,000}{\$450,000} = 33\frac{1}{3}$ per cent

2. (a) and (b)

	Sales Volume		
Units	100,000*	120,000	80,000
Sales, @ $4.50	$450,000	$540,000	$360,000
Variable costs, @ $1.00	$100,000	$120,000	$ 80,000
Fixed costs	200,000	200,000	200,000
Total expenses	$300,000	$320,000	$280,000
Net income	$150,000	$220,000	$ 80,000
Rate of return on $600,000 assets	25.0%	36.7%	13.3%

* Column not required.

A summary analysis of these three cases, in equation form, follows:

	Net income percentage on sales	× Turnover	= Rate of return
Volume 100,000:	33.3%	× .75	= 25.0%
Volume 120,000:	40.7%	× .90	= 36.7%*
Volume 80,000:	22.2%	× 60	= 13.3%*

* Rounded.

3. Average available assets would decrease by $100,000—from $600,000 to $500,000. Fixed overhead would be $180,000, $200,000 — $20,000. Results would be:

	Sell 70,000 units	Sell 100,000 units	Difference
Sales, 70,000 units @ $4.50 and 30,000 @ $2.25	$315,000	$382,500	$67,500
Variable costs, @ $1.00	$ 70,000	$100,000	$30,000
Fixed costs	180,000	200,000	20,000
Total expenses	$250,000	$300,000	$50,000
Net income	$ 65,000	$ 82,500	$17,500
Rate of return on $500,000 and $600,000 assets, respectively	13.0%	13.7%	.7%

Based on the information given, he should sell at the $2.25 price. Both divisions and the company as a whole will benefit from such a decision. Although the original over-all target rate of return of 25 per cent is unobtainable, the division will nevertheless earn a better rate of return with the intra-company business than without it. The additional units will earn an *incremental* rate of return which exceeds the 13.0 per cent rate earned on 70,000 units. This incremental rate would be 17.5 per cent (the additional net income of $17,500 divided by the additional investment of $100,000), and the over-all rate of return would increase from 13.0 per cent to 13.7 per cent, as shown in the table.

APPENDIX

Score Keeping and Internal Check

Nature of Internal Check

Accounting records are kept for other reasons besides the tally of performance for later appraisal and for income determination. Score keeping is necessary because operations would be in a hopeless tangle without the paper work that is so often regarded with disdain. The act of recording events has become as much a part of operating activities as the act of selling or buying. Even the simplest organization must keep some records, have some semblance of routine. And, as organizations become more complex, managers find themselves increasingly dependent on systematically compiled records for information and for help in planning and control.

Diverse terminology is used to describe various features of an accounting system. For example, *internal control* is frequently defined as the coordination of an organization's methods and measures designed to: (1) promote efficiency; (2) encourage adherence to prescribed management plans and policies; (3) check the accuracy and validity of organization data; and (4) safeguard assets. Such a definition is very broad; it is really an elaboration of this book's definition of *management control*, i.e., attaining adherence to plans. By *internal check*, we mean parts (3) and (4) of the above definition of internal control, those aspects of an over-all internal control system that are designed to maximize accuracy and reliability of data and to safeguard assets.

Our aim here is necessarily limited to developing an appreciation of why internal check is important for every organization. The aim is not to make an internal auditor out of every student of business. Comprehension of systems design requires specialized study and experience. However, the next time you eat in a restaurant, shop in a discount department store, or have an appliance repaired in your home, you may find it interesting, in light of the following ten rules, to notice what records are made and what procedures are followed to assure an accurate portrayal of events.

Rules of Internal Check

The use of the digital computer has changed many accounting systems so rapidly that a description of any specific system is likely to be out of date by the time it is off the press. We are concerned here with the general characteristics of internal check, those features which will continue to have wide applicability to a variety of organizations regardless of changes in their specific systems.

The following list of rules[13] may be used by any manager to appraise his organization's internal check:

1. *Reliable personnel.* Individuals should be given duties and responsibilities commensurate with their abilities, interests, experience, and dependability.

2. *Separation of powers.* Score keeping and physical handling of assets should not be combined in the hands of one person. For example, the bookkeeper should not handle cash; the cashier should not have access to ledger accounts such as subsidiary receivable records.

3. *Supervision.* Everyone has a boss who oversees and appraises performance. [Company organization charts (Exhibits 1-5 and 1-6) illustrate this point.]

4. *Responsibility.* Personal responsibility should be assigned as far down in the organization as possible (e.g., sales clerks sign the sales slips, inspectors initial the packing slips, and workmen sign their time cards and requisitions).

5. *Routine and automatic checks.* The use of prescribed routines permits specialization, division of duties, and built-in checks on previous steps in the routine. Forms, for example, are designed so that faulty recording is uncovered and corrected on the spot: the absence of a foreman's signature prevents payments of overtime pay; the omission of a receiving clerk's signature on a receiving report prevents the preparation of a check for payment to a supplier.

6. *Document control.* Recording should be immediate, complete, and tamper-proof. Devices used include cash registers with loud bells, pre-numbered source documents, and locked compartments in invoice-writing machines.

7. *Bonding, vacations, and rotation of duties.* Top executives, branch managers, cashiers, storekeepers, and others who may be subject to excessive temptation should be bonded, have understudies, and be forced to take vacations. It is also common practice to periodically rotate receivables and payables clerks. For instance, a receivables clerk may process accounts F to H for three months, M to P for the next three months, and so on.

8. *Reconciliation and audit.* All phases of the system should be subjected to a periodic review by independent external or internal auditors. Of course, other independent checks occur routinely. For example, the bank maintains an independent record of cash, which should be reconciled with the book balance;

---

[13] Also see William J. Vatter, *Managerial Accounting* (Englewood Cliffs, N.J.: Prentice-Hall, Inc., 1950), Chapter 11, for his ten principles of internal control, most of which are described here.

monthly statements are sent to credit customers; there are periodic physical counts of inventory which are checked against perpetual records.

9. *Physical safeguards.* Losses of cash, inventories, and records should be minimized by safes, locks, watchmen, and limited access.

10. *Balance and limits.* The complexity and cost of any accounting system should be compared with its benefits. The cost includes, besides explicit dollar outlays, possible detriment to employee morale. Highly complex systems which tend to strangle individuals in red tape (or, in this age of the computer, magnetic tape) impede rather than promote efficiency.

These ten rules are a guide to a positive objective—accurate recording—not a way of preventing swindlers from looting the assets. The latter objective is secondary. No set of procedures will block the astute individual who is intent upon beating the system by outright embezzlement. The purpose of internal checks is to help achieve positive objectives: smoothness of operations, accuracy and reliability of records, and minimization of temptation. No manager should overlook the subject of internal check when judging his accounting system.

ASSIGNMENT MATERIAL

ESSENTIAL ASSIGNMENT MATERIAL

12-1. *Terminology.* Define: profit center; asset turnover; transfer price; and negotiated market prices.

12-2. *Rate of return on assets: transfer pricing.* A company division manager has tentatively placed a selling price of $2 on his product. His division's asset and cost structure follows:

Cash	$ 10,000	
Receivables	20,000	
Inventories	70,000	
Fixed assets, net	100,000	
	$200,000	
Fixed overhead		$80,000
Variable costs		$1.50
Desired rate of return		
on average assets available		20%

Required:

1. (a) How many units must he sell in order to obtain the desired rate of return?
   (b) What would be the expected asset turnover?
   (c) What would be the net income percentage on dollar sales?
2. (a) What rate of return would be earned on available assets if the selling price were $1.90 and the sales volume 280,000 units?
   (b) If the selling price were $2.20 and sales volume 200,000 units?
3. Assume that 40,000 of a normal total volume of 240,000 units are usually

sold each year to another division of the same company. The two division managers are currently trying to agree on a transfer price for the coming year. The buying division manager has offered $1.80, claiming that he can buy the units from another company at that price. The selling division manager has decided that he can eliminate $10,000 of inventories, $10,000 of fixed assets, and $8,000 of fixed overhead if he does not sell to the other division. Should he sell for $1.80? Show computations.

4. Assuming that all cost data originally given are correct and that the unit selling price is $1.80 for the intracompany business, at what price must the 200,000 other units be sold in order for the division to achieve the 20 per cent desired rate of return?

12-3. *Motivation and salesmen's behavior.* The Frank Jones Brush Co. is a small local firm with three salesmen. Mr. Jones, being unable to decide on a payment plan for his salesmen, has assigned a different payment plan to each of his salesmen for a six-month period. The three plans assigned are:

Plan *A:* A flat salary of $400 per month.

Plan *B:* No base salary, but a $600 bonus if a monthly sales norm is met, plus 5 per cent commission on sales over the norm of $10,000.

Plan *C:* A base salary of $200 per month, plus 25 per cent commission on sales over the norm.

The sales record for the past six months is:

	Salesmen		
SALESMAN	*1*	*2*	*3*
January	$10,000	$10,200	$ 6,000
February	10,000	10,000	14,000
March	10,000	9,700	6,000
April	10,000	10,100	15,000
May	10,000	10,150	6,000
June	10,000	9,850	13,000

1. Analyze the sales patterns. Which payment plan (*A*, *B*, or *C*) was probably given to salesman No. 1, No. 2, and No. 3, respectively?
2. Which plan would be most desired by a conniving man?
3. Which of the three plans, if any, should Mr. Jones adopt on a permanent basis?

ADDITIONAL ASSIGNMENT MATERIAL

Note: Problems 12-21 and 12-22 deal with motivation and responsibility. Most of the remaining problems deal with various aspects of profit centers and transfer pricing. Problem 12-29 deals with internal check, a subject covered in the Appendix to this chapter.

12-4. What are the basic questions that need answers regarding the planning and controlling of current operations?

12-5. "There are other corporate objectives than profit." Name four.

12-6. What is the most important question in judging the effectiveness of a measure of performance?

12-7. What eight areas has General Electric Co. used to avoid overemphasis of one performance measure?

12-8. Give three examples of how managers may improve short-run performance to the detriment of long-run results.

12-9. Illustrate how a measurement system may engender faulty cost analysis.

12-10. What three guides are basic to the accountant's work in current planning and control?

12-11. What are the most glaring sources of error in source documents?

12-12. Why is attention directing such an important accounting function?

12-13. Distinguish between a profit center and a cost center.

12-14. What is the major benefit of the rate-of-return technique for measuring performance?

12-15. "There is an optimum level of investment in any asset." Explain.

12-16. "Just as there may be different costs for different purposes, there may be different rates of return for different purposes." Explain.

12-17. Why are cost-based transfer prices in common use?

12-18. Why are transfer pricing systems needed?

12-19. Why are interest expense and income taxes ordinarily excluded in computing incomes which are related to asset bases?

12-20. *Motivation and commissions for salesmen.* You have recently been elected president of a small specialized machine tool company. Your salesmen's commissions are, as in the past, based on a varying percentage of dollar sales; the higher the sales price, the higher the commission rate.
1. Evaluate the commissions plan.
2. What other methods deserve consideration?

12-21. *Responsibility for a stable employment policy.* The Sure-Weld Metal Fabricating Co. has been manufacturing machine tools for a number of years and has an industry-wide reputation for doing high quality work. The company has been faced with irregularity of output over the years. It has been company policy to lay off welders as soon as there was insufficient work to keep them busy, and to rehire them when demand warranted. The company, however, now has poor labor relations and finds it very difficult to hire good welders because of its lay-off policy. Consequently, the quality of the work has been continually declining.

The plant manager has proposed that the welders, who earn $3 per hour, be retained during slow periods to do menial plant maintenance work which is normally performed by men earning $1.85 per hour in the plant maintenance department.

You, as controller, must decide the most meaningful accounting procedure to handle the wages of the welders doing plant maintenance work. What department or departments should be charged with this work, and at what rate? Discuss the implications of your plan.

12-22. *Salesmen's compensation plan.* You are sales manager of a manufacturing firm whose sales are subject to month-to-month variations, depending upon the individual salesman's efforts. A new salary plus bonus plan has been in effect for four months and you are reviewing a sales performance report. The plan provides for a base salary of $400 per month, a $500 bonus each month if the salesman's monthly quota is met, and an additional commission of 5 per cent on all sales over the monthly quota.

		Salesman A	Salesman B	Salesman C
January	Quota	$30,000	$10,000	$50,000
	Actual	10,000	10,000	60,000
February	Quota	$10,300	$10,300	$61,800
	Actual	20,000	10,300	40,000
March	Quota	$20,600	$10,600	$41,200
	Actual	35,000	5,000	60,000
April	Quota	$36,050	$ 5,150	$61,800
	Actual	15,000	5,200	37,000

Evaluate the compensation plan. Be specific. What changes would you recommend?

12-23. *Management attitudes and profitability.* Comment critically on the following news story concerning an ocean shipping company:

This frugality has resulted in fantastic reserves of cash. Of the shipping company's total net worth of $220-million, about $170-million—nearly 80 per cent—is in retained earnings invested in government bonds, municipals, blue chips, and such.

A shipowner must build up reserves to meet huge lump sum costs of fleet replacement. The problem comes, says Nemec, "when rising costs and technical improvements require you to spend $250-million replacing a fleet that cost $50-million." So Lykes, in lieu of large dividends, makes additional voluntary payments into its replacement fund beyond government depreciation requirements.

In one decade (1948-57), these voluntary deposits exceeded $44-million; the total from 1936 to 1958 came to $56-million. Most of Lykes' rivals, without such close-knit stockholders, could not indulge in such stringent self-denial.

As a result, Lykes can finance its entire fleet replacement program—and its new mechanized ships—out of retained earnings. "We haven't borrowed money from a bank since 1933," says Turman proudly.[13]

12-24. *Simple calculations.* You are given the following data:

Sales	$100,000,000
Invested capital	$20,000,000
Return on investment	10%

Required:

1. Turnover of capital.
2. Net income.
3. Net income as a percentage of sales.

12-25. *Comparison of asset and equity bases.* Company A has assets of $1,000,000 and a long-term, 6-per cent liability of $500,000. Company B has assets of $1,000,000 and no long-term debt. The annual operating income (before interest) of both companies is $200,000.

---

[13] *Business Week*, Jan. 25, 1964, p. 94.

Compute the rate of return on:

1. Assets available.
2. Stockholders' equity.

Evaluate the relative merits of each base for appraising operating management.

12-26. *Using gross or net book value of fixed assets.* Assume that a particular plant acquires $400,000 of fixed assets with a useful life of four years and no residual value. Straight line depreciation will be used. The plant manager is judged on income in relation to these fixed assets. Annual net income, after deducting depreciation, is $40,000.

Assume that sales, and expenses except depreciation, are on a cash basis. Dividends equal net income. Thus, cash in the amount of the depreciation charge will accumulate each year. The plant manager's performance is judged in relation to fixed assets because all current assets, including cash, are considered under central company control.

1. Prepare a comparative tabulation of the plant's rate of return and the company's over-all company rate of return based on:
    (a) Gross (i.e., original cost) assets.
    (b) Net book value of assets. Assume (unrealistically) that any cash accumulated remains idle.
2. Evaluate the relative merits of gross assets and net book value of assets as investment bases.

12-27. *Margins and turnover.* Return on investment is often expressed as the product of two components—capital turnover and margin on sales. You are considering investing in one of three companies, all in the same industry, and are given the following information:

	Company		
	X	Y	Z
Sales	$5,000,000	$ 2,500,000	$50,000,000
Income	500,000	250,000	250,000
Capital	2,000,000	20,000,000	20,000,000

1. Why would you desire the breakdown of return on investment into margin on sales and turnover on capital?
2. Compute the margin on sales, turnover on capital, and return on investment for the three companies, and comment on the relative performance of the companies as thoroughly as the data permit.

12-28. *Fluctuations in rate of return.* The Standard Boating Co. sales volume is heavily influenced by general economic conditions which are uncontrollable by division managers. The company, over the long run, desires a rate of return of 25 per cent on invested capital. In pursuing this goal, the company has based selling prices on normal, or long-run, capacity. The prices, once established, are rarely changed except when wage rates or prices of material change drastically.

You are given the following data:

Variable costs	$800 per unit
Fixed costs	$20,000,000 per year
Long-run volume	100,000 units
Invested capital	$40,000,000

Required:

1. The required selling price, per unit, to attain the desired rate of return.

2. Return on sales, capital turnover, and return on invested capital at sales volumes of 60,000 and 140,000 units, respectively.

12-29. *Multiple choice: discovering irregularities.* In Questions 1 through 6 you are given a well-recognized procedure of internal control. You are to identify from among the lettered choices which follow, *the particular irregularity which will be discovered or prevented by each procedure.* Write the numbers 1 through 6 on an answer sheet. Then place your letter answer next to your numbers.

1. The general ledger control account and the subsidiary ledger of accounts receivable are reconciled monthly. The two bookkeepers are independent.

   a. The accounts receivable subsidiary ledger bookkeeper misreads a sales slip and charges a customer $72 instead of $74, the correct amount. The credit sales summary for the day has the correct amount of $74.

   b. The accounts receivable subsidiary ledger bookkeeper misreads a sales slip and charges merchandise to Mr. Smith instead of Mr. Smithe.

   c. The employee opening mail abstracts funds without making a record of their receipt. Customer accounts are not credited with their payments.

   d. The general ledger bookkeeper takes funds and covers the loss by charging Miscellaneous General Expenses.

   e. When friends purchase merchandise, the sales clerk allows them an employee discount by using an employee's name on the sales slip and deducting the discount on the slip. This is against company policy.

2. The voucher system requires that invoices be compared with receiving reports and freight bills before a voucher is prepared and approved for payment.

   a. Unrecorded checks appear in the bank statement.

   b. The treasurer takes funds and prepares a fictitious voucher charging Miscellaneous General Expenses.

   c. An employee in the purchasing department sends through fictitious invoices and receives payment.

   d. A cash shortage is covered by underadding outstanding checks on the bank reconciliation.

   e. A cash shortage is covered by omitting some of the outstanding checks from the bank reconciliation.

3. Both cash and credit customers are educated to expect a sales ticket, tickets being serially numbered and all numbers being accounted for daily.

   a. Customers complain that their monthly bills contain items which have been paid.

   b. Some customers have the correct change for the merchandise purchased. They pay and do not wait for a sales ticket.

   c. Customers complain that they are billed for goods which they did not purchase.

    d. Customers complain that goods ordered are not received.

    e. Sales clerks destroy duplicate sales tickets to the amount of cash stolen.

4. At a movie theatre box office, all tickets are prenumbered. At the end of each day, the beginning ticket number is subtracted from the ending number to give the number of tickets sold. Cash is counted and compared with the number of tickets sold.

    a. The box office gives too much change.

    b. The ticket taker admits his friends without a ticket.

    c. The manager gives theatre passes for personal expenses. This is against company policy.

    d. A test check of customers entering the theatre does not reconcile with ticket sales.

    e. Tickets from a previous day are discovered in the ticket taker's stub box despite the fact that tickets are stamped "Good on date of purchase only."

5. In Hutchinson Commons Cafeteria, the customers enter at an In door and choose their meals. Before leaving the serving rail, they are billed by a biller for the food taken. They eat, and then present their bills and payments to a cashier. At the end of the day, cash receipts are reconciled with billings.

    a. A friend of the biller and the cashier moves through the lines and takes a free meal without being billed or paying.

    b. A customer who has been billed goes out the In door without paying.

    c. Meat is stolen by an employee.

    d. The biller bills a meal at $1.15 instead of the correct amount, $1.35.

    e. A customer sneaks under the serving rail, takes an extra cup of coffee, sneaks back under the rail, and returns to his table.

6. The duties of cashier and accounts receivable bookkeeper should be separated.

    a. There are two cashiers. At the end of a certain day, there is a sizable cash shortage. Each cashier blames the other. It is impossible to fix responsibility.

    b. A cash shortage is covered by overfooting (overadding) cash in transit on the bank reconciliation.

    c. A cash shortage is covered by charging it to Miscellaneous General Expense.

    d. Customers who paid their accounts in cash complain that they still receive statements of balances due.

    e. The accounts receivable bookkeeper charges off the accounts of friends to Allowance for Bad Debts.

12-30. *Transfer pricing.* Viking Enterprises runs a chain of drive-in hamburger stands on Cape Cod during the ten-week summer season. The manager of each stand is told to act as if he owned the stand and is judged on his profit performance. Viking Enterprises has rented a soft ice cream machine for the summer, to supply its stands with ice cream for their frappés. Rent for the machine is $500. Viking is not allowed to sell ice cream to other dealers because it cannot obtain a dairy license. The manager of the ice cream machine charges the stands $1 per gallon. Operating figures for the machine for the summer are as follows:

Sales to the stands (5,000 gallons at $1)		$5,000
Variable costs, @ $.40 per gallon	$2,000	
Fixed costs		
Rental of machine	500	
Other fixed costs	1,500	4,000
Operating margin		$1,000

The manager of the Clam Bar, one of the Viking drive-ins, is seeking permission to make a contract to buy ice cream from an outside supplier at 80¢ a gallon. The Clam Bar uses 1,000 gallons of soft ice cream during the summer. Frank Redmond, controller of Viking Enterprises, refers this request to you. You determine that the Other Fixed Costs of operating the machine will decrease by $300 if the Clam Bar purchases from an outside supplier. He wants an analysis of the request in terms of over-all company objectives and an explanation of your conclusion.

12-31. *Profit centers and transfer pricing in an automobile dealership.* A large automobile dealership is installing a responsibility accounting system and three profit centers: parts and service; new vehicles; and used vehicles. Each department manager has been told to run his shop as if he were in business for himself. However, there are interdepartmental dealings. For example:

a. The parts and service department prepares new cars for final delivery and repairs used cars prior to resale.

b. The used car department's major source of inventory has been cars traded in in part payment for new cars.

The owner of the dealership has asked you to draft a company policy statement on transfer pricing, together with specific rules to be applied to the examples cited. He has told you that clarity is of paramount importance because your statement will be relied upon for settling transfer-pricing disputes.

12-32. *Transfer Pricing.* The Never Die Division of the Durable Motors Co. produces 12-volt batteries for automobiles. It has been the sole supplier of batteries to the automotive division, and charges $10 per unit, the current market price for very large wholesale lots. The battery division also sells to outside retail outlets, at $12.50 per unit. Normally, outside sales amount to 25 per cent of a total sales volume of 2,000,000 batteries per year. Typical combined annual data for the division follow:

Sales	$21,250,000
Variable costs, @ $8 per battery	$16,000,000
Fixed costs	2,000,000
Total costs	$18,000,000
Gross margin	$ 3,250,000

The Hot Shot Battery Co., an entirely separate entity, has offered the automotive division comparable batteries at a firm price of $9 per unit. The Never Die Division claims that it can't possibly match this price because it could not earn any margin at $9.

1. Assume you are the manager of the automotive division. Comment on the Never Die Division's claim. Assume that normal outside volume cannot be increased.

2. The Never Die Division feels that it can increase outside sales by 1,500,000 batteries per year by increasing fixed costs by $2,000,000 and variable costs by $1 per unit, while reducing the selling price to $12. Assume that maximum capacity is 2,000,000 batteries per year. Should the division reject intracompany business and concentrate on outside sales? YES

12-33. *Retail marketing methods and rate of return.* The Colonial Shop furniture store is considering a major change in its marketing methods. If it adopts the new plan, it would sell furniture at a discount of 20 per cent. In order to make up for the lost contribution margin, it would make the following changes: All advertising would be eliminated. All sales would be on a cash basis. The number of salesmen would be cut from three to two, and the sales commission would be lowered to 2 per cent of net sales.

Income Statement Items for 19x4

Assets (including $100,000 in accounts receivable)		$300,000
Sales		$500,000
Expenses:		
Merchandise	(V)	$250,000
Freight	(V)	20,000
Administrative	(F)	45,000
Rent	(F)	40,000
Advertising	(F)	48,000
Selling	(F)	12,000
	(V)	15,000
Handling	(F)	10,000
Delivery	(F)	10,000
	(V)	5,000
Bad debts	(V)	15,000
Miscellaneous	(F)	15,000
Total expenses		$485,000

V, Variable. *F*, Fixed.

The administrative costs of $45,000 include $10,000 which relate exclusively to accounts receivable. Salesmen are paid $4,000 in salary plus a commission of 3 per cent of net dollar sales.

1. Compare the present rate of return with the rate of return that would be achieved with the discount method if net sales under the new method are:
   (a) $320,000.
   (b) $400,000.
   (c) $480,000.

2. What other factors must the manager take into consideration?

CHAPTER 13

Relevant
Cost Analysis
for Problem Solving

MANAGERS' PROBLEM-SOLVING DECISIONS PERVADE A VARIETY
of areas and different spans of time. Examples are dropping
or adding products, setting prices, selecting equipment, selling manufactured products or processing them further, and
making parts internally or buying them from outside suppliers. Unique factors bear on particular decisions. However, there is a general approach that will help the executive
make wise decisions in *any* problem solving situation. In
this and in Chapter 14, we shall describe this *relevant cost*
approach. In this chapter, we concentrate on the notion of
relevancy, assuming a *short-run* planning horizon—that is,
a given amount of invested capital and of production or
sales capacity to be utilized. Unless otherwise stated, we
also assume that plant and equipment will neither be purchased nor sold. In the next chapter, we shall focus on long-
range planning—that is, changes in invested capital or in
production and sales capacity. In short, in this chapter we
consider the ultilization of existing resources; in Chapter
14 we consider commitments to additional resources.

THE ACCOUNTANT'S ROLE IN SPECIAL DECISIONS

Accuracy and Relevancy

Accountants have an important role in the problem-solving process, not as the decision makers but as collectors and reporters of relevant data. Their reports must provide valid data—numbers that measure the quantities which are pertinent to the decision at hand. Many managers want the accountant to offer recommendations about the proper decision, even though the final choice always rests with the operating executive.

The distinction between precision and relevancy should be kept in mind. Ideally, the data should be *precise* (accurate) and *relevant* (pertinent). However, as we shall see, figures can be precise but irrelevant, or imprecise but relevant. For example, the president's salary may be $100,000 per year, to the penny, but may have no bearing on the question of whether to make or buy a part.

Qualitative and Quantitative Factors

The aspects of each alternative may be divided into two broad categories, qualitative and quantitative. Qualitative factors are those whose measurement in dollars and cents is difficult and imprecise; yet a qualitative factor may easily be given more weight than a measurable saving in cost. For example, the opposition of a militant union to new labor-saving machinery may cause an executive to defer or even reject completely the contemplated installation. Or, the chance to manufacture a component oneself for less than the supplier's selling price may be rejected because of the company's long-run dependency on the supplier for other subassemblies. Quantitative factors are those which may more easily be reduced to dollars and cents—for example, projected costs of alternative materials, of direct labor, and of overhead. The accountant, statistician, and mathematician try to express as many decision factors as possible in quantitative terms. This approach reduces the number of qualitative factors to be judged.

MEANING OF RELEVANCY: THE MAJOR CONCEPTUAL LESSON

Problem solving is essentially choosing among several courses of action. The available courses of action are the result of an often time-consuming formal or informal search and screening process, perhaps carried on by a company team which includes engineers, accountants, and operating executives.

The accountant's role in problem solving is primarily that of a technical expert on cost analysis. His responsibility is to be certain that the manager is guided by relevant data, information that will lead him to the best decision.

Consider the final stages of the decision-making process. Two or more courses of action are aligned, and a comparison is made. The decision is based on the difference in the effect of the two on future performance. The key question is: What difference does it make? The relevant information is that *expected future data* which will *differ* between alternatives.

The ideas in the previous paragraph deserve elaboration because they have such wide application. Historical, or past, data have no direct bearing on the decision. Historical data may be helpful in the formulation of predictions, but past figures, in themselves, are irrelevant simply because they are not the expected future data that managers must use in intelligent decision making. Decisions affect the future. Nothing can alter what has already happened; all past costs are down the drain, as far as current or future decisions are concerned.

Of the expected future data, only those which will differ between alternatives are relevant. Any item is irrelevant if it will remain the same regardless of the alternative selected. For instance, if the department manager's salary will be the same regardless of the products stocked, his salary is irrelevant to the selection of products.

The following examples will help us summarize the sharp distinctions needed for proper cost analysis for special decisions.

EXAMPLE 1

You habitually buy gasoline from either of two nearby gasoline stations. Yesterday you noticed that one station is selling gasoline at $.30 per gallon; the other, at $.28. Your automobile needs gasoline, and, in making your choice of stations, you *assume* that these prices are unchanged. The relevant costs are $.30 and $.28, the expected future costs that will differ between the alternatives. You use your past experience (i.e., what you observed yesterday) for predicting today's price. Note that the relevant cost is not what you paid in the past, or what you observed yesterday, but what you *expect to pay* when you drive in to get gasoline. This cost meets our two criteria: (*a*) it is the expected future cost; and (*b*) it differs between the alternatives.

You may also plan to have your car lubricated. The recent price at each station was $1.50, and this is what you anticipate paying. This expected future cost is irrelevant because it will be the same under either alternative. It does not meet our second criterion.

EXAMPLE 2

A company is thinking of using aluminum instead of copper for the bases in the line of desk lamps that it produces. The cost of direct material will decrease from $.30 to $.20. A comparison of relevant costs follows:

	Aluminum	*Copper*	*Difference*
Direct material	$ .20	$ .30	$ .10

The cost of copper used for this comparison undoubtedly came from historical cost records, but note that the relevant costs in the above analysis are both expected future costs.

The direct labor cost will continue to be $.70 per unit regardless of the material used. It is irrelevant because our second criterion—an element of difference between the alternatives—is not met. Therefore, we can safely exclude direct labor from our cost comparisons. Of course, many companies would not bother to exclude direct labor. In such a case, the following comparison would be made:

	Aluminum	*Copper*	*Difference*
Direct materials	$ .20	$ .30	$ .10
Direct labor	.70	.70	—

There is no harm in including irrelevant items in a formal analysis, provided that they are included properly. However, clarity is usually enhanced by confining the reports to the relevant items only.

In sum, our definition of relevant costs for decision making has two criteria. In the matrix of Exhibit 13-1, the *AB* cross-hatched box is the

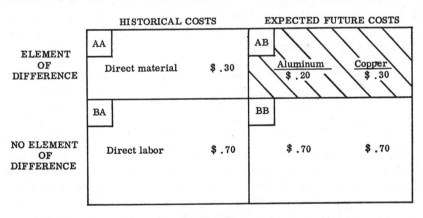

EXHIBIT 13-1

only relevant cost box. All other boxes fail to qualify. Historical costs, in Column *A*, are often used as a guide to prediction, but they are irrelevant *per se*. The expected future costs that are the same under all alternatives, Box *BB*, are also irrelevant.

This is a major conceptual lesson in this chapter. The remainder of the chapter will show how this notion of relevant costs may be applied to various special decisions.

IRRELEVANCY OF PAST COSTS

Obsolete Inventory

EXAMPLE 3

A company has 100 obsolete missile parts that are carried in inventory at a manufacturing cost of $100,000. The parts can be: (1) re-machined for $30,000, and then sold for $50,000; or (2) scrapped for $5,000. Which should be done?

This is an unfortunate situation; yet the $100,000 cost is irrelevant to the decision to re-machine or scrap. The only relevant factors are the expected future revenue and costs:

	Re-machine	Scrap	Difference
Expected future revenue	$ 50,000	$ 5,000	$45,000
Expected future costs	30,000	—	30,000
Relevant excess of revenue over costs	$ 20,000	$ 5,000	$15,000
Accumulated historical inventory costs*	100,000	100,000	—
Net over-all loss on project	$(80,000)	$(95,000)	$15,000

* Irrelevant because it is not an element of difference as between the alternatives.

We could completely ignore the historical cost and still arrive at the $15,000 difference, the key figure in the analysis.

Book Value of Old Equipment

Although we shall not consider all aspects of equipment replacement decisions, we shall now turn to one widely misunderstood facet of the replacement problem, the role of the book value of the old equipment.

EXAMPLE 4

An old machine originally cost $10,000, has accumulated depreciation of $6,000, and has four years of useful life remaining. It can be sold for $2,500 cash now, but will have no disposal value at the end of the four years. A new machine, which (to simplify the analysis) will also have a useful life of four years, is available for $6,000. The new machine will reduce cash operating costs (maintenance, power, repairs, coolants, etc.) from $5,000 to $3,000 annually, but it will have no disposal value at the end of four years. Prepare a comparative analysis of the two alternatives.

The most widely misunderstood facet of replacement analysis is the role of the book value of the old equipment in the decision. The book value, in this context, is sometimes called a *sunk cost,* which is really just another term for historical or past cost. All historical costs are always irrelevant. *Therefore the book value of the old equipment is always irrelevant in replacement decisions.* (This is true even if income taxes are considered, because the relevant item is then the tax cash outflow, not the book value. For elaboration, see Chapter 16.) We can apply our criteria to three separate items:

a. Book value of old equipment. Irrelevant, because it is a historical cost.
b. Disposal value of old equipment. Relevant, because it is an expected future inflow that will differ as between the alternatives.
c. Cost of new equipment. Relevant, because it is an expected future outflow that will differ as between the alternatives.

The situation in Example 4 may be analyzed as follows:

	Four Years Together			Annualized (Divided by 4)		
	Keep	*Replace*	*Difference*	*Keep*	*Replace*	*Difference*
Cash operating costs	$20,000	$12,000	$(8,000)	$5,000	$3,000	$(2,000)
Old equipment, depreciation*	4,000	—	—	1,000	—	—
Old equipment, lump-sum write-off *	—	4,000		—	1,000	
Disposal value of old equipment	—	(2,500)	(2,500)	—	(625)	(625)
New equipment	—	6,000	6,000	—	1,500	1,500
Total cost	$24,000	$19,500	$(4,500)	$6,000	$4,875	$(1,125)

* Irrelevant, because it is not an element of difference as between the alternatives.

The advantage in replacement is clearly $4,500 for the four years together; annually, it is $1,125.

The book value is irrelevant, no matter how it is allocated. The $4,000 may creep into an income statement as depreciation in four annual chunks of $1,000, or it may be written off in one year as a lump sum upon disposal of the old equipment. Regardless of how the cost is allocated, it is a historical cost and consequently irrelevant. Moreover, the amount of the book value will not affect the answer. To prove this, suppose that the book value of the old equipment is $1,000,000 rather than $4,000. Your final answer will not be changed.

Note that the same answer (the $4,500 net difference) will be produced even though the book value of the old equipment is completely omitted from the calculations:

	Four Years Together			Annualized (Divided by 4)		
	Keep	*Replace*	*Difference*	*Keep*	*Replace*	*Difference*
Cash operating costs	$20,000	$12,000	$(8,000)	$5,000	$3,000	$(2,000)
Disposal value of old equipment	—	(2,500)	(2,500)	—	(625)	(625)
New equipment	—	6,000	6,000	—	1,500	1,500
Total cost	$20,000	$15,500	$(4,500)	$5,000	$3,875	$(1,125)

IRRELEVANCY OF FUTURE COSTS THAT WILL NOT DIFFER

Sameness under All Alternatives

The past costs in Examples 3 and 4 were not an element of difference as between the alternatives. As we noted, the $100,000 inventory in Example 3 and the $4,000 book value in Example 4 were included under both alternatives and were irrelevant because they were the same for all alternatives under consideration.

There are also expected *future* costs that may be irrelevant because they will be the same under all feasible alternatives. These, too, may be safely ignored for a particular decision. The cost of lubrication in Example 1 and the direct labor cost in Example 2 are illustrations of expected future costs that will not be affected by the decision at hand.

Other examples include many fixed costs that will be unaffected by such considerations as whether Machine *A* or Machine *B* is selected or whether a special order is accepted. However, it is not merely a case of saying that fixed costs are irrelevant and variable costs are relevant. We have already seen, in Examples 1 and 2, that variable costs (lubrication and direct labor) can be irrelevant and, in Example 4, that fixed costs (cost of new equipment) can be relevant. Fixed costs are relevant whenever they differ under the alternatives at hand.

Joint Product Costs and Processing Further: Incremental Costs

Joint product cost is the term most often used to describe the costs of manufactured goods that are produced by a single process and that are not identifiable as different individual products up to a certain stage of production known as the split-off point. Examples include chemicals, lumber, petroleum products, flour milling, copper mining, meat packing, leather tanning, soap making, and gas manufacturing. A meat-packing company cannot kill a sirloin steak; it has to slaughter a steer, which supplies various cuts of dressed meat, hides, and trimmings.

Joint product costs are the costs of a single process, or a series of processes, that simultaneously produces two or more products of significant sales value. There are many elaborate schemes for assigning these joint costs to the various products. Most are based on the relative sales value of the products. But managers need not be concerned with how various joint products are costed for inventory purposes.

No technique for allocating joint product costs is applicable to decisions about whether a product should be sold at the split-off point or processed further. When a product results from a joint process, the decision to process further is not influenced either by the size of the joint costs or the portion of the joint costs which is assigned to the particular product. Joint costs are irrelevant to these decisions.

EXAMPLE 5

A company produces two petroleum products, X and Y, as a result of a particular joint process. Data are given in Exhibit 13-2.

EXHIBIT 13-2

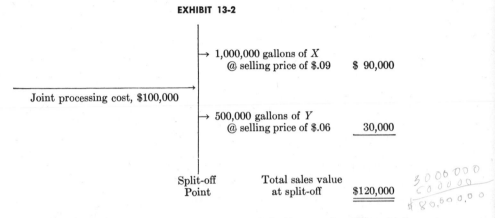

Joint processing cost, $100,000	→ 1,000,000 gallons of X @ selling price of $.09	$ 90,000
	→ 500,000 gallons of Y @ selling price of $.06	30,000
Split-off Point	Total sales value at split-off	$120,000

The 500,000 gallons of Y can be processed further and sold as high-octane gasoline at an additional cost of $.09 per gallon for manufacturing and distribution. The net sales price of the high-octane gasoline would be $.16 per gallon.

Product X will be sold at the split-off point, but management is undecided about Product Y. Should Y be sold or should it be processed into high-octane gasoline? The joint costs must be incurred to reach the split-off point, so they are completely irrelevant to the question of whether to sell or process further.* The sure-fire approach that will yield valid results is to concentrate on the *additional* costs and revenue after split-off:

EXHIBIT 13-3

	Sell at Split-off	Process Further	Difference
Revenue	$30,000	$80,000	$50,000
Separable costs beyond split-off, @ $ .09	—	45,000	45,000
Income effects	$30,000	$35,000	$ 5,000

* Conventional methods of joint cost allocation should be ignored. They are useful for inventory costing purposes *only*. Not only are they irrelevant, they may be downright misleading. Costing by gallonage would show allocated joint cost of $.06667 per gallon ($100,000 ÷ 1,500,000 gallons). This would indicate that Product Y is a loss product. Costing by relative sales value would show a profit for both products at split-off. Product X would bear $75,000 of the joint cost ($90,000/$120,000 × $100,000), and Product Y, $25,000 ($30,000/$120,000 × $100,000). Clearly, the indicated profitability of the individual products depends on the method used for allocating a joint cost which is unallocable by its nature: Product X cannot be obtained without obtaining Product Y, and vice versa.

In sum, it is profitable to extend processing or to incur additional distribution costs on a joint product if the difference in revenue exceeds the difference in expenses (including the cost of capital, which will be discussed in Chapter 14).

Two important points deserve mentioning here. First, the allocation of joint costs would not affect the decision:

EXHIBIT 13-4

	(1) Sell at Split-off	(2) Process Further	(3) Increment or Differential
Joint costs, no matter how allocated	(same for each alternative)		
Revenue	$30,000	$80,000	$50,000
Separable costs	—	45,000	45,000
Income effects	$30,000	$35,000	$ 5,000

Second, the title of the last column in Exhibit 13-4 contains terms that are frequently encountered in cost analysis for special decisions. *Incremental costs* (sometimes called *differential costs*) are, in any given situation, the difference between the total cost of each alternative. In this situation, the *incremental revenue* is $50,000, the *incremental cost* is $45,000, and the *incremental income* is $5,000. Each is the difference between the corresponding items under the alternatives being considered. An analysis that shows only the differences is called an *incremental analysis,* and only Column (3) is shown. In a *total analysis,* all three columns would be shown. The choice of an incremental or a total analysis is a matter of individual preference.

THE CONTRIBUTION APPROACH TO SPECIAL DECISIONS

We have already seen that the contribution approach to preparing income statements facilitates evaluation of performance. Now we shall see how the same approach facilitates analysis for special decisions regarding (1) the deletion or addition of product lines, departments, or territories; (2) the acceptance of orders or emphasis of products in relation to available capacity; (3) the making or buying of products; and (4) the thorny, everlasting problem of pricing a product.

Deletion or Addition of Products or Departments

EXAMPLE 6

A discount department store has three major departments: groceries, general merchandise, and drugs. Management is considering dropping groceries, which has consistently shown a net loss. The present annual net income follows:

Departments

	Total	Groceries	General Merchandise	Drugs
		(In thousands of dollars)		
Sales	$1,900	$1,000	$800	$100
Variable cost of goods sold and expenses	1,420	800	560	60
Contribution margin	$ 480(25%)	$ 200(20%)	$240(30%)	$ 40(40%)
Fixed expenses (salaries, depreciation, insurance, property taxes etc.)				
Separable*	$ 265	$ 150	$100	$ 15
Joint—but allocated	180	60	100	20
Total fixed expenses	$ 445	$ 210	$200	$ 35
Net income	$ 35	$ (10)	$ 40	$ 5

* Includes department salaries and other separable costs which could be avoided by not operating the specific department.

Assume that the alternatives are to drop or continue the grocery department. Assume further that the total assets invested will not be affected by the decision. The vacated space will be idle. Which alternative would you recommend?

SOLUTION

Income Statements	A Keep Groceries	B Drop Groceries	A − B Difference
Sales	$1,900	$900	$1,000
Variable expenses	1,420	620	800
Contribution margin	$ 480	$280	$ 200
Separable fixed expenses	265	115	150
Profit contribution to joint space and other costs	$ 215	$165	$ 50
Joint space and other costs	180	180	—
Net income	$ 35	$(15)	$ 50

The preceding analysis shows that matters would be worse, rather than better, if groceries were dropped and the vacated facilities left idle. In short, as the income statement shows, groceries bring in a contribution margin of $200,000, $50,000 more than the $150,000 separable fixed expenses which would be saved by closing the grocery department.

EXAMPLE 7

Assume now that the space made available by the dropping of groceries would be used by an expanded general merchandise department. The space would be occupied by merchandise that would increase sales by $500,000, generate a 30 per cent contribution margin percentage, and have separable fixed costs of $70,000. The operating picture would then be improved by an increase in net income of $30,000—from $35,000 to $65,000.

	Total	General Merchandise	Drugs
	(In thousands of dollars)		
Sales	$1,400	$800 + $500	$100
Variable expenses	970	560 + 350	60
Contribution margin	$ 430	$240 + $150	$ 40
Separable fixed expenses	185	100 + 70	15
Profit contribution to joint space and other costs	$ 245	$140 $ 80	$ 25
Joint space and other costs*	180		
Net income	$ 65		

* Former grocery fixed costs, which were allocations of joint costs that will continue regardless of how the space is occupied.

Required: Decide whether dropping the grocery department and expanding the general merchandise department would be more profitable than continuing with groceries.

As the following summary analysis demonstrates, the objective is to obtain, from a given amount of space or capacity, the maximum contribution to the payment of those costs which remain unaffected by the nature of the product sold:

		Profit Contribution of Given Space	
	Groceries	Expansion of General Merchandise	Difference
Sales	$1,000	$500	$500 U
Variable expenses	800	350	450 F
Contribution margin	$ 200	$150	$ 50 U
Directly separable fixed expense	150	70	80 F
Profit contribution to joint space costs	$ 50	$ 80	$ 30 F

F   Favorable difference resulting from replacing groceries with general merchandise.
U   Unfavorable difference.

In this case, the general merchandise will not achieve the dollar sales volume that groceries will, but the higher markups and the lower wages (mostly because of the diminished need for stockboys and checkout girls) will bring more favorable net results.

Contribution to Profit per Unit of Limiting Factor

When a multiple-product plant is being operated at capacity, decisions as to which orders to accept must often be made. The contribution approach is also applicable here, because the product to be pushed or the order to be accepted is the one that makes the biggest *total* profit contribution per unit of the limiting factor.

The contribution approach must be used wisely, however. A major pitfall is the erroneous tendency sometimes to favor those products with the biggest contribution margin ratios per sales dollar.

EXAMPLE 8

Assume that a company has two products:

	Product	
Per Unit	*A*	*B*
Selling price	$20	$30
Variable costs	16	21
Contribution margin	$ 4	$ 9
Contribution margin ratio	20%	30%

Required: Which is more profitable?

Product *B* apparently is more profitable than *A*. However, one important fact has been purposely withheld—the time that it takes to produce each product. If 10,000 hours of capacity are available, and three units of *A* can be produced per hour in contrast to one unit of *B*, your choice would be *A*, because it contributes the most profit per hour, the *limiting, critical,* or *scarce factor* in this example:

	A	*B*
Contribution margin per hour	$12	$9
Total contribution for 10,000 hours	$120,000	$90,000

The limiting, critical, or scarce factor is that item which restricts or constrains the production or sale of a given product. *Thus the criterion for maximum profits, for a given capacity, is the greatest possible contribution to profit per unit of the limiting or critical factor.* The limiting factor in the above example may be machine hours or labor hours. In Example 6 it was square feet of floor space. It may be cubic feet of display space. In such cases a ratio such as the conventional gross profit percentage (gross profit ÷ selling price) is an insufficient clue to profitability. The ratio must be multiplied by the stock turnover (number of times the average inventory is sold per year) in order to obtain comparable measures of product profitability.

The success of the suburban discount department stores illustrates the concept of the contribution to profit per unit of limiting factor. These stores have been satisfied with subnormal markups because they have been able to increase turnover and thus increase the contribution to profit per unit of space (Exhibit 13-5).

EXHIBIT 13-5

	Regular Department Store	Discount Department Store
Retail price	$4.00	$3.50
Cost of merchandise	3.00	3.00
Contribution to profit per unit	$1.00(25%)	$ .50(14+%)
Units sold per year	10,000	22,000
Total contribution to profit, assuming the same space allotment in both stores	$10,000	$11,000

Make or Buy and Idle Facilities

Manufacturers are often confronted with the question of whether to make or buy a product—whether, for example, to manufacture their own parts and subassemblies or buy them from vendors. The qualitative factors may be of paramount importance. Sometimes the manufacture of parts requires special knowhow, unusually skilled labor, rare materials, and the like. The desire to control the quality of parts is often the determining factor in the decision to make them. Then, too, companies hesitate to destroy mutually advantageous long-run relationships by erratic order-giving, which results from making parts during slack times and buying them during prosperous times. They may have difficulty in obtaining any parts during boom times, when there are shortages of materials and workers and no shortage of sales orders.

What are the quantitative factors relevant to the decision of whether to make or buy? The answer, again, depends on the context. A key factor is whether there are idle facilities. Many companies make parts only when their facilities cannot be used to better advantage.

EXAMPLE 9

Assume that the following costs are reported:

Cost of Making Part No. 300

	Per Unit	10,000 units
Direct materials	$1	$10,000
Direct labor	8	80,000
Variable overhead	4	40,000
Fixed overhead, separable	2	20,000
Fixed overhead, joint but allocated	3	30,000
Total costs	$18	$180,000

Another manufacturer offers to sell B Co. the same part for $16. Should B Co. make or buy the part?

Although the above figures indicate that the company should buy, the answer is rarely obvious. The key question is the difference in future costs as between the alternatives. If the $3 fixed overhead assigned to each unit represents those costs (e.g., depreciation, property taxes, insurance, reapportioned executive salaries) that will continue regardless of the decision, the entire $3 becomes irrelevant.

Again, it is risky to say categorically that only the variable costs are relevant. Perhaps all of the $2 of directly identifiable fixed costs will be saved if the parts are bought instead of made. In other words, fixed costs that may be avoided in the future are relevant.

For the moment, let us assume that the capacity now used to make parts will become idle if the parts are purchased. The relevant computations follow:

	Per Unit		Totals	
	Make	*Buy*	*Make*	*Buy*
Direct material	$ 1		$ 10,000	
Direct labor	8		80,000	
Variable overhead	4		40,000	
Fixed overhead that can be avoided by not making	2		20,000	
Total relevant costs	$15	$16	$150,000	$160,000
Difference in favor of making		$1		$10,000

Essence of Make or Buy: Opportunity Cost

The choice in Example 9 is really not whether to make or buy; it is how best to utilize available facilities. Although the data seemingly indicate that making the part is the better choice, the figures are not conclusive—primarily because we have no idea of what can be done with the manufacturing facilities if the component is bought. Only if the released facilities are to remain idle are the above figures valid.

On the other hand, if the released facilities can be used advantageously in some other manufacturing activity or can be rented out, there is an opportunity cost of continuing to make the part. An *opportunity cost* is the measurable sacrifice in rejecting an alternative; it is the amount foregone by forsaking an alternative; it is the earning that might have been obtained if the productive good, service, or capacity had been applied to some alternative use.

EXAMPLE 10

The decision to manufacture might entail the rejection of an opportunity to rent the given capacity to another manufacturer for $5,000 annually. The opportunity cost of making the parts is the sacrifice of the chance to get $5,000 rental.

SOLUTION

Although no dollar outlay is involved, the opportunity cost is relevant to the decision. It can be considered in two ways, depending on the preference of the analyst.

a. The two courses of action in Example 9 have become three, and can be analyzed in the following summary form:

	Make	Buy and not Rent	Buy and Rent
Obtaining of parts	$150,000	$160,000	$160,000
Rent revenue	—	—	(5,000)
Total relevant costs	$150,000	$160,000	$155,000

b. The opportunity cost approach yields the same results, but the format of the analysis differs:

	Make	Buy
Obtaining of parts	$150,000	$160,000
Opportunity cost: rent foregone	5,000	
Total relevant costs	$155,000	$160,000

Note that opportunity costs are not ordinarily incorporated in formal accounting systems. Such costs represent incomes foregone by rejecting alternatives; therefore, opportunity costs do not involve cash receipts or outlays. Accountants usually confine their recording to those events that ultimately involve exchanges of assets. Accountants confine their history to alternatives selected rather than those rejected, primarily because of the impracticality or impossibility of accumulating meaningful data on what might have been.

Policy Making for Make or Buy

Costs must be related to time. A cost which is fixed over a short period is variable over a longer period. Profits may increase momentarily by applying the contribution margin approach to decisions but, over the long run, profits may suffer by inordinate use of such an approach. Thus, companies develop long-run policies for the use of capacity:

> One company stated that it solicits subcontract work for other manufacturers during periods when sales of its own products do not fully utilize the plant, but that such work cannot be carried on regularly without expansion of its plant. The profit margin on subcontracts is not sufficiently large to cover these additional costs and hence work is accepted only when other business is lacking. The same company sometimes meets a period of high volume by purchasing parts or having them made by sub-contractors. While the cost of such parts is usually higher than the cost to make them in the company's own plant, the additional cost is less than it would be if they were made on equipment which could be used only part of the time.[1]

[1] *The Analysis of Cost-Volume-Profit Relationships,* National Association of Accountants, Research Series No. 17 (New York, 1949), p. 552.

Beware of Unit Costs

Unit costs should be analyzed with care in decision making. There are two major ways to go wrong: (a) the inclusion of irrelevant costs, such as the $3 allocation of joint costs in the make-or-buy comparison in Example 9, which would result in a unit cost of $18 instead of the relevant unit cost of $15; and (b) comparisons of unit costs not computed on the same basis. Generally, it is advisable to use total costs rather than unit costs. Then, if desired, the totals may be unitized. Machinery salesmen, for example, often brag about the low unit costs of using their new machines. Sometimes, they neglect to point out that the unit costs are based on outputs far in excess of the volume of activity of their prospective customer.

EXAMPLE 11

Assume that a new $100,000 machine with a five-year life can produce 100,000 units a year at a variable cost of $1 per unit, as opposed to a variable cost per unit of $1.50 with an old machine. Is the new machine a worthwhile acquisition?

SOLUTION

It is attractive at first glance. If the customer produces 100,000 units, unit cost comparisons would be valid, provided that new depreciation is also considered. Assume that the disposal value of the old equipment is zero. The book value of (and depreciation on) the old equipment is irrelevant and may be excluded from the analysis:

	Old Machine	New Machine
Units	100,000	100,000
Variable costs	$150,000	$100,000
Straight line depreciation	—	20,000
Total relevant costs	$150,000	$120,000
Unit relevant costs	$ 1.50	$ 1.20

However, if the customer's expected volume is only 30,000 units a year, the unit costs change:

	Old Machine	New Machine
Units	30,000	30,000
Variable costs	$45,000	$30,000
Straight line depreciation	—	20,000
Total relevant costs	$45,000	$50,000
Unit relevant costs	$ 1.50	$ 1.6667

Factors that Influence Prices

Many businessmen say that they use cost-plus pricing. That is, they compute an average unit cost and add a "reasonable" markup which will generate an adequate return on investment. This entails circular reasoning because price, which influences sales volume, depends upon full cost, which in turn is partly determined by the underlying volume of sales. Also, the plus in cost-plus is rarely an unalterable markup. Its magnitude depends on the behavior of competitors and customers. There are three major factors that influence pricing decisions: customers, competitors, and costs.

Customers always have an alternative source of supply, can substitute one material for another, and may make a part rather than buy it if the vendor's prices are too high.

Competitors will usually react to price changes made by their rivals. Tinkering with prices is usually most heavily influenced by the price setter's expectations of competitors' reactions.

The maximum price that may be charged is the one that does not drive the customer away. The minimum price is zero; companies may give out free samples to gain entry into a market. A more practical guide is that, in the short run, the minimum price to be quoted, *subject to consideration of long-run effects,* should be the costs that may be avoided by not landing the order—usually all variable costs.

Guiding Decisions: Target Pricing

When a company has little influence over price, it usually sells at the market price and tries, by controlling costs, to achieve profitable operations. When a company can set its own prices, its procedures are often a combination of shrewd guessing and mysterious folklore. Often the first step is to accumulate costs and add a markup. This is the target price. Subsequent adjustments may be made "in light of market conditions."

There are many ways to arrive at the same target price. They simply reflect different arrangements of the components of the same income statement.

However, when it is used intelligently, the contribution approach has distinct advantages over the traditional approach, which fails to highlight different cost behavior patterns:

First, the contribution approach offers more detailed information than the traditional approach.

Second, a normal or target pricing formula can be as easily developed by the contribution approach as by other approaches. Exhibit 13-6 shows a budgeted net income statement and various techniques for computing target prices for a hypothetical order. Initially, please concentrate on

DITTO

the budgeted income statement. Notice that various markup percentages may be constructed to suit the particular inclinations and habits of the managers concerned. Once this is decided, any of the techniques illustrated will yield a formula that will lead toward the *same* target price. But unless it is able to sell at this price consistently, the company will not achieve its $10,000 net income objective.

Third, the contribution approach helps to provide insight into pricing and cost-volume relationships. The Quote Sheets (the guide to the pricing decision) in Exhibit 13-6 contrast the contribution approach with the traditional approach. Note that no matter how fixed costs are allocated, if at all, the target price is unaffected. In some organizations, management may prefer a separate costing rate for fixed overhead; in others, the contribution margin markup percentage would be set high enough to automatically provide for a normal recovery of fixed costs. Either way, the data in the quote sheets prepared with the contribution approach are organized in a manner that will be more informative and more useful in pricing than the traditional approach, which fails to distinguish between variable and fixed costs.

A complete discussion of pricing is beyond the scope of this book. However, the contribution approach should clarify the major classes of information that bear on the pricing decision.

Robinson-Patman Act

The pricing decision is further complicated by the Robinson-Patman Act, which forbids quoting different prices to competing customers unless such price discrimination is justified by differences in costs of manufacturing, sale, or delivery. Decisions of courts and of the Federal Trade Commission have been based on allocation of full cost rather than on computation of incremental or differential cost.

Most of these price differentials are justified by differences in distribution costs (e.g., advertising, warehousing, and freight), rather than by differences in manufacturing costs. Companies with flexible pricing policies need to keep thorough records of distribution costs in order to be able to answer any government inquiries. However, cost justification is only one aspect of these cases. In most instances, it has been overshadowed by the issues of lessening competition and price cutting in good faith.[2]

Effects of Price Cutting

Why does the contribution approach offer insight into the pricing of special orders? Because it helps quantify the short-run versus long-run effects of possible price cuts. For example, assume the same cost behavior

---

[2] For an expanded discussion see H. Taggert, *Cost Justification* (Ann Arbor: Bureau of Business Research, University of Michigan, 1959).

CONTRIBUTION APPROACH

Budgeted Income Statement

		Per Cent of Sales	Per Cent of Total Variable Costs
Sales		$100,000 100	200
Variable factory cost of goods sold	$40,000		
Variable selling and administrative expenses	10,000	50,000 50	100
Contribution margin		$ 50,000 50	100
Fixed costs:			
Factory costs	$20,000		
Selling and administrative costs	20,000	40,000 40	80
Target net income		$ 10,000 10	20

Note: The target or normal markup percentage is $50,000 ÷ $50,000 = 100 per cent of total variable costs. This relationship can be subdivided, as in the quoting technique on the far right, into two steps, an 80 per cent provision for fixed costs plus a 20 per cent provision for target net income.

TRADITIONAL APPROACH

Budgeted Income Statement

		Per Cent of Sales	Per Cent of Factory Cost of Goods Sold
Sales		$100,000 100	166.7
Factory cost of goods sold (including $20,000 fixed costs)		60,000 60	100.0
Gross profit		$ 40,000 40	66.7
Operating expenses (including $20,000 fixed costs)		30,000 30	50.0
Target net income		$ 10,000 10	16.7

Note: The target or normal markup percentage is $40,000 ÷ $60,000 = 66.7 per cent of manufacturing cost. This relationship can be subdivided as illustrated in the quoting technique on the far right, into two steps, a 50 per cent provision for selling and administrative costs plus a 16.7 per cent provision for target net income.

13-6

and Traditional Approach to Pricing

Alternative Quote Sheets for a Particular Order

Technique A				*Technique B*		

	xxx				xxx	
Total variable costs (detailed)*	xxx	$ 500		Total variable costs (detailed)	xxx	$ 500
Add target markup, 100 per cent of variable costs		500		Add provision for fixed costs at 80 per cent of variable costs		400
				Total costs allocated to this order		$ 900
				Add markup, 20 per cent of variable costs†		100
Target selling price		$1,000		Target selling price		$1,000

* This figure, for any particular order, should include not only the routine variable costs, but all specific costs peculiar to the order that could be avoided by not taking the order. This figure represents the minimum price in the sense that any amount received above this figure would be a contribution margin.

† This can also be expressed as 11.1 per cent of the total costs allocated to this order ($100 ÷ $900)

Technique C				*Technique D*		

	xxx				xxx	
Total factory cost of goods (detailed)‡	xxx	$ 600		Total factory cost of goods (detailed)	xxx	$ 600
Add target markup, 66.7 per cent of factory costs		400		Add provision for selling and administrative costs, 50 per cent of factory costs		300
				Total costs allocated to this order		$ 900
				Add markup §		100
Target selling price		$1,000		Target selling price		$1,000

‡ Notice that no distinctions are made between cost behavior patterns.

§ Markup may be expressed as 16.7 per cent of factory costs ($100 ÷ $600) or 11.1 per cent of the total cost of the order ($100 ÷ $900).

patterns as above. Assume further that a customer offers $540 for some units that would have an ordinary target price of $1,000. Should the offer be accepted? No categorical answer can be given, but more information relevant to a decision can be generated by the contribution approach:

	Traditional Approach	Contribution Approach
Sales price	$540	$540
Factory cost of goods sold	600	
Total variable costs		500
Apparent decrease in net income	$—60	
Contribution margin		$ 40

Compare the two approaches. Under the traditional approach, the decision maker has no direct knowledge of cost-volume-profit relationships. He makes his decision by hunch. On the surface, the offer is definitely unattractive because the price of $540 is $60 below factory costs.

Under the contribution approach, the decision maker sees a short-run advantage of $40 from accepting the offer. Fixed costs will be unaffected by whatever decision is made and net income will increase by $40. Still, there are long-run effects to consider. Will acceptance of the offer undermine the long-run price structure? In other words, is the short-run advantage of $40 more than offset by high probable long-run financial disadvantages? The decision maker may think so and may reject the offer. But—and this is important—by doing so he is in effect saying that he is willing to forego $40 now in order to protect his long-run market advantages. Generally, he can assess problems of this sort by asking whether the probability of long-run benefits is worth an *investment* equal to the foregone contribution margin ($40 in this case).

SUMMARY

The accountant's role in problem solving is primarily that of a technical expert on cost analysis. His responsibility is to be certain that the manager uses *relevant data* in guiding his decisions. Accountants and managers must have a penetrating understanding of relevant costs.

To be relevant to a particular decision, a cost must meet two criteria: (1) it must be an expected *future* cost; and (2) it must be an element of *difference* as between the alternatives. All *past* (*historical* or *sunk*) costs are irrelevant to any decision about the future.

The combination of the relevant costing and contribution approaches may be applied to a vast range of problems. The following are among the more important generalizations regarding various decisions:

1. The book value of old equipment is always irrelevant in replacement decisions. This cost is often called a sunk cost. Disposal value, however, is generally relevant.

2. Joint product costs are irrelevant in decisions about whether to sell at split-off or process further.
3. Incremental costs or differential costs are the differences in the total costs under each alternative.
4. The key to obtaining the maximum profit from a given capacity is to obtain the greatest possible contribution to profit, per unit of the limiting or scarce factor.
5. Make or buy decisions are, fundamentally, examples of obtaining the most profitable utilization of given facilities.
6. Sometimes the notion of an opportunity cost is helpful in cost analysis. An opportunity cost is the measurable sacrifice in rejecting an alternative; it is the earning that might have been obtained if the productive good, service, or capacity had been applied to some alternative use. The opportunity cost approach does not affect the key final differences between the courses of action, but the format of the analysis differs.
7. Generally, it is advisable to use total costs, rather than unit costs, in cost analysis.
8. The contribution approach to pricing offers more helpful information because the foregone contribution can be quantified as the investment currently being made to protect long-run benefits.

SUMMARY PROBLEM FOR YOUR REVIEW

PROBLEM

Exhibit 13-7 contains data for the Block Co. for the year which has just ended. The company makes parts which are used in the final assembly of its finished product.

EXHIBIT 13-7

	A + B Company As a Whole	A Finished Product*	B Parts
Sales: 100,000 units, @ $100	$10,000,000		
Variable costs:			
Direct material	$ 4,900,000	$4,400,000	$ 500,000
Direct labor	700,000	400,000	300,000
Variable factory overhead	300,000	100,000	200,000
Other variable costs	100,000	100,000	—
Sales commissions, @ 10 per cent	1,000,000	1,000,000	—
Total variable costs	$ 7,000,000	$6,000,000	$1,000,000
Contribution margin	$ 3,000,000		
Separable programmed costs	$ 1,800,000	$1,450,000	$ 350,000
Separable committed costs	500,000	450,000	50,000
Joint programmed and committed costs	400,000	320,000	80,000
Total fixed costs	$ 2,700,000	$2,220,000	$ 480,000
Net income	$ 300,000		

* Not including the cost of parts (Column B).

Required:

1. During the year, a prospective customer in an unrelated market offered $82,000 for 1,000 finished units. The latter would be in addition to the

100,000 units sold. The regular sales commission rate would have been paid. The president rejected the order because "it was below our costs of $97 per unit." What would net income have been if the order had been accepted?

2. A supplier offered to manufacture the year's supply of 100,000 parts for $13.50 each. What would be the effect on net income if the Block Co. purchased rather than made the parts? Assume that the separable programmed costs assigned to parts would have been avoided if the parts were purchased.

3. The company could have had the parts made for $13.50 each and used the vacated space for the manufacture of a de luxe version of their major product. Assume that 10,000 de luxe units could have been made (and sold in addition to the 100,000 regular units) at a unit variable cost of $70, exclusive of parts and exclusive of the 10 per cent sales commission. The sales price would have been $110. The fixed costs pertaining to the parts would have continued, including the $350,000 separable programmed costs, because these costs related primarily to the manufacturing facilities utilized. What would net income have been if Block bought the necessary parts and made and sold the de luxe units?

SOLUTION

1. Costs of filling special order:

Direct material	$49,000
Direct labor	7,000
Variable factory overhead	3,000
Other variable cost	1,000
Sales commission, @ 10 per cent of $82,000	8,200
Total variable costs	$68,200
Selling price	82,000
Contribution margin	$13,800

Net income would have been $300,000 + $13,800, or $313,800, if the order had been accepted. In a sense, the decision to reject the offer implies that the Block Co. is willing to invest $13,800 in immediate gains foregone (an opportunity cost) in order to preserve the long-run selling price structure.

2. Assuming that the $350,000 separable programmed costs could have been avoided by not making the parts and that the other fixed costs would have been continued, the alternatives can be summarized as follows:

	Make	*Buy*
Purchase cost		$1,350,000
Variable costs	$1,000,000	
Separable programmed costs	350,000	
Total relevant costs	$1,350,000	$1,350,000

If the facilities used for parts were to become idle, the Block Co. would be indifferent as to whether to make or buy. Net income would be unaffected.

3. Net income would decline to $105,000 ($300,000 − $195,000, the disad-

vantage of selling the de luxe units). The de luxe units bring in a contribution margin of $290,000, but the variable costs of buying rather than making parts is $485,000, leading to a net disadvantage of $195,000:

Sales would increase by 10,000 units, @ $110		$1,100,000
Variable costs would increase by 10,000 units, @ $70	$ 700,000	
Plus the sales commission, 10 per cent of $1,100,000	110,000	810,000
Contribution margin on 10,000 units		$ 290,000
Parts: 110,000 rather than 100,000 would be needed		
Buy 110,000, @ $13.50	$1,485,000	
Make 100,000, @ $10 (only the variable costs are relevant)	1,000,000	
Excess cost of outside purchase		$ 485,000
Fixed costs, unchanged		—
Disadvantage of making de luxe units		$ (195,000)

Net income would decline to $105,000 ($300,000 — $195,000).

ASSIGNMENT MATERIAL

ESSENTIAL ASSIGNMENT MATERIAL

13-1. *Terminology.* Define: qualitative factor; relevant data for decision making; sunk cost; historical cost; joint product costs; incremental cost; differential cost; opportunity cost; and quote sheet.

13-2. *Role of old equipment in replacement.* On Jan. 2, 19x1, the Hartman Co. installed a brand new $81,000 special molding machine for producing a new product. The product and the machine have an expected life of three years. The machine's expected disposal value at the end of three years is zero.

On Jan. 3, 19x1 Bill Ferrara, a star salesman for a machine tool manufacturer, tells Mr. Hartman: "I wish I had known earlier of your purchase plans. I can supply you with a technically superior machine for $100,000. The old machine can be sold for $16,000. I guarantee that our machine will save $35,000 per year in cash operating costs, although it too will have no disposal value at the end of three years."

Mr. Hartman examines some technical data. Although he has confidence in Ferrara's claims, Hartman contends: "I'm locked in now. My alternatives are clear: (a) disposal will result in a loss; (b) keeping and using the 'old' equipment avoids such a loss. I have brains enough to avoid a loss when my other alternative is recognizing a loss. We've got to use that equipment till we get our money out of it."

The annual operating costs of the old machine are expected to be $60,000, exclusive of depreciation. Sales, all in cash, will be $900,000 per year. Other cash expenses will be $800,000 regardless of this decision. Assume that the equipment in question is the company's only fixed asset.

Note: The facts in this problem are probed more deeply in Problem 14-4 and Problem 16-4.

Required:

1. Prepare income statements as they would appear in each of the next three years under both alternatives. Assume straight line depreciation. What is the total difference in net income for the three years?

2. Prepare cash-flow statements (i.e., statements of cash receipts and disbursements) as they would appear for each of the three years under both alternatives. What is the total net difference in cash flow for the three years?

3. Assume that the cost of the "old" equipment was $1,000,000 rather than $81,000. Would the net difference computed in Parts (1) and (2) change? Explain.

4. As Bill Ferrara, reply to Hartman's contentions.

5. What are the irrelevant items in each of your presentations for (1) and (2)? Why are they irrelevant?

13-3. *Various costing techniques for pricing.* Budgeted income statement items for the Doyle Co. include: sales, $1,200,000; total factory cost of goods sold, $900,000; total selling and administrative expenses, $200,000; net income, $100,000; direct material, $350,000; direct labor, $200,000; fixed factory overhead, $300,000; and variable selling and administrative expenses, $100,000.

Operations were exactly in accordance with the budget. Target selling prices were achieved on every order.

Required:

1. Prepare two income statements for the year, one with a traditional format and a second with a contribution format. Show alternate percentage breakdowns of major items. Use both sales and factory cost of goods sold as a percentage base for the traditional approach, and both sales and total variable costs as a percentage base for the contribution approach.

2. For an item with total variable costs of $583 (including variable selling and administrative costs) and total factory costs of $750, show in detail four ways of cost analysis on a price quotation sheet that would yield the target price, two ways under the contribution approach and two ways under the traditional approach.

3. During the year, the president personally rejected an offer of $8,500 for some items whose total factory cost of goods was $9,000. The president said, "We never take orders for less than cost." What was the effect of his decision on net income for the year? Did he make a wise decision? Explain.

13-4. *Relevant cost analysis.* The following are the unit costs of making and selling a single product at a normal level of 5,000 units per month.

Manufacturing costs:	
Direct materials	$20
Direct labor	12
Variable overhead	8
Fixed overhead (total for the year, $300,000)	5
Selling and administrative expenses:	
Variable	15
Fixed (total for the year, $540,000)	9

Total FIXED $840 000

Consider each requirement separately. Label all computations, and present your solutions in a form that will be comprehensible to the company president.

DITTO

Required:

1. This product is usually sold at the rate of 60,000 units per year. Current selling price is $75. It is estimated that a rise in price to $80 will decrease volume by 5 per cent. How much may advertising be increased under this plan without having annual net profit fall below the current level?

2. The company has received a proposal from an outside supplier to make and ship this item directly to the company's customers, as sales orders are forwarded. Variable selling and administrative costs would fall 40 per cent. If the supplier's proposal is accepted, the company will use its own plant to produce a new product. The new product would be sold through manufacturer's agents at a 10 per cent commission based on a selling price of $20 each. The cost characteristics of this product, based on predicted yearly normal volume, are as follows:

USE FIXED OVERHEAD NUMBERS

	Per Unit
Direct material	$ 3
Direct labor	6
Variable overhead	4
Fixed overhead	3
Manufacturing costs	$16

Selling and administrative expenses:
Variable	10 per cent of selling price
Fixed	$ 1

What is the maximum price per unit that the company can afford to pay to the supplier for subcontracting the entire old product? Assume the following:

(a) Total fixed factory overhead and total fixed selling expenses will not change if the new product line is added.

(b) The supplier's proposal will not be considered unless the present annual net income can be maintained.

(c) Selling price of the old product will remain unchanged.

13-5. *Unit costs and choice of most profitable product.* The Dunkel Corp. sells two molding powders, known as *A* and *B*. A detail of the unit income and costs is as follows:

	Product A	Product B
Selling price	$12	$20
Direct material	$ 2	$ 4
Direct labor	2	1
Variable factory overhead*	2	4
Fixed factory overhead*	2	4
Total cost of goods sold	$ 8	$13
Gross profit per unit	$ 4	$ 7

* On a machine-hour basis.

As far as can be determined, the sales outlook is such that the plant could operate at full capacity on either or both products. Both *A* and *B* are processed through the same cost centers. Selling costs are completely fixed and may be ignored.

Which product should be produced? If more than one should be produced, indicate the proportions of each. Explain your answer briefly.

ADDITIONAL ASSIGNMENT MATERIAL

Note: The final three problems in this group are probably the most challenging.

13-6. "The distinction between precision and relevancy should be kept in mind." Explain.

13-7. Distinguish between the quantitative and qualitative aspects of decisions.

13-8. "Any future cost is relevant." Do you agree? Explain.

13-9. Why are historical or past data irrelevant in special decisions?

13-10. Which of the following items are relevant in replacement decisions? Explain.

 a. Book value of old equipment

 b. Disposal value of old equipment

 c. Cost of new equipment

13-11. "No technique applicable to the problem of joint-product costing should be used for management decisions regarding whether a product should be sold at the split-off point or processed further." Explain. Do you agree?

13-12. "Incremental cost is the addition to costs from the manufacture of one unit." Do you agree? Explain.

13-13. Give four examples of limiting or scarce factors.

13-14. "A ratio such as the conventional gross profit percentage is an insufficient clue to profitability." Do you agree? Explain.

13-15. "I had a chance to rent my summer cottage for two weeks for $150. But I chose to have it idle. I didn't want strangers living in my summer house." What term in this chapter describes the $150? Why?

13-16. "Accountants do not formally record opportunity costs in the accounting records." Why?

13-17. "There are two major reasons why unit costs should be analyzed with care in decision making." What are they?

13-18. What three major factors influence pricing decisions?

13-19. Why are customers one of the three factors influencing prices?

13-20. "I don't believe in assigning only variable costs to a job for guiding pricing. This results in suicidal under-pricing." Do you agree? Why?

13-21. "The contribution approach offers insight into the pricing of special orders. Why?

13-22. *Utilization of passenger jets.* In 19x2, Continental Air Lines, Inc. filled 50 per cent of the available seats on its Boeing 707 jet flights, a record about 15 per cent below the national average.

 Continental could have eliminated 4 per cent of its runs and raised its average load considerably. But the improved load factor would have reduced profits.

Give reasons for or against the above conclusion. What factors should influence an airline's scheduling policies?

13-23. *Profit per unit of space.*

1. Several successful chains of discount department stores have merchandising policies that differ considerably from the traditional downtown department stores. Name some characteristics of these discount stores that have contributed to their success.

2. Food chains have typically regarded, say, 20 per cent of selling price as an average target gross profit on canned goods and similar grocery items. What are the limitations of such an approach? Be specific.

13-24. *Special order: make or buy* (SICA Adapted.) A company which manufactures a range of products applies manufacturing overhead to production at a rate of 200 per cent of direct labor. This rate is based on:

Budgeted fixed expense	$32,000
Budgeted variable expense	48,000
Budgeted direct labor	40,000

DIVIDE

You have been asked to give your advice on the following problems confronting this company (in both instances, assume that fixed costs will not be changed):

a. The normal selling price of Product *A* is $12, and the cost of producing it is:

Raw materials	$ 4
Direct labor	2
Manufacturing overhead	4
Total cost	$10

20,000 normal output

The company has been asked to supply a special order for 2,000 units of Product *A* at $8 each. The supplying of this order will have no effect on the normal sales of this product, and the company has the capacity to produce the extra units.

Should this order be accepted? (Support your solution with cost analyses.)

b. The cost of manufacturing a component part of Product *B* is:

Raw materials	$ 2
Direct labor	4
Includeds: → Manufacturing overhead	8
FIXED Overhead Total cost	$14

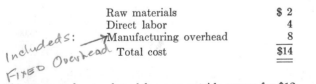
what will be our additional overhead cost?

This part can be purchased from an outside source for $12.

Should the company continue to make the part, or buy it from outside? (Support your solution with cost analyses.)

13-25. *Selection of product for special promotion.* The Foodly Co. produces three breakfast cereals, Wheatly, Cornly, and Oatly. A two-month sales promotion, during which a trinket costing 6¢ will be given away with the purchase of a box of one of the cereals, is being planned. The cereal to be promoted is being selected on the basis of the following figures:

	Wheatly	Cornly	Oatly
Regular selling price, per box	25¢	20¢	30¢
Standard cost of sales	22¢	14¢	26¢
Contribution margin ratio	20%	40%	30%
Anticipated increase in sales because of trinket	200,000 boxes	110,000 boxes	80,000 boxes

Which product should be chosen? Present appropriate figures to support your answer.

13-26. *Dropping of retail store* (SICA Adapted.) The Robertson Sales Company Ltd. statement of profit and loss year ending Dec. 21, 19x0.

THE ROBERTSON SALES COMPANY LTD.
Statement of Profit and Loss
Year Ending Dec. 31, 19x0

	Store A	Store B	Total
Net sales	$300,000	$1,000,000	$1,300,000
Cost of goods sold	250,000	550,000	800,000
Gross profit on sales	$ 50,000	$ 450,000	$ 500,000
Selling Expenses:			
Sales salaries	$ 60,000	$ 200,000	$ 260,000
Delivery truck driver's wages	1,000	2,000	3,000
Advertising expense	5,000	10,000	15,000
Store building depreciation expense	2,500	5,000	7,500
Store fixtures depreciation expense	2,000	8,000	10,000
Delivery equipment depreciation and maintenance expense	500	1,000	1,500
Miscellaneous selling expense	5,000	10,000	15,000
Total selling expense	$ 76,000	$ 236,000	$ 312,000
Net profit on sales	$ 26,000*	$ 214,000	$ 188,000
General expenses:			
Office salaries	$ 15,000	$ 40,000	$ 55,000
Management salaries	6,000	20,000	26,000
Insurance expense (building, stock and fixtures	4,000	10,000	14,000
Bad debts expense	10,000	35,000	45,000
Total general expense	$ 35,000	$ 105,000	$ 140,000
Net profit	$ 61,000*	$ 109,000	$ 48,000

* Loss.

The general manager of the company is considering closing Store *A* and asks your advice. The following information is made available to you:

   a. With the exception of one old employee in Store *A*, all other salesmen will be dismissed. This employee has three years till retirement and earns $6,000 per annum.
   b. Store *A* advertising expense will be eliminated, as there is no joint advertising program.
   c. Store *A* building will be put up for sale, and prospects of selling it are good.
   d. Fixtures will be transferred to Store *B*, where they can be used in space

which is available. No increase in staff will be needed in Store B, with the exception mentioned in a, above.

e. One truck driver presently services both stores, and he will be retained at the lower wage.   *means   wages of   3000 (total) + 2000 (for Store B)*

f. Insurance on fixtures amounts to 10 per cent of the present Store A expense for insurance.

g. Office salaries of Store A will be reduced by 50 per cent. Management salaries will not change.

h. Miscellaneous selling expense for Store A will be eliminated.

i. Store B is located in a new and expanding residential area.

lower of the two wages is 2000 so this is a reduction of $1000

Required:

Prepare the following reports for submission to the general manager:

1. A statement showing estimated reduction in expenses should Store A be closed.

2. A statement of estimated net income after Store A is discontinued.

3. Compile a brief report incorporating the advantages and/or disadvantages of the proposal to close Store A.

13-27. *Joint products: sell or process further.* Livingston Co. produced three joint products at a joint cost of $100,000. These products were processed further and sold as follows:

Product	Sales	Additional Processing Costs
A	$245,000	$200,000
B	330,000	300,000
C	175,000	100,000

The company has had an opportunity to sell at split-off directly to other processors. If that alternative had been selected, sales would have been: A, $56,000; B, $28,000; and C, $56,000.

The company expects to operate at the same level of production and sales in the forthcoming year.

Required:

Considering all the available information:

1. Could the company increase net income by altering its processing decisions? If so, what would be the expected over-all net income?

2. Which products should be processed further and which should be sold at split-off?

Assume that all costs incurred after split-off are variable.

13-28. *Elimination of drug store departments: joint effects.* A small drug store owner is considering dropping all services and items that are not of a pharmaceutical nature. This includes the soda fountain and various sundries (candy, magazines, stationery, cosmetics, etc.).

Other small store owners have reported that, after dropping the soda fountain, drug sales declined 10 per cent and sundry sales fell 5 per cent. Still others reported that after they dropped sundry items, drug sales dropped 5 per cent and soda fountain sales decreased 5 per cent.

At present, the store employs two pharmacists at yearly salaries of

$12,000 and a soda fountain man at $4,000 a year. Past experience has shown that one pharmacist is required for every $46,000 of drug sales. In 19x4, sales and cost of goods sold were as follows:

	Drugs	Soda Fountain	Sundry
Sales	$90,000	$8,000	$15,000
Cost of goods sold	45,000	7,000	12,000

The fountain man spends about 30 per cent of his time handling sundry items. If he were eliminated, a pharmacist would have to handle the sundry sales. Drug sales would decrease 1 per cent as a result of inconvenience to the customers. It would not be feasible to operate the fountain without a fountain man.

Required:

1. What is the net income of each operation?
2. Should any operation be dropped? What would be the saving, or the loss?
3. Assume that the owner considered the soda fountain a complete nuisance and has closed it. However, in an effort to regain lost drug sales, he is now considering cutting prices on certain manufactured drugs. He estimates that these discounts would amount to $1,000 a year, but that they would increase gross current drug sales by $10,000. This course of action would have an insignificant effect on sundry sales other than the effects already considered in part (2). Should he cut the prices?

13-29. *Make or buy.* The Dopuch Co.'s old equipment for making subassemblies is worn out. The company is considering two courses of action: (*a*) completely replacing the old equipment with new equipment; or (*b*) buying subassemblies from a reliable outside supplier who has quoted a unit price of $1 on a seven-year contract for a minimum of 50,000 units per year.

Production was 60,000 units in each of the past two years. Future needs for the next seven years are not expected to fluctuate beyond 50,000 to 70,000 units per year. Cost records for the past two years reveal the following unit costs of manufacturing the subassembly:

Direct material	$ .25
Direct labor	.40
Variable overhead	.10
Fixed overhead (including $.10 depreciation and $.10 for supervision and other direct departmental fixed overhead)	.25
	$1.00

The new equipment will cost $188,000 cash, will last seven years, and will have a disposal value of $20,000. The current disposal value of the old equipment is $10,000.

The salesman for the new equipment has summarized his position as follows: The increase in machine speeds will reduce direct labor and variable overhead by $.35 per unit. Consider last year's experience of one of your major competitors with identical equipment. They produced 100,000 units under operating conditions very comparable to yours and showed the following unit costs:

Direct material	$ .25
Direct labor	.10
Variable overhead	.05
Fixed overhead, including	
$.24 depreciation	.40
	$ .80

1. The president asks you to compare the alternatives on a total annual cost basis and on a per unit basis. Which alternative seems more attractive?

2. What factors, other than the above, should the accountant bring to the attention of management to assist them in making their decision? Include the considerations that might be applied to the outside supplier.

Note: For additional analysis, see Problem 14-23 and Problem 16-23.

13-30. *Traditional versus contribution approach to pricing.* The Standish Co. manufactures welding equipment. It has two product lines, a standard group of products and a custom group. The latter consists of special equipment designed especially for unique production processes. For example, the company made four special machines for the simultaneous welding of the grating on barbecue grills. These orders are usually acquired through competitive bidding.

The company has experienced a substantial decline in volume over the past three years, and the president is uneasy about pricing procedures, even though he often states proudly, "We use cost-plus pricing. If we cannot obtain a decent price, we don't want the business." He has asked you, an expert in cost analysis, to examine operations and advise him on pricing and other operating matters.

You analyze the financial statements for the past three years. A typical statement is the following, for the most recent year, 19x3:

Sales		$472,000
Direct material	$213,410	
Direct labor	44,029	
Factory overhead	138,917	
Total factory cost of goods sold		396,356
Gross profit		$75,644
Selling expenses	$ 68,884	
Administrative expenses	25,000	
Total operating expenses		93,884
Net operating loss		$— 18,240

A typical price quotation guide sheet appears as follows:

Direct materials: $25,000, plus a 10 per cent markup	$27,500
Direct labor: 3,000 hours, @ $2.40	7,200
Factory overhead: 3,000 hours, @ 300 per cent of	
direct labor	21,600
Sales commission	3,000
Total costs	$59,300
Add markup	2,700
Target selling price	$62,000

The bulk of your time is devoted to analyzing cost behavior patterns over the past three years. This is troublesome because the financial records and statements do not break costs down into variable and fixed categories. There are also many mixed costs that must be split into variable and fixed categories. This entails not only analysis by pencil, but interviewing of key personnel to discover management policies and how they affect various costs. Top management is perpetually optimistic, has a policy of retaining a stable administrative and engineering force, and is extremely reluctant to lay off such personnel when volume diminishes.

On the basis of your findings, you recast the 19x3 income statement as follows:

			Per Cent of Cost
Sales		$472,000	100
Direct material	$213,410		
Direct labor	44,029		
Variable factory overhead * (60 per cent of direct labor)	26,417		
Variable selling expense (mostly commissions)	32,384		
Total variable costs		316,240	67
Contribution margin		$155,760	33
Fixed costs:			
Engineering	$ 64,000		
Other fixed factory overhead	48,500		
Total fixed factory costs	$112,500		
Selling overhead	$36,500		
Administrative overhead	25,000	61,500	
Total fixed costs		174,000	
Net operating loss		$— 18,240	

* Mostly indirect labor and supplies.

Required:

1. Assuming an average contribution margin percentage of 33 per cent, what was the break-even sales volume in 19x3?

2. Assume that more flexibility in pricing would have resulted in $100,000 more sales at an average contribution margin percentage of 20 per cent; that is, quotes were lowered on jobs that were harder to get because of more intensive competition and craftier buyers. What would have been the net operating profit or loss for the year? Show computations.

3. Given the management attitude toward fixed costs, what general pricing policy should Standish follow?

4. In light of the above information, prepare a new price quotation sheet that you would recommend for use by Standish. Use the figures in the old price quotation sheet as a basis for your illustration, but also use any additional information that seems pertinent. Accompany your suggested quote sheet with a thorough explanation of how it is to be used as a guide to pricing decisions.

CHAPTER 14

Long-Range
Planning

SHOULD WE REPLACE THE EQUIPMENT NOW? WHAT TYPE OF equipment should we buy? Should we add this product to our line? Managers must make these and similar special decisions that have long-range implications. In this chapter we present a general approach to accounting's role in these long-range decisions. Therefore, we deal mostly with the accountant's problem-solving function.

CONTRASTS IN PURPOSES OF INTERNAL ACCOUNTING

At this stage, we again focus on purpose. Income determination and the planning and controlling of operations primarily have a *current time-period* orientation. Special decisions and long-range planning primarily have a *project* orientation.

William D. McEachron, Standard Oil Co. (Ind.), has illustrated these distinctions with a chart (Exhibit 14-1).

The project and time-period orientations of Exhibit 14-1 represent two distinct cross sections of the total corporate assets. The vertical dimension signifies the total investment (assets) of the company, which may be subdivided into divisions, product lines, departments, buildings, a fleet of trucks, or a machine. These parts of an organization's re-

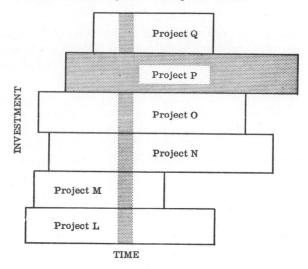

EXHIBIT 14-1

sources are individual *projects,* or investment decisions. The horizontal dimension represents successive years in a company's life.

The black horizontal rectangle shows that many projects entail commitments over a prolonged span of time, not just one year. The focus is on a single cross section, a lone investment venture, throughout its life. The interest which can be earned over a period of time (i.e., the time value of money) often looms large in special decisions and in long-range planning.

The black vertical rectangle illustrates the focus of income determination and current planning and control. The cross-sectional emphasis is upon the company's over-all performance and status for a year or less. The time period is relatively short, and the interest value of money is usually not directly involved.

The point of all this is that our ordinary accounting systems and techniques have been designed to determine the cost and income of products for current planning and control. There is a great danger of using the existing general-purpose accounting system incorrectly—that is, of using data indiscriminately for solving special problems.

So in this chapter, we shall shift gears. We shall take a fresh look at the purpose of the special decision, and then we will decide what tools seem best for achieving that purpose.

DEFINITION OF CAPITAL BUDGETING

Capital budgeting is long-term planning for making and financing proposed capital outlays. Most expenditures for plant, equipment, and other long-lived assets affect operations over a series of years. They are large, permanent commitments that influence long-run flexibility and earning power. Decisions in this area are among the most difficult, primarily because the future to be foreseen is distant and hard to perceive. Because the unknowable factors are many, it is imperative that all the knowable factors be collected and properly measured before a decision is reached.

The problem of measuring the potential profit of long-range investments has been receiving increased attention by management accountants. This trend is likely to grow as industrial mechanization and automation grow.

The profitability of a business decision depends on two vital factors: (1) future net increases in cash inflows or net savings in cash outflows; and (2) required investment. Thus, a chance to receive an annual return of $5,000 on a bond or stock can be judged only in relationship to how much money need be committed to obtain the $5,000. If the required capital is $10,000, the $5,000 (50 per cent) return may be extremely appealing. If the required investment is $1 million, the $5,000 (½ per cent) return probably will be unappealing. Depending on risk and available alternatives, individuals and corporate investors usually have some notion of a minimum rate of return that would make various projects desirable investments.

The quantitative approach to management problem-solving is, generally, to estimate the effect of the alternatives on cash flows in relation to the required investments. Thus, all projects whose rate of return exceeds the minimum rate of return would be desirable, and vice versa. A project which promises a return of 25 per cent would ordinarily be more desirable than one which promises a return of 12 per cent. The problem of choosing the minimum acceptable rate of return (more a problem of finance than of accounting) is extremely complex. In this book, we shall assume that the minimum acceptable rate of return is given to the accountant by management, and that it represents the rate that can be earned by alternative uses of investment capital.

There are several different ways of approaching the capital budgeting decision. Although we shall discuss: (a) discounted cash flow; (b) payback; and (c) the unadjusted rate of return, we shall concentrate on discounted cash flow because it is conceptually superior to the others.

DISCOUNTED CASH FLOW

Time Value of Money

The old adage that a bird in the hand is worth two in the bush is applicable to the management of money. A dollar in the hand today is worth more than a dollar to be received (or spent) five years from today. This is because the use of money has a cost (interest), just as the use of a building or an automobile may have a cost (rent). *Because the dis-*

counted-cash-flow method explicitly and automatically weighs the time value of money, it is the best method to use for long-range decisions.

Another major aspect of the cash-flow method is its focus on *cash* inflows and outflows rather than on *net income* as computed in the conventional accounting sense. As we shall see, the student without a strong accounting background has an advantage here. He does not have to unlearn the accrual concepts of accounting, which the accounting student often wrongly tries to inject into discounted cash flow analysis.

There are two main variations of the discounted-cash-flow method: (*a*) time-adjusted rate of return; and (*b*) net present value. A brief summary of the tables and formulas used is included in Appendix II at the end of this chapter. Do not be frightened by the mathematics of compound interest. We shall confine our study to present value tables, which may seem imposing but which are simple enough to be taught in many grade-school arithmetic courses. *Before reading on, be sure you understand Appendix II.*

The following example will be used to illustrate the concepts:

Example 1

A manager is contemplating the rearrangement of assembly line facilities. Because of rapid technological changes in the industry, he is using a four-year planning horizon as a basis for deciding whether to invest in the facilities for rearrangement, which should result in cash operating savings of $2,000 per year. In other words, the useful life of this project is four years, after which the facilities will be abandoned or rearranged again.

Required:

1. If the plant rearrangement will cost $6,074 now, what is the time-adjusted rate of return on the project?
2. If the minimum desired rate of return is 10 per cent, and the plant rearrangement will cost $6,074, what is the project's net present value? How much more would the manager be willing to invest and still earn 10 per cent on the project?

Requirement 1 deals with the time-adjusted rate of return, which we shall consider first.

Time-adjusted Rate of Return

The time-adjusted rate of return has been defined as "the maximum rate of interest that could be paid for the capital employed over the life of an investment without loss on the project." [1] This rate corresponds

---

[1] *Return on Capital as a Guide to Managerial Decisions,* National Association of Accountants, Research Report No. 35 (New York, December, 1959), p. 57.

to the effective rate of interest so widely computed for bonds purchased or sold at discounts or premiums. Alternatively, the rate of return can be defined as the discount rate that makes the present value of a project equal to the cost of the project.

EXHIBIT 14-2

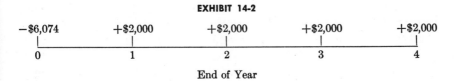

End of Year

The cash flows relating to our rearrangement problem are shown in Exhibit 14-2. The discounted cash flow analysis of these cash flows is shown in Exhibit 14-3.

EXHIBIT 14-3

Two Proofs of Time-adjusted Rate of Return

Original investment, $6,074
Useful life, 4 years
Annual cash inflow from operations, $2,000
Rate of return (selected by trial-and-error methods), 12 per cent

*Approach 1: Discounting Each Year's Cash Inflow Separately**

	Present Value of $1, Discounted at 12%	Total Present Value	Sketch of Cash Flows
End of Year			0 1 2 3 4
Cash flows:			
Annual savings	.893	$ 1,786	$2,000
	.797	1,594	$2,000
	.712	1,424	$2,000
	.636	1,272	$2,000
Present value of future inflows		$ 6,074‡	
Initial outlay	1.000	(6,074)	$(6,074)
Net present value (the zero difference proves that the rate of return is 12 per cent)		$ 0	

Approach 2: Using Annuity Table†

Annual savings	3.037	$ 6,074	$2,000 $2,000 $2,000 $2,000
Initial outlay	1.000	(6,074)	$(6,074)
Net present value		$ 0	

* Present values from Table 1, Appendix II to Chapter 14 (p. 378).
† Present values of annuity from Table 2, Appendix II to Chapter 14 (p. 380).
‡ Sum is really $6,076, but is rounded.

The exhibit shows that $6,074 is the present value, at a rate of return of 12 per cent, of a four-year stream of inflows of $2,000 in cash. Twelve per cent is the rate that equates the amount invested ($6,074) with the present value of the cash inflows ($2,000 per year for four years). In other words, *if* money were borrowed at an effective interest rate of 12 per cent, the cash inflow produced by the project would exactly repay the hypothetical loan plus the interest over the four years. If the cost of capital (minimum desired rate of return on the capital) is less than 12 per cent, the project will be desirable. If the cost of capital exceeds 12 per cent, the cash inflow will be insufficient to pay the interest and repay the principal of the hypothetical loan. Therefore, 12 per cent is the time-adjusted rate of return for this project.

Two Simplifying Assumptions

Two simplifying assumptions are being made here and throughout this book:

a. For simplicity in the use of tables, all operating cash inflows or outflows are assumed to take place at the *end* of the years in question. This is unrealistic because such cash flows ordinarily occur uniformly throughout the given year, rather than in lump sums at the end of the year. Compound interest tables especially tailored for these more stringent conditions are available,[2] but we shall not consider them here.

b. We assume that the cost of capital is known, is given; it is the minimum desired rate of return, an opportunity investment rate on alternative uses of the funds to be invested. The cost of capital is discussed in the literature on finance; but experts do not agree on how it should be computed. In any event, the cost of capital is *not* "interest expense" on borrowed money as the accountant usually conceives it. For example, a mortgage-free house still has a cost of capital—the amount that could be earned with the proceeds if the house were sold.

Explanation of Compound Interest

The time-adjusted rate of return is computed on the basis of the cash in use from period to period, rather than on the original investment. Exhibit 14-4 shows that the return is 12 per cent of the cash invested during the year. After 12 per cent of the cash invested is deducted, the remainder is the recovery of the original investment. Over the four years, the cash inflow equals the recovery of the original investment plus annual interest, at the rate of 12 per cent of the unrecovered capital.

---

[2] For example, J. C. Gregory, *Interest Tables for Determining Rate of Return* (The Atlantic Refining Company).

Depreciation and Discounted Cash Flow

Students are often mystified by the apparent exclusion of depreciation from discounted-cash-flow computations. A common homework error is to deduct depreciation. This is a misunderstanding of one of the basic ideas involved in the concept of the time-adjusted rate of return. Discounted-cash-flow techniques and tables *automatically* provide for recoupment of the principal. Therefore, *it is unnecessary to deduct depreciation from operating cash inflows before consulting present value tables.*

In Exhibit 14-4, at the end of Year 1, the $2,000 cash inflow represents a 12 per cent ($729) return on the $6,074 unrecovered investment at the beginning of Year 1 *plus* a $1,271 recovery of principal. The latter is similar to the depreciation provision in conventional accounting.

EXHIBIT 14-4

Rationale of Time-adjusted Rate of Return

Note. Same data as in Exhibit 14-3: Original investment, $6,074; Useful life, 4 years; Annual cash inflow from operations $2,000; Rate of return, 12 per cent. Unrecovered investment at the beginning of each year earns interest for the whole year. Annual cash inflows are received at the end of each year.

	(a) Unrecovered Investment at Beginning of Year	(b) Annual Cash Inflow	(c) Return: 12% per Year (a) × 12%	(d) Amount of Investment Recovered at End of Year (b) − (c)	(e) Unrecovered Investment at End of Year (a) − (d)
Year					
1	$6,074	$2,000	$729	$1,271	$4,803
2	4,803	2,000	576	1,424	3,379
3	3,379	2,000	405	1,595	1,784
4	1,784	2,000	216*	1,784	0

* Rounded.

This difficult point warrants another illustration. Assume that a company is considering investing in a project with a two-year life and no residual value. Cash inflow will be equal payments of $4,000 at the end of each of the two years. How much would the company be willing to invest to earn a time-adjusted rate of return of 8 per cent? A quick glance at the table for either the present value of $1 (Appendix II, Table 1, p. 378) or the present value of an ordinary annuity of $1.00 (Table 2, p. 380) will reveal:

Present Value of $4,000 at end of Year 1: $4,000 × .926 = $3,704
Present Value of $4,000 at end of Year 2: $4,000 × .857 = 3,428 $7,132
Present Value of annuity of $4,000 for 2 years at 8 per cent: $4,000 × 1.783 = $7,132

The following is an analysis of the computations that are automatically considered in the construction of present value tables.

Year	Investment at Beginning of Year	Operating Cash Inflow	Return, @ 8% per Year	Amount of Investment Received at End of Year	Unrecovered Investment at End of Year
1	$7,132	$4,000	.08 × $7,132 = $571	$4,000 − $571 = $3,429	$7,132 − $3,429 = $3,703
2	3,703	4,000	.08 × $3,703 = $297	$4,000 − $297 = $3,703	$3,703 − $3,703 = 0

A study of the above calculations will demonstrate that discounted-cash-flow techniques and tables have, built into them, the provisions for recovery of investment.

Net Present Value

Another type of discounted-cash-flow approach may be called the net present value method. Computing the exact time-adjusted rate of return entails trial-and-error and, sometimes, cumbersome hand calculations and interpolations within a compound interest table. In contrast, the net present value method assumes some minimum desired rate of return. All expected future cash flows are discounted to the present, using this minimum desired rate. If the result is positive, the project is desirable, and vice versa.

EXHIBIT 14-5

Net Present Value Technique

Original investment, $6,074; Useful life, 4 years; Annual cash inflow from operations, $2,000; Minimum desired rate of return, 10 per cent

*Approach 1: Discounting Each Year's Cash Inflow Separately**

	Present Value of $1, Discounted @ 10%	Total Present Value	Sketch of Cash Flows
End of Year Cash flows:			0 1 2 3 4
Annual savings	.909	$ 1,818	$2,000
	.826	1,652	$2,000
	.751	1,502	$2,000
	.683	1,366	$2,000
Present value of future inflows		$ 6,338	
Initial outlay	1.000	(6,074)	$(6,074)
Net present value		$ 264	

Approach 2: Using Annuity Table†

Annual savings	3.170	$ 6,340	$2,000 $2,000 $2,000 $2,000
Initial outlay	1.000	(6,074)	$(6,074)
Net present value		$ 264‡	

* Present values from Table 1, Appendix II to Chapter 14, p. 378.
† Present annuity values from Table 2, p. 380.
‡ Rounded.

Requirement (2) of Example 1 (p. 358) will be used to demonstrate the net present value approach. The problem assumes that the rearrangement will cost $6,074. Exhibit 14-5 shows a net present value of $264, so the investment is desirable. The manager would be able to invest $264 more, or a total of $6,338 (i.e., $6,074 + $264), and still earn 10 per cent on the project.

The higher the minimum desired rate of return, the less the manager would be willing to invest in this project. At a rate of 16 per cent, the net present value would be $−478 (i.e., $2,000 × 2.798 = $5,596, which is $478 less than the required investment of $6,074). (Present value factor, 2.798, is taken from Table 2, p. 380.) When the desired rate of return is 16 per cent, rather than 10 per cent, the project is undesirable at a price of $6,074.

THE NET PRESENT VALUE COMPARISON OF TWO PROJECTS

Incremental versus Total Project Approach

The mechanics of compound interest may appear formidable to those readers who are encountering them for the first time. However, a little practice with the interest tables should easily clarify the mechanical aspect. More important, we shall now blend some relevant cost analysis with the discounted-cash-flow approach.

EXAMPLE 2

A company owns a packaging machine, which was purchased three years ago for $56,000. It has a remaining useful life of five years, but will require a major overhaul at the end of its fifth year of life, at a cost of $10,000. Its disposal value now is $20,000; in five years its disposal value is expected to be $8,000. The cash operating costs of this machine are expected to be $40,000 annually.

A salesman has offered a substitute machine for $51,000, or for $31,000 plus the old machine. The new machine will slash annual cash operating costs by $10,000, will not require any overhauls, will have a useful life of five years, and will have a disposal value of $3,000.

Required:

Assume that the minimum desired rate of return is 14 per cent. Using the net present value technique, show whether the new machine should be purchased, using: (1) a total project approach; (2) an incremental approach.

EXHIBIT 14-6

Total Project versus Incremental Approach to Net Present Value
(Data from Example 2)

End of Year	Present Value Discount Factor, @ 14%	Total Present Value	0	1	2	3	4	5
						Sketch of Cash Flows		
TOTAL PROJECT APPROACH								
A. Replace								
Recurring cash operating costs, using an annuity table*	3.433	$(102,990)		($30,000)	($30,000)	($30,000)	($30,000)	($30,000)
Disposal value, end of Year 5	.519	1,557						3,000
Initial required investment	1.000	(31,000)	($31,000)					
Present value of net cash outflows		$(132,433)						
B. Keep								
Recurring cash operating costs, using an annuity table*	3.433	$(137,320)		($40,000)	($40,000)	($40,000)	($40,000)	($40,000)
Overhaul, end of Year 2	.769	(7,690)			(10,000)			
Disposal value, end of Year 5	.519	4,152						8,000
Present value of net cash outflows		$(140,858)						
Difference in favor of replacement		$ 8,425						
INCREMENTAL APPROACH								
A — B Analysis Confined to Differences								
Recurring cash operating savings, using an annuity table*	3.433	$ 34,330		$10,000	$10,000	$10,000	$10,000	$10,000
Overhaul avoided end of Year 2	.769	7,690			$10,000			
Difference in disposal values, end of Year 5	.519	(2,595)						(5,000)
Incremental initial investment	1.000	(31,000)	($31,000)					
Net present value of replacement		$ 8,425						

* Table 2, p. 380.

Solution

A difficult part of long-range decision making is the structuring of the data. We want to see the effects of each alternative on future cash flows. The focus here is on bona fide *cash* transactions, not on opportunity costs. Using an opportunity cost approach may yield the same answers, but repeated classroom experimentation with various analytical methods has convinced the author that the following steps are likely to be the clearest:

> *Step 1. Arrange the relevant cash flows by project, so that a sharp distinction is made between total project flows and incremental flows.* The incremental flows are merely algebraic differences between two alternatives. (There are *always* at least two alternatives. One is the *status quo*, the alternative of doing nothing.) Exhibit 14-6 shows how the cash flows for *each* alternative are sketched.
>
> *Step 2. Discount the expected cash flows and choose the project with the least cost or the greatest benefit.* Both the total project approach and the incremental approach are illustrated in Exhibit 14-6. Which approach you use is a matter of preference. However, to develop confidence in this area, you should work with both at the start. In this example, the $8,425 net difference in favor of replacement is the ultimate result under either approach.

Analysis of Typical Items under Discounted Cash Flow

1. FUTURE DISPOSAL VALUES. The disposal value at the date of termination of a project is an increase in the cash inflow in the year of disposal. Errors in forecasting disposal value are usually not crucial because the present value is usually small.

2. CURRENT DISPOSAL VALUES AND REQUIRED INVESTMENT. There are a number of correct ways to analyze this item, all of which will have the same ultimate effect on the decision. Probably the simplest way was illustrated in Example 2, where the $20,000 was offset against the $51,000 purchase price and the actual *cash* outgo was shown. Generally, the required investment is most easily measured by offsetting the disposal value of the old assets against the gross cost of the new assets.

3. BOOK VALUE AND DEPRECIATION. Depreciation is a phenomenon of accrual accounting that entails an allocation of cost, not a specific cash outlay. Depreciation and book value are ignored in discounted-cash-flow approaches for the reasons mentioned earlier in this chapter.

4. INCOME TAXES. In practice, comparison between alternatives is best made after considering tax effects, because the tax impact may alter the picture. (The effects of income taxes are considered in Chapter 16 (pp. 437 ff.), and may be studied now if desired.)

5. OVERHEAD ANALYSIS. In relevant cost analysis, only the overhead that will differ between alternatives is pertinent. There is need for careful study of the fixed overhead under the available alternatives. In practice,

this is an extremely difficult phase of cost analysis, because it is difficult to relate the individual costs to any single project.

6. UNEQUAL LIVES. Where projects have unequal lives, comparisons may be made either over the useful life of the longer-lived project or over the useful life of the shorter-lived project. For our purposes, let us estimate what the residual values will be at the end of the longer-lived project. We must also assume a reinvestment at the end of the shorter-lived project. This makes sense primarily because the decision maker should extend his time horizon as far as possible. If he is considering a longer-lived project, he should give serious consideration to what would be done in the time interval between the termination dates of the shorter-lived and longer-lived projects.

7. A WORD OF CAUTION. The foregoing material has been an *introduction* to the area of capital budgeting, which is, in practice, complicated by a variety of factors: unequal lives; major differences in the size of alternative investments; peculiarities in time-adjusted rate-of-return computations; various ways of allowing for uncertainty (see Chapter 17); changes, over time, in desired rates of return; the indivisibility of projects in relation to a fixed over-all capital budget appropriation; and more. These niceties are beyond the scope of this introduction to capital budgeting, but the Suggested Readings at the end of the chapter will help you pursue the subject in more depth.

8. THE GENERAL GUIDE TO CAPITAL BUDGETING DECISIONS. The following decision rule, subject to the cautionary words just stated, should guide the selection of projects: The net present value method should be used, and *any* project that has a positive net present value should be undertaken. When the projects are mutually exclusive, so that the acceptance of one automatically entails the rejection of the other (e.g., buying Dodge or Ford trucks) the project which maximizes wealth measured in net present value in dollars should be undertaken.

OTHER APPROACHES TO ANALYZING LONG-RANGE DECISIONS

Although discounted-cash-flow approaches to business decisions are being increasingly used, they are still relatively new, having been developed and applied for the first time, on any wide scale, in the 1950's. There are other techniques with which the manager should be at least somewhat familiar, because they are entrenched in many businesses.

The techniques we are about to discuss are conceptually inferior to discounted cash flow approaches. Then why do we bother studying them? First, changes in business practice occur slowly. Where older methods, such as payback or the accounting method, are in use, they should be used properly, even if there are better tools available. The situation is similar to using a pocket knife instead of a scalpel for removing a person's appendix. If the pocket knife is used by a knowledgeable and skilled surgeon, the chances for success are much better than if it is used by a bumbling layman.

One existing technique may be called the emergency-persuasion method. No formal planning is used. Fixed assets are operated until they crumble, product lines are carried until they are obliterated by competition, and requests by a manager for authorization of capital outlays are judged on the basis of his past operating performance regardless of its relevance to the decision at hand. These approaches to capital budgeting are examples of the unscientific management which eventually leads to the demise of many companies.

Payback Method

Payback, or *payout,* or *payoff,* is the measure of the time it will take to recoup in the form of cash inflow from operations, the initial dollars invested. Assume that $12,000 is spent for a machine with an estimated useful life of eight years. Annual savings of $4,000 in *cash* outflow are expected from operations. Depreciation is ignored. The payback calculations follow:

$$P = \frac{I}{O} = \frac{\$12,000}{\$ 4,000} = 3 \text{ years} \tag{1}$$

Where P is the payback time; I is the initial incremental amount invested; and O is the uniform annual incremental cash inflow from operations.

The payback method, by itself, does *not* measure profitability; it measures how quickly investment dollars may be recouped. This is its major weakness, because a shorter payback time does not necessarily mean that one project is preferable to another.

For instance, assume that an alternative to the $12,000 machine is a $10,000 machine whose operation will also result in a reduction of $4,000 annually in cash outflow. Then

$$P_1 = \frac{\$12,000}{\$ 4,000} = 3.0 \text{ years}$$

$$P_2 = \frac{\$10,000}{\$ 4,000} = 2.5 \text{ years}$$

The payback criterion indicates that the $10,000 machine is more desirable. However, one fact about the $10,000 machine has been purposely withheld. Its useful life is only 2.5 years. Ignoring the impact of compound interest for the moment, the $10,000 machine results in zero benefit, while the $12,000 machine generates cash inflows for five years beyond its payback period.

The main objective in investing is profit, not the recapturing of the initial outlay. If a company wants to recover its outlay fast, it need not spend in the first place. Then no waiting time is necessary; the payback time is zero.[1]

The payback approach may also be applied to Example 2. What is the payback time?

$$P = \frac{I}{O} = \frac{\$31,000}{\$10,000} = 3.1 \text{ years}$$

However, the formula may be used with assurance only when there are uniform cash inflows from operations. In this instance, $10,000 is saved by avoiding an overhaul at the end of the second year. When cash inflows are not uniform, the payback computation must take a cumulative form. That is, each year's net cash flows are accumulated until the initial investment is recouped:

		Net Cash Inflows	
Year	Initial Investment	Each Year	Accumulated
0	$31,000	—	—
1	—	$10,000	$10,000
2	—	20,000	30,000
2.1	—	1,000	31,000

The payback time is slightly beyond the second year. Straight-line interpolation within the third year reveals that the final $1,000 needed to recoup the investment would be forthcoming in 2.1 years.

UNADJUSTED RATE OF RETURN

Unadjusted Rate-of-Return Method

The label for this method is not uniform. It is also known as the *accounting method,* the *financial statement method,* the *book value*

---

[1] Businessmen have tempered their use of the payback method, the most widely used approach to capital budgeting, with common sense. They have used it in conjunction with estimated useful life. Professor Myron Gordon ["Payoff Period and Rate of Profit," *Journal of Business,* XXVIII, No. 4, October, 1955] has shown that the payback method may yield satisfactory indications of relative profitability, provided that the following two criteria are both met:

    a. Uniform cash inflows from operations occur throughout the project's useful life.

    b. The useful life of the project must be at least twice the payback time.

Coupling these criteria with the payback time effects a crude approximation of the relative time-adjusted profitability of various projects. The payback time is thus no longer being used nakedly, a dangerous approach that may lead to wrong decisions.

method, the *rate-of-return on assets method,* and the *approximate rate-of-return method.* Its computations supposedly dovetail most closely with conventional accounting methods of calculating income and required investment. However, the dovetailing objective is not easily attained because the purposes of the computations differ. The most troublesome aspects are depreciation and decisions concerning capitalization versus expense. For example, advertising and research are usually expensed, even though they often may be viewed as long-range investments.

The equations for the unadjusted rate of return are:

$$\text{Unadjusted rate of return} = \frac{\text{Increase in future average annual net income}}{\text{Initial increase in required investment}} \quad (2)$$

$$R = \frac{O - D}{I} \quad (3)$$

where R = Average annual rate of return on initial additional investment
O = Average annual incremental cash inflow from operations
D = Incremental average annual depreciation
I = Initial incremental amount invested

Assume the same facts as in our payback illustration: cost of machine, $12,000; useful life, eight years; estimated disposal value, zero; and expected annual savings in annual cash outflow from operations, $4,000. Substitute these values into Eq. (3).

$$R = \frac{\$4,000 - \$1,500}{\$12,000} = 20.83\%$$

Weighing Dollars Differently

The unadjusted method ignores the time value of money. Expected future dollars are unrealistically and erroneously regarded as equal to present dollars. The discounted-cash-flow method explicitly allows for the force of interest and the exact timing of cash flows. In contrast, the unadjusted method is based on *annual averages.* To illustrate, consider a petroleum company with three potential projects: an expansion of an existing gasoline station; an oil well; and a new gasoline station. To simplify the calculations, assume a three-year life for each project. Exhibit 14-7 summarizes the comparisons. Note that the unadjusted rate of return would indicate that all three projects are equally desirable and that the time-adjusted rate of return properly discriminates in favor of earlier cash inflows.

Thus, the conflict of purposes is highlighted in Exhibit 14-7. The unadjusted method "utilizes concepts of capital and income which were originally designed for the quite different purpose of accounting for periodic income and financial position." [3] In the unadjusted method, the

---

[3] *Return on Capital as a Guide to Managerial Decisions, op. cit.,* p. 64.

EXHIBIT 14-7

Comparison of Unadjusted Rates of Return and Time-adjusted Rates of Return

	Expansion of Existing Gasoline Station	Oil Well	New Gasoline Station
Initial investment	$ 90,000	$ 90,000	$ 90,000
Cash inflows from operations:			
Year 1	$ 40,000	$ 80,000	$ 20,000
Year 2	40,000	30,000	40,000
Year 3	40,000	10,000	60,000
Totals	$120,000	$120,000	$120,000
Average annual cash inflow	$ 40,000	$ 40,000	$ 40,000
Less: Average annual depreciation ($90,000 ÷ 3)	30,000	30,000	30,000
Increase in average annual net income	$ 10,000	$ 10,000	$ 10,000
Unadjusted rate of return on initial investment	11.1%	11.1%	11.1%
Time-adjusted rate of return, using discounted cash flow	16.0%*	23.2%*	13.8%*

* Computed by trial-and-error approaches using Tables 1 and 2, pp. 378, 380. See Appendix I to this chapter for a detailed explanation.

initial capital calculation is subject to questionable asset-versus-expense decisions (e.g., allocation of costs of research or of sales promotion outlays), while the effects of interest on the timing of cash flows may be ignored. The resulting unadjusted rate of return may be far from the real mark.[4]

Postaudit

The unadjusted method usually facilitates follow-up, because the same approach is used in the forecast as is used in the accounts. Yet exceptions to this ideal situation often occur. The most common exceptions arise from the inclusion, in the forecast, of some initial investment items that are not handled in the same manner in the subsequent accounting records. For example, the accounting for trade-ins and disposal values varies considerably. In practice, test checks are frequently used on key items. An interesting suggestion on the problem of postaudit follows:

> When a major project is undertaken, it seems desirable to prepare project cost and income budgets employing the usual accounting classifications so that subsequent actual figures drawn from the accounts can be compared

---

[4] Many managers use the unadjusted method because they regard it as satisfactory for their particular needs. In other words, they feel that the use of this tool is adequate for guiding their decisions even though the more refined discounted cash flow tools are available. In such cases, care should be taken so that the cruder tool is used properly. For illustrations of the details, subtleties, and complexities of the unadjusted (accounting) rate of return see Charles T. Horngren, *Cost Accounting: A Managerial Emphasis* (Englewood Cliffs, N.J.: Prentice-Hall, Inc., 1962), Chapter 13.

directly with estimates. Rates of return can also be computed by the [unadjusted method], using the budgeted and actual data. Thus . . . the discounted cash flow method would be used as a basis for project selection and rate of return based upon a financial budget for the project would be used as a goal against which to compare subsequent performance.[5]

THE PROBLEM OF UNCERTAINTY

It is vitally important to recognize that, throughout this and the previous chapter, we have assumed specific dollar amounts of future sales and operating costs in order to highlight and simplify various important points. In practice, the forecasting of these key figures is generally the most difficult aspect of decision analysis. (See Chapter 17 for a discussion of a probability approach to uncertainty.)

SUMMARY

Product costing, income determination, and the planning and controlling of operations have a current time-period orientation. Special decisions and long-range planning have primarily a project orientation. There is a danger in using ordinary accounting data for special purposes. Discounted-cash-flow techniques have been developed for the making of special decisions and for long-range planning because the time value of money becomes extremely important when projects extend beyond one or two years.

The field of capital budgeting is important because lump-sum expenditures on long-life projects have far-reaching effects on profit and on a business's flexibility. It is imperative that management develops its plans carefully and bases them on reliable forecasting procedures. Capital budgeting is long-term planning for proposed capital outlays and their financing. Projects are accepted if their rate of return exceeds a minimum desired rate of return.

Because the discounted-cash-flow method explicitly and automatically weighs the time value of money, it is the best method to use for long-range decisions. The overriding goal is maximum long-run net cash inflows.

The discounted-cash-flow approach has two variations: time-adjusted rate of return and net present value. Both approaches take into account the timing of cash flows and are thus superior to other methods.

The payback method is the most widely used approach to capital spending decisions. It is simple and easily understood, but it neglects profitability.

---

[5] *Return on Capital as a Guide to Managerial Decisions, op. cit.,* pp. 72-3.

The unadjusted rate-of-return method is also widely used in capital budgeting, although it is conceptually inferior to discounted-cash-flow methods. It fails to recognize explicitly the time value of money. Instead, the unadjusted method depends on averaging techniques that may yield inaccurate answers, particularly when cash flows are not uniform through the life of a project.

The difficulty of forecasting makes capital budgeting one of the most imposing tasks of management. Although judgment and attitudes are important ingredients of capital budgeting, the correct application of the techniques described here should crystallize the relevant factors and help management toward intelligent problem solving.

SUMMARY PROBLEM FOR YOUR REVIEW

PROBLEM

A toy manufacturer who specializes in making fad items has just developed a $50,000 molding machine for automatically producing a special toy. The machine has been used to produce one unit. It is planned to depreciate the $50,000 original cost evenly over four years, after which time production of the toy will be stopped.

Suddenly a machine salesman appears. He has a new machine which is ideally suited for producing this toy. His automatic machine is distinctly superior. It reduces the cost of material by 10 per cent and produces twice as many units per hour. It will cost $44,000 and will have zero disposal value at the end of four years.

Production and sales would continue to be at a rate of 25,000 per year for four years; annual sales will be $90,000. The scrap value of the toy company's machine is now $5,000 and will be $2,600 four years from now. Both machines will be useless after the 100,000-unit total market potential is exhausted.

With its present equipment, the company's annual expenses will be: direct materials, $10,000; direct labor, $20,000; and variable factory overhead, $15,000. Fixed factory overhead, exclusive of depreciation, is $7,500 annually, and fixed selling and administrative expenses are $12,000 annually.

Required:

1. Assume that the minimum rate of return desired is 18 per cent. Using discounted-cash-flow techniques, show whether the new equipment should be purchased. Use a total project approach and an incremental approach. What is the role of the book value of the old equipment in the analysis?
2. What is the payback period for the new equipment?

SOLUTION

1. The first step is to analyze all relevant operating cash flows and align them with the appropriate alternative:

Schedule of Annual Operating Cash Outflows

	(1) *Present* *Situation*	(2) *New* *Situation*	(3) *Increment*
Sales (irrelevant)			
Expenses:			
Direct materials	$10,000	$ 9,000	$ 1,000
Direct labor	20,000	10,000	10,000
Variable overhead	15,000	7,500	7,500
Fixed overhead (irrelevant)			
Selling and administrative expenses			
(irrelevant)			
Total relevant operating cash outflows	$45,000	$26,500	$18,500

The next step is to sketch the *other* relevant cash flows, as shown in Exhibit 14-8. Either the total project approach or the incremental approach results in the same $9,423 net present value in favor of replacement.

Note that the book value of the old machine is irrelevant, and so is completely ignored. In the light of subsequent events, nobody will deny that the original $50,000 investment could have been avoided, with a little luck or foresight. But nothing can be done to alter the past. The next question is whether the company will nevertheless be better off by buying the new machine. Management would have been much happier had the $50,000 never been spent in the first place, but the original mistake should not be compounded by keeping the old machine.

2. The payback formula can be used because the operating savings are uniform:

$$P = \frac{I}{O} = \frac{\$44,000 - \$5,000}{\$18,500} = 2.1 \text{ years}$$

SUGGESTED READINGS

Return on Capital as a Guide to Managerial Decisions, National Association of Accountants Research Report No. 35. New York, 1959.

Bierman, H., and S. Smidt, *The Capital Budgeting Decision*. New York: The Macmillan Company, 1960.

Solomon, E. (ed.), *The Management of Corporate Capital*. New York: Free Press of Glencoe, Inc., 1959.

Steiner, G. (ed.), *Managerial Long-range Planning*. New York: McGraw-Hill Book Company, 1963.

The National Association of Accountants Research Report No. 35 contains a good summary of capital budgeting. It also explains Prof. Myron Gordon's payback reciprocal, a practical technique that alters the payback method so that it may be used correctly in a wide variety of situations. Both this publication and Solomon's book contain extensive bibliographies.

EXHIBIT 14-8

Solution to Requirement 1 of Summary Problem for Your Review

End of Year	Present Value Discount Factor, @ 18%	Total Present Value	Sketch of Cash Flows				
			0	1	2	3	4
TOTAL PROJECT APPROACH							
A. New Situation							
Recurring cash operating costs, using an annuity table*	2.690	$ (71,285)		($26,500)	($26,500)	($26,500)	($26,500)
Disposal value of old equipment now	1.000	5,000	$ 5,000				
Cost of new equipment	1.000	(44,000)	($44,000)				
Present value of net cash outflows		$(110,285)					
B. Present Situation							
Recurring cash operating costs, using an annuity table	2.690	$(121,050)		($45,000)	($45,000)	($45,000)	($45,000)
Disposal value of old equipment four years hence	.516	1,342					$ 2,600
Present value of net cash outflows		$(119,708)					
Difference in favor of replacement		$ 9,423					
INCREMENTAL APPROACH							
A−B Analysis Confined to Differences							
Recurring cash operating savings, using an annuity table*	2.690	$ 49,765		$18,500	$18,500	$18,500	$18,500
Disposal value of old equipment now	1.000	5,000	$ 5,000				
Cost of new equipment	1.000	(44,000)	($44,000)				
Disposal value of old equipment foregone four years hence	.516	(1,342)					($ 2,600)
Net present value of replacement		$ 9,423					

* From Table 2, p. 380.

I. Calculations of Time-Adjusted Rates of Return Using Trial-and-Error Methods

(Data are from Exhibit 14-7)

Expansion

$90,000 = Present value of annuity of $40,000 at x per cent for three years, or what factor F in the table of the present values of an annuity will satisfy the following equation:

$90,000 = $40,000 F

$F = $90,000 \div $40,000 = 2.250

Now, on the Year 3 line of Table 2 (p. 380), find the column that is closest to 2.250. You will find that 2.250 is extremely close to a rate of return of 16 per cent—so close that straight-line interpolation is unnecessary between 14 per cent and 16 per cent. Therefore, the time-adjusted rate of return is 16 per cent.

Oil Well

Trial-and-error methods must be used to calculate the rate of return that will equate the future cash flows with the $90,000 initial investment. As a start, note that the 16 per cent rate was applicable to a uniform annual cash inflow. But now use Table 1 (p. 378), because the flows are not uniform, and try a higher rate, 22 per cent, because you know that the cash inflows are coming in more quickly than under the uniform inflow:

		Trial at 22 Per Cent		*Trial at 24 Per Cent*	
Year	*Cash Inflows*	*Present Value Factor*	*Total Present Value*	*Present Value Factor*	*Total Present Value*
1	$80,000	.820	$65,000	.806	$64,480
2	30,000	.672	20,160	.650	19,500
3	10,000	.551	5,510	.524	5,240
			$91,270		$89,220

The true rate lies somewhere between 22 and 24 per cent and can be approximated by straight-line interpolation.

Interpolation	*Total Present Values*	
22%	$91,270	$91,270
True rate		90,000
24%	89,220	
Difference	$ 2,050	$ 1,270

Therefore

$$\text{True rate} = 22\% + \frac{1,270}{2,050} \times 2\%$$

$$= 22\% + 1.2\% = 23.2\%$$

New Gasoline Station

In contrast to the oil well project, this venture will have slowly increasing cash inflows. The trial rate should be much lower than the 16 per cent rate applicable to the expansion project. Let us try 12 per cent.

		Trial at 12 Per Cent		*Trial at 14 Per Cent*	
Year	*Cash Inflows*	*Present Value Factor*	*Total Present Value*	*Present Value Factor*	*Total Present Value*
1	$20,000	.893	$17,860	.877	$17,540
2	40,000	.797	31,880	.769	30,760
3	60,000	.712	42,720	.675	40,500
			$92,460		$89,300

Interpolation	*Total Present Values*	
12%	$92,460	$92,460
True rate		90,000
14%	89,300	
	$ 3,160	$ 2,460

$$\text{True rate} = 12\% + \frac{2,460}{3,160} \times 2\%$$

$$= 12\% + 1.8\% = 13.8\%$$

II. Fundamentals of Compound Interest and the Use of Present Value Tables

Nature of Interest

Interest is the cost of using money. It is the rental charge for cash, just as rental charges are often made for the use of automobiles or boats.

Interest does not always entail an outlay of cash. The concept of interest applies to ownership funds as well as to borrowed funds. The reason why interest must be considered on *all* funds in use, regardless of their source, is that the selection of one alternative necessarily commits funds which otherwise could be invested in some other opportunity. The measure of the interest in such cases is the return foregone by rejecting the alternative use. For instance, a wholly owned home or business asset is not cost-free. The funds so invested could alternatively be invested in government bonds or in some other venture. The measure of this opportunity cost depends on what alternative incomes are available.

Interest cost is often unimportant when short-term projects are under consideration, but it becomes extremely important when long-run plans are being considered. The longer the time span, the higher the interest or rental charge. If you place $10,000 in a savings account at 4 per cent interest, compounded annually, the original $10,000 will grow to $10,400 at the end of Year 1 ($10,000 × 1.04); to $10,816 at the end of Year 2 ($10,400 × 1.04); to $11,249 at the end of Year 3 ($10,816 × 1.04); and to $21,911 at the end of Year 20 ($10,000 × 1.04^{20}$). If the rate of interest were 10 per cent compounded annually, the original $10,000 would grow to $13,310 at the end of Year 3, ($10,000 × 1.10^3$) ; and to $67,276 at the end of Year 20 ($10,000 × 1.10^{20}$).

Table 1: Present Value of $1

Two basic tables are used in capital budgeting. The first table (Table 1, p. 378), the Present Value of $1, deals with a single lump-sum cash inflow or out-flow at a given instant of time, the *end* of the period in question. An example should clarify the reasoning underlying the construction and use of the table.

Illustration: assume that a prominent corporation is issuing a three-year, non-interest-bearing, note payable which promises to pay a lump sum of $1,000 exactly three years from now. You desire a rate of return of exactly 6 per cent, compounded annually. How much would you be willing to pay now for the three-year note? The situation is sketched as follows:

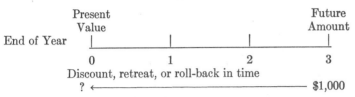

Let us examine the chart, period by period. First, let us assume that you are to purchase the $1,000 note at the end of Year 2 instead of at time zero. How much would you be willing to pay? If you wish to earn 6¢ annually on every $1 invested, you would want to receive $1.06 in one year for every $1 you in-vest today. Therefore, at the end of Year 2 you would be willing to pay $\frac{\$1.00}{\$1.06} \times$ $1,000 for the right to receive $1,000 at the end of Year 3, or $.943 × $1,000 = $943. Let us enter this in a tabular calculation:

End of Year	Interest per year	Cumulative Discount, Called Compound Discount	Present Value at the End of Year
3	$57	$ 57	$1,000
2	53	110	943
1	50	160	890
0	—	—	840

Note that what is really being done in the tabulation is a series of computa-tions that could be formulated as follows:

$$PV_2 = \$1,000 \left[\frac{1.00}{1.06}\right] = \$943$$

$$PV_1 = \$1,000 \left[\frac{1.00}{(1.06)^2}\right] = \$890$$

$$PV_0 = \$1,000 \left[\frac{1.00}{(1.06)^3}\right] = \$840$$

This can be written as a formula for the present value of $1:

$$PV = \frac{S}{(1 + i)^n}$$

TABLE 1:
Present Value of $1

$$PV = \frac{S}{(1+i)^n}$$

Periods	4%	6%	8%	10%	12%	14%	16%	18%	20%	22%	24%	26%	28%	30%	40%
1	0.962	0.943	0.926	0.909	0.893	0.877	0.862	0.847	0.833	0.820	0.806	0.794	0.781	0.769	0.714
2	0.925	0.890	0.857	0.826	0.797	0.769	0.743	0.718	0.694	0.672	0.650	0.630	0.610	0.592	0.510
3	0.889	0.840	0.794	0.751	0.712	0.675	0.641	0.609	0.579	0.551	0.524	0.500	0.477	0.455	0.364
4	0.855	0.792	0.735	0.683	0.636	0.592	0.552	0.516	0.482	0.451	0.423	0.397	0.373	0.350	0.260
5	0.822	0.747	0.681	0.621	0.567	0.519	0.476	0.437	0.402	0.370	0.341	0.315	0.291	0.269	0.186
6	0.790	0.705	0.630	0.564	0.507	0.456	0.410	0.370	0.335	0.303	0.275	0.250	0.227	0.207	0.133
7	0.760	0.665	0.583	0.513	0.452	0.400	0.354	0.314	0.279	0.249	0.222	0.198	3.178	0.159	0.095
8	0.731	0.627	0.540	0.467	0.404	0.351	0.305	0.266	0.233	0.204	0.179	0.157	0.139	0.123	0.068
9	0.703	0.592	0.500	0.424	0.361	0.308	0.263	0.225	0.194	0.167	0.144	0.125	0.108	0.094	0.048
10	0.676	0.558	0.463	0.386	0.322	0.270	0.227	0.191	0.162	0.137	0.116	0.099	0.085	0.073	0.035
11	0.650	0.527	0.429	0.350	0.287	0.237	0.195	0.162	0.135	0.112	0.094	0.079	0.066	0.056	0.025
12	0.625	0.497	0.397	0.319	0.257	0.208	0.168	0.137	0.112	0.092	0.076	0.062	0.052	0.043	0.018
13	0.601	0.469	0.368	0.290	0.229	0.182	0.145	0.116	0.093	0.075	0.061	0.050	0.040	0.033	0.013
14	0.577	0.442	0.340	0.263	0.205	0.160	0.125	0.099	0.078	0.062	0.049	0.039	0.032	0.025	0.009
15	0.555	0.417	0.315	0.239	0.183	0.140	0.108	0.084	0.065	0.051	0.040	0.031	0.025	0.020	0.006
16	0.534	0.394	0.292	0.218	0.163	0.123	0.093	0.071	0.054	0.042	0.032	0.025	0.019	0.015	0.005
17	0.513	0.371	0.270	0.198	0.146	0.108	0.080	0.060	0.045	0.034	0.026	0.020	0.015	0.012	0.003
18	0.494	0.350	0.250	0.180	0.130	0.095	0.069	0.051	0.038	0.028	0.021	0.016	0.012	0.009	0.002
19	0.475	0.331	0.232	0.164	0.116	0.083	0.060	0.043	0.031	0.023	0.017	0.012	0.009	0.007	0.002
20	0.456	0.312	0.215	0.149	0.104	0.073	0.051	0.037	0.026	0.019	0.014	0.010	0.007	0.005	0.001
21	0.439	0.294	0.199	0.135	0.093	0.064	0.044	0.031	0.022	0.015	0.011	0.008	0.006	0.004	0.001
22	0.422	0.278	0.184	0.123	0.083	0.056	0.038	0.026	0.018	0.013	0.009	0.006	0.004	0.003	0.001
23	0.406	0.262	0.170	0.112	0.074	0.049	0.033	0.022	0.015	0.010	0.007	0.005	0.003	0.002	
24	0.390	0.247	0.158	0.102	0.066	0.043	0.028	0.019	0.013	0.008	0.006	0.004	0.003	0.002	
25	0.375	0.233	0.146	0.092	0.059	0.038	0.024	0.016	0.010	0.007	0.005	0.003	0.002	0.001	
26	0.361	0.220	0.135	0.084	0.053	0.033	0.021	0.014	0.009	0.006	0.004	0.002	0.002	0.001	
27	0.347	0.207	0.125	0.076	0.047	0.029	0.018	0.011	0.007	0.005	0.003	0.002	0.001	0.001	
28	0.333	0.196	0.116	0.069	0.042	0.026	0.016	0.010	0.006	0.004	0.002	0.002	0.001	0.001	
29	0.321	0.185	0.107	0.063	0.037	0.022	0.014	0.008	0.005	0.003	0.002	0.001	0.001	0.001	
30	0.308	0.174	0.099	0.057	0.033	0.020	0.012	0.007	0.004	0.003	0.002	0.001	0.001	0.001	
40	0.208	0.097	0.046	0.022	0.011	0.005	0.003	0.001	0.001						

where $PV =$ Present value at time zero; $S =$ Future amount; $i =$ Interest rate; and $n =$ Number of periods.

Check the answers in the tabulation by using Table 1 (p. 378). For example, the Period 3 row and the 6 per cent column show a factor of .840. Multiply this factor by the future cash flow, $1,000, to obtain its present value, $840.

Use Table 1 (p. 378) to obtain the present values of:

1. $1,600, @ 20 per cent, at the end of 20 years.
2. $8,300, @ 10 per cent, at the end of 12 years.
3. $8,000, @ 4 per cent, at the end of 4 years.

Answers:

1. $1,600 (.026) = $41.60.
2. $8,300 (.319) = $2,648.
3. $8,000 (.855) = $6,840.

Table 2: Present Value of an Ordinary Annuity of $1

An ordinary annuity is a series of equal cash flows to take place at the *end* of successive periods of equal length. Assume that you buy a noninterest bearing serial note from a corporation which promises to pay $1,000 at the end of each of three years. How much should you be willing to pay, if you desire a rate of return of 6 per cent, compounded annually?

Exhibit 14-10 shows how the formula for PV_A, *the present value of an ordinary annuity*, is developed.

EXHIBIT 14-10

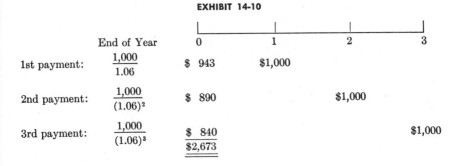

	End of Year	0	1	2	3
1st payment:	$\dfrac{1,000}{1.06}$	$ 943	$1,000		
2nd payment:	$\dfrac{1,000}{(1.06)^2}$	$ 890		$1,000	
3rd payment:	$\dfrac{1,000}{(1.06)^3}$	$\dfrac{$ 840}{$2,673}$			$1,000

$$PV_A = \text{Sum of present values of each item} \qquad (1)$$

For the general case, the present value of an ordinary annuity of $1 may be expressed as follows:

$$PV_A = \frac{1}{1 + i} + \frac{1}{(1 + i)^2} + \frac{1}{(1 + i)^3} \qquad (2)$$

Substituting values from our Illustration

$$PV_A = \frac{1}{1.06} + \frac{1}{(1.06)^2} + \frac{1}{(1.06)^3} \qquad (3)$$

Multiply by $\dfrac{1}{1.06}$ $\qquad PV_A\left(\dfrac{1}{1.06}\right) = \dfrac{1}{(1.06)^2} + \dfrac{1}{(1.06)^3} + \dfrac{1}{(1.06)^4} \qquad (4)$

TABLE 2:

Present Value of Ordinary Annuity of $1

$$PV_A = \frac{1}{i}\left[1 - \frac{1}{(1+i)^n}\right]$$

Periods	4%	6%	8%	10%	12%	14%	16%	18%	20%	22%	24%	25%	26%	28%	30%	40%
1	0.962	0.943	0.926	0.909	0.893	0.877	0.862	0.847	0.833	0.820	0.806	0.800	0.794	0.781	0.769	0.714
2	1.886	1.833	1.783	1.736	1.690	1.647	1.605	1.566	1.528	1.492	1.457	1.440	1.424	1.392	1.361	1.224
3	2.775	2.673	2.577	2.487	2.402	2.322	2.246	2.174	2.106	2.042	1.981	1.952	1.923	1.868	1.816	1.589
4	3.630	3.465	3.312	3.170	3.037	2.914	2.798	2.690	2.589	2.494	2.404	2.362	2.320	2.241	2.166	1.849
5	4.452	4.212	3.993	3.791	3.605	3.433	3.274	3.127	2.991	2.864	2.745	2.689	2.635	2.532	2.436	2.035
6	5.242	4.917	4.623	4.355	4.111	3.889	3.685	3.498	3.326	3.167	3.020	2.951	2.885	2.759	2.643	2.168
7	6.002	5.582	5.206	4.868	4.564	4.288	4.039	3.812	3.605	3.416	3.242	3.161	3.083	2.937	2.802	2.263
8	6.733	6.210	5.747	5.335	4.968	4.639	4.344	4.078	3.837	3.619	3.421	3.329	3.241	3.076	2.925	2.331
9	7.435	6.802	6.247	5.759	5.328	4.946	4.607	4.303	4.031	3.786	3.566	3.463	3.366	3.184	3.019	2.379
10	8.111	7.360	6.710	6.145	5.650	5.216	4.833	4.494	4.192	3.923	3.682	3.571	3.465	3.269	3.092	2.414
11	8.760	7.887	7.139	6.495	5.988	5.453	5.029	4.656	4.327	4.035	3.776	3.656	3.544	3.335	3.147	2.438
12	9.385	8.384	7.536	6.814	6.194	5.660	5.197	4.793	4.439	4.127	3.851	3.725	3.606	3.387	3.190	2.456
13	9.986	8.853	7.904	7.103	6.424	5.842	5.342	4.910	4.533	4.203	3.912	3.780	3.656	3.427	3.223	2.468
14	10.563	9.295	8.244	7.367	6.628	6.002	5.468	5.008	4.611	4.265	3.962	3.824	3.695	3.459	3.249	2.477
15	11.118	9.712	8.559	7.606	6.811	6.142	5.575	5.092	4.675	4.315	4.001	3.859	3.726	3.483	3.268	2.484
16	11.652	10.106	8.851	7.824	6.974	6.265	5.669	5.162	4.730	4.357	4.033	3.887	3.751	3.503	3.283	2.489
17	12.166	10.477	9.122	8.022	7.120	6.373	5.749	5.222	4.775	4.391	4.059	3.910	3.771	3.518	3.295	2.492
18	12.659	10.828	9.372	8.201	7.250	6.467	5.818	5.273	4.812	4.419	4.080	3.928	3.786	3.529	3.304	2.494
19	13.134	11.158	9.604	8.365	7.366	6.550	5.877	5.316	4.844	4.442	4.097	3.942	3.799	3.539	3.311	2.496
20	13.590	11.470	9.818	8.514	7.469	6.623	5.929	5.353	4.870	4.460	4.110	3.954	3.808	3.546	3.316	2.497
21	14.029	11.764	10.017	8.649	7.562	6.687	5.973	5.384	4.891	4.476	4.121	3.963	3.816	3.551	3.320	2.498
22	14.451	12.042	10.201	8.772	7.645	6.743	6.011	5.410	4.909	4.488	4.130	3.970	3.822	3.556	3.323	2.498
23	14.857	12.303	10.371	8.883	7.718	6.792	6.044	5.432	4.925	4.499	4.137	3.976	3.827	3.559	3.325	2.499
24	15.247	12.550	10.529	8.985	7.784	6.835	6.073	5.451	4.937	4.507	4.143	3.981	3.831	3.562	3.327	2.499
25	15.622	12.783	10.675	9.077	7.843	6.873	6.097	5.467	4.948	4.514	4.147	3.985	3.834	3.564	3.329	2.499
26	15.983	13.003	10.810	9.161	7.896	6.906	6.118	5.480	4.956	4.520	4.151	3.988	3.837	3.566	3.330	2.500
27	16.330	13.211	10.935	9.237	7.943	6.935	6.136	5.492	4.964	4.524	4.154	3.990	3.839	3.567	3.331	2.500
28	16.663	13.406	11.051	9.307	7.984	6.961	6.152	5.502	4.970	4.528	4.157	3.992	3.840	3.568	3.331	2.500
29	16.984	13.591	11.158	9.370	8.022	6.983	6.166	5.510	4.975	4.531	4.159	3.994	3.841	3.569	3.332	2.500
30	17.292	13.765	11.258	9.427	8.055	7.003	6.177	5.517	4.979	4.534	4.160	3.995	3.842	3.569	3.332	2.500
40	19.793	15.046	11.925	9.779	8.244	7.105	6.234	5.548	4.997	4.544	4.166	3.999	3.846	3.571	3.333	2.500

Subtract Eq. (4) from Eq. (3)

$$PV_A - PV_A \left(\frac{1}{1.06}\right) = \frac{1}{1.06} - \frac{1}{(1.06)^4} \tag{5}$$

Factor
$$PV_A \left(1 - \frac{1}{1.06}\right) = \frac{1}{1.06}\left[1 - \frac{1}{(1.06)^3}\right] \tag{6}$$

or
$$PV_A \left(\frac{.06}{1.06}\right) = \frac{1}{1.06}\left[1 - \frac{1}{(1.06)^3}\right] \tag{7}$$

Divide by $\frac{.06}{1.06}$
$$PV_A = \frac{1}{.06}\left[1 - \frac{1}{(1.06)^3}\right] \tag{8}$$

The general formula for the present worth of an annuity is:

$$PV_A = \frac{1}{i}\left[1 - \frac{1}{(1+i)^n}\right] \tag{9}$$

Solving
$$PV_A = \frac{1}{.06}(1 - .840) = \frac{.160}{.06} = 2.67 \tag{10}$$

This formula is the basis for Table 2 (p. 380). Check the answer in the table. Minor differences are due to rounding.

Use Table 2 to obtain the present values of the following ordinary annuities.

1. $1,600 at 20 per cent for 20 years.
2. $8,300 at 10 per cent for 12 years.
3. $8,000 at 4 per cent for 4 years.

Answers:

1. $1,600 (4.870) = $7,792.
2. $8,300 (6.814) = $56,556.
3. $8,000 (3.630) = $29,040.

ASSIGNMENT MATERIAL

ESSENTIAL ASSIGNMENT MATERIAL

14-1. *Terminology.* Define: capital budgeting; time-adjusted rate of return; net present value method; payback; payout; payoff; unadjusted rate of return; accounting method; book value method; total project approach; and incremental approach.

14-2. *Exercises in compound interest: answers supplied.** Use the appropriate interest tables to compute the following:

a. It is your sixty-fifth birthday. You plan to work five more years before retiring. Then you want to take $5,000 for a round-the-world tour. What lump sum do you have to invest now in order to accumulate the $5,000? Assume that your minimum desired rate of return is:

(1) 4 per cent, compounded annually.
(2) 10 per cent, compounded annually.
(3) 20 per cent, compounded annually.

* The answers appear after Problem 14-5.

b. It is your sixty-fifth birthday. You plan to work five more years before retiring. You want to spend $500 on a vacation each year. What lump sum do you have to invest now in order to take the five vacations? Assume that your minimum desired rate of return is:

(1) 4 per cent, compounded annually.
(2) 10 per cent, compounded annually.
(3) 20 per cent, compounded annually.

c. At age 60, you find that your employer is moving to another location. You receive termination pay of $5,000. You have some savings and wonder whether to retire now.

(1) If you invest the $5,000 now at 4 per cent, compounded annually, how much money can you withdraw from your account each year so that at the end of five years there will be a zero balance?
(2) If you invest it at 10 per cent?

d. At 16 per cent, compounded annually, which of the following plans is more desirable in terms of present values? Show computations.

	Annual Cash Inflows	
Year	Mining	Farming
1 .862	$10,000	$ 2,000
2 .743	8,000	4,000
3 .641	6,000	6,000
4 .552	4,000	8,000
5 .476	2,000	10,000
	$30,000	$30,000

14-3. *Comparison of capital budgeting techniques.* The Bower Co. is considering the purchase of a new packaging machine at a cost of $20,000. It should save $4,000 in cash operating costs per year. Its estimated useful life is eight years, and it will have zero disposal value.

Required:

1. Payback time.
2. Net present value if the minimum rate of return desired is 10 per cent. Should the company buy? Why?
3. Time-adjusted rate of return.

14-4. *Replacement of equipment.* Refer to Problem 13-2. Assume that the new equipment will cost $100,000 in cash, and that the old machine cost $81,000 and can be sold now for $16,000 cash.

Required:

1. Net present value of the proposed equipment, assuming that the minimum desired rate of return is 10 per cent.
2. Payback period for the proposed equipment.

14-5. *Replacement decision.* The Ajax Railroad has been operating a dining car on its lone passenger train. Yearly operations have shown a consistent loss, as follows:

Revenue (in cash)		$100,000
Expenses for food, supplies, etc. (in cash)	$50,000	
Salaries	60,000	110,000
Net loss (ignore depreciation on the dining car itself)		($10,000)

The Auto-vend Co. has offered to sell automatic vending machines to Ajax for $22,000, less a $3,000 trade-in allowance on old equipment (which is carried at $2,000 book value, and which can be sold outright for $2,000 cash) now used in the dining car operation.

The useful life of the vending equipment is estimated at ten years, with zero scrap value. The equipment will serve 50 per cent more food than the dining car handled, but prices will be 50 per cent less. A catering company will completely service and supply the machines. The variety of food will be the same as prevailed for the dining car. The catering company will pay 10 per cent of gross receipts to the Ajax Co. and will bear all costs of food, repairs, etc. All dining car employees will be discharged. Their termination pay will total $5,000. However, an attendant who has some general knowledge of vending machines will be needed for one shift per day. The annual cost to Ajax for the attendant will be $6,500.

The railroad will definitely not abandon its food service.

Required:

Using the above data, carefully compute the following. Label computations. Ignore income taxes.

1. Payback period.
2. The incremental net present value, in dollars, of the proposed investment. Assume a minimum desired rate of return of 20 per cent.

Solutions to Exercises in Compound Interest, Problem 14-2.

The general approach to these exercises centers about one key question: Which of the two basic tables am I dealing with? No calculations should be made until after this question is answered with assurance. If you made any errors, it is possibly because you used the wrong table.

a. From Table 1, p. 378.
   (1) $4,110
   (2) $3,105
   (3) $2,010

The $5,000 is an *amount* or *future worth.* You want the present value of that amount:

$$PV = \frac{S}{(1+i)^n}$$

The conversion factor, $\frac{1}{(1+i)^n}$, is on line 5 of Table 1.

Substituting:

(1) $PV = \$5,000 \,(.822) = \$4,110$
(2) $PV = \$5,000 \,(.621) = \$3,105$
(3) $PV = \$5,000 \,(.402) = \$2,010$

Note that the higher the interest rate, the lower the present value.
  b. From Table 2, p. 380.
    (1) $2,226.00
    (2) $1,895.50
    (3) $1,495.50

The $500 withdrawal is a uniform annual amount—an annuity. You need to find the present value of an annuity for five years:

$$PV_A = \text{Annual withdrawal } (F), \text{ where } F \text{ is the conversion factor.}$$

Substituting:

(1) $$PV_A = \$500 \ (4.452) = \$2,226.00$$
(2) $$PV_A = \$500 \ (3.791) = \$1,895.50$$
(3) $$PV_A = \$500 \ (2.991) = \$1,495.00$$

  c. From Table 2:
    (1) $1,123.97
    (2) $1,318.91

You have $5,000, the present value of your contemplated annuity. You must find the annuity that will just exhaust the invested principal in five years:

(1)
$$PV_A = \text{Annual withdrawal } (F)$$

$$\$5,000 = \text{Annual withdrawal } (4.452)$$
$$\text{Annual withdrawal} = \$5,000 \div 4.452$$
$$= \$1,123.97$$

(2)
$$\$5,000 = \text{Annual withdrawal } (3.791)$$
$$\text{Annual withdrawal} = \$5,000 \div 3.791$$
$$= \$1,318.91$$

  d. From Table 1. Mining is preferable; its present value exceeds farming by $3,852.

Year	Present Value Factors, @ 16 Per Cent, from Table 1	Present Value of Mining	Present Value of Farming
1	.862	$ 8,620	$ 1,724
2	.743	5,944	2,972
3	.641	3,846	3,846
4	.552	2,208	4,416
5	.476	952	4,760
		$21,570	$17,718

Note that the nearer dollars are more valuable than the distant dollars.

ADDITIONAL ASSIGNMENT MATERIAL

Note: Problems 14-25 and 14-27 are particularly challenging. Problems 14-28 and 14-29 provide a review. Those readers who want to compare the results of time-adjusted and unadjusted, or accounting, rate-of-return methods will be interested in Problems 14-23, 14-26 and 14-27.

  14-6. "Problem solving is project-oriented rather than time-period oriented." Explain.

14-7. Why is capital budgeting likely to receive increasing attention?

14-8. Why is discounted cash flow a superior method for capital budgeting?

14-9. Why should depreciation be excluded from discounted-cash-flow computations?

14-10. Can net present value ever be negative? Why?

14-11. "The higher the minimum rate of return desired, the higher the price that a company will be willing to pay for cost-saving equipment." Do you agree? Explain.

14-12. Why should the incremental approach to alternatives always lead to the same decision as the total project approach?

14-13. "Current disposal values of equipment are always relevant to a replacement decision." Do you agree? Explain.

14-14. "Discounted-cash-flow approaches will not work if the competing projects have unequal lives." Do you agree? Explain.

14-15. Some perceptive observer in ancient times said, "A little knowledge is a dangerous thing." How might this apply in capital budgeting?

14-16. State a rule that can serve as a general guide to capital budgeting decisions.

14-17. "If discounted-cash-flow approaches are superior to the payback and the accounting methods, why should we bother to learn the others? All it does is confuse things." Answer this contention.

14-18. What is the basic flaw in the payback method?

14-19. How can the payback method be adjusted to yield satisfactory indications of relative profitability?

14-20. Compare the unadjusted rate of return approach and the discounted-cash-flow approach to the time value of money.

14-21. *Discounted cash flow, uneven revenue stream, relevant costs.* Mr. Divot is the owner of a nine-hole golf course on the outskirts of a large city. He is considering the proposal that this golf course be illuminated and operated at night. Mr. Divot purchased the course early last year for $75,000. His receipts from operations during the 28-week season were $24,000. Total disbursements for the year, for all purposes, were $15,500.

The required investment in lighting this course is estimated at $20,000. 150 lamps of 1,000 watts each will be required. Electricity costs 3.2¢ per kilowatt-hour. The expected average hours of operation per night is five. Because of occasional bad weather and the probable curtailment of night operation at the beginning and end of the season, it is estimated that there will be only 130 nights of operation per year. Labor for keeping the course open at night will cost $15 per night. Lamp renewals are estimated at $300 per year; other maintenance and repairs, per year, will amount to 4 per cent of the initial cost of the lighting system. Property taxes on this equipment will be about 2 per cent of its initial cost. It is estimated that the average revenue, per night of operation, will be $90 for the first two years.

Considering the probability of competition from the illumination of other golf courses, Mr. Divot decides that he will not make the investment unless he can make at least 10 per cent per annum on his investment. Because of anticipated competition, revenue is expected to drop to $60 per night for Years 3 through 5. It is estimated that the lighting equipment will have a salvage value of $8,000 at the end of the five-year period.

Using discounted cash-flow techniques, determine whether Mr. Divot should install the lighting system.

14-22. *Replacing office equipment.* The Gardner Co. is considering replacing its present manual bookkeeping machines (NCR) with faster machines purchased from IBM. The administration is very concerned about the rising costs of operations during the last decade.

In order to convert to IBM, two operators would have to be sent to school. Required remodeling would cost $2,000.

Gardner's three NCR machines were purchased for $10,000 each, five years ago. Their expected life was ten years. Their resale value now is $3,000 each, and will be zero in five more years. The new IBM equipment will cost $30,000, and also has zero disposal value in five years.

The three NCR operators are paid $2 an hour each. They usually work a 40-hour week. Machine breakdowns occur monthly on each machine, resulting in repair costs of $25 per month and overtime of four hours, at time-and-one-half, per machine per month, to complete the normal monthly workload. Paper, supplies, etc., cost $25 a month for each NCR.

The IBM system will require only two regular operators, on a reduced work week of 30 hours each, to do the same work. Rates are $3 an hour and no overtime is expected. Paper, supplies, etc. will cost $1,200 annually. Maintenance and repairs are fully serviced by IBM for $150 annually.

Required:

1. Using discounted cash flow techniques, compute the present value of all relevant cash flows, under both alternatives, for the five-year period discounted at 12 per cent.

2. Should Gardner keep the NCR machines or replace them, if the decision is based solely on the given data?

3. What other considerations might affect the decision?

14-23. *Make or buy, discounted cash flow, and unadjusted rate of return.* Refer to Problem 13-29.

1. Using a net present value analysis, which alternative is most attractive? Assume that the minimum rate of return desired is 8 per cent.

2. Using the unadjusted (accounting) rate-of-return method, what is the rate of return on the initial investment?

14-24. *Cafeteria facilities.* The cafeteria of an office building is open 250 days a year. It offers typical cafeteria-line service. At the noon meal (open to the public), serving-line facilities can accommodate 200 people per hour for the two-hour serving period. The average customer has a thirty-minute lunch hour. Serving facilities are unable to handle the overflow of noon customers with the result that, daily, 200 dissatisfied customers who do not wish to stand in line choose to eat elsewhere. Projected over a year, this results in a considerable loss to the cafeteria.

To tap this excess demand, the cafeteria is considering two alternatives: (*a*) installing two vending machines, at a cost of $5,000 apiece; or (*b*) completely revamping present serving-line facilities with new equipment, at a cost of $80,000. The vending machines and serving-line equipment have a useful life of ten years and will be depreciated on a straight-line basis. The minimum desired rate of return for the cafeteria is 10 per cent. The average sale is $1.50, with a contribution margin of 30 per cent. This will remain the same if new serving-line facilities are installed.

Data for alternative *a* (vending machines) are as follows:

Service cost per year is $300; salvage value of each machine at the end of ten years is $500. The price of a sandwich is $.90; salad, $.20; dessert, $.20; milk or coffee, $.20. Contribution margin is 20 per cent. It is estimated that 60 per cent of the dissatisfied customers will use the vending machines and will have a full lunch. The estimated salvage value of the present equipment will net $2,000 at the end of the 10-year period.

Data for alternative *b* (new serving line facilities) are as follows:

Yearly salary for an extra check-girl, $4,000; salvage value of old equipment is $5,000; salvage value of new equipment, at the end of ten years, is $10,000; cost of dismantling old equipment is $1,000. It is estimated that all of the previously dissatisfied customers will use the new facilities.

All other costs are the same under both alternatives and need not be considered.

Using the discounted-cash-flow method, which is the better alternative?

14-25. *Desirability of cash offer for baseball pitcher.* The Los Angeles Mocking Birds of the Continental Baseball League have a pitcher by the name of Bo Peep. The Mocking Birds claim Bo is the fastest pitcher in organized baseball, and there is not an opposing batter in the Continental League who will contest this point. Bo has led the League in striking out opponents in each of the last three years. But he is inconsistent and has lost as many games as he has won.

Statistics furnished by the League indicate that attendance increases by 3,000 fans every time Bo is the starting pitcher. In the opinion of the League secretary and the general managers throughout the League, this rise in attendance is solely attributable to Bo's pitching. The additional 3,000 fans bring in an average of $2 each in gross ticket revenue—60 per cent of which is a contribution margin. There are ten teams in the League. Each team plays the other 18 times, for a total of 162 games. The contribution margin is kept by the home team, except that the visiting team receives 36 cents per ticket. Bo is expected to start 36 games a year. He faces each opposing team the same number of times; half at home, half at the opponents' stadium. Bo's salary for the coming year, 19x6, is $15,000, and an annual raise of $1,500 per year is virtually assured.

On Jan. 1, 19x6, Frank Bane, general manager of the San Francisco Midgets of the Continental Baseball League, made a cash offer of $200,000 for Bo Peep's services. Bane, if able to obtain Bo, plans to have him pitch in the same pattern and with the same frequency as he pitched for the Mocking Birds. The Mocking Birds have told Bane they will decide on his offer in 10 days.

If the Mocking Birds accept Bane's offer, they plan to purchase James Bushleague from a minor league team for $25,000 cash. The Mocking Birds feel certain that James can equal Bo's won-lost record. Bushleague's salary for 19x6, in the event of his purchase, would be $8,000, with an annual raise of $500 per year.

Assume that all salaries are paid at the end of the year (Dec. 31) and that all income from extra attendance attributable to Bo's pitching is received at the end of the year (Dec. 31). The minimum rate of return desired by the Los Angeles Mocking Birds is 10 per cent.

1. Should the Los Angeles Mocking Birds sell Bo Peep to the San Francisco Midgets? Base your answer on a five-year analysis, using discounted-cash-flow techniques.

2. What would be the effect on the transaction if the same offer was made for Bo's services from a team in another league?

3. List several possible benefits in retaining Bo which were not considered in this problem.

14-26. *Comparison of unadjusted method and time-adjusted method.* Tony's Pizza Co. makes and sells frozen pizzas to local retail outlets. Tony just inherited $10,000 and has decided to invest it in the business. He is trying to decide between:

   Alternative *a*: Buy a $10,000 contract, payable immediately, from a local reputable sales promotion agency. The agency would provide various advertising services, as specified in the contract, over the next ten years. Tony is convinced that the sales promotion would increase cash inflow from operations, through increased volume, by $2,000 a year for the first five years, and by $1,000 per year thereafter. There would be no effect after the ten years had elapsed.

   Alternative *b*: Buy new mixing and packaging equipment, at a cost of $10,000, which would reduce operating cash outflows by $1,500 per year for the next ten years. The equipment would have zero salvage value at the end of the ten years.

Neglect any tax effect.

1. Compute the rates of return on initial investment by the unadjusted (accounting) method for both alternatives.

2. Compute the rates of return by the discounted cash flow method for both alternatives.

3. Are the rates of return different under the discounted cash flow method? Explain.

14-27. *New equipment and analysis of operating costs: unadjusted rate of return.* The processing department of Hay Co. has incurred the following costs in producing 150,000 units, which is normal volume, during the past year:

Variable	$100,000
Fixed	50,000
	$150,000

The department has been offered some new processing equipment. The salesman says that the new equipment will reduce unit costs by 20¢. The department's old equipment has a remaining useful life of five years, has zero disposal value now, and is being depreciated on a straight-line basis at $5,000 annually. The new equipment's straight line depreciation would be $30,000 annually. It would last five years and have no disposal value. The salesman pointed out that over-all unit costs now are $1, while the new equipment is being used by one of Hay's competitors to produce an identical product at a unit cost of 80¢, computed as follows:

Variable costs	$ 80,000
Fixed costs*	80,000
Total costs	$160,000
Divide by units produced	200,000
Cost per unit	80¢

* Fixed costs include $30,000 depreciation on the new equipment. Hay's supervisory payroll is $10,000 less than this competitor's.

The salesman stated that a saving of 20¢ per unit would add $30,000 to Hay's annual net income.

1. Show *specifically* how the salesman computed Hay's costs and prospective savings.
2. As adviser to the Hay Co., evaluate the salesman's contentions and prepare a quantitative summary to support your recommendations for Hay's best course of action. Include the unadjusted rate-of-return method and the net-present-value method in your evaluation. Assume that Hay's minimum desired rate of return is 10 per cent. *I̶m̶p̶o̶r̶t̶a̶n̶t̶*

14-28. *Launching a new product: review of Chapters 13 and 14.* Barden Co. is trying to decide whether to launch a new household product. Through the years, the company has found that its products have a useful life of six years, after which the product is dropped and replaced by other new products. Data follow:

1. The new product will require new special-purpose factory equipment costing $900,000. The useful life of the equipment is six years, with a $140,000 estimated disposal value at that time. However, the Internal Revenue Service will not allow a write-off based on a life shorter than nine years. Therefore, the new equipment would be written off over nine years, using straight line depreciation and zero salvage value.

2. The new product will be produced in an old plant already owned. The plant has a book value of $30,000 and is being depreciated, on a straight-line basis, at $3,000 annually. It is currently being leased to another company at an annual rental of $9,000. This lease has six years remaining. It contains a cancellation clause whereby the landlord can obtain immediate possession of the premises upon payment of $6,000 in cash. The estimated sales value of the building is $80,000; this price should remain stable over the next six years. The plant is likely to be kept for at least ten more years. *irrelevant* *going to cost $9000 a year*

3. Certain nonrecurring market research studies and sales promotion activities will amount to $500,000 during Year 1. The entire amount will be deducted as an expense on the income statement for Year 1. *At the end of Year 1*

4. Additions to working capital will be $200,000 at the outset and an additional $200,000 at the end of Year 2. This total is fully recoverable at the end of Year 6. *Put in a end of year 2 column*

5. Net cash inflow from operations (before consideration of nonrecurring expenses) will be $400,000 in Years 1 and 2, $600,000 in Years 3 through 5, and $100,000 in Year 6.

The company uses discounted-cash-flow techniques for evaluating decisions. In this case, tabulations of differential cash flows would be made from Years 0 through 6. Yearly cash flows are estimated for all items, including capital outlays or recoveries. An applicable discount rate is used to bring all outlays, from Years 1 through 6, back to Year 0. If the summation in Year 0 is positive, the project is desirable, and vice versa.

The minimum rate of return desired is 12 per cent.

Required:

Using an answer sheet, show how you would handle the data listed above for purposes of the decision. Note that you are *not* being asked to apply discount rates. You are being asked for the detailed impact of each of items (1) through (5), in Years 0 through 6.

Each item is to be considered separately. *Do not combine your answers to cover more than one item.*

Assume that all cash flows take place at the end of each period.

Answer Sheet for Problem 14-28.

Item: Description and brief explanation of your computations:

Item	Description	Net Present Value		Cash Flows in Year					
			0	1	2	3	4	5	6
1.									
2.									
3.									
4.									
5.									

Totals for each year Then use TABLE 1 on totals

14-29. *Uses of warehouse: review of Chapters 13 and 14.*

a. The Devine Co. is currently leasing one of its warehouses to another company for $3,000 per year, on a month-to-month basis.

b. The estimated sales value of the warehouse is $12,000. This price is likely to remain unchanged indefinitely—even if a contemplated public expressway results in the building's condemnation. The building originally cost $20,000 and is being depreciated at $500 annually. Its net book value is $9,000.

c. The Devine Co. is seriously considering converting the warehouse into a retail outlet for selling furniture at ridiculously low discount prices. Such an endeavor would entail remodeling, at a cost of $15,000. The remodeling would be extremely modest because the major attraction will be flimsy furniture at rock-bottom prices. The remodeling can be accomplished over a single weekend.

d. The inventory, cash, and receivables needed to open and sustain the retail outlet would be $50,000. This total is fully recoverable whenever operations terminate.

e. The president, who paid an expressway engineer $1,000 to discover when and where the expressway will be built, is virtually certain that the warehouse will be available for no more than four years. He has asked you to give him an analysis of whether the company should continue to lease the warehouse or convert it to a retail outlet, assuming that the minimum annual rate of return desired is 14 per cent over a four-year planning horizon. Estimated annual operating data, exclusive of depreciation, are:

f. Sales	$200,000
f. Operating expenses	177,000
g. Nonrecurring sales promotion costs at *beginning* of year 1	20,000
h. Nonrecurring termination costs at *end* of year 4	10,000

The president has definitely decided not to sell the warehouse until forced to by condemnation proceedings.

Required:

1. Show how you would handle the *individual* items on the company's analysis form, which is set up as follows:

			Cash Flows in Year				
Item	*Description*	*Net Present Value*	*0*	*1*	*2*	*3*	*4*
a.							
b.							
.							
.							
.							
g.							
h.							

Use the following present value factors: *PV* of $1 = .60 and the *PV* of an annuity of $1 = 2.9. Ignore income taxes. If you think an item is irrelevant, leave the space blank.

2. After analyzing all the relevant data, compute the net present value. Indicate which course of action, based on the data alone, should be taken.

CHAPTER 15

Multipurpose Accounting Systems, Product Costing, and Overhead Application

THUS FAR, WE HAVE PAID LITTLE ATTENTION TO THE PRODUCT costing-income determination purpose of an accounting system. The purpose of this chapter is to show how data may be accumulated within an accounting system and how various alternative methods of applying costs to products affect inventories and income determination. These are essentially scorekeeping tasks. Management makes policy decisions, at one time or another, regarding methods of product costing. Because such decisions affect the way net income will be determined, managers should know the various approaches to product costing. Moreover, as we have seen previously, a knowledge of product costing techniques will enhance a manager's understanding of his product costs, particularly when the latter are used for pricing and evaluating product lines.

This chapter has the following major sections: I Actual-Normal Costing; II Problems of Overhead Application; III Direct or Variable Costing, and IV Standard Costs for Product Costing. The discussion is confined to manufacturing costs because accountants almost unanimously view selling, administrative, and other costs as being totally excludable from costs of *product*—that is, as being not inventoriable.

As you study the various product costing techniques in

this chapter, keep in mind that *product costing is separable from control*. That is, a good planning and control system may be coupled with any of a number of product costing theories. In short, how costs are held back in inventory and released to expense should have little bearing (except for income tax planning described in Chapter 16) on the planning and controlling decisions of intelligent managers.

This chapter contains many new terms and, for the first time in this book, deals with the details of journal entries and ledger postings. Consequently, your study may be eased by concentrating on one section at a time rather than by making one big sweep through the entire chapter.

For instance, it will be beneficial to study Section I and to solve Problem 15-2; then Section II and Problems 15-3 and 15-4; Section III and Problem 15-5; Section IV and Problem 15-6. Similarly, the Summary Problem for Your Review may best be approached in sections. Some readers will want to confine their study to only Sections I and II of the chapter; others will wish to study all four sections.

SECTION I: ACTUAL-NORMAL COSTING

Two Routine Purposes of Accounting System

In Chapter 1, we enumerated three purposes of an accounting system: (1) internal reporting for special decisions and long-range plans (the special decision purpose); (2) internal reporting for current planning and control (the control purpose); and (3) external reporting of results and financial position (the product costing-income determination purpose). The special-decision purpose is difficult to satisfy on a routine basis, primarily because the needed information is expected future data, not historical data. The second and third purposes, however, can be fulfilled on a routine basis by designing the accounting system to satisfy both purposes simultaneously.

Control can be achieved by initially charging costs to the particular departments, responsibility centers, or profit centers that have the major responsibility for control of the item in question. In turn, the product costing purpose can be achieved by applying (assigning) the costs to the products that physically flow through the production departments in question.

In principle then, the general system design is straightforward and rests on a rigid distinction between control and product costing (see Exhibit 15-1). There is wide agreement among accountants, managers, and systems experts that control is best attained in *any* organization by initially charging the departments with the costs subject to their control. There is a wide divergence in theory and practice, however, as to the best way for *applying* overhead costs to products. (The credit side of the Department Responsibility Cost Control account is often represented by a completely separate offsetting account, which could be termed "Department Responsibility Costs Applied." Such an *applied* account is similar to

EXHIBIT 15-1

General Systems Design:
Journal Entries for Cost Accumulation and Application

Purpose	*Journal Entries*		
	1. Direct Material Usage, $10,000		
Control	(1*a*) Department *A* responsibility cost control	10,000	
	Direct materials inventory		10,000
Product-costing	(1*b*) Work-in-process inventory	10,000	
	Department *A* responsibility cost control		10,000
	2. Direct Labor Usage, $8,000		
Control	(2*a*) Department *A* responsibility cost control	8,000	
	Accrued payroll or cash		8,000
Product-costing	(2*b*) Work-in-process inventory	8,000	
	Department *A* responsibility cost control		8,000
	3. Manufacturing Overhead Incurred, $4,500		
Control	(3*a*) Department *A* responsibility cost control	4,500	
	Accounts Payable, Allowance for Depreciation, Accrued Payroll, and various other accounts		4,500
Product-costing	(3*b*) Work-in-process inventory	4,500	
	Department *A* responsibility cost control		4,500

Allowance for Depreciation and Allowance for Bad Debts, which offset Fixed Assets and Accounts Receivable.)

Job Costing and Process Costing

The two major product costing techniques are job order costing and process costing. Job order costing is used in companies which produce unique, one-of-a-kind, specialized products or services (e.g., custom furniture, auto repairs, interior decoration, construction). Process costing is used in mass production situations (e.g., the manufacture of paints, rubber, plastics, chemicals, glass).

Unlike process costing, which deals with broad averages and vast quantities of like units, the job cost system is an attempt to apply costs to specific jobs or batches which may consist of a lone unit or of several like units in a separate batch or lot. Typically, different jobs receive varying attention, effort, and types of direct material. Of course, the more refined the costing objective, the more complicated the costing task: job order costing tends to require more score keeping than process costing.

The basic record for the accumulation of job costs is the *job order* or *job cost sheet*. Exhibit 15-2, a Job Cost Sheet, also shows the related source documents. A file of current job cost sheets becomes the subsidiary ledger for the general ledger account, Work-in-process Inventory.

While job cost sheets are the primary score-keeping vehicle for *product costing,* department responsibility control sheets serve *control* purposes. For example, Exhibit 15-3 shows how the details of various costs charged

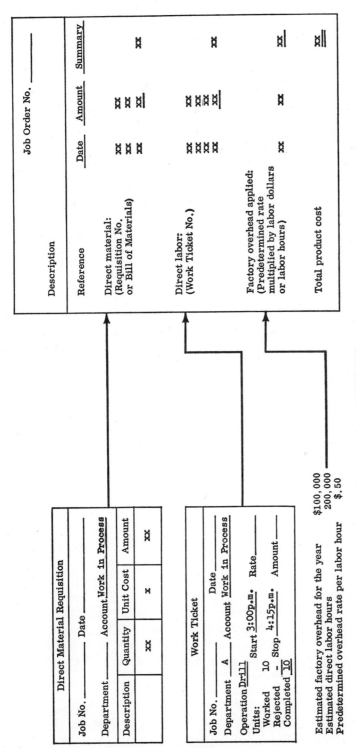

Direct Material Requisition

Job No. _____ Date _____

Department _____ Account Work in Process

Description	Quantity	Unit Cost	Amount
	xx	x	xx

Work Ticket

Job No. _____ Date _____

Department __A__ Account Work in Process

Operation __Drill__

Start __3:00p.m.__ Rate _____

Units:
Worked __10__ Stop __4:15p.m.__ Amount _____
Rejected __-__
Completed __10__

Estimated factory overhead for the year $100,000
Estimated direct labor hours   200,000
Predetermined overhead rate per labor hour $.50

Job Order No. _____

Description   Date   Amount   Summary

Reference

Direct material:
(Requisition No.
or Bill of Materials)   xx   xx
                          xx   xx   xx

Direct labor:
(Work Ticket No.)   xx   xx
                     xx   xx
                     xx   xx   xx

Factory overhead applied:
(Predetermined rate
multiplied by labor dollars
or labor hours)   xx   xx   xx

Total product cost   xxx

EXHIBIT 15-2

Job Cost Sheet

to a particular department may be accumulated. The file of these sheets forms a subsidiary ledger for the general ledger account, Department Responsibility Cost Control.

Illustration of Job Order Costing: Development of Overhead Application Rates

The Malin Company has a job order cost system, and has the following inventories on Dec. 31, 19x1:

Direct materials (12 types)	$110,000
Work in process	—
Finished goods (left-over units from 2 jobs)	12,000

The following manufacturing overhead budget has been prepared for the coming year, 19x2:

	Machining	Assembly
Indirect labor	$ 69,600	$ 28,800
Supplies	14,400	5,400
Utilities	20,000	9,000
Repairs	10,000	6,000
Factory rent	24,000	16,800
Supervision	18,600	20,400
Depreciation on equipment	114,000	14,400
Insurance, property taxes, etc.	7,200	2,400
	$277,800	$103,200

In order to cost units as they are worked on, a job cost sheet is prepared for each job as it begins. Three classes of costs are applied to the units as they pass through the departments: material requisitions are used to apply costs of direct material; work tickets are used to apply costs of direct labor; and predetermined overhead rates are used to apply manufacturing overhead. The overhead rates are as follows:

	Year 19x2	
	Machining	Assembly
Manufacturing overhead	$277,800	$103,200
Machine hours	69,450	
Direct labor cost		$206,400
Rate, per machine hour	$4	
Rate, per direct labor dollar		50%

Overhead is a conglomeration of items which, unlike direct material or direct labor, cannot conveniently be applied on an individual basis. But the commonly accepted theory is that overhead is an integral part of a product's cost. Therefore, it is applied in an indirect manner, using a base which is common to all jobs worked on and which is the best available index of the product's relative utilization of, or benefits from, the overhead items.

Two or more machines in the machining department can often be operated simultaneously by a single direct laborer. Since utilization of machines is the major overhead cost in the machining department,

MACHINING DEPARTMENT RESPONSIBILITY COST CONTROL SHEET

Month of _____

Date	Source Document	Direct Material	Direct Labor	Indirect Labor	Supplies	Utilities	Repairs	Rent	Supervision	Depreciation	Insurance
	Requisitions	xx			xx						
	Labor work tickets, analyses, or recapitulations		xx	xx					xx		
	Invoices					xx	xx	xx			
	Special memos on accruals, prepayments, etc.						xx			xx	xx

EXHIBIT 15-3

Machining Department Responsibility Cost Control Sheet

machine hours are the base for application of overhead costs. This necessitates keeping track of the machine hours used for each job, and thus creates an added clerical burden. Both direct labor costs and machine hours must be accumulated for each job.

In contrast, the assembly workers are paid uniform hourly rates, so the cost of direct labor is an accurate reflection of the relative attention and effort devoted to various jobs. No separate job records have to be kept of the labor *hours*. All that is needed is to apply the 50 per cent overhead rate to the cost of direct labor already applied to the job. Of course, if the hourly labor rates differed greatly for individuals performing identical tasks, hours of labor, rather than dollars spent for labor, would have to be used as a base. Otherwise, a $4 per hour worker would cause more overhead to be applied than a $3 per hour worker, despite the probability that the same time would be taken and the same facilities utilized by each employee to do the same work.

These overhead rates will be used throughout the year to cost the various jobs as they are worked on by each department. All overhead will be applied to all jobs worked on during the year, in proportion to either the machine hours or direct labor costs of each job. If management predictions are accurate, the total overhead applied to the year's jobs on the basis of these predetermined rates should be equal to the total overhead costs actually incurred.

In January, 19x2, several jobs were begun. For example, Job 404 was begun and completed. Exhibit 15-4 is the Completed Job Cost Sheet.

				Job Order No. _____	
		Machining Department			
Reference	Date	Quantity	Unit Cost	Amount	Summary
Direct material:					
Type M – Various requisitions Various		900	$2.00	$1,800	
Type N – Various requisitions Various		900	5.00	4,500	$ 6,300
Direct labor:					
Various work tickets Various		320 hours	2.50	$ 800	800
Factory overhead applied		425 machine hours	4.00	1,700	1,700
Total machining					$ 8,800
		Assembly Department			
(Entries would be similar to above)					xxx
Total assembly (assumed)					$ 2,000
Total product cost					$10,800

EXHIBIT 15-4

Completed Job Cost Sheet

EXHIBIT 15-5

Summary Effects of Job Costing: Actual-Normal Costing System

General Journal

		Debit	Credit
1.	Direct materials inventory	$1,900,000	
	Accounts payable or cash		$1,900,000
	Purchases		
2a.	Department responsibility cost control	1,890,000	
	Direct materials inventory		1,890,000
	Requisitions charged to departments for control purposes		
2b.	Work in process	1,890,000	
	Department responsibility cost control		1,890,000
	Requisitions applied to jobs for product costing purposes		
3a.	Department responsibility cost control	390,000	
	Accrued payroll or cash		390,000
	Work tickets charged to departments for control purposes		
3b.	Work in process	390,000	
	Department responsibility cost control		390,000
	Work tickets applied to jobs for product costing purposes		
4a.	Department responsibility cost control	392,000	
	Cash, accounts payable, and various accounts		392,000
	Overhead charged to departments as incurred for control purposes		
4b.	Work in process	375,000	
	Department responsibility cost control		375,000
	Overhead applied to products, using predetermined application rates		
5.	Finished goods	2,500,000	
	Work in process		2,500,000
	To transfer costs of goods completed		
6a.	Accounts receivable or cash	3,000,000	
	Sales		3,000,000
6b.	Cost of goods sold	2,480,000	
	Finished goods		2,480,000

General Ledger (Selected Accounts)

Department Responsibility Cost Control

Control Purpose:		Product Costing Purpose:	
2a. Direct material	$1,890,000	2b. Applied	$1,890,000
3a. Direct labor	390,000	3b. Applied	390,000
4a. Factory overhead	392,000	4b. Applied	375,000

Direct Materials

Bal. $	110,000	2a.	$1,890,000
1.	1,900,000		

Work in Process

2b.	$1,890,000	5.	$2,500,000
3b.	390,000		
4b.	375,000		

Finished Goods

Bal.	12,000	6b.	2,480,000
5.	2,500,000		

Cost of Goods Sold

6b.	2,480,000

Subsidiary Ledger (Selected)

Department Cost Sheets

Assembly

Machining

Direct Material	Direct Labor	In-direct Labor	Supplies	Various

Job Cost Sheets

Direct Material

Direct Labor

Applied Overhead

The bulk of the score keeping is a detailed recording and summarization of source documents such as requisitions, work tickets, invoices, and so on.

The following is a summary of events for the year 19x2:

Related to Journal Entry Number	Machining	Assembly	Total
1. Direct materials purchased	—	—	$1,900,000
2. Direct materials requisitioned	$1,000,000	$890,000	1,890,000
3. Direct labor costs incurred	200,000	190,000	390,000
4a. Factory overhead *incurred* (machine hours worked, 70,000)	290,000	102,000	392,000
4b. Factory overhead *applied* (50 per cent of direct labor costs, 70,000 machine hours @ $4)	280,000	95,000	95,000 280,000
5. Cost of goods completed	—	—	2,500,000
6a. Sales	—	—	3,000,000
6b. Cost of goods sold	—	—	2,480,000

Exhibit 15-5 shows how the general ledger acounts would be affected by the above transactions. A careful study of this exhibit should yield insight into many relationships, particularly those between the subsidiary ledgers and the general ledger. A file of department cost sheets supports the charges to Department Responsibility Cost Control, while a file of job cost sheets supports Work in Process.

Nature of Actual-Normal Costing

The over-all system we have just described is sometimes called an actual costing system, because every effort is made to trace the actual costs, as incurred, to the physical units benefited. However, it is only partly an actual system, because the overhead, by definition, cannot be definitely assigned to physical products. Instead, overhead is applied on an average or normalized basis, in order to get representative or normal inventory valuations. Hence, we shall label the system an *actual-normal* system. The cost of the manufactured product is composed of actual direct material, actual direct labor, and normal applied overhead.

Relationships Among Source Documents, Subsidiary Ledgers, and General Ledger

The source documents, such as material requisitions or work tickets, which were illustrated in Exhibit 15-2, are usually made in multiple copies, each being used for a specific task. For example, a materials requisition could be executed by a foreman in as many as five copies and disposed of as follows:

1. Kept by storekeeper who issues the materials.
2. Used by job order cost clerk to post the Job Cost Sheet (Exhibit 15-2).
3. Used by cost control clerk to post the Direct Material Used column of Department Responsibility Cost Control Sheet (Exhibit 15-3).

4. Used by general ledger clerk as a basis for a summary monthly entry for all of the month's requisitions (Exhibit 15-5).
5. Retained by the foreman. He can use the requisition as a cross check against the performance reports which show his usage of material.

Of course, machine accounting and electronic computer systems can use a single punched card as a requisition. Sorting, re-sorting, classifications, reclassifications, summaries, and re-summaries can easily provide any desired information. Because these source documents are the foundation for data accumulation and reports, the importance of accurate initial recording cannot be overemphasized.

Copies of these source documents are used for direct postings in subsidiary ledgers. Sometimes the subsidiary ledgers will contain summarized postings of daily batches of source documents, rather than individual direct postings. Accounting data are most condensed in the general ledger and most detailed on the source documents, as the following listing shows.

Item

Work in Process	General ledger (usually monthly totals only)
Job Cost Sheets	Subsidiary ledgers (perhaps daily summaries)
Material requisitions or work tickets	Source documents (minute to minute, hour to hour)

The daily score-keeping duties are accomplished with source documents and subsidiary ledgers. Copies of the source documents are independently summarized, and are usually posted to the general ledger only once a month. See Entry 2a, Exhibit 15-5, where, for convenience, a year was used, rather than a month.

In order to obtain a bird's-eye view of a system, we have been concentrating on general ledger relationships. However, keep in mind that the general ledger is a very small part of the accountant's daily work. Furthermore, current control is aided by hourly, daily, or weekly flash reports of material, labor, and machine usage. The general ledger itself is a summary device. Reliance on the general ledger for current control is ill-advised, because the resulting reports come too late and are often too stale for management control use.

Before reading on, you may find it helpful to prepare answers to the actual-normal phase of Requirements 1 and 2 of the Summary Problem for Your Review and also to solve Assignment Problem 15-2.

SECTION II: PROBLEMS OF OVERHEAD APPLICATION

Actual Overhead Rates

A few accountants favor delaying application of overhead until all overhead costs for the year are known. Then, using an average rate, they apply all these costs to all jobs that have been worked on throughout the year. In such a case, Entry 4*b* in Exhibit 15-5 would be $392,000 instead of $375,000. All costs incurred would be exactly offset by costs applied. All costs would be easily and neatly acounted for.

Most organizations would find this approach unsatisfactory because of management's need for a close approximation of the costs of different products before the end of a fiscal period. Essentially, this need is for pricing, income determination, and inventory valuation. Moreover, there is a growing objection to the view that all costs incurred must be fully applied to the products. Some costs result from inefficiency, and these can hardly be viewed as being inventoriable as assets. Customers are rarely willing to pay for inefficiency.

Normalized Overhead Rates

Basically, Exhibit 15-5 demonstrates the normalized approach. Overhead application rates are predetermined by dividing total *budgeted* overhead by an appropriate base like machine hours, direct labor hours, or direct labor dollars. The basic idea is to use an annual average overhead rate consistently throughout the year, for product costing, *without altering it from day to day and from month to month*. The resultant actual-normal product costs include an average or normalized chunk of overhead.

As actual overhead costs are incurred by departments from month to month, they are charged, in detail, to the Department Responsibility Cost Control Sheets and, in summary, to Department Responsibility Cost Control. These costs are accumulated weekly or monthly and are then compared with budgeted costs, to obtain budget variances for performance evaluation. This *control* process is completely divorced from the *product costing* process of applying overhead to specific jobs.

During the year and at year-end, it is unlikely that the amount incurred and applied will be equal. This variance between incurred and applied cost may be analyzed. The following are usually contributory causes: poor forecasting; inefficient use of overhead items; price changes in individual overhead items; erratic behavior of individual overhead items (e.g., repairs made only during slack time); calendar variations (i.e., 20 workdays in one month, 22 in the next); and, probably most important, operating at a different level of volume than the level used as a denominator in calculating the predetermined overhead rate (e.g., using 100,000 direct·labor hours as the denominator and then working 80,000 hours).

All of these peculiarities of overhead are commingled in an annual overhead pool. Thus, an annual rate is predetermined and used regardless of the month-to-month peculiarities of specific overhead costs. Such an approach is more defensible than, say, applying the actual overhead for each month, because an *actual-normal* product cost is more meaningful, and more representative for inventory costing purposes, than a so-called actual product cost that is distorted by month-to-month fluctuations in production volume and by the erratic behavior of many overhead costs. For example, the employees of a gypsum plant had the privilege of buying company-made items "at cost." It was a joke common among employees to buy "at cost" during high-volume months. Unit costs were then lower under the actual overhead application system in use, whereby fixed overhead rates would fall as volume soared, and vice versa:

	Actual Overhead			Direct Labor Hours	Actual Overhead Application Rate* per Direct Labor Hour
	Variable	*Fixed*	*Total*		
Peak volume month	$60,000	$40,000	$100,000	100,000	$1.00
Low volume month	30,000	40,000	70,000	50,000	1.40

* This over-all rate can be separated into two rates, one for variable overhead and one for fixed overhead.

Another example of the difficulties of product costing was cited by James Lorie, who, after completing a consulting task for Chrysler Corporation in the middle 1950's, asked some top Chrysler executives if he could buy an Imperial automobile directly from the company "at cost." The response was, "We'll be happy to sell an Imperial to you at cost, which this year happens to be 120 per cent of list price."

Disposition of Underapplied or Overapplied Overhead

When predetermined rates are used, the difference between incurred and applied overhead is typically untouched during the year. When the amount applied to product exceeds the amount incurred by the departments, the difference is called *over-applied* or *over-absorbed* overhead; when the amount applied is less than incurred, the difference is called *under-applied* or *under-absorbed*. The amounts incurred and applied accumulate on each side of the Department Responsibility Cost Control account, and the difference fluctuates from month to month. At year-end, however, the difference is eliminated by one *or* the other of the entries:

1. Cost of goods sold (or a separate charge against revenue)   17,000
    Department responsibility cost control   17,000

   To close ending under-applied overhead directly to Cost of Goods Sold where the bulk of the costs of the goods worked on are now lodged. This is the most widely used approach. Another justification for direct write-off against current income is the notion that unutilized overhead costs are not assets. They should be written off because they largely represent inefficiency or under-utilization of available facilities.

2. Work in process   994
   Finished goods   205
   Cost of goods sold   15,801
      Department responsibility cost control   17,000

   To prorate ending under-applied overhead among the accounts where the costs of the 19x2 jobs worked on are now lodged. Theoretically, if the objective is to obtain as accurate a cost allocation as possible, all of the costs of the individual jobs worked on should be recomputed, using the actual rather than the original predetermined rates. This approach is rarely feasible, so the best practical attack is probably to prorate on the basis of the costs of the 19x2 jobs in each of three accounts (Work in Process, $155,000; Finished Goods, $32,000; and Cost of Goods Sold, $2,480,000), assuming that the beginning Finished Goods Inventory was sold during 19x2:

	(1) *Unadjusted Balance,* *End of 19x2**	*(2)* *Deduct 19x1* *Jobs*	*(3)* *(1)-(2)* *Basis for* *Proration*
Work in process	$155,000	$ —	$155,000
Finished goods	32,000	—	32,000
Cost of goods sold	2,480,000	12,000	2,468,000
			$2,655,000

	(4) *Proration of Under-* *applied Overhead*		*(1) + (4)* *Adjusted* *Balance* *End* *of 19x2*
	$155/2,655 \times 17,000 =$	$994	$155,994
	$32/2,655 \times 17,000 =$	205	32,205
	$2,468/2,655 \times 17,000 =$	15,801	2,495,801
		$17,000	

* See Exhibit 15-5 for details.

The amounts prorated here are not significant. In practical situations, prorating is done only when inventory valuations would be significantly affected.

In sum, overhead application will rarely coincide with overhead incurrence (e.g., Entry 4b in Exhibit 15-5 will not exactly offset Entry 4a). A difference will arise (i.e., Entry 4b, compared with Entry 4a, shows a $17,000 under-application). This under- or overapplication is typically disposed of at year-end by a direct charge or credit to Income or to Cost of Goods Sold, even though it pertains to other accounts as well as Cost of Goods Sold and there may therefore be some conceptual justification for prorating it.

The Use of Variable and Fixed Application Rates

As we have seen, overhead application is the most troublesome aspect of product costing. The presence of fixed costs is the biggest single reason for the costing difficulties. Most companies have made no distinction between variable and fixed cost behavior in the design of their accounting systems. For instance, reconsider the development of overhead rates in the Illustration used on p. 396. The machining department developed the rate as follows:

$$\text{Overhead application rate} = \frac{\text{Expected total overhead}}{\text{Expected machine hours}} = \frac{\$277{,}800}{69{,}450}$$

$$= \$4 \text{ per machine hour}$$

Many companies distinguish between variable overhead and fixed overhead for product costing as well as for control purposes. This distinction could have been made in the machining department. Rent, supervision, depreciation, and insurance might have been considered the fixed portion of the total manufacturing overhead, and two rates could have been developed:

$$\text{Variable overhead application rate} = \frac{\text{Expected total variable overhead}}{\text{Expected machine hours}}$$

$$= \frac{\$114{,}000}{69{,}450} = \$1.64 \text{ per machine hour}$$

$$\text{Fixed overhead application rate} = \frac{\text{Expected total fixed overhead}}{\text{Expected machine hours*}}$$

$$= \frac{\$163{,}800}{69{,}450} = \$2.36 \text{ per machine hour}$$

* Alternatively, the denominator could be a measure of practical capacity.

Such rates can be used for product costing, and distinctions between variable and fixed overhead incurrence can also be made for control purposes.

At this point, prepare the actual-normal part of Requirement 3 of the Summary Problem for Your Review and solve Assignment Problems 15-3 and 15-4.

SECTION III: DIRECT OR VARIABLE COSTING

The distinctions between variable and fixed overhead rates have prompted many accountants to reexamine their procedures for product costing and have led to two opposing ideas. The first idea has been commonly labeled *absorption costing*. It is the notion described in the previous section, that *both* variable and fixed manufacturing overhead should be absorbed as a product cost. The opposing idea has been commonly called *direct costing*. It is the notion that *fixed* overhead should be excluded from product costs.

Direct costing is more accurately called *variable* or *marginal costing*, because in essence it is the product costing method which applies only the variable production costs to the cost of the product. Direct costing differs from absorption costing because fixed manufacturing overhead is regarded as a period cost (charged against revenue immediately) rather than as a product cost (assigned to units produced).

Direct costing has been the subject of heated controversy among ac-

EXHIBIT 15-5

Comparison of Absorption and Direct Costing
(Data assumed; there is no beginning inventory)

B CO.

Income Statements

For the Year Ending Dec. 31, 19x2

Absorption Costing

	Unit Cost		
Sales: 10,000 units, @ $14			$140,000
Cost of goods sold:			
Variable manufacturing costs, 12,000 units	$ 7	$ 84,000	
Fixed manufacturing costs	3	36,000	
Total cost of goods available for sale	$10	$120,000	
Less ending inventory, 2,000 units	10	20,000	100,000
Gross profit			$ 40,000
Less total selling and administrative expenses, including $20,000 of variable expenses			29,000
Net income			$ 11,000

Direct or Variable Costing

Sales		$140,000
Variable manufacturing cost of goods produced	$84,000	
Less ending inventory, 2,000 units, @ $7	14,000	
Variable manufacturing cost of goods sold	$70,000	
Variable selling and administrative expenses	20,000	
Total variable costs charged against sales		90,000
Contribution margin		$ 50,000
Less fixed costs, all of which are charged against sales:		
Fixed manufacturing costs	$36,000	
Fixed selling and administrative expenses	9,000	45,000
Net income		$ 5,000

Note: The $6,000 difference in net income is caused by the $6,000 (i.e., $20,000 − $14,000) difference in ending inventory. Under absorption costing, $6,000 of the $36,000 fixed manufacturing costs is held back in inventory; under direct costing, the $6,000 is released immediately as a charge against sales.

countants—not so much because there is disagreement about the need for delineating between variable and fixed cost behavior patterns for management planning and control, but because there is question about its theoretical propriety for external reporting. Proponents of direct costing maintain that the fixed part of factory overhead is more closely related to the *capacity* to produce than to the production of specific units. Opponents of direct costing maintain that inventories should carry a fixed cost component because both variable and fixed costs are necessary to produce goods; both these costs should be inventoriable regardless of their differences in behavior patterns. The public accounting profession and the Internal Revenue Service have not approved of direct costing as a generally acceptable method of inventory valuation.

The notion of direct costing blends easily with the contribution margin approach so heavily advocated in this text. Exhibit 15-6 illustrates the principal differences between direct costing and absorption costing. Note the following points about the exhibit:

1. Under absorption costing, fixed production costs are applied to the product, to be subsequently released to expense as a part of Cost of Goods Sold. Under direct costing, fixed production costs are regarded as period costs and are immediately released to expense along with the selling and administrative expenses.

2. Under direct costing, only the variable manufacturing costs are regarded as product costs. Variability with manufacturing volume is the criterion used for the classification of costs into product or period categories.

3. The term "direct costing" is misleading, compared with the use of the word "direct" in absorption product costing (e.g., direct material, direct labor). In direct costing, the variable manufacturing overhead is considered a direct cost of production; in absorption costing, the variable factory overhead is regarded, along with fixed manufacturing overhead, as an indirect cost.

4. The absorption costing statement in Exhibit 15-6 differentiates between the variable and fixed costs only to aid your comparison. Costs are seldom classified as fixed or variable in absorption costing statements.

5. If inventories increase during a period, the direct costing method will generally report less net income than absorption costing; when inventories decrease, direct costing will report more net income than absorption costing. The differences in net income, as the note at the bottom of Exhibit 15-6 indicates, are due *solely* to the difference in accounting for *fixed* manufacturing costs.

Whether direct costing should be acceptable for external reporting need not be of paramount importance to accountants or managers. Company systems can accommodate either method; the important point is that the internal reports should use the contribution approach, which incorporates direct costing, and which is the best available technique for evaluation and control.

Before reading on, you should solve Problem 15-5.

SECTION IV: STANDARD COSTS FOR PRODUCT COSTING

Over-all Approach

Under a standard costing system, much of the clerical effort of tracing requisitions and work tickets to jobs or batches of products is eliminated. Predetermined costs are used for *all* elements of manufacturing cost, not just overhead. Thus, instead of having just a difference between incurred and applied overhead, there will also be a difference between incurred and applied direct material and direct labor (see Exhibit 15-7).

EXHIBIT 15-7

Department Responsibility Cost Control		*Work in Process*
Control Purpose:	Product Costing Purpose:	
1. Actual quantities × actual unit prices	2. Standard quantities allowed × standard unit prices ↔	2. Standard quantities allowed × standard unit prices

The differences between the debit and credit sides of the Department Responsibility Cost Control account are the total variances for direct material, direct labor, variable overhead, and fixed overhead. These variances are analyzed for control purposes. They may be disposed of at year-end, being either directly written-off or prorated among the pertinent accounts, just like under-applied overhead. Work in Process, Finished Goods, and Cost of Goods Sold are recorded at the standard quantities allowed for the good units produced.

Isolation and Disposition of Variances

There is an endless variety of standard cost systems. A good system tries to isolate the variances earlier than might be indicated in the above conceptual scheme. For example, price variances for direct material may be isolated at the time of purchase, as follows:

Direct materials inventory (@ standard unit cost of $1,00)	100,000	
Purchase price variance	10,000	
Accounts payable		110,000
Purchased: 100,000 units, @ actual unit cost of $1.10		

In turn, the producing department may be charged for control purposes at standard unit costs rather than at actual unit costs. In this way, responsibility for *prices* is properly removed from the producing department:

EXHIBIT 15-8

Department Responsibility Cost Control

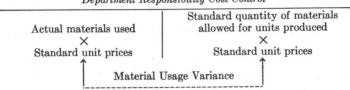

For instance, assume that a producing department used 100,000 units of direct material to produce 90,000 good finished units. It should take one unit of raw material per good finished unit. Entries follow:

Department responsibility cost control	100,000	
Direct materials		100,000
To charge departments with actual quantities at standard unit prices, 100,000 × $1		
Work in process	90,000	
Department responsibility cost control		90,000
To apply costs to product at standard quantities allowed at standard unit prices, 90,000 × $1		

The key account would appear as follows:

EXHIBIT 15-9

Department Responsibility Cost Control

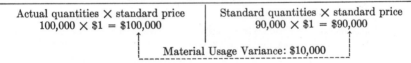

The usage variance can accumulate in Department Responsibility Cost Control, or, when convenient, it can be isolated in the ledger by the following entry:

Direct material usage variance	10,000	
Department responsibility cost control		10,000
To isolate usage variance, 10,000 × $1		

The advocates of currently attainable standard costs for product costing claim that the results are conceptually superior to the results under actual or normal product costing systems. They contend that variances are measures of inefficiency or abnormal efficiency. Therefore, variances are not inventoriable and should be completely charged or credited against the revenue of the period instead of being prorated over inventories and cost of goods sold. In this way, inventory valuations will be more representative of desirable and attainable costs.

In practice, the direct charging or crediting of variances to Cost of Goods Sold is considered acceptable as long as the standards are currently attainable or as long as the net income and inventory figures are not greatly distorted. Many accountants favor showing the variances as completely separate deductions after the gross profit on sales. This helps to distinguish between product costing (i.e., Cost of Goods Sold, at standard) and loss recognition (unfavorable variances are lost costs because inefficiencies are not inventoriable).

For a complete example of a standard costing system, see the Summary Problem for Your Review at the end of this chapter. If you understand the actual-normal system, you should be able to adapt yourself readily to a standard costing system. At this point, you should solve Problem 15-6.

SUMMARY

Accounting systems should be designed to satisfy *control* and *product costing* purposes simultaneously. Costs are initially charged to department responsibility centers; then they are applied to products in order to get inventory costs for balance sheets and income statements and in order to guide pricing and to evaluate product performance.

Many different product costing systems are in use. Four widely used approaches are compared in Exhibit 15-10.

1. *Actual-Normal Absorption Costing.* Includes actual prime costs (direct material and direct labor) plus predetermined variable and fixed overhead.
2. *Actual-Normal Direct Costing.* Includes actual prime costs plus predetermined variable overhead; excludes fixed overhead.
3. *Standard Direct Costing.* Includes predetermined prime costs plus predetermined variable overhead; excludes fixed overhead.
4. *Standard Absorption Costing.* Includes predetermined prime costs plus predetermined variable and fixed overhead.

As you can see from Exhibit 15-10, the term "absorption costing" signifies that fixed overhead is being inventoried. In contrast, direct costing signifies that fixed overhead is not being inventoried. These terms, thus, may be coupled with either an actual-normal costing system (1 and 2) or a standard costing system (3 and 4), depending solely on whether a particular system inventories fixed overhead. Absorption costing is much more widely used than direct costing, although the growing use of the contribution approach in performance measurement has led to increasing use of direct costing.

The variances (including under- or overapplied overhead) below the bottom line of Exhibit 15-10 are usually directly charged or credited to

EXHIBIT 15-10

Summary Comparison of Alternative Systems
for Accounting for Manufacturing Costs

Actual-Normal Costing System	*Standard Costing System*
"Actual" direct material usage $xx "Actual" direct labor xx Predetermined variable overhead xx	Predetermined direct material usage $xx Predetermined direct labor xx Predetermined variable overhead xx
Predetermined fixed overhead xx	Predetermined fixed overhead xx

*Under- or overapplied variable overhead	xx	**All* variable cost variances	xx
*Under- or overapplied fixed overhead	xx	**All* fixed cost variances	xx
Total factory costs accounted for	$xx	Total factory costs accounted for	$xx

* Usually not inventoried but written off immediately as expenses of the current period. Sometimes prorated so that ending inventories will better approximate "actual" cost.

The various items within the boxes are charged initially to Work in Process, transferred to Finished Goods as the goods are completed, and transferred to Cost of Goods Sold as the goods are sold under:

   (1) Actual-Normal Absorption Costing   (3) Standard Direct Costing
   (2) Actual-Normal Direct Costing   (4) Standard Absorption Costing

current operations, and not inventoried. Where such charges are likely to result in a flagrant misstatement of income and inventories, the variances are prorated.

Cost planning and control is not accomplished by journals and ledgers. Current control is an hour-to-hour, day-to-day task that is mainly achieved by prompt summaries of source documents.

SUMMARY PROBLEM FOR YOUR REVIEW

PROBLEM

The Delarez Co. began business on Jan. 2, 19x1. Its executives were experienced in the industry and had a standard cost system installed from the outset. A summary of results follows:

Related to Journal Entry Number

1.	Direct material purchased: 100,000 lbs. @ $1.10, $110,000	
2.	Pounds of direct material used: 90,000	
	Standard allowances per unit of finished output:	
	Direct material: 1 lb. @ $1.00	$1.00
3.	Direct labor: 1 hr. @ $3.00	3.00
4.	Variable factory overhead: 1 hr. @ $.50	.50
	Variable factory costs	$4.50
5.	Fixed factory overhead: 1 hr. @ $1.50	1.50
	Total standard cost per unit	$6.00
3.	Direct labor incurred: 85,000 hours @ $3.05, or $259,250	
4,5.	Factory overhead incurred: variable, $42,000; fixed, $150,000	
6.	Production in units: 80,000	
7.	Sales in units: 60,000	

Required:

1. The president is satisfied with standard costing for planning and control, but he desires to compare the income effects of his system with other product costing systems. In adjoining columns, prepare journal entries to record the above information under actual-normal costing (see Exhibit 15-10, p. 411) and under standard costing.

   Note that Work in Process is charged on the basis of standard allowances under standard costing; in contrast, it is charged on the basis of inputs under actual-normal costing. In a sense, standard cost systems may be regarded as being *output*-oriented, whereas actual-normal costing systems are *input*-oriented. For example, the factors of production are charged and credited to Work in Process at what they *should* cost for the good output, not at what they actually cost in terms of inputs.

2. Show the postings of the journal entries in Requirement 1 to T accounts for Department Responsibility Cost Control, for Work in Process, and for Finished Goods. What are their final balances before the isolation or disposition of year-end variances? Use a final compound journal entry to isolate a usage variance for direct material, a rate and efficiency variance for direct labor, a total variable overhead variance, and a total fixed overhead variance.

3. Assume that sales are $600,000; variable selling and administrative expenses, $60,000; and fixed selling and administrative expenses, $40,000. Prepare a comparative schedule showing net income computations under standard costing and actual-normal costing. Assume that all variances, including under- or overapplied overhead, are written off at year-end as adjustments to Cost of Goods Sold. Explain why net income differs under the two methods.

4. The executive has heard about direct costing. He wants you to compare net income under standard *absorption* costing (which you have just computed) with net income under standard *direct* costing. Explain the difference in net income briefly. As you know, absorption costing entails applying fixed overhead to product, as was done in the previous Requirements, and direct costing does not.

5. Without regard to the previous Requirements, would direct costing or absorption costing give a manager more leeway in influencing short-run net income through production scheduling decisions? Why?

SOLUTION:

1

Journal Entries

Actual-Normal Costing

		Debit	Credit
1.	Direct materials inventory	110,000	
	Accounts payable		110,000
2a.	Department responsibility cost control	99,000	
	Direct materials inventory		99,000
2b.	Work in process (direct material usage)	99,000	
	Department responsibility cost contro		99,000
3a.	Department responsibility cost control	259,250	
	Accrued payroll		259,250
3b.	Work in process (direct labor)	259,250	
	Department responsibility cost control		259,250
4a.	Department responsibility cost control	42,000	
	Miscellaneous accounts		42,000
4b.	Work in process (variable overhead)	42,500	
	Department responsibility cost contro		42,500
5a.	Department responsibility cost control	150,000	
	Miscellaneous accounts		150,000
5b.	Work in process (fixed overhead)	127,500	
	Department responsibility cost control		127,500
	85,000 hrs., @ $1.50		
6.	Finished goods	528,250	
	Work in process		528,250
7.	Cost of goods sold	396,188	
	Finished goods		396,188
	60,000 units, @ $6.603125		

(handwritten: 1 FINISHED GOODS C.P.U.)

Standard Costing

		Debit	Credit
1.	Direct materials	100,000	
	Direct material purchase price variance	10,000	
	Accounts payable		110,000
2a.	Department responsibility cost control	90,000	
	(90,000 lbs., @ $1)		
	Direct materials inventory		90,000
2b.	Work in process (80,000 lbs. allowed)	80,000	
	Department responsibility cost control		80,000
3a.	Department responsibility cost control	259,250	
	Accrued payroll		259,250
3b.	Work in process (direct labor)	240,000	
	Department responsibility cost control		240,000
4a.	Department responsibility cost control	42,000	
	Miscellaneous accounts		42,000
4b.	Work in process (variable overhead)	40,000	
	Department responsibility cost control		40,000
	80,000 standard hours allowed, @ $.50 = $40,000		
5a.	Department responsibility cost control	150,000	
	Miscellaneous accounts		150,000
5b.	Work in process (fixed overhead)	120,000	
	Department responsibility cost control		120,000
	80,000 hrs., @ $1.50		
6.	Finished goods	480,000	
	Work in process		480,000
7.	Cost of goods sold	360,000	
	Finished goods		360,000
	60,000 units @ $6		
8.	(See second part of the solution of Requirement 2 for entry on the isolation of variances.)		

2

Actual-Normal Costing				*Standard Costing*			

Department Responsibility Cost Control   **Department Responsibility Cost Control**

(2a)	99,000	(2b)	99,000	(2a)	90,000	(2b)	80,000
(3a)	259,250	(3b)	259,250	(3a)	259,250	(3b)	240,000
(4a)	42,000	(4b)	42,500	(4a)	42,000	(4b)	40,000
(5a)	150,000	(5b)	127,500	(5a)	150,000	(5b)	120,000
	550,250		528,250		541,250		480,000
		To bal.	22,000			To bal.	61,250
Bal.	22,000*			Bal.	61,250†		

Work in Process   **Work in Process**

(2b)	99,000	(6)	528,250	(2b)	80,000	(6)	480,000
(3b)	259,250			(3b)	240,000		
(4b)	42,500			(4b)	40,000		
(5b)	127,500			(5b)	120,000		
Bal.	0			Bal.	0		

Finished Goods   **Finished Goods**

(6)	528,250	(7)	396,188	(6)	480,000	(7)	360,000
		To bal.	132,062			To bal.	120,000
Bal.	132,062			Bal.	120,000		

* Under-applied overhead:
Variable $ 500 overapplied
Fixed   22,500 under-applied
Total $22,000 under-applied

† Variances: For isolation, see Journal Entry 8.

Journal Entry 8, Standard Costing

Direct material usage variance: 10,000 lbs., @ $1	10,000	
Direct labor rate variance: 85,000 hrs., @ 5¢	4,250	
Direct labor efficiency variance: 5,000 hrs., @ $3	15,000	
Variable overhead variance (under-applied overhead)	2,000	
Fixed overhead variance (under-applied overhead)	30,000	
Department responsibility cost control		61,250

All variances (except for the direct material price variance, which is isolated as material is purchased) may be isolated weekly, monthly, or at year-end. At year-end, the variances are either prorated or directly written off. Note that under this system, the $10,000 purchase price variance for direct materials was isolated earlier, in Entry 1. So the grand total of all variances is $71,250, unfavorable.

3

	Actual-Normal Costing	Standard Costing
Sales	$600,000	$600,000
Cost of goods sold	$396,188	$360,000
Add under-applied overhead	22,000	71,250*
Cost of goods sold, actual	$418,188	$431,250
Gross profit	$181,812	$168,750
Selling and administrative expenses	100,000	100,000
Net income	$ 81,812	$ 68,750
Difference in net income		$13,062

* Includes all variances, not just under-applied overhead. For a detailed breakdown of the $71,250 amount, see Journal Entry 8 (Solution to Requirement 2) and its explanation (p. 414).

Net income is higher under normal costing because its ending inventories are higher. That is, direct materials inventory is carried at an actual unit cost of $1.10 instead of $1.00, and finished goods is carried at a normal unit cost of $6.603125 instead of a standard unit cost of $6.00. These differences were written off as current expense under standard costing, but they are inventoried under actual-normal costing. A summary follows:

	Actual-Normal	Standard	Difference
Direct materials inventory, 10,000 units	$ 11,000	$ 10,000	$ 1,000
Finished goods, 20,000 units	132,062	120,000	12,062
Difference in net income	$143,062	$130,000	$13,062

Net Income Comparisons:
Standard Absorption Costing and Standard Direct Costing

Standard Absorption Costing

	Unit Cost		
Sales			$600,000
Cost of goods sold:			
Variable manufacturing costs, 80,000 units	$4.50	$360,000	
Fixed manufacturing costs	1.50	120,000	
Total cost of goods available for sale	$6.00	$480,000	
Ending inventory, 20,000 units	6.00	120,000	
Cost of goods sold, at standard		$360,000	
Add unfavorable variance (see Solution to Requirement 3)		71,250	
Cost of goods sold, "actual"			431,250
Gross profit			$168,750
Selling and administrative expenses			100,000
Net income			$ 68,750

* Total variance	$71,250
Fixed overhead variance	30,000
Variable cost variances	$41,250

Standard Direct Costing

Sales		$600,000
Variable manufacturing cost of goods produced: 80,000 units, @ $4.50	$360,000	
Less ending inventory: 20,000 units, @ $4.50	90,000	
Variable cost of goods sold, at standard	$270,000	
Add unfavorable variable cost variance*	41,250	
Variable cost of goods sold, at "actual"	$311,250	
Variable selling and administrative expenses	60,000	
Total variable costs charged against sales		371,250
Contribution margin		$228,750
Less fixed costs:		
Fixed manufacturing overhead	$150,000	
Fixed selling and administrative expenses	40,000	190,000
		$ 38,750

Note. The $30,000 difference in net income is caused by the $30,000 (i.e., $120,000 − $90,000) difference in ending inventory. Under absorption costing, $30,000 of the $150,000 fixed manufacturing overhead is held back in inventory, but under direct costing the $30,000 is released immediately as a charge against sales.

5

Some version of absorption costing will give a manager more leeway in influencing his net income via production scheduling. Net income will fluctuate in harmony with changes in net sales under direct costing, but it is influenced by both production and sales under absorption costing. For example, production schedules that increase inventory levels will result in more fixed costs being held back in inventory and in higher current net income than under direct costing. The comparison in the solution to Requirement 4 clearly shows that the higher the ending inventory, the higher the net income—because more fixed costs are being held back as an asset (inventory) instead of being released immediately as an expense.

APPENDIX

Reapportionment of Service Department Costs for Product Costing

Sharply Distinguish Control and Product-costing Purposes

Departments may be classified in two categories: production departments and service departments. Production departments are those that work directly on the manufacture of goods (e.g., machining, drill press, milling, boring, cleaning, painting, and assembly). Service departments are those that exist solely to aid the production departments by rendering specialized assistance with certain phases of the work (e.g., production planning and control, engineering, materials handling, and building maintenance).

Because these services are considered essential to smooth factory operations, the service department costs are commonly regarded as part of the manufacturing overhead that should be applied to the product, even though the products do not physically pass through the service departments. Service department costs are accumulated initially by departments, for *control* purposes, and they must be reapportioned to the producing departments before the computation of overhead application rates for *product costing* purposes. This reapportionment should be based on the relative benefits received by the producing departments from their utilization of the various other departments' services.

Since the utilization of services is often difficult to measure, the interpretation of the cost charged to the product should be tempered accordingly. Disputes over the proper way to reapportion service department costs are rampant in industry. Many of these disputes could be avoided by not reapportioning any service department costs that have questionable or arbitrary reapportionment bases. Above all, a sharp distinction should be made between control and product costing. Attempts to use a single reapportionment plan to satisfy both purposes simultaneously will fail. Supervisors of the producing departments will resist being held responsible for what they regard as uncontrollable service department costs.

The theme for control is: Reapportion, and with care, only those costs whose relative benefits may be measured with assurance. Use standard unit rates for charging the producing departments, so that the latter are responsible for the *quantity* of services consumed and not for interim price changes of the services.

The theme for product costing is: Reapportion on the same basis as the over-all costing system. For example, if direct costing is used, only the variable portion of the service department costs should be reapportioned. Confine these product-costing reapportionment rates to strictly inventory costing purposes.

Do not mix this repapportionment procedure with control efforts or management performance reports.

Procedures for Reapportionment

As you probably suspect, there are many ways to reapportion service department costs. They all are compromises, practical approximations of the ideal results which may be visualized in any given company as being theoretically best. The steps are as follows:

1. *Service department budgets* are prepared by the department for the forthcoming year in light of expected levels of production.

2. *Reapportionment bases* are chosen as the best common denominator for measuring the relative benefits received by the production departments. These bases are not changed each year. They are determined by policy decision, and then they may remain unchanged for years. Criteria for the selection of a base include: (*a*) physical identification or use, as evidenced by repair orders, requisitions, and power meters; (*b*) facilities provided, as evidenced by square feet occupied and rated capacity of electrical equipment; and (*c*) ease of reapportionment, as evidenced by using the number of employees as bases for reapportioning personnel, cafeteria, and medical costs when more refined theoretical bases could be developed. For example, labor turnover and types of skilled and unskilled employees may decidedly influence the personnel department's efforts, time, and costs. Still, it is expedient to use the number of employees as a base. The traditional refinement of the measuring stick seldom generates enough change in the final reapportionment to be worthwhile or meaningful. Some typical bases for reapportionment follow:

Service Department	*Basis for Reapportionment of Costs*
Building and grounds; Janitorial service	Square or cubic footage
Cafeteria; Personnel; Employment	Number of workers
Medical; Production planning and control	Periodic survey of proportion of services rendered to each producing department; total man hours
Material handling; Internal transportation	Units carried; tonnage; hours of service rendered
Power	Metered usage; capacity of equipment; machine hours; formula which weights capacity and machine hours; expected long-term use
Receiving; Shipping; Storeroom	Tonnage; requisitions; issues
Tool room	Requisitions; expected long-term use

3. *Reapportionment cost rates* are developed by dividing the service department budgets by the reapportionment base chosen. For example:

$$\text{Building and grounds reapportionment rate} = \frac{\text{Budgeted building and grounds department costs}}{\text{Reapportionment base: number of square feet}}$$

Then the costs are reapportioned to the producing departments on the basis of square feet occupied.

EXHIBIT 15-11

Computation of Reapportionment Rates for 19x2

	(1) Budgeted Department Costs	(2) Reapportionment Base	(1) ÷ (2) Reapportionment Rate	Reapportionment to					
				Machining		Assembly		Finishing and Painting	
				Base	Total	Base	Total	Base	Total
Cafeteria: Revenue of $100,000, less $220,000 expenses, equals net department costs to reapportion	$ 120,000	600 total production department employees	$200.00	100 employees	$ 20,000	450 employees	$ 90,000	50 employees	$ 10,000
Engineering	$ 480,000	60,000 expected engineering hours worked in production departments	$ 8.00	40,000 hours	$320,000	15,000 hours	$ 120,000	5,000 hours	$ 40,000
General factory administration	$2,480,000	6,200,000 man hours worked in production departments	$ .40	1,250,000 hours	$500,000	4,500,000 hours	$1,800,000	450,000 hours	$180,000

4. *The overhead application rate* is developed by adding the reapportioned overhead to the producing department's budgeted overhead and dividing the total by the application base (usually machine hours or direct labor hours).

Example of Reapportionment

Assume that Miller Co. has three service departments and three producing departments. Exhibit 15-11 shows the development of the service departments' reapportionment rates.

Exhibit 15-12 shows how the reapportioned costs from Exhibit 15-11 are added to the other manufacturing overhead to develop predetermined overhead rates for product costing.

EXHIBIT 15-12

Reapportionment and Computation of Overhead Application Rates

	Service Departments			Producing Departments		
	Cafeteria	Engineering	General Factory Administration	Machining	Assembly	Finishing and Painting
Overhead costs before reapportionment	$120,000	$480,000	$2,480,000	$6,000,000	$4,000,000	$500,000
Reapportionment:						
Cafeteria	(120,000)	—	—	20,000	90,000	10,000
Engineering	—	(480,000)	—	320,000	120,000	40,000
General factory administration	—	—	(2,480,000)	500,000	1,800,000	180,000
Total overhead costs to be applied				$6,840,000	$6,010,000	$730,000
Computation of predetermined overhead rates for product costing:						
Divide by machine hours				2,000,000		
Divide by direct labor hours*					4,000,000	420,000
Application rate				$3.42	$1.502	$1.737

* Man hours and direct labor hours are not the same. Man hours include both direct and indirect labor hours.

Some Complications

The foregoing example is a widely used straightforward approach to reapportionment. Such a method ignores the following complicating factors that are sometimes allowed for in more refined systems:

1. Certain items within a service department's budget may be obviously reapportioned in a manner different than the rest of the items. Such items are culled and are assigned on a basis different from that used for other costs in the same service department. For example, the costs of a special clean-up workforce under the jurisdiction of the Building and Grounds Department may be separately assigned to the Machining Department, if its work is confined to cleaning there.

2. There is always mutual or reciprocal service between service departments. For example, Personnel serves Buildings and Grounds, and vice versa. This reciprocity can be taken into account. Some companies use a se-

quential reapportionment plan, whereby reapportionment begins with the department that renders service to the greatest number of other service departments. Once a service department's costs have been reapportioned, no subsequent service department costs are recirculated. Other companies use the theoretically most accurate method for reapportioning reciprocal service: simultaneous linear equations that are quickly solved by digital computers.

Separate Reapportionment of Variable and Fixed Costs

In the illustration we have been considering, no distinctions were made between variable and fixed cost behavior. Where direct costing is used, such separations are needed. Even if direct costing is not used, reapportionments may be made more precise by delineating variable and fixed costs. Robert Beyer provides a scheme using these distinctions. He favors the allocation of fixed costs "on the basis of the expected amount of services in the long range." [1] That is, long-term readiness or capacity to serve should be the reapportionment base. In this way, the amount of fixed costs which are reapportioned will not fluctuate widely from year to year because of temporary shifts in volumes between departments or product lines.

The development of dual reapportionment rates also allows a complete separation of variable and fixed overhead application rates for product costing.

Beyer assigns only variable costs to products in the formal accounting records. He maintains that reapportionment of all manufacturing overhead costs to products and product lines should be accomplished entirely on a memorandum basis, apart from the formal accounting records. [2] He favors developing variable cost application rates only and contends that fixed costs should be allocated to product lines in lump sums.

Review Problem on Reapportionment

The American Institute of Certified Public Accountants has asked your advice on the following reapportionment problem. A power service department has the following budget for the coming year, 19x1:

Schedule of Horsepower Hours, 19x1

	Producing Departments				
	A	*B*	*C*	*D*	*Total*
Expected use	80,000	90,000	70,000	60,000	300,000
Needed at practical capacity production volume	100,000	200,000	120,000	80,000	500,000

The expected fixed costs of operating the department for 19x1 are $90,000; the variable costs are $60,000.

Required:

What dollar amounts should be reapportioned to each producing department? Show three different sets of answers.

---

[1] *Profitability Accounting for Planning and Control* (New York: The Ronald Press Company, 1963), pp. 196-203.

[2] *Ibid.*, pp. 195-6.

Reapportionment may be based on: (1) dual variable and fixed rates; (2) a single rate related to use; or (3) a single rate related to capacity provided.

1.   Variable cost rate $= \dfrac{\$60,000 \text{ expected costs}}{300,000 \text{ hrs. expected usage}} = 20\cancel{c}$

Fixed cost rate $= \dfrac{\$90,000 \text{ expected costs}}{500,000 \text{ hrs. capacity provided}} = 18\cancel{c}$

2.   Single rate $= \dfrac{\$150,000 \text{ expected costs}}{300,000 \text{ hrs. expected usage}} = 50\cancel{c}$

3.   Single rate $= \dfrac{\$150,000 \text{ expected costs}}{500,000 \text{ hrs. capacity provided}} = 30\cancel{c}$

EXHIBIT 15-13
Comparison of Three Methods of Reapportionment

	Departments				
	A	B	C	D	Total
Expected use	80,000	90,000	70,000	60,000	300,000
Needed at practical capacity	100,000	200,000	120,000	80,000	500,000
1. *Dual Rates:*					
Variable, @ 20¢	$16,000	$18,000	$14,000	$12,000	$ 60,000
Fixed, @ 18¢	18,000	36,000	21,600	14,400	90,000
	$34,000	$54,000	$35,600	$26,400	$150,000
2. *Single Rate:*					
Expected use, @ 50¢	$40,000	$45,000	$35,000	$30,000	$150,000
3. *Single Rate:*					
Capacity provided, @ 30¢	$30,000	$60,000	$36,000	$24,000	$150,000

Exhibit 15-13 is a comparison of the three reapportionments. The dual rate properly considers the $90,000 fixed costs as that of providing ability to serve all other departments at practical capacity. The fixed cost is unrelated to the amount of usage in a given year. On the other hand, the $60,000 variable cost is directly related to service rendered. Consequently, its proper reapportionment base is the horsepower hours expected to be used. One or the other of the single rate reapportionments is used more frequently than the dual rate. Exhibit 15-13 reveals the rather significant differences in results under the three alternatives.

ASSIGNMENT MATERIAL

ESSENTIAL ASSIGNMENT MATERIAL

15-1. *Terminology.* Define: job order costing; process costing; job order; actual-normal system; overapplied; absorption costing; direct costing; variable costing; marginal costing; reapportionment; service departments; standard absorption costing; standard direct costing.

15-2. *Section I Problem: Actual-normal system, journal entries, source documents.* The following data summarize the factory operations of the Bensmeier Manufacturing Co. for the year 19x1, its first year in business:

1. Direct materials purchased for cash	$230,000
2. Direct materials issued and used	220,000
3. Labor used directly on production	100,000
4. Indirect labor	80,000
5. Depreciation of plant and equipment	40,000
6. Miscellaneous factory overhead (ordinarily would be detailed)	30,000
7. Overhead: 180 per cent of direct labor	?
8. Cost of production completed	450,000
9. Cost of goods sold	300,000

Required:

1. General journal entries for an actual-normal cost system. Number your entries. After each entry indicate: (*a*) the most likely name of the source documents that would authorize the entry; and (*b*) how the subsidiary ledgers, if any, would be affected.

2. Present the T account for Department Responsibility Cost Control. Sketch how this account's subsidiary ledger would appear, assuming that there are four factory departments. You need not show any numbers in the subsidiary ledger.

15-3. *Section II Problem: accounting for overhead, predetermined rates.* Thomas Allan and Co. uses a predetermined overhead rate in applying overhead to individual job orders on a *machine hour* basis for Department No. 1 and on a *direct labor hour* basis for Department No. 2. At the beginning of 19x4, the company's management made the following budget estimates:

	Dept. No. 1	*Dept. No. 2*
Direct labor cost	$12,000	$25,000
Factory overhead	24,000	7,500
Direct labor hours	5,000	10,000
Machine hours	16,000	1,500

Cost records of recent months show the following accumulations for Job Order No. 455:

	Dept. No. 1	*Dept. No. 2*
Material placed in production	$11.75	$ 3.50
Direct labor cost	9.00	12.50
Direct labor hours	3	5
Machine hours	12	1

Required:

1. What is the predetermined overhead *rate* that should be applied in Department No. 1? In Department No. 2?

2. What is the *total overhead* cost of Job Order No. 455?

3. If Job Order No. 455 consists of 18 units of product, what is the *unit cost* of this job?

4. At the *end* of 19x4, actual results for the year's operations were as follows:

	Dept. No. 1	*Dept. No. 2*
Actual overhead costs incurred	$23,000	$ 8,300
Actual direct labor hours	5,000	10,000
Actual machine hours	16,000	1,500

Find the under- or overapplied overhead for each department and for the factory as a whole.

15-4. *Section II Problem: year-end disposition of overhead.*

1. Refer to Problem 15-2. Assume that under- or overapplied overhead is closed directly to Cost of Goods Sold. Show the journal entry. Show the T accounts and the closing balances for all inventories.

2. Assume that under- or overapplied overhead is prorated among the pertinent accounts in proportion to their ending balances. Show the journal entry and supporting calculations. Would net income be higher or lower than in Requirement 1? By how much?

(15-5.) *Section III Problem: comparison of direct costing and absorption costing.* From the following information pertaining to a year's operation, answer the questions below:

Units produced	2,400
Units sold	2,000
Selling and administrative expenses (all fixed)	$ 800
Fixed manufacturing overhead	$2,400
Variable manufacturing overhead	$1,100
Direct labor	$3,400
Direct materials used	$2,700
All beginning inventories	-0-
Gross margin	$2,000
Direct materials inventory, end	$ 300
Work in process inventory, end	-0-

Required:

1. What is the ending finished goods inventory cost under conventional costing procedures (absorption costing)?

2. What is the ending finished goods inventory cost under variable costing procedures (direct costing)?

3. Would net income be higher or lower under direct costing? By how much? Why? [Answer: $400 lower.]

15-6. *Section IV Problem: standard cost system journal entries.* The Berryman Co. isolates the variances in its standard cost system as early as is practical. Journalize the transactions for material and labor, using the following data for the month of February:

No beginning or ending work in process.
Direct material: standard allowance of 2 gallons per finished unit, @ $2 per gallon.

Direct labor: standard allowance of one-half hour per finished unit, @ $4 per hour.

	Actual Usage	Standard Allowed for Units Produced
Direct material	11,000 gallons	10,000 gallons
Direct labor	2,900 hours	2,500 hours

Direct labor costs incurred totaled $11,890. Direct materials purchased totaled $49,400, for 26,000 gallons.

15-7. *Summary comparison of alternative systems for accounting for manufacturing costs.* The following information pertains to operations for the year 19x2. There were no beginning inventories. There is no ending inventory of direct material. Total fixed manufacturing overhead costs incurred were $53,000. Balances in certain accounts, as of Dec. 31, 19x2, were as follows:

Variances (unfavorable):	
Direct material purchase price	$ 5,000
Direct material usage	20,000
Direct labor rate	4,000
Direct labor efficiency	-0-
Under-applied variable overhead	6,000
Under-applied fixed overhead	3,000
	$38,000

At standard unit prices using absorption costing:

Work in process (including fixed overhead applied, $2,500)	$10,000
Finished goods (including fixed overhead, $12,500)	50,000
Cost of goods sold (including fixed overhead, $35,000)	140,000

1. Compute the *unadjusted* cost of goods sold under the following costing methods: (a) standard absorption costing (given); (b) standard direct costing; (c) actual-normal absorption costing; (d) actual-normal direct costing. (Hint: see Exhibit 15-10.) That is, what balance would appear in the Cost of Goods Sold account at the end of the year under each method *before* adjusting for any variances (including under- or over-applied overhead) that might exist.

2. Where variances are not too huge, they are, as Exhibit 15-10 indicates, charged directly in total to current operations (either as separate items on the income statement or as adjustments to the ending balance in Cost of Goods Sold). However, in this part, assume that the variances are large enough to warrant proration on the basis of the final given balances of Work in Process, Finished Goods, and Cost of Goods Sold ($10,000, $50,000, and $140,000, respectively). Compute the adjusted cost of goods sold under each costing method (a) through (d) above.

3. Analyze the results in requirements (1) and (2). Which assumption

writes costs off to expense most quickly? What other generalizations about the four assumptions can be made? Do you think that the standards were currently attainable? Why or why not?

4. If sales were $220,000 and the only expenses are those shown in the problem, what would be the net income under the four methods, assuming (a) no proration of variances, (b) proration of variances.

15-8. *Chapter review: comparison of alternative income statements.* (Adapted from a problem prepared by Professor James March.) Alternative income statements for the same company for a given year follow:

	A	*B*	*C*
Sales	$100,000	$100,000	$100,000
Cost of goods sold	40,000	30,000	42,000
	$ 60,000	$ 70,000	$ 58,000
Variances:			
Direct material	(1,500)	(1,500)	—
Direct labor	(500)	(500)	—
Factory overhead	(4,000)	—	(4,000)
	$ 54,000	$ 68,000	$ 54,000
Other operating expenses (all fixed)	40,000	54,000	40,000
Net operating income	$ 14,000	$ 14,000	$ 14,000

Required:

Write a brief explanation for each of your answers:

a. Which cost system: (1) pure historical cost; (2) standard absorption cost; (3) standard variable cost; or (4) historical cost with predetermined overhead rates was used for *A*? For *B*? For *C*?

b. Did the inventory: (1) increase; (2) decrease; or (3) remain unchanged for *A*? For *B*? For *C*?

c. What was the selling and administrative expense for the year?

d. What would you expect the net operating income to be if sales volume increased 10 per cent and selling prices remained the same? Assume that all variable costs will be at standard—in other words, no variances are to be budgeted for material, labor, or variable overhead for any production.

e. Was the production volume for the year higher than, lower than, or equal to the predetermined volume?

f. What was the fixed factory overhead for the year?

g. Was the variable factory overhead for the year more than, less than, or equal to the budget?

ADDITIONAL ASSIGNMENT MATERIAL

Note: This material is sequentially related to the major sections of the chapter, including the Appendix. Problem 15-27 is a good check on the comprehension of general ledger relationships in a job cost system. In Problems 15-26, 15-28, 15-29, and 15-36 the topics are blended and compared. They require a maximum of thinking and a minimum of pencil-pushing.

15-9. "The special decision purpose of accounting is difficult to satisfy on a routine basis." Why?

15-10. "Cost application or absorption is terminology related to the product costing purpose." Why?

15-11. "I was looking at a trial balance the other day and was mystified by the account Department Responsibility Cost Applied. I just didn't know what it meant or where it fit." Briefly unravel the mystery.

15-12. What are some reasons for *incurred* and *applied* overhead differing?

15-13. Sometimes five copies of a stores requisition are needed. What are their uses?

15-14. "The general ledger is an incidental part of the accountant's daily work." Explain.

15-15. "Costs of inefficiency cannot be regarded as assets." Explain.

15-16. "Under actual overhead application, unit costs soar as volume increases, and vice versa." Do you agree? Explain.

15-17. What is the best theoretical method of allocating under- or overapplied overhead, assuming that the objective is to obtain as accurate a cost allocation as possible?

15-18. "Direct costing means that only direct material and direct labor are inventoried." Do you agree? Why?

15-19. Why do advocates of currently attainable standard costs method for product costing claim that it is conceptually superior to actual costing?

15-20. "If all variances, plus under- or overapplied overhead, are directly charged to Cost of Goods Sold, the effects on net income of standard costing systems and actual-normal costing systems should coincide where the basic data are the same." Do you agree? Explain.

15-21. Why do service department costs have to be reapportioned?

15-22. Name three criteria for reapportionment of service department costs.

15-23. What are mutual or reciprocal services?

15-24. *Journal entries for job costing.* Manders, Inc. has a job shop which uses a job-order system. At the start of 19x1, it was estimated that the corporation would incur overhead at the rate of $1.50 per direct labor hour.

1. Job 177 used $40 of raw material and 16 hours of direct labor @ $2 per hour. What is the total cost of Job 177?

2. Give the journal entries for charging costs to Job 177.

3. During 19x1, the following costs were incurred:

Raw materials purchased	$2,000
Indirect labor	1,000
Depreciation of equipment	500

Journalize these facts.

4. During 19x1 the company worked 20,000 hours and incurred $28,000 of overhead. Make the proper entry on Dec. 31, 19x1 to dispose of year-end under- or overapplied overhead.

15-25. *Disposition of year-end under-applied overhead.* A company that uses a normal cost system has the following balances at the end of its first year's operations:

Work in process control	$200,000
Finished goods control	300,000
Cost of goods sold	500,000
Department factory overhead control	360,000
Department factory overhead applied	300,000

Using journal entries, show two different ways to dispose of the year-end overhead balances. By how much would net income differ?

15-26. *Comparison of overhead accounting for control and for product costing.* The controller of the Ward Co. had prepared the following factory overhead budget for 19x2:

Supplies	$ 10,000
Indirect labor	32,000
Utilities (variable)	10,000
Repairs (variable)	12,000
Miscellaneous	8,000
Total variable overhead	$ 72,000
Utilities (fixed)	$ 10,000
Repairs (fixed)	8,000
Depreciation	60,000
Insurance	2,000
Property taxes	7,000
Supervision	21,000
Total fixed overhead	$108,000
Total budgeted overhead	$180,000

This budget had been prepared after careful consideration of the sales outlook for 19x2. The production schedules were geared to the forecasted sales pattern. Sales have seasonal peaks in the first and third quarters.

The controller wanted to spread overhead over the jobs in such a way that the total overhead for the year would be equal to the total overhead applied to jobs. Therefore, he developed a predetermined rate, to be used throughout the year as various jobs were performed. He decided that the 360,000 hours of direct labor which were forecasted would provide a reasonable base.

Quarterly data for actual operations in 19x2 are as follows:

Quarter	Direct Labor Hours	Overhead Costs Incurred *
1	120,000	$ 51,000
2	50,000	37,000
3	130,000	60,000
4	75,000	40,000
	375,000	$188,000

* Fixed costs were exactly equal to budgeted amounts, in every quarter.

Required:

1. What is the under- or overapplied overhead, by quarters and for the year-to-date?

2. During 19x2, the president asked for a quarterly written summary explanation of the reasons for the current quarter's and year-to-date under-

or overapplied overhead. Each report was to be 100 words or less, because the president detests wordiness. Prepare the four reports for the president.

3. From the information given, in which quarters should the president have gone to the factory superintendent with praise for good control of overhead or with inquiry about inferior control? Explain your answer briefly.

4. Summarize how the accountant resolves the problem of overhead accounting for control and of overhead accounting for product costing. What accounting tools, entries, and accounts serve primarily a control purpose? A product costing purpose?

5. What accounting treatment should be given to the under- or overapplied overhead which appears in the quarterly financial statements? At the end of the year? Be specific.

15-27. *Review of job costing: general ledger relationships. Note:* This problem is a bit more technically demanding than the others on the material in the first two sections of the chapter. The Weismer Co.'s job-order accounting system is on a calendar year basis. As of Jan. 31, 19x2, the following information is available:

a. Direct materials stores requisitions for January totaled $200,000.

b. The cost of goods sold during January was $500,000.

c. Stores (i.e., direct materials inventory), on Jan. 31, 19x2, were $9,000.

d. The cost of goods completed and transferred to finished goods during January was $600,000.

e. The predetermined factory overhead application rate for 19x2 is 180 per cent of direct labor costs.

f. The finished goods inventory, on Dec. 31, 19x1, was $42,000.

g. Gross factory wages paid in January totaled $195,000. (Ignore withholdings.)

h. All employees performing direct labor get the same rate of pay. Direct labor hours for January totaled 50,000. Indirect labor, supervision, and miscellaneous factory overhead payroll totaled $30,000.

i. Jobs No. 480 and No. 482 were uncompleted on Jan. 31, 19x2. Together, their total labor charges were $6,000 (2,000 direct labor hours). Their total direct material charges were $13,200.

j. The overapplied factory overhead, as of Jan. 31, was $14,000.

k. Direct materials purchased during January totaled $207,000.

l. Balance, Accrued Factory Payroll, as of Jan. 31, 19x2, was $4,000.

Required:

(1) Balance, Stores (direct materials inventory), on Dec. 31, 19x1.

(2) Balance, Finished Goods, on Jan. 31, 19x2.

(3) Direct labor costs incurred during January.

(4) Actual overhead incurred during January.

(5) Balance, Accrued Factory Payroll, on Dec. 31, 19x1.

(6) Balance, Work in Process, on Jan. 31, 19x2.

(7) Balance, Work in Process, on Dec. 31, 19x1.

15-28. *All-fixed costs.* (Suggested by Raymond P. Marple.) The Marple Co. has built a massive water-desalting factory next to an ocean. The factory is completely automated. It has its own source of power, light, heat, etc. The salt water costs nothing. All producing and other operating costs are fixed; they do not vary with output because the volume is governed by adjusting a few dials on a control panel. The employees have flat annual salaries.

The desalted water is not sold to household consumers. It has a special taste that appeals to local breweries, distilleries, and soft drink manufacturers. The price, 10¢ per gallon, is expected to remain unchanged for quite some time.

The following are data regarding the first two years of operations:

| | In Gallons | | Costs (All Fixed) | |
	Sales	Production	Manufacturing	Other
19x1	5,000,000	10,000,000	$450,000	$100,000
19x2	5,000,000	0	450,000	100,000

Orders can be processed in four hours, so management decided, in early 19x2, to gear production strictly to sales.

Required:

1. Prepare three-column income statements for 19x1, for 19x2, and for the two years together using: (a) direct costing; and (b) absorption costing.
2. What is the break-even point under: (a) direct costing; and (b) absorption costing?
3. What inventory costs would be carried on the balance sheets on Dec. 31, 19x1 and 19x2, under each method?
4. Comment on your answers in Requirements 1 and 2. Which costing method appears most useful?

15-29. *Semifixed costs.* The McFarland Co. differs from the Marple Co. (described in Problem 15-28) in only one respect: it has both variable and fixed manufacturing costs. Its variable costs are $.025 per gallon and its fixed manufacturing costs are $225,000 per year.

Required:

1. Using the same data as in the previous problem, except for the change in production cost behavior, prepare three-column income statements for 19x1, for 19x2, and for the two years together using: (a) direct costing; and (b) absorption costing.
2. Why did McFarland earn a profit for the two-year period while Marple suffered a loss?
3. What inventory costs would be carried on the balance sheets on Dec. 31, 19x1 and 19x2, under each method?

15-30. *Inventory costing: for income or liquidity.* Mr. X has completed plans to begin manufacture of a unique sports car on Jan. 1, 19x3. The banks are skeptical of his venture and will not consider any requests for short-term capital unless Mr. X can show a current ratio of 2 or higher. If his plan is successful, he anticipates a substantial need for funds on Jan. 1, 19x4. Mr. X also anticipates that, on that date, his current liabilities will be $500,000 and that his current assets, excluding inventories, will be $720,000.

Operating data:

Selling price per unit: $15,000
Prime costs:

Labor, @ $2 per hr.	500 hrs. per unit
Material	$5,000 per unit

Factory overhead:

Variable	$2 per direct labor hour
Fixed	$1,200,000 per year

Selling and administrative expenses:

Variable	$700 per unit sold
Fixed	$240,000 per year

Expected production volume: 400 units per year
Expected sales for 19x3: 370 units
Expected inventory on Jan. 1, 19x4: 30 finished units

Required:

1. What would be the minimum inventory valuation in order to show a current ratio of 2 on Jan. 1, 19x4?
2. Prepare income statements for the year 19x3:
   (a) using direct costing.
   (b) using absorption costing.
3. Which accounting system should Mr. X use, direct costing or absorption costing? Why?
4. Explain the differences in net income and inventory valuation under the two costing methods.

15-31. *Comparison of direct and absorption costing over five years.* Two corporations are hotly competitive in the manufacture and sale of farm machinery. Their sales volume, production volume, and their fixed indirect manufacturing costs have been practically identical.

Companies A and B	19x1	19x2	19x3	19x4	19x5
Units produced	100,000	120,000	126,000	90,000	85,000
Units sold	90,000	100,000	110,000	100,000	90,000
Fixed indirect manufacturing costs	$100,000	$108,000	$110,000	$107,000	$100,000

Company *A* uses absorption costing, and Company *B* uses direct costing. For each of the five years, would Company *A*'s net income be higher or lower than Company *B*'s? Assume that neither company had inventories at the beginning of 19x1. Assume a first-in, first-out flow of costs.

15-32. *Alternate systems for isolating direct material price variances.* Co. A has a standard cost system that isolates variances as quickly as possible. For example, price variances for direct material are isolated upon purchase. Usage variances are detected by issuing standard quantities of material at the start of production. If more material is needed to complete the scheduled production, *excess material requisitions* are used to obtain the additional material from the storeroom.

Co. *B* also has a standard cost system. However, its management is less concerned about price variances and prefers to have direct materials carried at actual cost. Co. *B* controls its usage variance in a manner similar to Co. *A* and carries its work in process at standard cost.

Each company had the following data during a recent month:

Standard price per pound	$1.00
Actual purchase price per pound	$ .90
Standard quantity allowed for good units produced	5,000 lbs.
Actual quantity used	5,400 lbs.
Actual quantity purchased	7,000 lbs.

Draw a line down the center of a sheet of paper. On one side show the journal entries that would summarize how Co. *A* accounts for materials; on the other side, show how Co. *B* accounts for materials.

15-33. *Standard absorption and standard direct costing.* Kohlberg Co. has the following results for a certain year. All variances are written off as additions to (or deductions from) Standard Cost of Sales. Find the unknowns, designated by letters.

Sales: 200,000 units, @ $22	$4,400,000
Net variance for standard variable manufacturing costs	$ 36,000, unfavorable
Variable standard cost of goods manufactured	$10.00 per unit
Variable selling and administrative expenses	$2.00 per unit
Fixed selling and administrative expenses	$1,000,000
Fixed manufacturing overhead	$240,000
Maximum capacity per year	240,000 units
Normal or standard capacity per year	200,000 units
Beginning inventory of finished goods	30,000 units
Ending inventory of finished goods	10,000 units
Beginning inventory: direct costing basis	*a*
Contribution margin	*b*
Net income: direct costing basis	*c*
Beginning inventory: absorption costing basis	*d*
Gross margin	*e*
Net income: absorption costing basis	*f*

15-34. *Reapportionment of service department costs.* A company has four departments. The two service departments are General Factory Administration and Engineering. The two production departments are Machining and Assembly. Budgeted data for the expected activity for the forthcoming year are:

	Overhead Costs before Reapportionment	Total Man Hours*	Engineering Hours Worked for Each Department
General administration	$ 600,000	—†	—†
Engineering	116,000	—†	—†
Machining	400,000	12,000	16,000
Assembly	200,000	36,000	2,000
Totals	$1,316,000	48,000	18,000

* Includes both direct and indirect hours.
† Although man hours and engineering hours are worked in these departments, they are ignored in the reapportionment process. (There are many ways of refining the reapportionment process. As the text points out, ideally all reciprocal services should be allocated by using simultaneous equations.)

Reapportion the service department costs to the producing departments. Compute the predetermined overhead rates for product-costing purposes. Assume that 40,000 machine hours are used as a base for overhead application in the Machining Department and that 30,000 direct labor hours are used as a base in the Assembly Department.

15-35. *Dual reapportionment.* The power plant that services all factory departments has a budget for the forthcoming year. This budget has been expressed in the following terms, for a normal month:

	Kilowatt Hours	
Factory Departments	Needed at Practical Capacity Production Volume	Expected Usage
A	10,000	8,000
B	20,000	9,000
X	12,000	7,000
Y	8,000	6,000
Totals	50,000	30,000

The expected monthly costs for operating the department during the budget year are $15,000—$6,000 variable and $9,000 fixed.

What dollar amounts should be reapportioned to each department? Show three different sets of answers.

15-36. *Inventory measures, production scheduling, and evaluating divisional performance. (Note.* This problem is more rigorous than previous problems, but the benefits should exceed the effort.)

The Odmark Co. stresses competition between the heads of its various divisions and rewards stellar performance with year-end bonuses that vary between 5 and 10 per cent of division net operating income (before considering the bonus or income taxes). The divisional managers have great discretion in setting production schedules.

Division *Y* produces and sells a product for which there is a long-standing demand but that can have marked seasonal and year-to-year fluctuations. On Nov. 30, 19x2, George Craft, the Division *Y* manager, is preparing a production schedule for December. The following data are available, for Jan. 1 through Nov. 30:

Beginning inventory, January 1, in units	10,000
Sales price, per unit	$ 500
Total fixed costs incurred for manufacturing	$11,000,000
Total fixed costs: other (not inventoriable)	$11,000,000
Total variable costs for manufacturing	$22,000,000
Total other variable costs (fluctuate with units *sold*)	$ 5,000,000
Units produced	110,000
Units sold	100,000
Variances	None

Production in October and November was 10,000 units each month. Practical capacity is 12,000 units per month. Maximum available storage space for inventory is 25,000 units. The sales outlook, for December through February, is 6,000 units monthly. In order to retain a core of key employees, monthly production cannot be scheduled at less than 4,000 units without special permission from the president. Inventory is never to be less than 10,000 units.

The expected capacity used for applying fixed factory overhead is regarded as 120,000 units annually. The company uses a standard absorption costing system. All variances are disposed of at year-end as an adjustment to Standard Cost of Goods Sold.

Required:

1. Given the restrictions as stated, and assuming that the manager wants to maximize the company's net income for 19x2:
    (a) How many units should be scheduled for production in December?
    (b) What net operating income will be reported for 19x2 as a whole, assuming that the implied cost behavior patterns will continue in December as they did throughout the year, to date? Show computations.
    (c) If December production is scheduled at 4,000 units, what would reported net income be?
2. Assume that standard direct costing is used rather than standard absorption costing.
    (a) What would net income for 19x2 be, assuming that the December production schedule is the one in Requirement (1-part a)?
    (b) Assuming that December production was 4,000 units?
    (c) Reconcile the net incomes in this Requirement with those in Requirement (1).
    Show compuations.
3. From the viewpoint of the long-run interests of the company as a whole, what production schedule should the division manager set? Explain fully. Include in your explanation a comparison of the motivating influences of absorption and direct costing in this situation.
4. Assume standard absorption costing. The manager wants to maximize his after-income-tax performance over the long run. Given the data at the beginning of the problem, assume that income tax rates will be halved in 19x3. Assume also that year-end write-offs of variances are acceptable for income-tax purposes.
    How many units should be scheduled for production in December? Why?

PART THREE

Selected Topics
for Further Study

CHAPTER 16

Impact
of Income Taxes
on Management Planning

INCOME TAXES INFLUENCE NEARLY ALL BUSINESS DECISIONS. In this chapter, we show how income taxes may be reckoned with in decision making. Our focus is on corporations, rather than on individuals or partnerships.

Managers have an obligation to avoid income taxes. Avoidance is not evasion. Avoidance is the use of legal means to minimize tax payments; evasion is the use of illegal means. Income tax problems are often exceedingly complex, so professional tax counsel should be sought whenever the slightest doubt exists.

We are especially concerned with the effect of income taxes on depreciation and on capital budgeting decisions. However, other topics will also be explored—the tax effects of last-in, first-out inventory valuations, of charitable contributions, and some miscellaneous matters. Obviously, in one chapter we can only scratch the surface of this vast and complicated subject.

INCOME TAXES AND CAPITAL BUDGETING

General Characteristics

Income taxes are cash disbursements. Income taxes can influence the *amount* and/or the *timing* of cash flows. Their basic role in capital budgeting is no different from any other cash disbursement. However, taxes tend to narrow the cash differences between projects. Cash savings in operations will cause an increase in net taxable income and, thus, an increase in tax outlays. A 60 per cent income tax rate reduces the net attractiveness of $1,000,000 in cash operating savings to $400,000.

Federal income tax rates on ordinary corporate net income, as of 1965, were 22 per cent on the first $25,000 and 48 per cent on the excess. State income tax rates vary considerably. In many instances, state plus federal income tax rates are more than 50 per cent. We use a 60 per cent rate in several examples to facilitate computations.

Effects of Depreciation Deductions

Exhibit 16-1 shows the interrelationship of net income before taxes, income taxes, and depreciation. Please examine this exhibit carefully

EXHIBIT 16-1

**Basic Analysis of Income Statement,
Income Taxes, and Cash Flows**

Traditional Income Statement

(A)	Sales	$130,000
(B)	Less: Expenses, excluding depreciation	$ 70,000
(D)	Depreciation (straight line)	25,000
	Total expenses	$ 95,000
	Net income before taxes	$ 35,000
(E)	Income taxes	21,000
(F)	Net income after taxes	$ 14,000

Net after-tax cash inflow from operations is
either $A - B - E = \$130,000 - \$70,000 - \$21,000 = \$ 39,000$
or $F + D = \quad \$14,000 + \$25,000 = \$39,000$

Analysis of the Above for Capital Budgeting

(A-B)	Cash inflow from operations: $130,000 − $70,000 =	$ 60,000
	Income tax effects, @ 60 per cent	36,000
	After-tax effects of cash inflow from operations	$ 24,000
	Tax-Shield	
(D)	Straight line depreciation: $100,000 ÷ 4 = $25,000	
	Income tax savings, @ 60 per cent	15,000
	Total cash provided by operations after consideration of tax shield	$ 39,000

before reading on. Assume that the company has a single fixed asset, purchased for $100,000 cash, which has a four-year life and zero disposal value. The purchase cost, less the estimated disposal value, is tax-deductible in the form of yearly depreciation. This deduction has been aptly called a *tax shield*, because that portion of income which is assigned to depreciation is protected from tax.

As Exhibit 16-2 shows, the asset represents a valuable future tax de-

EXHIBIT 16-2

Tax Shield Effects of Depreciation

Assume: Original cost of equipment $100,000; four-year life; zero disposal value; annual cash inflow from operations, $60,000; income tax rate, 60 per cent; minimum desired after-tax rate of return, 12 per cent.

Straight Line Depreciation

Annual depreciation: $100,000 ÷ 4 = $25,000
Tax shield: Savings in income tax disbursements,
@ 60% = .60 × $25,000 = $15,000

	12% Discount Factor, from Appropriate Tables	Total Present Value, @ 12%	Year 0	1	2	3	4
	3.037	$45,555	$ —	$15,000	$15,000	$15,000	$15,000

Sum-of-the-Years' Digits Depreciation

Year	Multiplier*	Deduction	Tax Shield: Income Tax Savings, @ 60%	12% Discount Factor, from Appropriate Tables	Total Present Value, @ 12%	Year 0	1	2	3	4
1	4/10	$40,000	$24,000	.893	$21,432	—	$24,000			
2	3/10	30,000	18,000	.797	14,346			$18,000		
3	2/10	20,000	12,000	.712	8,544				$12,000	
4	1/10	10,000	6,000	.636	3,816					$ 6,000
					$48,138					

* The *denominator* for the sum-of-the-digits method is:

1 + 2 + 3 + 4 = 10

or

$$S = \frac{n(n+1)}{2} \qquad (1)$$

$$S = \frac{4(4+1)}{2} = 4 \times 2.5 = 10$$

where S = sum of the digits
n = years of estimated useful life

duction of $100,000. The present value of this deduction depends directly on its specific yearly effects on future income tax payments. Therefore, the present value is influenced by the depreciation method selected, the tax rates, and the discount rate.

The Best Depreciation Method

The three most popular depreciation methods are straight line depreciation, sum of the years' digits, and the double-declining balance. The effects of the first two are shown in Exhibit 16-2. Note that the present value of the tax shield is greater if straight line depreciation is *not* used. As far as income tax planning is concerned, the general decision rule is to select sum-of-the-years' digits or the double-declining balance method because, as compared with the straight-line method, they maximize present values. The total *dollar* tax bills may not change when the years are taken together, but the early write-offs defer tax outlays to future periods. The measure of the latter advantage depends on the rate of return that can be gained from funds that otherwise would have been paid as income taxes. The mottoes in income-tax planning are: When there is a legal choice, take the deduction sooner rather than later; and recognize taxable income later rather than sooner.

Comprehensive Illustration: Effects of Income Taxes on Cash Flow

The easiest way to visualize the effects of income taxes on cash flow is by a step-by-step analysis of a concrete situation. The following Illustration is the same one used in Example 2 in Chapter 14 (p. 363). However, an after-tax discount rate is now going to be used, and all income tax effects—including gains and losses on disposals—will now be considered.

EXAMPLE

A company owns a packaging machine, which was purchased three years ago for $56,000. It has a remaining useful life of five years, providing that it has a major overhaul, at the end of its fifth year of life, at a cost of $10,000, fully deductible in that year for income tax purposes. Its disposal value now is $20,000; in five years its disposal value will be $8,000. The cash operating costs of this machine are expected to continue at $40,000 annually. The company has not used a residual value in allocating depreciation for tax purposes. Accumulated straight line depreciation is $21,000.

A salesman has offered a substitute machine for $51,000 in cash. The new machine will slash annual cash operating costs by $10,000, will not require any overhauls, will have a useful life of five years, and will have a disposal value of $3,000. The company would use sum-of-the-years' digits depreciation for tax purposes, with no provision for residual value.

Required:

Assume that the minimum desired rate of return, after taxes, is 6 per cent. Using the net present value technique, show whether the new machine should be purchased: (*a*) under a total project approach; (*b*) under an incremental approach. Assume that income tax rates are 60 per cent on ordinary income and 25 per cent on capital gains. Assume that the zero residual values used for tax purposes will not be challenged by the Internal Revenue Service.

SOLUTION. Exhibits 16-3 and 16-4 show the complete solution. The following steps are recommended. The pertinent income tax aspects will be considered as each step is discussed.

Step 1. General Approach. Review Example 2 in Chapter 14. The general approach to these decisions is unchanged by income tax considerations.

Step 2. Cash Operating Costs and Depreciation. Cash operating costs and their income tax effects are separated from the depreciation tax shield effects. *These can be combined, if preferred.* However, the approach illustrated facilitates comparisons of alternative depreciation effects and permits the use of annuity tables for the cash operating costs when they do not differ from year to year.

This illustration, in which we assume that any given cash flows and related tax flows occur in the same period, could be refined to account for any possible lags. For instance, some tax payments related to Year 1 may not actually occur until Year 2; the pre-tax operating cash inflows may occur in 19x1, and the related tax outflows may not occur until April, 19x2. For simplicity, we are neglecting this possibility.

Step 3. Disposals of Equipment. In general, gains and losses on disposals of equipment are taxed in the same way as ordinary gains and losses.[1]

Exhibit 16-3 is an analysis of the alternative dispositions of the asset. Disposal at the end of Year 5 entails the cash effect of the selling price, subject to a 60 per cent tax. The tax is on the *gain*, the excess of the selling price over book value; the book value was zero in this case.

---

[1] In this case, the old equipment was sold outright. Where there is a trade-in of old equipment for new equipment of like kind, special income tax rules result in the gain or loss being added to, or deducted from, the capitalized value of the new equipment. The gain or loss is not recognized in the year of disposal. Instead, it is spread over the life of the new asset as an adjustment of the new depreciation charges.

Before 1962, gains from disposal of equipment were taxed at the capital gains rate, 25 per cent. Since then, the general rule has been that gain on sale of equipment is not a capital gain except in special circumstances. This complicates the effect on taxes of gains arising on disposal, frequently resulting in part of the gain being taxed at ordinary income tax rates and part at capital gain rates. For simplicity, this chapter does not introduce the latter complication.

EXHIBIT 16-3

After-tax Analysis of Equipment Replacement: Total Project Approach

End of year	Present Value Discount Factors, @ 6%	Total Present Value	0	1	2	3	4	5
						Sketch of Cash Flows		
(A) Replace								
Recurring cash operating costs $30,000								
Income tax savings, @ 60 per cent 18,000								
After-tax cash operating costs $12,000	4.212	$(50,544)		($12,000)	($12,000)	($12,000)	($12,000)	($12,000)

Depreciation deductions (sum of digits $1 + 2 + 3 + 4 + 5 = 15$)

Year	Multiplied by $51,000	Deduction	Tax Shield: Income Tax Savings, @ 60%	Present Value Discount Factors, @ 6%	Total Present Value	1	2	3	4	5
1	5/15	$17,000	$10,200	.943	9,619	10,200				
2	4/15	13,600	8,160	.890	7,262		8,160			
3	3/15	10,200	6,120	.840	5,141			6,120		
4	2/15	6,800	4,080	.792	3,231				4,080	
5	1/15	3,400	2,040	.747	1,524					2,040

End of year	Present Value Discount Factors, @ 6%	Total Present Value	0	1	2	3	4	5
Residual value, all subject to tax because book value will be zero, $ 3,000								
Less: 60% income tax 1,800								
Net cash inflow $ 1,200	.747	896						1,200
Initial required investment, actual cash outflow: $51,000	1.000	(51,000)	($51,000)					
Disposal of old equipment:								
Book value now: $56,000 − $21,000 = $35,000								
Selling price 20,000								
Net loss $15,000								
× .60								
Tax savings 9,000								
Net immediate cash effects, including tax saving $29,000	1.000	29,000	29,000					
Total present value of all cash flows		$(44,871)						

Sketch of Cash Flows

End of year		Present Value Discount Factors, @ 6%	Total Present Value	0	1	2	3	4	5
(B) Keep									
Recurring cash operating costs	$40,000								
Income tax savings, @ 60%	24,000								
After-tax operating costs	$16,000	4.212	$(67,392)		($16,000)	($16,000)	($16,000)	($16,000)	($16,000)
Tax-shield: savings in income tax disbursements, @ 60% = .60 × $7,000	4,200	4.212	17,690		4,200	4,200	4,200	4,200	4,200
Residual value, all subject to tax	$ 8,000								
Less: 60% income tax	4,800								
Net cash inflow	$ 3,200	.747	2,390						3,200
Overhaul, end of Year 2	$10,000								
Income tax savings, @ 60%	6,000								
Net effect on cash flow	$ 4,000	.890	(3,560)			(4,000)			
Total present value of all cash flows			$(50,872)						
Difference in favor of replacement			$ 6,001						

EXHIBIT 16-4

After-tax Analysis of Equipment Replacement: Incremental Approach

End of year

Analysis Confined to Differences between (A) and (B) in Exhibit 16-3:

Recurring operating savings,
$40,000 − $30,000 $10,000
Income tax, @ 60%   6,000

		Present Value Discount Factors @ 6%	Total Present Values	Sketch of Cash Flows					
				0	1	2	3	4	5
After-tax operating savings	$ 4,000	4.212	$ 16,848		$4,000	$4,000	$4,000	$4,000	$4,000

Differences in depreciation:

Year	Replace	Keep	Difference	Income Tax Effect, @ 60%	Present Value Discount Factors @ 6%	Total Present Values	0	1	2	3	4	5
1	$17,000	$7,000	$10,000	$6,000	.943	5,658		6,000				
2	13,600	7,000	6,600	3,960	.890	3,524			3,960			
3	10,200	7,000	3,200	1,920	.840	1,614				1,920		
4	6,800	7,000	(200)	(120)	.792	(95)					(120)	
5	3,400	7,000	(3,600)	(2,160)	.747	(1,614)						(2,160)

	Present Value Discount Factors @ 6%	Total Present Values	0	1	2	3	4	5
Difference in disposal value, end of Year 5 (see Exhibit 16-3 for details): $1,200 − $3,200 = $(2,000)	.747	(1,494)						(2,000)
Overhaul avoided, end of Year 2, net of tax effects	.890	3,560			4,000			
Incremental initial investment (see Exhibit 16-3 for details): $51,000 − $29,000	1.000	(22,000)	($22,000)					
Net present value of replacement		$ 6,001						

Immediate replacement entails the disposal of the old equipment at a loss. This loss is fully deductible from current income, so the cash flow computations become a bit more subtle. The net loss must be computed, to isolate its effect on current income tax, but the *total* cash inflow effect is the selling price plus the current income tax benefit.

Step 4. Total Project or Incremental Approach? The relative merits of the total project and the incremental approaches were discussed in Chapter 14. Exhibits 16-3 and 16-4 demonstrate these approaches. Either yields the same net answer in favor of replacement. Note, however, that the incremental approach rapidly becomes unwieldy when computations become intricate. This becomes even more apparent when three or more alternatives are being considered.

Income Tax Complications

In the foregoing illustration, believe it or not, we deliberately avoided many possible income tax complications. As all tax-paying citizens know, income taxes are affected by many intricacies, including progressive tax rates, loss carrybacks and carryforwards, a variety of depreciation options, state income taxes, short- and long-term gains, distinctions between capital assets and other assets, offsets of losses against related gains, exchanges of property of like kind, exempt income, and so forth. Moreover, most fixed asset purchases in the 1960's have qualified for an "investment credit," which is an immediate income tax credit of 7 per cent of the initial cost; furthermore, the full original cost, less the estimated disposal value, is deductible in the form of yearly depreciation.[2]

MISCELLANEOUS TAX PLANNING MATTERS

Changes in Income Tax Rates

During World War II and during the Korean War, the United States imposed an excess profits tax which considerably boosted effective income tax rates. During this period, the prospect of changes in income tax rates in a given year or series of years influenced management planning extensively. If income taxes were going to rise in the next year, the tendency would be to postpone certain expenses (e.g., repairs, advertising, legal services, purchases of supplies not usually inventoried) and to accelerate revenue recognition by boosting production to fill any existing orders before the higher tax rates take effect.

---

[2] For a book-length discussion of these and other complications, see W. L. Raby, *The Income Tax and Business Decisions* (Englewood Cliffs, N.J.: Prentice-Hall, Inc., 1964).

Lifo or Fifo

The income tax planner does not have to be directly concerned with the relative conceptual merits of Lifo (last-in, first-out) or Fifo (first-in, first-out) inventory methods. The most desirable inventory method is that which postpones income tax payments, perhaps permanently. For instance, an expansion coupled with increasing price levels favors Lifo rather than Fifo. In this way, the highest (most recent) costs will be released to expense sooner rather than later.

The adoption of Lifo by one-third of the large American companies is directly attributable to the income tax benefits rather than to the conceptual justification of more "realistic" income measure so often cited. The only tax-planning reasons for not adopting Lifo would be: (1) the negligible prospect of income tax savings because of expected long-run declines in prices; (2) stability of prices; and (3) insignificance of inventories to particular organizations, such as service businesses.

If the prices of inventory are expected to rise, a company should adopt Lifo. The annual savings in cash flow will have compound effects and will result in a substantial financial advantage. Raby illustrates these effects as follows:

> Assume an effective income tax rate of 50 per cent and after-tax rate of return of 7 per cent. Inventory is $1,000,000 at time of adoption of Lifo. Prices increase in a straight-line, so that, inventory in Year 1 is $1,100,000 under Fifo but still $1,000,000 under Lifo; in Year 2 Fifo inventory is $1,200,000; in Year 3, $1,300,000; and so forth throughout twenty years. Meanwhile, Lifo inventory stays at $1,000,000, and income tax savings of $50,000 annually, invested at 7 per cent compounded annually, will accumulate to $2,049,750 more assets under Lifo.[3]

Effect of Lifo on Purchase Decisions

When prices are rising, it may be advantageous—subject to prudent restraint as to maximum and minimum inventory levels—to buy unusually heavy amounts of inventory near year-end, particularly if income tax rates are likely to fall. For example, assume that a company has made the following transactions during 19x1, its first year in business:

Sales: 10 units, @ $5   Purchases: 8 units, @ $2
                                       3 units, @ $3

Decision: Buy 6 more units, near year-end, @ $4? Current income tax rates, 50 per cent, are expected to decline to 40 per cent next year. Prices on inventory are not expected to decline next year.

---

[3] *Ibid.*, p. 226.

Comparison of Alternatives

		Do Not Buy	Buy 6 More Units
Sales: 10 units, @ $5		$50	$50
Cost of goods sold (Lifo basis):			
3 units, @ $3	= $ 9		
7 units, @ 2	= 14	23	
or			
6 units, @ $4	= $24		
3 units, @ 3	= 9		
1 unit, @ 2	= 2		35
Gross margin		$27	$15

Tax savings: 50 per cent of ($27 − $15) = $6.00 this year. The effects on later years' taxes will depend on inventory levels, prices, and tax rates.

Tax savings can be generated because Lifo permits management to influence immediate net income by its purchasing decisions. In contrast, Fifo results would be unaffected by this decision:

		Do Not Buy	Buy 6 More Units
Sales		$50	$50
Cost of goods sold (Fifo basis):			
8 units, @ $2	= $16		
2 units, @ $3	= 6	22	22
Gross margin		$28	$28

Contributions of Property Rather Than Cash

Donations to qualifying charitable educational and similar institutions are generally deductible in computing income taxes. Giving property (such as marketable securities or land) rather than cash is more beneficial to both the donor and the donee. The reason is that any gain accumulated on the property[4] is unrecognized, but the tax deduction is the fair market value of the contributed asset. For example:

Market price	$400,000
Cost of property	100,000
Capital gain	$300,000
Capital gain tax, @ 25 per cent	$ 75,000

[4] A capital gain on qualifying assets held more than six months is subject to tax at a rate of 25 per cent, rather than at ordinary income tax rates. The tax law specifies which assets are subject to the capital gains rate (the most notable are land and marketable securities). Gains on sales of inventories and receivables are taxed at ordinary rates, while gains on sales of depreciable property are now taxed as ordinary income in most cases.

NOT RESPONSIBLE FOR

	Sell, and Donate Cash	Donate Outright
Income tax effects of contribution:		
Deduction	$325,000	$400,000
Assumed income tax rate of 50 per cent	× .50	× .50
Income tax savings	$162,500	$200,000
Charitable institution can receive:		
Cash = $400,000 in cash − $75,000 tax	$325,000	
Property, and then sell it for cash		$400,000

As the tabulation suggests, charitable institutions have tried to attract donations by stressing the tax-saving features of giving property rather than cash.

Variable and Fixed Costs and Making Profits through Giving: Illustration

Orace Johnson has investigated the effects on net income of the merchandise contributions made by the drug companies to the 1962 ransom of Cuban prisoners. The merchandise was deductible for income tax purposes at the lowest price at which the goods are regularly sold to the contributor's usual customers. If, as in the case of the drug companies,

EXHIBIT 16-5

Comparative Effects of Sales and Donation of Extra Ten Units of Merchandise

Actions

1	Sell 1,010 units
2	Sell 1,000 units and have idle capacity of 10 units
3	Sell 1,000 units and give away 10 (same as Cuban ransom)
4	Sell 1,000 units and give away cash

	1*	2	3	4
Sales	$1,010	$1,000	(same	(same
Variable expenses	202	200	as if	as if
			1,000	1,000
Contribution margin	$ 808	$ 800	sales	sales
			were	were
Non-variable expenses	600	600	made)	made)
Net income before donation	$ 208	$ 200	$ 200	$ 200
Donation deduction for tax purposes	—	—	10	10
Net taxable income	$ 208	$ 200	$ 190	$ 190
Income taxes	146	140	133	133
Net income after taxes (before adjustment)	$ 62	$ 60	$ 57	$57
Adjustment for overstatement of cost of donations†	—	—	8	—
Net income, as adjusted	$ 62	$ 60	$ 65	$57

SOURCE: Adapted from O. Johnson, "Charity Begins at Home," University of Chicago, 1964. (Unpublished.)

* Practical capacity 1,010 units. Selling price, $1. Variable expenses, 20¢. Nonvariable expenses $600. Tax rate is 70 per cent.

† $1.00 market value − $.20 variable cost = $.80 per unit.

the variable costs of the merchandise are relatively small, the corporation's net income after taxes may be increased more by giving merchandise than by selling it. In other words, the tax savings from contributions can actually exceed the variable costs of the goods. These effects are illustrated in Exhibit 16-5. The lesson here is that it is generally better to donate merchandise rather than cash.

Operating Losses

The net operating loss of a corporation may be used to offset net income by being carried back to each of the three preceding years and carried forward to each of the five following years. This sequence must be followed strictly. No part of a given year's loss may be used to offset the second preceding year's income until all of the third preceding year's income has been absorbed. In sum, a net operating loss enables the corporation to obtain tax refunds related to past years' operations or to reduce tax disbursements in future years.

The tax effects of a 19x4 net operating loss may be illustrated as follows (note that any loss carryforward unused after five years becomes nondeductible):

	Net Income (Loss)	19x4 Carryback or Carryforward	Taxable Income
19x1	$ 5,000	$ (5,000)	—
19x2	15,000	(15,000)	—
19x3	35,000	(35,000)	—
19x4	(100,000)	—	—
19x5	5,000	(5,000)	—
19x6	8,000	(8,000)	—
19x7	10,000	(10,000)	—
19x8	10,000	(10,000)	—
19x9	5,000	(5,000)	—
Used		(93,000)	
Unused and nondeductable		(7,000)	
Accounted for		(100,000)	

Strangely enough, a company may properly view a loss carryforward as an "asset," for planning purposes. It represents a valuable tax deduction as long as profitable operations are forthcoming. If the tax rate is 48 per cent, a loss carryforward of $100,000 represents future tax savings of $48,000. In certain cases, this may prompt corporations to buy other profitable companies at higher-than-usual prices.

Suppose that Co. A has a potential net operating cash inflow of $200,-000 per year for the next five years. Suppose further that two companies, X and Y, are interested in buying Co. A. Company X has a $1,000,000 net operating loss carryforward that it can offset against the next five years' net taxable income. Company Y has no such loss carryforward.

Both companies are willing to buy all the capital stock of Company A at a price not to exceed the present value of the five years' after-tax cash inflows, discounted at 8 per cent. What are the maximum prices that Company X and Y are willing to pay? Calculations follow:

Company Y

After-tax net cash inflow of Company A is $200,000 less .48(200,000)	$= $104,000	
Present value of an annuity of $1, @ 8 per cent, for 5 years	$\times$	3.993
Maximum price		$415,272

Company X

After-tax net cash inflow of Company A would be the entire $200,000, because of the loss carried forward		$200,000
Present value of an annuity of $1, @ 8 per cent, for 5 years	$\times$	3.993
Maximum price		$798,600

The relevance of the loss carryforward in the Company X analysis depends on the available alternatives. Perhaps the carryforward can be used to offset Company X's future regular income. That is, there is danger of double-counting the carryforward. It cannot be used to offset both the Company A income and the Company X income.

Tax-free Interest

Interest on the bonds issued by a city, state, and certain nonprofit organizations is nontaxable to the investor. Because of this feature, such bonds have a lower pre-tax yield than industrial bonds. However, the high-bracket taxpayer will usually find tax-exempt bonds more attractive:

	Industrial Bond: Coupon Rate, 5%	Municipal Bond: Coupon Rate, 3%
Investment in bonds	$100,000	$100,000
Interest income before taxes	$ 5,000	$ 3,000
Income taxes, @ 50 per cent	2,500	—
Net income, after taxes	$ 2,500	$ 3,000

Other General Considerations

ɪ URCHASES OF ASSETS. When a group of assets is acquired for a single over-all price, care must be taken to see that as much of the total cost as possible is allocated to those assets whose costs will eventually be deductible for income tax purposes. Otherwise, the excess of the total cost over those parts allocated is assigned to land and/or goodwill, which are not subject to amortization for income tax purposes.

USE OF DEBT IN THE CAPITAL STRUCTURE. Interest is deductible as an expense; dividends are not. Therefore, the relative after-tax cash drains on corporations favor using as much debt in the capital structure as seems prudent. Assume a 50 per cent tax rate:

	Pre-tax Cost	After-tax Cost
4% Bonds Payable	4%	2%
6% Preferred Stock	6%	6%

RESEARCH AND DEVELOPMENT. There is conceptual merit in capitalizing many research costs. From a tax-planning standpoint, however, research costs should be deducted as quickly as possible.

CASH VERSUS ACCRUAL ACCOUNTING METHODS. The cash method of accounting allows more discretion in the timing of revenue and expense than the accrual method. However, where inventories exist, companies must use the accrual basis.

DEFERRAL OF INCOME. Among the many ways of deferring income are installment sales methods, whereby income is geared to cash receipts rather than point of sale.

For example, a furniture store's taxable income for its first year in business could be computed as follows:

	Regular Basis	Installment Basis
Installment sales	$500,000	
Cost of goods sold	300,000	
Gross profit, @ 40 per cent	$200,000	$160,000*
Expenses	150,000	150,000
Net taxable income	$ 50,000	$ 10,000

* 40 per cent of current installment collections of $400,000. Unrealized gross profit is 40 per cent of ending receivables: 40 per cent of $100,000, or $40,000.

If the owner chooses to report income on the installment basis, income tax on the uncollected gross profit—which is 40 per cent of $100,000 (i.e., $500,000 − $400,000), or $40,000—is deferred.

Also available is the discretionary timing of shipments. At year-end, shipment at Dec. 31 or Jan. 1 can have a significant impact on income taxes, because the sale can be included in either year.

DIVIDENDS RECEIVED. Corporations can generally deduct 85 per cent of dividends received from taxable domestic corporations; in other words, only 15 per cent of the dividend is taxable to the recipient. This provision enhances the attractiveness of investing excess cash in common stock rather than in federal or corporate bonds, whose interest is fully taxable.

TIMING OF GAINS AND LOSSES. Capital gains on the disposal of qualifying assets are taxed at 25 per cent; losses on these assets are fully deductible if they exceed the capital gains. Because the losses offset the gains dollar for dollar, the shrewd tax planner tries to time his transactions so that losses occur in one year and gains in another.

For example, assume that a company owns two parcels of land. One parcel can be sold at a capital gain of $500,000; the other, at a capital loss of $500,000. If both are sold in the same year, the loss would offset the gain, and there would be no impact on taxes. If they are sold in separate years, the tax bill would be 25 per cent of $500,000 in one year, or $125,000, and lower (assuming an ordinary tax rate of 48 per cent) by $240,000 in the next year. The second strategy would save the company $115,000 in income tax disbursements.

Desirability of Losses

The oft-heard expression, "What the heck, it's deductible," sometimes warps perspective. Even though losses bring income-tax savings and gains bring additional income taxes, gains are still more desirable than losses. For example, 100 shares of stock which cost $300 a few years ago and which are sold now, would have the following effect at two different selling prices:

	Gain		Loss	
Selling price	$1,000	$1,000	$ 100	$100
Cost	300		300	
Gain (loss)	$ 700		$(200)	
Tax, @ 25 per cent of $700		175		
Tax savings, @ 60 per cent of $200				120
Net cash effect		$825		$220

SUMMARY

The income tax is a significant cost of conducting business. No accountant or manager should be indifferent to its impact. Income taxes may be necessary evils, but this does not mean that management should be resigned to tax burdens. Intelligent planning, assisted by expert advice, can minimize income taxes.

Income taxes are sometimes too influential in business decisions. Their effects may be overemphasized. The ogre of the income tax may reduce the emphasis on efficiency and may unduly hamper risk taking. The income tax is only one of a number of variables that bear on business administration.

SUMMARY PROBLEM FOR YOUR REVIEW

PROBLEM

The Flan Co. estimates that it can save $2,500 per year in annual cash operating costs for the next five years if it buys a special-purpose machine at a cost of $9,000. Residual value is expected to be $1,000, although no residual value is being provided for in using sum-of-the-years' digits depreciation for tax purposes. The minimum desired rate of return, after taxes, is 10 per cent. Income tax rates are 40 per cent on ordinary income and 25 per cent on capital gains. Using discounted cash flow techniques, show whether the investment is desirable.

	Present Value Discount Factors, @ 10%	Total Present Values
End of year		
Recurring cash operating savings $2,500		
Income taxes, @ 40% 1,000		
After-tax cash operating savings $1,500	3.791	$ 5,686

Depreciation: Sum-of-the-years' digits,
$1 + 2 + 3 + 4 + 5 = 15$

Year	Multiplied by $9,000	Deduction	Tax Shield: Income Tax Savings, @ 40%	Present Value Discount Factors, @ 10%	Total Present Values
1	5/15	$3,000	$1,200	.909	1,091
2	4/15	2,400	960	.826	793
3	3/15	1,800	720	.751	541
4	2/15	1,200	480	.683	328
5	1/15	600	240	.621	149

	Present Value Discount Factors, @ 10%	Total Present Values
Residual value, all subject to tax because book value will be zero $1,000		
Less: 40% income tax on disposal gain* 400		
Net cash inflow $ 600	.621	373
Initial required investment		(9,000)
Net present value of all cash flows		$ (39)

Sketch of Cash Flows

	0	1	2	3	4	5
After-tax cash operating savings		$1,500	$1,500	$1,500	$1,500	$1,500
Tax Shield		1,200	960	720	480	240
Net cash inflow (residual)						600
Initial required investment	(9,000)					

* Ordinary income tax rates, not capital gains rates, apply.

There is a net disadvantage in purchasing because the net present value is slightly negative, indicating a time-adjusted rate of return a shade below the minimum desired rate of 10 per cent.

453

ESSENTIAL ASSIGNMENT MATERIAL

16-1. *Terminology.* Define: tax shield.

16-2. *Income taxes and disposal of assets.* Assume that income tax rates are 60 per cent on ordinary income and 25 per cent on capital gains.

    1. The book value of an old machine is $20,000. It is to be sold for $8,000. What is the effect of this decision on cash flows, after taxes?

    2. The book value of an old machine is $10,000. It is to be sold for $13,000. What is the effect on cash flows, after taxes, of this decision?

16-3. *Equipment purchase.* The Morax Co. expects to save $6,000 in cash operating costs for each of the next four years if it buys a special machine at a cost of $20,000. Residual value is expected to be $1,000, although no residual value is being provided for in using the sum-of-the-years' digits depreciation method for tax purposes. A major overhaul, costing $1,000, will occur at the end of the second year and is fully deductible, in that year, for income tax purposes. The minimum desired rate of return, after taxes, is 8 per cent. Income tax rates are 60 per cent on ordinary income and 25 per cent on capital gains. Using discounted-cash-flow-techniques, show whether the investment is desirable.

16-4. *Income taxes and replacement of equipment.* Refer to Problem 14-4. Assume that income tax rates are 60 per cent on ordinary income and 25 per cent on capital gains. The minimum desired rate of return, after taxes, is 6 per cent. Using the net present value technique, show whether the proposed equipment should be purchased. Present your solution on both a total project approach and an incremental approach. For illustrative purposes, assume that old equipment would have been depreciated on a straight-line basis and the proposed equipment on a sum-of-the-years' digits basis.

16-5. *Effects of Lifo, Fifo, and direct costing.* (Adapted from a problem originated by George H. Sorter.) The Cado Co. is starting in business on Dec. 31, 19x0. In each *half year*, from 19x1 through 19x4, they expect to purchase 1,000 units and sell 500 units for the amounts listed below. In 19x5, they expect to purchase no units and sell 4,000 units for the amount indicated below.

	19x1	19x2	19x3	19x4	19x5
Purchases:					
First 6 months	$ 2,000	$ 4,000	$ 6,000	$ 6,000	0
Second 6 months	4,000	9,000	6,000	8,000	0
Total	$ 6,000	$13,000	$12,000	$14,000	0
Sales (at selling price)	$10,000	$10,000	$10,000	$10,000	$40,000

Assume that there are no costs or expenses other than those shown above. The tax rate is 60 per cent, and taxes for each year are payable on Dec. 31 of each year. Cado Co. is trying to decide whether to use periodic Fifo or Lifo throughout the five-year period.

Required:

1. What was net income after taxes under Fifo for each of the five years? Under Lifo? Show calculations.
2. Explain briefly which method, Lifo or Fifo, seems more advantageous, and why. What kind of quantitative analysis, other than that performed in (1), might help you to reach a decision?
3. Suppose that this problem deals with goods being manufactured, rather than with goods being purchased. Assume that the Purchases shown in the above tabulation are Costs of Goods Manufactured, computed on a full absorption costing basis. Assume that fixed manufacturing costs are $3,000 per year. For each of the five years, would net income be higher or lower under direct costing than under absorption costing?

ADDITIONAL ASSIGNMENT MATERIAL

Note: These problems cover a wide range of assorted topics. Problem 16-23 explores the tax aspects of a problem from a previous chapter. Problem 16-24 demonstrates in stark fashion how the value of accelerated depreciation methods is affected by future increases in tax rates.

16-6. Distinguish between tax avoidance and tax evasion.
16-7. "Tax planning is unimportant because the total income tax bill will be the same in the long run, regardless of short-run maneuvering." Do you agree? Explain.
16-8. What are the major influences on the present value of a tax deduction?
16-9. Explain why accelerated depreciation methods are superior to straight-line methods for income tax purposes.
16-10. "Immediate disposal of equipment, rather than its continued use, results in a full tax deduction of the undepreciated cost now—rather than having such a deduction spread over future years in the form of annual depreciation." Do you agree? Explain, using the $35,000 cost of old equipment in Exhibit 16-3 as a basis for your discussion.
16-11. Name some income tax complications that were ignored in Exhibits 16-3 and 16-4.
16-12. What is an investment credit?
16-13. Why does Lifo save income taxes when prices are rising?
16-14. "If income tax rates are likely to rise, the tendency would be to increase year-end purchases of inventory under Lifo." Do you agree? Explain.
16-15. Why have charitable institutions tried to attract donations in the form of property rather than cash?
16-16. How was it possible that the drug companies' net income was increased in 1962 by their contribution to the ransom of Cuban prisoners?
16-17. "A loss carryforward has an economic value." Explain.
16-18. *Effects of Lifo on purchase decisions.* The Bjork Corp. is nearing the end of its first year in business. The following purchases of its single product have been made:

	Units	Unit Price	Total Cost
January	1,000	$10	$10,000
March	1,000	10	10,000
May	1,000	11	11,000
July	1,000	13	13,000
September	1,000	14	14,000
November	1,000	15	15,000
	6,000		$73,000

Sales for the year will be 5,000 units for $120,000. Expenses other than cost of goods sold will be $20,000.

The president is undecided about whether to adopt Fifo or Lifo for income tax purposes. The company has ample storage space for up to 7,000 units of inventory. Inventory prices are expected to stay at $15 per unit for the next few months.

Required:

1. If the president decided to purchase 4,000 units @ $15 in December, what would be the net income before taxes, the income taxes, and the net income after taxes for the year under: (*a*) Fifo; and (*b*) Lifo? Income tax rates are 30 per cent on the first $25,000 of net taxable income and 50 per cent on the excess.

2. If the company sells its year-end inventory in Year 2 @ $24 per unit and goes out of business, what would be the net income before taxes, the income taxes, and the net income after taxes under: (*a*) Fifo; and (*b*) Lifo? Assume that other expenses in Year 2 are $20,000.

3. Repeat (1) and (2), assuming that 4,000 units, @ $15, were not purchased until January of the second year. Generalize on the effects on net income of the timing of purchases under Fifo and Lifo.

16-19. *Donations of property rather than cash.* The Fantasy Co. has 100 shares of Florence common stock that were acquired four years ago at $70 per share. Current market price is $120 per share. Income tax rates are 60 per cent on ordinary income and 25 per cent on capital gains. Compare the effects on Fantasy's income taxes of: (1) selling the stock and donating the net cash after taxes to a university; and (2) donating the stock outright. How much cash will the university net under each plan, assuming that all donations of property are immediately converted into cash?

16-20. *Variable and fixed costs and donations.* A company has a practical capacity of 10,000 units of product. Sales for the year are 9,500 units. It is Dec. 31. Variable costs of production are 30¢, per unit. Nonvariable expenses are $6,000. The selling price is $1, per unit. The tax rate is 60 per cent.

The company is going to donate either $100 in cash or 100 units of product to a local charity.

Required:

Show the effects on: (1) taxable net income; (2) income taxes; and (3) net income after taxes of each alternative plus the following alternative: Donate nothing, but sell the 100 units through regular channels (in addition to the 9,500 units already sold).

16-21. *Loss carryforward and purchase of a business.* Company *G*'s potential net operating cash inflow, before taxes, for the next five years is $500,000 annually. Two companies, *P* and *Q*, are interested in buying all of the capital stock of Co. *G*. Company *P* has a $2,500,000 net operating loss which it can carry forward to offset the next five years' net taxable income. Company *Q* has no such loss carryforward. Both companies are willing to buy all the capital stock of Co. *G* at a price not to exceed the present value of the five years' cash inflow after taxes, discounted at 10 per cent. *Required:* What are the maximum prices that Co. *P* and Co. *Q* are willing to pay? Show calculations. The ordinary income tax rate is 40 per cent and the capital gains rate is 25 per cent.

16-22. *Timing of gains and losses.* A company owns 10,000 shares each of the common stock of Co. *A* and Co. *B*. The Co. *A* stock was acquired ten years ago for $100,000. It can now be sold for $400,000. The Co. *B* stock was purchased five years ago for $900,000. It can now be sold for $600,000. It is now near the end of year 19x1. Capital gains tax rate is 25 per cent, and ordinary income tax rate is 40 per cent.

Required:

1. If all the stock were sold in 19x1, what would be the effect on income taxes?

2. If the Co. *B* stock were sold in 19x1, and the Co. *A* stock were sold in 19x2, what would be the effect on income taxes? Assume that these are the only transactions affecting capital gains or losses. Which strategy will save the most income taxes? How much would be saved?

16-23. *Income taxes and make or buy.* Refer to Problem 13-29. Assume a tax rate of 40 per cent on ordinary income and 25 per cent on capital gains. The minimum desired rate of return, after taxes, is 6 per cent. Using the net present value technique, show whether the proposed purchase from the outside supplier is desirable. Use both a total project approach and an incremental approach. Assume straight line depreciation.

16-24. *Tax shield and depreciation methods.* A company has just paid $42,000 for some equipment that will have a six-year life and no residual value. The minimum rate of return desired, after taxes, is 10 per cent.

The president has attended a management conference luncheon where an accounting professor had adamantly stated: "Not using accelerated depreciation for tax purposes is outright financial stupidity." The president has a perpetual fear of rises in income tax rates and has favored straight line depreciation "to have greater deductions against future income when taxes are higher."

He is having second thoughts now, and has asked you to prepare a financial analysis of the dollar benefits of using sum-of-the-years' digits depreciation instead of straight line depreciation under the following assumptions: (*a*) income tax rates of 60 per cent throughout the coming six years; and (*b*) income tax rates of 60 per cent for the first three years and 80 per cent for the subsequent three years.

16-25. *Comprehensive problem on equipment replacement.* A manufacturer who specializes in making aircraft parts developed a $68,000 special-purpose molding machine for automatically producing a special part. The machine will be useless after the total market potential, spread evenly over four years, is exhausted. The machine has been used for one year. The $68,000 original cost is being depreciated on a straight line basis.

At the beginning of the second year, a machine salesman offers a new machine which is vastly more efficient. It will cost $45,000, will reduce annual cash operating costs from $45,000 to $26,500, and will have zero disposal value at the end of three years. Sum-of-the-years' digits would be the depreciation method used for tax purposes for this machine.

The scrap value of the old machine is $30,000 now and will be $2,000 three years from now; however, no scrap value has been provided for in calculating straight line depreciation for tax purposes.

Assume that income tax rates are 60 per cent on ordinary income and 25 per cent on capital gains. The minimum rate of return desired, after taxes, is 8 per cent. Using the net present value technique, show whether the new machine should be purchased: (a) under a total project approach; and (b) under an incremental approach.

CHAPTER 17

Influences
of Quantitative Techniques
on Management Accounting

THE DIGITAL COMPUTER HAS HAD A SWIFT AND VAST IMPACT on business. It has stimulated a trend toward: (1) the design of integrated business information systems; (2) the application of mathematical models to the solution of business problems via simulation, statistical probability techniques, linear programming, and sophisticated inventory control models; and (3) the realignment of organizational structures and executive responsibilities. Although the accounting system continues to provide the large bulk of the quantitative information used by managers in guiding their organizations, accountants and managers need to be aware of the current and potential impact of mathematical models and computers on business practice.

Because the branches of knowledge overlap, it is always an oversimplification to specify where the field of accounting starts and where it ends. Some accountants take the view that accounting should restrict itself to score keeping, the compilation of financial history. Others feel that if accountants do not move quickly to assimilate a working knowledge of computer technology and assorted mathematical techniques, their attention-directing and problem-solving functions will be seized by the burgeoning field of management science.

We need not be concerned with the controversy over what

is accounting and what is not. Regardless of its label, the subject matter of this chapter has a bearing on management planning and control and is therefore important to accountants and to managers. One of the marks of an educated man is his ability to recognize and accept changes that promise better ways of accomplishing objectives. The accountant is still the top quantitative expert in nearly all organizations, and few companies employ full time operations research specialists. To retain and improve his status, the accountant should be aware of how operations research techniques may improve his problem-solving abilities. The alert manager would naturally expect his accountants to keep abreast of the newer quantitative techniques.

This chapter is a survey. Technical competence in any of the areas mentioned can be achieved only by thorough specialized study.

OPERATIONS RESEARCH

Description of the Field

Operations research (often abbreviated hereafter as OR) is a diffused collection of mathematical and statistical models which are applied to decision making. It is characterized by: (1) a rigorous search for and definition of the central problem; (2) an over-all organizational approach; (3) mixed teams of mathematicians, statisticians, engineers, and, to a much lesser extent, accountants; and (4) the use of mathematical and statistical models as a framework for analysis.

Operations research techniques were initially developed in Great Britain during World War II. Groups of mathematicians, statisticians, physicists, chemists, and military commanders pooled their talents to solve complex problems throughout the war—problems such as convoy sizes, repair schedules for airplane engines, and deployment of ships to minimize losses from the suicidal attacks by Japanese kamikaze pilots.

Management science is a term that is often used interchangeably with OR, although the pioneers in the field have spent many frustrating hours splitting hairs about how the two differ. For our purposes, management science is a broader concept than OR because it embraces OR (i.e., the building of mathematical models) *and* digital computer techniques (i.e., practical applications of OR ideas).

OR is primarily a tool for *planning*, rather than *controlling*. It is a disciplined means for discovering feasible alternatives, evaluating them, and selecting the best alternative. Control is subordinate, in the sense that even poor decisions may be implemented in an efficient way. For example, an obsolete machine that needs replacement may be operated with supreme efficiency, but factory costs may nonetheless be too high.

Characteristics of Models

A model is a depiction of the interrelationships among the recognized factors in the real situation. Most models spotlight the key interrelationships and deemphasize the unimportant factors. Models take many forms. Museums contain model rockets and model ships. Automobile companies distribute miniature model cars. Accountants continually work with accounting systems and financial reports, which are models. Operations researchers principally use mathematical equations as models.

When OR models are an accurate portrayal of real relationships, they can replace hunches, guesses, and business folklore with an explicit collection and appraisal of a *large number* of relevant factors. The practical power of OR techniques is their ability to deal with a huge number of alternatives or restrictions (e.g., a set of many equations with many unknowns). Once the equations are formulated, the digital computer can solve them rapidly. Without the computer, OR's practical potential would be much more limited.

Models must conform to reality in two major respects. First, they must capture the factors relevant to the problem. For example, discounted cash flow models are appropriate for capital budgeting decisions, but unadjusted rate-of-return models are not. Historical depreciation costs, although relevant in income-statement models, are irrelevant to equipment-replacement problems. Second, the data must be accurate. Elaborate conceptual models may be constructed, but they may be impractical because the data needed to test the model cannot be isolated and measured. For example, there is some tendency to use unit costs which, when they are conglomerations of variable, fixed, and joint costs, may be inappropriate. Because operations researchers often depend on accounting data for testing their models, it is evident that OR men must comprehend the meaning and limitations of accounting data. Moreover, to maximize accounting's usefulness in the problem-solving function, accountants must comprehend the purposes and meaning of those OR models that use accounting data.

Some OR Techniques

The growth of OR has been accompanied by many new terms. The most widely used techniques in business are statistical probability theory, linear programming, and inventory planning and control systems. These will be described more fully in later sections. Other techniques include:

1. *PERT* (Program Evaluation and Review Technique) is a formal, probabilistic diagram of the interrelationships of a complex time series of activities. Its objective is to discover potential bottlenecks and to chart progress. PERT was initially used in missile research and development,

where time estimates are considered crucial, and many military contracts now specify that PERT be used. When PERT is combined with costs to determine optimum trade-offs between time and costs, it is called PERT-COST.

2. *Simulation* is the formulation of a detailed model of a system or process. It is valuable because it permits experimentation with different alternatives before a final course of action is selected.

Normal and Poisson distributions are widely used in model building by statisticians. The data may then be tested repeatedly on a digital computer, and average expected results obtained.

However, because normal and Poisson distributions often do not adequately describe the distribution of demand met in practice, a simulation is not necessarily repeated over and over and then averaged. In inventory control models, for example, a company's historical demand data may be fed into a simulation; the ingredients (combinations of various stock levels, purchase-order sizes, and sales) of the model may then be manipulated until the best (optimal) set is discovered. The solution can then be tested on a separate set of historical demand data, preferably from a different year.

3. *Waiting-line* or *queuing theory* deals with the problems of supplying facilities to meet a demand that comes in uneven spurts (e.g., cars at a toll booth, people using elevators in an office building, machines awaiting a limited number of repairmen).

4. *Competitive models* are applications of managerial economics which use probability theory in dealing with such relevant variables as a company's own costs, competitors' costs, and competitors' bids. The objective of this application of *game theory* is to help management follow an optimal pricing policy.

5. *Information theory* is a rigorous study of the interrelationships of capacity, noise, size, timing, and feedback in a communications network.

6. *Dynamic programming* is a technique for optimizing the overall effect of a time sequence of interrelated decisions, basically by working backward from the last point to the first point in a complex network of decisions.

STATISTICAL PROBABILITY THEORY

Probabilistic Approach to Uncertainty

Statistical probability theory is used in many OR techniques. Probability theory is a rigorous approach to the quantification of uncertainties. Decision making is crystal-ball gazing. The manager is seldom *certain* about the future. His choices are based on *expected* future outcomes, and these are subject to a number of influences that may generate different results. Under uncertainty, the correspondence of the actual outcome with the predicted outcome is purely random—that is, it is subject to the laws of chance.

Accountants tend to quantify predictions with single-figure estimates, without explicitly or formally reporting the uncertainties attached to the individual figures. The range of the possible outcomes is rarely stated.

Thus, comparisons of single-figure estimates may be insufficient or downright misleading.

Schlaifer[1] and others have developed an approach to these decisions that accountants and managers should find helpful. Probabilities are assigned to the possible range of outcomes by the executives. The probabilities of all possible events under consideration must be exhaustive—that is, they must add up to 100 per cent. If the chance of a flipped coin showing heads is fifty-fifty, the probability would be expressed as .5:

Event	Percentage Chance of Occurence	Probability
A: Heads	50%	.5
B: Tails	50	.5
	100%	1.0

For example, as an appliance dealer, you may be deciding on how to service your one-year warranty on the 1,000 color television sets that you have just sold to a large local hotel. You have three alternatives:

1. A reputable service firm has offered to service the sets, including all parts and labor, for a flat fee of $18,000.
2. For $15,000, another reputable service firm would furnish all necessary parts and provide up to 1,000 service calls at no charge. Service calls in excess of that number would be $4 each. The number of calls are likely to be:

Event	Chance of Occurrence	Probability of Occurrence	Total Cost
A: 1,000 calls or less	50%	.5	$15,000
B: 1,500 calls	20	.2	17,000
C: 2,000 calls	20	.2	19,000
D: 2,500 calls	10	.1	21,000
	100%	1.0	

3. You can hire your own labor and buy your own parts. Your past experience with similar work has helped you to formulate the following probabilities and costs:

Event	Chance of Occurrence	Probability of Occurrence	Total Cost
A: Little trouble	10%	.1	$ 8,000
B: Medium trouble	70	.7	10,000
C: Much trouble	20	.2	30,000
	100%	1.0	

Schlaifer would construct three *expected value tables,* as follows:

[1] R. Schlaifer, *Probability and Statistics for Business Decisions* (New York: McGraw-Hill Book Company, 1959), p. 25.

	(1)	(2)	(3)	(4)
			Value	
	Event	*Probability*	*Conditional*	*Expected*
1.	*A:* Certainty	1.0	$18,000	$18,000
2.	*A:* 1,000 calls or less	.5	$15,000	$ 7,500
	B: 1,500 calls	.2	17,000	3,400
	C: 2,000 calls	.2	19,000	3,800
	D: 2,500 calls	.1	21,000	2,100
		1.0		
	Expected value			$16,800
3.	*A:* Little trouble	.1	$ 8,000	$ 800
	B: Medium trouble	.7	10,000	7,000
	C: Much trouble	.2	30,000	6,000
		1.0		
	Expected value			$13,800

Note the steps for each alternative:
a. List every possible event in column (1).
b. Enter the probability of each event in column (2).
c. Enter the conditional value of each event in column (3).
d. Multiply the probability of each event by the conditional value. Enter the product in column (4), taking care to preserve the algebraic sign.
e. Add the products in column (4), with due regard for the algebraic sign.

This approach preferably uses objective probabilities based on historical evidence and tempered by business judgment. However, if no historical evidence is available, subjective probabilities, based on a consensus of the interested managers' best judgment, should be used. The use of subjective probabilities forces the executive to make an explicit statement of the intuitive judgments and hunches that he so often uses.

In this case, a decision based strictly on expected values would favor Alternative 3. However, reliance on a single number may bury information that the executive may need for a wise decision. There is a 20 per cent chance that the cost of Alternative 3 will soar to $30,000, whereas there is no uncertainty about Alternative 1. Comparison of the $18,000, $16,800, and $13,800 costs, by themselves, are not as informative as having these figures *plus* some idea of the probability distributions which they represent. The accountant should explicitly attempt to indicate the degree of uncertainty accompanying the budget or the relevant cost estimates.

The following example illustrates the essential techniques:

EXAMPLE

Once a day a retailer stocks bunches of fresh-cut flowers, which cost $.40 and sell for $1 each. The retailer never cuts the price; leftovers are given to a nearby church. He estimates demand as follows:

Demand	Probability
0	.05
1	.20
2	.40
3	.25
4	.10
5 or more	.00

He wants to know how many units he should stock in order to maximize profits. Try to solve his problem before consulting the following solution.

SOLUTION

The profit, per unit sold, is $.60; the loss, per unit unsold, is $.40. All of the alternatives may be assessed in the following *payoff table:*[2]

		Act: Units Purchased								
		0		*1*		*2*		*3*		*4*	
Event: Demand	Probability of Event	C.V.*	E.V.†	C.V.	E.V.	C.V.	E.V.	C.V.	E.V.	C.V.	E.V.
0	.05	0	0	$−.40	$−.02	$− .80	$−.04	$−1.20	$−.06	$−1.60	$−.08
1	.20	0	0	.60	.12	.20	.04	− .20	−.04	− .60	−.12
2	.40	0	0	.60	.24	1.20	.48	.80	.32	.40	.16
3	.25	0	0	.60	.15	1.20	.30	1.80	.45	1.40	.35
4	.10	0	0	.60	.06	1.20	.12	1.80	.18	2.40	.24
			$0		$ .55		$ .90		$ .85		$ .55

* Conditional value.
† Expected value.

The expected value (E.V.) of any act is computed by taking a weighted average of the appropriate conditional value (C.V.) of each act. The probabilities in Column two are used as the weighting factors. To maximize expected profit, the retailer should stock two units.

Obtaining Additional Information

Sometimes the executive is hesitant about making a decision. He would like to obtain more information before making a final choice. Some additional information is nearly always obtainable—at a price. Schlaifer has suggested a technique for computing the maximum amount that should be paid for such additional information. The general idea is to compute the expected value, under ideal circumstances—that is, circumstances which would permit the retailer to predict, with absolute certainty, the number of units to be sold on any given day. A payoff table *with perfect information* would appear as follows:

[2] Schlaifer, *op. cit.*

Event: Demand	Probability of Event	Perfect Information	
		Conditional Value	*Expected Value*
0	.05	$0	$0
1	.20	.60	.12
2	.40	1.20	.48
3	.25	1.80	.45
4	.10	2.40	.24
			$1.29

In this table, it is assumed that the retailer will never err in his forecasts and that demand will fluctuate from zero to four exactly as indicated by the probabilities. The maximum day-in, day-out profit is $1.29. Consequently, the most he should be willing to pay for perfect advance information would be the difference between the expected value with perfect information and the expected value with existing information, $1.29 − $.90, or 39¢. Schlaifer calls the latter the expected value of perfect information, the top price the retailer should pay for additional knowledge.

In the real world, of course, the retailer would not pay 39¢, because no amount of additional information is likely to provide perfect knowledge. But businesses often obtain additional knowledge through sampling, and sampling costs money. The executive needs a method, such as the one described at length by Schlaifer (a) of assessing the probable benefits, in relation to its cost, of additional information from sampling and (b) of determining the best sample size. In the present example, no sampling technique would be attractive if its cost, allocated to each day's operations, exceeded 39¢.

LINEAR PROGRAMMING

Characteristics

Linear programming is a potent mathematical approach to a group of business problems which contain many interacting variables and which basically involve the utilization of limited resources in such a way as to increase profit or decrease cost. There are nearly always limiting factors or scarce resources that are restrictions, restraints, or constraints on available alternatives. Linear programming has been applied to a vast number of business decisions, such as machine scheduling, product mix, raw material mix, scheduling flight crews, production routing, shipping schedules, transportation routes, blending gasoline, blending sausage ingredients, and designing transformers. In general, linear programming is the best available technique for combining materials, manpower, and facilities to best advantage, when all the relationships are approximately linear and many combinations are possible.

The Techniques, the Accountant, and the Manager

All of us are more or less familiar with linear equations (e.g., $X + 3 = 9$). We also know that simultaneous linear equations with two or three unknowns become progressively more difficult to solve with pencil and paper. Linear programming essentially involves: (1) constructing a set of simultaneous linear equations, which represent the model of the problem and which include many variables; and (2) solving the equations with the help of the digital computer.

The formulation of the equations—that is, the building of the model—is far more challenging than the mechanics of the solution. The model must be a valid and accurate portrayal of the problem. Computer programmers can then take the equations and process the solution.

As a minimum, accountants and executives should be able to recognize those types of problems in their organizations that are most susceptible to analysis by linear programming. Hopefully, the managers and accountants should be able to help in the construction of the model—i.e., in specifying the objectives, the constraints, and the variables. Ideally, they should understand the mathematics and should be able to talk comfortably with the operations researchers who are attempting to express their problem mathematically. However, the position taken here is that the accountant and the manager should concentrate on the formulation of the model and not worry too much about the technical intricacies of the solution. The latter may be delegated to the mathematicians; the ability to delegate the former is highly doubtful.

Product Mix

Machine 1 is available for 24 hours, and Machine 2 is available for 20 hours, for the processing of two products. Product X has a contribution margin of $2 per unit; Product Y, $1 per unit. These products must be sold in such combination that the quantity of X must be equal to or less than the quantity of Y. X requires 6 hours of time on Machine 1 and 10 hours of time on Machine 2. Product Y requires 4 hours of time on Machine 1 only. What production combination will produce the maximum profit?

The linear-programming approach may be divided into four steps, although variations and shortcuts are available in unique situations, notably in transportation problems:

1. Formulate the objectives. The objective is usually to increase profit or decrease cost.
2. Determine the basic relationships, particularly the constraints.
3. Determine the feasible alternatives.
4. Compare the optimum solution.

Techniques may differ. In the uncomplicated situation in our example, the graphic approach is easiest to understand. In practice, the *simplex method* is used—a step-by-step process that is extremely efficient. Basically, the simplex method begins with one feasible solution and tests it algebraically, by substitution, to see if it can be improved. These substitutions continue until further improvement is impossible. The optimum solution is therefore achieved.

These four steps may be applied to the example.

Step 1. Formulate the objectives. In our case, find the product combination that results in the maximum total contribution margin. Maximize:

$$\text{Total contribution margin} = \$2x + \$1y \tag{1}$$

This is called the *objective function.*

Step 2. Determine the basic relationships. The relationships may be depicted by the following inequalities:

For Machine 1:	$6X + 4Y \le 24$
For Machine 2:	$10X \quad\; \le 20$
Sales of X and Y:	$X - Y \le 0$
Because negative production is impossible:	$X \quad\quad \ge 0 \;\text{ and }\; Y \ge 0$

The three solid lines in Exhibit 17-1 will help you to visualize the machine constraints and the product mix constraint.

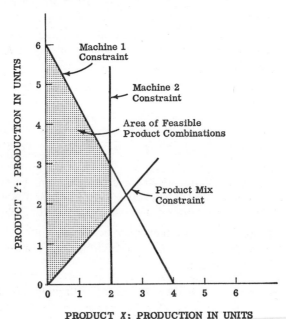

EXHIBIT 17-1

Linear Programming: Graphic Solution

Step 3. Determine the feasible alternatives. Alternatives are feasible if they are technically possible. We do not want to bother with computations for impossible solutions. The shaded area in Exhibit 17-1 shows the boundaries of the feasible product combinations.

Step 4. Compute the optimum solution. Steps 2 and 3 focused on physical relationships alone. We now return to the economic relationships expressed as the objective in Step 1. We test various feasible product combinations to see which one results in a maximum total contribution margin. It so happens that the best solution must lie on one of the corners of the Area of Feasible Product Combinations in Exhibit 17-1. The total contribution margin is calculated for each corner. The steps, which are similar to the simplex method, which uses digital computers, are:

a. Start with one possible combination.
b. Compute the profit.
c. Move to any other possible combination to see if it will improve the result in *b*. Keep moving from corner to corner until no further improvement is possible. (The simplex method is more efficient because it does not necessitate testing all possible combinations before finding the best solution.)

These steps are summarized below. They show that the optimum combination is two units of X and three units of Y:

| Trial | Corner | Combination | | $2X + $1Y =$ |
		Product X	Product Y	Total contribution margin
1	0,0	0	0	$2(0) + $1(0) = 0
2	0,6	0	6	$2(0) + 1(6) = 6$
3	2,3	2	3	$2(2) + 1(3) = 7$
4	2,2	2	2	$2(2) + 1(2) = 6$

Why must the best solution lie on a corner? Consider all possible combinations that will produce a total contribution margin of $1 ($2X + 1Y = 1). This is a straight line through (0,2) and (1,0). Other total contribution margins are represented by lines parallel to this one. Their associated total contribution margins increase the further the lines get from the origin. The optimum line is the one furthest from the origin which has a feasible point on it; intuitively, we know that this happens at a corner (2,3). Furthermore, if you put a ruler on the graph and move it parallel with the $1 line, the optimum corner becomes apparent.

As these trials show, the central problem of linear programming is to find the specific combination of variables that satisfies all constraints and achieves the objective sought. Moving from corner to corner (which is really moving from one possible solution to another) implies that the scarce resource, productive capacity, is being transferred between products. Each four-hour period that machine 1 is productively used to produce one unit of Y may be sacrificed (i.e., given or traded) for one six-hour period required to produce one unit of X. Consider the exchange of twelve hours of time. This means that three units of Y will be traded for two units of X. Will this exchange add to profits? Yes:

Total contribution margin at corner (0,6)		$6
Additional contribution margin from Product X:		
2 units, @ $2	$4	
Lost contribution margin, Product Y:		
3 units, @ $1	3	
Net additional contribution margin		1
Total contribution margin at corner (2,3)		$7

These substitutions are a matter of trading a given contribution margin per unit of a limiting factor (i.e., a critical resource) for some other contribution margin per unit of a limiting factor. It is not simply a matter of comparing margins per unit of *product* and jumping to the conclusion that the production of Product X, which has the greater margin per unit of product, should be maximized.[3]

INVENTORY PLANNING AND CONTROL SYSTEMS

Characteristics

Comprehensive inventory planning and control systems have been successfully installed in many companies. The major objective of inventory management is to discover and maintain the optimum level of invest-

EXHIBIT 17-2

Total Associated Costs of Inventories

Costs of Carrying
 1. Desired rate of return on investment.*
 2. Risk of obsolescence.
 3. Space for storage.
 4. Handling and transfer.
 5. Clerical.
 6. Personal property taxes.
 7. Insurance.

plus

Costs of Not Carrying Enough
 1. Foregone quantity discounts.*
 2. Foregone fortuitous purchases.*
 3. Contribution margins on lost sales.*
 4. Loss of customer goodwill.*
 5. Extra purchasing or transportation costs.
 6. Extra costs of uneconomic production runs, overtime, setups, and training.

   * Costs which ordinarily do not explicitly appear on formal accounting records.

---

[3] This point was also discussed in Chapter 13, pp. 332-334.

ment in the inventory. Inventories may be too high or too low. If too high, there are unnecessary carrying costs and risks of obsolescence. If too low, production may be disrupted or sales permanently lost. The optimum inventory level is that which minimizes all costs associated with inventory.

Exhibit 17-2 shows the many costs that must be considered. Some of these are not routinely recorded by the accounting system. For instance, operations researchers have had the challenging job of deciding the cost of an item being out of stock so that the seller's lack of inventory results in a lost order. Will the customer return later? Will he go elsewhere? Will he ever return? The appropriate cost is an opportunity cost—the profit lost on the orders lost.

How Much to Order

The two key questions in inventory control are how much to order at a time and when to order. The *economic standard order quantity* is that which minimizes the associated annual costs of the inventory. The two significant cost items tend to offset one another. The total costs of carrying, including interest, rise as orders grow in size, but the total costs of ordering, delivery, etc. decrease, and vice versa. Exhibit 17-3 is a graph of the relationships.

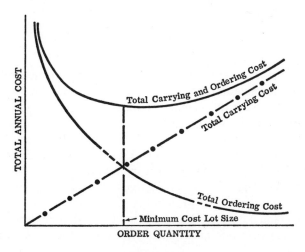

EXHIBIT 17-3

For example, suppose that a company incurred a cost of $200 per order for trucking, delivery, and relevant clerical costs, and an annual carrying cost of 20 per cent of average inventory (including 10 per cent for minimum rate of return desired, 5 per cent for obsolescence, 2 per cent for space costs, 1 per cent for insurance, and 2 per cent for property taxes). Monthly usage at cost amounts to \$3,000. A tabular comparison of possible standard order quantities follows:

Number of months' supply acquired with each order	1	2	3	4	6	12
Number of orders per year	12	6	4	3	2	1
Average inventory (assuming no safety stock)*	\$1,500	\$3,000	\$4,500	\$6,000	\$9,000	\$18,000
Yearly ordering cost, @ \$200 per order	\$2,400	\$1,200	\$ 800	\$ 600	\$ 400	\$ 200
Yearly carrying cost, @ 20 per cent	300	600	900	1,200	1,800	3,600
Total associated cost	\$2,700	\$1,800	\$1,700	\$1,800	\$2,200	\$ 3,800

* One-half the size of the standard order.

The economic order quantity is a three-month supply. Note, however, how the total associated costs tend to flatten out over a wide range of possible order-sizes.

Because the total cost curve tends to flatten over a wide range, errors in estimating individual cost factors are not crucial. Sometimes there is an unwarranted tendency to criticize various mathematical approaches to problems of inventory control and to problems of combinations of scarce resources (linear programming) because the relevant costs are impossible to measure. Such criticism is seldom valid. In OR, *sensitivity analysis* is used to gauge the impact of errors in cost data on the available course of action. Optimum inventory policies can be achieved without knowledge of "true" costs.[4]

When to Order

The *reorder point* is that inventory level at which a new order should be placed. It depends on the expected usage during the *lead time,* the time interval between the placing of an order and its delivery. Immediately before delivery, the inventory level should be equal to the *safety stock*—that is, the minimum inventory that provides a cushion against reasonably expected maximum demand and against variations in lead time. These relationships are graphed in Exhibit 17-4.

If demand and lead time were known with certainty, no safety stock would be needed. Statistical probability theory is used to analyze variations in demand and lead time. Again, the optimum level for safety stock is the one that minimizes the total expected costs associated with the inventory.

The foregoing discussion of inventory control revolved around the so-called two-bin policy: when inventory levels get down to *x*, order *y*. In practice, a fixed order *cycle* is often used. This entails somewhat different problems.

---

[4] For an interesting discussion see Miller and Starr, *Executive Decisions and Operations Research* (Englewood Cliffs, N.J.: Prentice-Hall, Inc., 1960), p. 405.

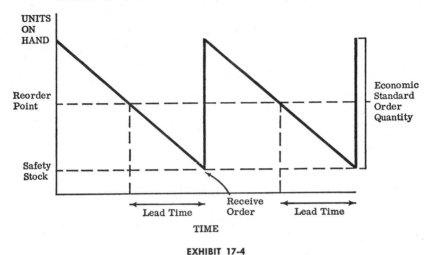

EXHIBIT 17-4

Reorder Point, Lead Time, and Safety Stock

The economic order quantity may be used for setting order cycles for various classes of products, but other inventory rules will also be used. One common rule is to have a predetermined order cycle time, with the size of each order depending on the target safety stock upon arrival of the next order. Demand forecasts and seasonal pattern adjustments are also very important aspects of altering the size of orders during the year.

COMPUTERS, SYSTEMS, AND ORGANIZATIONS

Computers and Organizational Changes

In 1964, over 14,000 electronic computers were being used by American businesses. Computers have enabled OR techniques to flourish, speeded accounting's score-keeping function, and tended to centralize and integrate organizational structures and information systems. Computers seize raw information, submit it to arithmetical operations, reach logical decisions with respect to it, and issue processed data. All this is accomplished with electronic swiftness, usually limited only by the mechanical abilities of input and output devices. The computer's speed, memory, and arithmetical operations free middle managers from preoccupation with data processing, facilitate the simulation of alternative courses of action, and indicate the optimum choice.

Organizations tend to be departmentalized by function or division, and many of the resulting departments have heavy clerical duties. For example, credit and purchasing departments normally devote more manpower to recordkeeping than to their primary functions. The installation of a computerized information system often captures data-processing functions from these departments, takes information from department filing cabinets and stores it on reels of magnetic tape, and disrupts long-standing organizational structures and duties.

The supervisor of most purchasing departments, for example, is concerned with statistics. He devotes much time to recordkeeping and to overseeing large clerical staffs. The computer takes this work over almost completely, and leaves him with the task of selecting suppliers—the essence of his management responsibility. In other words, the computer tends to reduce the drudgery in the middle manager's job, leaving him with fewer people to supervise and with more time to spend on his major duty. As you may imagine, many managers are likely to resent and resist such changes.

In addition to changing the individual manager's job, the computer tends to obliterate an organization's traditional compartmentalization and to integrate business functions. Many large companies (e.g., International Shoe, Standard Oil of New Jersey) have used computers as their central planning and control device. The computer relates sales to inventories of finished goods, to production schedules, to estimates of raw material, to estimates of labor requirements, etc. In brief, estimates are processed so that production, merchandising, and procurement no longer function as semi-independent entities. For example, International Shoe now has a vice-president of merchandising *and* production, whereas these had been separate functions before 1960.

On-Line, Real-Time Systems

The more advanced of today's computer systems provide better planning and control information than ever before, because relevant facts are being supplied "on-line" and in "real time." *On-line* means compiling information instantaneously, as events occur. *Real-time* means supplying the relevant information rapidly enough so that interested managers or other parts of the system may exert control. An "on-line, real-time" system is often abbreviated as an OLRT system.

An OLRT system has a central data-processing center consisting of computers, communications equipment, storage equipment, and input-output devices such as punched card or punched-tape readers, and punches and high-speed printers. Point of origin devices (POD) are physically located where the needed information originates or where it is required for operating decisions. POD devices are directly connected to the central processing center in a two-way communication pattern.

Among the users of OLRT systems are the federal, state, and local governments, banks, radio and television companies, telephone companies, stock brokerage firms, and airlines. Almost all the major American air carriers have an OLRT reservations system installed, or one on order. For instance, with American Airlines' $30-million SABRE system, a reservations clerk asks for space on a particular flight by punching a few buttons on a special console typewriter. If a certain light flashes, the agent knows that space is available and that, as of that instant, he has priority for that space over anyone else asking for that flight through any of the other 35 centers on line. There are many other clever features of SABRE which are too detailed to describe here. Computer pundits claim that, by the early 1970's, nearly all data-processing systems will be OLRT.

Implications for Information Systems

As operations research techniques and computers become more widely understood and more useful, information systems in organizations will be redesigned to take advantage of their powerful features for helping management to plan and control. Advanced business systems tend to break down traditional department walls and tend to redefine managers' duties—freeing them for more attention directing and problem solving.

Somebody has to manage the over-all business information system. The accountant, who has long dominated quantitative information systems, is the logical candidate for the job. But now he must know how to weld operations research techniques, computer technology, and modern accounting for management control so that the quality of management becomes better than ever. In short, such a person must be an astute combination score keeper, attention director, and problem solver—with a breadth of knowledge that extends beyond the traditional boundaries of accounting and into the fields of mathematics, statistics, and the behavioral sciences.

SUMMARY

Accountants and managers should be aware of the potential applications of operations research techniques to business problems. OR has flourished because the digital computer has facilitated the solutions of mathematical models. Statistical probability theory, linear programming, and inventory control systems have also found wide practical use.

OR techniques and digital computers encourage a total information systems viewpoint, as does modern management accounting. The future is sure to bring improved, tightly knit information systems that will better meet management needs. The chiefs of such information systems will be those accountants who have a grasp of all three functions—score keeping, attention directing and problem solving. The quality of the latter function will be particularly enhanced by a knowledge of operations research.

SUMMARY PROBLEM FOR YOUR REVIEW

PROBLEM

Review this chapter's examples on statistical probability theory and on linear programming by trying to solve them before studying their solutions.

SUGGESTED READINGS

Bierman, H., L. Fouraker, and R. Jaedicke, *Quantitative Analysis for Business Decisions.* Homewood, Ill.: Richard D. Irwin, Inc., 1961.

Bross, I. D. J., *Design for Decision.* New York: The Macmillan Company, 1953.

Buchan, J., and E. Koenigsberg, *Scientific Inventory Management.* Englewood Cliffs, N.J.: Prentice-Hall, Inc., 1963.

Glicksman, A., *Linear Programming and the Theory of Games.* New York: John Wiley & Sons, Inc., 1963.

Miller, D., and M. Starr, *Executive Decisions and Operations Research.* Englewood Cliffs, N.J.: Prentice-Hall, Inc., 1960.

Roberts, H., "The New Business Statistics," *Journal of Business* XXXIII, No. 1 (January, 1960), 21-30.

Schlaifer, R., *Probability and Statistics for Business Decisions.* New York: McGraw-Hill Book Company, 1959. Chapter 7 should be of special interest to accountants because it distinguishes between the total-cost approach and the incremental-cost approach. The cost of uncertainty is defined and demonstrated.

Stockton, R. S., *Introduction to Linear Programming* (2nd ed.). Boston: Allyn and Bacon, Inc., 1964.

ASSIGNMENT MATERIAL

ESSENTIAL ASSIGNMENT MATERIAL

17-1. *Terminology.* Define: operations research; model; management science; PERT; conditional value; expected value; payoff table; linear programming; economic standard order quantity; safety stock; and lead time.

17-2. *Fundamental approach of linear programming.* A company has two departments, machining and finishing. The company's two products require processing in each of two departments. Data follow:

Product	Contribution Margin per Unit	Daily Capacity in Units	
		Department 1: Machining	Department 2: Finishing
A	$2.00	200	120
B	2.50	100	200

Severe shortages of material for Product *B* will limit its production to a maximum of 90 per day. How many units of each product should be produced to obtain the maximum net income? Show the basic relationships as inequalities. Solve by using graphical analysis.

17-3. *Influence of uncertainty in forecasts.* The figures used in many examples and problems in the previous chapters were subject to uncertainty. For simplicity, the expected future amounts of sales, direct material, direct labor, and other operating costs were presented as if they were errorless predictions. For instance, in Example 1 in Chapter 14 (p. 358), we blithely said that a facilities rearrangement "should result in cash operating savings of $2,000 per year."

The industrial engineers who studied the situation had really prepared three estimates:

Event	Percentage Chance of Occurrence	Savings
Pessimistic	.1	$1,200
Most likely	.6	1,800
Optimistic	.3	2,500

Using an expected-value table, show how the estimate of $2,000 was probably computed.

17-4. *Inventory levels and sales forecasting.* Each day, an owner of a sidewalk stand stocks bunches of fresh flowers which cost 30¢ and sell for 50¢ each. Leftovers are given to a nearby hospital. Demand characteristics are:

Demand	Probability
Less than 20	.00
20	.10
21	.40
22	.30
23	.20
24 or more	.00

How many units should be stocked to maximize expected net income? Show computations.

17-5. *Costs and benefits of perfect information.* If the owner of the stand in Problem 4 were clairvoyant, so that he could forecast the demand each day and stock the exact number of flowers needed, what would be his expected profit per day? What is the maximum price that he should be willing to pay for perfect information?

ADDITIONAL ASSIGNMENT MATERIAL

Note: Problems 17-23 through 17-27 deal with probabilities; 17-28 through 17-30, with linear programming; and 17-31 through 17-34, with inventory planning and control.

17-6. "The management accountant must be technically competent in computer technology and modern mathematics." Do you agree? Explain.

17-7. What are the distinguishing features of operations research?

17-8. How does management science differ from operations research?

17-9. "OR is mainly a planning tool rather than a controlling tool." Why?

17-10. "Models must conform to reality in two major respects." Explain.

17-11. "Simulation is game-playing in the world of make-believe. It has no practical value." Do you agree? Explain.

17-12. "I'm not certain what uncertainty is." Explain uncertainty briefly.

17-13. What is the difference between a conditional value and an expected value?

17-14. Consider the following probability distribution:

Daily Sales Event in Units	Probability
1,000	.1
1,500	.5
2,000	.2
2,500	.1
3,000	.1
	1.0

A student commented: "If a manager has perfect information, he will always sell 3,000 units." Do you agree? Explain.

17-15. Which of the following are linear equations?

$$x + y + 4z + 6a = 8c + 4m$$
$$x^2 = y$$
$$x^2 - y = 4$$
$$4c = 27$$

17-16. What is the minimum competence in linear programming that managers should have?

17-17. What is an infeasible alternative?

17-18. What are the four basic steps in linear programming?

17-19. "The major objective of inventory management is to minimize cash outlays for inventories." Do you agree? Explain.

17-20. What are the principal costs of having too much inventory? Too little inventory?

17-21. "The safety stock is the average amount of inventory used during lead time." Do you agree? Explain.

17-22. "If demand and lead time were known with certainty, no safety stock would be needed." Do you agree? Explain.

17-23. *Probabilities and costs of rework versus costs of setup.* The Schlaifer Co. has an automatic machine ready and set to make a production run of 2,000 parts. For simplicity, only four events are assumed possible:

Faulty Parts	Probability
30	.6
200	.2
600	.1
900	.1

The incremental cost of reworking a faulty part is 20¢. An expert mechanic can check the setting. He can, without fail, bring the faulty parts down to 30, but this is time-consuming and costs $25 per setting.

Should the setting be checked?

17-24. *Probabilities: automatic or semi-automatic equipment.* The Click Co. is going to produce a new product. Two types of production equipment are being considered. The more costly equipment will result in lower labor and related variable costs:

Equipment	Total Original Cost	Salvage Value	Variable Costs, per Unit of Product
Semi-automatic	$40,000	—	$4
Automatic	95,000	—	3

Marketing executives believe that this unique product will be salable only over the next year. The unit selling price is $5. Their best estimate of potential sales follows:

Total Units	Probability
30,000	.2
50,000	.4
60,000	.2
70,000	.2

Prepare an analysis to indicate the best course of action.

17-25. *Probabilities and a professor's alternative uses of sabbatical leave* (prepared by William M. Voss). Professor Voss will receive a sabbatical leave for the next school year. He has two alternative plans for research and writing during this period:

a. He may write a workbook in Principles of Management, for which he would receive $1,500 in cash plus a royalty of 10 per cent based on sales. His publisher has studied the market and tells Professor Voss that he can be 75 per cent certain that his royalties from sales will be: Year 1 (the sabbatical year), $400; Year 2, $600; Year 3, $900; Year 4, $700; Year 5, $400. At the end of Year 5 he would have to revise the workbook completely to get further income from it. There is a 15 per cent chance that his royalties will be 10 per cent higher, and a 10 per cent chance that they will be 25 per cent lower than the figures given.

b. Professor Voss's alternative is to spend his time working on a research project, for which he will receive no direct compensation but which will enhance his professional reputation. He may expect, with a certainty of 90 per cent, that his professional status will change immediately from assistant to associate professor. Otherwise, Professor Voss will have to wait four years after the end of his sabbatical leave before receiving this promotion. The additional stipend would be $1,000 per year.

Assume that the $1,500 cash payment is made at the beginning of his sabbatical year and that all other payments are made at the end of the year in which they are earned.

Required:

1. What are the total expected values of the two alternatives, not considering the time-value of money?
2. Determine the present value of each alternative (discount @ 6 per cent).

17-26. *Probability assessment and new product.* A new manager, Emil Frang, has just been hired by the Nattelle Co. He is considering the market potential for a new toy, Marvo, which, like many toys, may have great fad appeal.

Frang is experienced in the fad market and is well qualified to assess Marvo's chances for success. He is certain that sales will not be less than 25,000 units. Plant capacity limits total sales to a maximum of 80,000 units during Marvo's brief life. Frang thinks that there are two chances in five for a sales volume of 50,000 units. The probability that sales will exceed 50,000 units is four times the probability that they will be less than 50,000.

If sales are less than 50,000, he feels quite certain that they will be 25,000 units. If sales exceed 50,000, unit volumes of 60,000 and 80,000 are equally likely. A 70,000 unit volume is four times as likely as either.

Variable production costs are $3 per unit, selling price is $5, and the special manufacturing equipment (which has no salvage value or alternate use) costs $125,000. Assume, for simplicity, that the above-mentioned are the only possible sales volumes.

Should Marvo be produced? Show detailed computations.

17-27. *Net present values, probabilities, and capital budgeting.* At the recent stockholders meeting of a large utility company, the question of the profitability of the satellite communications project undertaken by the company was raised by a stockholder. The project was undertaken two years ago. The president stated that $10 million had been invested in the project in each of the previous years and that an equal amount must be invested in each of the next three years. There would be no income from the project until the total investment was completed. At that time, the probability of receiving $4 million, cash inflow from operations, would be .8; the probability of receiving $8 million in the second year after completion would be .7; the probability of receiving $15 million in the third year after completion would be .6; the probability of receiving $30 million for the following seven years would be .5.

This company expects a minimum rate of return of 10 per cent on investments.

As a stockholder, would you have approved of this project when it was first undertaken? Support your answer with figures, using the net present value approach.

17-28. *Production scheduling and linear programming.* A factory can produce either Product A or Product B. Machine 1 can produce 15 units of B or 20 units of A, per hour. Machine 2 can produce 20 units of B or 12 units of A, per hour. Machine 1 has a maximum capacity of 10,000 hours and Machine 2 has a maximum capacity of 8,000 hours.

Product A has a unit contribution margin of 20¢; B, 16¢. There is an unlimited demand for either product; however, both products must be produced together through each machine in a combination such that the quantity of B is at least 20 per cent of the quantity of A.

Which combination of products should be produced? Solve by graphic analysis. Express all relationships as inequalities.

17-29. *Linear programming.* A company manufactures two kinds of precision tools, C (cheap) and E (expensive). The contribution margin of C is $4 per unit, while E's contribution margin per unit is $5. The tools are produced in three operations: machining, assembling, and finishing. The following is the average time, in hours, required for each tool.

	Machining	*Assembling*	*Finishing*
C	1	5	3
E	2	4	2
Maximum time available for each operation	700	1,700	850

Assume that the time available can be allocated to either type of tool. Express the relationships as inequalities. Using graphic analysis, show which product mix will result in the maximum total contribution margin.

17-30. *Linear programming and minimum cost.* The local agricultural center has advised George Junker to spread at least 4,800 pounds of a special nitrogen fertilizer ingredient and at least 5,000 pounds of a special phosphate fertilizer ingredient in order to increase his crops. Neither ingredient is available in pure form.

A dealer has offered 100-pound bags of VIM @ $1 each. VIM contains the equivalent of 20 pounds of nitrogen and 80 pounds of phosphate. VOOM is also available in 100-pound bags, @ $3 each; it contains the equivalent of 75 pounds of nitrogen and 25 pounds of phosphate.

Express the relationships as inequalities. How many bags of VIM and VOOM should Junker buy in order to obtain the required fertilizer at minimum cost? Solve graphically.

17-31. *Inventory control and economic lot size.* An aircraft manufacturer purchases some aluminum components from an outside supplier at $4 each. Total annual needs are 5,000, at a rate of 20 per working day. The minimum rate of return desired on inventory investment is 10 per cent of $4, or 40¢ per unit. Rent, insurance, personal property taxes, and miscellaneous storage costs are 10¢ per unit of inventory per year. The costs (clerical, stationery, postage, telephone, trucking, etc.) are $10 per purchase order.

What is the most economic order size? Tabulate in columnar form the total costs per year, using order sizes of 50, 100, 200, 400, 500, 600, 800, 1,000 and 5,000. Also graph the total costs as related to the various order sizes. Note that the $4 unit cost of inventory is common to all alternatives and hence may be ignored in the tabulation. Assume that stock is zero when each order arrives.

17-32. *Inventory control and television tubes.* The Nemmers Co. assembles private-brand television sets for a retail chain, under a contract requiring delivery of 100 sets per day for each of 250 business days per year. Each set requires a picture tube which Nemmers buys outside, for $20 each. The tubes are loaded on trucks at the supplier's factory door and are then delivered by a trucking service at a charge of $100 per trip, regardless of the size of the shipment. The cost of storing the tubes (including the desired rate of return on investment) is $2 per tube per year. Because production is stable throughout the year, the average inventory is one-half the size of the truck lot. Tabulate the relevant annual cost of various truck lot sizes at 5, 10, 15, 25, 50, and 250 trips per year. Show your results graphically. (Note that the $20 unit cost of tubes is common to all alternatives and hence may be ignored.)

17-33. *Reorder point.* A utility company uses 5,000 tons of coal per year to generate power at one of its plants. The company orders 500 tons at a time. Lead time for the orders is five days, and the safety stock is a three-day supply. Usage is assumed to be constant over a 360-day year. Calculate the reorder point.

17-34. *Channels of distribution and inventory control.* The Karlin Commodities Co. is located in Los Angeles. It maintains a warehouse and sales office in Chicago to serve customers in the Middle West. Management is considering eliminating the Chicago warehouse and sales office in favor of a well-known distributor. They believe that the average Middle West customer will receive comparable service and that sales will remain constant. Goods would be sold directly to the distributor FOB Los Angeles at prices 30 per cent below normal list price.

Elimination of the warehouse would save the following days of inventory in:

Transportation	3.5
Chicago warehouse inventory	33.0
Total days per year	36.5

The annual carrying charges in the Chicago warehouse, per dollar of inventory value, are:

Cost of capital	$ .10
Obsolescence	.02
Property taxes	.05
Insurance on inventory	.02
Breakage	.06
Total	$ .25

The present costs of shipping to the Chicago warehouse are:

Shipping	$ .06
Pickup and delivery	.02
	$ .08 per lb.

The costs of operating the Chicago warehouse and sales office are:

Rent	$ 70,000
Labor and salaries	325,000
Overhead	65,000
Shipping and delivery	84,000
	$544,000

The total annual sales of goods handled through the Chicago office is $5,840,000, weighing 11,260,000 pounds. It is estimated that using the distributor would also save $48,000 because of a reduction in telephone calls and other communications.

Required: The total saving or loss resulting from switching to the distributor.

Glossary

The terms included in this glossary pertain mainly to accounting for management planning and control. For a more elaborate description of each term, consult the chapter indicated in parentheses.

Absorption costing. That type of product costing which assigns fixed manufacturing overhead to the units produced as a product cost. Contrast with direct costing. (Chap. 15)

Accounting method. See unadjusted rate of return. (Chap. 14)

Activity accounting. See responsibility accounting. (Chap. 11)

Actual-normal system. A type of product costing which applies to units produced, as costs of production, the actual direct materials consumed, the actual direct labor used, and a portion of overhead calculated on the basis of a normal schedule of production. (Chap. 15)

Allocation. Assigning one or more items of cost or revenue to one or more segments of an organization according to benefits received, responsibilities, or other logical measure of use. (Chap. 11)

Appropriation. An authorization to spend up to a specified dollar ceiling. (Chap. 10)

Asset turnover. The ratio of sales to total assets available. (Chap. 12)

Attention directing. That function of the accountant's information supplying task which focuses on problems in the operation of the firm or which points out imperfections or inefficiencies in certain areas of the firm's operation. (Chap. 1)

Bill of materials. A specification of the quantities of direct materials allowed for manufacturing a given quantity of output. (Chap. 9)

Book value method. See unadjusted rate of return (Chap. 14)

Budget. A plan of action expressed in figures. (Chaps. 1, 6)

Capacity costs. An alternate term for fixed costs, emphasizing the fact that fixed costs are needed in order to provide operating facilities and an organization ready to produce and sell at a planned volume of activity. (Chap. 8)

Capital budgeting. Long-term planning for proposed capital outlays and their financing. (Chap. 14)

Cash budget. A schedule of expected cash receipts and disbursements. (Chap. 6)

Committed costs. Those fixed costs arising from the possession of plant and equipment and a basic organization and thus affected primarily by long-run decisions as to the desired level of capacity. (Chaps. 8, 10)

Common cost. See joint cost. (Chap. 11)

Comptroller. See controller. (Chap. 1)

Conditional value. The value which will ensue if a particular event occurs. (Chap. 17)

Continuous budget. A budget which perpetually adds a month in the future as the month just ended is dropped. (Chap. 6)

Contribution approach. A method of preparing income statements which separates variable costs from fixed costs in order to emphasize the importance of cost behavior patterns for purposes of planning and control. (Chap. 8)

Contribution margin. Excess of sales price over variable expenses. Also called marginal income. May be expressed as a total, a ratio, or on a per unit basis. (Chap. 7)

Controllable cost. A cost which may be directly regulated at a given level of managerial authority, either in the short run or in the long run. (Chap. 11)

Controller. The chief management accounting executive. Also spelled comptroller. (Chap. 1)

Controlling. Obtaining conformity to plans through action and evaluation. (Chap. 1)

Currently attainable standards. Standards expressing a level of economic efficiency which can be reached with skilled, diligent, superior effort. (Chap. 9)

Differential cost. See incremental cost. (Chap. 13)

Direct costing. That type of product costing which charges fixed manufacturing overhead immediately against the revenue of the period in which it was incurred, without assigning it to specific units produced. Also called variable costing or marginal costing. (Chap. 15)

Direct labor. All labor which is obviously related and specifically and conveniently traceable to specific products. (Chap. 8)

Direct material. All raw material which is an integral part of the finished good and which can be conveniently assigned to specific physical units. (Chap. 8)

Economic standard order quantity. The amount of inventory which should be ordered at one time in order to minimize the associated annual costs of the inventory. (Chap. 17)

Efficiency variance. Quantity variance, applied to labor. (Chap. 9)

Excess material requisitions. A form to be filled out by the production staff to secure any materials needed in excess of the standard amount allotted for output. (Chap. 9)

Expected idle capacity variance. The excess of practical capacity over the master budget sales forecast capacity expressed in physical or dollar terms. This variance is pertinent when the master budget is being prepared. (Chap. 10)

Expected value. A weighted average of all the conditional values of an act. Each conditional value is weighted by its probability. (Chap. 17)

Factory burden. See factory overhead. (Chap. 8)

Factory overhead. All factory costs other than direct labor and direct material. Also called factory burden, indirect manufacturing costs, manufacturing overhead, and manufacturing expense. (Chap. 8)

Fixed cost. A cost which, for a given period of time and range of activity called the relevant range, *does not change in total* but becomes progressively smaller on a *per unit* basis as volume increases. (Chap. 7)

Flexible budget. A budget, usually referring to overhead costs only, which is prepared for a range, rather than for a single level, of activity; one which can be automatically geared to changes in the level of volume. Also called variable budget. Direct materials and direct labor are sometimes included in the flexible budget. (Chap. 9)

Functional costing. Classifying costs by allocating them to the various functions performed, such as warehousing, delivery, billing, and so forth. (Chap. 11)

Historical cost. See sunk cost. (Chap. 13)

Ideal capacity. The absolute maximum number of units that could be produced in a given operating situation, with no allowance for work stoppages or repairs. Also called theoretical capacity. (Chap. 10)

Idle time. A classification of *indirect labor* which constitutes wages paid for unproductive time due to circumstances beyond the worker's control. (Chap. 8)

Incremental approach. A method of determining which of two alternative courses of action is preferable by calculating the present value of the difference in net cash inflow between one alternative and the other. (Chap. 14)

Incremental cost. The difference in total cost between two alternatives. Also called differential cost. (Chap. 13)

Indirect manufacturing costs. See factory overhead. (Chap. 8)

Internal check. The coordinated methods and measures in an organization designed to check the accuracy and validity of organization data and safeguard assets. This definition represents parts (*c*) and (*d*) of the definition of *internal control,* a more inclusive concept. (Chap. 12)

Internal control. The coordinated methods and measures in an organization designed to: (*a*) promote efficiency; (*b*) encourage adherence to prescribed management plans and policies; (*c*) check the accuracy and validity of organization data; and (*d*) safeguard assets. (Chap. 12)

Job cost sheet. See job order. (Chap. 15)

Job order. The basic record for the accumulation of job costs. Also called job cost sheet. (Chap. 15)

Job order costing. A system of applying manufacturing costs to specific jobs or batches of specialized or unique production in proportion to the amounts of materials, attention, and effort used to produce each unit or group of units. (Chap. 15)

Joint cost. A cost which is common to all the segments in question and which is not clearly or practically allocable except by some questionable allocation base. Also called common cost. (Chap. 11)

Joint product costs. Costs of two or more manufactured goods, of significant sales values, that are produced by a single process and that are not identifiable as individual products up to a certain stage of production known as the split-off point. (Chap. 13)

Lead time. The time interval between placing an order and receiving delivery. (Chap. 17)

Linear programming. A mathematical approach to a group of business problems which contain many interacting variables and which basically involve combining limited resources to maximize profits or minimize costs. (Chap. 17)

Line authority. Authority which is exerted downward over subordinates. (Chap. 1)

Long-run planning capacity. The rate of activity needed to meet average sales demand over a period long enough to encompass seasonal and cyclical fluctuations. Also called normal capacity. (Chap. 10)

Managed costs. See programmed costs. (Chaps. 8, 10)

Management by exception. The practice, by the executive, of focusing his attention mainly on significant deviations from expected results. It might also be called management by variance. (Chap. 1)

Management science. The formulation of mathematical and statistical models applied to decision making and the practical application of these models through the use of digital computers. (Chap. 17)

Manufacturing expenses. See factory overhead. (Chap. 8)

Manufacturing overhead. See factory overhead (Chap. 8)

Marginal costing. See direct costing. (Chap. 15)

Marginal income. See contribution margin. (Chap. 7)

Master budget. The budget which consolidates the organization's over-all plans. (Chap. 6)

Master budget sales forecast capacity. That rate of activity employed in formulating the master budget for the period. (Chap. 10)

Mixed cost. A cost that has both fixed and variable elements. (Chap. 8)

Negotiated market price. A transfer price negotiated by the buying and selling segments when there is no market mechanism to fix a price clearly relevant to the situation. (Chap. 12)

Net present value method. A method of calculating the expected utility of a given project by discounting all expected future cash flows to the present, using some predetermined minimum desired rate of return. (Chap. 14)

Normal capacity. See long-run planning capacity. (Chap. 10)

On-Line, Real-Time. Computer compilation of information as events occur (on-line) and supplying the relevant information rapidly enough so that interested managers may exert needed control (real-time). (Chap. 17)

Operations research. A diffused collection of mathematical and statistical models applied to decision making. (Chap. 17)

Opportunity cost. The maximum alternative earning that might have been obtained if the productive good, service, or capacity had been applied to some alternative use. (Chap. 13)

Order-filling cost. A marketing cost incurred in the storing, packing, shipping, billing, credit and collection, and other similar aspects of selling merchandise. (Chap. 10)

Order-getting cost. A marketing cost incurred in the effort to attain a desired sales volume and mix. (Chap. 10)

Overabsorbed overhead. See overapplied overhead. (Chap. 15)

Overapplied overhead. The excess of amount of overhead cost applied to product over the amount of overhead cost incurred. Also called overabsorbed overhead. (Chap. 15)

Overtime premium. A classification of *indirect labor costs,* consisting of the extra wages paid to *all* factory workers for overtime work. (Chap. 8)

Payback. The measure of the time needed to recoup, in the form of cash inflow from operations, the initial dollars invested. Also called payout and payoff. (Chap. 14)

Payoff. See payback. (Chap. 14)

Payoff table. A convenient technique for showing the total expected value of each of a number of contemplated acts in the light of the varying probabilities of the events which may take place and the varying values of each act under each of the events. (Chap. 17)

Payout. See payback. (Chap. 14)

Performance report. The comparison of actual results with the budget. (Chap. 1)

PERT (Program Evaluation and Review Technique). A formal probabilistic diagram of the temporal interrelationships of a complex series of activities. (Chap. 17)

Planning. Selecting objectives and the means for their attainment. (Chap. 1)

Practical attainable capacity. See practical capacity. (Chap. 10)

Practical capacity. The maximum level at which the plant or department can realistically operate most efficiently, i.e., ideal capacity less allowances for unavoidable operating interruptions. Also called practical attainable capacity. (Chap. 10)

Price variance. The difference between the actual price and the standard price, multiplied by the total number of items acquired. The term "price variance" is usually linked with direct materials; the term "rate variance," which is conceptually similar to the price variance, is usually linked with direct labor. (Chap. 9)

Problem solving. That function of the accountant's information supplying task which expresses in concise, quantified terms the relative advantages and disadvantages to the firm of pursuing a possible future course of action, or the relative advantages of any one of several alternative methods of operation. (Chap. 1)

Profitability accounting. See responsibility accounting. (Chap. 11)

Profit center. A segment of a business that is responsible for both revenue and expense. (Chap. 12)

Pro forma statements. Forecasted financial statements. (Chap. 6)

Programmed costs. Those fixed costs that arise from periodic, usually yearly, appropriation decisions that directly reflect top management policies. Also called managed costs. (Chaps. 8, 10)

Qualitative factor. A factor which is of consequence but which cannot be measured precisely and easily in dollars. (Chap. 13)

Quantity variance. The standard price for a given resource, multiplied by the difference between the actual quantity used and the total standard quantity allowed for the number of good units produced. (Chap. 9)

Quote sheet. An analysis of costs used as a basis for determining selling prices. (Chap. 13)

Rate variance. The difference between actual wages paid and the standard wage rate, multiplied by the total actual hours of direct labor used. See price variance. (Chap. 9)

Reapportionment. Allocation of the costs of operating the service departments to the various production departments in proportion to the relative benefits or services received by each production department. (Chap. 15)

Relevant data for decision making. Expected future data which will differ as between alternatives. (Chap. 13)

Relevant range. The band of activity in which budgeted sales and expense relationships will be valid. (Chap. 7)

Responsibility accounting. A system of accounting which recognizes various responsibility centers throughout the organization and which reflects the plans and actions of each of these centers by allocating particular revenues and costs to the one having the pertinent responsibility. Also called profitability accounting and activity accounting. (Chap. 11)

Safety stock. A minimum inventory that provides a cushion against reasonably expected maximum demand and against variations in lead time. (Chap. 17)

Sales forecast opportunity variance. A measure of the difference between the scheduled capacity and the master budget sales forecast capacity, expressed in physical terms or in dollars. When it is expressed in dollars, the applicable unit contribution margin is applied to the physical measure. (Chap. 10)

Sales mix. The relative combination of the quantities of a variety of company products that compose total sales. (Chaps. 7, 11)

Scheduled production. That rate of activity assigned for production in the current period. (Chap. 10)

Schedule variance. The difference between actual production and scheduled production, expressed in physical terms or in dollars. (Chap. 10)

Score keeping. That data accumulation function of the accountant's information supplying task which enables both internal and external parties to evaluate the financial performance of the firm. (Chap. 1)

Segment. Any line of activity or part of an organization for which separate determination of costs and/or sales is wanted. (Chap. 11)

Segment margin. The contribution margin for each segment less all separable fixed costs, both programmed and committed. A measure of long-run profitability. (Chap. 11)

Separable cost. A cost directly identifiable with a particular segment. (Chap. 11)

Service departments. Those departments that exist solely to aid the production departments by rendering specialized assistance with certain phases of the work. (Chap. 15)

Short-run performance margin. The contribution margin for each segment, less separable programmed costs. (Chap. 11)

Source document. The original record of any transaction, internal or external, which occurs in the firm's operation. (Chaps. 1, 12)

Spending variance. Basically, a price variance applied to variable overhead. However, other factors besides prices may influence the amount of the variance. (Chap. 9)

Staff authority. The authority to *advise* but not to command; may be exerted laterally or upward. (Chap. 1)

Standard absorption costing. That type of product costing in which the cost of the finished unit is calculated as the sum of the costs of the standard allowances for the factory overhead, without reference to the costs actually incurred. (Chap. 15)

Standard cost. A carefully predetermined cost that should be attained. Usually expressed per unit. (Chap. 9)

Standard direct costing. That type of product costing in which the cost of the finished unit is calculated as the sum of the costs of the *standard allowances* for the factors of production, *excluding* fixed factory overhead, which is treated as a period cost, and without reference to the costs actually incurred. (Chap. 15)

Static budget. A budget prepared for only one level of activity and, consequently, one which does not adjust automatically to changes in the level of volume. (Chap. 9)

Step-variable costs. Those variable costs which change abruptly at intervals of activity because their acquisition comes in indivisible chunks. (Chap. 8)

Sunk cost. A cost which has already been incurred and which, therefore, is irrelevant to the decision-making process. Also called historical cost. (Chap. 13)

Tax shield. The amount of depreciation charged against income, thus protecting that amount from tax. (Chap. 15)

Theoretical capacity. See ideal capacity. (Chap. 10)

Time-adjusted rate of return. The rate of interest at which the present value of expected cash inflows from a particular project equals the present value of expected cash outflow of that same project. (Chap. 14)

Total project approach. A method of comparing two or more alternative courses of action by computing the total expected inflows and outflows of each alternative and then converting these flows to their present value by applying some predetermined minimum rate of return. (Chap. 14)

Transfer price. The price charged by one segment of an organization for a product or service which it supplies to another segment of the same organization. (Chap. 12)

Unadjusted rate of return. An expression of the utility of a given project as the ratio of the increase in future average annual net income to the initial increase in required investment. Also called book value method and accounting method. (Chap. 14)

Usage variance. Quantity variance applied to materials. (Chap. 9)

Variable budget. See flexible budget. (Chap. 9)

Variable cost. A cost which is uniform *per unit,* but which fluctuates in total in direct proportion to changes in the related total activity or volume. (Chap. 7)

Variable costing. See direct costing. (Chap. 15)

Variance. The deviation of actual results from the expected or budgeted result. (Chap. 1)

Index

Note: See also the Glossary, pages 483-490.

493

Operations research (Cont.):
  defined, 460
  effects of computers, 473, 474
  origin, 460
  relationship to management science, 460
  sensitivity analysis, 472
  techniques, 461, 462
Opportunity cost:
  defined, 335
  make or buy decisions, 335
  measurement of variances, 253
OR (*see* Operations research)
Order-filling, defined, 238
Order-filling costs:
  examples, 241
  work measurement techniques, 241
Order-getting:
  advertising, 239
  defined, 238
  field selling, 239
Order-getting costs:
  explained, 239
  influential factors, 239
Over-absorbed overhead (*see* Over-applied
    overhead)
Over-applied overhead, defined, 403
Overhead:
  defined, 396
  job order costing, 396, 398
  over-under-applied, year-end balance
    as adjustment to cost of sales, 403,
    404
Overhead application:
  bases, 401, 402
  problems, 401-405
Overhead control budget (*see* Flexible
    budget)
Overhead rates:
  actual, 401
  actual vs. normal rates, 402, 403
  fixed, 404, 405
  normalized, 402
  variable, 404, 405
Overhead variances, causes, 402
Overtime premium, factory overhead, 190

Past cost (*see* Historical cost)
Payback, defined, 367
Payback method of project selection:
  defined, 367
  weakness, 367
Payoff (*see* Payback)
Payoff table, illustrated, 465
Payout (*see* Payback)
Performance margin, defined, 301
Performance report:
  aid in controlling, 5
  examples, 7, 8, 213, 270, 271
PERT, defined, 462
PERT-COST, defined, 462
Planning:
  defined, 7
  operations research, 460
  orientation, 355
  relationship to budgeting, 145
POD (*see* Computer systems)
Policy, for use of capacity, 336

Price-earnings ratio:
  defined, 109
  illustrated, 109
Price level:
  adjustments, 115
  effect of changes on firm, 115
  mechanics for adjustment, 118, 119
Prices, influencing factors, 338
Price variance:
  defined, 213
  mutual price-quantity effects, 216
  need, 212
  responsibility for, 213, 214
Pricing:
  contribution approach, 338, 339
  long-run vs. short-run decisions, 339,
    341, 342
  traditional approach vs. contribution
    approach, 338-340
Prime costs, defined, 189
Probabilities:
  source, 464
  use in determining expected value of
    information, 465, 466
Probability theory, defined, 462
Problem solving:
  accountant's role, 323
  defined, 5, 323
  examples of problems, 322
  quantitative approach, 357
Process costing, compared with job cost-
    ing, 394
Product costing:
  absorption costing, 405
  direct costing, 405
  overhead rates, 403
  relationship to control, 393, 402
  standard cost, 408, 409
  techniques, 394
Production, scheduled, defined, 249
Profitability:
  determining factors, 357
  measures, 275
Profitability accounting (*see* Responsi-
    bility accounting)
Profit center:
  defined, 297
  techniques for measuring performance,
    297
Profit maximization, probability appli-
    cation, 464, 465
Profits:
  evaluation, 107
  maximization criterion, 333
  per unit of limiting factor, 332, 333
Programmed costs:
  behavior, 237
  defined, 193, 237
  examples, 193, 237
  follow-up, 245
Project selection (*see* Capital budgeting)
Purchases budget, example, 153

Qualitative factors, defined, 323
Quantitative factors, defined, 323
Quantity variances:
  control, 215, 216
  defined, 214

Quantity variances (Cont.):
  illustrated, 214, 215
  mutual price-quantity effects, 216
Queuing theory, (see Waiting-line theory)
Quick ratio:
  illustrated, 112
  purpose, 113
Quote sheets, illustrated, 341

Rate of return:
  analytical uses, 298, 299
  bases for measurement, 299
  defined, 359
  formulas, 298
  minimum acceptable level, 357
  relationship to income, 301
  relationship to investment, 363
  relative change vs. absolute amount, 302
  short-run concept, 304
  time adjusted, 369
Rate of return on assets:
  advantage, 297
  used as measure of efficiency, 297
Rate of return on assets method of project selection (see Unadjusted rate-of-return method of project selection)
Rate of return on common stock, 107
Rate of return on investment, 104
Rate of return on stockholders' equity, 107
Rate of return on total assets, 104
Rate variances:
  causes, 214
  defined, 214
Ratios:
  acid-test ratio, 112
  bond interest coverage, 111
  book value per share of common stock, 110
  debt service coverage, 111
  dividend payout ratio, 109
  dividends per share of common stock, 109
  dividend yield ratio, 109
  current ratio, 112
  earnings per share of common stock, 108
  function, 102, 103
  interval measure, 114
  inventory turnover, 113
  preferred dividend coverage, 111
  price-earnings ratio, 109
  quick ratio, 112
  rate of return on common stock, 107
  rate of return on investment, 104
  rate of return on stockholders' equity, 107
  rate of return on total assets, 104
  total fixed charge coverage, 111
Real-time, defined, 474
Receivables, defined, 48
Record keeping, as part of measurement system, 294, 295
Relevant costs:
  book value, 326, 327
  criteria, 325
  fixed and variable costs, 328

Relevant costs (Cont.):
  future costs, 328
  illustration, 325
  make or buy decisions, 335
Relevant data:
  criteria, 324
  distinguished from precise data, 323
  explained, 324
  illustrated, 324, 325
Relevant range:
  defined, 186
  fixed costs, 164, 165
Reorder point, defined, 472
Reserves, types, 58-60
Responsibility accounting:
  characteristics, 267
  control, 273
  difficulties in assigning costs, 272, 273
  guide for assigning responsibility, 273
  illustration, 268, 269
  relative items, 269
  throughout organization, 294
Revenue:
  defined, 24
  recognition of, 21
  source, 24
Robinson-Patman Act, influence on pricing, 339
Routing sheet (see Master operations list)

Safety stock, defined, 472
Sales forecast:
  difficulties, 153
  example, 152
  important factors, 153
  relationship to budgets, 150
Sales forecast opportunity variances (see Variances)
Scarce factor (see Limiting factor)
Scharff, S., accuracy of time reports, 296
Schlaifer, R., probabilities, 463
Schedule variances (see Variances)
Score keeping:
  defined, 5
  importance of accuracy, 296
  use of source documents and subsidiary ledgers, 401
Securities Exchange Commission, 100
Segment:
  defined, 274
  illustrated, 276
Segment costs (see Segment)
Segment margin:
  defined, 301
  illustrated, 276
Self-liquidating loan, defined, 150
Semi-variable budget (see Flexible budget)
Senior securities:
  defined, 110
  nature, 110
Sensitivity analysis, use in operations research, 472
Separable costs:
  defined, 275
  examples, 275
Simplex method, defined, 468
Simulation, defined, 462
Sliding scale budget (see Flexible budget)

m